THE TAX INSTITUTE AT H&R BLOCK

Wiley Tax Preparer
A Guide to Form 1040

THE TAX INSTITUTE AT H&R BLOCK

Wiley Tax Preparer
A Guide to Form 1040

WILEY

THE TAX INSTITUTE™
AT H&R BLOCK

Published by John Wiley & Sons, Inc., Hoboken, New Jersey.
Published simultaneously in Canada.

Library of Congress Cataloging-in-Publication Data

Wiley tax preparer : a guide to Form 1040.
p. cm.
ISBN 978-1-118-07262-2 (pbk.); ISBN 978-1-118-41608-2 (ebk);
ISBN 978-1-118-41898-7 (ebk); ISBN 978-1-118-61587-4 (ebk)
1. Income tax—Law and legislation—United States—Examinations—Study guides. 2. Tax returns—United States—Examinations—Study guides. I. John Wiley & Sons.
KF6369.85.W58 2013
343.7305'2044—dc23

2013005222

Printed in the United States of America

10 9 8 7 6 5 4 3 2 1

Contents

PART 1

The Income Tax Return

CHAPTER 1

Filing Information

Filing an income tax return is a yearly obligation for most U.S. citizens and residents. However, not everyone is required to file a return, and even some who do not have to file may want to do so for various reasons. Tax returns are due by a set date—generally April 15 for most individual taxpayers. It is possible to obtain an automatic six-month extension if action is taken in a timely manner. If not, penalties can apply. There are different versions of Form 1040, *U.S. Individual Income Tax Return*, for individuals. The version to use depends on the taxpayer's income, deductions, credits, and other factors. Special rules apply to individuals who are not U.S. citizens or residents.

> **ALERT:** If the taxpayer's name has changed due to marriage or divorce, the taxpayer should report the change to the Social Security Administration before filing the return.

Personal Information

In order to complete a return, you need to know certain personal information about a taxpayer. You must enter some of the information directly on the tax return; other information is useful to you as a preparer.

> **ALERT:** If the taxpayer plans to move after the return is filed, the taxpayer should complete Form 8822, *Change of Address*, at the time of the move. This will ensure that refunds and other IRS communications reach the taxpayer at the new address.

Taxpayer's Name The name of the taxpayer and that of his or her spouse (if married and filing jointly) must be included on the return. See Chapter 2 for information on filing status. There is no requirement that the husband's name appear first.

Address Usually the address is a street address. However, a post office box number can be used if the post office does not deliver mail to the home. A foreign address may be used if the taxpayer is located outside of the United States.

Daytime Phone Number The phone number is optional information that can be entered at the end of the return. The IRS may use this phone number to contact the taxpayer to speed up the processing of the return.

Taxpayer Identification Number Enter the taxpayer's Social Security Number (SSN) (and the SSN of the taxpayer's spouse even if filing a separate return). Nonresident and resident aliens who are ineligible for a SSN must include their Individual Taxpayer Identification Number (ITIN).

> **ALERT:** An ITIN can be obtained by filing Form W-7, *Application for IRS Individual Taxpayer Identification Number*. The taxpayer generally submits Form W-7 to the IRS together with the first income tax return he or she files. See the form's instructions for more details.

Date of Birth The taxpayer's date of birth is not entered on the return but is used to determine eligibility for certain tax breaks, such as the additional standard deduction amount for those age 65 and over.

TIP: A taxpayer can elect to contribute to the presidential election fund. It does not change the taxpayer's tax liability in any way. If the taxpayer wants to contribute, this is indicated in a check box on Form 1040. Taxpayers using the married filing jointly filing status can each make their own decision.

DEFINITION: Gross income is all income received that is not specifically tax free, including income from sources outside the United States. Examples of gross income include gain on the sale of a principal residence (even though the gain may be all or partially excluded) and the taxable portion of Social Security benefits (see Chapter 9).

Disability Disability information is not entered on the return but may alert you to possible tax breaks, such as an additional standard deduction amount for blindness or exemption from an early distribution penalty for IRA withdrawals before age 59½.

Occupation List occupation information at the end of the return near the signature line.

Filing Requirements and Thresholds

Certain taxpayers *must* file a tax return while others *may* want to file even though they aren't required to do so.

A person *must* file a tax return if **gross income** is at least a threshold amount (called the "filing threshold") for the person's filing status (explained in Chapter 2) and age. This is so even if the person is a U.S. citizen or resident living outside of the United States.

General Filing Thresholds

Table 1.1 lists the filing threshold amounts.

Example

Stan is single, age 45, with interest income of $1,200 and wages of $20,000. He must file a return because his gross income ($1,200 + $20,000 = $21,200) exceeds the filing threshold of $9,750 for 2012.

TABLE 1.1 Filing Threshold Amounts

Filing status	Age at end of 2012[1]	2012 Gross income at least
Single	Under 65 65 or older	$9,750 $11,200
Married filing jointly	Both spouses under 65 One spouse 65 or older Both spouses 65 or older	$19,500 $20,650 $21,800
Married filing separately	Any age	$3,800
Head of household	Under 65 65 or older	$12,500 $13,950
Qualifying widow(er) with dependent child	Under 65 65 or older	$15,700 $16,850

[1]Those born on January 1 are treated as age 65 on the previous December 31. Thus, a person born on January 1, 1948, is treated as attaining age 65 in 2012.

Example

Sarah is single, age 70, with interest income of $1,200 and Social Security benefits of $20,000. She does not have to file a return. Her Social Security benefits are not counted as gross income because they are not taxable. Her gross income of $1,200 does not exceed the filing threshold for 2012 of $11,200 for a single taxpayer age 65 and over.

ALERT: If the only reason for filing a return is to report the additional tax on IRAs or other tax-favored accounts, a taxpayer can file Form 5329, *Additional Taxes on Qualified Plans (Including IRAs) and Other Tax-Favored Accounts,* by itself; no income tax return needs to be filed. See Chapter 35 for information on Form 5329.

The gross income thresholds reflect the standard deduction amount for each filing status plus the personal exemption amount.

A person *must* also file a tax return if he or she:

- Is self-employed and has net earnings from self-employment of at least $400.
- Had wages of $108.28 or more from a church or church-controlled organization that is exempt from employer Social Security and Medicare taxes.
- Owes any special taxes including
  - The alternative minimum tax (AMT).
  - Additional tax (penalties) on individual retirement accounts (IRAs) or other tax-favored accounts.
  - Employment taxes for household employees.
  - Social Security and Medicare tax on tips not reported to an employer or uncollected Social Security and Medicare or Railroad Retirement Tax Act (RRTA) tax on tips reported to an employer.
  - Recapture of the first-time homebuyer credit or other credit.
  - Additional taxes on Health Savings Accounts (HSAs), Archer Medical Savings Accounts, and Coverdell Education Accounts.

DEFINITIONS: Earned income is income from the performance of personal services. Examples include salary and wages, earnings from self-employment, tips, and taxable scholarships and grants.

Unearned income is income from investments and other sources not involving personal services. Examples include taxable interest, ordinary dividends, capital gain distributions, unemployment benefits, taxable Social Security benefits, pensions and annuities, and distributions of unearned income from trusts.

Special Rules for Dependents

The usual filing thresholds discussed above do not apply to a person who is treated as a dependent of another taxpayer. A dependent is an individual whose exemption may be claimed on another person's income tax return. The rules for dependents are discussed in Chapter 3. Filing requirements for dependents turn not only on gross income but also on **earned** and **unearned income**.

Table 1.2 shows the filing threshold for dependents.

ALERT: Even a dependent must file a return if any special taxes are due, such as if he or she had self-employment income of at least $400 or owed Social Security or Medicare tax on unreported tip income.

Example

A taxpayer's dependent child, who is single, age 17, and is not blind, earned $5,900 from a part-time job throughout the year and also received bank interest of $500. A tax return for the child must be filed because the child had gross income of $6,400 ($5,900 earned income and $500 unearned income) that exceeded the filing threshold of the larger of (1) $950, or (2) earned income up to $5,560, plus $300.

ALERT: If a dependent child under age 19 or a full-time student under age 24 at the end of the year has income only from interest, dividends, and capital gain distributions and is subject to the kiddie tax (the kiddie tax is a tax imposed on certain children with investment income of $1,900 or more), the child's parent may be able to elect to report the income on the parent's return (discussed in Chapter 34). In such a case, the child does not have to file a return.

TABLE 1.2 Filing Threshold for Dependents for 2012

Marital status	Under 65/not blind	65 or older or blind
Single	Unearned income over $950, or	Unearned income over $2,400 ($3,850 if 65 or older and blind), or
	Earned income over $5,950, or	Earned income over $7,400 ($8,850 if 65 or older and blind), or
	Gross income more than the larger of (1) $950, or (2) earned income up to $5,650, plus $300	Gross income more than the larger of (1) $2,400 ($3,850 if 65 or older and blind), or (2) earned income up to $5,650, plus $1,750 ($3,200 if 65 or older and blind)
Married	Unearned income over $950, or	Unearned income over $2,100 ($3,250 if 65 or older and blind), or
	Earned income over $5,950, or	Earned income over $7,100 ($8,250 if 65 or older and blind), or
	Gross income of at least $5 and spouse files a separate return and itemizes deductions, or	Gross income at least $5 and spouse files a separate return and itemizes deductions, or
	Gross income more than the larger of (1) $950, or (2) earned income up to $5,650, plus $300	Gross income was more than the larger of (1) $2,100 ($3,250 if 65 or older and blind) or (2) earned income up to $5,650, plus $1,450 ($2,600 if 65 or older and blind)

Filing a Return Even If Not Required

Even though a return is not required, there are some situations in which filing may still be a good idea:

ALERT: If a taxpayer is eligible for a refundable credit, a return must be filed to receive the refund. The IRS will not send the refund automatically.

- *Requesting a refund.* If the taxpayer overpaid tax (e.g., there was too much withholding from wages), the only way to obtain a refund is to file a return.
- *Obtaining refundable credits.* Some tax credits are refundable, which means they can be paid to the taxpayer in excess of taxes owed. Refundable credits include the earned income credit, the additional child tax credit, and the American Opportunity credit. Refundable credits are explained in Chapters 27 through 31.
- *Establishing a capital loss.* If a taxpayer had an overall capital loss on investments or other property transactions for the year, he or she should file a return, along with Schedule D, *Capital Gains and Losses,* and any other necessary forms or schedules, to show the loss. Doing this enables the taxpayer to establish a capital loss carryforward (explained in Chapter 13).

Deadlines, Extensions, and Penalties

Filing Deadline

The income tax return is due by the fifteenth day of the fourth month after the close of the tax year, which is April 15. However, this date is extended if

April 15 falls on a weekend or national holiday. Emancipation Day is a holiday in Washington, D.C., that is usually observed on April 16, and this occasionally extends the filing deadline.

U.S. citizens and resident aliens are allowed an automatic two-month extension of time to file (until June 15) if they are living outside the United States or Puerto Rico on the ordinary due date for filing the tax return and either: (1) their main place of business is outside the United States or Puerto Rico, or (2) they are on duty on military or naval service outside of the United States or Puerto Rico.

ALERT: Individuals serving in a combat zone have an automatic extension of time to file. This extension lasts at least 180 days after the later of (1) the last day they are in a combat zone, or (2) the last day they were hospitalized due to an injury in a combat zone.

Requesting an Extension

If, for any reason, a taxpayer cannot meet the filing deadline, he or she must make an extension request by the filing deadline. This request provides an automatic six-month extension. Thus, anyone who timely requests an extension will not be penalized if their return is filed by October 15. This date is extended if October 15 falls on a weekend.

Filing an extension does not extend the time to pay any balance due.

Request an extension by filing Form 4868, *Application for Automatic Extension of Time to File U.S. Individual Income Tax Return*. Form 4868 may be filed electronically or on paper. Taxpayers who are paying all or part of their taxes due can obtain an extension by paying using a credit or debit card through an IRS-approved processor. Paying by credit or debit card is discussed in Chapter 36.

TIP: The taxpayer should pay as much of the tax that is expected to be owed as possible by the original due date, usually April 15, in order to avoid or minimize a late payment penalty (explained in Chapter 36).

Penalty for Late Payment

When requesting an extension, estimate the taxes that will be due when the return is filed. It is advisable for taxpayers to pay as much of the amount expected to be owed in order to minimize or avoid a late-payment penalty. The late-payment penalty is usually ½ of 1% of the tax not paid by the due date. It is charged for each month or part of a month that the tax is unpaid; the maximum penalty is 25%.

Example

Edwin obtains a filing extension and files his return on August 1, 2012. He pays the balance of the taxes he owes, $3,000, when he files his return. The late payment penalty is $60 ($3,000 × 0.5% × 4 months).

Penalty for Late Filing

A late filing penalty can apply if the return is not filed on time (postmarked or e-filed by midnight of the filing deadline) and no filing extension is obtained. The penalty is usually 5% of the amount due for each month or part of a month that the return is late. The maximum penalty is 25%. If the return is more than 60 days late, the minimum penalty is $135 or the balance of the tax due on the return, whichever is smaller.

TIP: The IRS can waive the late filing penalty if there is reasonable cause for filing late. Attach a personal statement (there is no IRS form for this) to the late-filed tax return explaining the reasonable cause. Common reasonable causes are illness of the taxpayer or an immediate family member and incapacity. Whether the cause stated is reasonable is a subjective determination made by the IRS.

Which Version of Form 1040 to Use

There are three different base income tax returns for individuals: Form 1040EZ, *Income Tax Return for Single and Joint Filers with No Dependents*, Form 1040A, *U.S. Individual Income Tax Return*, and Form 1040. There is also Form 1040NR, *U.S. Nonresident Alien Income Tax Return*, for nonresident aliens (discussed later in this chapter). Use the return that will enable a taxpayer to report all the income and claim all the deductions and credits to which he or she is entitled.

Form 1040EZ

Form 1040EZ is the simplest return that can be filed. However, its utility is very limited.

- Only those who are single or married filing jointly and who are under age 65 and not blind can use this form.
- It cannot be used to claim dependents.
- These are the only types of income that can be reported:
  - Wages and salary
  - Interest income
  - Unemployment benefits
- Taxable income must be less than $100,000.
- The standard deduction is built into the return; no separate adjustments to gross income or other deductions can be claimed.
- The only credit that can be claimed is the earned income credit.

Form 1040A

Form 1040A is more extensive than Form 1040EZ but not as broad as Form 1040.

- It can be used regardless of filing status, and dependents may be claimed.
- These types of income are reported:
  - Wages and salary
  - Interest and ordinary dividends
  - Capital gain distributions
  - Unemployment compensation
  - Income from annuities, pensions, and IRAs
  - Social Security benefits
- Taxable income must be less than $100,000.
- These adjustments from gross income can be claimed:
  - An IRA deduction
  - Student loan interest deduction

- □ Tuition and fees deduction
- □ Deduction for educator expenses

- No itemized deductions are allowed.
- Only these credits can be claimed:
  - □ Child and dependent care credit
  - □ Earned income credit
  - □ Credit for the elderly and the disabled
  - □ Child tax credit
  - □ Adoption credit
  - □ Retirement savings contribution credit
  - □ Education credits
- Form 1040A can be used to report estimated tax payments and estimated tax penalties, the advance earned income credit, and the inclusion of a child's unearned income on a parent's return (explained in Chapter 34).

ALERT: If a taxpayer files an amended return, he or she must use Form 1040X, *Amended U.S. Individual Income Tax Return*, regardless of whether he or she filed a 1040EZ, 1040A, 1040, or 1040NR originally.

Form 1040

Form 1040 is the most comprehensive return. It must be used for anyone who itemizes deductions, reports business income, or has income, deductions, credits, and other taxes not allowed to be reported on either of the other tax return options. Anyone can use Form 1040, even if a simpler return is permissible.

Special Filing Rules for Aliens

The type of tax return to file depends on an alien taxpayer's status. There are three types of aliens: **resident aliens**, **nonresident aliens**, and **dual-status taxpayers**.

DEFINITIONS:
Resident aliens are non-U.S. citizens who have met either the green card test or the substantial presence test for the calendar year. This is explained in Figure 1.1.

Nonresident aliens are aliens who did not meet the green card test or the substantial presence test at any time during the calendar year.

Dual-status taxpayers are aliens (non-U.S. citizens) who are residents for part of the year.

See IRS Pub. 519, *U.S. Tax Guide for Aliens*, for a complete discussion on determining status. Figure 1.1 provides an overview.

Resident Aliens

Resident aliens generally are taxed the same as U.S. citizens. They follow the rules explained earlier in this chapter and can file Form 1040EZ, 1040A, or 1040 as appropriate.

Nonresident Aliens

Nonresident aliens with income that must be reported to the United States, including income effectively connected with a U.S. trade or business, file Form 1040NR, or Form 1040NR-EZ, *U.S. Income Tax Return for Certain Nonresident Aliens With No Dependents.*

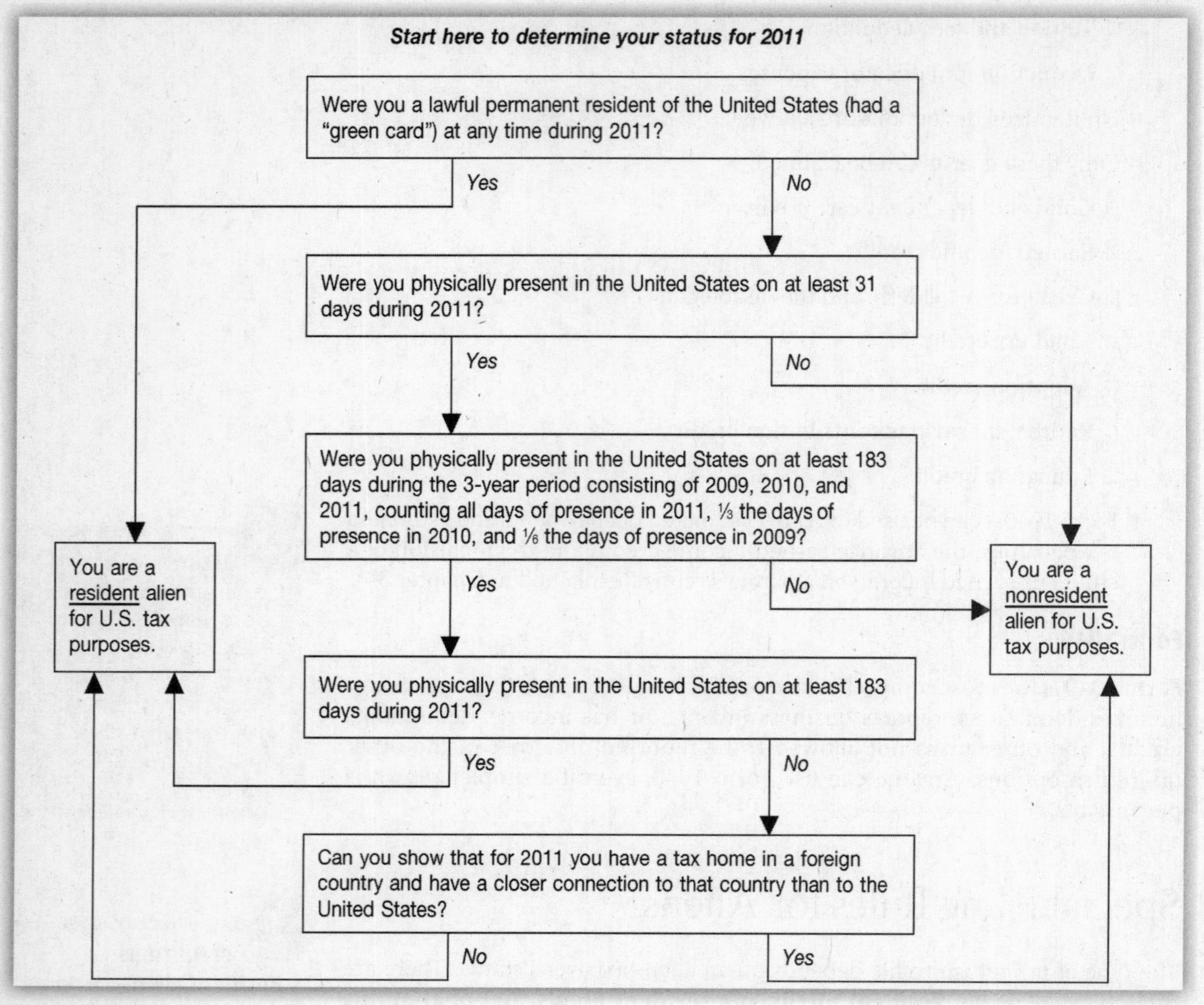

FIGURE 1.1 Nonresident Alien or Resident Alien?

Dual-Status Aliens

Dual status occurs most frequently in the year an alien taxpayer arrives or departs from the United States. Dual-status aliens are subject to different rules for the part of the year they are residents and the part of the year they are nonresidents. The rules for dual-status aliens are complex but are explained more thoroughly in IRS Pub. 519.

The base tax form a dual-status alien should file depends on residency status at the end of the year. A dual-status alien who is a resident at the end of the year must file Form 1040 (dual-status aliens are not allowed to file Form 1040A or 1040-EZ) and attach Form 1040NR or 1040NR-EZ as a statement. A dual-status taxpayer who is a nonresident at the end of the year may file either Form 1040NR or Form 1040NR-EZ, as appropriate, and attach Form 1040 as a statement.

Special Elections

First-Year Choice In some cases, a taxpayer who does not meet either the green card test or the substantial presence test in the current year, but who meets the substantial presence test in the following year, may elect to be treated as a resident for part of the current year.

Election for Nonresident Alien or Dual-Status Taxpayer Married to a U.S. Citizen or Resident Alien to Choose Resident Alien Status Normally, both spouses must be U.S. citizens and/or residents to file a joint U.S. income tax return. However, if married on the last day of the year, the nonresident alien spouse or dual-status taxpayer-spouse can elect to be treated as a resident alien and file a joint return. Doing this requires the nonresident alien/dual-status taxpayer to include his or her worldwide income for the entire year on the joint return. Refer to IRS Pub. 519 for more information.

Review Questions

1. Sara, who is single, has gross income of $7,000 and self-employment income of $500. Which statement **best** describes her filing situation? Sara:
   a. Must file a tax return.
   b. May file a tax return.
   c. Is not required to file a tax return.
   d. Should not file a tax return.

2. Carlos, who is required to file a tax return, wants to obtain a filing extension. Which of the following actions is required?
   a. Paying all of the taxes due.
   b. Giving a good reason for wanting the extension.
   c. Having a paid preparer submit the extension request.
   d. Requesting the extension no later than the filing deadline.

3. Harrison, an employee earning $75,000, does not file his return on time and does not obtain a filing extension. He files his return on August 15 and pays his balance due, $4,000 at that time. The $4,000 is 25% of his total tax liability. Harrison is:
   a. Subject to a late filing penalty.
   b. Subject to a late payment penalty.
   c. Subject to both a late filing penalty and late payment penalty.
   d. Not subject to any penalty because the return was filed and payment made before October 15.

4. Ed is a U.S. citizen who is single, age 70, and has gross income of $65,000 (including Social Security benefits of $20,000). He owns his home on which he pays mortgage interest and property taxes. He also makes charitable contributions. Because of these payments, it is beneficial for him to itemize his deductions. Which tax return should he use?
   a. Form 1040EZ
   b. Form 1040A
   c. Form 1040
   d. Form 1040NR

5. Madeline and Owen are U.S. residents who are married, with one dependent child. They do not have enough deductions to itemize. Based on these facts alone, which is the simplest tax return they can file?
   a. Form 1040EZ
   b. Form 1040A
   c. Form 1040
   d. Form 1040NR

6. Louisa, who is 42 years old and files as a head of household, has gross income in 2012 of $12,000. Assuming Louisa is eligible for the earned income tax credit, which of the following statements **best** describes her filing options?
   a. She must file a tax return because her gross income exceeds the filing threshold for her filing status.
   b. She should file a tax return in order to claim the earned income tax credit.
   c. She need not file a tax return to obtain the earned income credit; it will be sent to her automatically.
   d. She must file a tax return because she is claiming head of household status.

CHAPTER 2

Filing Status

One of the first and most important determinations you will make as you begin to prepare a tax return is the taxpayer's filing status.

Filing status affects many areas of the tax return, such as whether the taxpayer is eligible for certain tax benefits, the amount of the standard deduction, the tax table and rates used to determine tax liability, and other tax rules. Filing status also affects the version of Form 1040, *U.S. Individual Income Tax Return*, that can be filed, as noted in Chapter 1. You must be consistent and use the same filing status for all purposes on a return.

Filing status may sound simple, and in most cases you will be able to easily select the correct filing status. However, in some cases, a taxpayer may qualify for more than one filing status, and you may need to determine which is the most advantageous status for the taxpayer. Also, be aware that filing status is one of the most misunderstood areas of the tax law, and many errors are caused when taxpayers claim a status they do not qualify to use.

Five Filing Statuses

Taxpayers may use only one of five filing statuses shown in Figure 2.1.

On Form 1040, and Form 1040A, select filing status by checking the appropriate box on the tax return after determining the filing status for which the taxpayer qualifies.

Form 1040EZ, *Income Tax Return for Single and Joint Filers With No Dependents,* can be used only by those taxpayers who use either the single or married

Filing Status

Check only one box.

1 ☐ Single
2 ☐ Married filing jointly (even if only one had income)
3 ☐ Married filing separately. Enter spouse's SSN above and full name here. ▶
4 ☐ Head of household (with qualifying person). (See instructions.) If the qualifying person is a child but not your dependent, enter this child's name here. ▶
5 ☐ Qualifying widow(er) with dependent child

FIGURE 2.1 Filing Status on Form 1040

Form **1040EZ** | Department of the Treasury—Internal Revenue Service | **Income Tax Return for Single and Joint Filers With No Dependents** (99) | **2012** | OMB No. 1545-0074

Your first name and initial	Last name		**Your social security number**
If a joint return, spouse's first name and initial	Last name		**Spouse's social security number**
Home address (number and street). If you have a P.O. box, see instructions.		Apt. no.	▲ Make sure the SSN(s) above are correct.
City, town or post office, state, and ZIP code. If you have a foreign address, also complete spaces below (see instructions).			**Presidential Election Campaign** Check here if you, or your spouse if filing jointly, want $3 to go to this fund. Checking a box below will not change your tax or refund. ☐ **You** ☐ **Spouse**
Foreign country name	Foreign province/state/county	Foreign postal code	

FIGURE 2.2 Filing Status on Form 1040EZ

ALERT: The filing status used on the prior year's return may not be the same as that on the current return. Circumstances change: a person can get married or divorced, lose a spouse, be abandoned, or experience some other change affecting filing status. Determine filing status for the tax return each year.

filing jointly filing status. On Form 1040EZ, shown in Figure 2.2, filing status is indicated simply by including personal information for either one or two people.

Single

The taxpayer's filing status is single if, on the last day of the tax year, the taxpayer was unmarried, widowed, divorced, or legally separated from his or her spouse and does not qualify for another filing status.

A widow(er) is single if the spouse died prior to the current tax year and he or she does not qualify to file under the head of household or qualifying widow(er) status rules.

Example

Ellen's husband died last year, and she has not remarried. For the current year, Ellen is single (unless she qualifies for either the head of household or qualifying widow(er) statuses).

Married Filing Jointly

Married filing jointly (MFJ) is the filing status used by most married couples. A married couple can file a joint income tax return if they both agree to do so. This means that a couple's combined income and combined deductions are taken into account in figuring the couple's combined tax liability. A married couple can file jointly even if one spouse has no income.

A married couple *can* file a joint return even if:

- They live apart for part or all of the year.
- One spouse died during the year and the surviving spouse did not remarry during the year.

- One spouse is incapacitated or in a combat zone and cannot sign the joint return; the other spouse may sign on his or her behalf. Signing a joint return is discussed in Chapter 37.

A married person *cannot* file a joint return if:

- His or her spouse files a return using the married filing separately status.
- His or her spouse is a nonresident alien or dual-resident alien at any time during the year, and they do not elect to file jointly. (Filing jointly means including the worldwide income of both spouses on the return.)

The tax law in some instances penalizes married couples in comparison to unmarried couples; in other words, the tax liability for a married couple may be higher than the combined tax liabilities if the couple had not married and each taxpayer were to file as single. The 2001 Tax Act introduced temporary marriage penalty relief: (1) The MFJ 15% income tax bracket was expanded to exactly twice the size of the single income tax bracket, and (2) the MFJ standard deduction was increased to exactly twice the single deduction. Under the relief provisions, MFS amounts are exactly one-half the MFJ amounts, so MFS filers benefit too. The American Taxpayer Relief Act of 2012 made the marriage relief penalty permanent.

Married Filing Separately

Married filing separately (MFS) is the filing status with the least favorable tax rules.

A married person can *choose* to use this filing status even though he or she is eligible to use the MFJ status. Why would someone want to file separately if the least favorable tax rates apply? Filing separately may be advisable in two situations:

1. *To avoid joint and several tax liability on the joint return.* Each spouse is "jointly and severally liable" for the tax on the joint return, which means the IRS can look to either spouse for the full amount owed on the joint return, regardless of which spouse is responsible for the income or any omissions on the return.
2. *To save the couple income taxes (in special situations).* For example, if one spouse has lower income and higher medical deductions, casualty or theft losses, and/or miscellaneous itemized deductions, filing separately allows for greater deductions because these three itemized deductions all have an income threshold that must be exceeded. The income threshold is easier to meet for the taxpayer with lower income.

Example

The Longstreets' adjusted gross income is $105,000 ($90,000 attributable to Mr. Longstreet and $15,000 to Mrs. Longstreet). She had medical expenses of $10,000. If they file jointly, they can deduct only $2,125 of these costs ($10,000 – [$105,000 × 7.5%]) (see Chapter 20 for more details on deducting medical costs). If they file separately and itemize deductions, Mrs. Longstreet can deduct $8,875 ($10,000 – [$15,000 × 7.5%]), or $6,750 more than had the Longstreets filed jointly.

Limitations However, if taxpayers choose to file separate returns merely to avoid liability for the taxes on a joint return, they probably will pay higher taxes overall. This is because of the limitations on certain favorable tax rules. By filing using the MFS status:

- A spouse cannot claim the earned income credit, adoption credit, American Opportunity credit, or child and dependent care credit.
- The income levels for determining the child tax credit and retirement saving contribution credit are half of those for joint filers.
- A spouse cannot claim exclusions for employer-paid adoption expenses or interest on U.S. savings bonds redeemed for higher education purposes.
- A spouse cannot claim the deductions for student loan interest or tuition and fees.
- Half the capital loss deduction applies against ordinary income ($1,500 instead of the $3,000 for other filers).
- If one spouse itemizes deductions, the other spouse cannot use the standard deduction; instead, he or she must itemize as well. If one spouse uses the standard deduction and the other spouse wants to use it too, the amount is limited to half of that for joint filers.
- Half the alternative minimum tax (AMT) exemption amount applies for purposes of the AMT.
- If a spouse lived with the other spouse for any portion of the year, then 85% of Social Security benefits are taxable, regardless of other income; and such spouse cannot claim the credit for the elderly and disabled.
- If the taxpayers lived apart for the entire year, they can claim only one-half of the special rental loss allowance (up to $12,500 rather than $25,000). If the spouses lived together for any portion of the year and file separately, the spouses cannot claim any rental loss allowance.

A spouse *must* file a separate return (and cannot file a joint return) if the other spouse files as married filing separately or if either spouse is a nonresident alien or dual-resident alien at any time during the year and they do not elect to file jointly.

Community Property Rules If taxpayers file separately and are domiciled in a community property state—Arizona, California, Idaho, Louisiana, Nevada, New Mexico, Texas, Washington, or Wisconsin—their income must be characterized as either separate or community income. (Special rules apply to reporting community income and expenses on separate returns. See IRS Pub. 555, *Community Property,* for details.)

Example

Frank lives in California with his spouse, Gretchen, who works, while he does not. Gretchen files a separate return. Under state community property rules, half of Gretchen's wages are treated as Frank's income. Frank must report half of the wages on his separate return. Gretchen will report only half of the wages she earned on her return.

Head of Household

Head of household is a filing status that is more beneficial in many ways than the single status. As head of household, a taxpayer may use tax rates that are better than those for single or married persons filing separate returns, and the standard deduction is higher. To qualify for head of household status, a taxpayer must meet three conditions, discussed next.

I. Unmarried or Considered Unmarried A taxpayer must be unmarried (single) or considered to be unmarried on the last day of the year.

Even though married, a taxpayer is considered unmarried on the last day of the tax year if *all* these tests are met.

1. The taxpayer files a separate return.
2. The taxpayer paid more than half the cost of keeping up the home for the tax year.
3. Taxpayer's spouse did not live in the home during the last six months of the tax year. The taxpayer's spouse is considered to live in the home even if he or she is temporarily absent due to special circumstances.
4. The taxpayer's home was the main home of the taxpayer's child, stepchild, or eligible foster child for more than half the year. A "child" for this purpose is a son or daughter (including an adopted son or daughter). Grandchildren, parents, siblings, and others who may meet the relationship test for other purposes are *not* qualifying people for the "considered unmarried" test.
5. The taxpayer must be able to claim an exemption for the child. However, this test is met if the taxpayer cannot claim the exemption only because the noncustodial parent can claim the child using the rules for children of divorced or separated parents or parents who live apart. (The exemption rules are explained in Chapter 3.)

II. Cost of Keeping Up the Home The taxpayer must pay more than half the cost of keeping up a home for the entire year, whether he or she owns or rents the home. As shown in Figure 2.3, costs for keeping up the home include expenses such as rent, mortgage interest, real estate taxes, insurance on the home, repairs, utilities, and food eaten in the home.

Payments received under Temporary Assistance for Needy Families (TANF) or other public assistance programs that are used for upkeep do not count as the taxpayer's payment. However, they are included in the total cost of keeping up the home when figuring whether the taxpayer paid half of such cost. The following items are *not* considered payments for the upkeep of a home: clothing, education, life insurance, medical expenses, transportation, vacations, and the value of the taxpayer's services in maintaining the home.

III. Qualifying Person The taxpayer must have a qualifying person (someone listed in Figure 2.4) who lived in the home for more than half the year (discounting any temporary absences for attending school, taking a vacation, or other reasons, such as birth or death, during the year).

ALERT: If the qualifying person was born or died during the year, a different rule applies. Previously, IRS guidance indicated that a taxpayer may file as head of household as long as he or she provided more than half the cost of keeping up the home that was the qualifying person's main home for more than half the year, or if less, the entire period the person was alive. The IRS was considering a change to this rule when this edition went to print. Check IRS Pub. 501, *Exemptions, Standard Deduction, and Filing Information*, and the Form 1040 Instructions to verify current IRS guidance for situations when a qualifying person was born or died during the year.

Keeping Up a Home

To qualify for head of household status, you must pay more than half of the cost of keeping up a home for the year. You can determine whether you paid more than half of the cost of keeping up a home by using the worksheet shown on this page.

Cost of Keeping Up a Home

Keep for Your Records

	Amount You Paid	Total Cost
Property taxes	$	$
Mortgage interest expense		
Rent		
Utility charges		
Repairs/maintenance		
Property insurance		
Food consumed on the premises		
Other household expenses		
Totals	$	$
Minus total **amount you paid**		( )
Amount others paid		$

If the total amount you paid is more than the amount others paid, you meet the requirement of paying more than half the cost of keeping up the home.

FIGURE 2.3 Cost of Keeping Up the Home

If the taxpayer's parent is the dependent, the parent need not live with the taxpayer. However, the taxpayer must pay more than half the cost of keeping up the parent's home. Also, as explained earlier, for purposes of being considered unmarried, qualifying persons are more narrowly defined than in other areas (such as dependency exemptions, discussed in Chapter 3).

Example

Harriet is single and supported her child who lived in her home until the child's death in February. Harriet's child is her qualifying child and she claims a dependent exemption for the child. Harriet qualifies for head of household status because she paid more than half the cost of keeping up the home for her child while the child was alive (since the child was alive less than half the year). The same result would apply if Harriet had a child born in December; even though the child did not live with her for more than half the year, Harriet could still qualify for head of household status.

IF the person is your . . .	AND . . .	THEN that person is . . .
qualifying child (such as a son, daughter, or grandchild who lived with you more than half the year and meets certain other tests)	he or she is single	a qualifying person, whether or not you can claim an exemption for the person.
	he or she is married and you can claim an exemption for him or her	a qualifying person.
	he or she is married and you cannot claim an exemption for him or her	not a qualifying person.
qualifying relative who is your father or mother	you can claim an exemption for him or her	a qualifying person.
	you cannot claim an exemption for him or her	not a qualifying person.
qualifying relative other than your father or mother (such as a grandparent, brother, or sister who meets certain tests)	he or she lived with you more than half the year, and he or she is related to you in one of the ways listed under *Relatives who do not have to live with you* in Chapter 3, Pub. 501 and you can claim an exemption for him or her	a qualifying person.
	he or she did not live with you more than half the year	not a qualifying person.
	he or she is not related to you in one of the ways listed under *Relatives who do not have to live with you* in Chapter 3, Pub 501 and is your qualifying relative only because he or she lived with you all year as a member of your household	not a qualifying person.
	you cannot claim an exemption for him or her	not a qualifying person.

FIGURE 2.4 Qualifying Person

Example

Jane's 12-year-old child lived with the child's father for eight months of the year. Jane cannot use head of household status, regardless of whether she supported her child, because the child did not live with her for more than half the year.

Example

Cynthia is single and supports herself as well as her elderly parent who lives in a nursing home. Cynthia's parent is her dependent. Cynthia qualifies for head of household status.

Example

The same facts as in the last example except that Cynthia is married, although she has not lived with her husband for most of the year. Cynthia cannot be considered unmarried and therefore cannot file using the head of household filing status because a parent is not a qualifying person for this purpose. Cynthia must use either the MFJ or MFS status.

Qualifying Widow(er) with a Dependent Child

Qualifying widow(er)s use the same tax rates and standard deduction amount as those who are married filing jointly. This filing status applies only to the two years following the year of a spouse's death; it cannot be used for more than two years.

To be a qualifying widow(er), these tests must be met:

1. The taxpayer was eligible to file a joint return for the year of the spouse's death, whether the taxpayer actually did so or not.
2. The taxpayer's spouse died in either of the two prior tax years, and the taxpayer has not remarried.
3. The taxpayer has a child or stepchild who can be claimed as a dependent. A foster child does not count for this purpose. As with being considered unmarried for head of household purposes, children related to the taxpayer in other ways are not qualifying people for this status.
4. The taxpayer's child lived in the home for the full year, except for temporary absences. The taxpayer's child is treated as having lived in the home for the full year, even if the child was born or died during the year, so long as the child lived with the taxpayer the entire portion of the year the child was alive. Kidnapped children must have lived with the taxpayer more than half the portion of the year before the kidnapping.
5. The taxpayer paid more than half the cost of keeping up the home for the year, whether the taxpayer owns or rents the home.

Example

Edna's spouse died on April 20, 2010 and she has not remarried. She supported herself and her child, now ten years old, in the home since the death of the spouse. She qualifies for qualifying widow(er) status in 2011 and 2012.

For 2013, Edna can no longer use qualifying widow(er) status because of the two-year limit on this status. However, if Edna continues to support her child in the home and has not remarried, she may qualify to use the head of household status.

Determining Marital Status

For federal income tax purposes, marital status is determined under state law. Marital status depends on whether the taxpayer is married on the last day of the year.

Example

The taxpayer was single on January 1 but got married on December 31. The taxpayer is considered married for the entire year.

Example

The taxpayer was married throughout the year but the divorce was finalized on December 31. The taxpayer is not considered married for the year.

Legal Marriage

A marriage that is recognized by state law is usually recognized as a legal marriage for federal income tax purposes. Also, marriages performed outside the United States are usually recognized as legal marriages for federal income tax purposes. In common-law states, living together, no matter how long, does not create a marriage unless a couple meets all of the state's requirements to be considered a valid marriage under common law. These rules vary from state to state.

ALERT: Oklahoma's current common-law marriage rules differ somewhat from the rules in place before November 1, 1998. More information on this topic is beyond the scope of this book.

These states currently recognize common-law marriage: Alabama, Colorado, Iowa, Kansas, Montana, Oklahoma, Rhode Island, South Carolina, Texas, and the District of Columbia.

Five states recognize common-law marriages established before a certain date: Georgia (1/1/97), Idaho (1/1/96), Ohio (10/10/91), Oklahoma (11/1/98), and Pennsylvania (1/1/05). Utah recognizes common-law marriages only if they have been validated by a court or administrative order.

Example

A couple in Pennsylvania formed a common-law marriage in that state in 2002, meeting all the state's requirements. The couple can file a joint return because their arrangement is recognized as a legal marriage.

Example

Same facts as the last example except the couple began living together in Pennsylvania in 2008, claiming to be husband and wife. They cannot file a joint return; their arrangement, which was formed in 2008, is not recognized by Pennsylvania because the state only recognizes common-law marriages established before January 1, 2005.

ALERT: When this publication went to print, several court cases were challenging the Defense of Marriage Act. While President Obama has directed the U.S. attorney general not to defend the Act in court, the President did instruct federal administrative agencies to continue to enforce the law.

Federal Rules

While state law determines whether a couple is legally married, the federal government recognizes marriages only between a man and a woman (due to the Defense of Marriage Act, a federal law enacted in 1996). Same-sex couples that are recognized as married by a state are not viewed as married under federal law and cannot file joint federal tax returns.

Divorces

Taxpayers who are divorced under a *final* divorce decree as of December 31 of the tax year cannot file a joint return.

Example

Sue and Juan obtain an *interlocutory* divorce (a temporary court order) in December 2012, but the divorce will not be finalized until December 2013. Sue and Juan are still considered married in 2012 and can choose to file a joint return. However, because their divorce will be finalized in 2013, they cannot file a joint return for that year (unless they remarry by December 31, 2013).

Annulments

If a marriage is annulled, it is considered to have never existed. If a couple filed a joint return prior to an annulment, each taxpayer must file, for each year they filed as married, an amended return using a filing status other than one available only for married taxpayers.

Example

Julia and George married in 2010. They file joint returns for 2010 and 2011. In 2012, a court annuls their marriage. They cannot file a joint return in 2012. They also must amend their jointly filed tax returns for 2010 and 2011 to claim the filing status that applies as if the marriage had not occurred.

Separation

Spouses who are legally separated under a separate maintenance decree issued by a court are considered unmarried for federal tax purposes. They can file as single or as head of household (if head of household tests described earlier are met); they cannot file a joint return.

Spouses who live apart but are not legally separated can choose to file a joint return. Under certain conditions, they may be treated as unmarried for tax purposes and can file as head of household (if head of household tests are met).

Example

Ann moved out of the marital home with her young child in November 2012; husband Harry continued to live there. Neither spouse has filed for a legal separation. Ann and Harry can choose to file a joint return, or each may file a married filing separate return. They may not use the single or head of household filing statuses.

Example

Same as the last example except Ann moved out of the marital home in April 2012. Ann and Harry can choose to file a joint return or married filing separate returns. Or, because they each lived apart for the last six months of the year, it is possible that Ann may qualify to file as head of household.

Making Changes in Filing Status

Returns generally can be amended to change entries up to three years from the filing date of the return. The exact rules for time limits on filing amended returns are not discussed in this book but can be found in the Form 1040X instructions.

If an error was made on an original return, it should be corrected by filing an amended return.

In some cases, amended returns may be used to change filing status from one permissible filing status to another permissible filing status after the original return has been filed.

The taxpayer can make these changes in permissible filing statuses:

- From married filing separately to married filing jointly
- From single to head of household or qualifying widow(er) if eligibility conditions are met
- From married filing jointly to unmarried following an annulment of the marriage

However, a taxpayer generally cannot make a change from married filing jointly to married filing separately. Once a joint return has been filed, the status is final with one exception: a taxpayer can change from married filing jointly to married filing separately only if an amended return is filed *before* the original due date of the return.

Review Questions

1. During the current tax year, Harriet is single from January through October; she marries Charles on November 1. She has no dependents. They each have about the same amount of income and will use the standard deduction. For the current tax year, which filing status is **probably** best for Harriet (and allowable)?
   a. Single
   b. Married filing jointly
   c. Part single/part married
   d. Married filing separately

2. Stan married Inez several years ago after his first wife died but is separated from Inez under a court order of legal separation. They did not live together during the current year. Stan does not have any children or other dependents. Which filing status is the **most** favorable and allowable?
   a. Married filing jointly
   b. Single
   c. Head of household
   d. Qualifying widow(er)

3. Joan and Edwin are married and have no children or other dependents. Joan, a part-time bookkeeper who earns a comparably modest amount, has large medical expenses that were not covered by insurance. Edwin is a successful Wall Street broker with a comfortable six-figure income. Edwin also pays a large amount of home mortgage interest and real estate taxes. Which permissible filing status for Joan is most likely to result in the **smallest** total tax liability?
   a. Married filing jointly
   b. Married filing separately
   c. Single
   d. Head of household

4. Ellie, who is single, supports her elderly mother, who resides in a nursing home. Ellie pays all of the costs for her own household as well as more than half the costs for her mother. Her mother receives $10,000 of Social Security benefits and a $3,000 pension that pays the expenses not covered by Ellie. Which filing status is the **most** advantageous (and allowable) for Ellie?
   a. Single
   b. Head of household
   c. Qualifying widower(er)
   d. Married filing separately

5. Camila has two children who lived with her all year. Her husband, Mark, left the home in August. She has not been able to locate him, and they have not filed for divorce or legal separation. Mark did not work all year, and Camila provided all the support for the home and children. Which filing status can Camila use if she does not wish to file a return together with her husband?
   a. Single
   b. Head of household
   c. Married filing separately
   d. Married filing jointly

6. Margaret, a single mother who has never been married, lost her job in May of 2012. Margaret and her ten-year-old daughter, Samantha, moved in with Margaret's sister, Joanne, that same month and lived with her the rest of the year. Joanne provided more than half of the support for the household during the year. What is Margaret's filing status?
   a. Single
   b. Head of household
   c. Married filing jointly
   d. Married filing separately

7. Rose's spouse died in 2011 and she has not remarried. She supports and cares for her 12-year old daughter. What is the filing status for 2012 that typically will be **most** favorable to Rose?
   a. Single
   b. Head of household
   c. Qualifying widow(er)
   d. Married filing separately

CHAPTER 3

Personal and Dependency Exemptions

Personal and dependency exemptions reduce the amount of income subject to tax. Individuals are allowed to claim one exemption for themselves, their spouse, and any dependents claimed on the return. Each personal and dependency exemption is worth the same deduction amount. For 2012, each exemption is worth $3,800. While the exemption amount is the same, the rules for when an exemption can be claimed are different for personal and dependency exemptions.

Personal Exemptions

Each taxpayer, other than someone who can be claimed as a dependent of another taxpayer, is entitled to claim a personal exemption.

Joint Returns

When a married couple files a joint return, they can claim a total of two personal exemptions on their joint return (one exemption for each spouse).

Separate Returns

If a married couple files separately (as explained in Chapter 2), each spouse generally can claim only their own personal exemption on their own separate return. An exception allows one spouse to claim a personal exemption for the other spouse on a separate return but only if:

- The spouse has no income, AND
- The spouse is not filing a return, AND
- The spouse cannot be claimed as another taxpayer's dependent.

Example

A young wife files a separate return. Her husband, a student without any income, can be claimed as a dependent by his parents. The wife can claim her own exemption on her return, but she cannot claim an exemption for her husband because he can be claimed as a dependent by another taxpayer (his parents). This is true regardless of whether the husband's parents claim him as a dependent.

Deceased Spouse

If one spouse dies during the year, the surviving spouse may claim an exemption for the deceased spouse on a joint return if the survivor has not remarried by the end of the year. Alternatively, a surviving spouse may claim the deceased spouse's exemption on a separate return if the rules above for separate returns can be met.

Surviving spouses with no gross income who remarry in the same year can also be claimed as a dependent on both their current spouse's and their deceased spouse's returns if separate returns are filed. However, if the surviving spouse files a joint return with the new spouse, the surviving spouse may claim a personal exemption only on the joint return filed with the new spouse. The surviving spouse's exemption may not be claimed on the separate return of the deceased spouse.

Example

Linda's spouse Frank dies in May of 2012. Linda marries Ed in November of 2012. If Linda has no income for the year, an exemption for her can be claimed on both Frank's and Ed's 2012 tax returns if Frank's and Ed's returns are both filed using MFS. A (final) return for her deceased husband Frank has to be filed for 2012 even though he died. If Linda and Ed file a joint return, then no exemption for Linda can be claimed on Frank's return.

Dependency Exemptions

Taxpayers who support another person may be entitled to an exemption, known as a dependency exemption. The exemption amount for a dependent is the same as the amount for a personal exemption; in 2012, it is $3,800. There is no limit to the number of dependency exemptions that can be claimed. However, a dependent can be claimed by only one taxpayer.

Different criteria apply to determining eligibility for a dependency exemption for a qualifying child (typically the taxpayer's minor child), as compared with a qualifying relative exemption for any other person whom the taxpayer supports. In some cases, a taxpayer may be able to claim a child as a qualifying relative when the child cannot be claimed as a qualifying child.

Qualifying Child

In determining whether a taxpayer can claim a dependency exemption for a child, there is more at stake than just the dependency exemption. Eligibility to take the exemption may also be related to other tax breaks, such as the head of household filing status (Chapter 2), the earned income credit (Chapter 27), and the child tax credit (Chapter 29).

A noncustodial parent who is granted the dependency exemption may also be eligible for the child tax credit for that qualifying child. However, only a custodial parent can claim the EITC for that qualifying child. (The noncustodial parent may be eligible for EITC on the basis of another qualifying child, or even no qualifying children. (See Chapter 27 for more information on eligibility requirements for EITC.) Also, a noncustodial cannot claim head of household filing status or the child and dependent care credit solely on the basis of a child whose dependency exemption was released by the custodial parent.

All of the next seven tests must be met in order for a child to be claimed as a qualifying child by the taxpayer:

1. *Relationship.* The child is the taxpayer's son, daughter, stepchild, foster child, brother, sister, stepbrother, stepsister, half brother, half sister, or a descendant of any of them, such as the taxpayer's niece or grandson.
2. *Age.* The child is under age 19 at the end of the year or under age 24 if the child is a full-time student.

   No age limit applies if the child is permanently and totally disabled.

   The child also must be younger than the taxpayer. For example, if the qualifying child is the taxpayer's sister, the sister must be younger than the taxpayer. However, this rule does not apply if the dependent is permanently and totally disabled.
3. *Residency.* The child lived with the taxpayer for more than half of the year.
   - Temporary absences, such as stays at school, vacations, summer camp, or a hospital, are disregarded. Time spent serving in the military or serving detention in a juvenile facility is treated as a temporary absence.
   - If a child under age 18 is kidnapped by a nonfamily member, the absence is treated as temporary provided the child was living with the taxpayer at the time of the crime. If a child under age 18 is kidnapped by a member of the taxpayer's family or the child's family, the absence is not treated as temporary.
   - Children who are born or died during the year but lived with the taxpayer the entire time they were alive are considered to have lived with the taxpayer for the entire year.
4. *Support.* The child provided less than half of his or her own support. **Support** includes such items as food, lodging, medical expenses, education costs, recreation, and transportation. Social Security Administration (SSA) benefits (benefits paid under the old age, survivor's, and disability insurance programs) paid to a child are considered support provided by the child if the benefits are used for the child's support.

   Some types of income are *not* considered support provided by the child, such as:
   - Scholarships received by a full-time student (someone enrolled at school for any part of five calendar months) are not treated as support provided by the child.

ALERT: If the child is age 19 or older and not a full-time student under age 24, he or she still may be a dependent according to the rules for a qualifying relative discussed later in this chapter.

DEFINITION: Support means the total cost for a person's food, lodging, clothing, education, medical care, recreation, transportation, child care expenses, and other necessities. Tuition payments and allowances under the GI bill are treated as support. Capital items, such as appliances and furniture, can be counted as support. Life insurance premiums and scholarships received by a full-time student are *not* counted as support. Money that a qualifying relative receives but does not use for his or her own support is not factored into the individual's total support.

ALERT: "Support" includes only income the child uses for his or her own support. Thus, a child could earn enough money to be self-supporting but deposit all of the money into savings and use none of it for support. In this case, the child would still be a qualifying child because the money the child earned was not used for his or her own support.

DEFINITION: Supplemental Security Income (SSI) is a nontaxable federal income supplement program funded by general federal tax revenues (not Social Security taxes). It is designed to help aged, blind, and disabled people who have little or no income. It provides cash to meet basic needs for food, clothing, and shelter. SSI benefits are considered to have been provided by a third party.

- To the extent that Social Security benefits are not used for the child's support (e.g., the benefits are placed in the child's savings account), the benefits are not considered support provided by the child.
- Supplemental Security Income (SSI) is not considered support provided by the child.

Example

In 2012, Kevin is 17 and works a part-time job after school and a full-time job during the summer. During the year, he earned $8,000, all of which he uses for his own support. Kevin's parents also contribute $10,000 to his support. Total support is determined in this way:

$8,000 support provided by Kevin
<u>$10,000</u> support provided by Kevin's parents
$18,000 total support
$9,000 half support

Kevin meets the support requirement to be claimed as a qualifying child of his parents because he has not provided more than half of his own support for the year. He provided $8,000 toward his own support, which is less than half ($9,000) of his total support.

Example

Same facts as in the last example, but Kevin's parents provide only $7,000 of support.

$8,000 support provided by Kevin
<u>$7,000</u> support provided by Kevin's parents
$15,000 total support
$7,500 half support

Kevin no longer meets the support test to be a qualifying child because the $8,000 he provided for his own support is more than half ($7,500) of his total support.

Example

Same facts as in the last example, but Kevin places $4,000 of his earnings in a savings account for college and uses the remaining $4,000 for his own support.

$4,000 support provided by Kevin
<u>$7,000</u> support provided by Kevin's parents
$11,000 total support
$5,500 half support

Kevin meets the support requirement to be a qualifying child because only $4,000 of the $8,000 he earned was used for his own support, which is less than half ($5,500) of his total support.

Example

Bonnie's 11-year old daughter, Kim, received SSI benefits totaling $7,500 for the year. Kim also received a pension distribution of $1,200 in her name from her late father and used the funds for personal expenses. The pension is treated as support provided by Kim. Bonnie provided $6,000 toward Kim's support. Total support is determined in this way:

$1,200 support provided by Kim
$7,500 support provided by SSI (third party—general welfare)
$6,000 support provided by Bonnie
$14,700 total support
$7,350 half support

Under the support test to be a qualifying child, Kim must not provide more than one-half of her own support. Because the only support provided by Kim ($1,200) was less than half ($7,350) of her total support, the support test is met for Kim to be claimed as a qualifying child.

Note that for the qualifying child support test, it is not necessary for Bonnie to provide more than half of Kim's support as long as Kim did not provide it herself. The fact that much of Kim's support came from SSI payments did not prevent the test from being met.

5. *Not a dependent of another taxpayer.* The taxpayer, or the taxpayer's spouse, if filing jointly, is ineligible to be claimed as a dependent on someone else's tax return.
6. *Married filing a joint return.* If the child is married and filed a joint return, the child and the child's spouse filed the return only to obtain a tax refund (e.g., their income was below the filing threshold, but they filed a return to obtain a refund of withholding on wages).
7. *Citizenship or residency.* The child is a U.S. citizen, U.S. national, U.S. resident alien, or resident of Canada or Mexico.

If *all* of these tests are met, then a dependency exemption can be claimed. If the answer to *any* of the questions is no, then the child does not qualify as a dependent under the qualifying child rules.

If a child meets the requirements to be the qualifying child of multiple taxpayers, then the tie-breaker rules must be applied to determine who actually can claim the exemption.

Tie-Breaker Rules Apply If the Child Is a Qualifying Child of More than One Taxpayer

In some situations, a child may meet all of the conditions to be claimed as a qualifying child by more than one taxpayer. However, only one taxpayer can claim the exemption for the child; the exemption amount cannot be divided between taxpayers.

A tie-breaker rule must be applied when two or more taxpayers are eligible to claim the exemption for a child, even if the taxpayers agree as to which one can claim the exemption. However, there is an exception to this rule: If there are only two taxpayers who are eligible to claim the child and each taxpayer is the child's parent, the tie-breaker rules apply only if both parents actually claim the child on separate returns.

The four tie-breaker rules are listed next.

1. If only one of the taxpayers who can claim the exemption for the child is the child's parent, the parent is the taxpayer who can claim the exemption.
2. If parents do not file a joint return together but each claims the exemption for the child, the IRS will treat the child as the qualifying child of the custodial parent. The *custodial parent* is the parent with whom the child spent the most nights during the year. If the child spent an equal number of nights with each parent, then the exemption belongs to the parent with the higher adjusted gross income (AGI) for the year.

Example 1

The taxpayer lives the entire year with her five-year-old son and the son's father, to whom she is not married. The taxpayer has AGI of $19,000; the father's AGI is $20,000. Both the taxpayer and the son's father qualify for the exemption and do not file a joint return. (They cannot do so because they are not married.) If both claim the exemption, the IRS will disallow the taxpayer's claim because the father's AGI ($20,000) is higher than the taxpayer's AGI ($19,000). However, if the parties agree that the taxpayer may claim the child and the father does not claim him, then the taxpayer may claim the child as a dependent, and the claim would not be disallowed.

Example 2

Same facts as Example 1 except that the father moves out of the house in August, and the son continues to live with the taxpayer. Either parent is eligible to claim the exemption if they file separate returns. However, if both of them claim the child, the taxpayer is entitled to the exemption under the tie-breaker rules because the child lived with her for the greater number of nights. This is true even though the father had the higher AGI. The custodial parent rule applies before the higher AGI rule. In other words, the higher AGI rule comes into play only if both parents claim the child and the child lived with both an equal number of nights.

3. If no parent can claim the exemption, then the exemption belongs to the person with the highest AGI for the year.

Example 3

A child lives with her grandmother and her aunt. The aunt's AGI is $9,000; the grandmother's AGI is $20,000. Since neither the aunt nor the grandmother is the child's parent, only the person with the higher AGI can claim the exemption. The grandmother can claim the exemption because her AGI ($20,000) is higher than the aunt's AGI ($9,000), even though the child could be a qualifying child of both the aunt and the grandmother.

4. If a parent can claim the exemption but does not, a nonparent may claim the exemption only if the nonparent's AGI is higher than the parent's. If the child's parents file a joint return with each other, the AGI of the parents can be divided equally for purposes of this component of the tie-breaker rule.

Example 4

As a variation to Example 3, a child lives with his mother and grandmother. The mother is unmarried and has AGI of $9,000. The grandmother's AGI is $20,000. The child's father does not live with them. Under these circumstances, the child is a qualifying child of both the mother and the grandmother, and the grandmother can claim the exemption under the tie-breaker rules if the mother does not (and the son is not a qualifying child of anyone else).

Example 5

Same facts as in Example 4, except that both the mother and the grandmother each claim the exemption for the child. The IRS will disallow the grandmother's claim because the mother is the parent of the qualifying child.

Example 6

As a variation to Example 4, assume the mother's AGI is $22,000 (instead of $9,000). Only she can claim the exemption because her AGI ($22,000) is higher than the grandmother's AGI ($20,000). This is true even if the mother does not actually claim the child's exemption.

Example 7

As another variation to Example 4, assume the child's father is married to the mother and lives in the same household; they file jointly and have a combined AGI of $26,000. Because their AGI can be divided equally, the child's grandmother can claim the exemption because her AGI ($20,000) is higher than that of each of the child's parents ($13,000 [$26,000 ÷ 2]). However, the grandmother can claim the exemption only if neither parent actually claims the child.

Example 8

As a final variation to Example 4, assume the mother is only 18 years old and can be claimed by her mother (the child's grandmother) as a qualifying child herself. In this situation, only the child's grandmother can claim an exemption for the child; the mother cannot claim a dependency exemption because she is a dependent of another taxpayer (her mother).

Qualifying Relative

A dependency exemption for anyone other than a qualifying child is referred to as a "qualifying relative." This term can include a taxpayer's child who does not meet the earlier tests to be considered a qualifying child or someone who is not related to the taxpayer.

If each of the following seven tests is met, an exemption for a qualifying relative can be claimed for the individual in question.

1. *Not a qualifying child.* The person cannot be claimed as a qualifying child by the taxpayer or by any other taxpayer.
   - For this purpose, a "taxpayer" is someone who is required to file a return. A child is not the qualifying child of any other taxpayer if the child's parent (or other person for whom the child is defined as a qualifying child) is not required to file an income tax return and either:
     - □ Does not file an income tax return, OR
     - □ Files a return only to get a refund of income tax withheld or estimated tax paid.

Example 9

Debbie and Mike, who are not married, live together along with Debbie's son, age 6. Mike supports her son because Debbie's wages are not enough to fully support her child, but they are enough to require her to file a tax return. Mike wants to claim the exemption for Debbie's son because he provides most of the support and has a higher AGI. However, Mike cannot take a dependency exemption for Debbie's son because the son is a qualifying child of Debbie. Because Debbie earned enough income to require her to file a tax return, she is considered a taxpayer. As a taxpayer herself, Debbie is the only one who can claim a dependency exemption for her son.

2. *Relationship.* The person either:
   - Meets one of the relationship tests contained in Table 3.1, OR
   - If the person does not meet any of the relationship tests in Table 3.1, the person lived with the taxpayer all year as a member of the taxpayer's household (and their relationship did not violate local law).

ALERT: If a taxpayer is claiming an exemption for an individual who is not identified in Table 3.1, the taxpayer and the other person *must* be members of the same household for the entire year. For any individual with a relationship described in Table 3.1, the taxpayer can claim the exemption even if the individual lives in his or her own home, provided the other qualifying relative tests are met.

TABLE 3.1 Relationships that Qualify for Dependency Exemption under Qualifying Relative

1	Son or daughter (including legally adopted children), stepchild, foster child, or descendant of any of them (such as a grandchild)
2	Brother, sister, half brother, half sister, stepbrother or stepsister
3	Father, mother, grandparent, or other direct ancestor, but not a foster parent
4	Stepfather or stepmother
5	A son or daughter of the taxpayer's brother or sister
6	A son or daughter of the taxpayer's half brother or half sister
7	A brother or sister of the taxpayer's father or mother
8	The taxpayer's son-in-law, daughter-in-law, father-in-law, mother-in-law, brother-in-law, or sister-in-law

Example 10

Lucy and Mike fully support their unmarried 25-year-old son, Ben, who attends college full time out of state. Ben does not work and had no gross income in 2012. Because Ben is Lucy and Mike's son, the relationship test is met (Ben doesn't have to live with them all year to meet the relationship test). Lucy and Mike can claim Ben as a qualifying relative in 2012 because all the tests to claim a qualifying relative are met. However, Ben cannot be claimed as a qualifying child because he is over age 24 even though he is a full-time student.

Example 11

As a variation to Example 10, assume Ben is 23 years old instead of 25. Ben cannot be claimed as a qualifying relative of Lucy and Mike because he is under age 24 and is therefore a qualifying child. Lucy and Mike will claim Ben as a dependent under the rules for a qualifying child.

Example 12

Sarah provides 100% of her boyfriend's support. Sarah and her boyfriend moved in together in February 2012. Sarah's boyfriend does not meet the relationship test to be a qualifying relative because he is not related to Sarah and he did not live with her for the entire year.

3. *Gross income.* The person has gross income less than the exemption amount of $3,800 in 2012. "Gross income" for this purpose is any money, property, or services received that is not exempt from tax. In some cases, scholarship income may be included unless it is used to pay for tuition, fees, books, or equipment required for attendance. (See Chapter 10 for more information.)
4. *Support.* The taxpayer provided more than half of the qualifying relative's support for the year. In order to make this determination, the amount of support provided by the taxpayer must be totaled and compared against the total support for the qualifying relative for the year. Worksheet 3-1 in Chapter 3 of IRS Pub. 17, *Tax Guide for Individuals*, can be used to determine if the taxpayer provided more than half of the individual's support for the year.

Example 13

A daughter provides assistance to maintain her mother in the mother's own home. The mother's monthly rent, including utilities, is $1,200. Other monthly costs include food of $900; medical expenses of $1,500; and clothing, transportation, and recreation costs of $2,000 a month. The mother's total monthly support is $5,600 (half of which is $2,800). The mother's monthly Social Security check of $2,000 is used entirely for her support. The daughter pays the balance, or $3,600, which is more than half of the mother's support.

DEFINITION: The **fair rental value** is the amount that a stranger would reasonably expect to pay for similar furnished accommodations.

TIP: Documentation that substantiates the taxpayer's support payments includes:

- A statement of account from a child support agency or other government agency verifying the amount and type of benefit received by the taxpayer or dependent for the year
- Rental agreements or a statement showing the fair rental value of the home (proof of lodging cost)
- Utility and repair bills with canceled checks or receipts (proof of household expenses)
- Day care, school, medical records, clothing bills or other bills with canceled checks or receipts (proof of the dependent's support)

Support items that are not directly attributable to one member of a household, such as rent, utilities, and food, must be divided equally among all members of the household.

Example 14

Mom and Dad live with their three children, ages 16, 18, and 24. The monthly utility bill for the home is $200. The parents also buy a $150 television for the 24-year-old son, which is placed in the son's bedroom for his exclusive use. The parents may include only $40 of the utility bill in the total support for the 24-year-old because there are five members of the household and only one-fifth of the bill is attributable to this child. However, the parents may include the entire $150 cost of the television in the support of this child because the television was placed in his room for his exclusive use.

If the person providing support owns the house, the **fair rental value** of the lodging is treated as a support payment.

Example 15

A taxpayer's mother lives rent free with the taxpayer in a house that he owns. He also pays for all of the food. If he were to rent to a stranger the space that his mother uses, the rent would be $1,200 per month; this is treated as a support payment. The cost of the food for the entire household can be divided equally among the members of the household. In this case, two people live in the home, so half the monthly cost of food is treated as a support payment.

A person's own funds are not treated as support unless they are actually spent for support. Medical benefits received under insurance or a government program, such as Medicare, are not treated as support. Life insurance premiums are not treated as support.

5. *Taxpayer is not a dependent.* The taxpayer, or the taxpayer's spouse, if filing jointly, cannot be claimed as a dependent on someone else's tax return.
6. *Joint return.* If the qualifying relative is married and filing a joint return, the couple filed a return only to obtain a tax refund (e.g., their income was below the filing threshold, but they filed a return to obtain a refund of withholding on wages).
7. *Citizenship or residency.* The qualifying relative is a U.S. citizen, U.S. national, U.S. resident alien, or a resident of Canada or Mexico.

If *all* of the tests are met, then an exemption for a qualifying relative can be claimed.

Multiple Support Agreements

In some cases, more than one taxpayer may provide support for an individual, but no one individual provides more than half of the individual's support. Special rules apply when these individuals could claim the qualifying relative exemption except for the fact that they are unable to meet the support test.

Under the special rules, the taxpayers providing support can agree to allow any one of the individuals to claim the exemption, providing that individual provided *more than* 10% of the support to the qualifying relative.

TABLE 3.2 Summary of Qualifying Child and Qualifying Relative Requirements

A Qualifying Child OR	A Qualifying Relative
1. **Relationship.** The child must be the taxpayer's son, daughter, stepchild, foster child, brother, sister, half brother, half sister, stepbrother, stepsister, or a descendant of any of them.	1. **Not a Qualifying Child.** The person cannot be the taxpayer's qualifying child or the qualifying child of any other taxpayer.
2. **Age.** The child must be: • Under age 19 at the end of the year and younger than the taxpayer (or taxpayer's spouse, if filing jointly), • Under age 24 at the end of the year, a full-time student, and younger than the taxpayer (or taxpayer's spouse, if filing jointly), OR • Any age if permanently and totally disabled.	2. **Relationship.** The person must: • Be related to the taxpayer in one of the ways listed in Table 3.1, OR • Live with the taxpayer all year as a member of the taxpayer's household (and the relationship must not violate local law).
3. **Residency.** The child must have lived with the taxpayer more than half of the year.[1]	3. **Gross income.** The person's gross income for the year must be less than the personal exemption amount[2] ($3,800 in 2012).
4. **Support.** The child must not have provided more than half of his or her own support for the year.	4. **Support.** The taxpayer must provide more than half of the person's total support for the year.[3]
Tie-breaker rules apply. If the child meets the rules to be a qualifying child of more than one person, only one person can claim the child as a qualifying child under the tie-breaker rules.	
AND	
5. **Taxpayer Is Not a Dependent.** The taxpayer cannot claim any dependents if the taxpayer, or spouse if filing jointly, could be claimed as a dependent by another taxpayer. 6. **Joint return.** The taxpayer cannot claim a married person who files a joint return as a dependent unless that joint return is only a claim for refund and there would be no tax liability for either spouse on separate returns. 7. **Citizenship or Residency.** The taxpayer cannot claim a person as a dependent unless that person is a U.S. citizen, U.S. resident alien, U.S. national, or a resident of Canada or Mexico.[4]	

[1]There are exceptions for temporary absences: children who were born or died during the year, children of divorced or separated parents or parents who live apart, and kidnapped children.

[2]There is an exception if the person is disabled and has income from a sheltered workshop.

[3]There are exceptions for multiple support agreements: children of divorced or separated parents or parents who live apart, and kidnapped children.

[4]There is an exception for certain adopted children.

ALERT: A completed Form 2120 must be filed each year by the person claiming the exemption, even if it is the same person as the previous year. In addition, the person claiming the exemption must obtain a signed statement from each individual who provided more than 10% of support. The signed statement should indicate the year for which the agreement is being signed (i.e., the 2012 tax year).

Because only one exemption may be claimed and the exemption cannot be split, each of the other individuals providing support must sign a statement agreeing not to claim the exemption for that year. The taxpayer claiming the exemption keeps these signed agreements in his or her own records. Form 2120, *Multiple Support Declaration*, must be attached to the return of the individual claiming the exemption; this declaration identifies the names of all individuals that provided support.

To be eligible to claim the exemption, the qualifying relative of the taxpayer must meet *all* of the other requirements discussed earlier in this chapter, such as having gross income below a set amount ($3,800 in 2012) *and* satisfy all of these three conditions:

1. The taxpayer must contribute *more than* 10% of the other person's support.
2. The amount contributed by the taxpayer and other contributors totals *more than 50%* of the other person's support. Thus, the person being designated as a dependent cannot contribute more than half of his or her own support.
3. The multiple support agreement is signed by each person who could be designated as the taxpayer entitled to claim the exemption but is waiving the exemption.

Example 16

Paul, who is elderly and infirm, has three sons who contribute toward his support. The oldest son, Tom, contributes 35%; the middle son, Dick, contributes 20%; and the youngest son, Harry, contributes 5%. Since Tom and Dick each contribute more than 10%, and together contribute more than 50%, of Paul's support, either one can claim the exemption for Paul. They must decide between them who will claim the exemption, and both must sign the multiple support agreement. Since Harry did not contribute more than 10%, he is not eligible to claim the exemption, and his signature is not required.

Example 17

Michelle, Randal, and Kyle each contribute to support their mother, Mary. Mary resides in a nursing home. Michelle contributes 40% and Randal and Kyle each contribute 30%. All three siblings would be eligible to claim Mary as a qualifying relative except that none of them individually provides more than half of Mary's support. The siblings all agree that Michelle should be entitled to the exemption because she provides the most support. Michelle may therefore claim the exemption and must attach Form 2120 to her return and obtain a signed agreement from each of her two brothers confirming that they will not claim the exemption.

Example 18

Using Example 17, assume that Michelle provides 60% of Mary's support but is not related to Mary, and Kyle and Randal each contribute 20%. In this case, no one is entitled to claim the exemption because even though Michelle provides over 50% of Mary's support, she cannot meet the other tests for qualifying relatives (because Mary and Michelle did not live together the entire year), and thus she cannot claim the exemption. Also, because more than 50% of Mary's support is provided by a person who does not qualify to claim her as a qualifying relative, Kyle and Randal also cannot qualify to claim Mary under the multiple support agreement rules.

Special Rules for Parents Who Are Divorced, Separated, or Not Married

The child of parents who are divorced, separated, or not married usually qualifies as the qualifying child of one or both parents, but only one taxpayer can claim the exemption. Special rules apply to make this determination. In some situations, a tie-breaker rule, discussed earlier in this chapter, comes into play.

The custodial parent is the parent with whom the child spends the greater number of nights during the year. If the child lives with both parents some of the time, count the number of nights where the child sleeps. If the parents divorce or separate partway through a year, the custodial parent is the parent with whom the child spends the most nights for the period of time after the divorce or separation. If the child spends an equal number of nights with each parent, the parent with the higher AGI is the custodial parent. If a child is supposed to spend the night with a parent but sleeps at a friend's house or is away at camp, this counts as the parent's night.

Example 19

Sarah and Bill have two children. Sarah and Bill divorced in 2011 and agreed that the children would alternate weeks between each of their homes. Over the course of the year, the children alternate weeks but spend one extra week at Sarah's home when Bill is out of town on business. Sarah is the custodial parent because the children spent more nights with her during the year than they did with Bill.

Example 20

As a variation to Example 19, assume the children spend four weeks away at summer camp. The children will be treated as having spent two weeks with their mother and two weeks with their father because that is where the children would have stayed had they not been away at camp.

Example 21

As another variation to Example 19, assume the children spent exactly 182 nights with each parent (and 1 night with an aunt). Sarah has an AGI of $50,000, and Bill has an AGI of $45,000. Because Sarah has a higher AGI than Bill, she will be considered the custodial parent.

Waiver by Custodial Parent

The custodial parent can agree to let the noncustodial parent claim the exemption for their child. This waiver (also called a "release") can be made annually, for a certain number of years, or permanently.

Usually, a divorce decree or other legal document that awards the dependency exemption to the noncustodial parent is not sufficient for income tax purposes.

ALERT: If the noncustodial parent qualifies to claim the exemption by attaching certain pages of a divorce decree or agreement (which went into effect after 1984 and before 2009), instead of using Form 8332:

- The cover page of the agreement or decree must show the custodial parent's Social Security Number.
- The signature page showing the custodial parent's signature and date of agreement.

After 2008 If the divorce decree went into effect in 2009 or later, the noncustodial parent cannot attach pages from the divorce decree or agreement to the tax return in order to claim the child.

After 1984 but before 2009 If the divorce decree went into effect after 1984 but before 2009, the noncustodial parent may be able to attach certain pages from the divorce decree or agreement in order to claim the child. However, the divorce decree must state all of the following:

- The fact that the noncustodial parent is entitled to the exemption without regard to any condition, such as payment of child support, AND
- The custodial parent will not claim the exemption, AND
- The number of years that the noncustodial parent is entitled to claim the exemption.

Most of the time, the custodial parent must sign Form 8332, *Release/Revocation of Release of Claim to Exemption for Child by Custodial Parent* (or a substantially similar statement), to waive the right to the exemption and allow the noncustodial parent to claim it. The noncustodial parent must attach Form 8332 to the tax return when it is filed.

ALERT: Parents who have never been married to each other can use Form 8332 if:

(1) They lived apart at all times during the last six months of the year,
(2) together provided more than half the support of the child, AND
(3) the child was in the custody of one or both parents for more than half the year.

The pages of the agreement or decree that show all of this information: (1) The fact that the noncustodial parent is entitled to the exemption without regard to any condition, such as payment of child support, (2) the custodial parent will not claim the exemption, and (3) the number of years that the noncustodial parent is entitled to claim the exemption.

Example 22

Marlene and Vernon divorced in 2009. Marlene becomes the custodial parent of the couple's child, Hannah. Vernon is ordered to pay child support and is awarded the dependency exemption as long as he makes the required payments. Vernon cannot claim the dependency exemption merely by attaching the divorce decree documents because the divorce decree contains a condition (the payment of child support); he must have Marlene sign Form 8332 in order for him to claim the exemption.

Revoking a Waiver A custodial parent who has waived the right to claim the exemption can revoke it by signing Form 8332, naming the noncustodial parent on the form, and attaching it to the custodial parent's tax return.

The revocation will be effective no earlier than the tax year following the year in which the noncustodial parent is provided (or reasonable attempts to provide are made) with a copy of the revocation. Therefore, if a custodial parent revokes a waiver and provides a copy of the form to the noncustodial parent in 2011, the revocation is effective in 2012. The parent making the revocation must attach a copy of the revocation to his or her return for each tax year after the revocation has been made.

TIP: A custodial parent who had released a dependent exemption in a pre-2009 divorce decree can revoke the release using Form 8332 even if the exemption was originally released using the appropriate pages from the divorce decree.

Example 23

Leon and Eva are the divorced parents of a child. They divorced in 2007, and the divorce decree awarded the exemption to Leon. Eva, the custodial parent, agreed to waive the right to claim her child as her dependent for all future years. In 2011, Eva signs Form 8332, revoking her waiver of the right to claim the child as a dependent. The revocation entitles Eva to claim the child as her dependent in 2012.

Taxpayer Identification Numbers

Taxpayer identification numbers (TINs) include Social Security Numbers (SSNs), Individual Taxpayer Identification Number (ITINs), and Adoption Taxpayer Identification Number (ATINs). The taxpayer, spouse (if filing a joint return), and each dependent is required to have a TIN in order for the taxpayer to claim the dependent or personal exemptions.

If the dependent or spouse does not qualify for a Social Security Number (e.g., a child who is an undocumented alien or a nonresident alien may not qualify for an SSN), and the dependent or spouse does not yet have an ITIN, attach a completed Form W-7, *Application for IRS Individual Taxpayer Identification Number*, to the tax return. The IRS will process the ITIN application when it processes the return. Multiple W-7s can be attached if necessary (e.g., for two children). Form W-7 should also be used to obtain an ITIN for a foreign child who is being placed with a taxpayer for adoption.

If a U.S. citizen or resident alien child is placed with the taxpayer for a pending legal adoption and the taxpayer will not be able to obtain an SSN before the tax return is filed, then an Adoption Taxpayer Identification Number (ATIN) must be obtained by filing Form W-7A, *Application for Taxpayer Identification Number for Pending U.S. Adoptions*. If an ATIN is needed, Form W-7A should be filed before the tax return. The taxpayer should request a filing extension if necessary.

Review Questions

1. Art lives with his wife, Marie, who is a full-time homemaker with no outside income. They have no dependents and file a joint return. What is the **maximum** number of personal exemptions that can be claimed on this return?
   a. 0
   b. 1
   c. 2
   d. 3

2. George lives with his nephew, Sam, who is 18, a U.S. resident and in school in the United States. George, who is 17, dropped out of school so he could support himself and Sam. Sam does not provide more than half of his own support. George cannot claim his nephew as his qualifying child because:
   a. Sam is not his child.
   b. Sam is not younger than George.
   c. George has not shown he provides more than half of Sam's support.
   d. Sam is not a U.S. citizen.

3. Support items for a qualifying relative include all of the following amounts **except**:
   a. Food
   b. Tuition
   c. A vacation
   d. Life insurance premiums

4. Natalie lives with her seven-year-old daughter and the daughter's father to whom she is not married. Natalie's AGI is $21,000; the father's AGI is $25,000. Both Natalie and the father qualify for the dependency exemption for Natalie but cannot file a joint return because they are not married. Under IRS rules, which parent, if any, can claim the exemption for the daughter?
   a. Natalie
   b. The father
   c. Natalie and the father can split the exemption in half
   d. Either Natalie or the father

5. John and Phyllis are the divorced parents of Peter, age ten. Peter lives with Phyllis, who has signed a waiver to allow John to claim Peter's exemption. If Phyllis revokes the waiver and gives John the signed statement in 2011, she can claim the exemption for Peter in:
   a. 2011
   b. 2012
   c. 2013
   d. Never

6. Carlos supports his girlfriend and her young child (Carlos is not the child's biological father), both of whom live with him all year. Neither Carlos's girlfriend nor her child has any income. Carlos's girlfriend has not released the dependency exemption to the child's biological father, and the biological father does not provide any support for the child. Carlos can claim a dependency exemption for:
   a. Girlfriend only
   b. Girlfriend's child only
   c. Both girlfriend and child
   d. Neither girlfriend nor child

7. Mom's only income is Social Security benefits of $18,000 that she uses for her own support. Her three daughters help to support her in this way: Aline contributes $15,000, Betty contributes $10,000, and Carol contributes $3,000. Which daughter, if any, can claim an exemption for Mom?
   a. Aline, Betty, or Carol
   b. Aline or Betty
   c. Aline only
   d. No daughter

PART 2

Income and Assets

Wages, Salaries, and Other Earnings

Payments to employees for services rendered, such as wages, salaries, and commissions, are fully taxable. Fringe benefits, such as payments for vacation days and sick days, personal use of a company car, or gym memberships, are also taxable. However, many benefits are not taxable, such as employer-provided health insurance, qualified retirement plan contributions (although qualified retirement plan contributions may be taxable when withdrawn), and dependent care benefits.

Taxpayers who work in certain industries or receive non-regular wages, such as workers who earn tips, members of the clergy and the military, and U.S. citizens who live overseas and earn foreign income, are subject to specific rules.

Although an employer may pay a worker for services rendered, the worker may not be an employee but an independent contractor. Whether an employer–employee relationship exists depends on the facts and circumstances and the relationship between the two parties. Various factors are taken into account in determining this relationship.

Employee Compensation

"Employee compensation" generally refers to payments made by an employer to an employee for services rendered. The payments may be in the form of cash, property, or employer-paid benefits. Examples of different forms of employee compensation are described next.

> **TIP:** The employee's Form W-2 serves as a road map to the tax treatment of employee compensation. Codes to the entries on this form help identify taxable and tax-free amounts. See the instructions to Form W-2 at www.irs.gov/pub/irs-pdf/fw2.pdf for details.

Wages and Salaries

"Compensation" received by an employee usually refers to cash compensation based on an hourly wage or an annual salary. Compensation, including taxable benefits such as paid personal days, vested stock options, and bonuses, are also reported as wages and salaries on Form W-2, *Wage and Tax Statement* (see Figure 4.1). Generally, all amounts received from an employer in the form of cash or property are taxable *unless* there is a special tax rule for other treatment.

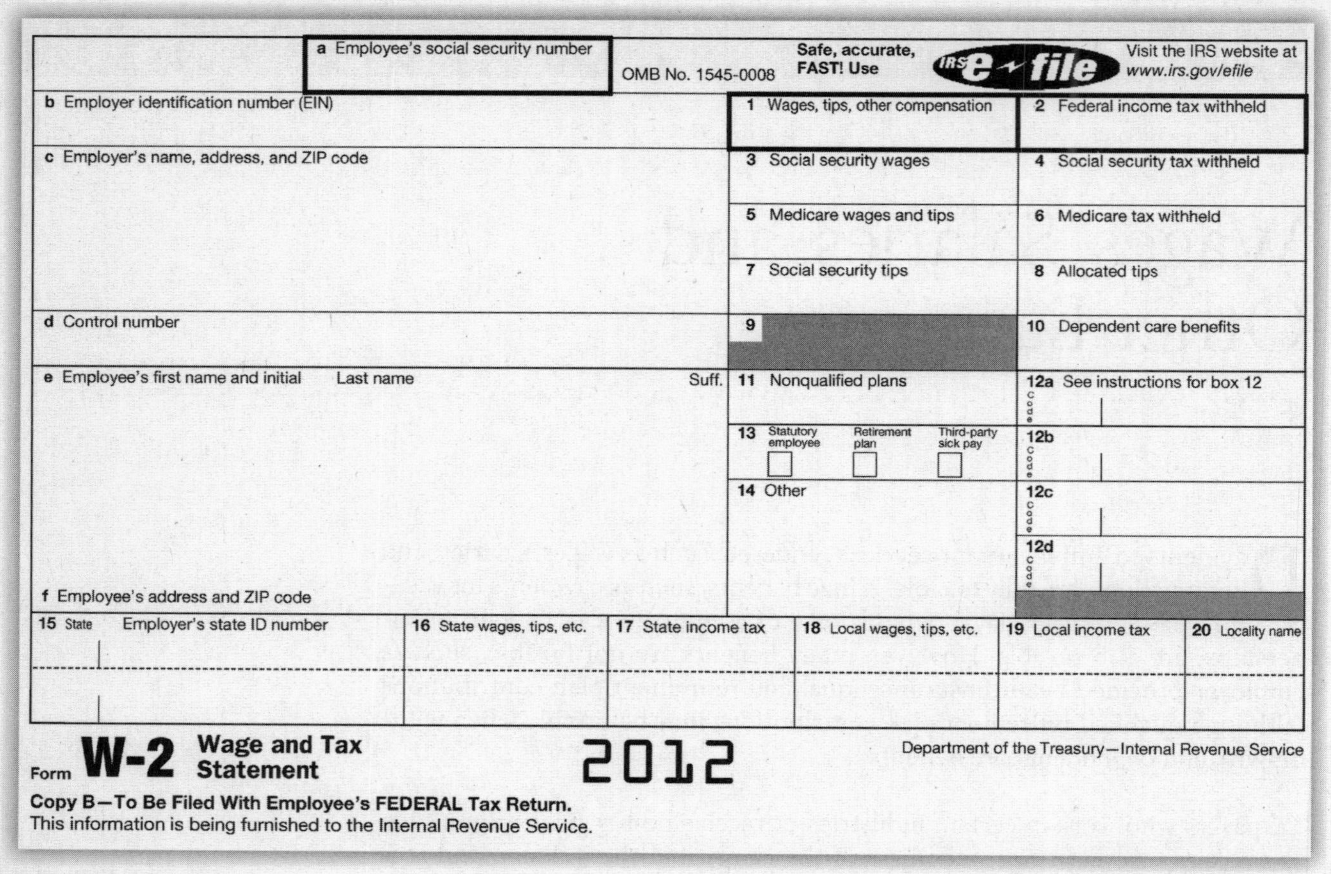

a Employee's social security number
OMB No. 1545-0008
Safe, accurate, FAST! Use IRS e-file
Visit the IRS website at www.irs.gov/efile
b Employer identification number (EIN)
1 Wages, tips, other compensation
2 Federal income tax withheld
c Employer's name, address, and ZIP code
3 Social security wages
4 Social security tax withheld
5 Medicare wages and tips
6 Medicare tax withheld
7 Social security tips
8 Allocated tips
d Control number
9
10 Dependent care benefits
e Employee's first name and initial Last name Suff.
11 Nonqualified plans
12a See instructions for box 12
13 Statutory employee Retirement plan Third-party sick pay
12b
14 Other
12c
12d
f Employee's address and ZIP code
15 State Employer's state ID number
16 State wages, tips, etc.
17 State income tax
18 Local wages, tips, etc.
19 Local income tax
20 Locality name
Form **W-2** Wage and Tax Statement **2012**
Department of the Treasury—Internal Revenue Service
Copy B—To Be Filed With Employee's FEDERAL Tax Return.
This information is being furnished to the Internal Revenue Service.

FIGURE 4.1 Form W-2

Supplemental Wages

"Supplemental wages" include such forms of compensation as bonuses, commissions, severance pay, sick pay, back pay, and vacations. These payments are fully taxable as ordinary wages and are reported like ordinary wages on the employee's Form W-2.

Fringe Benefits

An employee may receive a number of different fringe benefits, some of which may be fully taxable while others are partially or fully tax free. The instructions to Form W-2 list various types of benefits, and more information about fringe benefits may be found in IRS Pub. 15-B, *Employer's Tax Guide to Fringe Benefits* (www.irs.gov/pub/irs-pdf/p15b.pdf). Some of the more common fringe benefits are explained next.

Health and Long-Term Care Insurance Health insurance premiums paid by an employer to cover an employee, employee's spouse, dependent, and child under age 27 (even if not the employee's dependent) are not taxable to the employee. This rule applies to traditional health coverage, high-deductible health plans, and dental and vision coverage. Employers who were required to file 250 or more W-2 forms for the 2011 tax year report the cost of health insurance paid for employees in 2012 on W-2 forms for the 2012 tax year. Smaller employers may choose to report the cost of health insurance on Form W-2 for 2012. Reporting such costs is for information purposes only and does not change the nontaxable nature of employer-provided health insurance.

Other Health-Related Employer Contributions Other health-related employer contributions include contributions to such special medical plans as health savings accounts (HSAs), health reimbursement arrangements (HRAs), and Archer medical savings accounts (MSAs) generally are not taxable to the employee when the contribution was made. See Chapter 15 for information about when HSA distributions are taxable.

Retirement Plan Contributions Employer contributions to a qualified retirement plan on behalf of an employee are not taxed when the contributions are made. Instead, they are taxed as ordinary income when the employee takes distributions from the plan. There are annual limits on how much an employer can contribute each year to an employee's retirement plan. See Chapter 8 for more information about types of plans and deferral limits.

Group-Term Life Insurance The first $50,000 in coverage of group-term life insurance is tax free to the employee, regardless of the cost to the employer. Coverage over $50,000 generally is taxable to the employee based on a rate tied to the employee's age. The taxable portion of any life insurance premiums paid by the employer is shown on Form W-2, Box 12, code C.

Disability Insurance Long-term or short-term disability benefits either received by (1) a taxpayer from a disability policy directly purchased by that taxpayer with after-tax dollars or (2) an employee who has irrevocably elected, prior to the beginning of the plan year, to have the coverage paid by the employer on an after-tax basis for the plan year in which the employee becomes disabled are attributable solely to after-tax employee contributions. Thus, benefits received by a taxpayer under such a policy are excludable from the employee's gross income.

However, long-term or short-term disability benefits received by an employee whose coverage was paid by the employer on a pretax basis for the plan year in which the employee became disabled are attributable solely to pretax employer contributions. Thus, benefits received by a taxpayer under such a policy are includible in the employee's gross income.

Supplemental Unemployment Insurance Supplemental unemployment benefits received from a company-financed fund are considered wages and are subject to income tax withholding as wages. These benefits should be reported on Form W-2.

TIPS: Some forms of supplemental wages may not be paid in cash but are still fully taxable. For example, an employer may award a prize, an all-expenses-paid vacation, or personal use of a company vehicle as a bonus or award. All are taxable to the employee.

Employees who receive reimbursements for employee expenses in excess of the amount incurred are taxed on the excess amount. Although the excess reimbursement is included on Form W-2, it is not subject to Federal Insurance Contributions Act (FICA) taxes. See Chapter 26 for more information about employee expenses.

TIP: Income that is paid under a worker's compensation act or statute is generally not taxable to the recipient. Worker's compensation benefits are included in gross income only to the extent the benefits offset prior medical expense deductions claimed by the taxpayer.

TIP: Employer contributions to an employee's HSA plus the employee's own contributions (including employee contributions through a flexible spending account) must not exceed the annual limit. See Chapter 15 for additional information.

Dependent Care Benefits Taxpayers who receive dependent care benefits under a qualified plan may be able to exclude these benefits from income. Employer-paid dependent care benefits include amounts paid directly by the employer to the taxpayer or to the taxpayer's care provider. Benefits also may include the fair market value of care in a day care facility provided by or sponsored by the employer.

Adoption Assistance Amounts paid or reimbursed by an employer to cover qualified adoption costs of an employee may be tax free. Whether these payments are tax free or the extent to which they are tax free depends on the amount paid by the employer and the employee's adjusted gross income.

Moving Expense Reimbursements Moving expenses paid by an employer for an employee's personal moving expenses are tax free if an employee could have deducted the expenses if paid by him- or herself. Details on moving expenses are explained in Chapter 17.

ALERT: Designated Roth contributions to 401(k) or other plans that permit such contributions are not tax free.

Achievement Awards A noncash award given to an employee for length of service or safety achievement is tax free. However, the tax-free amount is limited to the cost of the item that is deductible by the employer. This amount cannot exceed $1,600 (or $400 if the award is not a qualified plan award).

TIP: Look at Form W-2, Box 13, to see whether "Retirement Plan" has been checked. A check indicates that the taxpayer is an active participant in an employer's qualified retirement plan. This limits the amount that a taxpayer can deduct when contributing to a traditional individual retirement account (IRA; explained in Chapter 15).

Car Usage Usage of a company car for business driving is not taxable to the employee. However, if the employee uses the car for personal driving (including commuting to and from work), the value of this benefit is taxable.

De Minimis (Minimal) Benefits Cash, including gift certificates or gift cards, is always taxable pay. However, some products or services may be so small that they are difficult to value and unreasonable to require an employer to account for them, such as coffee in a company break room. Such benefits are not taxable to the employee.

Educational Assistance Payments by an employer for courses or training may be tax free to the employee, regardless of an employee's income. The maximum annual exclusion is $5,250 and applies to either undergraduate- or graduate-level courses. The payment must be made under an employer's educational assistance plan.

ALERT: The exclusion does not apply to awards of cash, cash equivalent items, gift certificates or gift cards, or other intangible property such as vacations or theater tickets.

Example

Charlene is a computer programmer. Her employer sends her for a course to learn new programming applications; it costs $6,000. It is fully excludable as a working condition fringe benefit because it is job related and she could have deducted it if she had paid for it herself. If her employer reimburses her for a creative writing course under the company's employer educational assistance plan, the tax-free reimbursement is limited to $5,250.

Transportation Certain transportation fringe benefits are not taxable. These include monthly transit passes, free parking, and transportation in a commuter highway van. For 2012, the value of parking provided to an employee that does not exceed $240 per month is tax free. Similarly, the value of monthly transit passes and van pooling that does not exceed $240 per month is tax free. Employees may also receive up to $20 per month tax free for commuting by bicycle, to offset the cost of storage and repairs.

> **TIP:** If courses are job related, there is no cap on the excludable amount. The courses are viewed as a working condition fringe benefit (explained later in this chapter).

Working Condition Benefits Working condition benefits are benefits paid by an employer that, if the employee had paid for them, would be deductible by the employee as an employee benefit expense. The benefits are tax free without dollar limits or income limits.

Stock Options Generally, employees can receive two forms of stock options: statutory (incentive) stock options and nonstatutory stock options. In the case of nonstatutory stock options, the recipient could have taxable income on the grant date, on the exercise date, and/or on the date of sale, depending on several different factors. In the case of statutory stock options, the recipient generally has taxable income (for regular tax purposes) only on the date of sale. A detailed discussion of stock options is beyond the scope of this book. For more information, see IRS Pub. 525, *Taxable and Nontaxable Income.*

Special Topics

Compensation earned by certain types of employees or employees in specific occupations are explained in this section. Such income includes tip income and income earned by members of the clergy, members of the military, statutory employees, and U.S. citizens working in foreign countries.

Tip Income

"Tips" are discretionary payments made by customers to employees. All tips, whether paid in cash or in property (such as tickets, passes, or other items of value), are income and must be reported on the tax return. They are included on the return as wages; there is no separate line on the return for reporting tips.

In addition, an employee must keep a daily record of tips received and report the tips to the employer. Employees whose reported tips are below a certain threshold may be allocated tips by their employers. See "Allocated Tips" later in this section.

Tip Record Employees earning tips must use a tip record to accurately report tip income to their employers for Social Security and Medicare (FICA) tax purposes and for preparation of the tax return.

The record can be an employee's tip diary or the IRS Form 4070A, *Employee's Daily Record of Tips* (shown in IRS Pub. 1244, *Employee's Daily Record of Tips and Report to Employer*). The record should reflect:

- Cash tips received directly from customers or from other employers.
- Tips on credit and debit cards that the employer pays to the employee.

- The value of noncash tips.
- Amounts that the employee paid to other employees ("tip-outs") through tip pools, tip splitting, or other arrangements. Employees reporting tip-outs must include the names of the other employees to whom tips were paid.

ALERT: Mandatory service charges imposed by a restaurant, such as 18% for parties of eight or more, are *not* treated as tips. The employer reports them to the worker as wages.

Reporting to the Employer Even though all tips are taxable, employees must report tips totaling at least $20 per month to the employer by the tenth day of the following month. If this day is a Saturday, Sunday, or legal holiday, reporting is the next business day.

Example

A hairdresser receives over $20 in tips in February 2012 and must report these tips by March 10, 2012. However, because March 10 is a Saturday, she must submit the report by Monday, March 12, 2012.

TIP: An employee can avoid the penalty for not reporting tips to an employer by showing reasonable cause. The employee must attach a statement to the return explaining why the tips were not reported.

There is no specific form required for reporting tips to an employer. The employer may provide a form, or the employee may use Form 4070, *Employee's Report of Tips to Employer*. An employee also may submit his or her own report, either in writing or electronically, but it must show the employee's name, Social Security Number, address, the date of the report, the dates covered by the report, and the total amount of tips received by the employee during the period. The employee also must sign the report.

An employee who does not timely report tips to an employer may be subject to a penalty of 50% of the FICA taxes or equivalent Railroad Retirement tax.

ALERT: Form 1040 must be used for an employee with allocated tips; do not use Form 1040A or 1040-EZ.

Allocated Tips Special rules apply to tips that an employer assigns to a worker in addition to any tips reported by the worker to the employer. Allocated tips occur if:

- The employee worked in an establishment (restaurant, cocktail lounge, etc.) that must allocate tips to employees.
- The tips reported by the worker to the employer were less than the worker's share of 8% of food and drink sales.
- The worker did not participate in the employer's Attributed Tip Income Program (ATIP).

ALERT: Chapter 35 explains how to figure Social Security and Medicare (FICA) taxes on allocated tips.

Allocated tips are reported in Box 8 of Form W-2. They are reported as income on the return *unless* either of the following applies:

- The employee's daily tip record is credible and reliable. If so, report only the amount in the employee's record.
- The employee's tip record is incomplete but the employee shows by other credible evidence that actual tips were more than the tips reported to the employer plus the allocated tips. Again, report only the amount in the employee's record.

No income or FICA taxes are withheld on allocated tips, so the employee must pay the taxes directly to the government.

Clergy

The term "clergy" includes priests, ministers, rabbis, cantors, and anyone else "duly ordained, licensed, or commissioned" who performs service in the exercise of his or her ministry. Generally, income earned by a member of the clergy is taxable. This includes wages as well as offerings and fees received for performing marriages, baptisms, funerals, masses, and other rites.

TIP: If the offering is made to the religious institution, it is not taxable to the clergy member. Members of the clergy who donate to their religious organizations offerings and fees earned outside of their employment are taxed on the earnings but may be able to deduct the contributions (see Chapter 27).

Housing Special rules apply to housing provided to a duly-ordained member of the clergy as compensation for services (parsonage allowance). The rental value of housing (including utilities) or a designated housing allowance is excludable from taxable income provided it is used to pay for rent (including furnishings and utilities) that does not exceed the fair rental value of the home or apartment.

Example

A minister and his family live in his church parsonage. He is not taxed on the rental value of this fringe benefit. If, instead, he is given a monthly allowance of $1,500 for housing and his housing costs (rent and utilities) are no more than this amount, that allowance also would be tax free.

ALERT: The rental value of the home or the housing allowance is treated as self-employment income for purposes of self-employment tax (see Chapter 35).

Vow of Poverty Members of religious orders who take a vow of poverty (renounce earnings and turn them over to the orders) can be treated in one of two ways:

1. If the member receives payments for services performed for the order and turns the amounts over to the order, the payments are *excluded* from income. Also, any payments received for services performed at another associated institution are excludable from income if the services were performed at the direction of the member's order.
2. If services are performed outside the order, the earnings are not income only if (a) they are the kind of services that are ordinarily the duties of members of the order and (b) they are part of the duties that the member must exercise for, or on behalf of, the religious order as its agent.

If a member is an employee of a third party, the earnings are taxable even if the member has taken a vow of poverty.

Military

Payments received by a member of the military generally are taxable as wages. However, certain payments may be tax free.

Taxable payments include:

- Basic pay for active duty, back pay, drills, reserve training, and training duty
- Special pay for hazardous duty, hostile fire or imminent danger, aviation career incentives, diving duty, foreign duty, medical and dental officers, nuclear-qualified officers, and special duty assignments
- Enlistment and reenlistment bonuses

TIP: Distributions from a military retirement plan are taxable as pension and annuity income, not as wages, if the payments are based on the service member's age or length of service.

TIP: An election can be made to treat combat pay as taxable in order to qualify for the earned income credit (see Chapter 27). Combat pay, even though excluded from income, can be considered income for the purpose of contributing to an IRA (see Chapter 15).

- Pay for accrued leave
- Personal money allowances for high-ranking officers
- Student loan repayment programs

Tax-free payments include:

- Combat pay
- Basic Allowance for Housing (BAH; a living allowance)
- Basic Allowance for Subsistence (BAS; a living allowance)
- Housing and cost-of-living allowances abroad
- Variable housing allowance (VHA)
- Family allowances for the education of dependents, emergencies, evacuation to a safe place, and separation
- Death allowances for burial
- Dislocation allowances (essentially temporary living allowances for a hotel)
- Temporary lodging expense allowance to offset the added living expenses of temporary lodging within the United States for up to 10 days and up to 60 days abroad
- Moving-in housing allowance for certain moving-related costs
- Travel allowances for annual round trips for dependent students
- Defense counseling payments
- Reserve Officers' Training Corps (ROTC) educational and subsistence allowances
- Survivor and retirement protection plan premium payments
- Uniform allowances
- Forfeited pay on the order of a court-martial
- Foreign currency adjustments
- Payments to former prisoners of war
- Benefits under Servicemembers' Group Life Insurance
- Dividends on GI insurance and interest on dividends left on deposit with the Veterans Administration
- State and local government bonuses to active or former military personnel
- Payments from Compensated Work Therapy programs

Military differential pay (sometimes called supplemental military leave pay) are payments made voluntarily by an employer to a employee to make up the difference between the employee's regular salary and the employee's military pay while on active duty. Such payments are fully taxable to the employee. However, if the employee is on active duty for more than 30 days, the payments are not subject to FICA taxes.

Statutory Employees

Statutory employees are workers who are treated under statutory rules instead of common law rules. Statutory employees include:

- Full-time life insurance salespersons
- Certain agent or commission drivers
- Traveling salespersons
- Certain homeworkers

Earnings of statutory employees are reported on Form W-2 (Box 13 is checked to indicate a statutory employee), but the earnings are not taxed as wages for income tax purposes. Instead, they are taxed as self-employment income on Schedule C of Form 1040, *Profit or Loss From Business*, or Schedule C-EZ, *Net Profit From Business (Sole Proprietorship)*, of Form 1040. (See Chapter 11 for more information about Schedule C.)

ALERT: A statutory employee who has Schedule C income outside his or her position as a statutory employee must file a separate Schedule C for that income. That is, income earned as a statutory employee cannot be combined with other Schedule C income earned in a different capacity.

A statutory employee can also deduct expenses on Schedule C (or C-EZ) that are related to the employee's work as a statutory employee. The expenses are not treated as miscellaneous unreimbursed employee business expenses deductible on Schedule A, *Itemized Deductions*, and subject to the 2% AGI threshold.

The earnings of a statutory employee are subject to Social Security and Medicare (FICA) taxes. Because Social Security and Medicare taxes should have already been withheld and shown on the employee's Form W-2, statutory employees do *not* pay self-employment tax on their earnings.

U.S. Citizens with Foreign Income

Generally, a U.S. citizen or resident is taxed on his or her worldwide income. If a U.S. citizen or resident alien works abroad, some or all of the earnings may be excludable from gross income. For 2012, U.S. citizens with foreign income may exclude up to $95,100 under the foreign earned income exclusion.

ALERT: The exclusion is not automatic; it must be elected by filing Form 2555, *Foreign Earned Income* (or a simplified version where appropriate, titled Form 2555-EZ, *Foreign Earned Income Exclusion*), and attaching it to Form 1040.

The U.S. citizen or resident who claims the foreign earned income exclusion cannot claim the foreign tax credit on excluded foreign earnings. Full details on the foreign earned income exclusion are available in IRS Pub. 54, *Tax Guide for U.S. Citizens and Resident Aliens Abroad*.

Eligibility for the Exclusion To qualify for the exclusion, a taxpayer must have a tax home in a foreign country and meet either the bona fide resident test or physical presence test, as follows:

- *Bona fide resident test.* The taxpayer is a bona fide resident of a foreign country for an uninterrupted period that includes one full tax year (for calendar-year taxpayers, from January 1 through December 31). For details about the bona fide residence, see IRS Pub. 54. Once a taxpayer establishes a bona fide residence in a foreign country for an uninterrupted period that includes an entire tax year, the taxpayer is considered a bona fide resident starting on the date the taxpayer began the residency and ending on the date the taxpayer abandons the residency.

Example

A taxpayer is a bona fide resident of Spain from November 1, 2010, through March 12, 2012. Because the taxpayer was a bona fide resident for an entire uninterrupted calendar year (tax year 2011), the taxpayer can use the foreign earned income exclusion for the period beginning on the date he actually began the residence (November 1, 2010) and ending on the date he abandoned the foreign residence (March 12, 2012).

- *Physical presence test.* A taxpayer is physically present in a foreign country for 330 full days during a 12-month period. A full day is a period of 24 consecutive hours, beginning at midnight. The 330 days do not have to be consecutive. Days spent traveling between foreign countries and on vacation in foreign countries are to be counted. Special rules apply to time spent traveling on or over international waters.

Example

A taxpayer works in New Zealand for a 20-month period from January 1, 2011, through August 31, 2012, except that she spends 28 days in February 2011 and 29 days in February 2012 on vacation in the United States. She is present in New Zealand 330 full days during each of these two 12-month periods: January 1, 2011, to December 31, 2011, and September 1, 2011, to August 31, 2012. By overlapping the 12-month periods in this way, she meets the physical presence test for the whole 20-month period.

Housing Exclusion and Deduction A taxpayer with foreign earned income and foreign housing expenses may be able to elect to exclude or deduct a housing amount. Eligibility for the exclusion or deduction depends on whether the taxpayer is an employee or is self-employed.

- The housing exclusion applies only to amounts considered paid for with employer-provided amounts (such as wages and salary), subject to limits to be described next.
- The foreign housing deduction applies only to amounts considered paid for with self-employment earnings, subject to the limits to be described next.

"Housing" expenses for this purpose include rent, the fair rental value of housing (if provided by an employer and included in gross income), utilities (other than telephone charges), real and personal property insurance, rental of furniture and accessories, repairs, and residential parking.

Calculating the Housing Amount The housing amount is the excess of reasonable housing expenses over a base housing amount. The base housing amount is 16% of the maximum Foreign Earned Income Exclusion, computed on a daily basis for the number of days that the taxpayer meets the bona fide residence test or the physical presence test. In 2012, the base housing amount is $15,216 (16% of $95,100). If a taxpayer qualifies under the bona fide residence or physical presence test for only part of the year, the base housing amount is $41.57 for each qualifying day ($15,216 ÷ 366).

Limit on Housing Expenses Also, housing expenses generally are limited to 30% of the maximum Foreign Earned Income Exclusion for the tax year. For 2012, the maximum foreign housing expenses taken into account are $28,530 (30% of $95,100), or $77.95 for each qualifying day ($28,530 ÷ 366).

Thus, the maximum housing exclusion for most foreign locations is $13,314 ($28,530 – $15,216). However, the exclusion may be higher where the cost of living is higher; there are about 275 high-cost areas, and these designated areas change annually.

For more information about how to calculate the exclusion or deduction, see IRS Pub. 54.

Employee or Independent Contractor

It is important to distinguish an employee from a worker who is an independent contractor. The difference in classification is critical because so many aspects of taxation are affected, including reporting (Form W-2 or Form 1099-MISC, *Miscellaneous Income*), income tax withholding, FICA withholding or self-employment taxes paid by the independent contractor, and eligibility for employee benefits.

This classification is scrutinized closely by the IRS to ensure that employers properly classify workers who perform services. An employer may misclassify employees as independent contractors to avoid paying the employer portion of FICA taxes, reduce employer-paid benefits costs, or other reasons. An employer may also misclassify employees as independent contractors because the employer lacks knowledge about the factors that determine a true employer–employee relationship.

Employer Control

An "employee" is a worker who functions under the control of an employer. "Control" can mean control over the employee's activities (such as providing instructions and supervision) as well as financial control (such as reimbursement for employee business expenses, or providing the employee with the tools or equipment necessary to perform the job).

The nature of the relationship between the parties also influences whether a valid employer–employee relationship exists. Generally, if an employer controls when, where, and how the work is to be performed ("right to direct and control"), the worker is an employee. The IRS has provided guidance for making this determination, including:

- Proper Worker Classification Audio Program from IRS at www.irsvideos.gov/ProperWorkerClassification.
- Rev. Proc. 87-41 lists 20 factors, including instructions, training, supervision, and setting hours, used in making a determination about worker classification.

An employee's wages are subject to income tax withholding (both federal and state), and an employee pays one-half (the employee's share) of FICA taxes. The employer issues an employee a Form W-2, reporting wages and other benefits.

In contrast, an independent contractor operates outside the control of the party for whom the work is performed. The independent contractor is responsible for his or her own taxes. An employer who pays at least $600 to an independent contractor must report such payments on Form 1099-MISC (not Form W-2) as nonemployee compensation. The independent contractor is self-employed and therefore pays the employer and employee share of FICA (explained in Chapter 35).

If a taxpayer has been treated by a business as an independent contractor but believes that he or she should have been classified as an employee, take these actions:

- File Form SS-8, *Determination of Worker Status for Purposes of Federal Employment Taxes and Income Tax Withholding,* with the IRS to ask that the government determine the taxpayer's proper worker classification. The taxpayer can file as an independent contractor. If the IRS determines that the taxpayer is an employee, the taxpayer files an amended return to claim a refund of self-employment tax paid as an independent contractor. An amended return can be filed *only* for an open tax year (generally within three years from the date the original return was filed or within two years from the date the tax was paid, whichever is later).
- Include what has been called "nonemployee compensation" on the income tax return as wages and do not pay self-employment tax (explained in Chapter 35). The worker should also file Form 8919, *Uncollected Social Security and Medicare Tax on Wages,* to report FICA taxes due on the compensation. This can be done while a determination on a Form SS-8 is pending.

Review Questions

1. All of the following factors show that a worker is an employee rather than an independent contractor **except**:

a. The company tells the worker how to do the job.

b. The worker can profit from an assignment, depending on how the work is done.

c. The company gives the worker the tools to do the job.

d. The company decides what hours and where the worker will perform duties.

2. Cecilia receives vacation pay, sick pay, and employer-paid health coverage. She also receives a year-end bonus. Which of these payments is **not** taxable on Cecilia's 2012 return?

a. Vacation pay

b. Sick pay

c. Employer-paid health coverage

d. Year-end bonus paid on December 24, 2012

3. Ann, a server at Joe's Diner who keeps poor records of her tips, reported to Joe that she earned $375 in tips last month. Joe allocated $25 in tips to Ann. Ann reports gross income from tips of:

a. $375

b. $400

c. $350

d. $340

4. Mark is a pastor at a church where he works as an employee. The church pays for his housing with a fair rental value of $15,000. He pays for utilities and does not receive reimbursement. Which statement about this payment is correct?

a. All of the $15,000 is includible in Mark's gross income.

b. Part may be excludable, depending on his income.

c. He can exclude the cost of utilities from gross income.

d. The $15,000 is subject to self-employment tax.

5. Greg is out of work in 2012. Which of the following benefits is tax free if he receives them?

a. Severance pay

b. Unemployment benefits

c. Workers' compensation

d. Supplemental unemployment benefits received from a company-financed fund

6. Caroline becomes disabled and receives benefits under a disability insurance policy for which she paid the premiums. How are the benefits treated for tax purposes?

a. All of the benefits are taxable.

b. None of the benefits are taxable.

c. Benefits are tax free to the extent of the premiums she paid.

d. Some of the benefits are tax free, depending on her age at time of disability.

7. Fred works for a company that pays him exclusively on commission for sales of its products (insurance policies). His Form W-2 shows $78,000 earned as "Wages, tips, other compensation." He also has unreimbursed employee expenses of $2,400. Which of the following is a true statement about Fred?

a. Because Fred is a statutory employee who reports expenses on Schedule C, his Form W-2 would show no Social Security or Medicare taxes withheld.

b. Fred is a statutory employee, and because he must file Schedule C, he must also file Schedule SE to report his self-employment taxes.

c. Fred can reduce the $78,000 shown on his Form W-2 by his unreimbursed expenses, so his tax return will show $75,600 in taxable compensation.

d. Fred reports his unreimbursed employee expenses on Schedule C, and he should not file Schedule SE because Social Security and Medicare taxes were withheld from his gross earnings.

8. Jaime is in the military. Which of the following payments is **always** taxable?

a. Reenlistment bonus

b. Combat pay

c. Basic Housing Allowance

d. Uniform allowance

Interest Income

Interest is a fee charged by a lender to a borrower for the use of money. Interest may be earned from many different sources, including bank accounts, loans, bonds, and notes. For tax purposes, interest may be taxable or nontaxable.

Interest income is reported to the taxpayer (lender) on Form 1099-INT, *Interest Income*, when the amount of interest received for the year is at least $10. Interest under $10 is still taxable to the taxpayer, although it is not formally reported on Form 1099-INT. Generally, interest income is taxable unless a special rule or exemption applies, such as interest from municipal bonds.

Interest income usually is not subject to withholding. However, in certain situations, the payments may be subject to backup withholding and will be reported as such on Form 1099-INT.

There are special reporting rules for interest earned on foreign accounts or through foreign trusts. These rules are designed to ensure that such interest is reported on U.S. tax returns by those who are U.S. citizens or residents and are required to report their worldwide income.

Taxable Interest Income

Banks, savings and loans, and credit unions are just a few of the entities that pay and report annual interest payments made to taxpayers on Form 1099-INT. Taxpayers must report all interest for the year, even interest that is not taxable or when no Form 1099-INT is issued.

TIP: Taxpayers should retain Form 1099-INT with their tax records; it is *not* attached to the tax return.

Sources of Taxable Interest

Taxable interest typically is paid on bank accounts and certificates of deposit (CDs). Other sources of taxable interest are listed next.

TIP: The interest on U.S. obligations, while taxable for federal income tax purposes, is exempt from any state and local income taxes.

U.S. Obligations Interest on U.S. Treasury bills, notes, and bonds issued by any agency or instrumentality of the United States is taxable.

ALERT: Payments from money market funds offered by brokerage firms and mutual funds are generally dividends, not interest, even though the underlying instruments in the funds produce interest income (see Chapter 6).

Interest Labeled by Payers as Dividends Certain payments labeled as dividends are actually interest and are reported as such. These payments include dividends from cooperative banks, credit unions, domestic savings/buildings and loan associations, federal savings and loans associations, and mutual savings banks.

Interest on Life Insurance Dividends and Prepaid Premiums Interest may accrue on policy dividends that are left to accumulate with an insurance company. Similarly, prepaid premiums may accrue interest before the premiums are applied to the cost of the policy. In either case, the interest is taxable whether paid to the taxpayer (policyholder) or not.

Interest on Federal and State Tax Refunds and Legal Settlements Funds owed to the taxpayer that have not been paid may accrue interest for the taxpayer. These funds include interest that accrues on refunds of tax payments that have not been made in a timely way by a taxing authority or interest deemed to have accrued on funds that are paid after a legal settlement or court award.

Example

In June 2012, Simon receives a settlement for a car accident in which he sustained serious physical injuries. The settlement was $1.2 million for physical injuries and 10,000 in interest. While the amount for physical injuries is tax free (see Chapter 10), the 10,000 interest is taxable.

Gift for Opening Account Any gift valued at more than $10 that is given for opening a bank account or other deposit of less than $5,000 in a savings institution (more than $20 for deposits of $5,000 or more) is treated as taxable interest.

Example

Eric opens a savings account at the local bank, deposits $4,000, and receives a $15 toaster. The account earns $40 in interest for the year. Eric's Form 1099-INT reports interest of $55 ($40 interest on the account plus the $15 toaster).

Bonds Traded Flat When bonds are purchased at a discount because the issuer has not paid accrued interest on them, the bonds are said to be *traded flat*. In this situation, the unpaid interest is not taxable as interest income if paid at a later time. Instead, it is treated as a return of capital and reduces the basis of the bond. However, any interest that accrues *after* the bond has been purchased is treated as taxable interest income.

Interest on Below-Market Loans If a taxpayer makes a loan at a rate below the IRS-set applicable federal rate (AFR), the interest that should have been charged but was not charged is taxable to the taxpayer (lender) as interest income (*imputed* interest). However, the interest is not taxable if the loan is a gift loan not more than $10,000 (or a gift loan not more than $100,000 and the borrower's net investment income is not more than $1,000).

Example

In July 2012, a mother lends her son $60,000 to make a down payment on his house. She expects him to pay her back over 10 years but does not charge him any interest. Assume the AFR for this loan is 3.8%. Ordinarily, under the below-market loan rules, she would have to report interest of $2,280 ($60,000 × 3.8%). However, the loan qualifies under the $100,000 gift loan exception if the son's net investment income does not exceed $1,000. Thus, no interest income would be imputed to the mother.

When to Report Interest

Interest generally is reported in the year it is actually or constructively received (meaning the taxpayer has the right to the interest regardless of whether the taxpayer has taken possession of the interest or not).

The interest on a savings account is reportable in the year it is credited. In the case of interest on CDs or deferred interest accounts of one year or less, interest generally is includible in income when actually or constructively received. If the term is more than one year, interest is reportable according to original issue discount (OID) rules discussed later in this chapter.

Example

Alice has a six-month CD that she took out in August 2011 and held to its maturity date. In February 2012, she received her original cash deposit and the accrued interest. Alice reports no interest in 2011 because the term of the CD was less than one year. All of the interest on the CD is reported in 2012.

There may be an interest penalty if the taxpayer withdraws funds from a savings deposit before maturity. *All* of the interest is reported as income. However, any penalty for the early withdrawal is deductible as an adjustment to gross income.

Frozen Bank Accounts Typically a bank account is frozen when the financial institution is bankrupt or insolvent or when the state where the institution is located has placed limits on withdrawals because other institutions in that state are bankrupt or insolvent.

Interest on a frozen deposit that cannot be withdrawn is *not* includible in income. It is included in income in the year in which it can be withdrawn.

Example

Carlos had interest of $100 credited to a frozen bank deposit in 2011; he was able to withdraw $80 by the end of the year. For 2011, $80 is reported as interest income. In 2012, he can withdraw the remaining $20 in interest, so he includes it in income in 2012.

Original Issue Discount

What Is OID?

Original issue discount (OID) is interest that accrues over the life of a debt instrument and is taxable as it accrues, even if not currently paid to the taxpayer. A debt instrument has OID when it is issued at a price below its redemption price at maturity. OID, which begins when the debt instrument is issued, is the difference between the issue price and redemption price. All instruments (other than short-term obligations that have a term of one year or less) that pay no interest out before maturity are presumed to have OID.

Example

Linda buys a zero coupon bond issued at $940. It matures in ten years to $1,000, with no interest payable currently. OID is $60 ($1,000 – $940). The $60 OID would be included in income as it accrues over the ten years and be reported to the taxpayer on Form 1099-OID (Figure 5.1).

If debt instruments are co-owned, nominee reporting rules that apply to jointly owned bank accounts apply to OID.

De Minimis OID If OID is de minimis (minimal), the discount can be treated as zero. De minimis OID is a discount of less than $\frac{1}{4}$ of 1% (0.0025) of the stated redemption price at maturity, multiplied by the number of years to maturity.

Continuing the Previous Example

For the discount to be considered de minimis, it would have to be less than $25 (.0025 × $1,000 redemption price × 10 years to maturity). If Linda (in the previous example) purchased the bond for $980 (OID of $20), she would not need to report the OID over the life of the bond because it would be de minimis.

☐ CORRECTED (if checked)

PAYER'S name, street address, city, state, ZIP code, and telephone no.

1 Original issue discount for 2012* $

2 Other periodic interest $

OMB No. 1545-0117

2012

Form 1099-OID

Original Issue Discount

PAYER'S federal identification number

RECIPIENT'S identification number

3 Early withdrawal penalty $

4 Federal income tax withheld $

Copy B For Recipient

RECIPIENT'S name

5 Description

Street address (including apt. no.)

6 Original issue discount on U.S. Treasury obligations* $

City, state, and ZIP code

7 Investment expenses $

* This may not be the correct figure to report on your income tax return. See instructions on the back.

Account number (see instructions)

8 State

9 State identification no.

10 State tax withheld $

This is important tax information and is being furnished to the Internal Revenue Service. If you are required to file a return, a negligence penalty or other sanction may be imposed on you if this income is taxable and the IRS determines that it has not been reported.

Form **1099-OID** (keep for your records) Department of the Treasury - Internal Revenue Service

FIGURE 5.1 Form 1099-OID

OID is reported to the taxpayer on Form 1099-OID, *Original Issue Discount*, if OID is $10 or more. However, even if no form is issued, OID is still taxable unless one of the exceptions apply. OID reporting rules do *not* apply to these debt instruments:

- Tax-exempt obligations
- U.S. savings bonds
- Short-term debt instruments (term of one year or less)
- Loans between individuals where the lender is not in the business of making loans, the amount outstanding is $10,000 or less, and no tax avoidance is intended

Taxable Bond Interest

What Is a Bond?

Bonds are a type of loan—the bond owner lends money to the issuer and receives interest in return. Interest on corporate bonds and federal bonds usually is taxable. Interest on state and local (municipal) bonds usually is not taxable.

TIP: The interest on U.S. savings bonds is exempt from state and local income taxes.

Bonds Sold between Interest Dates

Most bonds pay interest semiannually. For example, a $10,000 bond at a 5% coupon rate pays $250 twice per year ($10,000 × 5% = $500 per year, and $250 every six months). However, if a taxpayer sells a bond between scheduled interest payment dates, part of the sales price represents interest accrued to the date of sale and is taxable to the seller in the year of the sale. Interest that accrues after the date of sale is taxable to the buyer.

TIP: The rules for EE bonds also apply to Series E bonds. The last year Series E bonds were issued was 1980, the same year in which Series EE bonds were first offered. Taxpayers who did not elect to report interest ratably over the life of the bond on a Series EE bond issued in 1982 must report the entire amount of accrued interest on their 2012 tax return.

U.S. Savings Bonds

Interest on savings bonds generally is taxable for federal income tax purposes.

Series EE and I Bonds For cash-basis taxpayers, the face value and accrued interest on Series EE and I bonds is payable to the taxpayer when the bonds are redeemed at the maturity date. Both Series EE and I bonds have a maturity date of 30 years. The taxpayer must report the accrued interest either when the bond matures or when the bond is redeemed, whichever comes first.

However, a taxpayer can elect to report the interest over the life of the bond as it accrues annually. The election applies to all bonds owned by the taxpayer. If the election is not made, no interest is reported until the bonds mature (or are redeemed, if earlier).

ALERT: At the time of the exchange for the HH bonds, the taxpayer could have elected to treat all previously accrued interest on the EE or E bonds as income in the year of exchange and would be required to report interest income from the HH bonds ratably over the life of the new bonds.

Example

Steven received a $100 Series EE bond as a gift when he was born in 1985. (This bond is sold at a 50% discount to face value, or $50.) His parents did not elect to report the increase in the redemption value each year as interest. Thus, if Steven holds the bond until maturity in 2015 and then redeems it, all of the proceeds received in excess of $50 are treated as taxable interest at that time.

Series HH Bonds Series HH bonds were issued as a way to continue deferral of interest on Series E and EE bonds. Instead of redeeming Series E and EE bonds at their maturity date, a taxpayer could exchange them for HH bonds, allowing him or her to continue deferring the interest until the Series HH bond matured.

When the series HH bonds are redeemed, taxpayers report as interest income the difference between the redemption value (face value and accrued interest) of the Series HH bond and the cost of the Series EE or E bonds.

For Series HH bonds that were purchased (and not acquired through an exchange of Series E or EE bonds), interest is paid semiannually and cannot be deferred. The last HH bonds were sold in August 2004 with a 20-year maturity, so some taxpayers still may have semiannual interest income to report.

Education Redemptions Interest on qualified U.S. savings bonds that would otherwise be taxable can qualify for an exclusion if the proceeds are used to pay for certain education expenses.

These qualified bonds must be:

- Series EE or I bonds issued after 1989.
- Acquired by the bondholder (or bondholder's spouse), each of whom was at least 24 years old before the bond was issued. *Note:* A bond purchased by a parent and issued in the name of his or her child who is under age 24 does not qualify for the exclusion by either the parent or child.

Other qualifications for tax-free treatment include:

- Redemption must be to pay for qualified higher education costs for the bondholder, spouse, or dependent for whom an exemption is claimed.
- The proceeds are used to pay for tuition and fees that are required by an eligible educational institution. This includes only colleges and universities that are eligible to participate in the Department of Education student aid programs.
- Married couples must file jointly.
- Taxpayer's modified adjusted gross income (MAGI) cannot exceed a limit. For 2012, the MAGI limit for a full exclusion is $72,850 for single filers and heads of household and $109,250 for joint filers or qualifying widow(ers). A partial interest exclusion applies for single filers and heads of household with MAGI between $72,850 and $87,850. For taxpayers filing jointly or qualified widow(ers), the phase-out range is between $109,250 and $139,250. If MAGI exceeds these limits, no exclusion can be claimed.

TIP: The exclusion is claimed on Form 8815, *Exclusion From Series EE and I Savings Bonds Issued After 1989*, in the year the bonds are redeemed. If the exclusion is claimed, the taxpayer must keep a written record of the qualified higher education expenses paid and the bonds redeemed, including each bond's serial number, issue date, face value, and redemption value. Form 8818, *Optional Form to Record Redemption of Series EE and I U.S. Savings Bonds Issued After 1989*, can be used to record this information, although the form is not filed with the return; it is retained in the taxpayer's records.

ALERT: Qualified expenses must be reduced by tax-free scholarships, fellowships, expenses used in figuring education credits, or any other tax-free programs (e.g., veterans' educational assistance benefits, employer-paid assistance). Qualified expenses also must be reduced by any tax-free distributions from a qualified tuition program or Coverdell education savings account.

Example

In 2012, a married couple cash in Series EE bonds and receive proceeds of $8,124, consisting of $5,000 in principal (cost) and $3,124 of interest. They paid their child's college tuition of $4,000 and do not claim any education credit. The child does not receive any financial assistance. Assuming the bonds are qualified and the couple's MAGI is $100,000, the interest that can be excluded is $1,538 ($3,124 × [$4,000 ÷ $8,124]). The remaining balance of the interest, $1,586 ($3,124 – $1,538), is taxable.

If the couple's MAGI was between $109,250 and $139,250, they would be entitled to a reduced deduction, as figured on Form 8815. If their MAGI exceeded $139,250, no exclusion would be allowed, and all of the interest income would be taxable.

ALERT: Even though the interest on state and municipal bonds is not taxable, it must be reported on the tax return. Taxable interest is reported on line 8a while tax-exempt interest is reported on line 8b of Form 1040 (see Figure 5.2). In addition, tax-exempt interest may affect the taxation of Social Security benefits (see Chapter 9).

Treasury Inflation-Protection Securities (TIPS)

TIPS are securities that pay interest twice a year at a fixed rate as well as adjust the principal amount for inflation. The interest earned as well as the increase of the principal value is taxable currently even though the taxpayer does not receive the adjusted principal value until the bond's maturity.

State and Municipal Bonds

Interest paid by state and local governments or agencies on their bonds or other instruments is not taxable for federal income tax purposes.

TIP: The interest on state and local government obligations may be taxable or tax free for state and local income tax purposes if the obligations are issued by that state. Rules vary by state.

Interest on certain private activity bonds, such as qualified student loan bonds, exempt facility bonds (e.g., New York Liberty bonds, Gulf Zone bonds, midwestern disaster and Hurricane Ike bonds), and qualified mortgage bonds, are tax free. Interest on other private activity bonds, such as those used to build athletic stadiums, is not taxable for income tax purposes but is an adjustment to income for purposes of the alternative minimum tax (AMT; see Chapter 33 for more information about the tax). However, there is no adjustment to the AMT for interest on private activity bonds issued before August 8, 1986, and on bonds issued in 2009 and 2010.

ALERT: Form 1040EZ, *Income Tax Return for Single and Joint Filers With No Dependents*, cannot be used if taxable interest is more than $1,500.

Reporting Interest on the Return

Interest of $10 or more annually is reported to taxpayers on Form 1099-INT, as shown in Figure 5.3.

Interest is reported on line 8a of Form 1040. However, if interest is more than $1,500, a taxpayer must first enter the interest on Schedule B of Form 1040 (or Form 1040A) and then enter the total on line 8a.

Income	7	Wages, salaries, tips, etc. Attach Form(s) W-2		7	
	8a	**Taxable** interest. Attach Schedule B if required		8a	
	b	**Tax-exempt** interest. **Do not** include on line 8a	8b		
Attach Form(s) W-2 here. Also attach Forms W-2G and	9a	Ordinary dividends. Attach Schedule B if required		9a	
	b	Qualified dividends	9b		
	10	Taxable refunds, credits, or offsets of state and local income taxes		10	

FIGURE 5.2 Form 1040—Taxable and Tax-Exempt Interest (lines 8a and 8b)

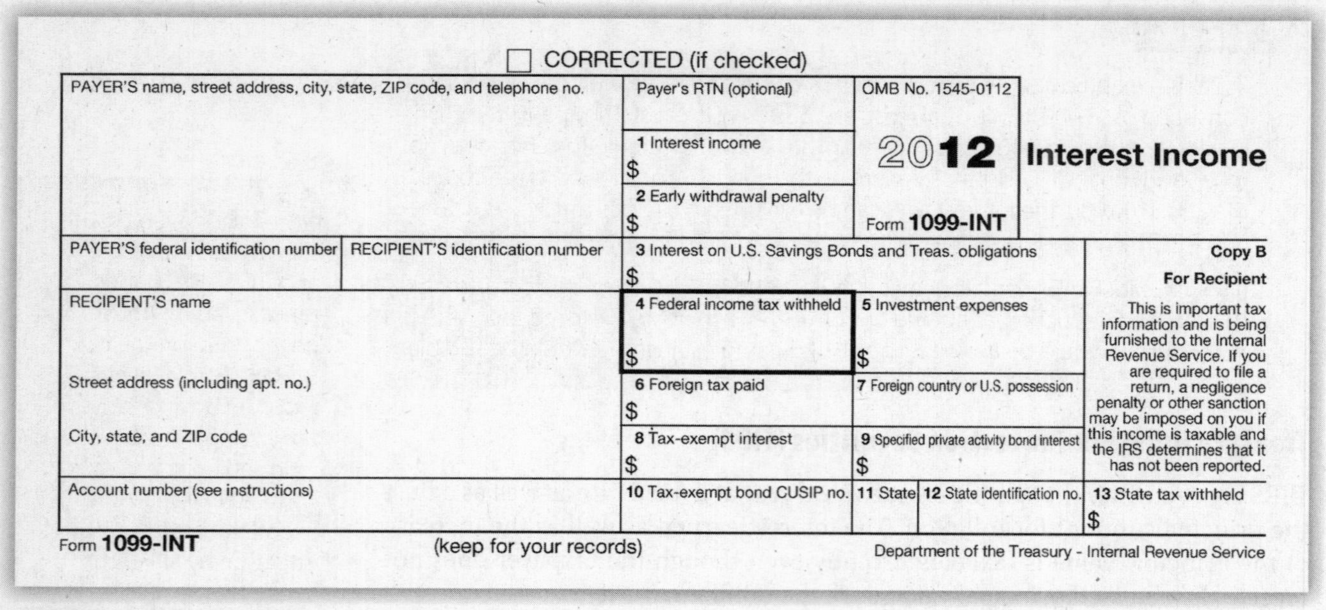

☐ CORRECTED (if checked)

PAYER'S name, street address, city, state, ZIP code, and telephone no.	Payer's RTN (optional)	OMB No. 1545-0112	
	1 Interest income $	2012	Interest Income
	2 Early withdrawal penalty $	Form 1099-INT	
PAYER'S federal identification number / RECIPIENT'S identification number	3 Interest on U.S. Savings Bonds and Treas. obligations $		Copy B For Recipient
RECIPIENT'S name	4 Federal income tax withheld $	5 Investment expenses $	This is important tax information and is being furnished to the Internal Revenue Service. If you are required to file a return, a negligence penalty or other sanction may be imposed on you if this income is taxable and the IRS determines that it has not been reported.
Street address (including apt. no.)	6 Foreign tax paid $	7 Foreign country or U.S. possession	
City, state, and ZIP code	8 Tax-exempt interest $	9 Specified private activity bond interest $	
Account number (see instructions)	10 Tax-exempt bond CUSIP no.	11 State / 12 State identification no.	13 State tax withheld $

Form 1099-INT (keep for your records) Department of the Treasury - Internal Revenue Service

FIGURE 5.3 Form 1099-INT

> **DEFINITION:** A **nominee** is a person who receives interest that partially or fully belongs to another owner. This typically occurs when two or more people co-own a bank account. All of the interest is paid to the individual whose SSN appears on the account even though the individual does not own the entire account.

> **TIP:** The *total* interest on savings bonds is reported to taxpayers on Form 1099-INT. If an exclusion applies, the total interest must still be reported by the taxpayer on Schedule B of Form 1040 (see Figure 5.4) even though the total amount may not be taxable. The excludable interest (line 3 of Schedule B) is subtracted from the total interest (line 2 of Schedule B), to arrive at the taxable interest (line 4 of Schedule B).

Joint Accounts When two or more people own a bank account, bond, or other property paying interest, each person's share of interest from the property is determined by local law. The way the property is titled—as joint tenants, tenants by the entirety, or tenants in common—can affect taxation.

Nominees When co-owners of an interest-bearing account are not spouses, the interest is reported to the person whose name and Social Security Number (SSN) was listed on Form W-9, *Request for Taxpayer Identification Number and Certification*, when the account was opened. This does not change who is actually taxable on the interest. The person receiving this type of Form 1099-INT is called a **nominee.**

The nominee should complete a Form 1099-INT to report the co-owner's share of interest; a Form 1096 transmittal should be sent to the IRS.

Example

Sisters Janice and Joyce are equal co-owners of a CD that paid interest in 2012 of $1,200. The bank reported all of the interest to Janice because her name and SSN were furnished to the bank on Form W-9 when the CD was obtained. Janice should give Joyce a Form 1099-INT reporting interest of $600, Joyce's share. Janice should also file a copy of Form 1099-INT and Form 1096, *Transmittal Form*, with the IRS. Each sister should report $600 on her tax return.

Custodial Accounts for Children Cash and other property given to a child under the Uniform Gifts to Minors Act, the Model Gifts of Securities to Minors Act, or other similar law becomes the property of the child. Income from the property is taxable to the child, even though there is a custodian managing the funds for the benefit of the child. The same is true of savings accounts with the parent or other person acting as trustee.

Backup Withholding

Backup withholding is a way for the government to ensure that taxes are paid on income. Backup withholding on interest income functions like withholding on wages. Withholding on interest is a flat 28% of the amount paid. The amount of interest for the year, along with backup withholding (referred to as federal income tax withheld), is reported to the taxpayer on Form 1099-INT.

Backup withholding is required only in certain situations:

- The taxpayer does not provide the payer a tax identification number (TIN) in the required manner or furnishes an obviously incorrect TIN (one with fewer than 9 numbers or one containing letters).
- The IRS or broker notifies the payer that the TIN given by the taxpayer is incorrect.
- The taxpayer is required, but fails, to certify that he or she is not subject to backup withholding.
- The IRS notifies the payer to start withholding on interest or dividends because the taxpayer has underreported interest or dividends on an income tax return.

ALERT: Depending on the amount of interest and other income, a tax return may have to be filed for the child. Alternatively, a parent may be able to report the child's investment income on his or her return, eliminating the need to file a return for the child. See Chapter 34 for more information on reporting the child's investment income on the parent's return.

SCHEDULE B (Form 1040A or 1040)
Department of the Treasury Internal Revenue Service (99)

Interest and Ordinary Dividends

► Attach to Form 1040A or 1040.
► Information about Schedule B (Form 1040A or 1040) and its instructions is at *www.irs.gov/form1040*.

OMB No. 1545-0074
2012
Attachment Sequence No. 08

Name(s) shown on return | Your social security number

Part I Interest

(See instructions on back and the instructions for Form 1040A, or Form 1040, line 8a.)

Note. If you received a Form 1099-INT, Form 1099-OID, or substitute statement from a brokerage firm, list the firm's name as the payer and enter the total interest shown on that form.

			Amount
1	List name of payer. If any interest is from a seller-financed mortgage and the buyer used the property as a personal residence, see instructions on back and list this interest first. Also, show that buyer's social security number and address ►	1	
2	Add the amounts on line 1	2	
3	Excludable interest on series EE and I U.S. savings bonds issued after 1989. Attach Form 8815	3	
4	Subtract line 3 from line 2. Enter the result here and on Form 1040A, or Form 1040, line 8a . . . . ►	4	

Note. If line 4 is over $1,500, you must complete Part III. | Amount

FIGURE 5.4 Schedule B Part 1

ALERT: A taxpayer cannot choose to have withholding taken on interest income. Where interest income is substantial, estimated taxes may be necessary to avoid tax underpayments.

Foreign Account Reporting

Interest on foreign bank accounts generally is taxable similar to the rules discussed above on domestic accounts. However, because foreign financial institutions may not be subject to the same reporting requirements as domestic financial institutions, a taxpayer with a foreign bank account is subject to special reporting rules. Reporting to the IRS is required for specified foreign financial assets. Reporting to the Treasury is required for foreign bank accounts. Both types of reporting may be required with respect to the same accounts or assets.

TIP: The federal income tax withheld and shown on Form 1099-INT is reported as a tax payment on Form 1040.

Foreign Taxes

If interest on a foreign account has been taxed in a foreign country, a taxpayer is eligible to claim either a deduction for foreign taxes or a foreign tax credit.

Information Reporting

A taxpayer with an interest in a foreign bank account is required to notify the IRS. Taxpayers may need to complete Part III of Schedule B, Form 1040 (see Figure 5.5) if any of the following apply:

- Taxpayer received over $1,500 of taxable interest or ordinary dividends.
- Taxpayer owned or had an interest in a foreign account, or had signature authority over such an account.
- Taxpayer received a distribution from, or was a grantor of, or a transferor to, a foreign trust.

ALERT: The IRS is on the hunt for taxpayers who fail to report their holdings in foreign accounts. The IRS's Large Business and International (LB&I) Division has specially trained agents just for this purpose. The IRS has the right to seek information from third-party sources, such as foreign banks, if the IRS has reason to believe that taxpayers are underreporting their income.

Foreign Bank Account Reporting (FBAR) If the taxpayer at any time during 2012 had an interest in or a signature or other authority over a financial account in a foreign country, such as a bank account, securities account, or other financial account, the taxpayer must answer "yes" to Question 1 on line 7a of Schedule B. Question 2 on line 7a asks the taxpayer whether he or she is required to report the financial interest or signature authority by filing Form

			Yes	No
Part III Foreign Accounts and Trusts (See instructions on back.)		You must complete this part if you **(a)** had over $1,500 of taxable interest or ordinary dividends; **(b)** had a foreign account; or **(c)** received a distribution from, or were a grantor of, or a transferor to, a foreign trust.		
	7a	At any time during 2012, did you have a financial interest in or signature authority over a financial account (such as a bank account, securities account, or brokerage account) located in a foreign country? See instructions		
		If "Yes," are you required to file Form TD F 90-22.1 to report that financial interest or signature authority? See Form TD F 90-22.1 and its instructions for filing requirements and exceptions to those requirements		
	b	If you are required to file Form TD F 90-22.1, enter the name of the foreign country where the financial account is located ▶		
	8	During 2012, did you receive a distribution from, or were you the grantor of, or transferor to, a foreign trust? If "Yes," you may have to file Form 3520. See instructions on back		

For Paperwork Reduction Act Notice, see your tax return instructions. Cat. No. 17146N **Schedule B (Form 1040A or 1040) 2012**

FIGURE 5.5 Schedule B, Part III

TD F 90-22.1, *Report of Foreign Bank and Financial Accounts*. If the taxpayer is required to file Form TD F 90-221, the name of the foreign country must be reported on line 7b.

Even if there was an interest or signature authority over a foreign account, the taxpayer does not have to report it on Form TD F 90-22.1 if any of the following applies:

ALERT: There are substantial civil and/or criminal penalties for not reporting foreign bank accounts.

- The combined value of the accounts was not more than $10,000 during any part of the year.
- The accounts were with a U.S. military banking facility operated by a U.S. financial institution.
- The taxpayer was an officer or employee of a commercial bank that is supervised by the Comptroller of the Currency, the Board of Governors of the Federal Reserve System, or the Federal Deposit Insurance Corporation; the account was in the taxpayer's employer's name; and the taxpayer did not have a personal financial interest in the account.
- The taxpayer was an officer or employee of a domestic corporation with securities listed on any United States national securities exchange.

TIP: Records related to Form TD F 90-22.1 must be retained for a minimum of five years from June 30 of the year following the calendar year reported and must be available for inspection as provided by law.

See the instructions to Form TD F 90-22.1 for other exceptions.

If a taxpayer checks "yes" in box 7a, then Form TD F 90-22.1 must be filed. This form is not filed with a taxpayer's income tax return and is *not* filed with the IRS. Instead, it is filed separately with the Department of the Treasury.

Form TD F 90-22.1 must be *received* by June 30 of the following year (e.g., June 30, 2013, for 2012 accounts). No extension can be obtained.

Also in Part III of Schedule B, Form 1040, a taxpayer must disclose whether he or she received a distribution from, or was the grantor of, or transferor to, a foreign trust. If the taxpayer checks "yes," Form 3520, *Annual Return to Report Transactions with Foreign Trusts and Receipt of Certain Foreign Gifts*, or Form 3520-A, *Annual Information Return of Foreign Trust with a U.S. Owner*, may need to be filed. Neither form is to be attached to Form 1040. They must be filed separately.

Statement of Specified Foreign Financial Assets Individuals who have an interest in specified foreign financial assets (SFFAs) may be required to file Form 8938, *Statement of Specified Foreign Financial Assets*, with Form 1040. An SFFA includes a financial account held with a foreign financial institution or other assets held for investment that are not at a foreign financial institution, such as stock or securities issued by someone other than a U.S. person or an interest in a foreign entity.

ALERT: There are substantial civil and/or criminal penalties for not reporting SFFAs.

Reporting is required if the value of the SFFAs on the last day of the year exceed $50,000 or at any time during the year exceed $75,000. Higher dollar limits apply for married taxpayers filing joint returns and for certain individuals living abroad. Asset value must be reported in U.S. dollars. See the instructions for Form 8938 for more information.

Review Questions

1. Joann lives in Florida and receives the following payments. Which of these payments is **not** reported as taxable interest on her federal tax return?
   a. Interest on a savings account of $8 that is not reported on Form 1099-INT
   b. Dividends from a savings and loan association
   c. Interest on a U.S. Treasury bond
   d. Interest on a California state bond

2. Olga had interest of $200 credited to a frozen bank deposit in 2012; she was able to withdraw $180 by the end of the year. For 2012, $180 is reported as interest income. In 2013, Olga is able to withdraw the remaining $20 in interest. How much interest is included in Olga's income in 2013?
   a. $0
   b. $20
   c. $180
   d. $200

3. A taxpayer has a bank account in the Cayman Islands. Assuming this is the taxpayer's only foreign account, which is the correct threshold for FBAR reporting the account to the Treasury?
   a. More than $1,500 interest income
   b. More than $1,500 account value
   c. More than $10,000 interest income
   d. More than $10,000 account value

4. Gil was subject to backup withholding on his interest income of $1,000. The withholding was $280. Backup withholding on interest means that Gil:
   a. Can opt to have taxes withheld
   b. Can claim a credit for taxes withheld
   c. Is subject to an additional tax (penalty)
   d. Reports interest income of $720 on the return

5. A grandmother gives her grandchild a $10,000 gift that is used to open a custodial account under the Model Gifts of Securities to Minors Act. The grandchild's father acts as custodian/trustee of the account. Interest on the account for 2012 is $200. Who reports the interest?
   a. Grandmother
   b. Father
   c. Grandchild
   d. No one because income under this type of account is tax free

6. In 1995, Lidia, age 30, purchased a Series EE bond for $1,000. In 2012, she redeemed it and used all of the proceeds to pay for qualified education expenses of her daughter, who is her dependent. On redemption, she received $1,450, $975 of which is principal and $475 of which is interest. If Lidia's modified adjusted gross income in 2012 is $90,000, how much, if any, of the interest is excludable? (Assume Lidia is a single mother filing as head of household.)
   a. $0
   b. $475
   c. $975
   d. $1,000

Dividends and Other Corporate Distributions

A taxpayer who owns stock in a corporation may receive cash distributions from the corporation, whether it is publicly traded or privately held. Mutual funds that hold corporate stock may distribute to their shareholders dividends received on corporate stock held by the mutual funds. Generally, dividend payments to a shareholder in annual amounts of at least $10 are reported on Form 1099-DIV, *Dividends* (see Figure 6.1). Taxpayers must report all dividends received during the year, even if they did not receive a dividend form.

Although cash dividends are taxable, certain types of dividends may offer favorable tax treatment. For example, "qualified" dividends and dividends that are distributions of capital gains entitle the shareholder recipient to favorable tax treatment on those dividends.

ALERT: In the case of preferred stock, the holding period is more than *90 days* during the *181-day* period that begins 90 days before the ex-dividend date.

Ordinary versus Qualified Dividends

Qualified Dividends

Dividends that are "qualified" enjoy special tax treatment. Instead of being subject to ordinary tax rates, they are taxed at a top rate of 15% (0% to the extent the taxpayer's qualified dividends would have been in the 10% or 15% tax bracket if treated as ordinary income). Qualified dividends are those paid by a U.S. corporation or a qualified foreign corporation (see IRS Pub. 550, *Investment Income and Expenses*, for details).

In addition, the taxpayer must meet a special holding period for the dividends to be qualified dividends. The taxpayer must have owned the stock for more than 60 days during the 121-day period that begins 60 days before the ex-dividend date. (The *ex-dividend date* is the first date after the date that a buyer of the stock is *not* entitled to a dividend.) The holding period includes the date the stock was sold but not the date it was acquired.

ALERT: The corporation or mutual fund company paying the dividend makes the initial determination of whether a dividend is qualified and reports it in box 1b of Form 1099-DIV (see Figure 6.1). However, the payer does not know whether taxpayers' holding periods allow them to treat the dividends as qualified. Therefore, ultimately taxpayers must determine whether they can treat the dividend as qualified based on their holding period.

☐ CORRECTED (if checked)

PAYER'S name, street address, city, state, ZIP code, and telephone no.		1a Total ordinary dividends $	OMB No. 1545-0110 2012	Dividends and Distributions
		1b Qualified dividends $	Form 1099-DIV	
		2a Total capital gain distr. $	2b Unrecap. Sec. 1250 gain $	Copy B For Recipient
PAYER'S federal identification number	RECIPIENT'S identification number	2c Section 1202 gain $	2d Collectibles (28%) gain $	
RECIPIENT'S name		3 Nondividend distributions $	4 Federal income tax withheld $	This is important tax information and is being furnished to the Internal Revenue Service. If you are required to file a return, a negligence penalty or other sanction may be imposed on you if this income is taxable and the IRS determines that it has not been reported.
			5 Investment expenses $	
Street address (including apt. no.)		6 Foreign tax paid $	7 Foreign country or U.S. possession	
City, state, and ZIP code		8 Cash liquidation distributions $	9 Noncash liquidation distributions $	
Account number (see instructions)		10 Exempt-interest dividends $	11 Specified private activity bond interest dividends $	
		12 State / 13 State identification no.	14 State tax withheld $	

Form 1099-DIV (keep for your records) Department of the Treasury - Internal Revenue Service

FIGURE 6.1 Form 1099-DIV

Example

Gabriel bought 1,000 shares of Android Inc. stock on July 8, 2012, with an ex-dividend date of July 16, 2012. He sold the shares on August 11, 2012. Even though the Form 1099-DIV for the dividends he received showed that they were qualified dividends, he held the stock for only 34 days and therefore cannot treat the dividends as qualified. (Instead, the dividends will be taxed as ordinary income.)

Had Gabriel held the stock for more than 60 days between May 17 and September 14 (60 days before and after July 17, the date the stock went ex-dividend), he would have been able to treat the dividends as qualified.

Example

Same facts as the previous example except that Gabriel sold the shares on September 6, 2012. In this case, he may treat the dividends as qualified dividends because he held the stock for more than 60 days within the 121-day period.

TIP: Brokerage firms are now required to report basis to shareholders for shares of stock purchased on or after January 1, 2011. Similarly, the basis of stock in a mutual fund or stock acquired through a dividend reinvestment plan on or after January 1, 2012 must also be reported.

Nonqualified Dividends

Certain dividends cannot be treated as qualified dividends (even if listed in box 1b of Form 1099-DIV; see Figure 6.1). These include capital gain distributions, dividends paid on deposits in savings banks and similar institutions, and payments in lieu of dividends that the taxpayer knows are not qualified dividends.

Dividend Reinvestments

Many corporations and mutual funds have dividend reinvestment plans that allow shareholders to use dividends to purchase additional shares. Even though the shareholder may not receive a dividend check, the dividend is taxable as if received. Thus, the dividend reinvestment is treated as if the shareholder received the dividend and then immediately purchased additional shares. If the plan deducted a service charge from the reinvestment, taxpayers must include this service charge in their dividend income. (The service charge may be deductible, as explained in Chapter 25.)

ALERT: Distributions from money market funds are dividends, even though the underlying investments in the funds may produce interest income.

Reinvested dividends add to the basis of the shares held by the taxpayer because they have been taxed. By adding them to basis, capital gain is reduced or capital loss is increased when the shares are eventually sold or exchanged. If the dividend reinvestment plan allows cash investments to buy shares at a price less than fair market value, dividend income results. The income is the difference between the cash invested and the fair market value of the stock purchased with the cash.

Capital Gain Distributions

Capital gain distributions are amounts paid from a mutual fund or a real estate investment trust (REIT) and are reported in box 2a of Form 1099-DIV (see Figure 6.1). These distributions are reported as long-term capital gains, not as dividends. Moreover, these capital gain distributions are classified as long-term gains regardless of how long the taxpayer held the shares in the mutual fund or REIT.

TIP: Capital gain distributions enjoy the same favorable tax treatment as qualified dividends: The maximum tax rate is 15%, and taxpayers pay 0% to the extent the taxpayer's capital gains income would have been in the 10% or 15% tax bracket if treated as ordinary income).

Undistributed Capital Gains of Mutual Funds and REITs

If the funds or REITs earned the capital gains but held onto them rather than distributing them to shareholders, they are still taxable to shareholders as long-term capital gains (not as dividends).

The difference between the long-term capital gain reported on the tax return and a tax credit claimed for taxes paid by the mutual fund or REIT on these amounts *increases* the shareholder's basis in the stock.

ALERT: Undistributed capital gains are not reported on Form 1099-DIV. Instead, they are reported on Form 2439, *Notice to Shareholder of Undistributed Long-Term Capital Gains*.

Nondividend Distributions

Corporations that do not have earnings and profits, either currently or accumulated from prior years, still may make distributions to shareholders. However, these distributions are nondividend distributions. They are reported to shareholders in box 3 of Form 1099-DIV (see Figure 6.1) and usually are not taxable. A nondividend distribution is a return of the shareholder's capital and therefore reduces the shareholder's basis in the stock invested.

TIP: Any tax paid by the mutual fund or REIT on these undistributed amounts entitles the taxpayer to claim a tax credit. Box 2 of Form 2439 shows the taxes paid by the mutual fund or REIT.

Once the basis has been reduced to zero, any additional distributions are taxed as long-term or short-term capital gains, depending on the shareholder's holding period.

ALERT: If a shareholder does not receive a Form 1099-DIV reporting a nondividend distribution, the amount received is reported as ordinary income rather than as a reduction in basis (or capital gain).

Example

Several years ago, Sherry bought 100 shares in the XYZ Corporation that pays her a nondividend distribution in 2012. Her basis in the stock (what she paid for it) is $1,000 before any distribution in 2012. The 2012 distribution is $400, as reported on Form 1099-DIV. She does not include the $400 in income; instead, she reduces her stock basis to $600 ($1,000 – $400). In 2013, she receives a nondividend distribution of $700. She reduces her basis to zero and reports $100 as long-term capital gain.

Other Distributions

In addition to ordinary dividends, capital gain distributions, and nondividend distributions, corporations may pay their shareholders other amounts. These other types of distributions have different tax treatments.

Liquidating Distributions

When a corporation partially or completely liquidates (sells off its assets, winds up business, and closes its doors), distributions called *liquidating distributions* may be made to shareholders. Usually at least some part of the distributions is a return of capital. Liquidating distributions are reported to shareholders in box 8 or 9 of Form 1099-DIV (see Figure 6.1).

Distributions of Stock and Stock Rights

Dividends paid in stock rather than in cash generally are not taxable. Distributions of rights to acquire stock (stock options) usually are not taxable and are not reported on the tax return.

However, as listed next, some stock dividends and stock rights are taxable:

- When a shareholder can choose to receive cash or other property instead of stock or stock rights
- A distribution that gives some shareholders cash or other property while increasing the ownership percentage for other shareholders
- A distribution of convertible preferred stock that has the same result as the bullet immediately above
- A distribution of preferred stock to some common stock shareholders and common stock to other common stock shareholders
- Generally, a distribution on preferred stock

TIP: The basis in stock or stock rights received in a taxable distribution is the fair market value of the stock or stock rights. The basis in stock or stock rights that are not taxable is more complicated (see Chapter 12 for more information).

Stock distributions also may be made in fractional shares (a percentage that is less than a full share of stock).

Stock splits are not taxable as dividends or otherwise. Stock splits change the total number of shares that the taxpayer owns but do not change the value of shareholder's interest in the corporation.

Example

Joan owns 100 shares of stock in which she has basis of $6,000 (basis of $60 per share). If the corporation splits its stock 2 for 1, Joan then owns 200 shares, and her total basis of $6,000 is allocated to 200 shares (basis of $30 per share). The stock split results in no taxable income or gain to Joan.

ALERT: Exempt-interest dividends must be reported on the return, even though they are not taxable.

Exempt-Interest Dividends

Exempt-interest dividends, which are reported in box 8 of Form 1099-DIV (see Figure 6.1), are *not* taxable.

ALERT: Form 1040EZ, *Income Tax Return for Single and Joint Filers With No Dependents*, cannot be used if a taxpayer has *any* dividend income.

Backup Withholding

Backup withholding applies to dividends as it does to interest. Please see Chapter 5 for a discussion of backup withholding.

TIP: If the dividends are paid on securities that are held by a brokerage firm, use the name of the brokerage firm, not the name of the individual securities, when reporting the income on Schedule B.

Reporting Dividends on the Tax Return

Dividends of $10 or more annually are reported to taxpayers on Form 1099-DIV. Even if they did not receive a form, taxpayers still must report all taxable dividends.

Ordinary dividends are reported on line 9a of Form 1040. However, if ordinary dividends are more than $1,500, a taxpayer must first enter the dividends on Schedule B, *Interest and Ordinary Dividends*, of Form 1040 (or Form 1040A). See Figure 6.2.

ALERT: If a taxpayer has any qualified dividends, taxes are not figured using the tax tables or rate schedules.

Qualified dividends are reported on line 9b of Form 1040. In order to apply the special tax treatment to these dividends, figure taxes using the *Qualified Dividends and Capital Gains* Worksheet instead of the regular income tax tables or rate schedules. (See Chapter 32 for a full explanation.)

Capital gain distributions have different reporting rules.

- If the taxpayer has no other capital gains or losses for the year (or any loss carryovers from prior years), capital gain distributions are reported directly on line 13 of Form 1040.

Part II

Ordinary Dividends

(See instructions on back and the instructions for Form 1040A, or Form 1040, line 9a.)

5 List name of payer ▶

5

FIGURE 6.2 Schedule B, Part II

- If, in addition to capital gain distributions, the taxpayer has capital gains or losses for the year (or any loss carryovers from prior years), Schedule D of Form 1040 must be completed.

When to Report Dividends

Dividends generally are reported in the year in which they are actually or constructively received (meaning the taxpayer has the right to the dividends whether they have been received in cash or not).

Stock Sold If stock is sold or otherwise disposed of after a dividend has been declared but before it is paid, whoever owns the stock on the record date is entitled to the dividend payment.

Mutual Funds If a mutual fund or a REIT declares a dividend in October, November, or December but pays it in January of the following year, the shareholder of record is treated as having received the dividend on December 31 and includes it in income in the year the dividend was declared.

Example

The ABC Mutual Fund declares a dividend on November 15, 2012, and pays the dividend to the shareholder of record on January 8, 2013. The shareholder includes the dividend in income in 2012.

Nominees Dividends received by a nominee are reported using the same procedure as with interest income received by a nominee. The nominee should complete Form 1099-DIV (instead of Form 1099-INT) and send it to the co-owner to report the co-owner's share of dividends. The nominee should also send a Form 1096, *Annual Summary and Transmittal of U.S. Information Returns*, transmittal with a copy of the 1099-DIV to the IRS. (See Chapter 5 for more information about nominees.)

Review Questions

1. On August 1, Michael buys 100 shares of ABC Corporation, a profitable domestic corporation. On September 1, ABC Corporation declares a dividend. On September 14, Michael sells his shares. To Michael, the dividend is:
   a. Ordinary
   b. Qualified
   c. A capital gain distribution
   d. A nondividend distribution

2. Which of the following is **not** a dividend?
   a. Cash distributions on preferred stock
   b. Dividends from mutual savings banks
   c. Cash dividends reinvested in additional stock
   d. Dividends from Sony, a Japanese corporation

3. What is the tax treatment for capital gain distributions?
   a. Ordinary dividends
   b. Qualified dividends
   c. Long-term capital gain treatment
   d. Tax-free treatment (regardless of the taxpayer's tax bracket)

4. Humphrey bought 100 shares in the DCE Corporation a number of years ago for $5,000. This year, the corporation made a nondividend distribution to him of $600 (reported in box 3 of Form 1099-DIV). How is the distribution taxed?
   a. Ordinary dividend
   b. Qualified dividend
   c. Return of capital (basis reduction)
   d. Long-term capital gain

5. All of the following dividends are tax free **except**:
   a. Dividends on life insurance policies kept by the insurer to pay the premiums
   b. Exempt-interest dividends
   c. Dividends received from nonprofitable corporations
   d. Dividends consisting entirely of shareholder's basis

6. Geraldo owns 100 shares of stock. His basis is $8,000 (basis of $80 per share). If the corporation splits its stock 2 for 1, he then owns 200 shares, and his total basis of $8,000 is allocated to 200 shares (basis of $40 per share). How much of this is taxable when the split is made?
   a. $0
   b. $40
   c. $4,000
   d. $8,000

CHAPTER 7

Rental Income and Expenses

A taxpayer who owns property and rents it out generally must report rental income. Expenses related to the property may be fully or partially deductible against rental income.

Special rules apply to rentals of property used for personal purposes, such as vacation homes. The time the property is used, along with other factors, dictates the tax treatment for reporting rental income and expenses.

Converting a personal residence to a rental property requires that the taxpayer begin depreciating the property. Converting a rental property to a principal residence requires that a taxpayer stop depreciating the property when the property is taken out of service. Special rules apply to calculate allowable depreciation in the year the property is converted.

Passive activity rules and at-risk limitations can prevent a taxpayer from deducting rental losses against ordinary income.

Rental Income

Rental income is any payment received for the use or occupancy of property. Payment in addition to the usual rent checks may also be treated as rental income. Rental payments are included in a cash-basis taxpayer's income when actually or constructively received. Thus, a rent check is income when received, regardless of when the taxpayer deposits it in a bank account or cashes it.

Advance Rents

Advance rents are rental payments made before the rent is due. An example of advance rents would be a payment at the beginning of a lease of the first and final months' rent. Advance rents are included in gross income unless they are treated as **security deposits**. However, once the landlord has the right to retain the security deposit, it is included in gross income.

DEFINITION: A **security deposit** is an amount left with the landlord to cover damage to the property or nonpayment of rent that may have to be returned to the tenant at the end of the lease. It does *not* represent a prepayment of rent.

Expenses Paid by the Tenant

If a tenant pays any of the landlord's expenses, these payments are rental income and includible in the landlord's gross income. However, a landlord may be able to claim a deduction for these expenses, effectively offsetting the income.

Property or Services

Payments made by a tenant in property or services are treated the same as cash payments and included in the landlord's gross rental income. Generally, property and services are valued at fair market value. However, if there is an agreed-on price for the services, that price usually becomes the fair market value.

Payments for Canceling a Lease

If a tenant pays a landlord a lump sum to cancel a lease, that payment is rental income in the year it is received.

Rental Expenses

Expenses related to the rental of property are generally deductible on Form 1040, Schedule E, *Supplemental Income and Loss*. However, certain limitations may apply for:

- Property not rented for profit
- Property used partly for personal purposes
- Passive loss limitations
- At-risk loss limitations

Deductible Rental Expenses

Deductible rental expenses include:

- Advertising the rental property
- Car and travel costs to and from the property
- Cleaning, maintenance, and repairs
- Commissions to real estate agents for renting the property and management fees for managing the property for the owner
- Insurance
- Interest on a mortgage on the property
- Legal and professional fees (e.g., attorney's fee for preparing a lease)
- Real estate and other taxes
- Utilities

ALERT: Even though a rental expense may be deductible, a taxpayer may not be able to deduct a loss on rental property in the current year due to passive loss and other limitations described later in this chapter.

This list is not exhaustive; any expense that is an ordinary and necessary business expense for the rental property, such as security costs, is deductible.

Mortgage Interest

Mortgage interest paid on rental property that is not the taxpayer's personal residence is deductible. Unlike the mortgage limit for deducting interest on personal residences (see Chapter 22), there is no limit to the size of the mortgage on rental property. Mortgage interest on a personal residence that is partially rented out must be allocated between rental and personal portions. (See the section "Rental of Property that Is Used Personally" later in this chapter for details.)

Points to Acquire a Mortgage

Points paid to a lender to obtain a mortgage on rental or investment property are deducted ratably over the term of the loan.

Example

On January 1, a landlord obtains a $360,000, 30-year mortgage for a building and pays 1 point (1% of the mortgage amount), or $3,600. The landlord can deduct $10 per month (total points of $3,600 ÷ 360 months), or $120 per year.

Insurance

Unlike insurance premiums on a personal residence, insurance premiums paid on rental property are fully deductible. However, if a taxpayer rents part of his or her home out, only the portion of insurance premiums that is allocated to the rental is deductible.

Insurance premiums paid for more than one year (12 months) in advance are deductible in the year to which they apply. In other words, they are not fully deductible in the year they were paid. Even a cash-basis taxpayer cannot deduct the total premium if premiums are paid more than one year in advance.

Example

A landlord pays $3,000 on July 1, 2012, for insurance that is effective immediately for three years (36 months). However, only $500 (6/36 × $3,000) is deductible in 2012, $1,000 (12/36 × $3,000) is deductible in 2013, $1,000 (12/36 × $3,000) is deductible in 2014, and the remaining $500 is deductible in 2015.

Example

A landlord pays $10,000 on July 1, 2012, for insurance that is effective for only one year beginning on July 1, 2012. The full $10,000 is deductible in 2012 because the coverage does not extend beyond 12 months.

DEFINITION: Depreciation is an expense reflecting the normal use and decline in value of an asset over time. It is the method for recovering the cost of income-producing property through periodic tax deductions. Depreciation begins when the item is considered placed in service or when the property is ready and available for use in a business or income-producing activity.

ALERT: *Residential* real property (such as an apartment building) placed in service after 1986 is depreciated using a straight-line method over 27½ years. The straight-line method provides for equal yearly deductions (except for the first and last years).

Nonresidential real property (such as an office building) placed in service on or after May 13, 1993, is depreciated using the straight-line method over 39 years. Nonresidential real property placed in service after 1986 and before May 13, 1993, is depreciated over 31½ years using the straight-line method.

Real property usually is subject to the *midmonth convention*. Half of a full month's depreciation is taken in the month the property is placed in service, and half of a full month's depreciation is taken in the month the property is disposed of.

Travel Expenses

Local transportation and other travel expenses may be deducted if incurred to collect rental income or to manage, conserve, or maintain the rental property. If a taxpayer uses a personal vehicle to perform these activities, the actual costs or the standard mileage rate can be used to figure mileage deductions. (The rate is 55.5¢ per mile for 2012.) However, if the purpose of the travel is primarily to improve the property, the travel costs must be capitalized and recovered through depreciation rather than current deductions.

Depreciation

An allowance must be claimed each year based on the cost of income-producing property (not including land). **Depreciation** is determined based on the property's basis, recovery period, and the depreciation method used. Depreciation deductions are allowed only on the part of the property that is used for rental purposes. Owners claiming depreciation deductions may need to file Form 4562, *Depreciation and Amortization*.

Land is not depreciable, so an allocation of the owner's basis between the land and the building is required.

Example

Harlan buys a four-family building for $800,000; the purchase contract does not make any allocation between the building and the land on which the building sits. A recent real estate assessment shows that 85% of the assessed value represents the building. Thus, the depreciable basis of the building is $680,000 ($800,000 × 85%). The basis in the land is $120,000 ($800,000 × 15%). Land may not be depreciated.

For more information about depreciation, see Chapter 11. For more information about basis, see Chapter 12. For depreciation tables, see IRS Pub. 946, *How to Depreciate Property*.

Repairs and Improvements

Repairs and maintenance expenses incurred after the property is placed in service to keep the property in good condition are deductible.

However, under a temporary regulation first effective in 2012, the cost of repairs and maintenance incurred before the property is placed in service must be capitalized.

The cost of improvements and additions that add to the property's value, prolong the life of the property, or adapt the property to a new use must be **capitalized**. (See Table 7.1.)

TABLE 7.1 Examples of Repairs and Improvements

Repairs (deductible*)	Improvements (capitalized)
Painting or repainting a room or building	Adding a room
Cleaning or fixing gutters	Adding or replacing appliances
Plastering	Changing wiring or plumbing
Servicing boilers, furnaces, and air-conditioning units	Paving a driveway
Replacing broken windows	Putting on a new roof
Fixing leaky pipes	Putting up fencing

*Repair expenses are deductible after the property is placed in service but must be capitalized if they are incurred before the property is placed in service.

Example

Continuing with the previous, Harlan placed the building in service in 2011. Harlan does the following to the building in 2012:

- Fixes a leaky faucet for $100
- Paints the outside of the building for $10,000
- Replaces the windows throughout the building for $24,000

For 2012, he can deduct $10,100, the cost of repairs (leaky faucet and paint job). The cost for replacing the windows ($24,000) is not an ordinary repair that is immediately deductible; it is an improvement and is depreciated as separate property. Thus, Harland may also deduct in 2012 that portion of the capitalized amount that is scheduled for depreciation under the depreciation convention used.

DEFINITION: Capitalizing a cost means adding it to the basis of the property. (Basis of property is explained in Chapter 12.) A capitalized cost can be recovered through depreciation in some instances. Otherwise, a capitalized cost reduces gain or increases loss when the property is sold. (See Chapter 13.)

TIP: A taxpayer must capitalize all the direct costs of an improvement and all the indirect costs (including repair costs that would otherwise be deductible) that directly benefit or are incurred by reason of an improvement. Repairs that do not directly benefit or are not incurred because of an improvement may be deducted, regardless of whether they are made at the same time as an improvement.

Tax Return Preparation

A landlord may deduct as a rental expense the portion of tax preparation fees paid to complete Schedule E. Expenses (other than federal taxes and penalties) paid to resolve tax underpayments related to rental activities may also be deducted.

Deducting Rental Expenses—Special Rules

Expenses of Property Not Rented for Profit

If the taxpayer (landlord) does not rent the property to make a profit, or if the property is not rented at a fair rental price (what an unrelated person would pay), the landlord is viewed as lacking a profit motive. Not-for-profit rental income is reported as Other Income. Rental expenses are deductible on Form 1040, Schedule A, *Itemized Deductions*, only to the extent of rental income. Excess deductions cannot be carried forward to subsequent years.

ALERT: If a tenant fails to pay a landlord, the uncollected rent is not a deductible expense or loss if the landlord is a cash-basis taxpayer. If, however, the landlord is on the accrual method, then uncollected rent can be treated as a bad debt.

DEFINITION: Leasehold improvements are improvements made by the landlord, lessee, or sublessee that are placed in service more than three years after the building is placed in service and do not involve enlarging the building, installing an elevator or escalator, any structural component benefiting a common area, or an internal structural framework of the building.

DEFINITION: Restaurant improvements are improvements made to a building in which more than 50% of its square footage is devoted to the preparation of and on-premises consumption of meals.

Retail improvements are improvements made more than three years after the building was placed in service where the building is used in the retail trade and open to the public.

Expenses Incurred When the Property Is Vacant

Even if a property is not generating rental income, expenses related to the property may still be deducted in certain circumstances:

- Pre-rental expenses can be deducted in the year paid. These include ordinary and necessary expenses for managing, conserving, or maintaining the property from when it is made available for rental.
- Expenses incurred while rental property is listed for sale can also be deducted in the year they are paid.

Local Benefit Taxes

Charges for local benefits that increase the value of property, such as charges for constructing streets, sidewalks, or water and sewer systems, are not deductible. Instead, they are nondepreciable capital expenditures that increase the owner's basis in the property. However, local benefit taxes for maintaining, repairing, or paying interest charges for the benefits are currently deductible.

Other Improvements

Most improvements must be capitalized and added to the basis of the property. The cost of improvements usually is recovered through depreciation. However, special rules may apply to **qualified leasehold**, **restaurant**, and **retail improvements**.

The cost of qualified leasehold improvements qualifies for bonus depreciation. *Bonus depreciation* allows a taxpayer to deduct in the current year a portion of the cost of the property that would otherwise be capitalized and deducted over a period of years through regular depreciation.

A taxpayer who elects not to use bonus depreciation for qualified leasehold improvements, or who has restaurant or retail improvements, may have other ways in which to treat the cost of these improvements.

- *Section 179 deduction.* Similar to bonus depreciation, Section 179 allows a taxpayer to deduct a portion of property in the current year instead of depreciating it.
- *15-year recovery period.* The costs of improvements can be depreciated ratably over 15 years. This applies to costs for which no Section 179 deduction has been made or for costs in excess of the deduction limit.

Rental of Property that Is Used Personally

When a taxpayer owns property that is used personally and also rented out for some part of the year, the amount of expenses that can be deducted may be limited. A determining factor is the number of days that the property is used personally as well as the number of days it is rented out at a fair rental value.

Multifamily Homes

If a taxpayer owns property in which a unit is used for personal purposes while one or more other units are rented at a fair rental price, the units are treated separately as personal and rental units. Expenses are allocated based on the proportion of the property used for rental and for **personal use**. Deductions for the rental portion are allowed (subject to the passive loss and at-risk limits discussed later).

Example

A taxpayer owns a three-family home in which all units are of the same size. The taxpayer and his family live in one unit, and he rents out the other two units. Two-thirds of the expenses are allocated to the rental portion of the home.

DEFINITION: Personal use includes usage not only by the owner but also by the owner's family members or any other person who does not pay a fair rental price. Personal use does *not* include days that the owner works substantially full time repairing and maintaining (not improving) the property, even if a family member also uses it at the same time for recreational purposes.

Rental of Personal Residence for Less than 15 Days

A taxpayer who rents his or her personal residence for less than 15 days during the year may exclude all related rental income. The taxpayer's deductions on the property are limited to normal homeowner deductions, such as mortgage interest, real estate taxes, and so on. Other related rental expenses are not deductible.

Example

A homeowner living near Augusta, Georgia, rents out her condo for 12 days to a golf fan who attends the Masters Tournament in April. Regardless of the amount of rent charged, it is tax-free income. The cost of advertising, cleaning, and other related expenses for rental of the condo is not deductible.

Rental of Personal Residence for More than 14 Days

In this situation, a taxpayer rents his home out for more than 14 days a year and personally uses it for more than 14 days or 10% of the rental days, whichever is greater. All rental income is taxable but may be reduced by rental expenses, which are allocated between rental and personal-use. Expenses allocated to the rental cannot exceed rental income.

Example

Jenny owns a house in the mountains near a popular resort. This past year, she stayed in the house for 30 days and rented it at fair rental value for 240 days. The house was vacant for the remainder of the year. Because Jenny used the house personally for more than 24 days (the greater of 14 days or 24 days [10% × 240 days rented out at fair rental value = 24 days]), the house is considered to be a residence. Jenny can deduct allocable rental expenses to the extent of her rental income.

The expenses related to the rental period are subject to the ordering rules explained next.

Ordering Rule for Claiming Deductions for Personal-Use Property

When the property is used for personal purposes, expenses may be deducted according to certain ordering rules. A worksheet that appears in IRS Pub. 527, *Rental Real Estate,* may be used for this purpose. The worksheet—Worksheet 5.1, *Worksheet for Figuring Rental Deductions for a Dwelling Unit Used as a Home*—helps determine the percentage of the home used for rent and allowable rental expenses.

Expenses allocated to the rental use are deductible on Schedule E in the following order:

1. Qualified home mortgage interest, real estate taxes, deductible casualty and theft losses, and expenses directly related to the rental activity (e.g., advertising expenses). These are fully deductible expenses.
2. Expenses indirectly related to the rental activity (e.g., repairs, insurance, and utilities). Expenses that exceed rental income may not be deducted in the current year but may be carried forward.
3. Depreciation. Depreciation that exceeds rental income may not be deducted in the current year but may be carried forward.

> **TIP:** The IRS prorates expenses using the ratio of rental-use days to the total of rental-use and personal-use days. This method applies to all rental expenses.
>
> However, the Tax Court and the 9th and 10th Circuit Courts of Appeals have held that the correct ratio to use for mortgage interest, real estate taxes, and casualty losses is the days of rental use to the total number of days owned during the year. The other expenses are prorated using the IRS method.
>
> Personal use is disregarded if the homeowner rented or tried to rent the home for 12 consecutive months (or less if the home is sold before the end of 12 months). Thus, if a homeowner converts a personal residence to rental property, the part of the year used for personal purposes is not taken into account. Expenses related to the rental period are deductible (subject to the passive loss limitations).

Example

A taxpayer owns a condominium apartment in a resort area that is rented at a fair rental price for a total of 170 days during the year. For 12 of those days, the tenant is not able to use the unit and allows the taxpayer to use it even though there is no rent refund. The taxpayer's family actually uses the apartment for 10 of those days as well as 7 other days not covered by the rental agreement. The apartment is treated as having been rented for 160 (170 – 10) days, which makes 10% of the total days rented to others at a fair rental price 16 days. The taxpayer uses the unit as a home because it is used for personal purposes for 17 days, which is more than the greater of 14 days or 10% of the 160 days it was rented (16 days).

Conversions of Rental Property

Conversion of a Personal-Use Property to Rental Property Generally, when property used for personal purposes is converted from personal use to rental property, the depreciation allowance for the year of change, and any subsequent tax year is determined as if the property were placed in service on the date on which the conversion occurs. The depreciable basis of the property for the year of change is the lesser of its fair market value or its adjusted depreciable basis at the time of the conversion to rental property.

Conversion of Rental Property to Personal-Use Property When rental property is converted to personal use during a tax year, the taxpayer must stop depreciating the property; it is treated as if the property was sold or a disposed of during the tax year. The depreciation allowance is determined by first multiplying the adjusted depreciable basis of the property as of the first day of the year of change by the applicable depreciation rate for that tax year. This amount is then multiplied by a fraction, the numerator of which is the number of months (including fractions of months) the property is considered to be placed in service during the year of change and the denominator of which is 12.

Example

Bill purchased a rental home in January of 2009. After the tenants moved out on March 28, 2012, Bill moved into the house and used it as his principal residence beginning on April 15, 2012. His depreciation deduction for 2012 is determined by multiplying the adjusted basis of the home on January 1, 2012, by 3.5/12.

TIP: Residential real estate uses the midmonth convention for depreciation under the Modified Accelerated Cost Recovery System (MACRS). This means that the middle of the month is used as the date of acquisition or disposition for depreciation purposes. In Bill's example, April 15 is considered the date of conversion for any date in April that Bill started using the home as his personal residence.

Passive Loss Limitations

Introduction

The **passive activity loss** rules prohibit a taxpayer from deducting against ordinary income a loss from activities in which the taxpayer does not *actively* or *materially* participate.

Thus, a casual investor in an apartment building cannot deduct losses on that property against ordinary income, such as wages or business income. Instead, losses from the property may either be used to offset gains from other passive activities or may be carried forward ("suspended") to future years when the passive losses may be offset against future passive gains (or deducted in full when the property is sold or disposed of).

ALERT: Active participation and material participation have specific rules defined in the Internal Revenue Code.

Passive Activities

Generally, all rental real estate activities (except those meeting the exception for real estate professionals explained later) are passive activities by definition and are subject to the passive loss limitation rules. Deductions for losses (expenses in excess of income) from passive activities are limited to passive activity income. Similar rules apply to credits from passive activities.

DEFINITION: A **passive activity loss** is a loss from an activity in which the taxpayer does not materially participate in a regular, continuous, or substantial basis during the year. The rental of real estate is automatically considered a passive activity regardless of participation (except for real estate professionals, defined later).

Carryforwards

Any excess loss is carried forward (suspended) to the next tax year and can be used to the extent of passive activity income in that year. The carryforward continues indefinitely until the losses are used up or until there is a disposition of the property in a fully taxable transaction.

Example

An owner of a rental residence in 2011 had income of $36,000 and expenses of $60,000. Under the passive activity loss rules, she could deduct only $36,000 of the expenses in 2011, so there was a carryforward of $24,000 ($60,000 – $36,000). In 2012, she sells the property to an unrelated party at a gain of $78,000. The carryforward can be used in full in 2012, regardless of rental income or income from other passive activities in 2012.

Active Participation Exception

DEFINITION: Active participation means owning at least 10% of the rental property for which the taxpayer makes management decisions, such as approving new tenants, deciding on rental terms, approving expenditures, and the like. Active participation is a less stringent participation rule than the material participation rule for real estate professionals.

If the taxpayer or the taxpayer's spouse **actively participates** in a rental activity, losses are currently deductible up to $25,000 against passive and nonpassive income. (The limit is $12,500 for married individuals who file separate returns for the year and live apart from their spouses at all times during the year.) Losses over this amount are carried forward to subsequent years.

To claim the $25,000, modified adjusted gross income (MAGI) must be $100,000 or less ($50,000 if married filing separately [MFS]). If MAGI is more than $100,000 ($50,000 if MFS), the allowance is limited to 50% of the difference between $150,000 ($75,000 if MFS) and MAGI. If MAGI exceeds the phaseout range, no part of the applicable $25,000 or $12,500 allowance can be claimed. Thus, the phaseout range for the allowance is for MAGI between $100,000 and $150,000 ($50,000 and $75,000 for MFS).

For this purpose, MAGI is adjusted gross income (AGI) calculated without taking into account:

- Passive activity income or loss on Form 8582, *Passive Activity Loss Limitations*
- Any rental real estate loss allowed because the taxpayer materially participated in the rental activity as a real estate professional
- Taxable Social Security and tier 1 railroad retirement benefits
- The deduction for one half of self-employment tax
- The deduction for qualified tuition and fees
- The deduction for student loan interest
- Deductible contributions to IRAs and Section 501(c)(18) pension plans
- The exclusion of interest income for qualified U.S. savings bonds used to pay higher education expenses
- The exclusion for amounts received under an employer's adoption assistance program
- The deduction for domestic production activities
- Any loss from a publicly traded partnership

Example

Jane, a single taxpayer with MAGI less than $100,000, has $70,000 in wages, $15,000 income from a limited partnership (passive income), and a $26,000 loss from rental real estate activities (passive losses) in which she actively participated. She can use $15,000 of her $26,000 rental real estate loss to offset her $15,000 passive income from the partnership. Because she actively participated in her rental real estate activities, Jane can use the remaining $11,000 rental real estate loss to offset $11,000 of her nonpassive income (wages).

Special Rules for Real Estate Professionals

A real estate professional is not subject to the passive loss limitations for rental real estate activities in which he or she materially participates; the activities are not treated as passive activities. In effect, the real estate activity constitutes an "active" business that is not subject to the passive loss rules.

To determine a real estate professional's rental real estate activities, each interest in a rental real estate activity is a separate activity, unless the taxpayer chooses to treat all interests in rental real estate activities as one activity.

Qualifying as a Real Estate Professional

To qualify as a real estate professional, the taxpayer must meet two tests:

1. More than half of the personal services performed by the taxpayer in all trades or businesses during the tax year are performed in real property trades or businesses in which the taxpayer **materially participates**.
2. The taxpayer performs more than 750 hours of services during the tax year in real property trades or businesses in which he or she materially participates.

DEFINITION:
Material participation means working on a regular, continuous, and substantial basis in operations. Material participation requires more work than active participation, described earlier. There are seven tests for material participation, listed in the text.

Material Participation

A taxpayer materially participates if one of these seven tests is satisfied:

1. Participation in the activity for more than 500 hours.
2. Participation by the taxpayer is substantially all the participation in the activity of all individuals involved in the activity for the tax year, including the participation of individuals who do not own any interest in the activity.
3. Participation in the activity for more than 100 hours during the tax year, and the taxpayer participates at least as much as any other individual (including those who did not own any interest in the activity) for the year.
4. The activity is a significant participation activity, and the taxpayer participates in all significant participation activities for more than

TIP: *Material participation* includes a spouse's participation. This applies even if the spouse does not own any interest in the activity and the taxpayer and spouse do not file a joint return for the year.

500 hours. (A *significant participation activity* is any trade or business activity in which the taxpayer participated for more than 100 hours during the year and in which the taxpayer did not materially participate under any of the material participation tests, other than this test.)

5. The taxpayer materially participated in the activity for any five (whether consecutive or not) of the ten immediately preceding tax years.

6. The activity is a personal service activity in which the taxpayer materially participates for any three (whether consecutive or not) preceding tax years. (An activity is a *personal service activity* if it involves the performance of personal services in the fields of health, including veterinary services, law, engineering, architecture, accounting, actuarial science, performing arts, consulting, or any other trade or business in which capital is not a material income-producing factor).

7. Based on all the facts and circumstances, the taxpayer participates in the activity on a regular, continuous, and substantial basis during the year.

A real estate professional may file a written election to group all rental real estate activities as one activity. If the professional elected to group his rentals as a single activity, then he must prove material participation in the grouped rental activity.

At-Risk Limitations

Losses from real estate activities are also subject to at-risk limitations before any losses can be deducted. These rules generally state that losses are allowed only to a taxpayer who has amounts at risk in the activity at the end of the tax year. Taxpayers generally are considered at risk to the extent of:

- Money (cash)
- The adjusted basis of property contributed to the activity
- Amounts borrowed for use in the activity (for which the taxpayer is personally liable for repayment)
- Amounts borrowed for use in the activity, to the extent of the fair market value of the taxpayer's property pledged as security (the property pledged as security must not be used in the activity)

Financing for which the taxpayer is not personally liable and the lender's recourse is only against the taxpayer's interest in the activity or the property used in the activity is generally considered nonrecourse and not at risk.

At-risk rules apply to businesses held directly by the taxpayer (e.g. sole proprietorships) as well as to interests a taxpayer has in a pass-through entity (such as a partnership or S corporation). Form 6198, *At-Risk Limitations*, is used to determine the amount at risk and the taxpayer's deductible loss.

Example

Gene started a solo consulting business in 2012. To get the business started, he contributed $20,000 in cash and a vehicle he owned with a fair market value of $27,000. To ensure the new business had enough cash to meet the operating expenses he expected during the first year, he also took out a $40,000 loan and contributed the proceeds to the business. He pledged his personal residence as collateral for the loan. He does not use his personal residence in the consulting business. Gene's at-risk amount is $87,000 ($20,000 + $27,000 + $40,000).

Reporting Rental Income and Expenses

Generally, rental income and expenses are reported on Schedule E (Part I) of Form 1040 (see Figure 7.1). As the schedule explains, the income and expenses for more than one property must be listed separately.

If a landlord provides substantial services that are primarily for the tenant's convenience, such as regular cleaning, changing linen, or maid service, the rental income and expenses are reported as business income and expenses on Form 1040, Schedule C, *Profit or Loss From Business,* or Schedule C-EZ, *Net Profit From Business (Sole Proprietorship).*

SCHEDULE E (Form 1040)
Department of the Treasury
Internal Revenue Service (99)

Supplemental Income and Loss
(From rental real estate, royalties, partnerships, S corporations, estates, trusts, REMICs, etc.)
▶ Attach to Form 1040, 1040NR, or Form 1041.
▶ Information about Schedule E and its separate instructions is at *www.irs.gov/form1040.*

OMB No. 1545-0074
2012
Attachment Sequence No. **13**

Name(s) shown on return | **Your social security number**

Part I **Income or Loss From Rental Real Estate and Royalties** **Note.** If you are in the business of renting personal property, use **Schedule C** or **C-EZ** (see instructions). If you are an individual, report farm rental income or loss from **Form 4835** on page 2, line 40.

A Did you make any payments in 2012 that would require you to file Form(s) 1099? (see instructions) ☐ Yes ☐ No
B If "Yes," did you or will you file required Forms 1099? ☐ Yes ☐ No

1a	Physical address of each property (street, city, state, ZIP code)
A	
B	
C	

1b	Type of Property (from list below)	**2** For each rental real estate property listed above, report the number of fair rental and personal use days. Check the **QJV** box only if you meet the requirements to file as a qualified joint venture. See instructions.		**Fair Rental Days**	**Personal Use Days**	**QJV**
A			**A**			
B			**B**			
C			**C**			

Type of Property:
1 Single Family Residence | 3 Vacation/Short-Term Rental | 5 Land | 7 Self-Rental
2 Multi-Family Residence | 4 Commercial | 6 Royalties | 8 Other (describe)

Income:	**Properties:**	**A**	**B**	**C**
3 Rents received	**3**			
4 Royalties received	**4**			
Expenses:				
5 Advertising	**5**			
6 Auto and travel (see instructions)	**6**			

FIGURE 7.1 Schedule E (Form 1040)

Not-for-Profit Rentals

If a taxpayer is not renting property for the purpose of making a profit, rental income is reported on Form 1040, line 21, as other income. Related rental expenses are deducted on Schedule A as miscellaneous itemized deductions subject to the 2% of AGI threshold, and only to the extent of rental income. If a taxpayer has rental income in excess of rental expenses for three of five consecutive years, the taxpayer is considered to be renting for the purpose of making a profit and should report the rental income and expenses on Schedule E.

Passive Losses

If the passive activity loss limitation applies, as described earlier, Form 8582 must also be filed.

At-Risk Losses

If the at-risk loss limitation applies, Form 6198 must also be filed.

Review Questions

1. On December 1, 2012, Stan, the landlord of a three-family house, rents out one unit for $800 per month for one year (starting December 1, 2012). The tenant pays him $2,400—the first month's rent plus a $1,600 security deposit that will be used to pay the last two months' rent. How much of the payment is taxable to Stan in 2012?
   a. $0
   b. $800
   c. $1,600
   d. $2,400

2. Which of the following is **not** taxable to a landlord?
   a. A security deposit held for purposes of protecting the property
   b. Payments made in property or services
   c. A landlord's expenses paid by the tenant
   d. A payment by the tenant for canceling the lease

3. What payment is currently deductible?
   a. Replacing the roof
   b. Putting up a fence
   c. Fixing a leaky pipe
   d. Installing new appliances

4. Darren rents out his home. What is the maximum rental period that would make the rent tax free?
   a. All rent is taxable, regardless of the rental period.
   b. The rental period is less than 10% of the time that Darren uses his home.
   c. 14 days.
   d. Any period as long as it is less than the time that Darren uses his home.

5. Miriam, a head of household, has $80,000 in wages, $12,000 income from a limited partnership (passive income), and a $30,000 loss from rental real estate activities (passive losses) in which she actively participated. (Her MAGI does not exceed $100,000.) What part of the $30,000 loss can she use in 2012?
   a. $0
   b. $12,000
   c. $25,000
   d. $30,000

6. A landlord owns an apartment building for which he paid $1 million. The purchase contract did not make any allocation for the land, but the most recent tax assessment shows that the building is 80% of the total assessed value. What is the depreciable basis of the building?
   a. $0
   b. $200,000
   c. $800,000
   d. $1,000,000

CHAPTER 8

Retirement Plans, Pensions, and Annuities

A taxpayer may receive income from a retirement plan, pension plan, individual retirement account (IRA), or annuity. The income may be derived from personal, employee, or employer contributions; or the taxpayer may inherit benefits in such plans or accounts.

As a general rule, income from retirement plans, IRAs, and annuities is taxable in full or in part. However, certain rules apply to limit immediate taxation of benefits. There are also various rules that impose penalties on distributions taken too early or too late, or for certain other actions.

Qualified Retirement Plans

A "qualified retirement plan" is a generic term that includes such plans as 401(k), 403(b), simplified employee pensions (SEPs), and pension plans. These plans are "qualified" because of the favorable tax advantages they offer. In return, specific rules must be followed regarding plan contributions and distributions, required communications with plan participants, and antidiscrimination rules for participating in the plans.

ALERT: An IRA is *not* a qualified retirement plan even though it may share some of the features of qualified plans.

Distributions received from qualified plans, whether received periodically or in a lump sum, are generally taxable. However, the taxable portion of a distribution does not include any portion of the taxpayer's investment, or basis.

Form 1099-R, *Distributions From Pensions, Annuities, Retirement or Profit-Sharing Plans, IRAs, Insurance Contracts, etc.* (see Figure 8.1), may be used to help determine the taxability of a distribution and whether any penalty applies to the distribution. The form contains much information about the nature of distributions, such as the kind of plan from which the distribution was made, how much of the distribution is taxable, and whether there are any known exceptions to a distribution penalty (which may apply). A detailed description of the form and the meaning of its boxes and codes is beyond the scope of this book. However, this information is readily available on the form instructions available on the IRS Web site.

☐ VOID ☐ CORRECTED

PAYER'S name, street address, city, state, and ZIP code		1 Gross distribution $ 2a Taxable amount $	OMB No. 1545-0119 **2012** Form **1099-R**	**Distributions From Pensions, Annuities, Retirement or Profit-Sharing Plans, IRAs, Insurance Contracts, etc.**
		2b Taxable amount not determined ☐	Total distribution ☐	**Copy 1 For State, City, or Local Tax Department**
PAYER'S federal identification number	RECIPIENT'S identification number	3 Capital gain (included in box 2a) $	4 Federal income tax withheld $	
RECIPIENT'S name		5 Employee contributions /Designated Roth contributions or insurance premiums $	6 Net unrealized appreciation in employer's securities $	
Street address (including apt. no.)		7 Distribution code(s) — IRA/ SEP/ SIMPLE ☐	8 Other $ %	
City, state, and ZIP code		9a Your percentage of total distribution %	9b Total employee contributions $	
10 Amount allocable to IRR within 5 years $	11 1st year of desig. Roth contrib.	12 State tax withheld $ $	13 State/Payer's state no.	14 State distribution $ $
Account number (see instructions)		15 Local tax withheld $ $	16 Name of locality	17 Local distribution $ $

Form **1099-R** www.irs.gov/form1099r Department of the Treasury - Internal Revenue Service

FIGURE 8.1 Form 1099-R

If a taxpayer receives payments that are derived entirely from employer contributions (and thus not previously taxed to the taxpayer), then generally *all* of the distributions are taxable. This rule applies whether the payments are made periodically or in a lump sum.

A taxpayer is *not* taxed on distributions representing amounts that have already been taxed (the taxpayer's investment, or basis, in the plan). These include taxpayer and employer contributions that were already included in the taxpayer's gross income (i.e., after-tax contributions).

Periodic Payments

Periodic payments are amounts received at regular intervals (such as monthly or annually) for a period of time greater than one year. These payments are also called amounts received as an annuity.

If the taxpayer (plan participant) has an investment in the plan, then part of each periodic payment represents a return of that investment and is not taxed; the balance is taxable. For payments from qualified retirement plans with an **annuity starting date** after November 18, 1996, the Simplified Method is used to calculate the portion of each distribution that is taxable.

DEFINITION: The **annuity starting date** is either the first day of the first period for which a taxpayer receives an annuity payment under the plan (or annuity contract) or the date on which the obligation under the plan (or annuity contract) becomes fixed, whichever is later.

Simplified Method

Divide the taxpayer's investment in the plan by the total number of anticipated monthly payments or, if payable for life (or the lives of the taxpayer and spouse), then according to a number based on the taxpayer's age (or the age of the taxpayer and spouse) as provided in an IRS table (see Table 8.1).

TABLE 8.1 Simplified Method Table

Annuity Start Date after November 18, 1996			
Taxpayer's Age at Annuity Starting Date		**Combined Ages of Taxpayer and Spouse**	
55 or under	360	110 or under	410
56–60	310	111–120	360
61–65	260	121–130	310
66–70	210	131–140	260
71 or older	160	141 or older	210

Example

Jesse, who is single, retired late last year and will receive a pension for life. He is 58 years old on the annuity starting date in January, when he receives his first payment. His investment in the contract is $31,000. For the year, he receives $14,400 from his pension. He figures his exclusion of $100 per month by dividing his investment in the contract ($31,000) by the number in the table corresponding to his age (310). He can exclude $1,200 each year ($100 exclusion x 12 monthly payments). Thus, of the $14,400 received, $1,200 is tax free and $13,200 is taxable.

ALERT: Distributions from IRAs or retirement plans may be subject to both income tax and penalties. For example, penalties may apply if distributions are taken too early (before the participant reaches age 59½) or too late (failing to take required minimum distributions after age 70½). Penalties, which are additions to tax, are discussed later in this chapter and in greater detail in Chapter 35. Monthly benefits paid from a qualified plan are taxable to the extent they include earnings. However, any part of the benefit that includes the taxpayer's investment in the plan, or basis, is not taxable. The taxable amount of benefits is reported to the taxpayer on Form 1099-R.

Outliving or Dying before Recovery of Cost

Once all of the taxpayer's cost has been recovered (e.g., after 310 payments have been made in the last example), all additional monthly payments are fully taxable.

If a taxpayer dies before fully recovering his or her cost in the plan, the unrecovered cost may be deducted as a miscellaneous itemized deduction on his or her final income tax return. This miscellaneous itemized deduction is *not* subject to the 2%-of-adjusted-gross-income (AGI) floor (see Chapter 25).

Nonperiodic Payments

In certain situations, a plan participant receives nonperiodic payments from the plan. Any payment that is not a periodic payment or corrective distribution is a nonperiodic payment (also referred to as amounts not received as an annuity).

Examples of nonperiodic payments include:

- Cash withdrawals
- Most types of current earning (dividend) distributions from the investment

- Certain loans
- The value of annuities transferred for less than full and adequate consideration

The tax treatment of a nonperiodic payment depends on whether the payment was made before or after the annuity starting date and whether the plan was qualified or nonqualified.

Corrective Distributions of Excess Plan Contributions

DEFINITION: A **corrective distribution** is made to undo an excess contribution, which can result from contributing more to a plan than is allowed. For instance, an employee makes a contribution to his or her plan based on anticipated earnings of $40,000. However, the employee earns only $35,000. The employee makes a corrective distribution to reduce the excess contribution.

While nonperiodic in nature, **corrective distributions** of excess plan contributions, which are reported on Form 1099-R, are *not* considered nonperiodic distributions and thus are not subject to the nonperiodic distribution rules. If contributions exceed annual limits, the excess contributions (plus any earnings on them) are distributed to the taxpayer and are fully taxable.

Determining the Taxable Amount

The amount taxable for nonperiodic distributions depends on whether the distribution is made before the annuity starting date or on or after the annuity starting date.

- *For distributions before the annuity starting date.* The tax treatment depends on whether the distribution is made under a qualified or nonqualified plan.
  - *Nonqualified plan.* If the distribution is made under a nonqualified plan the distribution is allocated first to earnings, then to the cost in the contract (i.e., the basis, or investment).
  - *Qualified plan.* If the distribution is made under a qualified plan, the tax-free amount is calculated as follows:

$$\text{Amount received} \times (\text{Cost of contract/Account balance}) = \text{Tax-free amount}$$

- *For distributions on or after the annuity starting date.* Generally distributions on or after the annuity starting date are includible in gross income.

DEFINITION: A **lump-sum distribution** is a distribution in a tax year consisting of a plan participant's entire balance from all of the employer's qualified plans of one kind (e.g., all profit-sharing plans). Deductible voluntary employee contributions made after 1981 and before 1987, along with forfeited amounts, are not taken into account.

Lump-Sum Distributions

Special tax rules apply to **lump-sum distributions** that can limit the tax that would otherwise apply to such distributions. These special tax rules apply only for participants born before January 2, 1936. If the participant was born after this date, lump-sum distributions are taxed as nonperiodic payments.

Options for Tax Treatment of Lump-Sum Distributions

If the taxpayer was born before January 2, 1936, and received a lump-sum distribution from a qualified plan, the taxpayer may elect to have a portion of the distribution taxed as a capital gain at a rate of 20%. The portion of the distribution that qualifies for this treatment relates to the taxpayer's active participation in the plan before 1974.

Another option for a taxpayer born before January 2, 1936, who receives a lump-sum distribution is the 10-year tax option. Under this option, the distribution is taxed at 1986 single rates as if one-tenth of the distribution is received in a tax year, and the result is multiplied by 10. The tax is paid only once, for the year of the distribution, and not over a 10-year period.

Either election for special tax treatment of lump-sum distributions is made on Form 4972, *Tax on Lump-Sum Distributions.*

Lump-sum distributions for purposes of choosing capital gains treatment or the 10-year tax option do *not* include:

- Any distribution that is partially rolled over to another qualified plan or an IRA.
- Any distribution if an earlier election to use either the 5- or 10-year tax option had been made after 1986 for the same plan participant.
- U.S. Retirement Plan Bonds distributed with a lump sum.
- Any distribution made during the first five tax years that the participant was in the plan, unless it was made because the participant died.
- The current actuarial value of any annuity contract included in the lump sum.
- Any distribution to a 5% owner that is subject to certain penalties.
- A distribution from an IRA.
- A distribution from a 403(b) plan.
- A distribution of the redemption proceeds of bonds rolled over tax free to a qualified pension plan and the like from a qualified bond purchase plan.
- A distribution from a qualified plan if the participant or his or her surviving spouse previously received an eligible rollover distribution from the same plan (or another plan of the employer that must be combined with that plan for the lump-sum distribution rules) and the previous distribution was rolled over tax free to another qualified plan or an IRA.
- A distribution from a qualified plan that received a rollover after 2001 from an IRA (other than a conduit IRA), a governmental section 457 plan, or a 403(b) annuity on behalf of the plan participant.
- A distribution from a qualified plan that received a rollover after 2001 from another qualified plan on behalf of that plan participant's surviving spouse.
- A corrective distribution of excess deferrals, excess contributions, excess aggregate contributions, or excess annual additions.
- A lump-sum credit or payment from the federal Civil Service Retirement System (or the Federal Employees Retirement System).

Summary of Methods for Taxation of Lump-Sum Distributions for Taxpayers Born before January 2, 1936

The taxable amount of lump-sum distributions generally includes employer contributions and income that is greater than the investment in the contract. Use these methods to determine the taxable part of the distribution:

- Report pre-1974 participation as a capital gain (if applicable) and post-1973 participation as ordinary income.
- Report pre-1974 participation as a capital gain (if applicable) and post-1973 using the 10-year averaging option (if applicable).
- Use the 10-year averaging option (if applicable).
- Roll over all or part of the distribution. Any part not rolled over is reported as ordinary income.
- Report the entire taxable part of the distribution as ordinary income.

Net Unrealized Appreciation

Net unrealized appreciation (NUA) is the net increase in value of employer securities while such securities were held in the plan. NUA included in a lump-sum distribution generally is not taxable until the securities are sold or exchanged if the securities are distributed to the taxpayer. However, the taxpayer may elect to include NUA in taxable income in the year received. The NUA is reported to the taxpayer on Form 1099-R, box 6.

Example

Edgar uses tax-deferred funds in the plan to purchase employer stock for $10,000. When he takes a distribution from the plan, the stock is worth $100,000 (and the NUA is $90,000). If he takes a distribution of all the stock, he is taxed on $10,000 (assuming he does not elect to include the $90,000 NUA in the current year). When he sells the stock, all appreciation is taxable as capital gains.

Losses

Participants receiving a lump-sum distribution entirely in cash or worthless securities can claim a loss on the difference between the investment in the plan (basis) and the amount of the cash distribution, if any. These losses are claimed on Schedule A, *Itemized Deductions*, and are subject to the 2% AGI limitation.

ALERT: Participants cannot claim a loss unless securities distributed are *totally* worthless, even if the value is less than the participant's basis.

IRA Distributions

Whether a distribution from an IRA is taxable, or the extent to which it is taxable, depends on the kind of IRA from which the distribution was made and whether the taxpayer has *basis* in the IRA. For IRA purposes, "basis" refers to after-tax (nondeductible) contributions made by the taxpayer to the IRA. A nondeductible IRA is one funded with after-tax dollars, but unlike a Roth IRA, earnings are not tax free. Therefore, each distribution includes a partially tax-free return of cost basis and a partially taxable distribution.

Traditional IRA Distributions

Distributions from traditional IRAs (also referred to as deductible or taxable IRAs) are generally fully taxable because the taxpayer has already derived a tax benefit—an adjustment to gross income—by contributing to the IRA in a prior year (see Chapter 15 for more information). The IRA trustee reports distributions to the beneficiary (taxpayer) on Form 1099-R, and the taxpayer reports the distributions on Form 1040 or Form 1040A, *U.S. Individual Income Tax Return.* Taxpayers receiving an IRA distribution cannot file Form 1040EZ, *Income Tax Return for Single and Joint Filers With No Dependents.*

TIP: Because IRAs are not considered qualified retirement plans, the rules regarding periodic, nonperiodic, and lump-sum distributions are not applicable.

Roth IRA Distributions

Distributions from a Roth IRA are generally tax free because the dollars used to fund the Roth IRA were already taxed. If a Roth IRA distribution is a *qualified distribution,* the entire distribution is tax free. However, if the distribution is *not* a qualified distribution, the portion of the distribution that includes earnings is taxed. The portion of a Roth IRA distribution that includes the taxpayer's basis is *never* taxed.

TIP: Even though a qualified Roth IRA distribution is fully tax free, it must be reported on Form 1040 or Form 1040A, with a zero shown for the taxable amount. Part IV of Form 8606, *Nondeductible IRAs,* must also be filed.

A **qualified distribution** is any distribution from a Roth IRA that meets all of these requirements:

- It is made after the 5-year period beginning with the first taxable year for which a contribution was made to a Roth IRA set up for the taxpayer's benefit, AND
- The payment or distribution is one of the following:
  - □ Made on or after the date the taxpayer reaches age 59½, OR
  - □ Made because the taxpayer is disabled, OR
  - □ Made to a beneficiary or to a taxpayer's estate after the taxpayer's death, OR
  - □ Meets the requirements of the first-time homebuyer exception.

ALERT: The 5-year period begins on January 1 of the year *for which* the contribution is first made to the Roth IRA. Because IRA contributions may be made up through the due date for the return, the year *for which* a contribution is made may be different than the calendar year *in which* the contribution is made.

Example

On November 1, 2007, Audrey contributed $2,500 to a Roth IRA. The 5-year period begins on January 1, 2007 (the beginning of the year for which the contribution was first made) and extends through 2011. Thus, Audrey can take tax-free distributions from her Roth IRA beginning in 2012 if she is at least age 59½ on or before the date of the distribution (or if she is disabled or makes a first time homebuyer distribution).

Example

Same information as the previous example, except that Audrey contributed the $2,500 to the Roth IRA on March 1, 2007 and designated those contributions for tax year 2006. The 5-year period begins on January 1, 2006 (the beginning of the year *for which* the contribution was first made) and extends through 2010. Thus, Audrey can take tax-free distributions from her Roth IRA beginning in 2011 if she is at least age 59½ on or before the date of distribution (or if she is disabled or makes a first time homebuyer distribution).

Nondeductible IRAs

Taxpayers who have made nondeductible contributions to IRAs may take distributions that will be partially taxed depending on the value and their basis in their IRAs. Taxpayers making nondeductible contributions and distributions from these accounts should report them on Form 8606, *Nondeductible IRAs* (*Part I*).

Distributions from IRAs into which nondeductible contributions have been made are partly tax free. The taxable and tax-free portions of the distribution are calculated on Form 8606.

To determine the taxable amount, divide the nondeductible contributions by the total value of all IRAs (including the amount withdrawn for the year) to arrive at the tax-free percentage for the current withdrawal. Multiply total withdrawals by this percentage to determine what amount is excludable; the balance is taxable.

Example

This year, Betsy withdrew $5,000 from her Traditional IRA, which contained $6,000 in nondeductible contributions she had made in earlier years. The account value (including the $5,000 withdrawal) was $30,000 on the last day of the previous year. The tax-free percentage is 20% ($6,000 ÷ $30,000). Of the $5,000 withdrawn, 20% ($1,000) is tax free, and the rest of the distribution ($4,000) is taxable.

DEFINITION: **Required minimum distributions (RMDs)** are amounts calculated to distribute the entire amount of an employee's interest in a plan or an account owner's IRA over his or her lifetime.

TIP: RMDs are not required from a Roth IRA while the account owner is alive, regardless of the account owner's age.

Required Minimum Distributions

Taxpayers who are at least age 70½ must take **required minimum distributions (RMDs)** from their IRAs each year. RMDs must also be taken from qualified retirement plans, such as 401(k)s. Failure to do so results in a hefty penalty: 50% of the distribution that should have been taken. A required minimum distribution may be taken at any time during the year to avoid the penalty. See Chapter 35 for more information about the penalty.

An RMD is the amount figured using the taxpayer's life expectancy, which is taken from an IRS table based on the taxpayer's age. The balance of the account at the end of the previous year is divided by this life expectancy figure. Usually a taxpayer uses Table III (Uniform Lifetime Table) from Appendix C in IRS

Pub. 590, *Individual Retirement Arrangements (IRAs).* However, if the taxpayer has named his or her spouse as beneficiary and the spouse is more than 10 years younger than the taxpayer, Table II from Appendix C in IRS Pub. 590 should be used.

Example

Warren, who was born on November 2, 1941, reaches age 70½ in 2012. The account balance of his IRA on December 31, 2011, was $53,000. Because he is 71 years old, his life expectancy from Table III of Appendix C in Pub. 590 is 26.5 years. His RMD for 2012 is $2,000 ($53,000 ÷ 26.5).

Taxpayers who turn age 70½ may take their first RMD for that year as late as April 1 of the following year. However, taxpayers who wait to take distributions in the year following the year in which they turn 70½ are required to take two distributions for that year (i.e., the previous *and* the current year's RMDs).

Example

Wesley turned 70½ in September 2012. He may take his required distribution for 2012 as late as April 1, 2013. However, he must also take a 2013 distribution no later than December 31, 2013.

The RMD for the second year is figured by using the next (lower) life expectancy (called the "distribution period" in the table) based on the taxpayer's additional year of age.

Example

Returning to the example above with Warren, at the end of 2012, assume his account balance is $54,000 ($53,000 – $2,000 RMD + $3,000 in earnings). His life expectancy (at age 72) from Table III of Appendix C in Pub. 590 is 25.6. His RMD for 2013 is $2,109 ($54,000 ÷ 25.6).

Rules for Inherited Benefits

Taxpayers who inherit IRAs are required to take RMDs but are subject to different rules on how to figure them. Spouses who inherit IRAs have an option to roll over some or all of the inherited IRA to their own IRA. If this is done the surviving spouse does not have to begin RMDs until they reach age 70½. They must begin RMDs for any IRA or portion of an IRA that is not rolled over, using the rules for beneficiaries that follow.

Beneficiaries must begin to take RMDs from an inherited IRA no later than the end of the year following the year of death. Generally beneficiaries will base their RMDs on their own life expectancy found in Table I *(Single Life Expectancy Table for Use by Beneficiaries)* of Appendix C in Pub. 590. Each year, they reduce the initial life expectancy by 1. However, if the decedent (from which the account was inherited) died on or after beginning his or her own RMDs and the beneficiary is older than the decedent was at death, then the decedent's life expectancy would be used.

Example

Rose is 52 years old when her mother dies in 2011. She is the only beneficiary to inherit her mother's IRA, which was valued at $100,000 on December 31 2011. Rose's RMD, which must be taken no later than December 31, 2012, is based on Rose's life expectancy in 2012 in Table I, or 31.4 years (she is age 53 in 2012). To calculate the RMD, she divides the value of the IRA as of December 31, 2011, by 31.4, for an RMD of $3,185. For her 2013 RMD, she divides the value of the account as of December 31, 2012, by 30.5, which is the life expectancy which corresponds to her age (54) in 2013.

ALERT: If a taxpayer receives a distribution from an IRA and immediately contributes it to a qualified charitable organization, the distribution is *not* a qualified charitable distribution (QCD). A QCD requires that the funds flow *directly* from the IRA to the charitable organization.

Qualified Charitable Distributions

Taxpayers who are at least age 70½ may transfer up to $100,000 from their IRA directly to a qualified charitable organization. The amount transferred is not taxable, but no charitable contribution deduction is allowed for the transfer. Such a transfer, called a qualified charitable distribution, counts toward the RMD requirement.

Example

Lynn's RMD was $8,000 in 2012. She arranged for her IRA trustee to transfer $6,000, as a charitable contribution, to a cancer research organization. Lynn is not taxed on the transfer, nor can she deduct the $6,000 as a charitable contribution. However, the qualified charitable distribution reduced her remaining RMD in 2012 to $2,000.

ALERT: The direct rollover method is highly preferred because any distribution taken from a qualified plan or IRA that is not rolled over within 60 days is taxed and may also be subject to the 10% penalty. The 60-day period begins on the date when the taxpayer receives the funds. Further, there is no mandatory withholding on direct rollovers.

Rollovers

A rollover is a transfer of funds between one retirement plan or IRA to another retirement plan or IRA. The rollover may occur in one of two ways:

1. Direct transfer of funds between plan trustees or custodians within 60 days, known as a direct rollover or a trustee-to-trustee transfer, OR
2. Distribution of the funds from one plan to the taxpayer, followed by depositing the funds into the new plan or IRA by the taxpayer within 60 days, known as an indirect rollover.

Qualified plans for rollover purposes include a:

- Qualified employee plan, such as a profit-sharing plan or 401(k) plan
- Qualified employee annuity

- 403(b) plan
- 457 plan

Not all funds in a plan may be eligible for rolling over into another plan. For example, RMDs are not eligible for rollovers: A taxpayer who takes a RMD cannot deposit the RMD into another qualified plan or IRA.

Example

Len takes a distribution of $100,000 from his 401(k), from which $20,000 income tax must be withheld. To make an indirect rollover of the entire $100,000 distribution, he must deposit the $80,000 distribution, plus $20,000 from his own funds, to a new or existing qualified plan or IRA within 60 days. When he files his return, he reports the $20,000 as income tax withheld. If, for example, he makes a rollover to a Roth IRA, he will likely use some or all of the $20,000 withholding to cover the tax on the conversion. Any withholding *not* applied toward the tax liability would be refunded upon filing.

TIP: The IRS has the authority to extend the 60-day rollover period. An extension may be granted when the failure to meet the time limit is deemed beyond the taxpayer's control (such as due to health issues of the tax-payer or immediate family, problems with the mail, mistakes by the financial institution, etc.). Generally a private letter ruling must be submitted requesting the extension. However, an automatic waiver may be granted if the 60-day requirement was not met solely due to financial institution error.

Rollovers to Designated Roth Accounts

A designated Roth account, sometimes called a Roth 401(k), is a qualified plan containing after-tax dollars, similar to a Roth IRA. Because dollars in both designated Roth accounts and Roth IRAs have already been taxed, rollovers can be made only from one designated Roth account to another or from one designated Roth account to a Roth IRA.

In-plan rollovers from a non-Roth qualified plan (such as a traditional 401(k)) to a designated Roth account are allowed. These in-plan rollovers are treated as conversions and are discussed later in this chapter.

ALERT: Unless there is a direct rollover, distributions are subject to a mandatory 20% income withholding tax. Therefore, if a taxpayer receives a distribution, only 80% of the requested funds will be distributed. Therefore, to avoid any tax or penalty, the taxpayer must replace the 20% tax withholding to make a full rollover into the new plan or IRA.

Rollovers that Include Nontaxable Amounts

Rollovers that include nontaxable amounts are permissible as direct rollovers as long as the nontaxable amounts are accounted for separately. (A separate account is not necessary to hold the taxable and nontaxable amounts, just a separate accounting.)

IRA Rollovers

Funds in a traditional IRA can be rolled over, with no tax effect, to another IRA (other than a Roth) or to a qualified retirement plan that accepts rollovers. A taxable event occurs only when funds in the IRA are distributed and are not rolled over. (The same 60-day rollover period that applies to rollovers from qualified plans applies to IRA rollovers.)

Rollovers by Someone Other than the Taxpayer

Special rules apply to spouses or other individuals who receive qualified retirement funds or IRA benefits as an inheritance or a marital settlement.

ALERT: Although generally one qualified plan may be rolled over into another qualified plan, some qualified plan documents do not allow such rollovers. For example, an employee who changes jobs cannot transfer her 401(k) balance to her new employer's 401(k) plan unless the new employer's plan allows such a rollover.

Qualified Domestic Relations Orders A qualified domestic relations order (QDRO) is a judgment, decree, or court order issued under state domestic relations law that provides rights to an "alternate payee" to receive benefits from the qualified plan. The "alternate payee" is the plan participant's spouse, former spouse, child, or other dependent of the participant.

Thus, the alternate payee may continue the tax-deferred status of the qualified plan by rolling over funds from the plan to another qualified retirement plan or to an IRA.

Surviving Spouse IRA funds transferred pursuant to divorce to a spouse or former spouse may be tax free if certain requirements are met. A spouse can elect to roll over some or all of inherited funds to his or her own account. A QDRO is not needed for these types of IRA transfers to be tax free.

Nonspouse Beneficiary A person other than a spouse who inherits funds from a qualified plan as a designated beneficiary can defer taxation by rolling over some or all of the funds to a traditional or Roth IRA. However, the rollover must be a direct trustee-to-trustee transfer that is set up to receive the distribution; the new account is treated as an inherited IRA rather than as the beneficiary's own plan. Because beneficiaries cannot treat the account as their own, they may not make any contributions to the inherited IRA nor roll other amounts into or out of the IRA.

TIP: Rollovers can be made from a qualified plan or traditional IRA to a Roth IRA, but the taxpayer must pay tax on the converted amount. Conversions are explained next.

Conversions

Any taxpayer owning a traditional IRA may convert some or all of the account balance to a Roth IRA. The taxpayer is taxed on the amount converted in the year of conversion.

TIP: If a rollover is made from a taxable account to a designated Roth account or Roth IRA, Form 8606 must be completed and attached to the return.

Designated Roth Accounts

If an employer's 401(k) or 403(b) plan permits designated Roth contributions, funds in the plan can be converted to the designated Roth portion of the account. These accounts are called "designated Roth accounts." Previously non-taxed amounts are included in income when they are included in an in-plan rollover to the designated Roth account.

TIP: A special tax rule applies to conversions made in 2010. The resulting income is reported half in 2011 and half in 2012 unless the taxpayer elected to include it all on the 2010 return. This information should appear in Part II of the taxpayer's 2010 Form 8606.

Special Additional Taxes

Certain actions or inactions can result in penalties, which are treated as additional taxes. These additional taxes are covered in more detail in Chapter 35; they are mentioned here because they are related to contributions to and distributions from IRAs and qualified plans. Many of these penalties are age related, such as a taxpayer taking an early distribution before age 59½ or failing to take required minimum distributions after age 70½.

Early Distributions

As noted, distributions from traditional IRAs and qualified plans before the taxpayer is age 59½ result in a 10% penalty unless certain exceptions apply. See Chapter 35 for more information.

> **TIP:** If nontaxable amounts are rolled over into an IRA, they become part of the taxpayer's cost basis in the account. They are not taxed when IRA distributions are made to the extent explained earlier in this chapter. The taxpayer must maintain good records to support his or her basis in such IRAs. Form 8606 may be used for this purpose.

Excess Contributions

Contributions that exceed annual limits result in a 6% penalty. For example, a taxpayer under age 50 who contributes $6,000 to a traditional IRA in 2012 has an excess contribution of $1,000. The penalty applies to the excess contribution each year until it (and related earnings) is withdrawn or applied as a contribution the following years. See Chapter 35 for more information.

Excess Accumulations

Generally, a taxpayer must begin to take required minimum distributions from qualified plans or IRAs starting in the year the taxpayer reaches age 70½.

Failure to take a required minimum distribution results in an excess accumulation penalty. The excess accumulation penalty is 50% of the amount that should have been taken out but was not. See Chapter 35 for more information.

> **ALERT:** Of the numerous exceptions to the 10% penalty, some apply only to qualified plans, some only to IRAs, and some to both. (For more information, see Chapter 35, Table 35.1, Exceptions to the 10% Early Distribution Penalty.)

Commercial Annuities

Commercial annuities are generally acquired from an insurance company and are not part of a qualified retirement plan. (Individuals can create private annuities, but these are very rare because of current tax rules.)

Taxpayers who hold nonqualified annuities (generally, annuities held outside of a qualified plan or IRA, such as commercial annuities and life insurance contracts) may elect to receive a portion of the contract as an annuity and leave the remaining portion to accumulate on a tax-deferred basis. The taxable portion of each annuity payment is figured using the General Rule. Under this rule, the tax-free amount of the annuity payment is the investment in the contract compared to the expected return. The expected return is the total amount the owner and other eligible persons expect to receive under the contract.

Calculation of Taxable Portion of Annuity Payment

1. Start by figuring the taxpayer's investment in the contract. Generally, this is what was paid to acquire the annuity. If the annuity was a gift, then use the donor's cost basis. Reduce the investment in the contract by any premium refunds, rebates, or dividends; additional premiums for double indemnity or disability coverage; amounts received before the annuity starting date (explained earlier in this chapter); or the value of a refund feature (which depends on life expectancy).

ALERT: The ability to avoid the excess accumulations penalty by delaying distributions until retirement does not apply to someone who owns more than 5% of the company maintaining the plan.

ALERT: Cash withdrawals from a commercial annuity before age 59½ usually are subject to a 10% penalty.

TIP: Annuities can be exchanged tax free for other annuities (see Chapter 13).

2. Determine the taxpayer's expected return from the annuity by totaling all payments to be received under the term of the contract or, if for life, by reference to IRS-set life expectancy tables. (See the Appendices in IRS Pub. 590 for these tables.)
3. Divide the investment in the contract by the total expected return to derive the "exclusion percentage." Apply this percentage to annuity payments for the year to determine the excludable portion; the balance of the payments is taxable.

Example

Ellen's commercial annuity begins paying her $1,000 month in June 2012, and she receives $7,000 for the year. Following the steps just outlined, assume that her tax-free amount is 10%. For 2012, $6,300 of her $7,000 income is taxable ($7,000 × 90%) and $700 ($7,000 × 10%) is tax free. In 2013, when she receives 12 monthly payments, $10,800 of her annual income of $12,000 will be taxable ($12,000 × 90%) and $1,200 ($12,000 × 10%) will be tax free. The tax-free percentage of 10% remains constant for the life of the annuity.

Life Insurance

Proceeds paid on account of the death of the insured generally are tax free; there is no limit on the amount excluded. However, life insurance may result in taxable income under certain situations.

Policies Acquired for Value

If a taxpayer buys a policy on an individual who dies, and the taxpayer receives proceeds on account of the death of the insured, the exclusion is limited to the amount paid for the policy, plus any premiums paid subsequent to purchasing the policy. If a policy is transferred and the policy has a loan outstanding, the amount of the loan is treated as a payment to acquire the policy.

Example

A father owns a $100,000 whole life policy on himself with a $20,000 policy loan outstanding. The father gives the policy to his adult child. The child is treated as buying the policy for $20,000. When the child receives the proceeds at the father's death, the child can exclude only $20,000, plus any premiums paid after the transfer; the balance of the proceeds is taxable to the child.

Proceeds Paid in Installments

Part of each installment represents interest, which is taxable. Divide the face amount of the policy by the number of years installments will be received; this is the amount tax free each year. Excess amounts are taxable as interest income (see Chapter 5).

Example

A beneficiary of a $100,000 life insurance policy elects to receive installments over 10 years. Each year, $10,000 ($100,000 ÷ 10) is tax free; additional amounts are taxable interest.

TIP: Form 1099-R indicates the taxable portion of life insurance proceeds.

TIP: Life insurance policies can be exchanged tax free for certain other insurance contracts (see Chapter 13).

Proceeds Not Paid in Installments

Lump-sum or nonregular interval payments are excludable from income to the extent that they represent amounts payable at the time of the death of the insured (original death payments). If this amount is not specified, then taxable payments are those that exceed the present value of the payments at the time of death.

Cancellation, Sale, or Surrender of a Policy

The type of policy (term or whole life or other permanent coverage) affects the tax treatment.

Surrender of a Whole Life Policy Money received from the insurance company representing the cash surrender value of the policy is ordinary income in excess of the premiums paid; the recovery of an amount equal to premiums is not taxable.

Sale of a Whole Life Policy Amounts received in excess of premiums paid are taxable. The portion of the gain that would have been ordinary income if the policy had been surrendered instead of sold (cash surrender value) continues to be ordinary income; any excess gain is capital gain.

Sale of a Term Policy All of the gain is capital gain; there is no cash surrender value for a term policy.

Accelerated Death Benefits

Amounts paid to an insured who is terminally ill are fully excludable. Amounts paid to an insured who is chronically ill (see Chapter 20) are excludable to the extent they are used to pay long-term care expenses.

Review Questions

1. This year, Seymour starts to receive a pension from his employer under a defined benefit (pension) plan. The plan was funded entirely by the employer. What portion of the benefits is taxable?
   a. 0%
   b. A portion based on the simplified method
   c. A portion based on the general method
   d. 100%

2. Joan retires and receives a pension for her lifetime. She is 62 years old on the annuity starting date (the total number of anticipated monthly payments for a 62-year-old is 260). Her investment in the contract is $26,000. She receives monthly payments of $1,500. How much of her annual payments of $18,000 is tax free?
   a. $1,200
   b. $1,500
   c. $16,800
   d. $18,000

3. Which is a lump-sum distribution (assume the recipient was born before January 2, 1936)?
   a. A distribution from an IRA
   b. A lump-sum credit or payment from the federal Civil Service Retirement System
   c. A distribution from a participant's entire account in a profit-sharing plan
   d. A total distribution from a 403(b) annuity

4. Alice, who is now 60 years old, contributed to a Roth IRA on March 12, 2010, for the 2009 plan year. She files her income tax return for 2009 on April 15, 2010. What is the date that the 5-year period for tax-free Roth IRA withdrawals begins for Alice?
   a. January 1, 2009
   b. April 15, 2010
   c. January 1, 2010
   d. March 12, 2010

5. Eduardo sells a $100,000 term life policy for $18,000. He paid premiums of $10,000. What taxation results?
   a. Nothing is taxable.
   b. All of the gain is ordinary income.
   c. Part of the gain in excess of premium payments is ordinary income; the balance is capital gain.
   d. All of the gain is capital gain.

6. Olivia, age 55, has $100,000 in an IRA (not a Roth) funded entirely by deductible contributions. She wants to convert $50,000 this year to a Roth IRA. What are her tax results?
   a. No part of the distribution is currently taxable to her.
   b. Half the distribution is taxed next year and the other half in the following year.
   c. $50,000 is included in her gross income this year.
   d. Only a portion of the $50,000 is includible in gross income because of her basis in the account.

Social Security and Equivalent Railroad Retirement Benefits

A taxpayer may receive Social Security benefits as a retiree, as a disabled person, or as a beneficiary. The benefits may be totally or partially tax free. Up to 50% or 85% of the total benefits may be taxable, depending on whether the taxpayer's other income exceeds certain base amounts.

Similar tax treatment applies to tier 1 Railroad Retirement benefits but not to tier 2 Railroad Retirement benefits (the discussion of which is beyond the scope of this book).

ALERT: Although Supplemental Security Income (SSI) benefits are paid by the Social Security Administration (SSA), they should not be confused with Social Security benefits (i.e., typical Social Security income reported on SSA-1099).

SSI benefits are funded through general tax revenues, not through Social Security taxes, and are paid to eligible recipients who have limited income and limited resources. As with any payments made from a public welfare fund based on need, SSI benefits are not taxable and are not reported on Form SSA-1099 or on the recipient's tax return.

Social Security Benefits

Whether any benefits are taxable depends on the amount of benefits as well as other income, including tax-exempt interest, and the taxpayer's filing status. The age of the recipient has no bearing on whether the benefits are taxable. Thus, a taxpayer who starts receiving benefits at age 60 based on the former spouse's earnings, a ten-year old child who receives benefits as a survivor, a 45-year old who receives Social Security benefits on account of disability, or a retiree at age 75 all figure their taxable portion of benefits using the same steps.

Social Security benefits are reported on Form SSA-1099, *Social Security Benefit Statement* (see Figure 9.1). Determining the taxable portion of Social Security benefits begins with the net amount of benefits received by the taxpayer, shown in box 5 of the form. Generally, each taxpayer receiving benefits will receive his or her own form.

Determining the Taxable Portion of Social Security Benefits

Taxpayer income that exceeds the base amount for the taxpayer's filing status will subject as much as 85% of the benefits to taxation. The taxable amount depends on how much **provisional income** the taxpayer has and how much the taxpayer's provisional income exceeds the base amount for the taxpayer's filing status (see Table 9.1).

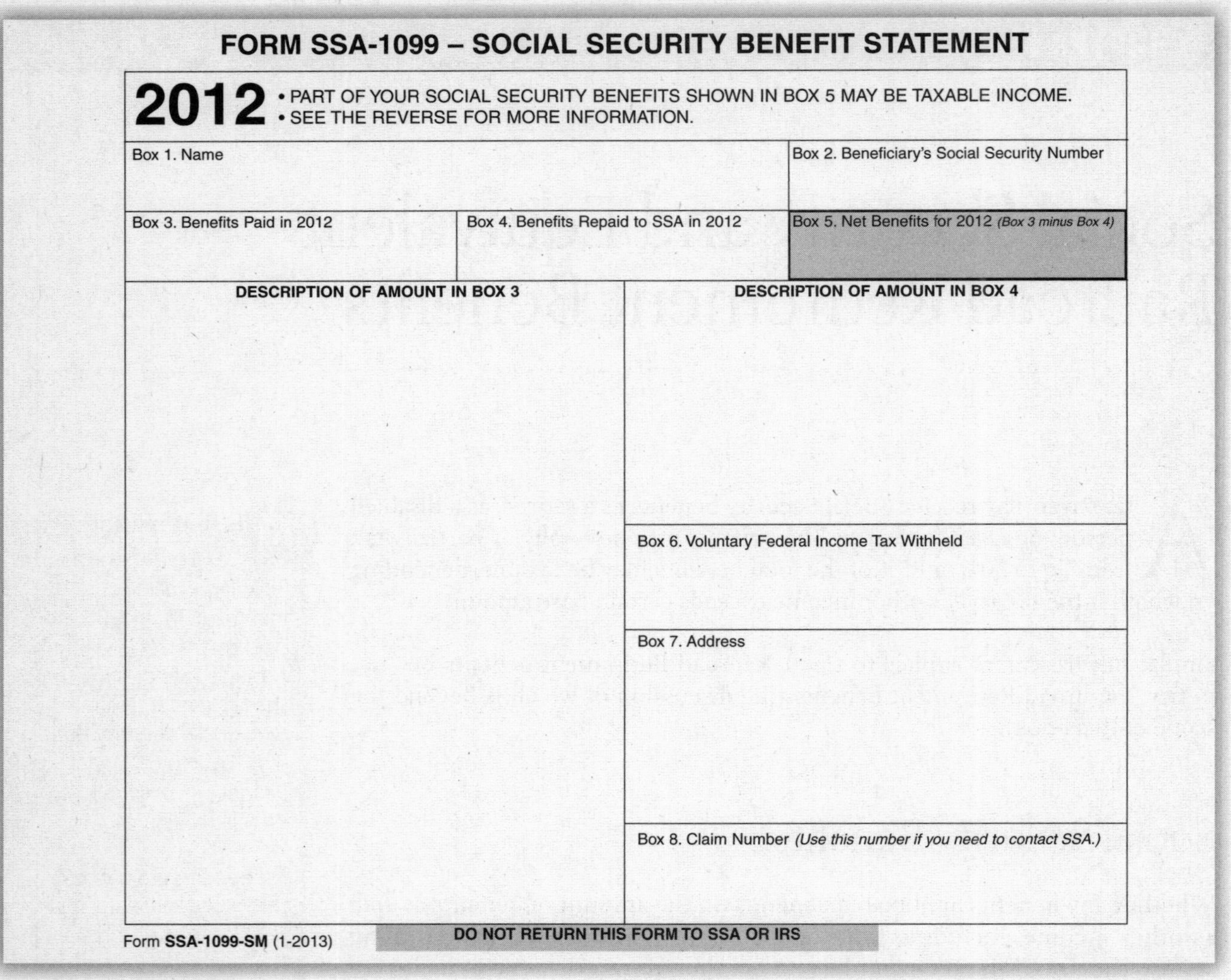

FORM SSA-1099 – SOCIAL SECURITY BENEFIT STATEMENT

2012 • PART OF YOUR SOCIAL SECURITY BENEFITS SHOWN IN BOX 5 MAY BE TAXABLE INCOME.
• SEE THE REVERSE FOR MORE INFORMATION.

Box 1. Name

Box 2. Beneficiary's Social Security Number

Box 3. Benefits Paid in 2012

Box 4. Benefits Repaid to SSA in 2012

Box 5. Net Benefits for 2012 *(Box 3 minus Box 4)*

DESCRIPTION OF AMOUNT IN BOX 3

DESCRIPTION OF AMOUNT IN BOX 4

Box 6. Voluntary Federal Income Tax Withheld

Box 7. Address

Box 8. Claim Number *(Use this number if you need to contact SSA.)*

Form **SSA-1099-SM** (1-2013)

DO NOT RETURN THIS FORM TO SSA OR IRS

FIGURE 9.1 Form SSA-1099

Income for purposes of calculations to determine the taxable portion of Social Security benefits includes:

- One-half of Social Security benefits, plus
- All tax-exempt interest (reported on line 8b of Form 1040, *U.S. Individual Income Tax Return*), plus
- All other taxable income (wages, interest, dividends, pensions, etc.)

DEFINITION: Provisional income, which is *not* defined in the Internal Revenue Code, is a technical term used to describe the sum of modified adjusted gross income plus one-half of the Social Security benefits reported to the taxpayer on Form SSA-1099.

Example

Ray, a single taxpayer, receives Social Security benefits of $12,000. His other income is $14,000 of taxable interest and $2,000 tax-exempt interest. Ray's income for purposes of figuring the taxable portion of Social Security benefits is $22,000 [($12,000 × 50%) + $14,000 taxable interest + $2,000 tax-exempt income].

For married taxpayers filing jointly, income of both spouses must be included in the calculation, even if only one spouse is receiving Social Security benefits.

Compare Income with a Base Amount

The base amount depends on the taxpayer's filing status. Find the base amount in Table 9.1.

TABLE 9.1 Base Amounts

Filing status	Base amount
Single, head of household, or qualifying widow(er)	$25,000
Married filing jointly	$32,000
Married filing separately *and* lived apart from the spouse for the entire year	$25,000
Married filing separately but did not live apart	0

ALERT: In determining whether Social Security benefits are taxable, do *not* reduce income by any of the following: exclusions for interest on U.S. savings bonds redeemed for higher-education purposes, employer-provided adoption assistance, foreign earned income or foreign housing, or income earned by residents in American Samoa or Puerto Rico.

Excess Income

If provisional income exceeds the base amount, then benefits will be partially taxable. Generally, when the base amount is exceeded, up to 50% of benefits are included in income. However, up to 85% of benefits may be includible in the income of some taxpayers when income exceeds the maximum amount.

Determining the Taxable Portion of Benefits

The amount of benefits included in income (50% or 85%) for a taxpayer, other than a married person filing separately who did not live apart from his or her spouse, depends on whether provisional income exceeds the maximum amount listed in Table 9.2.

If provisional income exceeds the maximum amount shown, 85% of the Social Security benefits received are included in income. If provisional income is between the base amount and the maximum amount, 50% of the Social Security benefits are taxable.

TIP: In the case of a married person filing separately who did not live apart from his or her spouse for the entire year, 85% of benefits are automatically included in gross income.

TABLE 9.2 Maximum Amount

Filing status	Maximum amount
Married filing jointly	$44,000
Single, head of household, qualifying widow(er), married filing separately and lived apart from spouse for the entire year.	$34,000
Married filing separately but did not live apart	0

TABLE 9.3 Summary of Taxable Social Security Benefits

	Provisional Income		
Filing Status	**None of Benefits Taxable**	**Up to 50% of Benefits Taxable**	**Up to 85% of Benefits Taxable**
Single, head of household, qualifying widow(er)	$0–$25,000	$25,001–$34,000	$34,001 & over
Married filing jointly	$0–$32,000	$32,001–$44,000	$44,001 & over
Married filing separately*			$1 & over

* If married filing separately and did not live with spouse at any time during the year, use single.

The computation of the taxable portion of benefits is made using Worksheet 1 in IRS Pub. 915, *Social Security and Equivalent Railroad Benefits*.

Example

Whitney is single and received Social Security benefits of $5,980, as shown in box 5 of Form SSA-1099. In addition, she received a fully taxable pension of $18,600, wages from a part-time job of $9,400, and taxable interest income of $990. Income for purposes of figuring the taxable portion of Social Security benefits is $31,980 ($5,980 x 50%) + $28,990 of other income]. To figure her taxable benefits, Whitney completes Worksheet 1: Whitney's taxable benefits are $2,990.

Special Payment Issues

Next are common situations regarding Social Security payments.

Check Covering Multiple Individuals If a check includes benefits for both a parent and child, the parent determines whether any of their benefits are taxable based only on his or her portion of the benefits; the remainder is considered the child's income. Whether the child's benefits are taxable depends on the child's income.

Receiving Benefits while Residing Abroad A U.S. citizen who is a resident of Canada, Egypt, Germany, Ireland, Israel, Italy (if also a citizen of Italy), Romania, or the United Kingdom is not taxed on Social Security benefits.

Canadian or German Benefits Paid to U.S. Residents Equivalent benefits paid by Canada or Germany to a U.S. resident are treated the same as U.S. Social Security benefits and are potentially subject to U.S. tax.

Repayment of Benefits Benefits repaid in the current year must be subtracted from the gross benefits to determine the amount of taxable benefits. Repaid benefits are reported to the taxpayer in box 4 of Form SSA-1099. The gross benefits are shown in box 3 and the net benefits in box 5 (gross benefits minus repayments). If there is a negative figure in box 5, a deduction or credit may be allowed (explained later in this chapter).

ALERT: Although the lump-sum election allows the taxpayer to determine the tax using the previous year's income, the taxpayer does not amend the previous year's return.

Lump-Sum Election Benefits for a prior year that are paid in a lump-sum to the taxpayer in the current year are part of the current year's taxable benefits, unless the lump-sum election is made. If the election is made, the taxable benefits for the previous year are calculated using that prior year's income (including the lump-sum payment for that prior year) rather than the current year's income. This election should be made if it lowers the tax on the benefits (e.g., if income in the prior years was below the taxable level but income in the current year makes benefits partially taxable it would be in the taxpayer's best interest to make the election). Worksheets 1 to 4 in IRS Pub. 915 may be used to determine whether the election provides a benefit. The previous year's returns are not amended, even if the election is made. Once the election is made, it can be revoked only with IRS consent.

Worksheet **Figuring Your Taxable Benefits**

Before you begin:

- If you are married filing separately and you lived apart from your spouse for all of 2012, enter "D" to the right of the word "benefits" on Form 1040, line 20a, or Form 1040A, line 14a.
- Do not use this worksheet if you repaid benefits in 2012 and your total repayments (box 4 of Forms SSA-1099 and RRB-1099) were more than your gross benefits for 2012 (box 3 of Forms SSA-1099 and RRB-1099). None of your benefits are taxable for 2012. For more information, see *Repayments More Than Gross Benefits*.
- If you are filing Form 8815, Exclusion of Interest From Series EE and I U.S. Savings Bonds Issued After 1989, do not include the amount from line 8a of Form 1040 or Form 1040A on line 3 of this worksheet. Instead, include the amount from Schedule B (Form 1040A or 1040), line 2.

1. Enter the total amount from box 5 of ALL your Forms SSA-1099 and RRB-1099. Also enter this amount on Form 1040, line 20a, or Form 1040A, line 14a **1.** 5,980

2. Enter one-half of line 1 . . . . . **2.** 2,990

3. Combine the amounts from:
Form 1040: Lines 7, 8a, 9a, 10 through 14, 15b, 16b, 17 through 19, and 21
Form 1040A: Lines 7, 8a, 9a, 10, 11b, 12b, and 13 . . . . . **3.** 28,990

4. Enter the amount, if any, from Form 1040 or 1040A, line 8b . . . . . **4.** -0-

5. Enter the total of any exclusions/adjustments for:
- Adoption benefits (Form 8839, line 24),
- Foreign earned income or housing (Form 2555, lines 45 and 50, or Form 2555-EZ, line 18), and
- Certain income of bona fide residents of American Samoa (Form 4563, line 15) or Puerto Rico . . . . . **5.** -0-

6. Combine lines 2, 3, 4, and 5 . . . . . **6.** 31.980

7. ***Form 1040 filers:*** Enter the amounts from Form 1040, lines 23 through 32, and any write-in adjustments you entered on the dotted line next to line 36.
Form 1040A filers: Enter the amounts from Form 1040A, lines 16 and 17 . . . . . **7.** -0-

8. Is the amount on line 7 less than the amount on line 6?
No. (STOP) None of your social security benefits are taxable. Enter -0- on Form 1040, line 20b, or Form 1040A, line 14b.
Yes. Subtract line 7 from line 6 . . . . . **8.** 31.980

9. If you are:
- Married filing jointly, enter $32,000
- Single, head of household, qualifying widow(er), or married filing separately and you **lived apart** from your spouse for all of 2012, enter $25,000 . . . . . **9.** 25,000

Note. If you are married filing separately and you lived with your spouse at any time in 2012, skip lines 9 through 16; multiply line 8 by 85% (.85) and enter the result on line 17. Then go to line 18.

10. Is the amount on line 9 less than the amount on line 8?
No. (STOP) None of your benefits are taxable. Enter -0- on Form 1040, line 20b, or on Form 1040A, line 14b. If you are married filing separately and you **lived apart** from your spouse for all of 2012, be sure you entered "D" to the right of the word "benefits" on Form 1040, line 20a, or on Form 1040A, line 14a.
Yes. Subtract line 9 from line 8 . . . . . **10.** 6,980

11. Enter $12,000 if married filing jointly; $9,000 if single, head of household, qualifying widow(er), or married filing separately and you **lived apart** from your spouse for all of 2012 . . . . . **11.** 9,000

12. Subtract line 11 from line 10. If zero or less, enter -0- . . . . . **12.** -0-

13. Enter the **smaller** of line 10 or line 11 . . . . . **13.** 6,980

14. Enter one-half of line 13 . . . . . **14.** 3,480

15. Enter the **smaller** of line 2 or line 14 . . . . . **15.** 2,990

16. Multiply line 12 by 85% (.85). If line 12 is zero, enter -0- . . . . . **16.** -0-

17. Add lines 15 and 16 . . . . . **17.** 2,990

18. Multiply line 1 by 85% (.85) **18.** 5,083

19. **Taxable benefits.** Enter the **smaller** of line 17 or line 18. Also enter this amount on Form 1040, line 20b, or Form 1040A, line 14b **19.** 2,990

TIP *If you received a lump-sum payment in 2012 that was for an earlier year, also complete Worksheet 2 or 3 and Worksheet 4 to see if you can report a lower taxable benefit.*

FIGURE 9.2 Whitney's Worksheet.

Railroad Retirement Benefits

Equivalent tier 1 railroad retirement benefits are the part of tier 1 benefits that a railroad employee or beneficiary would have been entitled to receive under the Social Security system. They are commonly called the Social Security Equivalent Benefit (SSEB) portion of tier 1 benefits. Tier 1 benefits are reported on Form RRB-1099, *Payments by the Railroad Retirement Board* (Figure 9.3).

UNFOLD TO SEE ALL TAX STATEMENT FORMS - SEE REVERSE SIDE FOR GENERAL INFORMATION

PAYER'S NAME, STREET ADDRESS, CITY, STATE, AND ZIP CODE **UNITED STATES RAILROAD RETIREMENT BOARD** 844 N RUSH ST CHICAGO IL 60611-2092	**2012**		**PAYMENTS BY THE RAILROAD RETIREMENT BOARD**
PAYER'S FEDERAL IDENTIFYING NO. 36-3314600	3. Gross Social Security Equivalent Benefit Portion of Tier 1 Paid in 2012		
1. Claim Number and Payee Code	4. Social Security Equivalent Benefit Portion of Tier 1 Repaid to RRB in 2012		**COPY C -**
2. Recipient's Identification Number	5. Net Social Security Equivalent Benefit Portion of Tier 1 Paid in 2012		FOR RECIPIENT'S RECORDS.
Recipient's Name, Street Address, City, State, and Zip Code	6. Workers' Compensation Offset in 2012		
	7. Social Security Equivalent Benefit Portion of Tier 1 Paid for 2011		THIS INFORMATION IS BEING FURNISHED TO THE INTERNAL REVENUE SERVICE.
	8. Social Security Equivalent Benefit Portion of Tier 1 Paid for 2010		
	9. Social Security Equivalent Benefit Portion of Tier 1 Paid for Years Prior to 2010		
	10. Federal Income Tax Withheld	11. Medicare Premium Total	

FORM RRB-1099 DO NOT ATTACH TO YOUR INCOME TAX RETURN

FIGURE 9.3 Form RRB-1099

TIP: A taxpayer can elect to have income taxes withheld on Social Security benefits by completing Form W-4V, *Voluntary Withholding Request*. The taxpayer can choose a withholding rate of 7%, 10%, 15%, or 25% from each payment. There is no withholding on Social Security benefits for a U.S. citizen whose benefits are exempt because of residence in one of the countries listed earlier.

ALERT: Benefits payable to a U.S. citizen residing in a country listed earlier in this chapter are subject to withholding unless the taxpayer files with the RRB Form RRB-1001, *Nonresident Questionnaire*. If the form is not filed, withholding is taken at the rate of 30% of benefits.

Tier 1 SSEB benefits are treated the same for tax purposes as Social Security benefits.

Social Security Disability Benefits

Disability benefits paid by the Social Security Administration are taxable in the same way as benefits paid to retirees, discussed earlier in this chapter. No special rules apply to Social Security disability benefits.

Deductions Related to Benefits

Some amounts paid by a taxpayer may be deductible. These include repayments of previously taxed disability payments, legal fees, and repayments of more than the gross benefits received during the year.

Example

Fred, a single taxpayer, receives $15,000 Social Security income in 2012. In 2012, Fred also repaid $5,000 of Social Security benefits that were overpaid to him in 2011. Fred will first reduce the current-year benefits received ($15,000) by the amount repaid during the year ($5,000). Fred then determines his taxable Social Security on $10,000. Fred is not eligible for a deduction or credit because the amount repaid in the current year did not exceed the current-year benefits received.

However, if Fred had repaid $20,000 in 2012 (rather than $5,000), Fred would report zero Social Security benefits for 2012 and would use the repayment rules discussed below for the remaining $5,000 repayment (to the extent previously included in income).

Social Security Repayment of More than Gross Benefits A taxpayer's repayment of Social Security benefits is reported on Form SSA-1099. If the amount repaid (shown in box 4) exceeds the gross benefits received (box 3), net benefits (box 5) are negative and the benefits are not taxable. A deduction or tax credit may be allowed for the excess repayment amount (repayments minus gross benefits).

ALERT: When Social Security benefits repaid during the year are *less than* the total benefits received during the year, the taxpayer simply reduces the current-year benefits by the repayment before determining taxable benefits. This occurs when there is an amount in Form SSA-1099 box 4 (benefits repaid) and a positive amount in box 5 (net benefits received).

There is a special rule for joint filers who both receive Social Security benefits (or to a taxpayer who receives more than one Form SSA-1099 in a taxable year). If one spouse's Form SSA-1099 has a negative number but the other has a positive number, combine the numbers to arrive at net benefits reported on the joint return.

Repayment of Disability Payments (and Other Previously Taxed Income) A deduction or credit may be allowed for a taxpayer who is required to repay amounts that were previously included in taxable income. For example, if the taxpayer receives taxable disability payments from an employer or an insurance company and is required to repay those amounts in a later year because of the receipt of Social Security benefits, then the taxpayer may be entitled to a deduction or credit in the year the amounts are repaid.

Whether a deduction or credit can be claimed depends on whether the amount of the repayment was $3,000 or less or more than $3,000.

Example

Wilma is expected to receive $18,000 of Social Security benefits in 2012. She was also required to repay $10,000 to a disability insurance company in 2012. Wilma receives $18,000 of Social Security benefits but uses $10,000 of the benefits to repay the disability insurance company. Wilma must use the full $18,000 to determine her taxable Social Security for the year, even though she made a $10,000 repayment to the disability insurance company. Wilma may choose either a deduction or a credit for the $10,000 repaid to the insurance company, assuming those amounts were previously included in taxable income.

Repayment of $3,000 or Less If the amount repaid was $3,000 or less, deduct it from income in the year it is repaid to the extent it was previously included in income. The deduction is an itemized deduction subject to the 2%-of- adjusted-gross-income (AGI) floor for miscellaneous itemized deductions.

Repayment of More than $3,000 If the taxpayer repaid more than $3,000, he or she may choose to take a deduction or credit. Figure both the deduction and the credit, and choose the method that provides the greater tax benefit. First, figure the deduction as an itemized deduction not subject to the 2% limit. Then figure the credit by refiguring the tax for the prior year in which the benefits were received without the benefits included. Then subtract the refigured tax from the actual tax on the return which included the benefits. If the first alternative is better, deduct it as a miscellaneous itemized deduction. If the second alternative is better, claim it as a tax credit on the return (enter "IRC 1341" in

ALERT: If part of the benefits is taxable, the taxpayer cannot use Form 1040EZ, *Income Tax Return for Single and Joint Filers with No Dependents*. If the benefits are not taxable, the taxpayer can use Form 1040EZ, but no benefits are reported on the return.

the margin on the Total Payments line of Form 1040). See Chapter 25 for more information about repayments of more than $3,000.

Legal Fees Legal fees for collecting the taxable benefits are deductible as a miscellaneous itemized deduction (subject to the 2%-of-AGI floor). Thus, taxpayers must itemize in order to deduct legal fees. Legal fees paid to collect nontaxable income are not deductible. If the benefits received contain amounts that are both taxable and nontaxable, the legal fees that are deductible are prorated based on the same ratio as the taxable portion of the benefits to the total benefits received. Please see Chapter 25.

Reporting Benefits on the Return

Benefits received (as shown on Forms SSA-1099 or RRB-1099) and the taxable portion of the benefits are reported on Form 1040 or 1040A.

If a married taxpayer is filing a separate return, 85% of the benefits will not automatically be included in income if the taxpayer lived apart from his or her spouse for the entire year. The taxpayer indicates this by entering "D" to the right of the word "benefits" on the return (Form 1040, line 20a, or on Form 1040A, line 14a). As shown in Table 9.3, whether the benefits are taxable will depend on the taxpayer's provisional income.

Review Questions

1. In figuring the taxable portion, if any, of Social Security benefits, "income" includes all of the following **except**:

a. All of Social Security benefits

b. All of tax-exempt interest

c. All of pension income

d. An employer's payment of adoption assistance

2. What is the maximum portion, if any, of Social Security benefits includible in gross income?

a. Zero

b. 50%

c. 85%

d. 100%

3. As a result of a claim, Julia receives lump-sum payments in 2012 for Social Security benefits that should have been paid to her in 2011. She makes no special election. How is the lump sum taxed?

a. It is automatically tax free.

b. It is treated as benefits paid in 2011.

c. It is treated as benefits paid in 2012.

d. She can claim a tax credit for the payments.

4. How are Social Security disability benefits treated for tax purposes?

a. They are always tax free.

b. They are taxed in the same manner as Social Security benefits paid to retirees.

c. They are always included in gross income at the rate of 85%.

d. They are fully taxable.

5. Bruce receives Social Security benefits of $12,340, taxable interest of $8,320, wages from a part-time job of $6,250, and tax-exempt interest of $200. What is Bruce's income for purposes of figuring the taxable portion of Social Security benefits?

a. $20,740

b. $20,940

c. $26,910

d. $27,110

6. Sue receives Social Security benefits of $8,670 on behalf of her dependent child, Tom. Which of the following statements is correct?

a. The benefits are taxed to Tom based on Sue's income.

b. The benefits are taxed to Tom based on his income.

c. The benefits are taxed to Sue based on Tom's income.

d. The benefits are taxed to Sue based on Sue's income.

CHAPTER 10

Other Types of Income

All income, from whatever source, is included in gross income *unless* there is a special rule that makes the income partially or fully excludable.

This chapter covers other types of income, such as alimony, taxable recoveries, income from S corporations and partnerships, and unemployment compensation that are reported on their own lines on the return but have not been discussed in a previous chapter.

However, there need not be a specific line on the tax return or a specific information document reporting the income in order for income to be taxable. Some of the most common types of taxable "other income" are income from cancellation of debt, gambling winnings, and jury duty pay. Line 21 on Form 1040, *U.S. Individual Income Tax Return*, is the line where most "other income" is reported.

Some types of income are specifically treated as tax free, including gifts and inheritances, life insurance proceeds from the death of the insured, and child support.

Scholarships and Grants

A scholarship or fellowship grant generally is not taxable if received by a taxpayer who is a candidate for a degree and if used for qualified education expenses. Qualified education expenses include:

- Tuition and fees
- Supplies and books if required by the institution for all students enrolled in the course

Room and board, travel, and equipment (that is not required for enrollment or attendance at the institution) are *not* qualified education expenses. Scholarships are taxable to the extent that funds are used for these purposes.

Tax-free scholarships reduce qualified education expenses for purposes of the education credits (see Chapter 30), whereas taxable scholarships do not. (Note that although a scholarship or grant may be taxable, it is *not* reported on Form 1040, line 21, Other Income. Instead, it is reported on line 7, Wages. If the taxable amount was not reported on Form W-2, *Wage and Tax Statement*, enter "SCH" on the dotted line next to line 7.)

Example

Lisa receives a $30,000 scholarship from Princeton for the spring semester, with $25,000 designated for tuition and $5,000 specifically designated for living expenses. Her tuition is $26,000. Lisa may exclude $25,000 of the scholarship, but the remaining $5,000 is taxable.

Taxable Recoveries

When a taxpayer deducts an expense in one year but receives a refund or recovers the expense in a later year, the receipt (recovery) is considered income to the extent it reduced taxes in the prior year. This is called the "tax benefit rule."

The most common example of a taxable recovery occurs when a taxpayer itemizes deductions (see Chapter 19) and deducts state and local income taxes one year and then receives a state tax refund in the following year. A taxable recovery is not limited to this example; it can occur when medical expenses or casualty or theft losses deducted in one year are reimbursed by an insurance company in the following year.

A recovery may be nontaxable, fully taxable, or only partially taxable, depending on the extent to which the recovery exceeded the prior-year tax benefit.

Example

Giovanni deducted state income taxes of $5,000 on his 2011 federal income tax return. In 2012, after filing his 2011 state income tax return, he receives a refund of $900. All of the $900 reduced his federal income taxes in 2011 (i.e., he received a full benefit from the deduction). Therefore, all of the $900 is taxable income in 2012.

TIP: Use the *Recoveries of Itemized Deductions* worksheet in IRS Pub. 525, *Taxable and Nontaxable Income*, to determine the extent to which a recovery is taxable.

Determine whether none, some, or all of the recovery is taxable:

- *Nontaxable recovery.* If the taxpayer received no benefit from the initial amount, a recovery is not taxable. For example, if a taxpayer did not itemize deductions (and did not receive any federal tax benefit from paying state taxes), any state income tax refund is not taxable.

- *Partially or fully taxable recovery.* If the taxpayer received a tax benefit from the initial amount, the recovery is taxable to the extent of the prior tax benefit received.

Example

Gus is single and itemized deductions on his 2011 tax return. The total of his itemized deductions was $5,900, of which $1,300 was for state and local income taxes. In 2012, Gus received a state income tax refund of $400.The standard deduction in 2011 for a taxpayer filing single was $5,800. By itemizing deductions, Gus reduced his taxable income by $100 (the excess of his itemized deductions over the standard deduction). Therefore, only $100 of his $400 state tax income tax refund is taxable.

TIP: S corporation shareholders who are also employees of the corporation may also receive wages from their business. These wages are reported as such (see Chapter 4). Wages paid by an S corporation are deducted as a corporate expense effectively reducing corporate income that is reported by shareholders on their personal returns. Owners of partnerships and LLCs are self-employed and do not receive wages; all of the net earnings from these businesses are passed through to owners and reported as business income on the owners' personal returns.

Alimony

Alimony is a payment made to or on behalf of a spouse or former spouse under a divorce or separation instrument. Alimony is fully taxable to the recipient spouse, and the spouse who pays the alimony can deduct the payments as an adjustment to gross income. See Chapter 18 for more information regarding which payments qualify as alimony.

A taxpayer who receives alimony reports it as income on Form 1040, and the taxpayer who pays the alimony deducts the payments as an adjustment to gross income on Form 1040. The alimony is symmetric: If the payments do not qualify as alimony, the ex-spouse making the payments cannot deduct them, and the ex-spouse receiving the payments does not report them.

S Corporation and Partnership Income

ALERT: An LLC with two or more owners is, by default, taxed as a partnership for federal income tax purposes *unless* the owners elect to be taxed as a corporation by filing Form 8832, *Entity Classification.* An LLC that elects to be taxed as a corporation also may elect to be taxed as an S corporation by filing Form 2553, *Election by a Small Business Corporation.*

S corporations, partnerships, and limited liability companies (LLCs) taxed as partnerships are "pass-through" entities. This means that owners of these entities report their share of business income ("profits") on their personal returns; they claim their share of business losses on their personal returns. The businesses themselves are not taxed on this income (or loss).

Shareholders in S corporations, partners in partnerships, and members in LLCs taxed as partnerships report their share of business income as it is reported to them on Schedule K-1, *Partner's Share of Income, Deductions, Credits, etc.* This is an informational form provided by the entity. S corporations and partnerships have different Schedule K-1s. (See Figure 10.1 for an example of Schedule K-1.)

651111

☐ Final K-1 ☐ Amended K-1 OMB No. 1545-0099

Schedule K-1 (Form 1065) **2011**

Department of the Treasury
Internal Revenue Service

For calendar year 2011, or tax year beginning ________, 2011 ending ________, 20 ____

Partner's Share of Income, Deductions, Credits, etc. ▶ **See back of form and separate instructions.**

Part I Information About the Partnership

A Partnership's employer identification number

B Partnership's name, address, city, state, and ZIP code

C IRS Center where partnership filed return

D ☐ Check if this is a publicly traded partnership (PTP)

Part II Information About the Partner

E Partner's identifying number

F Partner's name, address, city, state, and ZIP code

Part III Partner's Share of Current Year Income, Deductions, Credits, and Other Items

1	Ordinary business income (loss)	15	Credits
2	Net rental real estate income (loss)		
3	Other net rental income (loss)	16	Foreign transactions
4	Guaranteed payments		
5	Interest income		
6a	Ordinary dividends		
6b	Qualified dividends		
7	Royalties		
8	Net short-term capital gain (loss)		
9a	Net long-term capital gain (loss)	17	Alternative minimum tax (AMT) items
9b	Collectibles (28%) gain (loss)		
9c	Unrecaptured section 1250 gain		
10	Net section 1231 gain (loss)	18	Tax-exempt income and nondeductible expenses
11	Other income (loss)		

FIGURE 10.1 Schedule K-1 from a Partnership

TIP: Pass-through tax treatment applies to beneficiaries of trusts and estates. Some or all of the income from these entities are taxed to the beneficiaries, not to the entities. These entities issue Schedule K-1 to beneficiaries detailing the type and amount of income passed through to them.

Royalties

Royalties are payments received by a taxpayer based on ownership of certain intangible assets, such as copyrights for literary, musical, or artistic works, or patents for an invention or process. Royalties may also be received because of ownership of such properties as oil wells, natural gas reserves, or mineral deposits.

Royalties generally are reported on Schedule E, *Supplemental Income and Loss.* However, if the royalties are derived from a business that the taxpayer operates, they are reported on Schedule C, *Profit or Loss from Business* (*Sole Proprietorship*). A taxpayer is treated as having a business if he or she holds an interest in an operating oil, gas, or mineral property, or is a self-employed artist, musician, or writer.

Unemployment Compensation

Unemployment compensation includes state unemployment insurance benefits, railroad unemployment benefits, and disability benefits paid as a substitute for unemployment compensation.

Taxation of Unemployment Benefits

Unemployment compensation is fully taxable at the federal level. There is no exclusion for unemployment income.

Supplemental unemployment benefits received from a company-financed fund are not considered unemployment compensation. They are taxable as wages and subject to income tax withholding.

ALERT: If royalties are reported on Schedule E, the deduction for expenses related to the royalties may be limited by the passive activity loss (PAL) rules. See Chapter 7 for more information about these rules.

Reporting Unemployment Compensation

Unemployment compensation is reported to the taxpayer on Form 1099-G, *Certain Government Payments* (see Figure 10.2). Report these amounts as gross income on Form 1040, line 19. (A taxpayer can opt to have income tax withheld from unemployment benefits at a flat rate of 10% by filing Form W-4V, *Voluntary Withholding Request.* If a taxpayer receives unemployment compensation and federal income tax has been withheld, the withholding is reported as a tax payment.) (See Chapter 36.)

ALERT: Unemployment compensation does not include workers' compensation.

Damages

If a taxpayer files a lawsuit and receives a court award or settlement, it is taxable if it replaces income. Examples of amounts taxed as ordinary income include:

- Back pay and damages for emotional distress received to satisfy a claim under Title VII of the Civil Rights Act of 1964
- Compensation for lost wages or lost profits (in most cases)

☐ CORRECTED (if checked)

PAYER'S name, street address, city, state, ZIP code, and telephone no.		1 Unemployment compensation $ 2 State or local income tax refunds, credits, or offsets $	OMB No. 1545-0120 2012 Form 1099-G	Certain Government Payments
PAYER'S federal identification number	RECIPIENT'S identification number	3 Box 2 amount is for tax year	4 Federal income tax withheld $	Copy B For Recipient
RECIPIENT'S name		5 ATAA/RTAA payments $	6 Taxable grants $	This is important tax information and is being furnished to the Internal Revenue Service. If you are required to file a return, a negligence penalty or other sanction may be imposed on you if this income is taxable and the IRS determines that it has not been reported.
Street address (including apt. no.)		7 Agriculture payments $	8 If checked, box 2 is trade or business income ► ☐	
City, state, and ZIP code		9 Market gain $		
Account number (see instructions)		10a State / 10b State identification no.	11 State income tax withheld $	

Form 1099-G (keep for your records) Department of the Treasury - Internal Revenue Service

FIGURE 10.2 Form 1099-G

- Damages for breach of contract
- Damages for infringement of a copyright or patent
- Interest on any award or settlement
- Punitive damages (except in certain wrongful death claims)

Damages for a *physical* injury or sickness are tax free. For example, damages for a wrongful death claim are not included in income. Damages for nonphysical injury (e.g., injury to reputation) are taxable.

Damages on account of emotional distress are taxable unless the emotional distress is due to a physical injury or sickness.

Cancellation of Debt Income

When a lender or creditor forgives some or all of an outstanding debt or loan, the borrower/debtor is viewed as receiving cancellation of debt (COD) income. (It is also referred to as discharge of indebtedness income or income from "loan discounts.") Key examples of COD income include the cancellation of debt from credit cards and auto, student, and home loans. Generally, COD income is taxable unless specifically excluded by law, as discussed below.

Example

Vivian owes $42,500 on her credit card. She negotiates with the credit card company, which agrees to accept $35,000 in satisfaction of the amount owed. Vivian realizes $7,500 of COD income ($42,500 – $35,000).

ALERT: When a taxpayer's property is foreclosed or repossessed, there is also a "sale" of the property to the lender. This sale results in gain (or loss) to the taxpayer.

Forms Issued by the Lender/Creditor

Lenders/creditors use two different forms to report information to the IRS about canceled debts or abandoned property.

- Form 1099-A, *Acquisition or Abandonment of Secured Property*, is issued by a lender to a borrower when the lender has foreclosed or repossessed the property that is the security for the loan or the lender learns that the borrower has abandoned the property.
- Form 1099-C, *Cancellation of Debt*, is issued by the lender to the borrower when the lender has discharged or canceled debt owed by the borrower (see Figure 10.3).

Exclusion for Certain COD Income

Not all COD income is taxable. COD income is excludable from gross income in certain situations, including:

- *Bankruptcy*. If the taxpayer is bankrupt, a court-ordered discharge of debt is not taxable.

☐ CORRECTED (if checked)

CREDITOR'S name, street address, city, state, ZIP code, and telephone no.	1 Date of identifiable event 2 Amount of debt discharged $ 3 Interest if included in box 2 $	OMB No. 1545-1424 **2012** Form **1099-C**	**Cancellation of Debt**
CREDITOR'S federal identification number / DEBTOR'S identification number	4 Debt description		**Copy B** **For Debtor** This is important tax information and is being furnished to the Internal Revenue Service. If you are required to file a return, a negligence penalty or other sanction may be imposed on you if taxable income results from this transaction and the IRS determines that it has not been reported.
DEBTOR'S name Street address (including apt. no.) City, state, and ZIP code	5 If checked, the debtor was personally liable for repayment of the debt . . . . ▶ ☐		
Account number (see instructions)	6 Identifiable event code	7 Fair market value of property $	

Form **1099-C** (keep for your records) Department of the Treasury - Internal Revenue Service

FIGURE 10.3 Form 1099-C

- *Insolvency.* If the taxpayer's total liabilities immediately before the time of the debt discharge exceed the fair market value of his or her assets, making the taxpayer insolvent, the COD income is excludable to the extent of insolvency.

Example

A creditor reduced the debt on one of Woody's loans by $80,000 and sent to Woody Form 1099-C showing the canceled debt. Immediately before the debt was canceled, the fair market value of Woody's assets totaled $250,000 and his liabilities totaled $275,000. Thus, he was insolvent by $25,000. Woody may exclude from income up to $25,000 of the canceled debt under the insolvency exception. Thus, he is taxed on $55,000 of the canceled debt ($80,000 – $25,000).

- *Home mortgage debt.* Cancellation in 2012 of some or all of the outstanding principal of a mortgage on a principal (main) residence is not taxable. The limit is up to $2 million ($1 million if married filing separately) of **acquisition indebtedness**.
- *Cancellation of student loans.* Cancellation of student loans may be excluded from income if, as a condition of cancellation, the graduate is required to work in a certain profession and/or within a certain location for a specified period of time.

DEFINITION: Acquisition indebtedness is a mortgage secured by a residence and obtained for the purpose of buying, building, or substantially improving the residence.

Form 982, *Reduction of Tax Attributes Due to Discharge of Indebtedness (and Section 1082 Basis Adjustment)* should be filed if the taxpayer claims the bankruptcy, insolvency, or home mortgage debt exclusions listed previously. See IRS Pub. 4681, *Canceled Debts, Foreclosures, Repossessions, and Abandonments* for more information.

Gambling Winnings

Gambling winnings are fully taxable regardless of whether they are paid from legal or illegal sources. Gambling winnings also must be reported in full, whether they are reported on Form W-2G, *Certain Gambling Winnings*, or not, and cannot be netted against gambling losses for the year. Instead, losses are taken as a deduction against the winnings which is discussed later in this section.

Examples of gambling winnings include:

- State lotteries
- Raffles
- Casino winnings

ALERT: To be classified as a professional gambler, a taxpayer must be able to demonstrate that the level of gambling activity is the taxpayer's trade or business. Facts to consider include whether the gambling activity is full time and whether the taxpayer has another full-time job. Relatively few taxpayers qualify as professional gamblers.

Reporting Gambling Winnings

All gambling winnings are included in gross income and must be reported on the taxpayer's return. Gambling establishments report gambling winnings that meet a reporting threshold on Form W-2G, *Certain Gambling Winnings* (see Figure 10.4). However, even if a taxpayer wins an amount below the threshold for the gambling establishment to issue Form W-2G, the winnings are still taxable and must be reported as other income.

Report a taxpayer's gross gambling winnings on Form 1040 as other income. However, if the taxpayer is a professional gambler, report winnings (and losses, as explained next) on Schedule C of Form 1040.

3232 ☐ VOID ☐ CORRECTED

PAYER'S name	1 Gross winnings	2 Federal income tax withheld	OMB No. 1545-0238
Street address	3 Type of wager	4 Date won	2012
City, state, and ZIP code	5 Transaction	6 Race	Form W-2G
Federal identification number Telephone number	7 Winnings from identical wagers	8 Cashier	Certain Gambling Winnings
WINNER'S name	9 Winner's taxpayer identification no.	10 Window	For Privacy Act and Paperwork Reduction Act Notice, see the **2012 General Instructions for Certain Information Returns.**
Street address (including apt. no.)	11 First I.D.	12 Second I.D.	
City, state, and ZIP code	13 State/Payer's state identification no.	14 State income tax withheld	**File with Form 1096.**

Under penalties of perjury, I declare that, to the best of my knowledge and belief, the name, address, and taxpayer identification number that I have furnished correctly identify me as the recipient of this payment and any payments from identical wagers, and that no other person is entitled to any part of these payments.

Copy A For Internal Revenue Service Center

Signature ► **Date ►**

Form **W-2G** Cat. No. 10138V Department of the Treasury - Internal Revenue Service

FIGURE 10.4 Form W-2G

Other Miscellaneous Deductions	**28**	Other—from list in instructions. List type and amount ▶	28	
Total Itemized Deductions	**29**	Add the amounts in the far right column for lines 4 through 28. Also, enter this amount on Form 1040, line 40	29	
	30	If you elect to itemize deductions even though they are less than your standard deduction, check here ▶ ☐		

For Paperwork Reduction Act Notice, see Form 1040 instructions. Cat. No. 17145C **Schedule A (Form 1040) 2012**

FIGURE 10.5 Deducting Gambling Losses

Reporting Gambling Losses

Losses from gambling activities can be deducted only to the extent of gambling winnings. This is true for both professional and casual gamblers. In other words, a casual gambler cannot deduct a net loss from gambling activity. While the same rule applies to a professional gambler, a professional gambler may also deduct travel and other business expenses related to his or her trade or business as a gambler, potentially causing a net loss from the trade or business of professional gambling.

The losses and wins need not be from the same gambling activity.

Example

Frank wins $5,000 in a state lottery after buying $200 in tickets for the year. He also bet at the track and lost $1,000. Frank reports $5,000 as "other income." If he can document the losses, he can deduct all $1,200 of losses ($200 + $1,000) because they do not exceed his winnings for the year.

Claim gambling losses as miscellaneous itemized deductions on Schedule A, *Itemized Deductions*, of Form 1040, *not* subject to the 2%-of-AGI limit (see Figure 10.5). (See Chapter 25.)

ALERT: Whether a gambling establishment must issue a Form W-2G to a winner depends on the type of gambling and the amount of the winnings. For example, a gambler must win at least $1,200 from bingo or slot machines before the gambling establishment must issue Form W-2G. The threshold is $1,500 for keno and above $5,000 from a poker tournament. See the instructions to Form W-2G for more information.

Jury Duty Pay

Jury duty pay is taxable income and is reported as "other income" on line 21 of Form 1040.

If the taxpayer continues to receive the usual amount of wages from his or her employer and is required to turn over jury duty pay to the employer, then the jury pay, while still included in income, can be deducted as an adjustment to gross income (see Chapter 17).

ALERT: A taxpayer who receives jury duty pay cannot file Form 1040EZ, *Income Tax Return for Single and Joint Filers with No Dependents*, or 1040A, *U.S. Individual Income Tax Return*.

TIP: Reimbursement for mileage to and from jury duty is tax free. It is viewed as a reimbursement for out-of-pocket expenses. This treatment applies whether the taxpayer is selected for jury duty or not.

Barter

Barter is the exchange of goods and services for other goods and services. The amount taxable is the fair market value (FMV) of the goods at the time they are received.

TIP: If a taxpayer exchanges services with another person and both have agreed ahead of time as to the value of the services, usually the IRS will accept that value as the FMV unless the true value can be shown to be something else.

Example

Bob mows Anna's yard in exchange for a rare coin. Bob's reportable barter income for the mowing service is the value of the coin. Anna is considered to have sold the coin for the value of the lawn mowing.

If a taxpayer belongs to a barter club, he or she must include in income the value of the credit units added to the member's account, even if no goods or services are received until a later year. The club reports the credit units to the member on Form 1099-B, *Proceeds from Broker and Barter Exchange Transactions* (see Figure 10.6).

If a taxpayer barters his services in the course of a business, he must report the income on Schedule C (or C-EZ, *Net Profit From Business (Sole Proprietorship),*) of Form 1040. If the taxpayer's activity is a hobby, he must report the income from the services as "other income" on Form 1040. If barter involves the exchange of property, report the transaction as a sale of that item (see Chapter 13).

☐ CORRECTED (if checked)

PAYER'S name, street address, city, state, ZIP code, and telephone no.	1a Date of sale or exchange 1b Date of acquisition 1c Type of gain or loss Short-term ☐ Long-term ☐	OMB No. 1545-0715 2012 Form 1099-B	**Proceeds From Broker and Barter Exchange Transactions**
		1d Stock or other symbol	1e Quantity sold
PAYER'S federal identification number / RECIPIENT'S identification number	2a Stocks, bonds, etc. $	Reported to IRS ☐ Sales price ☐ Sales price less commissions and option premiums	2b If box checked, loss based on amount in 2a is not allowed ☐
RECIPIENT'S name	3 Cost or other basis $	4 Federal income tax withheld $	**Copy B For Recipient**
	5 Wash sale loss disallowed $	6 Checked if: a☐ Noncovered security b☐ Basis reported to IRS	This is important tax information and is being furnished to the Internal Revenue Service. If you are required to file a return, a negligence penalty or other sanction may be imposed on you if this income is taxable and the IRS determines that it has not been reported.
Street address (including apt. no.)	7 Bartering $		
City, state, and ZIP code	8 Description		
Account number (see instructions) / 2nd TIN not. ☐	9 Profit or (loss) realized in 2012 on closed contracts $	10 Unrealized profit or (loss) on open contracts—12/31/2011 $	13 State 14 State identification no.
CUSIP number	11 Unrealized profit or (loss) on open contracts—12/31/2012 $	12 Aggregate profit or (loss) on contracts $	15 State tax withheld $

Form **1099-B** (keep for your records) Department of the Treasury - Internal Revenue Service

FIGURE 10.6 Form 1099-B

Other Types of Income

Some other types of income may be taxable and others can be tax free. Next is a roundup of some common items of income, grouped according to their tax treatment.

ALERT: All "other income" - damages, cancellation of debt income, gambling winnings, barter income, etc. - are reported on Form 1040 line 21.

Other Taxable Income Items

Benefits Received from a Credit Card Insurance Program A credit card account owner may buy an insurance plan to make monthly payments on amounts owed if the owner becomes injured, sick, or unemployed. If the insurance plan makes payments, they are taxable to the account owner as "other income" to the extent that the benefits exceed the premiums paid for the insurance. It does not matter whether benefits are paid to the taxpayer or directly to the credit card company.

Bribes and Kickbacks Bribes and kickbacks are fully taxable, even if they are illegal.

Found Property A taxpayer who keeps lost or abandoned property (called treasure trove) is taxed on the FMV of the property in the first year it is in the taxpayer's undisputed possession.

Prizes and Awards Prizes, such as the Pulitzer and Nobel, are fully taxable. Employee awards generally are included in income. Certain noncash employee achievement awards may be tax free (see Chapter 4).

TIP: A prize winner can avoid taxation of the prize money by *disclaiming* it (not taking receipt of the money).

Rewards Amounts paid as rewards (e.g., to whistleblowers, tipsters, etc.) are taxable.

Strike and Lockout Benefits Benefits paid by a union are usually included in gross income unless it can be clearly shown that they were gifts.

Nontaxable Income Items

Welfare and Other Government Benefits Welfare benefits received from the taxpayer's state are not taxable, regardless of the amount. These include amounts paid based on need and amounts paid to crime victims from state funds if they are in the nature of welfare benefits.

Payments from Supplemental Security Income (SSI), a federal supplemental program for needy individuals, are not taxable.

ALERT: For purposes of the dependency exemption (explained in Chapter 3), SSI payments used for the support of the recipient are treated as support provided by a third party.

Examples of other tax-free public assistance benefits include:

- Disaster relief grants or payments and disaster mitigation payments
- Energy conservation subsidies and payments for winter energy usage

- Home Affordable Modification Program (HAMP) benefits
- Mortgage assistance payments
- Medicare or Medicaid
- Nutrition Program for the Elderly
- Veterans' benefits

Examples of taxable benefits include:

- Alternative trade adjustment assistance (ATAA) payments. These are reported to the taxpayer on Form 1099-G and entered on Form 1040 as "other income."
- Foster care payments from a state, political subdivision, or qualified foster care placement agency for the care of more than five individuals age 19 or older and certain difficulty-of-care payments. Payments to maintain space in the home for emergency foster care are also taxable.

ALERT: Calling something a "gift" does not necessarily make it so. For example, a "free gift" received for opening a bank account is taxable as interest if its fair market value exceeds certain levels. If the deposit is $5,000 or more, any gift by the bank that is worth $20 or less is not taxable. If the deposit is less than $5,000, any gift worth $10 or less is not taxable. A gift that is tax free is one given without anything of value in return. In the example, the bank gets the new account in exchange for the gift.

Other Tax-Free Income Items

Car Pools Contributions for gas, tolls, and parking received from passengers are not taxable.

Gifts The receipt of a gift, in any amount, is tax free. (The fact that the person making the gift [the donor] may owe gift taxes has no impact on the recipient of the gift. The $13,000 annual gift tax exclusion for the donor does not affect the recipient.)

Inheritances The receipt of an inheritance, in any amount, is tax free. However, if an heir who acts as an executor or other personal representative for the deceased's estate receives compensation for services for the estate, it is taxable as other income. Also, if an heir inherits an individual retirement account (IRA) or qualified retirement benefits, distributions are taxable to the heir when and to the extent the distributions are taken. In addition, income received from property after it is inherited is taxable.

Example

Mike inherits a traditional IRA worth $100,000 from his father, who died in 2012 at age 69. (Assume the father funded this account solely with tax-deductible contributions.) In 2012, Mike takes no distributions. In 2013, Mike takes $12,000 from the IRA. In 2012, Mike reports no income because the $100,000 inheritance is tax free and there were no IRA distributions. In 2013, Mike reports $12,000 in income from the IRA distribution. For more about inherited IRAs, see Chapter 8.

TIP: Income received from an estate or trust is taxed according to instructions in the Schedule K-1 provided by the estate or the trust.

Rebates Consumer rebates, including those earned on credit cards, are not taxable. They are viewed as a reduction in the purchase price (basis) of items. Similarly, utility rebates, whether received as a reduction in the purchase price of electricity or a nonrefundable credit against the purchase price of energy, are tax free.

Review Questions

1. Mr. Brown, a college student working on a degree in accounting, received the following during the year to pay his expenses:

   $4,000 scholarship used for tuition at State University

   $1,000 scholarship used for fees and books required by the college

   $8,000 fellowship used for his room and board

   What amount does Mr. Brown include in taxable income for the year?

   a. $8,000
   b. $5,000
   c. $13,000
   d. $9,000

2. John, a cash-basis taxpayer, had borrowed $5,000 from his local credit union. He lost his job and was unable to make payments on the loan. The credit union determined legal fees to collect might be more than John owed, so it canceled $3,000 of the balance due. John did not file bankruptcy and was not insolvent. How much does John report as income from cancellation of the debt?

   a. $5,000
   b. $3,000
   c. $0
   d. $8,000

3. Sherwood received disability income of $6,000. All premiums on the health and accident policy were paid by his employer and included in Sherwood's income. In addition, he received compensatory damages of $10,000 as a result of inadvertent poisoning at a restaurant. He received no other income during the year. How much income does Sherwood report on his tax return?

   a. $16,000
   b. $10,000
   c. $6,000
   d. $0

4. Lydia, age 28, is single and received $10,000 unemployment benefits from the state. She also received $3,000 from the state to reduce the cost of her winter fuel bill. What amount of income does she report for the year?

   a. $10,000
   b. $13,000
   c. $3,000
   d. $0

5. Which of the following is taxable to the recipient?

   a. $10,000 gift from mother to daughter
   b. $1 million inheritance
   c. $100 portable music player for opening a bank account
   d. $50 rebate for buying a laptop

CHAPTER 11

Self-Employment Activities

A large number of taxpayers have full-time or sideline businesses. More than 17% of all taxpayers filed a Schedule C (or C-EZ), *Profit or Loss From Business,* in 2009 to report their income and expenses from self-employment (SE) activities.

If a taxpayer has not incorporated his or her business, report all business income on Schedule C (or C-EZ). Generally, income that is reported by the business must match income reported to the IRS on information documents such as Form 1099-MISC, *Miscellaneous Income,* or Form 1099-K, *Merchant Card and Third Party Network Payments.* However, sole proprietorships may have income that is not traceable to one or more 1099 forms.

Recall from Chapter 4 that taxpayers who are employees do *not* file Schedule C (except for statutory employees). Although a taxpayer who is a full-time employee may also have a business, only income generated by the business must be reported on Schedule C.

Expenses in a business are deductible if they are ordinary and necessary expenses to operate the business. Sometimes taxpayers use assets in their businesses (such as a car) personally as well. These taxpayers must keep adequate records to differentiate business expenses from personal expenses. Moreover, numerous limitations and special rules apply to restrict deductible expenses. For example, a sole proprietor cannot deduct on Schedule C a contribution for his or her own retirement savings. Also, some business expenses may qualify a taxpayer for a tax credit.

This chapter covers some key information for self-employed individuals. More information can be found in IRS Pub. 334, *Tax Guide for Small Business.*

Who Files Schedule C (or Schedule C-EZ)?

Business owners who are sole proprietors file Schedule C (or C-EZ). (Farmers who are sole proprietors file Schedule F, *Profit or Loss From Farming,* as explained later in this chapter.) Sole proprietors include individuals who are independent contractors.

ALERT: If the LLC has any employees, it must file Schedule C using an Employer Identification Number (EIN) for the business; it cannot use the owner's EIN (Social Security Number). If the LLC has not previously obtained an EIN, it must do so when it hires any employees.

Limited liability companies (LLCs) owned by one person that do not elect to be taxed as corporations are called "disregarded entities." In effect, these entities are disregarded, or ignored, as taxable entities. The owners of these LLCs also file Schedule C as their business return.

Husband–Wife Partnerships

Generally, a husband and wife who jointly own and operate an unincorporated business are partners in a partnership, requiring the filing of Form 1065, *U.S. Return of Partnership Income*. However, the spouses may elect to form a "qualified joint venture" (QJV) enabling them to file two Schedule Cs (one for each spouse) instead of filing a partnership return and reporting their income on two Schedule K-1, *Partner's Share of Income, Deductions, Credits, etc.*, that the partnership issues to each of them.

Certain conditions must be met to file as a QJV:

- The spouses are the only owners of the business.
- The business is not merely a joint ownership of property but an actual business.
- Both spouses materially participate in the business (material participation is explained in Chapter 7).
- The spouses elect to divide in accordance with their interests in the venture all items of income, gain, loss, deduction, and credits attributable to the business.

ALERT: If spouses live in a community property state (see Chapter 2) and one spouse is treated as an owner because of community property rules but does not participate in the business, all of the income is the SE earnings of the spouse who participates.

(The election to be a QJV and file two Schedule Cs does not change the couple's total income taxes. However, it does allow each spouse to earn Social Security and Medicare credits. Each spouse must complete Schedule SE, *Self-Employment Tax*, to figure SE tax.)

The election to be a QJV and file two Schedule Cs is revocable once it is made. However, it can be revoked only with IRS permission.

Schedule C or Schedule C-EZ?

File Schedule C-EZ, the simplified Schedule C, only if *all* of these conditions are met; otherwise, file Schedule C:

- Business expenses are $5,000 or less (and none requires the filing of Form 4562, *Depreciation and Amortization*, explained later in this chapter).
- The business uses the cash method of accounting.
- The business does not have any inventory during the year.
- The business does not have a net loss (and does not have any passive activity loss carryovers from a prior year).
- The taxpayer has only one business (as a sole proprietor, statutory employee, or QJV).

- The business does not have any employees during the year.
- The business does not deduct expenses for business use of the home.

Starting Schedule C

Describe the taxpayer's type of business on the schedule: the general field or activity, the type of product or service, and the type of customer or client (see Figure 11.1). The IRS gives these examples:

- Wholesale sale of hardware to retailers
- Appraisal of real estate for lending institutions

Also enter the business code, a six-digit number that identifies the business activity. Business codes can be found in the instructions to Schedule C.

> **DEFINITIONS:** Under the **cash method** of accounting, income is reported when actually or constructively received (i.e., when the taxpayer has control over the funds). Expenses are deducted when paid.
>
> Under the **accrual method** of accounting, income and expenses are reported when all the events necessary to earn the income or owe the expense have occurred and the amount is determinable.

Accounting Method

Indicate the accounting method used by the business. Most Schedule C filers use the **cash method**. However, some inventory-based businesses may use the **accrual method**.

Material Participation

Indicate whether the taxpayer materially participates in the business activities. Material participation occurs when the taxpayer is involved in an activity on a regular, continuous, and substantial basis during the year.

Reporting Income

Report all business income (other than amounts that are excludable) on the return (see Figure 11.2).

SCHEDULE C (Form 1040)
Department of the Treasury Internal Revenue Service (99)

Profit or Loss From Business
(Sole Proprietorship)
► **For information on Schedule C and its instructions, go to *www.irs.gov/schedulec*.**
► **Attach to Form 1040, 1040NR, or 1041; partnerships generally must file Form 1065.**

OMB No. 1545-0074
2012
Attachment Sequence No. **09**

Name of proprietor | **Social security number (SSN)**

A Principal business or profession, including product or service (see instructions) | **B Enter code from instructions** ►

C Business name. If no separate business name, leave blank. | **D Employer ID number (EIN),** (see instr.)

E Business address (including suite or room no.) ►
City, town or post office, state, and ZIP code

F Accounting method: **(1)** ☐ Cash **(2)** ☐ Accrual **(3)** ☐ Other (specify) ►

G Did you "materially participate" in the operation of this business during 2012? If "No," see instructions for limit on losses . ☐ **Yes** ☐ **No**

H If you started or acquired this business during 2012, check here . . . . ► ☐

I Did you make any payments in 2012 that would require you to file Form(s) 1099? (see instructions) . . . ☐ **Yes** ☐ **No**

J If "Yes," did you or will you file required Forms 1099? . . . ☐ **Yes** ☐ **No**

FIGURE 11.1 Schedule C, *Profit or Loss From Business*

Part I	Income		
1	Gross receipts or sales. See instructions for line 1 and check the box if this income was reported to you on Form W-2 and the "Statutory employee" box on that form was checked . . . . ▶ ☐	1	
2	Returns and allowances (see instructions)	2	
3	Subtract line 2 from line 1	3	
4	Cost of goods sold (from line 42)	4	
5	**Gross profit.** Subtract line 4 from line 3	5	
6	Other income, including federal and state gasoline or fuel tax credit or refund (see instructions)	6	
7	**Gross income.** Add lines 5 and 6 . . . . ▶	7	

FIGURE 11.2 Schedule C, Part I

DEFINITION: The **cost of goods sold** represents the business owner's cost to purchase inventory. When a business owner purchases inventory for resale, the cost of the inventory is not a deductible expense until it is sold. Different methods can be used to determine the cost of goods sold. A discussion of inventory valuation methods can be found in IRS Pub. 538, *Accounting Periods and Methods*.

- For service-based businesses, income usually is in the form of fees.
- For inventory-based businesses, report gross receipts (proceeds from the sale of inventory). Gross receipts are reduced by the **cost of goods sold**, which is the business owner's cost to purchase the inventory. The cost of goods sold is calculated on part III of Schedule C.

Information Returns

Some types of income are reported to the IRS on information returns. The IRS uses information returns to check that taxpayers are reporting their income. Two key information returns of note for 2012 are:

- *Form 1099-MISC, Miscellaneous Income.* Payers use this information return to report payments to independent contractors for services of $600 or more in total for the year.
- *Form 1099-K, Merchant Card and Third Party Network Payments.* Financial institutions use this information return to report merchant transactions on credit cards, debit cards, and electronic transactions. However, no reporting is required unless the taxpayer exceeds $20,000 in total transactions *and* exceeds 200 transactions processed during the year.

ALERT: The taxpayer must report income even if no information return has been received (e.g., services were only $500 for the year).

Other Income

A business may earn interest on accounts receivable, recover a bad debt, or have other income that is not the mainstay of the business activity. Report this other income on a catchall line on Schedule C called "other income."

Business Expenses

Schedule C has a number of lines for listing various types of business expenses (see Figure 11.3). It also has a catchall line for expenses that do not fit within the enumerated lines, such as banking fees and business-related education costs. The catchall line is the total of expenses entered in Part V of Schedule C.

Part II Expenses — **Enter expenses for business use of your home only on line 30.**

8	Advertising	8		18	Office expense (see instructions)	18	
9	Car and truck expenses (see instructions)	9		19	Pension and profit-sharing plans .	19	
				20	Rent or lease (see instructions):		
10	Commissions and fees .	10		a	Vehicles, machinery, and equipment	20a	
11	Contract labor (see instructions)	11		b	Other business property . . .	20b	
12	Depletion	12		21	Repairs and maintenance . . .	21	
13	Depreciation and section 179 expense deduction (not included in Part III) (see instructions)	13		22	Supplies (not included in Part III) .	22	
				23	Taxes and licenses	23	
				24	Travel, meals, and entertainment:		
14	Employee benefit programs (other than on line 19) . .	14		a	Travel	24a	
15	Insurance (other than health)	15		b	Deductible meals and entertainment (see instructions) .	24b	
16	Interest:			25	Utilities	25	
a	Mortgage (paid to banks, etc.)	16a		26	Wages (less employment credits) .	26	
b	Other	16b		27a	Other expenses (from line 48) . .	27a	
17	Legal and professional services	17		b	**Reserved for future use** . . .	27b	

FIGURE 11.3 Schedule C, Part II, Expenses

Many of the expenses that have their own line on Schedule C are self-explanatory, such as advertising, insurance (other than health insurance), and rental expenses.

ALERT: A self-employed individual cannot deduct his or her own health insurance premiums as a business expense. Deduct the premiums as an adjustment to gross income on Form 1040 on the line labeled *Self-employed health insurance deduction*. Similarly, contributions to a qualified retirement plan for the self-employed person are not a business deduction; they also are deducted as an adjustment to gross income. These deductions are explained in Chapter 17.

Car and Truck Expenses

If a taxpayer drives his or her personal car, truck, or van for business, costs related to the business driving are deductible. (Special recordkeeping requirements for business driving are discussed later in this chapter.) There are two ways to figure the expense, and a taxpayer can select the method that produces the larger deduction:

1. Actual expenses, OR
2. An IRS standard mileage rate

Actual Expense Method Determine the portion of driving that is for business use; only this portion of expenses (gasoline, oil, repairs, maintenance, etc.) is deductible. For vehicles that are owned, an allowance for depreciation may be claimed (as explained later in this chapter under "Depreciation").

Example

Simon drives his car 18,000 miles during the year. Of these miles, 12,000 miles are for business. Thus, two-thirds of vehicle expenses for this car are deductible.

ALERT: The IRS mileage rate can be used only if the taxpayer elects to use it for the first year the vehicle is owned and placed in service or leased. After the first year, the taxpayer can elect to use either actual expenses or the IRS mileage rate. The IRS mileage rate cannot be used if the business operates five or more vehicles at the same time (fleet operations).

Standard Mileage Rate Instead of tracking all the expenses of vehicle usage for the year, a business owner can deduct vehicle expenses based on an IRS mileage rate. This rate takes the place of depreciation or lease payments, maintenance and repairs, tires, gasoline (including all taxes), oil, insurance, and license and registration fees. For 2012, the rate is 55.5¢ per mile.

Example

Simon drives his car 18,000 miles in 2012, of which 12,000 miles are for business. Using the standard mileage rate, his deduction for 2012 is $6,660 (12,000 × 55.5¢).

Deducting Vehicle Expenses

A taxpayer who deducts business expenses for a personal vehicle may be required to complete Part IV of Schedule C (see Figure 11.4). This part attests to whether the taxpayer has written records for the usage. (Recordkeeping is explained later in this chapter under "Recordkeeping".)

TIP: Regardless of which method is used, a taxpayer can also deduct parking fees, tolls, and interest on vehicle financing. These expenses are not included in the standard mileage rate.

Contract Labor, Wages, and Employee Benefits

A self-employed individual does *not* receive wages. (He or she is not an employee of the business.) If a self-employed individual has any employees or independent contractors, labor costs are deductible.

If the self-employed individual provides employees with any fringe benefits (such as health insurance and/or retirement plan contributions), these too are deductible.

Part IV **Information on Your Vehicle.** Complete this part **only** if you are claiming car or truck expenses on line 9 and are not required to file Form 4562 for this business. See the instructions for line 13 to find out if you must file Form 4562.

43 When did you place your vehicle in service for business purposes? (month, day, year) ► ____ / ____ / ____

44 Of the total number of miles you drove your vehicle during 2010, enter the number of miles you used your vehicle for:

a Business ____________ **b** Commuting (see instructions) ____________ **c** Other ____________

45 Was your vehicle available for personal use during off-duty hours? . . . . . ☐ **Yes** ☐ **No**

46 Do you (or your spouse) have another vehicle available for personal use? . . . . . ☐ **Yes** ☐ **No**

47a Do you have evidence to support your deduction? . . . . . ☐ **Yes** ☐ **No**

b If "Yes," is the evidence written? . . . . . ☐ **Yes** ☐ **No**

FIGURE 11.4 Schedule C, Part IV

Start-Up Costs

Start-up costs include expenses such as:

- An analysis or survey of potential markets, products, labor supply, transportation facilities. etc.
- Advertisements for the opening of the business
- Salaries and wages for training employees
- Travel and other necessary costs for securing prospective distributors, suppliers, or customers
- Salaries and fees for executives and consultants, or for similar professional services

(See IRS Pub. 535, *Business Expenses* for more information about start-up costs.)

Generally, start-up costs must be capitalized and amortized (reduced ratably) over 180 months, starting with the month the business begins operations. However, an election can be made to deduct start-up costs, subject to these restrictions:

- Up to $5,000 of start-up costs may be deducted in the current tax year. If start-up costs exceed $5,000 but not $55,000, the first $5,000 is deductible, with the balance deducted ratably over 180 months. However, if costs exceed $50,000, the up-front deduction is reduced by each dollar above this limit.

Example

Suzanne has start-up costs in 2012 of $52,000. She can deduct $3,000 immediately ($5,000 – [$52,000 – $50,000]). She can deduct the $49,000 balance ratably over 180 months ($272 per month).

- If costs exceed $55,000, they must be deducted ratably over the 180-month (15-year) amortization period starting in the month that the business begins (i.e., 1/180 × 5 months is deductible in 2012 if the business begins in August 2012).

ALERT: If the self-employed individual is an employer, use the EIN in place of the taxpayer's Social Security Number on Schedule C. The employer also is responsible for payroll taxes (not discussed in this book).

TIP: View the taxpayer's records, whether a paper log book or a printed copy of an electronic record.

Depreciation

Depreciation is an allowance that is deducted on long-lived assets that the business purchases. No depreciation is claimed on property that is leased.

The property can be tangible *personal property* items, such as furniture or computers. The property can be *real property*, such as an office building or factory.

Some types of property cannot be depreciated. For example, land is not depreciable. Similarly, in most cases antiques may not be depreciated because there is no determinable life for such items. Property that is bought and sold within the same year is not depreciated. Intangible assets, such as patents, copyrights, and covenants not to compete, are not depreciated; their cost may be deducted through amortization.

A brief explanation about the rules for depreciation follows. A more in-depth explanation can be found in IRS Pub. 946, *How to Depreciate Property*.

MACRS The Modified Accelerated Cost Recovery System (MACRS) is the system used for depreciating property. The system has various classes of assets; each class has its own recovery period over which depreciation is claimed.

There are regular depreciation tables for each class of property (general depreciation system [GDS]) and tables for the alternative depreciation system (ADS). For full table listings, see IRS Pub. 946.

Depreciation conventions (special rules) also affect the timing of depreciation. Under the *half-year convention*, it is assumed that all personal property is placed in service midyear, regardless of when the property is actually purchased and put to use in the business. This convention alters the depreciation deduction that can be taken for the first year. Under the *mid-quarter convention*, depreciation begins at the midpoint of the quarter of the tax year in which the asset is placed in service if more than 40% of tangible personal property is placed in service during the last quarter of the year. There are also special rules for short years (when a business starts or ends in midyear).

Listed Property The tax law classifies certain business property as "listed property." Generally, listed property includes items that can be used personally as well as for a business. Included in this category are vehicles (rated at 6,000 pounds or less of unloaded gross weight for passenger vehicles, or 6,000 pounds or less of gross vehicle weight for trucks and vans), computers, and video-recording equipment. Cell phones, which had been listed property, were delisted in 2010.

If the property is not used *more than* 50% for business, the taxpayer cannot use the Section 179 deduction (explained later in this chapter under "Section 179 Deduction and Bonus Depreciation") or a special depreciation allowance. The business portion of the property must be depreciated using only the ADS.

Claiming Depreciation Depreciation can be first claimed when property is placed in service. This means when property is ready and available to be used in the business, not merely ordered or paid for.

Depreciation ends when the property has been fully depreciated or when it is retired from service (sold, exchanged, abandoned, etc.).

Example

Seymour bought a machine for his business in December 2011. It was delivered and put into service in January 2012. He can start to depreciate it in 2012, the year it was placed in service. In July 2013, the machine becomes obsolete, and he simply disposes of it. He must stop claiming depreciation at this time.

Basis for Depreciation The basis of the property for depreciation generally is its adjusted basis. In most cases, adjusted basis is the original cost of the property, reduced by depreciation previously allowed or allowable. Basis is discussed in detail in Chapter 12.

When personal property is converted to business use, the basis for depreciation is the *lower of* its adjusted basis or the fair market value (FMV) at the time of conversion.

Example

Vernon starts a business from a home office in the house that he owns. (Assume the home office is 10% of the entire home.) He paid $150,000 for the house (exclusive of the land), which is now worth $225,000. He also converts his personal computer to business use. He paid $2,500 for the computer; it is now worth $900. For depreciation purposes, the basis of the home is $15,000 (10% of the adjusted basis of the home because it is lower than its current FMV). The basis of the computer is its FMV of $900 because this is lower than its adjusted basis.

Section 179 Deduction and Bonus Depreciation In order to encourage business purchases of property to help stimulate the economy, the tax law provides special deductions for the year of these purchases. For 2012, there are two types of special deductions (both of which can be used for the same item where applicable):

1. *Section 179 deduction.* This is a deduction of the cost of tangible personal property up to $500,000. However, if the cost of all qualifying property placed in service during the year exceeds $2 million, the $500,000 limit is reduced dollar for dollar for each dollar over this limit. The deduction applies to both new and used property purchased. However, there is a taxable income limit so that the deduction can be claimed only if the business is profitable. The Section 179 deduction applies only if the taxpayer elects to use it by completing Part I of Form 4562.
2. *Bonus depreciation.* This is a deduction for 50% of the cost of tangible MACRS property with a class life of 20 years or less, computers, and certain building improvements. Bonus depreciation applies only to new property. However, there is no taxable income requirement, so the deduction can be used to create or increase a net operating loss (NOL). Bonus depreciation applies automatically unless the taxpayer elects not to claim it. (Financing the purchase of property in whole or in part does not affect the Section 179 deduction or bonus depreciation.)

Depreciating Business Vehicles Special limits apply to depreciation for cars, trucks, and vans used in business. Depreciation cannot exceed a set dollar limit, based on the year in which the vehicle is first placed in service. Table 11.1 shows the dollar limits for vehicles placed in service in 2012. (Dollar limits for vehicles placed in service in prior years can be found in IRS Pub. 463, *Travel, Entertainment, Gift, and Car Expenses*).

For heavy sport utility vehicles (SUVs; weighing more than 6,000 pounds), there is a $25,000 first-year expensing limit; the dollar limits in Table 11.1 do *not* apply.

TABLE 11.1 Dollar Limits on Depreciation of Vehicles Placed in Service in 2012

Year	Passenger cars	Light trucks and vans
First year (2012)	$3,160 for used cars; $11,160 for cars eligible for bonus depreciation	$3,360 for used trucks and vans; $11,360 for trucks and vans eligible for bonus depreciation
Second year (2013)	$5,100	$5,300
Third year (2014)	$3,050	$3,150
Succeeding years (2015 and later)	$1,875	$1,875

There are no special depreciation limits for non–personal use vehicles (such as trucks with gross weight over 14,000 pounds). Either of the special write-offs (Section 179 deduction or bonus depreciation) can be used if applicable. Non–personal use vehicles are those that do not readily accommodate personal driving, such as a van with a jump seat and special built-in shelving. However, merely adding a business sign to the vehicle's exterior does not make it a non–personal use vehicle.

Recapture When tangible personal property that has been depreciated is sold at a gain, the amount of depreciation that has been claimed is reported as ordinary income. This is called "recapture." It applies to:

- Any Section 179 deduction
- Bonus depreciation
- MACRS allowance

In the case of real property, such as depreciation claimed on a home office, depreciation recapture is called "unrecaptured depreciation." All such depreciation claimed after May 6, 1997, to the extent of gain, is taxed at up to 25%.

Example

Vernon, in the earlier example, started his home business and claimed depreciation on $15,000. Assume depreciation for three years totaled $1,138, and he sold his home in 2015 at a gain of $130,000. If he uses the home sale exclusion, he is not taxed on his gain *except* that he must report $1,138 as unrecaptured depreciation, which is taxed at 25% (if he is in a tax bracket of at least this rate). Thus, he effectively pays a tax of $285 (25% of $1,138).

Home Office Deduction If a taxpayer uses a portion of his or her home to run a business, expenses related to the home are deductible as a business expense. Use Form 8829, *Expenses for Business Use of Your Home*, to figure the home office deduction, and enter the amount on Schedule C.

To qualify for a home office deduction, which is the total of the allocable expenses, the home must be used regularly and exclusively as:

- *The principal place of business.* If the home is used for administrative tasks, the home office can qualify even if business is conducted primarily at client/customer locations. For example, a plumber who uses a home office to keep books, schedule appointments, and order supplies can claim a home office deduction, OR

- *A place to meet or deal with clients, customers, or patients in the normal course of business.* For example, an attorney with an office downtown who uses space in her suburban home to meet with clients to sign papers can claim a home office deduction.

A home office deduction is also available if a separate structure (not attached to the home) is used in connection with the business or if space is used on a regular basis to store inventory or product samples.

Once you determine that a taxpayer can deduct home office expenses, segregate them into "direct" and "indirect" expenses.

- *Direct expenses* are those that relate solely to the home office (e.g., painting the home office). All of the direct expenses are deductible.
- *Indirect expenses* are those that relate to the entire home (e.g., painting the outside of the home, a security monitoring service, and monthly rent if the home is rented rather than owned). Only the portion of indirect expenses that relate to the home office are claimed as part of the home office deduction. The portion is determined by the amount of square footage of the office as it relates to the home. For example, if the home is 2,800 square feet and an area of 280 square feet is used for the office, 10% of the home is the home office; 10% of indirect expenses may be deducted. The balance of otherwise deductible indirect expenses may be deducted as personal itemized deductions (such as home mortgage interest, real estate taxes, and casualty losses); other expenses may be nondeductible (such as insurance, maintenance, and repairs).

TIP: Special rules apply to day care services provided in the home. For more details, see the instructions to Form 8829.

Depreciation (as explained earlier in this chapter) on the home office is also allowed if the taxpayer owns the residence.

Example

Vernon, in our continuing example, has mortgage interest of $8,000 and real estate taxes of $5,400. His other indirect expenses for homeowner's insurance, repairs, and other related expenses total $2,200. His total indirect expenses are $15,600. Since 10% of this home (determined on a square-footage basis) is used for his home office, 10% of these indirect expenses, or $1,560, may be deducted as part of his home office deduction. To this amount he can add any direct expenses for the office. Finally, he can claim depreciation on the $15,000 basis in his home, as explained earlier in an earlier example.

ALERT: Not all homeowner expenses can be taken into account in figuring the home office deduction. For example, the basic charge for the first phone line into a home and landscaping costs are not deductible. For more details about the home office deduction, see IRS Pub. 587, *Worksheet to Figure the Deduction for Business Use of Your Home.*

The home office deduction cannot exceed income earned from the home office activity for the year. In other words, a sole proprietor cannot incur a loss for his or her business by including all home office expenses. If the taxpayer has a loss, the deduction for home office expenses is limited. IRS Pub. 587 provides a worksheet to calculate the allowable deduction for home office expenses.

Generally, home office expenses that exceed gross income may be carried forward and used in a subsequent year, limited again to gross income in that year. There is no time limit on the carryforward.

Example

Jerry runs a business from his home office. His home office expenses for 2012 are $8,360. His gross income from the home office activity is $4,920. In 2012, his home office deduction is limited to $4,920; his carryforward is $3,440. In 2013, gross income from his home office activity is $45,110, and his home office expenses are again $8,360. He can claim all of his current home office expenses, plus the $3,440 carryforward, in 2013.

Casualty and Theft Losses If the business suffers an unreimbursed casualty or theft, the loss is fully deductible. Any partially reimbursed loss may be deducted to the extent of any reimbursement. This is in contrast to the deduction for personal casualty and theft losses, which is subject to limitations (explained in Chapter 24.)

However, a casualty or theft loss that involves inventory can be either deducted as a casualty or theft loss or deducted by including the amount of the inventory loss in cost of goods sold expense. To deduct the loss through cost of goods sold, simply record ending inventory at the actual amount of inventory. This causes the cost of goods sold expense to increase. If a taxpayer opts to deduct the loss as a casualty or theft loss, the items must be removed from inventory so they are not counted twice. In this case, either remove the items from the opening inventory (attach a statement explaining the adjustment to opening inventory) or adjust the amount of purchases made during the year.

Business Losses

If business expenses exceed business income, a net loss results. The loss may produce an NOL that can be carried back for a certain number of years to offset income in those years and generate a tax refund. A complete discussion of NOLs is beyond the scope of this book. To learn more, see IRS Pub. 536, *Net Operating Losses.*

Farmers

Farmers and ranchers who are self-employed use Schedule F, *Profit or Loss From Farming,* rather than Schedule C, to report their income and expenses. More information about tax returns for farmers and ranchers is available in IRS Pub. 225, *Farmer's Tax Guide.*

Much of the general information (name of the proprietor, EIN) that must be reported on Schedule F is the same as that reported on Schedule C (see Figure 11.5). See Part IV of Schedule F for the principal agricultural activity codes.

Who Files Schedule F?

A taxpayer who cultivates, operates, or manages a farm for profit, either as owner or tenant, must file Schedule F. For this purpose, a *farm* includes livestock, dairy, poultry, fish, fruit, and truck farms as well as plantations, ranches, ranges, and orchards.

The same rules for Schedule C for qualified joint ventures and community property apply to Schedule F.

> **ALERT:** Report on Form 4797, *Sales of Business Property,* and then enter directly on Form 1040 sales of farm products that are not held primarily for sale, such as livestock held for draft, breeding, sport, or dairy purposes.

Farm Income

Farm income includes amounts received for operating a stock, dairy, poultry, fish, fruit, or truck farm as well as income from operating a plantation, ranch, range, or orchard. Report income from the sale of crop shares if the taxpayer materially participates in producing the crop.

Report income that is reported to the taxpayer on information returns, including Form 1099-PATR, *Taxable Distributions Received From Cooperatives* (for patronage dividends, which are distributions that cooperatives pay to their members). Some other special types of farm income include:

- Crop insurance and crop disaster payments
- Agricultural payments (cash, materials, services, or commodity certificates from Commodity Credit Corporation loans)
- National Tobacco Settlement payments
- Forest health protection payments

(Farmers who receive crop insurance and crop disaster payments can opt to have income taxes withheld at the rate of 7%, 10%, 15%, or 25% by filing Form W-4V, *Voluntary Withholding Request*)

Income generally is reported according to the taxpayer's method of accounting (cash or accrual, as explained earlier in this chapter). Separate sections on Schedule F are used to report income, depending on the accounting method. Part I is for farm income on the cash method; Part III is for farm income on the accrual method (see Figures 11.5–11.7).

> **TIP:** The income of a taxpayer who is a farmer or a fisherman can be "income averaged." In such a case, the income is effectively taxed as if it were received evenly over three years. Income averaging has the effect of reducing the tax on the income. Income averaging is figured on Schedule J, *Income Averaging for Farmers and Fishermen,* of Form 1040.

Farming Expenses

Farmers can claim business expenses discussed earlier in connection with Schedule C (Figure 11.3).

However, farmers may have some special expenses, which include the following (the list is not all-inclusive; for more details see IRS Pub. 225):

- *Farm supplies (feed, seed, fertilizer, and similar supplies).* Cash-method farmers who prepaid for these supplies may not be able to deduct these costs in the year they were purchased; instead, they must allocate part of the costs to the year that the supplies are used.

SCHEDULE F (Form 1040)
Department of the Treasury
Internal Revenue Service (99)

Profit or Loss From Farming

▶ Attach to Form 1040, Form 1040NR, Form 1041, Form 1065, or Form 1065-B.
▶ Information about Schedule F and its separate instructions is at *www.irs.gov/form1040*.

OMB No. 1545-0074
2012
Attachment Sequence No. **14**

Name of proprietor			Social security number (SSN)
A Principal crop or activity	B Enter code from Part IV ▶	C Accounting method: ☐ Cash ☐ Accrual	D Employer ID number (EIN), (see instr)

E Did you "materially participate" in the operation of this business during 2012? If "No," see instructions for limit on passive losses ☐ Yes ☐ No

F Did you make any payments in 2012 that would require you to file Form(s) 1099 (see instructions) ☐ Yes ☐ No

G If "Yes," did you or will you file required Forms 1099? ☐ Yes ☐ No

Part I **Farm Income—Cash Method.** Complete Parts I and II (Accrual method. Complete Parts II and III, and Part I, line 9.)

1a	Sales of livestock and other resale items (see instructions)	1a		
b	Cost or other basis of livestock or other items reported on line 1a	1b		
c	Subtract line 1b from line 1a		1c	
2	Sales of livestock, produce, grains, and other products you raised		2	
3a	Cooperative distributions (Form(s) 1099-PATR)	3a	3b Taxable amount	3b
4a	Agricultural program payments (see instructions)	4a	4b Taxable amount	4b
5a	Commodity Credit Corporation (CCC) loans reported under election			5a
b	CCC loans forfeited	5b	5c Taxable amount	5c
6	Crop insurance proceeds and federal crop disaster payments (see instructions)			
a	Amount received in 2012	6a	6b Taxable amount	6b
c	If election to defer to 2013 is attached, check here ▶ ☐		6d Amount deferred from 2011	6d
7	Custom hire (machine work) income			7
8	Other income (see instructions)			8
9	**Gross income.** Add amounts in the right column (lines 1c, 2, 3b, 4b, 5a, 5c, 6b, 6d, 7, and 8). If you use the accrual method, enter the amount from Part III, line 50 (see instructions) ▶			9

FIGURE 11.5 Schedule F, Part I

Part II **Farm Expenses—Cash and Accrual Method.** Do not include personal or living expenses (see instructions).

10	Car and truck expenses (see instructions). Also attach **Form 4562**	10	23	Pension and profit-sharing plans	23
11	Chemicals	11	24	Rent or lease (see instructions):	
12	Conservation expenses (see instructions)	12	a	Vehicles, machinery, equipment	24a
13	Custom hire (machine work)	13	b	Other (land, animals, etc.)	24b
14	Depreciation and section 179 expense (see instructions)	14	25	Repairs and maintenance	25
15	Employee benefit programs other than on line 23	15	26	Seeds and plants	26
16	Feed	16	27	Storage and warehousing	27
17	Fertilizers and lime	17	28	Supplies	28
18	Freight and trucking	18	29	Taxes	29
19	Gasoline, fuel, and oil	19	30	Utilities	30
20	Insurance (other than health)	20	31	Veterinary, breeding, and medicine	31
21	Interest:		32	Other expenses (specify):	
a	Mortgage (paid to banks, etc.)	21a	a		32a
b	Other	21b	b		32b
22	Labor hired (less employment credits)	22	c		32c
			d		32d
			e		32e
			f		32f

33	**Total expenses.** Add lines 10 through 32f. If line 32f is negative, see instructions ▶	33
34	**Net farm profit or (loss).** Subtract line 33 from line 9	34

If a profit, stop here and see instructions for where to report. If a loss, complete lines 35 and 36.

35 Did you receive an applicable subsidy in 2011? (see instructions) ☐ Yes ☐ No

36 Check the box that describes your investment in this activity and see instructions for where to report your loss.

a ☐ All investment is at risk. b ☐ Some investment is not at risk.

FIGURE 11.6 Schedule F, Part II

Schedule F (Form 1040) 2011 — Page 2

Part III Farm Income—Accrual Method (see instructions).

37a	Specified sales of livestock, produce, grains, and other products (see instructions)			37a	
b	Sales of livestock, produce, grains, and other products not reported on line 37a			37b	
38a	Cooperative distributions (Form(s) 1099-PATR)	38a	38b Taxable amount	38b	
39a	Agricultural program payments	39a	39b Taxable amount	39b	
40	Commodity Credit Corporation (CCC) loans:				
a	CCC loans reported under election			40a	
b	CCC loans forfeited	40b	40c Taxable amount	40c	
41	Crop insurance proceeds			41	
42a	Specified custom hire (machine work) income from merchant card or third party payments (see instructions)			42a	
b	Other custom hire income not reported on line 42a			42b	
43a	Specified other income (see instructions)			43a	
b	Other income not reported on line 43a			43b	
44	Add amounts in the right column for lines 37a through 43b (lines 37a, 37b, 38b, 39b, 40a, 40c, 41, 42a, 42b, 43a, and 43b)			44	
45	Inventory of livestock, produce, grains, and other products at beginning of the year. Do not include sales reported on Form 4797	45			
46	Cost of livestock, produce, grains, and other products purchased during the year	46			
47	Add lines 45 and 46	47			
48	Inventory of livestock, produce, grains, and other products at end of year	48			
49	Cost of livestock, produce, grains, and other products sold. Subtract line 48 from line 47*			49	
50	**Gross income.** Subtract line 49 from line 44. Enter the result here and on Part I, line 9 ▶			50	

*If you use the unit-livestock-price method or the farm-price method of valuing inventory and the amount on line 48 is larger than the amount on line 47, subtract line 47 from line 48. Enter the result on line 49. Add lines 44 and 49. Enter the total on line 50 and on Part I, line 9.

FIGURE 11.7 Schedule F, Part III

- *Breeding fees.* Farmers can deduct breeding fees. Farmers using the cash method can deduct them as a farm business expense. Farmers on an accrual basis must capitalize the costs and add them to the cost basis of the offspring.
- *Soil and water conservation expenses.* Generally these expenses must be capitalized (although there is an election to deduct expenses up to 25% of gross income from farming immediately).

TIP: Special rules apply to fuels used in farming (e.g., to run a tractor). For more details, see IRS Pub. 225.

Expenses generally are deducted according to the taxpayer's method of accounting (cash or accrual, as explained earlier in this chapter). Whichever method of accounting is used, report farm expenses in Part II of Schedule F. However, there are certain variations on these accounting methods for farmers.

TIP: For purposes of SE income, crop shares are not taken into account unless the taxpayer materially participates in the farming operations. If the taxpayer does not materially participate, enter the income on Form 4835, *Farm Rental Income and Expenses* and carry the net amount to Schedule E, *Supplemental Income and Loss* of Form 1040 so that it is not part of SE income.

Farm Rental Income and Expenses

Rental income for the use of farmland generally is reported as *rental* income (see Chapter 7), not farm income. However, if the taxpayer materially participates in the farming operations, the rents are farm income.

A taxpayer who is paid in crop shares reports the income when the crop is turned into cash or a cash equivalent, regardless of the taxpayer's method of accounting.

Self-Employment Tax

To ensure that self-employed individuals earn credits for Social Security and Medicare, they pay SE tax. This tax reflects both the employer and employee share of the Federal Insurance Contributions Act (FICA; explained in Chapter 4), even though a self-employed individual is neither an employer of him- or herself nor an employee.

The net earnings from SE, which are the profits reported on Schedule C or F, are the basis for SE tax.

TIP: The employer portion of the tax is deductible as an AGI adjustment. Usually it is 50% of the tax, but for 2012, the adjustment generally is 57.51% of the self-employment tax. This is because self-employed taxpayers taking the above-the-line deduction for one-half of self-employment tax can still deduct 7.65% for Social Security taxes (7.65% ÷ 13.3% = 57.51%). (See Form 1040-SE instructions and Chapter 17 for more information).

Figuring Self-Employment Tax

The SE tax is figured on Schedule SE, *Self-Employment Tax*, of Form 1040. Both a short version and a long version of Schedule SE are available for computing the tax. Use the flowchart on page 1 of Schedule SE to determine if you can use the short version of the form. An optional method (Part II, Section B of Schedule SE) can be used to pay more tax than would otherwise be due in order to earn Social Security and Medicare credits.

While sole proprietors pay income tax on 100% of their net profit, they deduct 7.65% of net earnings before figuring SE tax. Thus, they pay SE tax on 92.35% of their net profit (100% – 7.65%).

For 2012, the Social Security portion of the tax is figured on net earnings up to $110,100. There is no limit on the amount of net earnings taken into account in figuring the Medicare portion of the tax. The tax rates for 2012 are:

- 10.4% for the Social Security portion (after 2012, the rate is 12.4%.)
- 2.9% for the Medicare portion

Thus, the total for Social Security and Medicare is 13.3% in 2012 (10.4% + 2.9%).

Example

In 2012, Mark earned $50,000 net profit from his SE activity. His SE tax is $6,141 [$50,000 × 92.35% × 13.3%]. He can deduct 57.51% of this tax ($3,532) as an above-the-line adjustment to gross income (see Chapter 17 for more information), so his AGI is $46,468 [$50,000 – $3,532].

In 2013, the 13.3% is set to return to 15.3%. When this occurs, Mark's SE tax will be $7,065 [$50,000 × 92.35% × 15.3%] instead of $6,141.

Hobby Loss Limitation

If an activity has an operating loss for the year (expenses exceed income), the loss is deductible only if the activity is operated with a profit motive. If there is no profit motive, then the activity is classified as a hobby and the hobby loss limitations apply:

- Losses cannot be more than income earned for the year from the activity. Excess losses do not carry over and are never deductible.
- Expenses to the extent of income are deductible only as a miscellaneous itemized deduction on Schedule A, *Itemized Deductions,* subject to the 2%-of-AGI floor for all miscellaneous itemized deductions; they are not deductible on Schedule C or F.
- Expenses from a hobby activity are not deductible for purposes of the alternative minimum tax (see Chapter 33).

Determining Profit Motive

There is no objective standard to prove that a taxpayer has a profit motive. The IRS looks at nine factors to subjectively assess whether a taxpayer has a profit motive:

1. The manner in which the taxpayer carries out the activity
2. The expertise of the taxpayer, or his or her advisors
3. The time and effort expended by the taxpayer in carrying out the activity
4. Expectations that assets used in the activity may appreciate in value
5. The success of the taxpayer in carrying out other similar or dissimilar activities
6. The taxpayer's history of income or losses with respect to the activity
7. The amount of occasional profits, if any, that are earned
8. The financial status of the taxpayer
9. Any elements of personal pleasure or recreation

No single factor is determinative. The IRS looks at all of the factors to decide whether the taxpayer has a realistic expectation of making a profit.

ALERT: If a taxpayer believes that he or she can prove a profit motive by relying on the nine factors if the IRS questions a loss on the return, it is probably not advisable to file Form 5213. Filing this form keeps the IRS away for the five (or seven) years but essentially guarantees that the IRS will review the returns at the conclusion of this term to see that the presumption period has been satisfied.

Presumption of Profit Motive

A taxpayer can rely on a presumption to establish a profit motive. If a taxpayer can show a profit for three out of the first five years in business (two out of seven years in the case of horse-related activities, such as breeding, training, showing, or racing horses), then the IRS will agree that the taxpayer had a profit motive in all of the years.

To postpone the determination as to whether the presumption applies, the taxpayer must file Form 5213, *Election to Postpone Determination as to Whether the Presumption That an Activity is Engaged in for Profit,* within three years after the due date of the return for the first year of the business.

Benefits

A self-employed individual may be able to take advantage of certain benefits that reduce income, such as deducting premiums for health coverage and retirement plan contributions. As mentioned earlier, deductions for these benefits are not treated as business expenses; they are deductible as adjustments to gross income (see Chapter 17).

TIP: A SEP-IRA can be set up and funded up to the extended due date of the taxpayer's return. For example, a self-employed individual obtains a filing extension for her 2012 return. In August 2013, when she completes the return, she has net income of $90,000. She can set up and fund the SEP-IRA at any time through October 15, 2013.

Retirement Savings Options

Retirement plans for employees were covered in Chapter 8. Self-employed individuals can use many of the plans to save for retirement on a tax-deductible basis. Favored plans include:

- Simplified Employee Pension Individual Retirement Accounts (SEP-IRAs)
- Savings Incentive Match Plan for Employees Individual Retirement Accounts (SIMPLE IRAs)
- Solo 401(k)s

IRS Pub. 560, *Retirement Plans for Small Business (SEP, SIMPLE, and Qualified Plans)*, covers retirement plans for self-employed individuals in detail.

Recordkeeping

A taxpayer in business is required to keep books and records to substantiate income and deductions. If the IRS challenges a taxpayer's deductions and the taxpayer cannot substantiate them, the IRS can reject those deductions. However, tax law does not dictate specifically how the records must be kept. Today, many self-employed individuals use software or online solutions for recordkeeping.

Regardless of the format for such recordkeeping, records showing gross receipts should indicate amounts and sources of income, such as:

- Cash register tapes
- Bank deposit slips
- Receipt books
- Invoices
- Credit card charge slips
- Forms 1099-MISC

Documents for recording expenses include (but are not limited to):

- Canceled checks
- Cash register tapes
- Account statements
- Credit card sales slips
- Invoices

Special recordkeeping rules apply for certain purposes:

- Charitable contributions (see IRS Pub. 526, *Charitable Contributions*)
- Travel and entertainment expenses (see IRS Pub. 463)

Review Questions

1. All of the following taxpayers file Schedule C **except**:
   a. An independent contractor.
   b. A sole proprietor running a boutique
   c. A sole proprietor running a farm
   d. A statutory employee

2. Which of the following expenses of a sole proprietor is **not** deducted on Schedule C?
   a. Advertising
   b. Work-related education costs
   c. Liability and property insurance for the business
   d. Health insurance for the sole proprietor

3. The IRS standard mileage rate for a vehicle used for business takes the place of deducting the actual cost of all of the following **except**:
   a. Tolls
   b. Insurance
   c. Depreciation for a vehicle that is owned by the sole proprietor
   d. Registration fees

4. George starts a business in2012. He pays $7,700 for research, travel, and other costs before he opens his doors. He begins operations on December 31, 2012. What is the most he can deduct in 2012?
   a. $0
   b. $5,000
   c. $7,700
   d. $10,000

5. Which of the following is **not** "listed property"?
   a. Vehicles (under a certain weight)
   b. Cell phones
   c. Video equipment
   d. Computers

6. Which of the following statements regarding the home office deduction is correct?
   a. There is a dollar limit on what can be deducted annually.
   b. The deduction is composed only of direct expenses, such as the cost of painting the office.
   c. There is an unlimited carryover of the deduction in excess of the taxable income limit.
   d. A sole proprietor who uses a home office only to schedule appointments, order supplies, and keep the books can never claim the deduction.

7. Which of the following types of farm income are **not** included on Schedule F?
   a. Patronage dividends
   b. Sales of livestock held for breeding purposes
   c. Commodity Credit Corporation loans
   d. Sales of crops

8. A sole proprietor has net earnings from SE in 2012 of $56,000. What is the maximum SE tax rate?
   a. 2.9%
   b. 10.4%
   c. 13.3%
   d. 15.3%

9. In 2012, a sole proprietor buys used office furniture at a cost of $4,200. He has a net loss from his business activities of $9,600. Which of the following options applies to him for purposes of writing off the cost of the furniture in 2012?
   a. Section 179 deduction only
   b. Bonus depreciation only
   c. Section 179 deduction and/or bonus depreciation
   d. Neither the section 179 deduction nor bonus depreciation

10. A sole proprietor runs a business from home. In 2012, he has income from the home office activity of $3,300 and expenses for the home office of $6,100. Which of the following statements **best** describes his tax treatment of the home office expenses?

a. None of the home office expenses is deductible.

b. $3,300 is deductible in 2012; the balance becomes permanently nondeductible.

c. $3,300 is deductible in 2012, and the balance can be carried forward indefinitely.

d. $6,100 is deductible in 2012.

11. In 2012, Sharon started a gift basket business. In 2012, she has income of $7,700 and expenses of $10,440. Assuming that the IRS successfully establishes that his is a hobby activity, how are Sharon's income and expenses reported?

a. On Schedule C, she reports income of $7,700 and expenses of $10,440.

b. On Form 1040 (line 21), she reports income of $7,700 and on Schedule A she reports expenses of $7,700.

c. On Form 1040 (line 21), she reports income of $7,700, and on Schedule A, she reports expenses of $10,440.

d. On Form 1040 (line 21), she reports income of $7,700; no expenses can be deducted.

Basis of Property

The basis of property—tangible personal property, intangible property, or real property—is important because it is used to help determine the amount of any gain or loss when property is disposed of or sold. Basis is also used to calculate depreciation, amortization, and depletion.

The rules for basis depend on the nature of the property and how the property is acquired, such as by purchase or by gift.

Basis also can be adjusted for various reasons while the taxpayer owns the property.

Knowing how basis is determined is essential to understanding how the sale of property generates gains and losses and how to report these gains and losses (Chapter 13). IRS Pub. 551, *Basis of Assets*, provides more information about basis.

What Is Basis?

A taxpayer's *basis* in property reflects his or her investment in that property. For example, if a taxpayer purchases a car for $25,000, his basis in the car is $25,000. If the car is a personal vehicle, the taxpayer's basis generally remains $25,000. However, if the same vehicle is used in a business, the taxpayer depreciates the vehicle, which reduces his basis in the vehicle by the amount of the depreciation. The "adjusted basis" is original basis plus or minus adjustments that reflect certain events, as described later in this chapter.

Basis is the starting point that is used to figure:

- Gain or loss on the sale or other disposition of property
- Casualty losses
- Depreciation, amortization, and depletion

The taxpayer must retain records to support the determination of basis. In the absence of records (or other means of establishing basis), the IRS can require the taxpayer to report zero basis, meaning that all the proceeds received when the asset is sold will be taxed.

Example

Three years ago Fred purchased a lathe for his woodworking business for $3,000. He has no receipt or other document supporting how much he paid for the lathe, when he bought it, or from whom. Fred sold the lathe for $2,000 last month. If Fred cannot establish his basis in the asset, the entire $2,000 is taxed. If Fred is able to demonstrate his basis of $1,800 (original cost of $3,000 – $1,200 in depreciation), his gain on the sale is only $200 ($2,000 – $1,800). Only the $200 gain on the sale would have been subject to tax, as the return of basis is not taxed.

TIP: Brokerage firms and mutual funds are now required to keep records on taxpayers' basis for investments they hold. Brokerage firms must report the basis of certain types of securities sold during the year on Form 1099-B, *Proceeds From Broker and Barter Exchange Transactions,* for securities acquired on or after January 1, 2011. Mutual funds must do the same for assets acquired on or after January 1, 2012. These investment institutions *may*, but are not required to, provide taxpayers with basis information on earlier purchases.

Example

Annette has 500 shares of Apple common stock that she bought many years ago. However, she has no record showing how much she paid for the stock. Annette could contact the brokerage firm where she bought the stock and ask if it has records. If she did not purchase the stock through a broker, she might contact Apple to make a lost or missing stock certificate request. If she can determine the date of purchase and the stock's market price at the time she purchased it, she also may be able to reconstruct her basis. The IRS may accept a reasonable attempt to reconstruct basis in an asset rather than assign a zero basis.

Cost Basis

The basis of purchased property is generally its cost, determined by the taxpayer's payment for the property by cash, check, credit or debit card, financing, or other purchase arrangement. Thus, if a taxpayer buys realty for $1 million and finances $800,000, the cost basis of the property is $1 million.

Cost basis includes:

- Excise taxes
- Freight
- Installation and testing costs
- Legal and accounting fees (if they must be capitalized, as explained in increases to basis later in this chapter)
- Revenue stamps
- Sales tax

For the purchase of real property, there may be other additions to basis.

Basis is increased by:

- Real estate taxes owed by the seller that are paid by the buyer and not separately reimbursed
- Settlement costs (including abstract fees, charges for installing utility services, legal fees, title searches, recording fees, surveys, transfer taxes, and title insurance)

If a home or other building is constructed, the basis of the property includes:

- Architect's fees
- Building permit charges
- Inspection fees
- Labor and materials (but not the value of the taxpayer's own labor if he constructs his own home)
- Land
- Payments to contractors
- Payments to rent equipment

If more than one asset is purchased at the same time in a lump sum, the total cost must be allocated between or among the assets acquired. If the group of assets makes up a trade or business where goodwill or going concern is valued, or could be valued, or is subject to the rules on distribution of stock in a controlled corporation, the buyer and seller must agree on the allocation and each file Form 8594, *Asset Acquisition Statement,* which allocates the sales price among the assets. The reported allocation is binding unless the IRS determines that the amounts are not appropriate.

TIP: If a taxpayer buys a sole proprietorship, the purchase price is allocated among the assets of the business (e.g., inventory, office furniture, computers, and possibly goodwill). For more information about this allocation, see Form 8594.

When real property is purchased, the taxpayer must make an allocation between the land and the building if these assets are not shown separately on the purchase documents. The reason is that only the building must be depreciated. The allocation is made according to fair market value (FMV).

Example

June buys an apartment building as an investment for $1 million. In order to figure depreciation on the building, she must allocate the $1 million between the building itself and the land. The basis of the building is the FMV of this asset divided by the FMV of the entire property times the purchase price (investment in the property).

Thus, if the apartment building is valued at $800,000 at the time of purchase, this becomes the basis of the building for depreciation, with the remaining $200,000 as the basis in the land.

TIP: If a taxpayer does not know the FMV of a building, use the property's assessed value to make an allocation between the land and the building.

Adjusted Basis

Adjusted basis is the amount used to determine gain or loss on the sale, exchange, or other disposition of property. Adjusted basis is the cost (or other basis) of property increased or decreased by certain items. Table 12.1 shows examples of increases and decreases to basis.

TABLE 12.1 Adjustments to Basis

Increases to basis	Decreases to basis
Capital improvements: • Putting an addition on your home • Replacing an entire roof • Paving your driveway • Installing central air conditioning • Rewiring your home Assessments for local improvements: • Water connections • Extending utility service lines to the property • Sidewalks • Roads Casualty losses: • Restoring damaged property Legal fees: • Cost of defending and perfecting a title • Fees for getting a reduction of an assessment • Zoning costs	• Exclusion from income of subsidies for energy conservation measures • Casualty or theft loss deductions and insurance reimbursements • Postponed gain from the sale of a home • Residential energy credits (Form 5695, *Residential Energy Credits*) • Depreciation and Section 179 deduction • Nontaxable corporate distributions • Certain canceled debt excluded from income • Easements

Example

Patrick owned a two-family home, which he bought for $400,000 on January 1, 2002. The land was allocated $50,000 of the purchase price. He immediately made capital improvements (a new roof, new appliances, rewiring, and converting the garage to another room) totaling $100,000, and then rented out the units.

Early last year, there was storm damage that was partially compensated by insurance ($19,700), and Patrick deducted $3,000 as a casualty loss. He used $18,000 of the insurance proceeds to repair the storm damage. Total depreciation deducted before the storm occurred was $162,946. To calculate Patrick's adjusted basis at the end of last year, his initial cost in the home is adjusted by these increases and decreases:

Original cost of home (not including land)	$350,000
Increase: capital improvements	100,000
Total adjusted basis for depreciation (including the amount claimed on last year's tax return)	$450,000
Decrease: Depreciation claimed for 10 years	(162,946)
Adjusted basis before casualty	$287,054
Decrease:	
Insurance proceeds ($19,700)	
Casualty loss deduction ($3,000)	($22,700)
Adjusted basis after casualty	$264,354
Increase: Cost of restoring home	18,000
Adjusted basis after restoration	$282,354

Basis Other than Cost

Acquisition of property other than through purchase may affect the taxpayer's basis in the property. The basis rules vary depending on whether the property was received for services, acquired in a like-kind exchange, received as a gift, or inherited. Once the taxpayer's original basis in the property is established, adjustments to the property will increase or decrease the original basis, as described earlier in this chapter.

ALERT: Ordinary repairs, such as painting or wallpapering to keep property in the same condition, do not increase basis. If the painting or wallpapering were part of a project that increased the value of the property, these would be capitalized and would increase basis.

Property Received for Services

Property received for services is valued and taxed as income based on its FMV. The taxpayer's basis in the property is its FMV.

Example

Ariel designed a website for her neighbor, who gave her a watch worth $1,200 for Ariel's work. Ariel's basis in the watch is $1,200, which is the property's FMV and the amount Ariel includes in her income.

If a taxpayer receives restricted property, such as stock from an employer, the basis of the stock is its FMV when the taxpayer is substantially vested (i.e., has the right to sell the property). However, if the taxpayer makes a special election (called a Section 83(b) election) to include the FMV of the stock in income when received, that amount becomes the taxpayer's basis in the stock. IRS Pub. 525, *Taxable and Nontaxable Income,* explains restricted stock.

DEFINITION: Like-kind properties are properties with the same nature or character, even if they have a different grade or quality. For example, the exchange of real estate for other real estate is like-kind even if the properties are different. A warehouse exchanged for an apartment building or improved land exchanged for unimproved land would both qualify as like-kind exchanges.

Property Received in Exchanges

Exchanges of property may be fully taxable, partly taxable, or fully tax free. Although the details of **like-kind** exchanges are beyond the scope of this book, the tax on the future sale of property received in an exchange is based on the taxpayer's basis in that property.

The basis of property received in a *taxable* exchange is the FMV of the property received on the date of the exchange.

The basis of property received in a *nontaxable* exchange is the adjusted basis of the property given up. If the taxpayer pays cash, the amount of cash is added to the basis of the property given up.

If money is paid in addition to property given up, the amount of the money paid is added to the basis of the property received.

TIP: A nontaxable like-kind exchange is also known as a Section 1031 exchange or simply a 1031 exchange, based on the Internal Revenue Code section authorizing it. A 1031 exchange involves the transfer of business or investment property in exchange for the same kind of property.

Example

Aaron trades in his old car for a new one, which is used in his business. The adjusted basis of the old car was $2,700 before the trade. The new car costs $28,000. The dealer gives him a trade-in credit of $3,000, and Aaron pays $25,000. His basis in the new car is $27,700 (the adjusted basis of the old car $2,700, plus the $25,000 he paid).

If there is a partially nontaxable exchange in which the taxpayer receives cash (generally called "boot") or unlike property in addition to the like-kind property, the basis is:

- Decreased by any boot received and any loss recognized on the exchange (with respect to the unlike property)
- Increased by any additional costs incurred and any gain recognized on the exchange (with respect to the unlike property)

IRS Pub. 551, *Basis of Assets*, contains more information about like-kind exchanges.

In a taxable exchange (one that does not qualify as a like-kind exchange), the FMV of the property the taxpayer receives at the time of the exchange is used as the basis.

Gifts

To determine the basis of property received as a gift, information required includes the donor's (giver's) adjusted basis at the time of the gift, the FMV of the property at the time of the gift, and the amount of gift tax paid on the gift.

TIP: As a practical matter, many recipients never learn the basis of gifts received. In such cases, they may be able to reasonably reconstruct the basis from known information or use the FMV as their basis if it is impossible to obtain facts about the basis from the donor.

The basis of the gift can differ, depending on whether the recipient later sells the property at a gain or a loss.

FMV Less than the Donor's Adjusted Basis If, at the time of the gift, the FMV of the property is less than the donor's adjusted basis, the taxpayer's basis for purposes of figuring gain is the *donor's* adjusted basis (including any adjustments while the taxpayer owned the property). The taxpayer's basis for determining loss is its FMV when received (including any adjustments while the taxpayer owned the property).

TIP: The taxpayer's basis in a gift when received is referred to as a "carryover basis." Essentially, the taxpayer steps into the shoes of the donor, taking over the donor's basis [except when the FMV becomes basis].

Example

Stan received a painting as a gift from his uncle. At the time of the gift, the painting's FMV was $8,000; his uncle paid $10,000 for it. Stan sells the painting for $12,000. Because there is a gain, Stan's basis is the donor's adjusted basis ($10,000), so Stan's gain is $2,000 ($12,000 – $10,000).

If Stan had sold the painting for $6,500, his basis would have been the FMV at the time of the gift ($8,000), which results in a loss to Stan of $1,500 ($8,000 – $6,500).

If the price Stan receives for the painting is between $8,000 and $10,000, he has neither a gain nor a loss.

FMV Equal to or Greater than the Donor's Adjusted Basis If, at the time of the gift, the FMV of the property is more than or equal to the donor's adjusted basis, the recipient's basis becomes the donor's adjusted basis. Depending on when the gift was made, this basis can be increased by any gift tax paid by the donor. IRS Pub. 950, *Introduction to Estate and Gift Taxes*, explains the gift tax.

Inheritances

Generally, the basis of inherited property is its FMV on the date of the decedent's death. The decedent's adjusted basis is **stepped up** (or down) to FMV.

DEFINITION: An heir's basis in inherited property is called **stepped-up basis** because the basis is stepped up, or increased to the property's fair market value. In some cases, of course, the value of the decedent's property may have declined.

Example

Veronica inherits a brooch from her aunt. The aunt bought the brooch 40 years ago for $1,000. On the date of the aunt's death, it is worth $28,000. Veronica's basis in the brooch is $28,000.

Special rules determine basis for jointly owned property. For nonspouse joint owners, the basis is the value of the property included in the co-owner's estate. In the absence of information that the surviving co-owner contributed toward the purchase price, the basis usually is the full value of the property.

When spouses are joint owners and a surviving spouse inherits property when the other spouse (joint owner) dies, the surviving spouse's basis usually is made up of two parts: one-half belonging to the surviving spouse (e.g., the surviving spouse's cost basis) and one-half from the deceased spouse (e.g., a stepped-up basis). However, a special rule applies to property acquired before 1977.

Example

Stanley jointly owned a vacation home with his wife, Thelma, which they bought in 1995 for $46,000. When Thelma died in 2012, it was worth $72,000. Stanley's basis in the home is $59,000 (his half of $46,000, or $23,000, plus the stepped-up basis in the other half, or $36,000).

DEFINITION: Under the **modified carryover basis** rules, the heir's basis in an inherited asset is the lower of (1) the decedent's adjusted basis or (2) the FMV on the date of death (no step-up in basis to the FMV at the date of death). However, the estate has a $1.3 million general basis step-up that the executor may allocate among the estate's assets. If the decedent has a surviving spouse, an additional $3 million step-up in basis is available for a total of $4.3 million basis step-up. For more information about the modified carryover basis rules, see IRS Pub. 4895, *Basis of Inherited Property Held by Decedents Who Died in 2010.*

An executor or administrator of the estate may elect to value the decedent's property at an alternate valuation date, which is the earlier of six months after the date of death or the date of distribution or sale of the property. The details of this election are beyond the scope of this book; see the instructions to Form 706, *United States Estate (and Generation-Skipping Transfer) Tax Return*, for more information.

Property Inherited from a Decedent Who Died in 2010 If the decedent died in 2010, the executor could elect to use the 2010 **modified carryover basis rules** instead of the general rules. If this election was made, the basis of assets acquired from the decedent is a modified carryover basis rather than FMV.

Community Property When a spouse in a community property state inherits property from the deceased spouse, each is considered to own half of the community property. As such, the total value of the community property, even the part belonging to the surviving spouse, is the basis of the property for the surviving spouse. This rule applies only if at least half the value of the community property interest is includible in the decedent's gross estate, whether an estate tax return is filed or not.

Example

A couple owned community property with a basis of $100,000. The wife dies, and half of the property is included in her gross estate. The FMV of the property was $120,000. The husband's basis in the property is now $120,000 (half the FMV of the property, or $60,000, + the other half of $60,000).

See IRS Pub. 555, *Community Property*, for more information about community property rules.

Converting Property to Business Use

When property that has been owned personally is put ("converted") to business use, the basis for depreciation is the *lower of* its adjusted basis or the FMV at the time of conversion.

Example

Jane starts a business using a room in her house as her home office, whose area is 10% of the entire home. She paid $250,000 for the house (exclusive of the land) that is now worth $325,000. For depreciation purposes, the basis of the home office is $25,000, which is 10% of the adjusted basis of the home and lower than its current FMV.

Review Questions

1. The "basis" of property is the starting point for determining all of the following **except**:

a. Depreciation

b. Excise taxes

c. A casualty loss

d. Gain or loss on the disposition of property

2. A taxpayer builds his own personal residence. What **cannot** be added to basis?

a. The value of his labor

b. The cost of materials

c. Architect's fees

d. Payments to contractors

3. Which of the following is an **increase** to basis?

a. Residential energy credits that have been claimed for a principal residence

b. A casualty loss

c. Depreciation

d. Capital improvements

4. Two years ago, Felicia received as a gift from her aunt a bracelet worth $5,000. Her aunt bought it many years ago for $800. If Felicia sells the bracelet for $4,000, her basis for figuring gain or loss is:

a. $0

b. $800

c. $4,000

d. $5,000

5. Same facts as in Question 4 except that Felicia inherited the bracelet instead of receiving it as a gift. It is worth $5,000 at the time of the aunt's death. Felicia sells it six months later for $4,000. Her basis for determining gain or loss is:

a. $0

b. $800

c. $4,000

d. $5,000

6. Adelaide sells her personal residence, which she has owned and lived in since 1988. For purposes of determining her gain or loss on the sale, which of the following expenses does **not** increase the basis of her home:

a. Adding a new roof

b. Adding aluminum siding to her home

c. Painting the living room

d. Adding a garage on her property

Sale of Property

Sales, exchanges, and other transfers of property enjoy special tax treatment. Gains from the sale of property may be taxed at favorable capital gains rates compared to ordinary income rates. Losses may be used to offset gains, but only $3,000 of net capital losses may be deducted against ordinary income.

Before applying the special capital gain and loss rules, it is necessary to determine whether there is a gain or loss for tax purposes. The gain or loss then must be classified as short term or long term before applying a netting process, as described later in this chapter.

In some situations, capital gains may not be immediately taxable. For example, gains are deferred when property used in a business or held for investment is exchanged in a like-kind exchange.

Special rules apply to dispositions of business assets where depreciation had been claimed. If there is a capital gain, a portion of the gain may be characterized as ordinary income to the extent of depreciation claimed on the property. In some cases, losses can be treated as ordinary losses.

Special rules govern where to report gains and losses on the tax return. These rules dictate the forms and schedules that must be used for various types of capital asset transactions.

Sales, Exchanges, and Transfers

A *sale* is a transfer of property by a seller for money or the buyer's promise for payment (a mortgage or a note). An *exchange* (trade) is a transfer of property for other property or services. An exchange is taxed in the same way as a sale unless it is considered a tax-free (like-kind) exchange.

FYI: Throughout this chapter, when the rules for a sale are being discussed, they also apply to exchanges unless otherwise noted.

Types of transactions that are treated like sales for tax purposes include:

- *Nonbusiness bad debts.* A nonbusiness bad debt may be deducted as a short-term capital loss in the year the debt becomes *completely* worthless.

- *Redemption of stock.* Redemption of a taxpayer's stock by the issuing corporation is treated as a sale *unless* the redemption qualifies as a dividend or other distribution on stock.
- *Redemption or retirement of bonds.* The redemption or retirement of bonds generally is treated as a sale.
- *Worthless securities.* Stock, stock rights, and bonds that become *completely* worthless during the year are treated as if they had been sold on the last day of the tax year. Securities that are abandoned because the taxpayer gives up all rights in them are also treated as worthless securities.

ALERT: A taxpayer who is a U.S. citizen and sells property abroad must report the gains and losses from foreign transactions. This rule applies whether the taxpayer resides abroad or not and whether the taxpayer receives or does not receive an information document reporting the transaction.

Sale Proceeds

In order to determine gain or loss on a sale or exchange, it is necessary to determine the amount realized on the transaction. The amount realized generally is the sale proceeds. Sale proceeds include cash and the fair market value (FMV) of any property received in an exchange. Sale proceeds can also include a note or other debt owed to the seller and any debt of the seller that the buyer assumes and agrees to pay off.

The taxpayer's basis is increased by expenses of the sale. Examples of sale expenses include:

- Redemption fees
- Sales commissions (e.g., brokerage commissions; real estate agent commissions)
- Sales charges
- Exit fees

ALERT: The amount of the gain that is recognized for tax purposes is calculated as the amount realized minus the taxpayers adjusted basis in the property (see Chapter 12 for calculating adjusted basis).

Example

Gus has property with a FMV of $15,000 and a cost basis of $8,000. Gus sold the property for $5,000 cash, and the buyer assumed the remaining balance owed on the property of $4,000. Total selling expenses were $500. The gain is calculated as:

Amount Realized:		
Cash	$5,000	
Debt assumed by the buyer	4,000	
		$9,000
Adjusted Basis:		
Cost	$8,000	
Selling Expenses	500	
		($8,500)
Recognized gain on the sale		$500

Calculating Gain or Loss

Gain or loss is determined by comparing the sale proceeds with the taxpayer's adjusted basis in the property.

Example

Wayne sells 100 shares of stock for $10,000 (sale proceeds). He paid $4,200 (his basis) for the stock. His gain is $5,800 ($10,000 – $4,200).

Capital or Ordinary Gains and Losses

Gains (or losses) can be treated either as capital or ordinary, depending on the type of property involved. Capital gains are taxed at different rates from ordinary gains.

As a general rule, the sale of a capital asset results in a capital gain or loss. A capital asset is any asset other than:

- Accounts receivable or notes receivable related to a trade or business
- Property held for sale to customers (inventory)
- Depreciable property used in a business, even if fully depreciated
- Real property used in a business
- U.S. government publications
- Certain commodity derivative financial instruments held by dealers
- A hedging transaction if identified as such before the close of the day on which the transaction is acquired, originated, or entered into
- Supplies used or consumed in the regular course of the taxpayer's business.
  - A self-created copyright, literary, musical, or artistic composition, a letter or memorandum, or similar property (or such property created for the taxpayer or acquired by gift or inheritance entitling the acquirer to the same rights as the creator)

TIP: While self-created works are not capital assets, creators of such works may elect to treat sales of such assets as capital gains or losses.

Thus, most assets are capital assets. Examples of capital assets include:

- Stocks, bonds, and mutual funds (stock in a small corporation is a capital asset but may receive ordinary loss treatment if it qualifies as Section 1244 stock, as explained in IRS Pub. 550.)
- Household furnishings
- A house, condominium, or shares in a cooperative apartment if the residence is used by the taxpayer (this includes a principal residence as well as additional homes or vacation properties)
- A car used for personal purposes, such as commuting
- Coin or stamp collections
- Jewelry
  - Gold, silver, or other metals (the metals are not capital assets but inventory when held by dealers in these metals)

TIP: If a taxpayer sells less than all of his or her holding of a stock or mutual fund that was acquired at different times for different prices, there are several methods available to determine which shares have been sold: first-in, first-out method; specific identification method; and the average cost method. If no special method is selected, the first-in, first-out method applies by default. The method used will affect the amount of gain or loss reported and can also determine whether the gain or loss is short or long term. These methods are discussed in IRS Pub. 550, *Investment Income and Expenses.*

ALERT: Even though the sale of a capital asset can generate a loss, a capital loss on the sale of a personal-use asset is not recognized for tax purposes. For example, if a taxpayer sells a principal residence at a loss, the loss is not deductible or otherwise taken into account. The same is true for sales of a personal car or household items. However, a gain from a personal asset must be reported (unless a special rule applies).

Special rules apply for determining the basis and amount realized for property that is abandoned, foreclosed, or repossessed. The rules for these transactions are discussed in IRS Pub. 4681, *Canceled Debts, Foreclosures, Repossessions, and Abandonments*.

Related Party Sales

The related party rules are intended to prohibit taxpayers from receiving favorable capital gain treatment and deducting losses on transactions with persons and entities with whom they have close ties, such as with relatives or with businesses they own.

Therefore, if sales are made between certain related parties, the gain may be treated as ordinary income rather than as a capital gain. This rule applies if the property sold can be depreciated by the party receiving it. Also, no loss can be taken when the transaction involves related parties.

For purposes of the restrictions on capital gains and losses, a *related party* includes:

- Family members, including only: siblings, half siblings, spouses, parents, grandparents, children, and grandchildren (in-laws, nieces, and nephews are *not* treated a related parties for these special rules)
- A partnership in which the taxpayer owns (directly or indirectly) more than 50% of the capital interest or profits interest
- A corporation in which the taxpayer owns (directly or indirectly) more than 50% in the value of the outstanding stock
- A tax-exempt charitable or educational organization controlled (directly or indirectly) by the taxpayer or the taxpayer's family

For purposes of the nondeductible loss rule, a related party also includes:

- A grantor and a fiduciary (trustee) of any trust
- A beneficiary and a fiduciary (trustee) of any trust
- A beneficiary and an executor of an estate (other than a sale to satisfy a pecuniary bequest)
- Certain transactions between businesses

For a complete list of related parties, see IRS Pub. 544, *Sales and Other Dispositions of Assets*.

Although the seller of property to a related party cannot claim the loss, the buyer can offset his or her gain by the amount of the disallowed loss if the property is sold at a later date. This rule applies only if the related party is the original transferee and he or she acquired the property by purchase or exchange. This rule does not apply if the related party's loss was disallowed because of the wash sale rules, discussed later in this chapter.

Example

Kristen sells stock that cost her $11,000 to her sister Kate for $8,600. Kristen cannot claim the $2,400 loss. However, if Kate later sells the stock to an unrelated party for $11,500, Kate can then use Kristen's disallowed loss to offset her gain. Kate's realized gain on the transaction is $2,900 ($11,500 – $8,600) but can be reduced by the $2,400 loss not taken by Kristen, making her recognized gain only $500. However, if Kate had sold the stock for only $7,900, she could claim only her own loss of $700 ($8,600 – $7,900). Kate would not be able to increase the amount of her loss ($700) by Kristen's disallowed loss.

Holding Period for Capital Assets

The period during which a taxpayer holds a capital asset before selling it determines whether the gain or loss is short term or long term.

- A short-term holding period is one lasting one year or less.
- A long-term holding period is one lasting more than one year.

To determine holding period, generally start counting the day *after* the date on which the property is acquired and include the day on which the property is sold.

TIP: Long-term capital gains rates are preferable to short-term capital gains rates. Long-term gains are taxed at a maximum rate of 15%. Short-term gains are taxed as ordinary income and subject to the taxpayer's marginal tax rate.

Example

Blossom bought stock on February 5, 2011, and sold it on February 5, 2012. Blossom's holding period is short term because it lasted exactly one year. Her holding period started on February 6, 2011 (the day after the stock was bought) and ended on February 5, 2012 (the day of the sale). Had Blossom sold the stock one day later, on February 6, 2012, her holding period would have been long term.

Special Holding Periods

In certain situations, the holding period is *not* determined by how long the taxpayer owned the property. Some common examples of other rules for determining the holding period include:

- *Gift.* The holding period for a gift depends on whether the recipient's basis is determined using the FMV or the donor's adjusted basis when the gift was made:
  - If the donor's adjusted basis is used to figure the recipient's adjusted basis in the gift, the recipient's holding period begins on the date the *donor* acquired the property.
  - If the FMV of the property is used to figure the recipient's adjusted basis in the gift, the recipient's holding period begins the day after the gift was received.
- *Inheritance.* The holding period of an inherited asset is *automatically* long term, regardless of how long the heir or the decedent owned the property.

ALERT: For securities sales, the holding period is determined by the trade date on which the security is purchased and the trade date on which it is sold. The "settlement date" for securities is not used in determining the holding period.

Example

In 2012, Buck inherits his uncle's gun. His uncle bought it one week before his death. Buck sells it two months after his uncle's death. Buck's holding period is long term, even though neither the uncle nor Buck owned the gun for more than one year.

- For property inherited from a decedent who died in 2010 only, a different holding period may apply, depending on whether the executor of the estate made a special basis election (very few do so). If the estate did not make this election, the normal inherited property holding period will apply.
- *Like-kind exchange.* When capital assets are exchanged, the holding period for the new property includes the holding period of the property that the taxpayer gave up.
- *Divorce.* When assets are transferred pursuant to divorce, the transferor spouse's holding period carries over to the recipient spouse.

Example

Arlen exchanges his vacant land that he bought years ago as an investment for $24,000 for Sam's vacant land worth $43,000. This qualifies as a tax-free exchange (discussed later in this chapter), and Arlen defers his gain. Arlen's holding period in the land he acquired from Sam includes his own holding period in the land he exchanged.

Nontaxable or Tax-Deferred Transactions

In some situations, an exchange of property may not be taxable immediately. The gain may be postponed until a later time. Examples of nontaxable transactions include:

- *Exchanges of life insurance policies and annuity contracts* (see Chapter 8).
- *Involuntary conversions.* These result when property is damaged or destroyed by a casualty event, such as a storm, and the insurance proceeds received exceed the basis of the property. A taxpayer may opt to defer the gain by reinvesting the proceeds in replacement property within a set time limit. Rules for involuntary conversions are discussed in IRS Pub. 544.
- *Like-kind exchanges.* When qualified like-kind property is exchanged, gain is automatically postponed until the property acquired in the exchange is sold or otherwise disposed of. Rules for like-kind exchanges are also discussed in IRS Pub. 544.
- *Transfers to a spouse incident to divorce.* When property is transferred to a spouse or former spouse according to the terms of a divorce decree or separation agreement, the transferor spouse does not report any gain. The recipient spouse reports the gain, if any, when he or she sells or disposes of the property. The nontaxable rule does not apply if the recipient spouse is a nonresident alien.

Example

Anita and Harrison divorce. Harrison transfers ownership of the home that had been solely in his name to Anita; he had owned it for many years. Harrison's basis in the home is $300,000. At the time of the transfer, the home is worth $500,000. Anita takes Harrison's basis and long-term holding period for the home. If she sells the home for any amount over $300,000, she will have a long-term capital gain.

Reporting Sales on the Tax Return

Reporting sales on a tax return requires that all the following information be identified:

- Whether the gain or loss results in capital or ordinary tax treatment
- Whether the gain or loss is short term or long term
- Whether the gain or loss is taxable or nontaxable
- The correct form or schedule to report each transaction

For example, identify whether a transaction is a capital gain or loss transaction reported on Schedule D, *Capital Gains and Losses*, or a gain or loss on business assets reported on Form 4797, *Sales of Business Property.*

TIP: To collect information that must be reported about the transactions, check information returns issued to the taxpayer. Note that all sales or exchanges must be reported by the taxpayer (unless a special rule applies), even if the taxpayer does not receive an information return.

Information Returns

Information returns or documents that a taxpayer may receive reflecting the sales of assets include:

- *Form 1099-A,* Acquisition or Abandonment of Secured Property. This form is used to report a lender's acquisition of property on which there is a mortgage where the borrower abandoned the property or the lender acquired it through foreclosure.
- *Form 1099-B,* Proceeds from Broker and Barter Exchange Transactions. This form lists the date of the sale or exchange, the date of acquisition, the quantity sold, the type of asset (e.g., stock, bonds), how proceeds have been reported to the IRS (e.g., gross proceeds or gross proceeds less commissions and option premiums), the cost or other basis (if known), and whether the gain or loss is short term or long term.
- *Form 1099-DIV,* Dividends and Distributions. This form is used to report dividends paid and capital gain distributions of $10 or more, section 1202 gain (from the sale of qualified small business stock in a C corporation), unrecaptured depreciation, and collectibles gain.
- *Form 1099-S,* Proceeds from Real Estate Transactions. This form lists the gross proceeds on the sale as well as other information about the transaction (e.g., closing date; description of the property sold).

TIP: Brokerage firms must include on Form 1099-B the cost or other basis of securities acquired from a firm on or after January 1, 2011. They may (but are not required to) include the basis of securities acquired before 2011. Similarly, mutual funds must report the basis of shares acquired on or after January 1, 2012; they may (but are not required to) include the basis of shares acquired before 2012. All other securities (including commodities, derivatives, options, bonds, and other financial instruments, are covered by this rule beginning January 1, 2013.

> **ALERT:** Do not overlook any foreign taxes reported on Form 1099-DIV that were paid on dividends or other distributions. If there are any foreign taxes, they can be claimed as an itemized deduction on Schedule A, *Itemized Deductions*, or as a tax credit directly on Form 1040, *U.S. Individual Income Tax Return*. (In some cases, Form 1116, *Foreign Tax Credit*, may be required to figure the foreign tax credit).

- *Schedule K-1,* Partner's Share of Income, Deductions, Credits, etc. Partnerships, S corporations, trusts, and estates issue this information return to an owner or beneficiary. The schedule reports the taxpayer's share of transactions, such as short-term and long-term gains and losses. The amounts are then reported on the taxpayer's personal return.

The income and other items on these information return documents should be reported *exactly* as they appear. If the information is incorrect, the taxpayer has two options:

1. The taxpayer can request that the payer issue a corrected information return. This option is appropriate if an amount is incorrect (e.g., sale proceeds of $10,200 are reported on Form 1099-B when the taxpayer received only $1,020) or the taxpayer's personal information is incorrect (name, Social Security Number, etc.)
2. The incorrect information can be reported with a correction and explanation on the taxpayer's return. This option is appropriate if the payer cannot or will not issue a new document.

Reporting Gains and Losses on Form 8949

Sales and other dispositions of capital assets are first entered on Form 8949, *Sales and Other Dispositions of Capital Assets*. A taxpayer may have to complete up to three such forms, depending on how basis is determined. Form 8949 is a two-page form. Part I is used to list short-term transactions, and Part II is used to list long-term transactions as shown in Figure 13.1. One Form 8949 is required for *each* of the following:

(A) Transactions reported on Form 1099-B with basis reported to the IRS,

(B) Transactions reported on Form 1099-B without basis reported to the IRS, AND

(C) Transactions that are not reported on Form 1099-B.

The taxpayer selects the check box for the type of transaction(s) being reported. For example, if the taxpayer receives a 1099-B that does not report basis, then the taxpayer will check box (B) and report the sale information in either Part I or Part II, depending on whether the holding period was short term or long term.

Short-term and long-term transactions using the same check box (A, B, or C) may be reported on the same Form 8949. For example, the taxpayer may report both short and long term (B) transactions on one Form 8949. However, the taxpayer cannot report transactions using different check boxes together. For example, a taxpayer could not report a short-term (A) transaction on the same Form 8949 as she reports a short-term (B) transaction. The totals of short-term transactions and long-term transactions (sales price, cost or other basis, and any adjustments to gain or loss) from each Form 8949 are then reported on the appropriate lines of Schedule D.

Form **8949** | Department of the Treasury Internal Revenue Service

Sales and Other Dispositions of Capital Assets

▶ Information about Form 8949 and its separate instructions is at *www.irs.gov/form8949.*
▶ File with your Schedule D to list your transactions for lines 1, 2, 3, 8, 9, and 10 of Schedule D.

OMB No. 1545-0074 | 2012 | Attachment Sequence No. 12A

Name(s) shown on return | Social security number or taxpayer identification number

Most brokers issue their own substitute statement instead of using Form 1099-B. They also may provide basis information (usually your cost) to you on the statement even if it is not reported to the IRS. Before you check Box A, B, or C below, determine whether you received any statement(s) and, if so, the transactions for which basis was reported to the IRS. Brokers are required to report basis to the IRS for most stock you bought in 2011 or later.

Part I **Short-Term.** Transactions involving capital assets you held one year or less are short term. For long-term transactions, see page 2.

You *must* check Box A, B, *or* C below. Check only one box. If more than one box applies for your short-term transactions, complete a separate Form 8949, page 1, for each applicable box. If you have more short-term transactions than will fit on this page for one or more of the boxes, complete as many forms with the same box checked as you need.

☐ **(A)** Short-term transactions reported on Form(s) 1099-B showing basis **was** reported to the IRS
☐ **(B)** Short-term transactions reported on Form(s) 1099-B showing basis was **not** reported to the IRS
☐ **(C)** Short-term transactions not reported to you on Form 1099-B

1 (a) Description of property (Example: 100 sh. XYZ Co.)	(b) Date acquired (Mo., day, yr.)	(c) Date sold or disposed (Mo., day, yr.)	(d) Proceeds (sales price) (see instructions)	(e) Cost or other basis. See the **Note** below and see *Column (e)* in the separate instructions	**Adjustment, if any, to gain or loss.** If you enter an amount in column (g), enter a code in column (f). **See the separate instructions.** (f) Code(s) from instructions	(g) Amount of adjustment	**(h) Gain or (loss).** Subtract column (e) from column (d) and combine the result with column (g)

FIGURE 13.1 Form 8949 Part I

Schedule D

Schedule D of Form 1040 is used to consolidate the reporting of a taxpayer's capital transactions.

- Part I is for carrying over the three types (As, Bs, and Cs) of short-term transactions from Form 8949 (see Figure 13.2). It also includes an entry for any short-term capital loss carryover from the previous year. Short-term gains are netted against short-term losses to find a net short-term gain or loss.

SCHEDULE D (Form 1040) | Department of the Treasury Internal Revenue Service (99)

Capital Gains and Losses

▶ Attach to Form 1040 or Form 1040NR.
▶ Information about Schedule D and its separate instructions is at *www.irs.gov/form1040.*
▶ Use Form 8949 to list your transactions for lines 1, 2, 3, 8, 9, and 10.

OMB No. 1545-0074 | 2012 | Attachment Sequence No. 12

Name(s) shown on return | Your social security number

Part I **Short-Term Capital Gains and Losses—Assets Held One Year or Less**

Complete Form 8949 before completing line 1, 2, or 3. This form may be easier to complete if you round off cents to whole dollars.	(d) Proceeds (sales price) from Form(s) 8949, Part I, line 2, column (d)	(e) Cost or other basis from Form(s) 8949, Part I, line 2, column (e)	(g) Adjustments to gain or loss from Form(s) 8949, Part I, line 2, column (g)	(h) Gain or (loss) Subtract column (e) from column (d) and combine the result with column (g)
1 Short-term totals from all Forms 8949 with **box A** checked in **Part I**				
2 Short-term totals from all Forms 8949 with **box B** checked in **Part I**				
3 Short-term totals from all Forms 8949 with **box C** checked in **Part I**				

FIGURE 13.2 Schedule D Part I

Part II **Long-Term Capital Gains and Losses—Assets Held More Than One Year**

Complete Form 8949 before completing line 8, 9, or 10. This form may be easier to complete if you round off cents to whole dollars.	**(e)** Sales price from Form(s) 8949, line 4, column (e)	**(f)** Cost or other basis from Form(s) 8949, line 4, column (f)	**(g)** Adjustments to gain or loss from Form(s) 8949, line 4, column (g)	**(h) Gain or (loss)** Combine columns (e), (f), and (g)
8 Long-term totals from all Forms 8949 with **box A** checked in **Part II**		( )		
9 Long-term totals from all Forms 8949 with **box B** checked in **Part II**		( )		
10 Long-term totals from all Forms 8949 with **box C** checked in **Part II**		( )		

FIGURE 13.3 Schedule D, Part II

- Part II is for carrying over the three types (As, Bs, and Cs) of long-term transactions from Form 8949 (see Figure 13.3). It also includes an entry for any long-term capital loss carryover from the previous year and capital gain distributions from mutual funds (see Chapter 6). Long-term gains are netted against long-term losses to find a net long-term gain or loss. The rates on different types of long-term capital gains are discussed in Chapter 34.
- Part III is a summary of the totals from Parts I and II. This part of Schedule D is discussed later in this chapter.

ALERT: If a taxpayer has sales of business property, involuntary conversions, or depreciation recapture, Form 4797, not Schedule D, must be used. See "Gains and Losses on Business Assets" later in this chapter.

Netting Capital Gains and Losses

Capital losses are netted against capital gains in a certain order. For example, short-term capital losses first offset short-term capital gains. If there is a net short-term capital loss (the short-term losses exceed the short-term gains), they are ultimately used to offset long-term capital gains.

Part III of Schedule D is used to figure the net amount of capital gains or losses. This netting is required because only one net amount—a net capital gain or a net capital loss—results. The net amount (subject to the loss limit discussed later in this chapter) from this part of Schedule D is reported on Form 1040.

Net Short-Term Capital Gain If net short-term capital gains are in excess of the net long-term loss (if any), the resulting short-term gain is entered on Form 1040 and is taxed with other ordinary income at the taxpayer's marginal tax rates.

Net Long-Term Capital Gain If the amount of the taxpayer's net long-term gain exceeds the net short-term loss (if any), the resulting long-term capital gain is reported on Form 1040. However, special worksheets are used to compute the tax so that the special rates for capital gains can be applied.

- A 15% tax rate for long-term capital gains and qualified dividends applies to the taxpayer's long-term capital gains and qualified dividends which are otherwise in a 25% or higher ordinary tax bracket (zero tax rate for the taxpayer's long-term capital gains and qualified dividends which are otherwise in the 10% or 15% ordinary tax brackets). For 2012, the 10% and 15% ordinary tax brackets apply to taxable income not exceeding \$70,700 (married filing jointly or qualifying widow(er)), \$47,350 (head of household), $35,350 (single or married filing separately). If there are gains subject to the special 15% or 0% capital gains rates, use the *Qualified Dividends and Capital Gain Tax Worksheet* (found in the Form 1040 instructions) to figure the tax.

Example

Beverly, a single taxpayer, has total taxable income of $50,000, of which $15,000 is ordinary income and $35,000 is long-term capital gain income. For a single taxpayer in 2012, the 15% bracket ends and the 25% rate begins at taxable income of $35,350, so $20,350 ($35,350 – $15,000) of Beverly's long-term capital gain will be taxed at 0%. The remaining $14,650 ($35,000 – $20,350) will be taxed at 15%.

- A 25% rate applies for unrecaptured gains (e.g., depreciation on a home office). If there are such gains, use the *Unrecaptured Section 1250 Gain Worksheet* to figure the tax.
- A 28% rate applies for collectibles gains and the nonexcluded portion of gain from the sale of Qualified Small Business Stock (section 1202 stock). If there are such gains, use the *28% Rate Gain Worksheet* to figure the tax.

These special tax computations are discussed in Chapter 32.

TIP: The wash sale rules do not apply to dealers in stock or securities if the loss is from a transaction made in their ordinary course of business.

Wash Sale Rule

If a sale of securities results in a loss, the loss may not be taken if it triggers the wash sale rule. Under this rule, losses cannot be claimed if substantially identical securities are acquired within 30 days before *or* after the date of sale. Instead, the disallowed losses on a wash sale increase the basis of the newly acquired securities. The holding period of the new securities includes the holding period of the securities that were sold.

ALERT: The wash sale rules cannot be avoided by having a related party acquire substantially identical securities within the wash sale period. For this purpose, a related party includes a taxpayer's individual retirement account (IRA). Thus, Gretchen could not sell the shares and then have her IRA reacquire the shares on August 10.

Example

Gretchen sold 100 shares of LTCG, Inc. on August 4, 2012. She paid $6,900 and received $2,400; her loss on the sale is $4,500. On August 10, 2012, she bought 100 shares of LTCG for $2,200. She cannot claim the $4,500 loss, although her basis in the new shares is $6,700 ($2,200 paid + $4,500 disallowed loss).

ALERT: In the year a taxpayer dies, capital loss carryovers can be reported on the taxpayer's (decedent's) final income tax return. However, any remaining loss carryforward attributable to the decedent cannot be used by the decedent's estate or a surviving spouse (beyond the couple's final joint return).

Capital Loss Limits and Carryovers

Depending on a taxpayer's capital gains and losses and carryovers of losses from prior years, he or she may not be able to use any part of the current year's capital losses.

Capital losses are used in these ways:

- *As an offset to capital gains.* If capital gains exceed capital losses, then the capital losses are used up completely in the current year.

- *As an offset to ordinary income (e.g., wages, interest income).* If the capital losses exceed the capital gains, then up to $3,000 ($1,500 if married filing separately) can be used to offset ordinary income.
- *As a capital loss carryover.* If capital losses exceed both capital gains *and* the ordinary income offset amount, then excess capital losses can be carried forward and used in a future year. There is no time limit on this carryforward. An individual taxpayer cannot carry back a capital loss to a prior year, but only forward to future years.

TIP: An individual taxpayer cannot carry *back* a capital loss to earlier years. However, an individual taxpayer can carry *forward* a capital loss indefinitely, until it is fully absorbed by future capital gains, or by ordinary income up to $3,000 per year. By contrast, a corporate taxpayer can carry back a capital loss up to three years, and forward up to only five years.

Example

Henry sold stock in 2012 that results in a long-term capital loss of $12,876. He has no other capital gains or losses for the year. He can use $3,000 to offset his ordinary income from taxable interest and other sources. His long-term capital loss carryover to 2013 is $9,876 ($12,876 – $3,000).

Special Reporting Situations

Some transactions do not necessarily fit neatly into the categories described earlier in this chapter:

Gains from Involuntary Conversions of Assets Held for Personal Purposes Involuntary conversions occur when property is destroyed, stolen, condemned, or disposed of under threat of condemnation. If a taxpayer's insurance proceeds or other reimbursements exceed the adjusted basis of the damaged or destroyed property, there is a gain. The gain is reported on Form 8949 *unless* the taxpayer opts to postpone the gain.

ALERT: If a taxpayer elected to postpone reporting the gain in the year of the involuntary conversion and failed to acquire replacement property within the specified amount of time, the taxpayer must amend the return for the tax year in which the election was made and recognize the gain.

The gain is postponed by reinvesting the proceeds in replacement property within a set time limit, which is generally two years after the end of the first tax year in which any part of the gain on the condemnation is realized. The time limit begins on the earlier of:

- The date when the property was disposed of, OR
- The date when the threat of condemnation began.

The two-year replacement period is extended in certain circumstances, such as replacing destroyed property or a principal residence located in a federally declared disaster area. For more information, see IRS Pub. 544.

Gains and Losses on Business Assets

The disposition of property used in business or certain property held for investment may be subject to different tax rules. This property includes stock in certain closely held corporations. Certain situations produce results that differ from the discussion earlier in this chapter.

Section 1244 Stock *Section 1244 stock* is stock in a small business (C or S corporation) that meets certain requirements (see IRS Pub. 550 for details). Sale of section 1244 stock may produce favorable tax treatment when it is disposed of at a loss. Instead of the loss being treated as a capital loss, it may be classified as an ordinary loss up to a set dollar limit. Ordinary loss treated is limited to $100,000 for joint filers (regardless of which spouse owns the stock) and $50,000 for other filers. The remaining balance of the loss is treated as a capital loss.

Example

Arnold, who is single, sells 100 shares of section 1244 stock for $10,000. He paid $75,000 for the stock 10 years ago. His loss is $65,000 ($75,000 – $10,000). Of this loss, he can treat $50,000 as an ordinary loss on section 1244 stock. The remaining balance of $15,000 is a capital loss, which can be used to offset capital gains up to $3,000 of ordinary income.

The taxpayer must retain records showing that the stock is section 1244 stock. These records need not be attached to the return.

Qualified Section 1202 Stock If a taxpayer disposes of *qualified small business stock* held more than five years at a gain, some or all of the gain may be excluded from income. Section 1202 stock is stock in a C (but not S) corporation that meets different criteria from section 1244 stock. See IRS Pub. 550 for details.

The exclusion for qualified small business stock depends on when the stock was acquired:

- *50% exclusion for stock acquired before February 18, 2009, and after December 31, 2011.* The other 50% of the gain is taxed at up to 28%. However, there is a 60% exclusion for empowerment zone business stock of an empowerment zone business acquired after December 21, 2000, and before February 18, 2009.
- *75% exclusion for stock acquired after February 17, 2009, but before September 28, 2010.* The other 25% of the gain is taxed at up to 28%.
- *100% exclusion for stock acquired after September 27, 2010, but before January 1, 2014.*

TIP: Because of the more-than-five-year holding period requirement, the only exclusion to be used on 2012 returns is the 50% exclusion, unless the 60% exclusion applies (i.e., gain from the sale of empowerment zone stock).

The dollar amount of the exclusion is limited to (1) 10 times the taxpayer's basis in all qualified stock of the corporation sold or exchanged during the year, or (2) $10 million ($5 million for a married person filing separately) minus the eligible gain from stock of the same corporation excluded in earlier years.

Section 1231 Gains and Losses Gain or loss on **section 1231 transactions** has favorable results, depending on whether the net results are gains or losses. That is, net gains are taxed as capital gains while net losses are treated as ordinary losses.

DEFINITION: **Section 1231 transactions** are business-related transactions of certain types of property.

Section 1231 transactions include:

- Sales or exchanges of real property or depreciable personal property used in a trade or business and held longer than one year

- Sales or exchanges of leaseholds used in a trade or business and held longer than one year
- Sales or exchanges of cattle and horses held for draft, breeding, dairy, or sporting purposes and held for two years or longer
- Sales or exchanges of other livestock (other than poultry) held for draft, breeding, dairy, or sporting purposes and held for one year or longer
- Sales or exchanges of unharvested crops sold, exchanged, or involuntarily converted at the same time and to the same person and the land must be held longer than one year
- Cutting of timber or disposal of timber, coal, or iron ore
- Condemnations of business or investment property held longer than one year
- Casualties and thefts affecting business or investment property that is held longer than one year. (However, if casualty or theft losses are more than casualty or theft gains, neither the gains nor the losses are taken into account in the section 1231 computation.)

To determine whether there is a net gain or loss, combine all of the section 1231 gains and losses for the year. If there is a net section 1231 loss, it is ordinary loss. If there is a net section 1231 gain, it is ordinary income up to the amount of any nonrecaptured section 1231 losses (net section 1231 losses for the previous five years that have not been applied against a net section 1231 gain); the balance, if any, is long-term capital gain. More details about section 1231 gains and losses can be found in IRS Pub. 544.

Example

In 2011, Ben has a $2,000 net section 1231 gain. To figure how much he has to report as ordinary income and long-term capital gain, he must first determine any section 1231 gains and losses from the previous five-year period. From 2006 through 2010, he had these section 1231 gains and losses:

Year	Amount
2006	-0-
2007	-0-
2008	($2,500)
2009	-0-
2010	$1,800

Ben uses this information to figure how to report his net section 1231 gain for 2011 as shown:

1)	Net section 1231 gain (2011)		$2,000
2)	Net section 1231 loss (2008)	($2,500)	
3)	Net section 1231 gain (2010)	$1,800	
4)	Remaining net section 1231 loss from prior 5 years	($700)	
5)	Gain treated as ordinary income		$700
6)	**Gain treated as long-term capital gain**		**$1,300**

His remaining net section 1231 loss from 2008 is completely recaptured in 2011. Had there been no section 1231 gain for 2010, the entire $2,000 net section 1231 gain for 2011 would be treated as ordinary income. Also, there would be $500 in net section 1231 losses remaining.

Depreciation Recapture

When depreciated property used in business or held for investment is sold at a profit, **depreciation recapture** may be triggered. Even though a sale may produce a capital gain, a portion of the gain may be treated as ordinary income to the extent of allowable depreciation.

Depreciation recapture recharacterizes gain as ordinary income in cases where the taxpayer claimed:

- A section 179 deduction
- Bonus depreciation
- Modified Accelerated Cost Recovery System (MACRS) allowance

In the case of residential real property, depreciation recapture applies only to the amount of the taxpayer's depreciation allowance that exceeds the amount of depreciation that would have been allowed under the straight-line method. Because residential rental property and nonresidential real property placed in service after December 31, 1986 is depreciated using the straight-line method, depreciation recapture rules (requiring part of the gain to be treated as ordinary income) generally will not apply to real property placed in service after that date.

DEFINITION: **Depreciation recapture** is a recharacterization of a gain that would normally be taxed at a favorable capital gain rate of 15% as ordinary income subject to a higher tax rate. The recharacterization depends on whether the property is tangible personal property or real property.

Unrecaptured Depreciation

In the case of depreciated real property, such as depreciation claimed on a home office, "unrecaptured depreciation" may apply. Any gain on property that is attributable to the depreciation but is not subject to the depreciation recapture rules discussed above is taxed at a maximum capital gains rate of 25%; it is not treated as ordinary income.

Example

Samantha sells her office furniture that she had depreciated in her business. She paid $6,000 for the furniture and had claimed total depreciation of $3,376. She sold the furniture for $4,000. Her gain is the difference between the sale proceeds ($4,000) and her adjusted basis of $2,264 (initial basis of $6,000 – depreciation of $3,376), or $1,376. However, because the total depreciation taken ($3,376) exceeds her gain ($1,376), the entire gain is treated as ordinary income.

If she had sold the office furniture for $6,500 instead of $4,000, her total gain would have been $3,876 ($6,500 – ($6,000 – $3,376)). The amount treated as ordinary income would be $3,376 (total depreciation), and the remaining gain of $500 ($3,876 – $3,376) would be treated as a capital gain.

DEFINITION: For residential real property, **unrecaptured depreciation** is usually the total depreciation expense that was deducted prior to the sale of the set. Unrecaptured depreciation is recognized as income when the property to which it relates is sold. This prevents taxpayers from converting ordinary income into capital gains by depreciating an asset and then selling it at a gain that is then taxed at favorable capital gain rates.

In the case of depreciated real property, such as depreciation claimed on a home office, depreciation recapture is called **unrecaptured depreciation.** All such depreciation claimed after May 6, 1997, to the extent of gain, is taxed at up to 25%; it is not treated as ordinary income.

Example

Arthur uses a room in his home as a home office for which he claims deductions. Depreciation allowances on the home office total $1,800. Arthur sells his home at a gain of $220,000 and uses the sale of home exclusion to exclude the gain. He still must pay tax of 25% on the $1,800 of depreciation that he claimed.

Reporting Gains and Losses on Business Assets

Gains and losses on most business assets are reported in Parts I and II of Form 4797. Part I is used for listing sales or exchanges of business property held more than one year as well as for reporting gains from involuntary conversions (other than casualties and thefts). Part II is used for listing ordinary gains and losses, which include property held one year or less that is not listed in another part of the form. For example, this part is used to report the ordinary loss of up to $50,000 ($100,000 on joint returns for section 1244 stock, described earlier and explained more fully in IRS Pub. 550) as shown in Figure 13.4.

Gain from the sale of property subject to depreciation recapture is reported in Part III of Form 4797 (see Figure 13.5).

Recapture of first-year expensing (the section 179 deduction) or when the use of listed property for business purposes declines below 50% is reported in Part IV of Form 4797 (see Figure 13.6).

Form **4797**

Department of the Treasury
Internal Revenue Service

Sales of Business Property
(Also Involuntary Conversions and Recapture Amounts Under Sections 179 and 280F(b)(2))
► Attach to your tax return.
► Information about Form 4797 and its separate instructions is at *www.irs.gov/form4797.*

OMB No. 1545-0184
2012
Attachment Sequence No. **27**

Name(s) shown on return | **Identifying number**

1 Enter the gross proceeds from sales or exchanges reported to you for 2012 on Form(s) 1099-B or 1099-S (or substitute statement) that you are including on line 2, 10, or 20 (see instructions) 1

Part I **Sales or Exchanges of Property Used in a Trade or Business and Involuntary Conversions From Other Than Casualty or Theft—Most Property Held More Than 1 Year** (see instructions)

2 (a) Description of property	(b) Date acquired (mo., day, yr.)	(c) Date sold (mo., day, yr.)	(d) Gross sales price	(e) Depreciation allowed or allowable since acquisition	(f) Cost or other basis, plus improvements and expense of sale	**(g) Gain or (loss)** Subtract (f) from the sum of (d) and (e)

Part II **Ordinary Gains and Losses** (see instructions)

10 Ordinary gains and losses not included on lines 11 through 16 (include property held 1 year or less):

FIGURE 13.4 Form 4797, Parts I and II

Part III **Gain From Disposition of Property Under Sections 1245, 1250, 1252, 1254, and 1255** (see instructions)

						(b) Date acquired (mo., day, yr.)	(c) Date sold (mo., day, yr.)
19	(a) Description of section 1245, 1250, 1252, 1254, or 1255 property:						
A							
B							
C							
D							

	These columns relate to the properties on lines 19A through 19D. ▶		Property A	Property B	Property C	Property D
20	Gross sales price (**Note:** *See line 1 before completing.*)	20				
21	Cost or other basis plus expense of sale	21				
22	Depreciation (or depletion) allowed or allowable	22				
23	Adjusted basis. Subtract line 22 from line 21	23				
24	Total gain. Subtract line 23 from line 20	24				

FIGURE 13.5 Form 4797, Part III

Part IV **Recapture Amounts Under Sections 179 and 280F(b)(2) When Business Use Drops to 50% or Less** (see instructions)

			(a) Section 179	(b) Section 280F(b)(2)
33	Section 179 expense deduction or depreciation allowable in prior years	33		
34	Recomputed depreciation (see instructions)	34		
35	Recapture amount. Subtract line 34 from line 33. See the instructions for where to report	35		

Form **4797** (2012)

FIGURE 13.6 Form 4797 Sales of Business Property, Part IV

Review Questions

1. Which of the following is a capital asset?
   a. Inventory
   b. U.S. government publications
   c. Mutual fund shares
   d. Real property used in business

2. Daniel has stock that has declined in value. He can report the loss if he sells it to:
   a. His wife
   b. His mother-in-law
   c. His daughter
   d. His mother

3. On February 1, 2012, a taxpayer buys 10 shares of X Corp. What is the earliest date that the stock can be sold to qualify for long-term treatment?
   a. Any time after 2012
   b. February 1, 2013
   c. February 2, 2013
   d. February 5, 2013

4. A taxpayer sells stock in 2012. Where is the sale **first** reported by the taxpayer?
   a. Schedule D
   b. Form 1040
   c. Form 4797
   d. Form 8949

5. A taxpayer sells 100 shares of X Corp. at a loss on December 15, 2012. Which of the following acquisition dates for acquiring substantially identical stock will **not** trigger the wash sale rule?
   a. November 15, 2012
   b. January 1, 2013
   c. January 14, 2013
   d. January 15, 2013

6. In 2012, a taxpayer's home is completely destroyed by a tornado. She receives insurance proceeds that exceed the adjusted basis of the home. She decides not to rebuild or buy a new home, relocates to another state, and rents an apartment. Where is the transaction reported?
   a. Directly on Form 1040
   b. Schedule A of Form 1040
   c. Schedule D of Form 1040
   d. Form 4797

Sale of Home

The sale of a home may generate gain or loss. To figure gain or loss, you need to determine the taxpayer's basis in the home, which may be adjusted upward or downward for certain items.

Special rules apply to exclude some or all of the gain from the sale of a principal residence. No loss can be recognized on the sale of a principal residence or any other home used for personal purposes (e.g., a vacation home that is not rented out).

If a home is foreclosed on, the taxpayer is considered to have sold the property to the lender even though the action is involuntary on the part of the taxpayer.

Taxpayers who claimed a first-time homebuyer credit may have to repay a portion of the credit if the home is sold.

Determining Basis

To determine whether there is a gain or a loss on the sale of a home, the homeowner's basis first must be calculated. Generally, this is the homeowner's cost basis, which is what the taxpayer paid to buy the home (cash and property plus any mortgage obtained to close the sale). Adjustments to basis, such as those described in this chapter, must also be considered. If the home is acquired other than by purchase (e.g., by gift or inheritance), special basis rules apply. See Chapter 12 for determining basis.

Settlement Costs

Basis also includes settlement (closing) costs that are not deductible, such as:

- Abstract fees
- Legal fees
- Recording fees
- Surveys

DEFINITION: Points are a form of prepaid interest. A buyer may opt to pay points in order to reduce the interest rate on the mortgage. Each point represents 1 percent of the amount borrowed, so 1 point on a $200,000 mortgage is $2,000. Points are also referred to as loan origination fees or discount points.

DEFINITION: A **personal residence** may include a house, houseboat, mobile home, cooperative apartment, or a condominium.

- Title insurance for the owner
- Transfer or stamp taxes

If a homeowner pays points to obtain a mortgage to acquire the home, the **points** may be fully deductible in the current year, or the taxpayer may choose to amortize them over the life of the mortgage (explained in Chapter 22). Deductible points do not increase basis, but if the points are not deductible, they are added to the basis of the home. Points paid by the seller usually reduce the homeowner's basis.

Adjustments to Basis

The basis of the home is increased or decreased for certain items (see Chapter 12). Here are some adjustments to basis that are unique to **personal residences.** These adjustments are made to determine the taxpayer's adjusted basis. Some increases (or decreases) to basis are found in Table 14.1. This table lists examples of some items that generally will increase or decrease basis in a home.

TABLE 14.1 Adjusted Basis

Increases to basis	Decreases to basis
• Putting an addition on your home • Replacing an entire roof • Paving your driveway • Installing central air conditioning • Rewiring your home • Assessments for local improvements • Amounts spent to restore damaged property	• Insurance or other reimbursement for casualty losses • Deductible casualty loss not covered by insurance • Payments received for easement or right-of-way granted • Depreciation allowed or allowable if home is used for business or rental purposes • Value of subsidy for energy conservation measure excluded from income

Basis must also be decreased if any of the following credits have been claimed:

- First-time homebuyer credit that has not previously been recaptured
- Nonbusiness energy property credit for improvements that increased the basis of the home
- Residential energy efficient property credit for improvements that increased the basis of the home

Figuring Gain or Loss

Gain or loss is the sale price minus the adjusted basis of the home. The sale price can be reduced by selling expenses to arrive at the amount realized on the sale. These expenses include advertising costs, brokers' commissions, legal fees, and loan charges paid by the seller to sell the home.

Figure gain or loss using this formula:

	Selling price
–	Selling expenses
	Amount realized
–	Selling expenses
	Gain or loss

Example

Alicia sells her home for $276,000 without help from a broker. She spent $2,000 to advertise the home in order to sell it. She bought it 10 years ago at a cost of $123,000 (including settlement costs) and made major (capital) improvements that cost $88,000, bringing her adjusted basis to $211,000. Her gain is $63,000 [($276,000 – $2,000) – ($211,000)]. If Alicia qualifies for the home sale exclusion, discussed next, the gain will not be taxed.

A loss on a personal residence cannot be recognized because it is a personal asset, not a business asset or investment property (even though a homeowner may view the home as an investment).

Home Sale Exclusion

Homeowners may be able to exclude gain on the sale of a **principal residence** of up to $250,000 for a single taxpayer ($500,000 for certain married taxpayers who file a joint return).

DEFINITION:
A **principal residence** is the personal residence that the taxpayer ordinarily lives in most of the time.

Individual taxpayers can exclude gain if all of the next points are true:

- The taxpayer owned the home for at least two years during the five-year period ending on the date of sale;
- The home was the taxpayer's principal residence for at least two years during the five-year period ending on the date of sale; AND
- The taxpayer did not exclude gain from the sale of another home during the two-year period ending on the date of sale.

Short temporary absences, for vacations, sabbaticals, or other seasonal absences, are treated as periods of use, even if the home is rented for that period. (Special time limits apply to the military and foreign service personnel, as explained later.)

The two years for ownership and use do not have to be continuous, nor do they have to occur at the same time.

Example

Elise bought her home in July 2008 and had lived there for 13 months when she moved in with her boyfriend. She moved back to her home in 2011 and lived there for 12 months until she sold the home in July 2012. She meets the ownership and use test. She owned the home for four years (July 2008 to July 2012). She used the home as her personal residence for 25 months (13 + 12 months), which is more than two years.

An individual taxpayer may exclude only up to $250,000 of gain.

Example

Herman sold his principal residence for $308,600. He bought the home 20 years ago and his adjusted basis is $110,000. Herman can exclude his gain of $198,600 ($308,600 – $110,000). If he had sold the home for $408,600, his exclusion would have been limited to $250,000; the other $48,600 of capital gain would be taxed as long-term capital gain. (For more information on capital gain, see Chapter 13.)

If two or more unmarried homeowners jointly own their principal residence that they sell, each owner can exclude up to $250,000 of gain.

For a married taxpayer who files a joint return, an exclusion of up to $500,000 applies if:

- Both spouses meet the use test;
- Either spouse meets the ownership test; AND
- Neither spouse claimed the exclusion for gain from the sale of another home during the two-year period ending on the date of sale.

If either one of the spouses does not meet all of these requirements, the couple must calculate their individual exclusion amounts separately (as if they were not married). They can exclude the total amount on their joint return.

Example

Betty sells her home in June 2012 and marries Freddy in December. Freddy never lived in the home, which was sold before the marriage. Betty can exclude only up to $250,000 of gain because Freddy did not meet the two-year use test. If Freddy also sold a home in 2012 (before the marriage) and he met the two-year use test for his home, they could claim an exclusion on their joint return of up to $250,000 each.

A surviving spouse who does not remarry before the sale of the couple's residence is considered to have owned and used the home as his or her principal residence for any period owned and used by the deceased spouse. The exclusion for a surviving spouse can be up to $500,000 if *all* of these conditions are met:

- The sale takes place no later than two years after the death of the spouse;
- The surviving spouse has not remarried;
- Both spouses met the use test at the time of the deceased spouse's death;
- Either spouse met the ownership test at the time of the deceased spouse's death;
- Neither spouse excluded gain from the sale of a principal residence within the last two years before the date of death; AND
- The sale or exchange took place after 2008.

If a residence is transferred from one spouse to the other spouse (or to a former spouse incident to divorce), any period of ownership for the former owner carries over to the new owner. The new owner is considered to have used the home for any period that he or she owned it and for any period in which the spouse or former spouse is allowed to live in the home as his or her principal residence under a divorce decree or separation agreement.

Example

Arnold and Anne, who are married to each other, jointly own a home they bought and lived in since 2002. Anne died on July 1, 2011, and Arnold sold the home on November 1, 2012. He can use the $500,000 home sale exclusion because the sale took place within two years of Anne's death, and he had not remarried at the time of the sale.

Exceptions to Ownership and Use Tests

If a homeowner becomes physically or mentally incapable of self-care after owning and living in the home for at least one year during the five-year period prior to sale and moves to a nursing home or other licensed care facility, the time in the facility counts as personal use. The two-year requirements for ownership and use must still be met.

If a home is destroyed or condemned and a replacement home is acquired, the period of ownership and use in the old home is added to the period of ownership and use in the new home.

Members of the military, Foreign Service or intelligence community personnel, and Peace Corps employees and volunteers can choose to suspend the five-year test period for ownership and use while they serve on "qualified official extended duty." The period of suspension cannot be more than 10 years, but this effectively produces a 15-year period (the 10-year suspension plus the normal 5 years for testing).

> **TIP:** A homeowner can opt to *not* use the exclusion and instead report all of the gain. There are limited situations when this is advisable. For example, a homeowner who realizes gains on the sale of two principal residences within two years can exclude the gain on only one. The taxpayer can elect to recognize the smaller gain.

Example

Harold bought a home on March 1, 1996. He used it as his main home until August 31, 1999. On September 1, 1999, he went on qualified official extended duty with the Air Force. He did not live in the house again before selling it on July 31, 2012. Harold chooses to use the entire 10-year suspension period, which extends back from July 31, 2012, to August 1, 2002. He also uses the 5-year test period, which extends back to August 1, 1997. Harold owned the house all 5 years and lived in it as his main home from August 1, 1997, until August 31, 1999, which is more than 24 months. Under the exception, Harold is able to meet the ownership and use test.

Partial Exclusion

If the homeowner sells before satisfying the two-year test for ownership and use, a partial exclusion is allowed if the sale is due to one of these reasons:

- *A change in the place of employment or self-employment of a qualified individual* (the taxpayer, taxpayer's spouse, a co-owner of the home, or a person whose primary residence is the same as the taxpayer's) that is at least 50 miles farther from the home sold than was the former place of work.

- *Health reasons of a qualified individual or the taxpayer's close family member,* including to obtain a diagnosis, cure, mitigation, or treatment, or to obtain or provide medical or personal care.

> **TIP:** This list of unforeseen circumstances is not exhaustive. The IRS has recognized many other situations as acceptable, including extreme bullying of a child, being a victim of violence in a neighborhood, being unable to pay basic living expenses because of a change in employment (being furloughed), receiving death threats, and needing to accommodate a blended family.

- *Unforeseen circumstances.* Examples of unforeseen circumstances include:
  - □ An involuntary conversion of the home (e.g., destruction or condemnation)
  - □ Natural or man-made disasters (e.g., terrorism)
  - □ An event that occurs to a qualified individual, including:
    - □ Death
    - □ Unemployment (if the individual is eligible for unemployment compensation)
    - □ Divorce or legal separation
    - □ Multiple births resulting from the same pregnancy (requiring more living space to accommodate the larger family)

If one of these conditions applies, the maximum partial exclusion is the applicable exclusion amount for the period in which the taxpayer met the ownership and use tests.

Example

Heddy had to sell her home in Maine because her doctor advised her to move to a warm, dry climate for health reasons (to mitigate her chronic asthma symptoms). She had owned and lived in her Maine residence for only one year when she sold it. Her gain on the sale was $28,000, which she can exclude. Her exclusion is limited to $125,000 ($250,000 × 50%) because she met the ownership and use tests for 12 of the 24 months required. This exclusion covers all of her gain.

> **TIP:** Note that the exclusion *limit* is prorated, not the gain itself. In the example above, Heddy can fully exclude her gain of $28,000 because the maximum exclusion was reduced from $250,000 to $125,000. Her gain of $28,000 is not reduced to $14,000 ($28,000 × 50%).

Nonqualified Use

The exclusion cannot be claimed for gain allocable to nonqualified use, even though the homeowner meets the two-year ownership and use tests. Nonqualified use means any period after 2008 where neither the taxpayer nor spouse used the property as a main home. However, nonqualified use does not include:

- Any portion of the five-year period ending on the date of sale after the last date the taxpayer or spouse used the property as a principal residence
- Any period during which the taxpayer is serving on qualified extended duty in the uniformed services, Foreign Service, or intelligence community (not to exceed ten years)
- Temporary absences (not to exceed two years) due to a change in employment or self-employment, health reasons, or unforeseen circumstances

The portion of the gain that is allocated to nonqualified use and cannot be excluded is figured by multiplying the gain by the next fraction:

$$\frac{\text{Total nonqualified use in 2009 and later}}{\text{Total period of ownership}}$$

Example

Ted buys a vacation home on January 1, 2007, for $500,000. On January 1, 2011, he converts the home to his principal residence, and on January 1, 2013, he sells the home for $800,000. Of the $300,000 gain, $100,000 is not eligible for the exclusion and is taxable in the year of sale (24 months of nonqualified use ÷ 72 months of total ownership/use) because it is allocable to nonqualified use. The remaining $200,000 is eligible for the exclusion.

Business Use or Rental of a Personal Residence

Gain on the sale of a home for which a taxpayer claimed an office in home deduction is treated as a single sale even though the taxpayer used part of the home for business purposes. The same principle applies to renting rooms or any other partial business use of the dwelling unit. Taxpayers can exclude gain on the sale if they meet the requirements for the sale of home exclusion. However, any depreciation allowed or allowable with respect to the home office or other business/rental use after May 6, 1997, is subject to unrecaptured section 1250 gain treatment, which is generally taxed at 25%. Unrecaptured section 1250 gain is explained in Chapter 13.

If the entire home was rented out after 2008 but before the taxpayer converted it to his or her personal residence, any gain allocated to the nonqualified use may not be excluded, as explained earlier. Again, any allowed or allowable depreciation is subject to the unrecaptured section 1250 gain rule, as explained in Chapter 13. Gain attributable to depreciation is applied before applying the exclusion and nonqualified use rules.

Example

Alison and Alex buy a home for $500,000 on January 1, 2010, and rent it out for one year before moving in and using it as their principal residence. They claim a $10,000 depreciation deduction for 2010. They remain in the home until January 1, 2015, when they sell it for $800,000. The $10,000 allowed/allowable depreciation is unrecaptured section 1250 gain, taxed at a maximum rate of 25%. For exclusion purposes, 20% of the gain on the sale cannot be excluded (12 months nonqualified use ÷ 60 months total use). The remaining $248,000 gain on the sale (80% × ($800,000 – $490,000 basis) is excludable.

ALERT: Note that in this case, the percentage of nonqualified use is applied against the *gain*, whereas with a partial exclusion, the exclusion *limit* is prorated (see the Heddy example above).

If the taxpayer owns a multifamily home and uses one unit for personal purposes while renting out the other unit or units, the sale can be separated and treated as the sale of two or more distinct properties. Taxpayers can exclude the portion of gain allocated to the personal use unit if they meet the requirements for the sale of home exclusion. Gain allocated to other units is nonexcludable and therefore taxable. Some or all of this taxable gain is subject to the unrecaptured section 1250 gain rules.

Abandonments, Foreclosures, and Repossessions

If a taxpayer "walks away" from his or her residence or the home is foreclosed on or repossessed, a taxable event occurs. The transaction usually is treated as a disposition. Generally, gain or loss is figured in the same way as if the home had been sold. However, the selling price used in this computation depends on whether the taxpayer was or was not personally liable for repaying the debt.

- If the taxpayer is *not* personally liable for the debt (nonrecourse debt), then the selling price includes the full amount of the debt canceled by the foreclosure or repossession.
- If the taxpayer is personally liable for the debt (recourse debt, as is usually the case), the selling price includes the amount of the debt canceled up to the home's fair market value (FMV). There may also be ordinary income to the taxpayer (explained later).

> **TIP:** The abandonment of a home is reported by the mortgagee (e.g., the bank) on Form 1099-A, *Acquisition or Abandonment of Secured Property*. If there is any cancellation of debt, it is reported on Form 1099-C, *Cancellation of Debt*. If an abandonment and cancellation occur in the same year, the lender may report all the information on Form 1099-C. These information returns contain the information needed to determine gain, loss, and ordinary income from abandonments, foreclosures, and repossessions of homes.

If the canceled debt is more than the home's FMV and the taxpayer is personally liable for the debt, the difference may be taxed as ordinary income to the taxpayer if the creditor cancels the remaining debt. However, the taxpayer may be eligible for an exclusion, such as the qualified principal residence indebtedness exclusion or the bankruptcy or insolvency exclusions (exclusions for cancellation of debt [COD] income are explained in Chapter 10).

More information about abandonments and how to figure gain, loss, and ordinary income, is in IRS Pub. 4681, *Canceled Debts, Foreclosures, Repossessions, and Abandonments.*

Reporting Home Sales

The sale of a principal residence does *not* have to be reported on the tax return if there is a gain and all of it can be excluded. However, the sale must be reported if:

- Some or all of the gain is not excluded.
- There is a gain but the taxpayer chooses not to exclude it.
- The taxpayer received Form 1099-S, *Proceeds from Real Estate Transactions.*

No special form is used to figure gain or loss or to report gain from the sale of a principal residence. IRS Pub. 523, *Selling Your Home*, includes a series of worksheets that can be used to figure gain or loss.

If there is taxable gain that cannot be excluded on the sale of the main home, the entire gain is reported on Form 8949, *Sales and Other Dispositions of Capital Assets*, which is carried to Schedule D, *Capital Gains and Losses*. The gain is reported as short-term or long-term capital gain depending on how long the taxpayer owned the home. Any excluded gain is shown as a loss (in parentheses) on the schedule. If the home was used for business (other than a home office) or for rental purposes, the sale may have to be reported on Form 4797, *Sales of Business Property*.

If the taxpayer sells the home through an installment sale (a sale where the taxpayer receives at least one payment after the tax year of the sale), the taxpayer may be able to use Form 6252, *Installment Sale Income*, to report the sale (see IRS Pub. 537, *Installment Sales*, for details). The installment method can be used only if there is unexcluded gain.

If the lender cancels part of the taxpayer's mortgage, the COD income generally is reported on line 21 of Form 1040, *U.S. Individual Income Tax Return*. Chapter 10 discusses COD income and when it can be excluded.

Recapture

When a home is sold, there may be certain types of recapture in addition to any depreciation recapture discussed earlier in this chapter.

First-Time Homebuyer Credit

The first-time homebuyer credit was created to stimulate the housing market at the beginning of the housing slump in 2008. However, a taxpayer who claimed the credit may have to recapture (repay as an additional tax) part of the credit if the home is sold or ceases to be used as the taxpayer's principal residence. Whether and to what extent the credit must be repaid depends on when the home was purchased and the reason for it not remaining the taxpayer's principal residence. See Chapter 35 for more details about repayment of the first-time homebuyer credit.

Federal Mortgage Subsidy

If a taxpayer sells a home on which he or she received a **federal mortgage subsidy** provided after December 31, 1990, a recapture of this benefit may apply. Form 8828, *Recapture of Federal Mortgage Subsidy*, is used to figure recapture if the home is sold or given away. Recapture applies only if there is a sale or disposition within nine years of when the subsidy was received and the taxpayer's income for the year of disposition is greater than that year's adjusted qualifying income for the taxpayer's family size. Special rules apply to refinancing of the original loan within four years.

DEFINITION:
A **federal mortgage subsidy** is either (1) a mortgage with a lower interest rate than usually charged because it is financed with a qualified mortgage bond, or (2) a mortgage credit certificate used to reduce the taxpayer's income taxes.

However, there is no recapture for:

- The transfer of a home to a spouse or former spouse incident to divorce
- The destruction of a home by a casualty
- A qualified home improvement loan up to $15,000 used to repair or improve the home or make it more energy efficient

Review Questions

1. Basis of a home is increased by all of the following **except**:
   a. Points that are fully deductible in the year of payment
   b. Legal fees to buy the home
   c. Surveys of the home
   d. Title insurance for the home

2. Basis of a home is decreased by all of the following **except**:
   a. Deductible casualty loss not covered by insurance
   b. Assessments for local improvements
   c. First-time homebuyer credit
   d. Subsidy for conservation measures that was excluded from income

3. A taxpayer, who is single, sells his condo in February 2012. He buys a new home, weds in June 2012, and his new bride moves in at that time. Gain on the sale of his condo is $275,000. Assuming he owned and used the condo as his main home for two out of the last five years, he can:
   a. Exclude gain of $250,000 and report no further gain
   b. Exclude gain of $275,000
   c. Exclude gain of $500,000
   d. Exclude gain of $250,000 and report $25,000 as long-term capital gain

4. Which of the following unforeseen circumstances would **not** entitle a homeowner to a partial home sale exclusion?
   a. The unexpected birth of triplets
   b. Winning the lottery
   c. Being a victim of a crime in the neighborhood
   d. Losing a job and being unable to pay the household bills

5. On February 1, 2010, Kevin, a single taxpayer, buys a condo in North Dakota. On April 3, 2011, he suffers a stroke and following hospitalization, is transferred to a nursing home. While he was living in the nursing home, his daughter, acting under a power of attorney, sells the condo in December 2012 for a gain of $48,000. How is the gain treated?
   a. It is fully excludable.
   b. It is excludable for the portion of the time Kevin lived in the condo.
   c. It is excludable for the portion of the time he lived in the condo, plus the time in the hospital.
   d. It is fully taxable.

IRA and HSA Contributions

The tax law encourages savings—for retirement, medical costs, and other purposes—by offering special tax incentives. These incentives generally are claimed as adjustments (reductions) to gross income, which are available regardless of whether a taxpayer uses the standard deduction or itemizes deductions.

Claiming these adjustments means that Form 1040, *U.S. Individual Income Tax Return,* generally must be used. A taxpayer cannot use Form 1040A to deduct a contribution to a health savings account (HSA) or Form 1040-EZ to deduct contributions to either an HSA or an individual retirement account (IRA).

IRAs are a tax-advantaged way to save for retirement. A taxpayer can make deductible or nondeductible contributions to a traditional IRA. Earnings in the IRA grow tax deferred. Distributions from IRAs, which are discussed in Chapter 8, generally are taxed in the year of distribution. However, if a nondeductible contribution was made to an IRA, it is not taxed again upon distribution.

One form of after-tax, or nondeductible, IRA, is the Roth IRA. Unlike contributions to a traditional IRA, taxpayers may not deduct their contributions to a Roth IRA. However, taxpayers can take tax-free distributions from Roth IRAs if certain conditions are met.

Another tax-advantaged savings account is an HSA, used to pay for medical costs. This account offers triple tax savings: Taxpayers may deduct contributions to the HSA, earnings on the funds are tax deferred, and withdrawals are tax free if used for qualified medical expenses.

Traditional IRAs

IRAs originally were created to enable taxpayers to save for their retirement on a tax-deductible basis. They were intended to supplement employer-provided pensions. Today, IRAs can be used even when taxpayers have other qualified retirement savings, such as 401(k) plans or tax-sheltered annuities, through employers.

Contributions

Taxpayers must meet age and earned income requirements in order to make contributions to an IRA. A taxpayer who is covered by an employer-provided retirement plan may qualify for only a partial deduction or for none at all if the taxpayer's income exceeds certain thresholds. See "Contribution Limits" later in this chapter.

ALERT: For purposes of calculating a self-employed taxpayer's earned income qualifying for purposes of IRA contributions, self-employment income must be reduced by one-half of the adjustment for self-employment tax, plus any deductions the taxpayer made to a qualified retirement plan, such as a solo 401(k).

Earned Income Taxpayers must have earned income in order to contribute to an IRA. Earned income for purposes of an IRA contribution includes wages, tips, and self-employment income.

For IRA purposes, earned income also includes:

- Alimony received
- Combat pay (even if excluded from income)

Earned income does *not* include foreign earned income that is excluded, pensions and annuities, or unemployment compensation.

For married couples, if one spouse works and the other does not, the working spouse can contribute to an IRA for the nonworking spouse based on the working spouse's earnings.

Example

Jon and Sandy, both age 45, are married and file a joint return. Sandy does not work and has no earned income, while Jon earned a salary of $45,000. Jon may contribute up to $5,000 to his own traditional IRA as well as $5,000 to Sandy's traditional IRA (known as a spousal IRA). The IRAs must be separate for each individual.

Age There is no minimum age for making IRA contributions. A teenager with a summer job can contribute to an IRA based on those earnings, up to the $5,000 limit.

Taxpayers can contribute to traditional IRAs only as long as they are under age 70½ at the end of the year; after reaching age 70½, taxpayers cannot contribute to a traditional IRA even if they continue to work and have earned income.

Contribution Limits

General Limit Contributions must be made only in cash (not in stock or other property). The maximum amount that can be contributed to an IRA for 2012 is $5,000. If the taxpayer is at least 50 years old by December 31, 2012, an additional $1,000 can be contributed. However, the contribution cannot exceed earned income for the year.

Example

Liz, a college student, has a summer job in which she earns $3,200. She has no other earned income for the year. Her maximum IRA contribution is $3,200 (the lesser of earned income and $5,000).

Limit for Active Participants A taxpayer who **actively participates** in a qualified retirement plan can contribute and deduct the maximum amount only if his or her modified adjusted gross income (MAGI) does not exceed the low end of the MAGI phase-out range for the taxpayer's filing status. Part of the contribution is deductible if the taxpayer's MAGI falls within the MAGI phase-out range. No part of the contribution is deductible if MAGI equals or exceeds the high end of the phase-out range.

DEFINITION: For purposes of IRA contributions, a taxpayer is an **active participant** if contributions or allocations are made on behalf of the taxpayer to an account including a qualified pension; 401(k); profit-sharing, or stock bonus plan; a Savings Incentive Match Plan for Employees Individual Retirement Account (SIMPLE IRA); a Simplified Employee Pension Individual Retirement Account (SEP-IRA); a qualified annuity plan; or a tax-sheltered annuity; or a federal, state, or local government plan that is not a 457(b) plan. Active participation status is indicated on the taxpayer's Form W-2, *Wage and Tax Statement* (box 13).

For married taxpayers, each spouse must calculate his or her deduction separately based on the MAGI on their joint return. This is because IRAs are *individual* accounts and *cannot* be jointly owned.

The 2012 MAGI thresholds and phase-out ranges are shown in Tables 15.1 and 15.2. Table 15.1 shows MAGI limits for taxpayers who *are* active participants in an employer plan, and Table 15.2 shows MAGI limits for taxpayers who *are not* active participants in an employer plan.

TABLE 15.1 2012 MAGI Limits for Taxpayers Who Are Active Participants in an Employer Plan

Filing status	Full deduction if MAGI is:	Partial Deduction for MAGI:	No deduction if MAGI is:
Single or head of household	$58,000 or less	Over $58,000 but under $68,000	$68,000 or more
Married filing jointly	$92,000 or less	Over $92,000 but under $112,000	$112,000 or more
Married filing separately (MFS)*		Under $10,000	$10,000 or more

*If the spouses lived together at any time during the year and file MFS, the use the limits in the MFS row. If the spouses did not live together at any time during the year, they can each use the limits in the single row.

ALERT: If a taxpayer is eligible to participate in a defined benefit plan, the taxpayer is considered to be an active participant even if he or she declined to participate in the plan.

MAGI means AGI with the following amounts added back:

- IRA deduction
- Any deduction for student loan interest, tuition and fees, or excluded qualified savings bond interest
- Foreign earned income exclusion or foreign housing exclusion or deduction
- Any exclusion for employer-provided adoption benefits
- Domestic production activities deduction (see the instructions to Form 8903, *Domestic Production Activities Deduction,* for more information)

Calculating the Maximum Deductible Contribution To calculate the maximum deductible contribution amount if the taxpayer's MAGI falls within the phase-out range:

1. Find the taxpayer's MAGI and compare it to the appropriate phase-out range in Table 15.1 or 15.2.
2. Subtract the taxpayer's MAGI from the high end of the phase-out range.

TIP: If a taxpayer makes a contribution to an IRA, he or she may be entitled to a credit for retirement plan contributions as well as the tax deduction. The credit is discussed in Chapter 31.

TABLE 15.2 2012 MAGI Limits for Taxpayers Who Are Not Active Participants in an Employer Plan

Filing status	Full deduction if MAGI is:	Partial Deduction for MAGI:	No deduction if MAGI is:
Single or head of household	Any amount		
Married filing jointly or separately with a spouse who is also not an active participant	Any amount		
Married filing jointly with a spouse who *is* an active participant	$173,000 or less	Over $173,000 but under $183,000	Over $183,000
Married filing separately* with a spouse who *is* an active participant		Under $10,000	Over $10,000

*If the spouses did not live together at any time during the year, the nonparticipating spouse is eligible for a full deduction.

3. Multiply the result by the next amount to determine the maximum deductible contribution:

- Married filing jointly (MFJ) or Qualifying widow(er) (QW) and an active participant: 0.25
- MFJ or QW, age 50 or older and an active participant: 0.30
- Single, head of household (HH), or MFS: 0.50
- Single, HH or MFS, and age 50 or older: 0.60

Example

Amelia is a single taxpayer who is 42 years old. She is an active participant in her employer plan, and her MAGI is $60,000. Because her MAGI is between $58,000 and $68,000 (the phase-out range for her filing status as shown in Table 15.1), her deduction is limited. The high end of Amelia's phase-out range exceeds her MAGI by $8,000 ($68,000 – $60,000). Her maximum deductible contribution is $4,000 ($8,000 × 0.5).

Another way of calculating the allowable contribution is to consider the percentage of the phase-out range where the taxpayer's MAGI lies. For example, Amelia's MAGI of $60,000 is 20% over the bottom of the $10,000 phase-out range ($60,000 – $58,000 = $2,000), so her maximum contribution is reduced by 20%. Thus, her maximum contribution allowed is 80% (100% – 20%) of the allowable maximum: $5,000 × 80% = $4,000.

ALERT: Obtaining an extension of time to file the return does not extend the time to make an IRA contribution. Contributions must be made by the due date of the return.

Different calculations are required if the taxpayer (or the taxpayer's spouse) receives Social Security benefits or if the taxpayer has deductions for self-employment (SE) tax or a deduction for a self-employed retirement plan contribution. See IRS Pub. 590, *Individual Retirement Arrangements*, for more information.

Deadline for Making Contributions Contributions can be made up to the deadline (without extensions) for filing the income tax return for the year. For example, if the deadline for filing a tax return is April 15, the deadline for making an IRA contribution is April 15. A deduction can even be claimed on the return prior to actually making a contribution, as long as the contribution is made by the filing deadline.

> **TIP:** A taxpayer may apply a tax refund toward an IRA contribution by means of a direct transfer from the government to the account. Any time a taxpayer makes a contribution between January 1 and the due date of the return (generally April 15), the taxpayer should advise the IRA custodian or trustee which year the contribution relates to: the current year or the previous year. For example, a taxpayer files her 2012 return in February 2013 and directs her refund to be sent to her IRA. If she wants it applied toward her 2012 contribution, she must tell her IRA custodian. If not, the funds will be treated as a 2013 contribution by default.

Reporting Contributions

Deductible Contributions Deductible IRA contributions are reported in the Adjusted Gross Income section of Form 1040 or on Form 1040A, *U.S. Individual Income Tax Return*. See Figure 15.1.

Because the deduction for an IRA contribution is made "above the line," a taxpayer does not have to itemize deductions to claim the IRA deduction. No separate form or schedule is required to figure the IRA deduction.

Nondeductible Contributions If nondeductible IRA contributions are made, they must be designated on Form 8606, *Nondeductible IRAs*. Form 8606 should be filed with the taxpayer's return. Form 8606 becomes the record of the taxpayer's basis in the IRA and is used to determine the nontaxable portion of future distributions.

IRA distributions are discussed in further detail in Chapter 8.

Roth IRAs

Roth IRAs are retirement savings accounts funded with after-tax contributions. As mentioned in the introduction to this chapter, there is no deduction when funds are contributed to a Roth IRA. However, earnings accrue tax-deferred. Earnings are tax-free when they are held in the account at least five years and withdrawn only if certain conditions are met.

Adjusted Gross Income	23	Educator expenses	23		
	24	Certain business expenses of reservists, performing artists, and fee-basis government officials. Attach Form 2106 or 2106-EZ	24		
	25	Health savings account deduction. Attach Form 8889 .	25		
	26	Moving expenses. Attach Form 3903	26		
	27	Deductible part of self-employment tax. Attach Schedule SE .	27		
	28	Self-employed SEP, SIMPLE, and qualified plans . .	28		
	29	Self-employed health insurance deduction	29		
	30	Penalty on early withdrawal of savings	30		
	31a	Alimony paid **b** Recipient's SSN ▶	31a		
	32	IRA deduction	32		
	33	Student loan interest deduction	33		
	34	Tuition and fees. Attach Form 8917	34		
	35	Domestic production activities deduction. Attach Form 8903	35		
	36	Add lines 23 through 35		36	
	37	Subtract line 36 from line 22. This is your **adjusted gross income** . . . . ▶		37	

For Disclosure, Privacy Act, and Paperwork Reduction Act Notice, see separate instructions. Cat. No. 11320B Form **1040** (2012)

FIGURE 15.1 Form 1040 Adjustments to Gross Income

Contributions

As explained earlier, IRA contributions may be limited based on the taxpayer's earned income. However, unlike a traditional IRA that prohibits contributions if the taxpayer is over age 70½, there is *no* age limit on funding a Roth IRA. A taxpayer who is age 80 and who continues to work can still contribute to a Roth IRA.

While there is no active participant limit, there is a MAGI limit for Roth contributions, as shown in Table 15.3.

TABLE 15.3 2012 MAGI Limits for Roth IRA Contributions

Filing status	Full contribution if MAGI is:	Contribution phased-out for MAGI:	No contribution if MAGI is:
Single, head of household, or married filing separately and did not live with spouse at any time during the year	Below $110,000	At least $110,000 but under $125,000	$125,000 or more
Married filing jointly	Below $173,000	At least $173,000 but under $183,000	$183,000 or more
Married filing separately, lived with spouse at some time during the year		Under $10,000	$10,000 or more

The maximum contribution amount is the same for traditional IRAs and Roth IRAs: $5,000 ($6,000 if age 50 or older) for 2012. Although taxpayers can make contributions to both a traditional and a Roth IRA for the same year, contributions made to a traditional IRA reduce the amount a taxpayer can contribute to a Roth IRA dollar for dollar.

Example

Brad, single and age 45, has $75,000 of wages. His MAGI is $100,000. Brad wants to maximize his retirement savings. Assuming he is not eligible to participate in a qualified retirement plan, he can contribute a total of $5,000 to an IRA for 2012. If Brad contributes $2,000 into a tax-deductible traditional IRA, he can contribute only $3,000 into a Roth IRA. If Brad were an active participant, he could contribute $5,000 to a Roth IRA; he could not contribute anything to a deductible IRA because his MAGI exceeds the maximum limit for single taxpayers ($68,000) found in Table 15.1.

Other IRAs

In addition to traditional and Roth IRAs, some taxpayers may be able to establish other IRA-like plans to save for retirement.

SEP-IRAs

If a taxpayer has net earnings from self-employment, the taxpayer can set up a retirement savings account called a Simplified Employee Pension (SEP). Taxpayers can then make contributions to individual SEP-IRAs for themselves and their employees. For 2012, the maximum contribution to a SEP-IRA is the lesser of $50,000 or 25% of the participant's compensation. A complete discussion of SEPs can be found in IRS Pub. 560, *Retirement Plans for Small Business*. Here are some key facts about SEPs:

- A SEP can be set up through the *extended* due date of the return. For example, if a self-employed individual obtains a filing extension for the 2012 return, the SEP for 2012 can be set up through October 15, 2013.
- Contributions can be made through the *extended* due date of the return.
- If a self-employed individual has employees, contributions must be made on their behalf (with some exceptions) using the same percentage of earnings used for the self-employed individual.
- A deduction for a SEP-IRA contribution on behalf of the self-employed individual is claimed as an adjustment on Form 1040 as a self-employed contribution to a SEP; it is not included on the line for IRA contributions. Contributions on behalf of employees are a deductible business expense and claimed on Schedule C, *Profit and Loss From Business*, of Form 1040.
- SEPs are not restricted to sole proprietors. Partnerships and corporations can use them as well.

SIMPLE IRAs

A Savings Incentive Match Plan for Employees (SIMPLE) is another retirement plan option that an employer can offer for his or her employees and that can be used by a self-employed individual. This plan can be used only by a business with no more than 100 employees. Employees can contribute to their accounts in much the same way as those who work for companies with 401(k) plans. Because employees make pretax contributions, their contributions are not deductible. For 2012, the maximum *employee* contribution is $11,500 ($14,000 if at least 50 years old by the end of the year).

Under a SIMPLE plan, the employer *must* make a contribution for each eligible employee. The amount of the employer contribution depends on the employer's choice of contribution formulas and other factors.

More information about SIMPLE plans is in IRS Pub. 560. Here are some key facts about SIMPLE plans:

- A SIMPLE plan for an existing business must be set up no later than October 1 of the year of the plan (e.g., October 1, 2012, for 2012 contributions). A business that starts after this date must set up the plan as soon as it is practical to do so.

- A self-employed individual can make both the employee and employer contributions to his or her own account.
- Any salary reduction amounts must be contributed within 30 days after the end of the month during which the amounts would have been payable to employees. Employer matching contributions can be made through the *extended* due date of the return.
- Like SEPs, SIMPLE plans are not restricted to sole proprietors; they can also be used by small partnerships and corporations.

Health Savings Accounts

Health savings accounts (HSA) provide a tax free way to save money to pay for medical expenses. An HSA offers an unusual tax benefit in that contributions, earnings, and distributions are completely tax free if all the rules are followed.

Eligibility

DEFINITION: A high-deductible health plan is an insurance plan that meets the minimum annual deductible and maximum annual deductible and out-of-pocket limits shown in Table 15.4. HDHP plan limits are set by law and are adjusted annually for inflation.

In order to contribute to a health savings account, a taxpayer must have health insurance coverage under a **high-deductible health plan** (HDHP) and have no other coverage (including Medicare) on the first day of the month for which a contribution is being made. The minimum and maximum annual deductible limits on an HDHP for 2012 are shown in Table 15.4.

TABLE 15.4 2012 High-Deductible Health Plan Limits

Type of coverage	Minimum annual deductible	Maximum annual deductible and out-of-pocket limits
Self-only coverage	$1,200	$6,050
Family coverage	$2,400	$12,100

Contributions

ALERT: A person who can be claimed as a dependent on another taxpayer's return cannot set up an HSA.

The annual HSA contribution limits are set by law and adjusted annually for inflation. The limits are shown in Table 15.5.

TABLE 15.5 2012 HSA Contribution Limits

Type of coverage	Maximum annual contribution
Self-only coverage	$3,100
Family coverage	$6,250

A taxpayer who is at least 55 years old at the end of the year can contribute an additional $1,000. Thus, if a taxpayer has family coverage and both spouses are at least 55 years old, the deductible contribution for 2012 is $8,250 ($6,250 + $1,000 + $1,000).

HSA contributions for the year can be made up to the regular due date of the return. They can also be made using tax refunds, as discussed earlier in this chapter in connection with IRAs.

Contributions are recorded in Part I of Form 8889, *Health Savings Accounts (HSAs)*. They are deducted in the Adjusted Gross Income section of Form 1040 (Form 1040A cannot be used); the taxpayer does not need to itemize to deduct the HSA contribution.

Under the last-month rule, a taxpayer is eligible to make an HSA contribution equal to the maximum annual limit if the taxpayer is eligible for an HSA on the first day of the last month of the year (December 1 for most taxpayers). For example, a taxpayer with self-only coverage may contribute the maximum amount ($3,100; see Table 15.5) even if he or she first became eligible to set up an HSA on December 1. This is true even if the taxpayer had other coverage earlier in the year.

However, if a contribution is made using the last-month rule, the taxpayer must continue to remain eligible during a testing period. The testing period starts on the first day of the last month of the tax year and ends on the last day of the next year (e.g., December 1, 2012, through December 31, 2013).

Example

Hilda, age 48, becomes eligible for an HSA on December 1, 2012. She contributes $3,100 for self-only coverage for 2012 and claims a $3,100 deduction on her return. In June 2013, she takes a new job, receives employer-provided health coverage, and stops her HDHP. Because she did not remain eligible during the testing period (through December 2013), she must include in income for 2013 the portion of the contribution that would not have been made but for the last-month rule. She was eligible to make a contribution only for December 2012, so only 1/12th of the total contribution made in 2012, or $258 ($3,100 ÷ 12), should have been deducted; the balance, or $2,842 ($3,100 – $258), is included in income for 2013. There is also a 10% additional tax on the income.

ALERT: If an employer maintains an HDHP and makes contributions to the taxpayer's HSA for the year, the taxpayer can make an additional contribution only up to the annual limit. Contributions made by an employer or through an employer plan are usually made on a pretax basis. Taxpayers may not claim a deduction for contributions made on a pretax basis. For example, if an employer contributes $3,100 for each employee, but an employee with family coverage wants to add $3,150 (the additional amount needed to reach the maximum deduction for family coverage of $6,250), the employee can contribute this amount. If the employer contribution is made through a pretax arrangement, the $3,150 is not deductible by the employee. Employer and employee contributions made through a pretax arrangement are shown on Form W-2, box 12, Code W, and are not deductible on the employee's tax return.

Distributions

Distributions can be taken from the HSA at any time for any reason. However, distributions taken for reasons other than qualified medical expenses are fully taxable. Moreover, if these nonqualified distributions are taken before age 65, or if the taxpayer is not disabled, they are also subject to a 20% penalty. (Nonqualified distributions taken after attaining age 65 or after the taxpayer becomes disabled are not subject to penalty but are still taxable.)

Qualified distributions include the same expenses that qualify for an itemized medical deduction (see Chapter 20). Over-the-counter medications can be a qualified medical expense for HSA purposes, provided they are purchased with a doctor's prescription.

ALERT: A taxpayer who relies on the last-month rule and fails to remain eligible for the testing period must include in income the portion of the deduction that would not have been claimed but for the last-month rule and pay an additional tax on the amount.

Review Questions

1. Earned income for purposes of an IRA contribution includes all of the following **except**:
   a. Tips
   b. Alimony
   c. Unemployment compensation
   d. Self-employment income

2. A taxpayer obtains an extension of time to file her 2012 tax return, but she actually files on April 14, 2013, before the filing deadline. What is the deadline for making a 2012 IRA contribution?
   a. December 31, 2013
   b. April 14, 2013
   c. April 15, 2013
   d. October 15, 2013

3. Roth IRAs are similar to traditional IRAs in all of the following ways **except**:
   a. There is no maximum age limit for contributions.
   b. Distributions on account of disability are not penalized.
   c. The contribution limit for 2012 is $5,000 ($6,000 for those 50 and older by year-end)
   d. Taxpayers must have earned income in order to make a contribution.

4. Which of the following statements about a SEP is **not** correct?
   a. The maximum deductible contribution for 2012 is $50,000.
   b. A self-employed individual must make contributions for all employees based on the same percentage of the employees' earnings
   c. A SEP can be used only by a self-employed individual, not by a business operated as a corporation.
   d. The deadline for making contributions is the extended due date of the tax return.

5. What is an eligibility requirement for contributing to a health savings account (HSA)?
   a. Attaining a minimum age
   b. Being covered by a high-deductible health plan
   c. Having earned income
   d. Having MAGI below set limits

6. What is the maximum contribution for 2012 to a health savings account (HSA) for a taxpayer who has family coverage under a high-deductible health plan?
   a. $2,400
   b. $3,100
   c. $6,250
   d. $12,100

Education-Related Adjustments

Certain education-related deductions can be claimed as an adjustment to gross income (above the line). Thus, they are deductible regardless of whether the taxpayer itemizes other personal deductions.

A taxpayer can choose to deduct tuition and fees as an above-the-line deduction rather than to use such fees for calculating a tax credit, or as a miscellaneous itemized deduction for work-related costs. For example, if a taxpayer does not qualify to claim an education credit (see Chapter 30), the taxpayer may still deduct tuition and fees. The amount of the above-the-line deduction, if any, depends on a taxpayer's modified adjusted gross income (MAGI) and filing status.

A taxpayer who is a qualified educator may deduct up to $250 of out-of-pocket classroom expenses as an adjustment to income with no limit to MAGI.

A taxpayer who is repaying student loans may be able to deduct up to $2,500 of student interest each year. Again, this deduction is claimed as an above-the-line deduction. However, an MAGI limitation may limit or bar any interest deduction.

Tuition and Fees Deduction

A deduction from gross income of up to $4,000 ($2,000 for some higher-income taxpayers) can be claimed for tuition and fees for higher education. Qualified expenses can be paid out of pocket or with borrowed funds.

The amount of the deduction, if any, depends on a taxpayer's MAGI. For this purpose, MAGI is adjusted gross income (AGI) without regard to the deduction for tuition and fees, the domestic production activities deduction, or the foreign earned income exclusion. The dollar limit applies regardless of the number of eligible students for whom a deduction can be claimed.

ALERT: Qualified tuition and fees must be reduced by any expenses paid for using tax-free educational assistance, such as a scholarship or employer-provided educational assistance. Qualified tuition and fees must also be reduced by any tax-free earnings in distributions taken from a qualified tuition plan (section 529 plan), the tax-free portion of a distribution from an Educational Savings Account (ESA), or by expenses used to exclude interest on U.S. savings bonds.

Eligibility

To claim the deduction, the taxpayer must pay qualified tuition and fees for himself or herself, a spouse, or a dependent. Qualified education expenses include:

- Tuition
- Activity fees if required for attendance and paid directly to the institution
- Expenses for course-related books, supplies, and equipment required for attendance and paid directly to the institution

Nondeductible expenses include:

- Course-related books, supplies, and equipment not required for attendance and required to be paid directly to the institution
- Personal living expenses
- Room and board
- Student health fees
- Transportation

The educational institution must be qualified. Most accredited schools in the United States that participate in the U.S. Department of Education financial aid program are considered qualified.

The taxpayer's MAGI determines the deduction limit, as shown in Table 16.1.

ALERT: The deduction does not phase out when MAGI exceeds a certain threshold. Instead, even $1 of MAGI over the limit means that no deduction is allowed or that the lower deduction limit applies.

Claiming the Deduction

The deduction for qualified education expenses is figured first on Form 8917, *Tuition and Fees Deduction*. The applicable deduction amount is claimed as an adjustment to gross income.

The amount of tuition and fees paid by the taxpayer is reported by the school to the IRS and the taxpayer on Form 1098-T, *Tuition Statement*. The school has a choice about how to report the tuition: Box 1 is for amounts paid, and box 2 is for amounts billed. However, only amounts *paid*, and not amounts merely *billed*, are deductible by the taxpayer. The taxpayer must use only the amounts paid as a basis for the deduction, even if the school reports the amounts billed. Payments made in the previous year for classes starting in

TABLE 16.1 MAGI Limit for Tuition and Fees Deduction

Filing status	MAGI limit—$4,000 deduction	MAGI limit—$2,000 deduction
Married filing jointly	Not more than $130,000	More than $130,000 but not more than $160,000
Other taxpayers[1]	Not more than $65,000	More than $65,000 but not more than $80,000

[1]Married persons filing separately cannot claim the deduction.

the first three months of the current year are deductible in the previous year (the year they were paid).

Example

Jesse, who is single, paid tuition and fees on December 15, 2012, for the spring semester starting in January 2013. His deductible expenses for 2012 include all such payments made in 2012, including the amounts paid for the 2013 spring semester.

ALERT: Instead of claiming a deduction, the tuition and fees paid during the year may be used to claim an education credit (the American Opportunity Credit or the Lifetime Learning Credit, explained in Chapter 30). Each education credit has its own MAGI limit; these limits differ from the limits for the tuition and fees deduction. Figure both the deduction and the credit(s), then claim the one that gives the taxpayer a greater benefit. Because of MAGI limitations and phase-outs, the deduction may be the better (or only) choice for some taxpayers.

Recapture

Recapture applies when tax-free educational assistance for, or a refund of, an expense used to figure a tuition and fees deduction is received after the return has been filed. The recapture rules may require that all or part of the deduction be reported as income to the extent that the tax-free assistance or refund lowered the tax liability on the return. Recapture applies to assistance and refunds received by the taxpayer claiming the deduction. If the taxpayer is the student, recapture applies to refunds received by anyone else who paid expenses on behalf of the student.

Under the recapture rules, the tuition and fees deduction must be refigured as if the tax-free assistance or refund has been received in the year in which the deduction was claimed. Income from recapture is the difference between the tax benefit received from the deduction claimed and the tax benefit received from the deduction that would have been claimed if the refund had been received in the year of the deduction. The recaptured amount is entered as "other income" on line 21 of Form 1040, *U.S. Individual Income Tax Return*, for the year the tax-free assistance or refund is received.

ALERT: Do not amend the return for the year in which the deduction (before the refund) was claimed.

Example

Mr. and Mrs. Smith paid $3,000 tuition in December 2011 for their child who began college in January 2012. They filed their 2011 tax return in March, showing MAGI of $150,000. They claim a $2,000 above-the-line deduction (because of the MAGI limit). The child dropped some courses after the return was filed, and the college refunded $1,400 of tuition. After refiguring their 2011 taxes using $1,600 of fees ($3,000 minus the $1,400 tuition refund), they must include the difference of $400 ($2,000 original deduction minus the $1,600 refigured deduction) as "other income" on line 21 of Form 1040 of their 2012 tax return. They should not amend their 2011 return.

ALERT: If there is no change in tax liability when the prior-year return is refigured with the lower tuition amount, no income results from the tuition refund (an example of the tax benefit rule; see Chapter 10).

Educator Expenses Deduction

A taxpayer who is considered to be an **educator** can deduct up to $250 of qualified expenses as an adjustment to gross income (above-the-line deduction). If both spouses are educators and both have qualified expenses of at least $250, the total deduction on a joint return is $500.

DEFINITION: An **educator** is a person who is a teacher, instructor, counselor, principal, or aide for grades kindergarten through 12 and who works at least 900 hours during the school year. An educator does *not* include a parent who home-schools his or her child.

Qualified expenses include ordinary and necessary expenses for the classroom, such as:

- Athletic supplies for athletic activities (but not other supplies for courses in health or physical education)
- Books
- Equipment (including computer equipment, software, and related services)
- Supplies

There is no special form or schedule needed to claim this deduction; it is entered directly as an adjustment on Form 1040 or Form 1040A, *U.S. Individual Income Tax Return.*

TIP: If a taxpayer's qualified expenses exceed the $250 annual limit, the excess amount can be claimed as an unreimbursed employee business expense. This is taken as a miscellaneous itemized deduction on Schedule A, *Itemized Deductions,* subject to the 2%-of-adjusted gross income floor.

Student Loan Interest Deduction

A taxpayer can deduct up to $2,500 in interest paid on student loans each year if certain conditions are met. The deduction is an adjustment to gross income (above-the-line deduction). No deduction can be claimed for repayment of the principal on student loans.

Who Can Claim the Deduction

The deduction can be claimed by a taxpayer who is legally obligated to pay interest on a student loan for him- or herself or for a student who is a spouse or who was a dependent at the time the loan was taken out. For purposes of this deduction, the student can be treated as a dependent of an individual even though:

- The taxpayer could not claim the student as a dependent because the taxpayer was the dependent of another taxpayer in the year the loan was taken out;
- The student files a joint return with a spouse; OR
- The student has gross income over the exemption amount ($3,800 in 2012) that prevents the taxpayer from claiming a dependency exemption.

The student must be enrolled at least half time in a degree program. Interest continues to be deductible for the remaining period of the student loan.

ALERT: Two classes of taxpayers cannot claim the deduction: a married person filing separately and a person who is claimed as a dependent on another taxpayer's return.

To be eligible for the deduction, a taxpayer's MAGI cannot exceed a set amount. MAGI for this purpose is adjusted gross income without regard to the student loan interest deduction and the foreign earned income exclusion. If MAGI is within a phase-out range, a partial deduction may be taken. The MAGI limits for 2012 can be found in Table 16.2.

TABLE 16.2 MAGI Limit for the Student Interest Deduction

Filing status	Full deduction if MAGI is	Deduction phases out if MAGI is between:
Married filing jointly	Not more than $125,000	$125,000 to $155,000
Other taxpayers[1]	Not more than $60,000	$60,000 to $75,000

[1]Married persons filing separately cannot claim the deduction.

Use the worksheet in Figure 16.1 to figure the phase-out of the deduction for a taxpayer with MAGI in the phase-out range.

What Type of Loan Qualifies

Only interest on a loan that is obtained *solely* to pay for qualified education expenses can be deductible. Again, the expenses must be for the taxpayer, spouse, or dependent.

1. Enter the total interest you paid in 2011 on qualified student loans. **Do not enter more than $2,500** . . . . . 1. ______
2. Enter the amount from Form 1040, line 22 . . . . . 2. ______
3. Enter the total of the amounts from Form 1040, lines 23 through 32 . . . . . 3. ______
4. Enter the total of any amounts entered on the dotted line next to Form 1040, line 36 . . . . . 4. ______
5. Add lines 3 and 4 . . . . . 5. ______
6. Subtract line 5 from line 2 . . . . . 6. ______
7. Enter any foreign earned income exclusion and/or housing exclusion (Form 2555, line 45, or Form 2555-EZ, line 18) . . . . . 7. ______
8. Enter any foreign housing deduction (Form 2555, line 50) . . . . . 8. ______
9. Enter the amount of income from Puerto Rico you are excluding . . . . 9. ______
10. Enter the amount of income from American Samoa you are excluding (Form 4563, line 15) . . . . . 10. ______
11. Add lines 6 through 10. This is your **modified adjusted gross income** . . . . . 11. ______
12. Enter the amount shown below for your filing status . . . . . 12. ______
    - Single, head of household, or qualifying widow(er)—$60,000
    - Married filing jointly—$120,000
13. Is the amount on line 11 more than the amount on line 12?
    - ☐ **No.** Skip lines 13 and 14, enter -0- on line 15, and go to line 16.
    - ☐ **Yes.** Subtract line 12 from line 11 . . . . . 13. ______
14. Divide line 13 by $15,000 ($30,000 if married filing jointly). Enter the result as a decimal (rounded to at least three places). If the result is 1.000 or more, enter 1.000 . . . . . 14 ___.___
15. Multiply line 1 by line 14 . . . . . 15. ______
16. **Student loan interest deduction.** Subtract line 15 from line 1. Enter the result here and on Form 1040, line 33. **Do not** include this amount in figuring any other deduction on your return (such as on Schedule A, C, E, etc.) . . . . . 16. ______

FIGURE 16.1 Student Loan Interest Deduction Worksheet

DEFINITION: The term **qualified education expenses** is broadly defined, for the purpose of deducting student loan interest, to include tuition and fees; room and board; books, supplies, and equipment; and other necessary expenses, such as transportation.

The **qualified education expenses** must be paid within a reasonable period before or after the loan was obtained. ("Reasonable period" is explained next.)

Any qualified education expenses paid with the proceeds of a federal student loan are automatically treated as paid within a reasonable period. Expenses paid with other types of loans meet the reasonableness test if both of the next conditions are met:

- The expenses are related to a specific academic period.
- The loan proceeds are disbursed within a period beginning 90 days before the start of the academic period and ending 90 days after the end of the same academic period.

Loans from a related person or a qualified employer plan do not qualify for this interest deduction. "Related persons" for this purpose include a spouse, siblings, parents, grandparents, children, grandchildren, or certain corporations, partnerships, trusts, and exempt organizations.

ALERT: Expired! The tuition and fees deduction and the educator expense deduction have expired as of January 1, 2012. As of this writing, Congress has not extended these provisions. Review questions 4, 5, and 6 cover these expired provisions.

Claiming the Deduction

The institution to which student loan interest is paid must issue to the taxpayer (and the IRS) Form 1098-E, *Student Loan Interest Statement,* if the interest it receives is $600 or more. Use the information reported on Form 1098-E to help figure the deduction for student loan interest. However, even if no form is received (e.g., interest is only $500), a deduction still may be allowed.

There is no special form or schedule needed to claim this deduction; it is entered directly as an adjustment on Form 1040 or on Form 1040A.

Review Questions

1. A taxpayer is single, graduated college and is now repaying her student loans. She paid $2,800 in interest on her loans in 2012. Her MAGI before considering any student loan interest deduction is $67,500. How much of an above-the-line deduction can she claim?

a. $0

b. Part of the interest she paid ($1,250)

c. All interest paid ($2,800)

d. $2,500 of the interest she paid

2. The student loan interest statement issued by the institution to which interest is paid is:

a. Form 1099-C

b. Form 1099-B

c. Form 1099-E

d. Form 1099-T

3. Which statement concerning the deduction for student loan interest is **not** correct?

a. The amount of the deduction depends on modified adjusted gross income.

b. No deduction can be claimed for the repayment of principal on a student loan.

c. Qualified education expenses must be paid within a reasonable period before or after the loan was obtained

d. It can be claimed on Form 1040 only.

4. Which education-related tax break does **not** depend on MAGI?

a. Tuition and fees deduction

b. Education credits

c. Deduction for educator expenses

d. Student loan interest deduction

5. Which type of expense qualifies for the tuition and fees deduction?

a. Room and board

b. Activity fees

c. Student health fees

d. Personal living expenses

6. Which taxpayer does **not** qualify as an educator for purposes of deducting educator expenses up to $250?

a. A parent who home-schools her child

b. A principal of an elementary school

c. A classroom aide in a middle school

d. A teacher in a high school

Business-Related Adjustments

Most business deductions are claimed on business schedules such as Schedule C, *Profit or Loss From Business (Sole Proprietorship)*, and Schedule F, *Profit or Loss From Farming*. However, some specific business deductions are treated like personal expenses and are claimed as adjustments to gross income. For example, contributions made on behalf of a self-employed taxpayer to a Simplified Employee Pension (SEP) individual retirement account (IRA) are treated as an adjustment to gross income (see Chapter 15) while contributions to a plan for employees are treated as a business expense deductible on Schedule C.

Self-employed taxpayers can deduct a portion of the self-employment tax they pay. This deduction allows a self-employed taxpayer (who is both the employer and employee) to receive a deduction similar to the deduction allowed employers for their share of employment taxes.

A self-employed taxpayer can also deduct as an adjustment to gross income the health insurance premiums paid for self, a spouse, a dependent, or a child under age 27 as of the end of the tax year. An employer claims a deduction for health insurance premiums paid for employees on Schedule C (see Chapter 11).

The cost of a work-related move is also deductible as an adjustment to gross income. Although it is not a business deduction, it is business-related.

Finally, there are several other business-related adjustments to gross income. Some have their own lines on Form 1040, *U.S. Individual Income Tax Return*, while others do not.

Deduction for a Portion of Self-Employment Tax

A self-employed taxpayer pays both the employee and employer shares of Social Security and Medicare taxes on net earnings from self-employment (i.e., profits). Self-employment tax is explained in Chapter 35. However, as employers normally deduct their portion of employment tax paid for employees, one-half of a self-employed taxpayer's employment tax is deductible as an adjustment to gross income. This allows the self-employed taxpayer to receive the same employment tax adjustment as other employers.

Generally, the deduction is one-half of the self-employment tax figured on Schedule SE, *Self-Employment Tax*. However, for 2012, the adjustment to gross income is not as simple because there is a 2-percentage-point reduction in the employee share of Social Security taxes.

TIP: The $14,643.30 is the product of the maximum earnings subject to Social Security and Medicare tax for 2012 ($110,100) and 13.2%, which is the total of employer (6.2% + 1.45%) and employee (4.2% + 1.45%) portion of these taxes.

The deduction for the employer-equivalent portion of the self-employment tax for 2012 is:

- 57.51% of the tax if the self-employment tax is $14,643.30 or less
- 50% of the self-employment tax plus $1,100 if the self-employment tax is more than $14,643.30

The deduction is claimed in the adjustments section of Form 1040, and Schedule SE must be attached to the return.

Self-Employed Health Insurance Deduction

A deduction for health insurance premiums covering a self-employed taxpayer, and his or her spouse, dependents, and child under age 27 by the end of the year is claimed as an adjustment to gross income. The full amount of the premiums can be deducted if certain conditions are met.

Health insurance premiums include not only amounts typically deducted for health coverage but also coverage for dental and vision care, Medicare, and long-term care insurance premiums. While premiums paid generally are fully deductible, in the case of long-term care insurance, the deduction may be limited based on the covered person's age.

Health insurance coverage paid with retirement plan distributions that are tax free because the taxpayer is a public safety officer does not qualify for the self-employed health insurance deduction. Also, amounts paid with an advance payment of the health coverage tax credit do not qualify for the self-employed health insurance deduction.

TIP: Health insurance premiums paid to cover employees are deducted as business expenses (not as adjustments to gross income). These premiums may entitle the taxpayer to the small employer health insurance credit (see Chapter 31).

Who Can Claim the Deduction

The deduction is allowed for taxpayers who pay qualified health insurance costs and who are considered self-employed. A self-employed taxpayer for purposes of the deduction is defined as a taxpayer with net profit on Schedules C, C-EZ, *Profit or Loss from Business*, or F; a general partner (or limited partner receiving guaranteed payments); or an S corporation shareholder who receives wages on Form W-2, *Wage and Tax Statement*, and owns more than 2% of the stock of the S corporation.

Conditions for the Deduction

In order to claim the deduction, all of these conditions must be met:

- *Net earnings from a trade or business.* The deduction can be claimed only if the taxpayer has a profit for the year.
  - For a sole proprietor, partner, or limited liability company member, the individual's net self-employment earnings less any adjustment for the employer portion of self-employment tax (Form 1040, Line 27) and any adjustment for contributions to s self-employed Simplified Employee Pension (SEP) plan, Savings Incentive Match Plan for Employees (SIMPLE), or qualified plans (Form 1040, Line 28) are considered net earnings from a trade or business.
  - For a shareholder owning more than 2% of an S corporation, net earnings means wages reported in Box 5 of Form W-2 by the corporation under which the health insurance plan was established.
  - If a taxpayer has two or more businesses, they cannot be aggregated to determine profitability; only the profits of the company to which the coverage relates are taken into account.

Example

Bill owns two separate businesses, a lawn service and a custom cabinet shop. Net earnings from the lawn service are $1,500, and net earnings from the cabinet shop are $2,500. His lawn service pays health insurance premiums of $1,800 to cover Bill and his wife. He can deduct only $1,500 of these premiums, limited to the net earnings from the business that pays the premiums.

- *No other health coverage.* The deduction can be claimed only if the taxpayer is not eligible to participate in a health plan subsidized by the taxpayer's employer or spouse's employer. The same rule applies for long-term care insurance. This requirement is determined on a month-to-month basis.

Example

Reggie, who is single, operates his own business until he starts a job in September 2012. His employer provides health coverage, which Reggie is eligible to participate in beginning in September. He can deduct the premiums he paid through August, to the extent his business is profitable for 2012.

- *Plan established under the trade or business.* Insurance plans must be established, or considered to be established, using the name of the business in order to be deductible. A sole proprietor filing Schedule C, C-EZ, or F can deduct the premiums whether the policy is purchased in the name of the business or the individual. For a more-than-2% S corporation shareholder, however, a deduction is allowed only if the corporation purchases the policy or the corporation reimburses the shareholder for the premiums and includes these premiums in the shareholder's gross income on the W-2 form.

Figuring the Deduction

The deduction is figured using the *Self-Employed Health Insurance Deduction Worksheet—Line 29* (from the instructions to Form 1040) (Figure 17.1).

The worksheet effectively limits the deduction to the smaller of the health insurance premiums or the taxpayer's net earnings from the business. For purposes of the health insurance deduction, net earnings are reduced by the employer-equivalent portion of the self-employment tax and any deduction for contributions to a SEP, SIMPLE, or other qualified retirement plan; see Chapter 15.

Note that the *Self-Employed Health Insurance Deduction Worksheet—Line 29* cannot be used if the taxpayer:

- Had more than one source of self-employment income (e.g., multiple unincorporated businesses)
- Claimed the foreign earned income exclusion using Form 2555, *Foreign Earned Income*
- Claimed a deduction for long-term care insurance premiums

If the *Self-Employed Health Insurance Deduction Worksheet—Line 29* cannot be used, then the deduction is figured on Worksheet 6-A, *Self-Employed Health Insurance Deduction Worksheet,* in IRS Pub. 535, *Business Expenses.*

Self-Employed Health Insurance Deduction Worksheet

Before you begin:

√ If, during 2011, you were an eligible trade adjustment assistance (TAA) recipient, alternative TAA (ATAA) recipient, reemployment TAA (RTAA) recipient, or Pension Benefit Guaranty Corporation pension recipient, see the instructions for Form 8885 to figure the amount to enter on line 1 of this worksheet.

√ Be sure you have read the **Exception** in the instructions for this line to see if you can use this worksheet instead of Pub. 535 to figure your deduction.

1. Enter the total amount paid in 2012 for health insurance coverage established under your business (or the S corporation in which you were a more-than-2% shareholder) for 2012 for you, your spouse, and your dependents. Your insurance can also cover your child who was under age 27 at the end of 2012, even if the child was not your dependent. But do not include amounts for any month you were eligible to participate in an employer-sponsored health plan or amounts paid from retirement plan distributions that were nontaxable because you are a retired public safety officer . . **1.** ______

2. Enter your net profit* and any other earned income** from the business under which the insurance plan is established, minus any deductions on Form 1040, lines 27 and 28. Do not include Conservation Reserve Program payments exempt from self-employment tax . . . . **2.** ______

3. Self-employed health insurance deduction. Enter the **smaller** of line 1 or line 2 here and on Form 1040, line 29. **Do not** include this amount in figuring any medical expense deduction on Schedule A . . . . **3.** ______

**If you used either optional method to figure your net earnings from self-employment, do not enter your net profit. Instead, enter the amount from Schedule SE, Section B, line 4b.*

*****Earned income** includes net earnings and gains from the sale, transfer, or licensing of property you created. However, it does not include capital gain income. If you were a more-than-2% shareholder in the S corporation under which the insurance plan is established, earned income is your Medicare wages (box 5 of Form W-2) from that corporation.*

FIGURE 17.1 Self-Employed Health Insurance Deduction Worksheet—Line 29

Moving Expenses

If a taxpayer relocates because of a new job or a new business, the cost of moving the family and personal effects is allowed as an adjustment to gross income. The deduction is figured first on Form 3903, *Moving Expenses,* and then entered in the adjustments section of Form 1040. In order to claim this deduction, certain conditions must be met.

TIP: If an employer reimburses a taxpayer's moving costs under an *accountable plan*, the reimbursement may be tax free (see Chapter 4). If moving costs are reimbursed under a *non-accountable plan* (or reimbursements exceed the amount of moving expenses), then the costs may be deductible by the taxpayer if the rules in this section are met. The taxpayer's Form W-2 should indicate the reimbursement plan in box 12 under code P. For more information, see IRS Pub. 521, *Moving Expenses*, and Table 2 in that publication.

Business-Related Move

Moving for personal reasons usually is not sufficient to support this deduction. The move must be motivated because of a new job, a new job location, or a new business and must be closely related to the new position in terms of time and location.

Generally, moving expenses incurred within one year of the date of starting the new position are considered to be closely related in time. If the move is delayed beyond one year of starting a new position, the taxpayer must show good reason for the delay.

Example

A family delays a move for 18 months to allow their child to complete high school. Moving expenses are deductible as this is an allowable delay.

The move is treated as closely related in location if the distance from the taxpayer's new home to the new job location is not more than the distance from the taxpayer's old home to the new job location. If this test is not met, then the move can still be considered closely related in location if:

- The taxpayer is required to live in the new home as a condition of employment, OR
- The taxpayer spends less time or money commuting between the new home and new job location.

For purposes of this deduction, a home is defined as a taxpayer's main home (residence). This includes a house, apartment, condominium, houseboat, or similar dwelling. Seasonal, vacation, or summer homes are not main homes. An old home is the home before the taxpayer left for the new job location. A new home is the home in the area of the new job location.

Retirees usually cannot deduct the cost of a move because it is not work-related; it is a matter of personal choice. However, a taxpayer who had worked outside the United States may be eligible to deduct expenses for a move back to the United States (see IRS Pub. 521).

Distance Test

The taxpayer's new main job location must be at least 50 miles farther from the old home than the old work location was from the old home. In other words, the taxpayer's commute to a new job location must be at least 50 miles farther than if the taxpayer did not move and stayed in his or her old home. The location of the new home is not factored into the distance test. The worksheet in Figure 17.2 is used to figure whether the taxpayer meets the distance test.

Example

Julie's former company was just 5 miles from her old home. To deduct moving expenses, her new company must be located at least 55 miles from the old home.

In figuring distance, use the shortest of the more commonly traveled routes. Taxpayers who are members of the armed forces may not have to meet the distance test if the taxpayers moved because of a permanent change of station (see IRS Pub. 521).

Time Test

There are two time tests: one for employees and another for self-employed individuals. The taxpayer (or the taxpayer's spouse) must meet the appropriate test:

- Employees must work full time for at least 39 weeks during the first 12 months after arriving in the general area of the new job location.
- Self-employed individuals must work full time for at least 39 weeks during the first 12 months and at least 78 weeks during the first 24 months after arriving in the general area of the new job location.

Example

DeeDee takes a new job starting on June 4, 2012, that requires her to move across the country. She satisfies the 39-week test on March 3, 2013, when she has completed 39 weeks of work in the new location. If DeeDee had been self-employed, her 78 weeks would be completed on December 1, 2013.

For purposes of the time test, these rules apply to employees:

- An employee counts only full-time work on a job.
- An employee need not work for the same employer throughout the 39 weeks.

Distance Test

Note. Members of the Armed Forces may not have to meet this test. See *Members of the Armed Forces.*

1.	Enter the number of miles from your old home to your new workplace	**1.**	______ miles
2.	Enter the number of miles from your old home to your old workplace	**2.**	______ miles
3.	Subtract line 2 from line 1. If zero or less, enter -0-	**3.**	______ miles
4.	Is line 3 at least 50 miles? ☐ Yes. You meet this test. ☐ No. You do not meet this test. You cannot deduct your moving expenses.		

FIGURE 17.2 Distance Test Worksheet

- An employee does not have to work 39 consecutive weeks.
- An employee must work full time within the same general commuting area for all 39 weeks.

For purposes of the time test, these rules apply to self-employed taxpayers:

- A self-employed individual counts any full-time work as an employee or as a self-employed individual.
- A self-employed individual does not have to work for the same employer or be self-employed in the same trade or business for the 78 weeks.
- A self-employed individual must work within the same general commuting area for all 78 weeks.

Temporary absences, such as vacation, sick days, or strikes, count as work. Seasonal work can count as work for the time test. However, in order to count off-season time when no work is required, for an employee, the contract or agreement must cover the off-season, and the off-season cannot be more than six months. For a self-employed taxpayer, if the nature of the business is seasonal, the off-season counts as weeks worked as long as it is less than six months and the taxpayer performed full-time services both before and after the off-season.

Example

Sheldon operates a candy store on the boardwalk in a resort area. It closes during the winter months. As long as the store is open for six months or more, the time that the store is closed counts toward the 78 weeks of full-time work.

Special Rule for Spouses If a couple files a joint return and both spouses work full time, either one can meet the time test. However, weeks worked by one spouse cannot be added to weeks worked by the other spouse in order to satisfy the time test.

Exceptions to the Time Test The time test does not have to be satisfied for any of these situations:

- A taxpayer is transferred for the employer's benefit or laid off (other than for willful misconduct) and had expected to complete the time test when the job started.
- A taxpayer is in the armed forces and moves because of a permanent change of station.
- A taxpayer who worked abroad retires back to the United States.
- A survivor of someone who worked abroad moves back to the United States within six months following the death of the worker.
- Work ends because of disability or death.

Deductible Moving Expenses

The only moving costs that are deductible are those for moving household goods and personal effects and for travel to the new home (including lodging on the trip, but not meals). All costs must be reasonable, but there are no dollar limits fixed by law. Examples of some deductible moving expenses include:

- Costs of connecting or disconnecting utilities
- Costs of storing and insuring household goods within any 30 consecutive days after moving from a home (before they are delivered to the new home) (however, this time limit does not apply if the move is outside the United States)
- Shipping a vehicle
- Shipping household pets

If a taxpayer drives to the new location, he or she can use a standard mileage rate rather than claiming actual costs. For 2012, the standard mileage rate is 23¢ per mile.

Nondeductible expenses include:

- Any part of the purchase price of a new home
- Car tags and new driver's licenses
- Cost of moving an employee who is a member of your household
- Cost of refitting carpets and drapes
- Cost of side trips during the course of a move
- Expenses of buying the new home
- Expenses of selling the old home, including improvements to help sell it
- Loss on the sale of the old home
- Losses from canceling club memberships
- Meals during the move
- Mortgage penalties
- Pre-move house-hunting expenses
- Real estate taxes
- Return trips to the old home
- Security deposits

Claiming the Deduction

The moving expense deduction is figured on Form 3903 and reported in the adjustments section of Form 1040. Taxpayers have different options regarding how to claim the deduction depending on whether they receive a reimbursement for the moving expenses or not. Taxpayers who are not reimbursed claim the deduction in the year the expenses were paid or incurred.

The moving expense deduction can be claimed on the current return even though the time test will not be satisfied until after the year ends. The taxpayer must expect to meet the time test in the next year. For example, a taxpayer moves in 2012. She must expect to meet the time test in 2013 if she is an employee or in 2013 or 2014 if she is self-employed in order to claim the deduction on her 2012 return.

A taxpayer who claims a deduction and then fails to meet the time test has two options to handle the previously claimed deduction:

1. Report the deduction as income on Form 1040 for the year in which the test is not met (e.g., on the 2013 return for an employee who moved in 2012); OR
2. File an amended return for 2012 on Form 1040X, *Amended U.S. Individual Income Tax Return,* and eliminate the moving expense deduction.

ALERT: If a taxpayer claims the foreign earned income exclusion or foreign housing exclusion, the part of moving expenses that relate to the excluded income is not deductible. IRS Pub. 54, *Tax Guide for U.S. Citizens and Resident Aliens Abroad*, explains how to figure the amount of moving expenses related to excluded income.

A taxpayer who is reimbursed for moving expenses and uses the cash method of accounting may deduct them either in the year the expenses are paid or in the year the taxpayer receives the reimbursement. Reimbursements received in a year after a deduction is claimed are reported as other income on line 21 of Form 1040. A deduction cannot be claimed for moving expense reimbursements that were not included in income.

Other Business Adjustments

There are several other business-related adjustments to gross income. These include:

- *Expenses of reservists.* National Guard and reservist members who travel more than 100 miles from home to perform services in their military capacity can deduct travel expenses as an adjustment to gross income (even though they technically are unreimbursed employee business expenses normally claimed on Schedule A, *Itemized Deductions,* of Form 1040). The amount deductible as an adjustment to income is limited to the regular federal per diem rate for lodging, meals, and incidental expenses and the IRS standard mileage rate for car expenses (plus parking fees and tolls).
- *Expenses of performing artists.* If the taxpayer performs services in the performing arts for at least two employers and receives wages of at least $200 from at least two of those employers, business expenses may be deducted as an adjustment to gross income to the extent they exceed 10% of income from the performing arts. To claim an adjustment, adjusted gross income (AGI) must not be more than $16,000 before the deduction.

TIP: Complete Form 2106, *Employee Business Expenses,* or Form 2106-EZ, *Unreimbursed Employee Business Expenses,* to figure the amount deductible for reservists, performing artists, and fee-based government officials. This form must be attached to the return. The deduction is reported in the adjustments section of Form 1040.

- *Expenses of fee-based government officials.* If the taxpayer is a fee-based official with a state or political subdivision, expenses incurred in performing the job are deductible as an adjustment to gross income.

A number of the write-in deductions listed below can be claimed as adjustments to gross income. Enter the amount and the abbreviation or term appearing in the parentheses that follow:

- Archer MSA deductions (MSA)
- Jury duty pay turned over to an employer who continues paying salary to the taxpayer while on jury duty (Jury Pay)
- Deductible expenses related to the rental of personal property engaged in for profit, the income from which is reported on line 21 as other income (PPR)
- Reforestation amortization and expenses (RFST)
- Repayment of certain supplemental unemployment benefits in order to qualify for trade readjustment allowances under the Trade Act of 1974 (Sub-Pay TRA)
- Contributions to 501(c)(18)(D) pension plans (501(c)(18)(D))
- Contributions by certain ministers to 403(b) plans (403(b))
- Attorney fees and court costs for certain discrimination actions, but only to the extent of gross income from the actions (UDC)
- Attorney fees and court costs related to a whistleblower reward received by the taxpayer from the IRS (WBF)

See the instructions for Form 1040 for more information about these write-in deductions.

Review Questions

1. The deduction for a portion of self-employment tax is taken:
   a. As a business deduction on Schedule C
   b. As a personal miscellaneous itemized deduction on Schedule A
   c. As an adjustment to gross income directly on Form 1040
   d. As an adjustment to self-employment tax owed on Schedule SE

2. For purposes of deducting health insurance premiums from adjusted gross income, which business owner bases the deduction on compensation?
   a. More-than-2% S corporation shareholder
   b. Sole proprietor
   c. General partner
   d. Limited liability company member

3. A sole proprietor has health insurance for herself and has no employees. In figuring the deductible portion of the premiums, which of the following statements is correct?
   a. All premiums are deductible as an adjustment to gross income without any limitations.
   b. The premiums are limited to the net profits shown on Schedule C.
   c. The premiums cannot exceed the net profits reduced by the employer-equivalent portion of the self-employment tax.
   d. The premiums cannot exceed the net profits reduced by both the employer-equivalent portion of the self-employment tax and a deduction for contributions to a qualified retirement plan for the sole proprietor.

4. A self-employed individual who relocates because of a new business must work in the new location for how long before the individual can deduct moving expenses?
   a. 12 months
   b. 24 months
   c. 39 weeks
   d. 78 weeks

5. Which of the following moving expenses is **not** deductible?
   a. The cost of connecting or disconnecting utilities
   b. The expenses of selling the old home
   c. The cost of shipping a household pet
   d. The cost of driving to the new home

CHAPTER 18

Alimony

Alimony is a series of regular payments made under a divorce or separation agreement from one former spouse to the other. Alimony is included in the gross income of the recipient spouse and claimed as an above-the-line deduction by the payer spouse. The payments must meet certain requirements to be treated as alimony.

Payments made for a couple's child or children are not alimony but rather child support. Child support is not deductible by the payer spouse and is not income to the recipient spouse.

Payments representing a property settlement are not alimony. There is no immediate gain recognized when property is transferred to a spouse or former spouse because of divorce or legal separation. The recipient spouse essentially takes over the basis of the other spouse and will report gain when the property is eventually sold.

If alimony payments are structured in such a way that the payments are too large in the first few years, there may be recapture required by the payer spouse. The recipient spouse may be entitled to a deduction for the recaptured amount.

A divorce may also affect tax issues other than alimony and child support payments. For example, if a divorce becomes final before the end of the year, it changes the taxpayers' filing status (see Chapter 2). Dependency exemptions may also be an issue for a child of divorced parents (see Chapter 3).

Payments that Are Alimony

To be considered alimony, *all* of these conditions must be met:

- The payments must be in cash (which includes payments by check or by electronic funds transfer).
- The payments must be made under a decree of divorce or separate maintenance or under a written separation agreement. Payments made under oral agreements do not qualify as alimony.
- The payer and recipient spouse cannot file a joint return with each other.

> **ALERT:** Different tax rules apply to payments made under a divorce decree or other instrument (e.g., a separation agreement) made before 1985. These rules are not explained here.

- The decree or instrument requiring payments does not label the payments as something other than alimony (e.g., as child support or a property settlement).
- The payment is not treated as child support (discussed later in this chapter).
- Spouses who are legally separated under a decree of divorce or separate maintenance may not be members of the same household at the time the payments are made. The separate household requirement does not apply to alimony paid under a written separation agreement for spouses who are not legally separated.
- There is no requirement to make any payment after the death of the recipient spouse. The decree or other instrument need not specify that payments cease at death if, under state law, they would have ended at death anyway. However, if there is a requirement to pay cash or property after the death of the recipient spouse as a substitute for continuing payments, some or all of the payments will not be treated as alimony.

Example

Roy is required by a divorce decree to pay Rita $30,000 annually for 15 years or until her death, whichever comes first. However, the decree also stipulates that if she dies before the end of 15 years, Roy must pay her estate the difference between the $450,000 ($30,000 × 15) and the payments he had made to date. If Rita dies at the end of 10 years, Roy would have to pay her estate $150,000 ($450,000 – $300,000). Under these facts, Roy is really making a property settlement in installments rather than alimony payments. As such, *none* of Roy's payments is deductible as alimony because he must pay out the same amount as if Rita's death did not end his alimony obligation.

Payments need not be made directly to the recipient spouse in order to qualify as alimony. Payments to a third party are treated as alimony if they are required under the terms of a decree or written agreement. Payments to a third party can also be treated as alimony if there is a written request from the recipient spouse and *all* of the next requirements are met:

- The payments are made in lieu of direct payments to the recipient spouse.
- The written request states that both spouses intend to treat the third-party payments as alimony.
- The payer spouse receives the written request before he or she files the tax return for the year to which the payments relate.

Example

Hugo is required under the terms of a divorce decree to pay his former wife's rent, which he does by sending a check each month to the landlord. The rent payments can be treated as alimony.

Payments that Are Not Treated as Alimony

Certain payments are never treated as alimony. In addition, certain payments that normally would be considered alimony may not be treated as alimony if they are specifically excluded under a written divorce decree or separation agreement or are excluded by a subsequent statement making the election. These payment types are not considered alimony:

- Child support
- Property settlements
- Payments that are the other spouse's share of community income
- Payments to keep up or for the use of the payer's property

Example

A divorce decree requires Milton to pay Pricilla $200,000 in monthly installments of $20,000. Milton's obligation does not end if Pricilla dies before the $200,000 has been paid. Thus, the monthly payments are not alimony because they do not end at Priscilla's death. The monthly payments are a property settlement, not alimony, and therefore not deductible by Milton.

Child Support

Payments that are child support are not deductible as alimony or taxable to the recipient spouse. There are no dollar limits on amounts that can be treated as child support. Child support is a payment specifically designated as such in the divorce decree or separation agreement.

Payments not specifically designated as child support are also treated as child support if payments to the recipient spouse are reduced for either the occurrence of an event or a contingency that can be clearly associated with the recipient spouse's child:

- Payments will be deemed child support if upon the occurrence of an event or contingency relating to the child, such as becoming employed, dying, leaving the household, leaving school, marrying, joining the military, or reaching a certain age or income level the payments are reduced or terminated.
- Payments will be deemed child support if the payment is reduced at a time that can be clearly associated with one of the contingencies just mentioned. For instance, reducing payments six months before or after a child reaches age 18 creates a presumption that the payments are child support.

TIP: The presumption that the reduction in payments is based on or clearly associated with a contingency can be overcome if the taxpayer can establish that the reduction was not because of a contingency. For example, the taxpayer may establish that under the laws of the taxpayer's state, the alimony period is customarily one-half of the duration of the marriage.

ALERT: If both alimony and child support are required to be paid and the payer spouse pays less than the total amount required, the payments are first applied to child support and then to alimony.

Property Settlements

When a couple divorces or separates, property may pass from one spouse to another. There is no gain or loss recognized on transfers under a property settlement incident to divorce or separation.

The spouse receiving property assumes the basis and holding period of the spouse transferring the property. (See Chapter 12.)

Example

As required by the divorce decree, Justin transferred 100 shares of XYZ Corp. to Marian. He bought them some years ago for $10,000, and they are worth $50,000 at the time of the transfer. Marian's basis in the shares is $10,000 (Justin's basis). If she sells the shares, she will report gain or loss as the difference between the fair market value of the shares at the time of the sale and her $10,000 carryover basis.

TIP: Special rules apply to the marital residence when related to the home sale exclusion (see Chapter 14).

Community Income

Payments that represent a spouse's portion of community income are not alimony.

Payments to Keep Up or for the Use of the Payer's Property

Amounts paid to keep up property owned by the payer spouse are not considered alimony. For example, if the payer spouse owns a car used by the recipient spouse, then payments made on the car loan are not considered alimony, even if agreed to by both parties in the decree.

Alimony Deduction

A deduction from gross income (an above-the-line deduction) can be claimed for payments that meet the definition of alimony. There is no dollar limit on this deduction, although there is a rule which prevents frontloading of payments. (This rule, called the alimony recapture rule, is discussed later in this chapter.) There are no restrictions on the alimony deduction based on the payer's income.

ALERT: The failure to include the recipient spouse's SSN on the return can result in a $50 penalty and a possible disallowance of the alimony deduction.

No special form or schedule is used to figure deductible alimony. The total amount deductible is claimed in the adjustments section of Form 1040, *U.S. Individual Income Tax Return*. Form 1040A, *U.S. Individual Income Tax Return,* or 1040EZ, *Income Tax Return for Single and Joint Filers with No Dependents,* cannot be used to claim an alimony deduction.

Also enter the recipient spouse's Social Security Number (SSN) on the alimony deduction line. The IRS uses this information to check that the recipient spouse has reported the payments as alimony income.

Alimony Income

The recipient spouse must include in gross income the receipt of payments that meet the definition of alimony. No information document (such as Form 1099-MISC, *Miscellaneous Income*) is issued to the recipient spouse reporting the total payments for the year. Alimony income is reported in the income section of Form 1040. Form 1040A or 1040EZ cannot be used if a taxpayer is reporting alimony income.

The recipient spouse must provide his or her SSN to the person making the alimony payments.

ALERT: The recipient spouse's failure to provide the SSN to the payer spouse can result in a $50 penalty.

Alimony Recapture

If during the first three years of alimony payments, the payments decrease by more than $15,000 or end, some or all of the alimony must be recaptured. "Recapture" means that amounts previously deducted must be included in gross income of the payer spouse in the third year. Conversely, the payee spouse may claim a deduction for recaptured amounts. The three-year period starts with the first calendar year in which alimony payments are made under the divorce decree or written separation agreement. Payments made under any temporary support orders are disregarded for purposes of the recapture rule.

TIP: Alimony income is considered earned income for individual retirement account (IRA) or Roth IRA contribution purposes (see Chapter 15). However, alimony income is *not* considered earned income for the earned income tax credit (see Chapter 27).

Although the alimony recapture rule is generally meant to deter spouses from disguising property settlements, alimony may be reduced or ended for a variety of reasons, any one of which can trigger recapture. These reasons include:

- A change in the decree or separation agreement
- A failure to make the payments required under the decree or separation agreement
- A reduction because of the payer spouse's ability to provide support
- A reduction in the recipient spouse's need for support

Alimony recapture applies when alimony paid in the third year decreases by more than $15,000 from the second year or when alimony paid in the second and third years decreases significantly from the alimony paid in the first year. Whether a decrease is "significant" is based on a formula (not discussed in this chapter). Use Worksheet 1, *Recapture of Alimony*, from IRS Pub. 504, *Divorced or Separated Individuals*, to figure the amount of alimony recapture.

Example

Edward paid his former spouse $60,000 of alimony in year 1, $42,000 in year 2, and $32,000 in year 3. Edward appears to be subject to alimony recapture because the alimony payments in the second and third years decreased significantly from the amount paid in the first year. However, to determine whether Edward actually is subject to alimony recapture (and if so, the amount), his tax preparer completes the recapture of alimony worksheet as shown in Figure 18.1.

In year 3, Edward is subject to alimony recapture and must report income from recapture of $8,000 (Form 1040, line 11). He also deducts alimony of $32,000 (line 31a). Edward's former spouse does the reverse—she reports alimony income of $32,000 and deducts $8,000. They do not net the amounts on their year 3 tax returns.

Note. *Do not enter less than -0- on any line.*

1. Alimony paid in **2nd year**		1. $42,000	
2. Alimony paid in **3rd year**	2. $32,000		
3. Floor	3. **$15,000**		
4. Add lines 2 and 3		4. $47,000	
5. Subtract line 4 from line 1			5. -0-
6. Alimony paid in **1st year**		6. $60,000	
7. Adjusted alimony paid in **2nd year** (line 1 minus line 5)	7. $42,000		
8. Alimony paid in **3rd year**	8. $32,000		
9. Add lines 7 and 8	9. $74,000		
10. Divide line 9 by 2	10. $37,000		
11. Floor	11. **$15,000**		
12. Add lines 10 and 11		12. $52,000	
13. Subtract line 12 from line 6			13. $8,000
14. **Recaptured alimony**. Add lines 5 and 13			*14. $8,000

* If you deducted alimony paid, report this amount as income on Form 1040, line 11.
If you reported alimony received, deduct this amount on Form 1040, line 31a.

FIGURE 18.1 Edward's Recapture of Alimony Worksheet

TIP: There is no recapture if alimony payments decrease because of the death of either spouse or the remarriage of the recipient spouse. Also, there is no recapture if payments vary within the three-year period because they are tied to an agreed-to percentage of income from a business or property or from a portion of wages or self-employment income.

If there is alimony recapture, the spouse who previously deducted the payments must report the recapture as income in the income section of Form 1040 line 11. Cross out "received" and enter "recapture." Also include the recipient spouse's last name and SSN.

The spouse who previously included the payments in income may deduct the recapture amount in the adjustments section of Form 1040 (line 31a). Cross out "paid" and enter "recapture" and include the other spouse's SSN.

Review Questions

1. Which of the following is **not** a condition for deducting alimony?
   a. Payments must be in cash.
   b. The spouse paying alimony must have modified adjusted gross income below a set level.
   c. The obligation to make payments must end on the recipient spouse's death.
   d. Spouses who are divorced are not members of the same household.

2. Alimony recapture applies when payments in the third year decrease by more than $15,000 from the second year as a result of:
   a. The payer spouse's ability to provide support.
   b. The death of the recipient spouse.
   c. The remarriage of the recipient spouse.
   d. The demise of the payer spouse's business upon which alimony payments were based.

3. Which statement about child support is **not** correct?
   a. It is not deductible by the payer spouse.
   b. It need not be designated as such in the divorce decree if payments are contingent on an event related to the child, such as reaching the age of majority.
   c. It is not income to the recipient spouse.
   d. There are dollar limits on amounts paid as child support.

4. This year, Janet transfers 100 shares of stock to Ben as part of their divorce decree. Janet paid $10,000 for the shares. They are worth $18,000 on the day they are transferred to Ben. He sells the shares six months later for $22,000. What is his gain on the sale of the stock?
   a. $0
   b. $4,000
   c. $12,000
   d. $22,000

5. Sylvia and Joel divorce. Joel obtains custody of their child, Stu, age 16. Sylvia is ordered to pay Joel $500 per month until Stu turns age 18. At that time, her payments decline to $200 per month for the next three years. What, if anything, can Sylvia deduct?
   a. $0
   b. $200 per month as long as she makes such payments
   c. $500 per month as long as she makes such payments
   d. $500 per month until Stu is age 18

PART 3

Deductions and Credits

Standard and Itemized Deductions

The calculation of a taxpayer's tax liability includes the subtraction from adjusted gross income of either a standard deduction or the total of various allowable expenses known as itemized deductions. Generally, taxpayers may choose either method, but they usually choose the method that provides the greater tax benefit. Taxpayers in some situations are required to itemize deductions.

The standard deduction is an inflation-adjusted amount based on filing status. Taxpayers who are at least 65 years old and/or blind can add an additional amount to the standard deduction.

Itemized deductions are allowed for various personal expenses, including medical costs, taxes, interest, charitable contributions, personal casualty and theft losses, and various miscellaneous expenses. Certain thresholds and limitations apply to some itemized deductions. Taxpayers must keep adequate records to support deductions claimed.

Itemized deductions are explained further in Chapters 20 through 26.

Standard Deduction

The standard deduction is a fixed dollar amount that can be deducted from adjusted gross income (AGI) to arrive at taxable income. Table 19.1 presents the standard deduction amounts for 2012.

Additional Standard Deductions

Taxpayers who claim the standard deduction may qualify for additions to their standard deduction for age and blindness. The additional amounts are based on filing status, as shown in Table 19.1.

TIP: Taxpayers who itemize deductions are not eligible to claim any additional standard deductions based on age or blindness.

TABLE 19.1 2012 Standard Deduction Amounts

Filing status	Standard deduction	Additional standard deduction (per person, per event) for age or blindness
Married filing jointly and qualifying widow(er) with dependent child	$11,900	$1,150
Head of household	$8,700	$1,450
Single and married filing separately	$5,950	$1,450 for singles; $1,150 for married filing separately

A taxpayer may claim an additional standard deduction amount if he or she is at least 65 years old. For tax purposes, a person is treated as being age 65 on the day before his or her 65th birthday. Thus, a person born on January 1, 1948, is treated as attaining age 65 on December 31, 2012, and the additional standard deduction for age can be claimed on a 2012 tax return for someone born on or before January 1, 1948.

TIP: Taxpayers should retain with their tax records the statement certifying partial blindness.

A taxpayer may claim an additional standard deduction amount for blindness if he or she is totally or partially blind on the last day of the year. *Partial blindness* means that the taxpayer cannot see better than 20/200 in the better eye with glasses or contact lenses *or* the taxpayer's field of vision is not more than 20 degrees. A taxpayer must obtain a certified statement from an eye doctor or registered optometrist if the taxpayer is partially blind.

A taxpayer who is both 65 or older *and* blind can claim two additional standard deductions. Married couples filing a joint return can claim additional standard deduction amounts for each spouse who qualifies.

Example

Cynthia is 68 years old and totally blind. Her filing status is single. She can claim a total standard deduction of $8,850 ($5,950 + $1,450 + $1,450).

Mr. and Mrs. Jones, who are each in their 90s *and* totally blind, can claim a total standard deduction of $16,500 ($11,900 + $1,150 + $1,150 + $1,150 + $1,150) on their joint return.

Standard Deduction for Dependents

A person who can be claimed as a dependent by another taxpayer may claim a limited standard deduction. In 2012, it is the greater of:

- $950 OR
- Earned income plus $300 (but not more than a total of $5,950, the standard deduction for single filers). Earned income includes wages, tips, professional fees, and self-employment income.

Example

Jane, age 20, is a full-time college student. Jane's parents claim a dependent exemption for her. Jane has interest income of $840 and wages of $1,750. Her standard deduction is $2,050 (earned income of $1,750 + $300).

Now assume instead that Jane's interest income is $1,750, but her wages are only $350. In this case, her standard deduction is $950, which is the greater of $950 or $650 ($350 earned income plus $300).

If the dependent is blind or age 65 or older, and the dependent is filing a return, he can increase his standard deduction by the applicable additional standard deduction amount.

Example

Reggie, who is 68 years old, is his daughter's dependent. He has no earned income but has investment income of $2,500. His standard deduction amount is $2,400 ($950 + $1,450).

TIP: Although taxpayers usually benefit by itemizing deductions when their total itemized deductions exceed the standard deduction amount for their filing status, in some situations, choosing the standard deduction can actually result in lower overall tax. For example, this can occur if the taxpayer's state disallows a deduction allowed on the federal return.

However, the standard deduction is not allowed for federal alternative minimum tax purposes (see Chapter 33), so the net effect of choosing the standard deduction or itemized deductions may need additional analysis.

Overview of Itemized Deductions

Taxpayers typically choose to itemize when their total itemized deductions exceed the standard deduction amount for their filing status (see Table 19.1).

There are a variety of itemized deductions. The next list summarizes some common deductions and the chapter where more information can be found.

Medical and Dental Expenses (Chapter 20)
Some examples include amounts paid for medical insurance (including Medicare premiums), travel to and from medical institutions for medical treatment, and certain expenditures for medical reasons (e.g., installing a chair lift for a disabled taxpayer). For 2012, only the portion of unreimbursed medical expenses that exceed 7.5% of AGI is deductible.

Tax Payments (Chapter 21)
A taxpayer can choose to deduct *either* state and local income taxes or state and local sales taxes. Real estate taxes on personal homes can be deducted without limit, while other taxes, such as personal property taxes, may also be deductible if based on the property's value.

Interest Payments (Chapter 22)
Interest on a home mortgage, line of credit secured by a home, or a home equity loan on a primary residence (and a second home owned by the taxpayer) is deductible up to a dollar limit. Investment interest is also deductible, but only to the extent of net investment income. However, interest on student loans is not an itemized deduction; it is claimed as

an adjustment when figuring AGI (see Chapter 16). No deduction is allowed for personal interest, such as interest paid on credit card debt or car loans.

Charitable Contributions (Chapter 23)

Donations of cash and property are deductible up to a set percentage of AGI. Donations exceeding the AGI limit can be carried forward up to five years. Special substantiation rules apply and no deduction is allowed if these rules are not met.

Nonbusiness Casualty and Theft Losses (Chapter 24)

Unreimbursed losses on personal property due to casualties, disasters, and theft may be deductible. Such losses are subject to two limits: (1) The loss for each event must be reduced by $100; (2) only the total of all personal casualty and theft losses exceeding 10% of AGI are deductible.

Miscellaneous Itemized Deductions (Chapter 25)

A taxpayer may have various expenses that are deductible as miscellaneous itemized deductions. Some of these include tax preparation fees, certain legal fees, and investment expenses. Hobby expenses and gambling losses are also deductible, but only to the extent of income and winnings. Some miscellaneous itemized deductions are deductible only to the extent they exceed 2% of AGI (the 2%-of-AGI floor), while others may be fully deductible.

TIP: Taxpayers who itemize at the federal level generally must itemize at the state level. Even if a taxpayer's itemized deductions are less than the federal standard deduction, it still may be better to itemize if doing so produces an advantage for state income taxes. In other words, if the savings from itemizing deductions for state tax purposes is greater than the additional federal income tax that results from not using the standard deduction, itemizing makes sense. The election to itemize, even though the taxpayer's itemized deductions are less than the standard deduction, must be made by checking the box at the bottom of Schedule A (1040), *Itemized Deductions*, and listing the applicable itemized deductions on the schedule.

Employee Business Expenses (Chapter 26)

An employee who incurs expenses for business-related travel, entertainment, and other ordinary and necessary expenses incurred on the job may deduct such costs as a miscellaneous itemized deduction subject to the 2%-of-AGI floor. Such costs may include work-related education, uniforms, union dues, and subscriptions. However, only those expenses that are not reimbursed by the employer may be deducted. Special substantiation rules apply to transportation, travel, and entertainment costs.

Taxpayers Who Must Itemize

- Most taxpayers have the choice of using the standard deduction or itemizing deductions. However, in certain cases, the standard deduction cannot be used: Married persons who file separate returns must both itemize if either spouse chooses to itemize. That is, a married person filing separately cannot use the standard deduction if the other spouse itemizes.
- A taxpayer who files a return for a short tax year because of a change in the annual accounting period (this is a *very* rare occurrence for individuals) must itemize.
- A nonresident or dual-status alien (a person is considered a dual-status alien if he or she was both a nonresident and resident alien during the year) must itemize. However, if the taxpayer is eligible to and makes a choice to be treated as a resident alien for the entire year (see IRS Pub. 519, *U.S. Tax Guide for Aliens*), the taxpayer can claim the standard deduction.

Advantages of Itemizing

There are many situations where a taxpayer may benefit by choosing to itemize instead of claiming a standard deduction. Itemizing typically benefits:

- Taxpayers incurring large medical expenses that were not covered by insurance
- Homeowners with mortgage interest and real estate tax expenses
- Taxpayers making large donations to charity
- Taxpayers who have property damage or destruction that was not covered (or fully covered) by insurance or other reimbursements
- Employees with substantial employee business expenses that were not reimbursed by an employer
- Taxpayers who have high state or local income taxes

A taxpayer who claimed the standard deduction on an original tax return may amend that return to itemize, as long as the statute of limitations for filing an amended return (Form 1040X), *Amended U.S. Individual Income Tax Return,* has not expired. The statute of limitations is generally three years from the return's due date or two years from when the tax was paid, whichever is later.

ALERT: A taxpayer using the married filing separately filing status can change to or from itemizing *only* if the other spouse also does so.

Review Questions

1. In 2012, Sally, age 45, is single and has no dependents. Her earned income is $45,000. Sally's standard deduction is:
   a. $950
   b. $5,950
   c. $8,700
   d. $11,900

2. In 2012, Ed, who is single and age 67, fully supports his 90-year-old mother and claims a dependent exemption for her. He can claim a standard deduction of:
   a. $5,950
   b. $8,700
   c. $10,150
   d. $11,600

3. In 2012, Jimmy, who is 21 years old and a full-time college student, earns $2,500 at a summer job. He also has interest income of $250 and capital gain distributions from a mutual fund of $800. His parents claim a dependent exemption for him on their return. Jimmy's standard deduction is:
   a. $950
   b. $2,800
   c. $5,950
   d. $6,250

4. Which of the following individuals can use the standard deduction?
   a. A married person filing a separate return whose spouse itemizes deductions
   b. A taxpayer who files a return for a short tax year because of a change in the annual accounting period
   c. A nonresident or dual-status alien
   d. A dependent who is claimed on another taxpayer's return

5. Matt received a certified statement from his optometrist on December 1, 2012, confirming that he cannot see better than 20/200. Matt does not itemize deductions. Matt is:
   a. Not eligible for an additional standard deduction because he is only partially blind.
   b. Eligible for an additional standard deduction because he was partially blind beginning in 2012.
   c. Eligible for an additional standard deduction beginning in 2013, the first full year after he is declared partially blind.
   d. Not eligible for an additional standard deduction because he was not blind during the entire year.

6. A taxpayer **must** itemize in each of the following situations **except**:
   a. The taxpayer is married filing separately and the other spouse itemizes deductions.
   b. When itemized deductions are greater than the standard deduction amount.
   c. The taxpayer has a short year (his tax year has fewer than 12 months).
   d. The taxpayer is a dual-resident alien.

CHAPTER 20

Medical and Dental Expenses

A taxpayer who has qualified medical expenses may be able to deduct them as an itemized deduction. Medical expenses are subject to a 7.5% of adjusted gross income (AGI) limitation. The amount of the deduction for medical expenses will be limited to only the amount exceeding 7.5% of the taxpayer's AGI.

ALERT: Starting in 2013, the deduction will be limited to medical expenses exceeding 10% of AGI. However, if the taxpayer (or the taxpayer's spouse, whether filing a joint return or not) is age 65 or older, the taxpayer can continue to deduct expenses that exceed 7.5% of AGI through 2016.

Medical insurance premiums (that are not already excluded from income) are deductible as medical expenses and are subject to the 7.5% AGI floor. Self-employed taxpayers with a net profit for the year may deduct the premiums paid for themselves, their spouse, and children under age 27 as an adjustment to income without itemizing (see Chapter 17).

Itemized Deduction

Medical and dental expenses may be deducted without limit (see the "Qualified Medical Expenses" section later in this chapter for which expenses qualify). However, only those qualified expenses that exceed 7.5% of the taxpayer's AGI may be deducted.

Before calculating the limitation, the amount paid for medical expenses must first be reduced by any reimbursements from an insurance policy or other plan before the 7.5% of AGI limitation is applied.

Example

June, a single taxpayer with an AGI of $67,000, paid $18,000 in unreimbursed fees to a psychotherapist to treat a medical condition. Only $12,975 ($18,000 – $5,025 [7.5% of $67,000]), the amount that exceeds the 7.5% threshold, is deductible as a medical expense. The amount under the 7.5% threshold ($5,025) is not deductible.

Whose Medical Expenses Are Deductible

A taxpayer's medical expenses include his or her own expenses and those of a spouse or dependent.

TIP: If one spouse has sizable medical costs and low AGI, the couple should consider filing separately so that the spouse with the low AGI can get the maximum benefit of the deduction. In this case, the married filing separately status may be beneficial because the spouse with the lower AGI will have a lower threshold, which may allow medical expenses to be deducted.

Medical expenses are deductible by the taxpayer as long as the spousal or dependency relationship existed when the services were provided or paid for. Thus, the expenses can be deducted provided that the spousal or dependency relationship existed when the services are rendered or paid for even though the relationship of the parties may change before the deduction is taken on the return.

Example

Derek paid the medical expenses of his new wife, Lucille. She had received the medical treatment before they were married, but because he paid the expenses while they were married, he may deduct the expenses on either a joint or separate return.

A taxpayer can treat the medical expenses of another individual as being those of a dependent, even when the individual does not meet all requirements to be claimed as a dependent, as long as the individual *would* qualify to be a dependent *except that*:

- The individual's gross income exceeds $3,800 in 2012,
- The individual files a joint return for 2012, OR
- The individual or his or her spouse, if filing jointly, can be claimed as a dependent on someone else's 2012 return.

The dependent must be a U.S. citizen or national or a resident of the United States, Canada, or Mexico. However, this rule does not apply to an adopted child who lived with the taxpayer as a member of the household for 2012 so long as the taxpayer is a U.S. citizen or national.

Example

Amanda, who is single, pays more than half of the cost of supporting her elderly father, including all of his out-of-pocket medical costs. Her father's gross income for 2012 is $11,000. The only reason her father is not Amanda's dependent is that his gross income exceeds the 2012 personal exemption amount of $3,800. Amanda can add her father's medical expenses to her own and deduct them on her own return (subject to the 7.5% AGI threshold).

There are some special situations for deducting medical costs:

- *Child of divorced or separated parents.* Each parent can deduct the medical expenses that he or she paid for their qualifying child, regardless of which parent claims the dependency exemption, provided that:
  - The child is in the custody of one or both parents for more than half the year,
  - The child receives over half of his or her support from the parents, AND
  - The parents are divorced or legally separated under a decree of divorce or separate maintenance, separated under a written separation agreement, or living apart at all times during the last six months of the year.

- *Adopted child.* A legally adopted child is treated as the taxpayer's own child (i.e., the taxpayer can deduct the dependent's medical expenses). If the taxpayer repays the adoption agency or other person for medical expenses under an agreement related to the adoption, the expenses may be deductible. The taxpayer must clearly substantiate that any payments made to the adoption agency are directly attributable to the medical care of the child.
- *Dependent under a multiple support agreement.* A taxpayer who is treated as providing more than half of a qualifying relative's support under a multiple support agreement (see Chapter 3) can deduct medical expenses the taxpayer paid for such person. The medical expenses paid by other individuals participating in the multiple support agreement are not deductible by the taxpayer or by the other participating individuals.
- *Medical costs of a deceased taxpayer.* Medical expenses paid through the date of death are deducted subject to the normal 7.5% floor on the decedent's final income tax return. However, an election can be made to treat expenses paid by the decedent's estate within one year of death as having been paid by the decedent at the time the medical services were provided. Making this election allows the expenses to be deducted on the decedent's final return. The survivor or personal representative making this election must attach a statement to the decedent's return stating that the medical expenses have not and will not be claimed on the estate tax return.
- *Medical expenses of a deceased spouse or dependent.* If a taxpayer pays medical expenses for a deceased spouse or dependent, the expenses are included on the taxpayer's Form 1040, *U.S. Individual Income Tax Return*, in the year paid, whether they are paid before or after death. The taxpayer is allowed to take this deduction as long as the deceased individual was the taxpayer's spouse or dependent at the time the services were rendered or paid for.

Example

Continuing the earlier Derek *and Lucille* example, now assume that Derek dies and next year Lucille pays his medical bills for care provided to Derek before his death. Because she was married to Derek when the medical services were received, she can deduct the medical expenses on her return for the year of payment.

Qualified Medical Expenses

Qualified medical expenses are amounts paid for the diagnosis, cure, mitigation, treatment, or prevention of disease and costs for treatments affecting any part or function of the body.

Medical expenses must be for treatments primarily to alleviate or prevent a physical or mental defect or illness. Expenses incurred to maintain or promote general good health are not deductible. For instance, the cost of a weight loss program prescribed by a doctor to alleviate morbid obesity is deductible, while the cost of a weight loss program to look and feel better is not.

Deductible Medical Expenses

Examples of commonly deductible medical costs include:

- Costs for diagnostic services (e.g., blood screening).
- Fees to doctors, therapists, and other medical practitioners.
- Health insurance premiums, including any Medicare premiums under Parts A, B, or D, and premiums for Consolidated Omnibus Budget Reconciliation Act (COBRA) coverage. Health insurance premiums also include coverage for dental care, insurance to replace lost or damaged contact lenses, and long-term care insurance (with limits based on age of the taxpayer).
- Hospitalization and surgical charges.
- Qualified long-term care costs include the cost of a nursing home or similar facility. The cost of services, meals, and lodging is deductible if the principal reason for the stay at the nursing home or similar facility is to obtain medical care for a chronically ill individual pursuant to a plan of care prescribed by a licensed health care practitioner. (Limitations on long-term care insurance are explained later in this chapter.)
- Medical equipment and supplies.
- Prescription medications and insulin.
- Smoking cessation programs. The taxpayer cannot include the cost of drugs that do not require a prescription, such as over-the-counter nicotine gum or patches.
- Travel for medical purposes. The standard mileage rate of 23¢ per mile can be used to calculate the cost of deductible medical travel expenses in 2012. Lodging costs incurred for medical reasons are deductible at a maximum rate of $50 per person per night.

A more extensive list of deductible medical expenses can be found in IRS Pub. 502, *Medical and Dental Expenses.*

Premiums for long-term care insurance are deductible only up to a set dollar amount based on the taxpayer's age at the end of the year, as shown in Table 20.1.

TABLE 20.1 2012 Deduction for Long-Term Care Insurance Premiums

Age	Deductible limit
40 or less	$350
More than 40 but less than 50	$660
More than 50 but less than 60	$1,310
More than 60 but less than 70	$3,500
More than 70	$4,370

Nondeductible Medical Expenses

Not every medical cost is deductible. Examples of nondeductible costs include, but are not limited to:

- Controlled substances that violate federal law, such as medical marijuana, even if prescribed by a doctor and legal under state law.
- Cosmetic surgery or cosmetic dentistry to improve one's appearance. However, surgery to correct a medical condition is deductible. For example, a nose job merely to improve appearance is not deductible, but the procedure is deductible if undertaken to correct a deviated septum. Teeth-whitening treatments are nondeductible because they are solely cosmetic.
- Costs reimbursed from health plans, including flexible spending accounts (FSAs), health savings accounts (HSAs), medical savings accounts (MSAs), and health reimbursement accounts (HRAs).
- Funeral, burial, or cremation expenses.
- Over-the-counter medications, vitamins, and other supplements.
- Toiletries, including toothpaste.

A more extensive list of nondeductible medical expenses can be found in IRS Pub. 502 or in IRS Pub. 17, *Your Federal Income Tax for Individuals.*

Home (Capital) Improvements

A taxpayer may need to make modifications to a home because of health reasons, such as installing a ramp for wheelchair access for a wheelchair-bound individual living in the home. Normally, improvements to one's home are not deductible, although they can increase the taxpayer's basis in the home (see Chapter 12). However, an improvement made for medical reasons may be deductible—subject to the limitation described below—if its purpose is to accommodate a disability. Examples include the installation of an elevator for a heart patient, central air conditioning for someone with cystic fibrosis, or an air cleaning system for a person with asthma.

Only the costs that do not increase the home's fair market value (FMV) may be fully deducted (subject to the 7.5% AGI floor). For example, installing a wheelchair ramp generally does not increase the FMV of the home, so the expense is usually fully deductible. However, adding a Jacuzzi to a bathroom for treating a child with congenital muscular problems may add to the home's value, so the deductible portion of the expenditure is limited to the part of the cost that exceeds any increase in the value of the property.

Example

Sharon has polio and, upon her physician's recommendation, installs a swimming pool on her property for therapeutic purposes. The pool costs $40,000. The installation of the pool increases the value of her home by $30,000. Therefore, only $10,000 can be deducted as a medical expense (subject to the 7.5% of AGI threshold) because that amount exceeds the additional value the pool added to the home.

Worksheet A. **Capital Expense Worksheet**

Keep for Your Records

Instructions: Use this worksheet to figure the amount, if any, of your medical expenses due to a home improvement.

1. Enter the amount you paid for the home improvement . . . . **1.** ______

2. Enter the value of your home immediately after the improvement . . . . **2.** ______

3. Enter the value of your home immediately before the improvement . . . . **3.** ______

4. Subtract line 3 from line 2. This is the increase in the value of your home due to the improvement. . . . . **4.** ______

- If line 4 is more than or equal to line 1, you have no medical expenses due to the home improvement; stop here.
- If line 4 is less than line 1, go to line 5.

5. Subtract line 4 from line 1. These are your medical expenses due to the home improvement . . . . **5.** ______

FIGURE 20.1 IRS Pub. 502, Worksheet A

Deducting Medical Expenses

Medical expenses are deducted on Schedule A (Form 1040), *Itemized Deductions*. No additional form or schedule is required.

Reimbursements

Generally, most reimbursements, including amounts from insurance, flexible spending accounts, or other sources, reduce deductible medical expenses. However, no reduction is necessary for amounts received for permanent loss or loss of the use of a member or function of the body, such as the loss of an arm or leg, vision, or hearing. Additionally, no reduction is required for amounts received due to disfigurement to the extent that the payment is based on the injury, and with no regard to time lost at work. Amounts paid for dismemberment or disfigurement may be paid by workers' compensation or the U.S. Department of Veterans Affairs, or through private insurance. No reduction is required for payments received for lost earnings, but the payments are taxable (see Chapter 4).

A reimbursement received in a later year for medical expenses deducted in an earlier year is treated as income up to the amount the taxpayer previously deducted as medical expenses. The reimbursement is included in income for the year the reimbursement is received; the earlier tax containing the deduction is not amended.

Example

Adelaide had medical expenses of $12,000 in 2011. She deducted $6,700 of these medical expenses on her 2011 return. In 2011, her standard deduction was $5,800, and her itemized deductions were $15,500. In 2012, she receives a reimbursement of $500. The $500 reimbursement is reported as income in 2012, the year she received the reimbursement. If, however, her AGI was too high to allow for any medical deduction in 2011 (or if she did not itemize deductions in 2011), then the 2012 reimbursement of $500 is not taxable. In other words, the reimbursement is taxable income only to the extent she had previously deducted the medical expense.

Damages

Damages received in a lawsuit for a personal physical injury or illness are not taxed (see Chapter 10). The part of the award or settlement covering medical expenses is not deductible. However, if the taxpayer previously deducted the medical expense and a portion of the award received is paid to reimburse him or her for the deducted medical expenses, the taxpayer must include that part of the award or settlement in income to the extent of any previous medical deduction taken, as explained earlier.

The portion of an award or settlement covering future medical expenses is applied against future medical costs until it has been completely used.

Special Situations

A taxpayer may have a unique situation that results in special treatment for medical expenses.

Impairment-Related Work Expenses

A taxpayer with a disability can deduct work-related expenses as a business expense rather than as a medical expense, thereby avoiding the 7.5%-of-AGI threshold. Unlike other work-related expenses, impairment-related work expenses are *not* subject to the 2%-of-AGI floor.

A taxpayer has a disability for purposes of **impairment-related work expenses** if either:

- The taxpayer has a physical or mental disability, such as blindness, that functionally limits the taxpayer from being employed, OR
- The taxpayer has a physical or mental impairment—for example, a missing limb—that substantially limits one or more major life activities. (A major life activity includes breathing, learning, performing manual tasks, speaking, walking, or working.)

DEFINITION:
Impairment-related work expenses are ordinary and necessary business expenses required for the taxpayer to work satisfactorily, for goods and services not required or used in personal activities, and costs not covered in other tax laws. Example: The cost of a reader for a blind person when at work.

Health Insurance for the Self-Employed

A taxpayer who is self-employed (or who owns more than 2% of an S corporation and receives wages from the S corporation) may be able to deduct the full amount of health insurance premiums from gross income as an adjustment to income rather than treating the premiums as an itemized medical expense. Premiums include regular health coverage (including Medicare) as well as long-term care insurance. This deduction is explained in Chapter 17.

Health Coverage Tax Credit

TIP: More information about the HCTC is available in the instructions to Form 8885, *Health Coverage Tax Credit,* and on the IRS website at http://www.irs.gov/Individuals/The-Health-Coverage-Tax-Credit-(HCTC)-Program.

A taxpayer may claim the Health Coverage Tax Credit (HCTC) if he or she is a trade adjustment assistance (TAA) recipient, an alternative TAA recipient, a reemployment TAA recipient, or a Pension Benefit Guaranty Corporation pension payee who is at least age 55. The refundable credit offsets 72.5% of the premiums paid for health insurance coverage.

Eligibility for the HCTC is determined on a monthly basis. An eligible taxpayer can claim the credit if these requirements are met:

1. The taxpayer must pay the premium for qualified health insurance coverage for himself or herself or a qualifying family member.
2. The taxpayer must not be imprisoned under federal, state, or local authority.
3. The taxpayer must not have other specified coverage (discussed in Pub. 502).
4. The taxpayer was the qualifying family member of an eligible individual.
5. An individual who can be claimed as a dependent of another taxpayer is not eligible for the credit.

An eligible taxpayer may receive advance payments of the credit, which are sent by the HCTC Program directly to the insurance provider to be applied directly toward the taxpayer's insurance premiums. Advance payments made by the HCTC Program to the insurance provider are reported to the taxpayer on Form 1099-H, *Health Coverage Tax Credit (HCTC) Advance Payments.*

Review Questions

1. In 2012, Jorge, who is single with no dependents, has AGI of $48,000 and unreimbursed medical costs of $8,900. How much of his medical expenses can be claimed as an itemized deduction?
   a. $0
   b. $5,300
   c. $8,900
   d. $3,600

2. Edwina can add the medical costs of all of the following people to her own in determining her medical deduction **except**:
   a. Her spouse
   b. Her sister, whom she claims as a dependent under a multiple support agreement
   c. Her grandchild, who lives with her for two months while her parents resolve their marital issues
   d. Her dependent son

3. Which of the following is **not** a deductible medical expense?
   a. Fees to a chiropractor
   b. The cost of teeth-whitening treatments
   c. The cost of a prescribed smoking cessation program
   d. A nursing home bill for medical care, lodging, and meals when the principal reason for being in the nursing home is for medical care

4. Which of the following over-the-counter items is a deductible medical expense?
   a. Insulin
   b. Multivitamins
   c. Aspirin
   d. Cough syrup

5. Rita, who is 68 years old, pays $3,600 for long-term care insurance in 2012. She is not self-employed. How much of the premiums qualify as a deductible medical expense?
   a. $0
   b. $1,310
   c. $3,500
   d. $3,600

6. Harvey suffers from severe cystic fibrosis. His doctor advised him to install central air conditioning in his home to alleviate his condition by controlling temperature and regulating humidity. It cost him $12,000 and increased the value of his home by $10,000. Assuming the total of his other medical costs already exceed the 7.5% AGI limit, how much of the cost of the air conditioning installation can Harvey deduct as a medical expense?
   a. $0
   b. $2,000
   c. $10,000
   d. $12,000

Tax Payments

There are various types of taxes, including income, property, and sales. Some taxes are deductible and some are not.

Deductible taxes that are personal in nature, such as a taxpayer's state income taxes, are deductible only as an itemized deduction on Form 1040, *U.S. Individual Income Tax Return*, Schedule A, *Itemized Deductions*. However, taxes related to rental real estate or to a trade or business do not have to be itemized to be deducted on other appropriate forms or schedules (e.g., Schedule E, *Supplemental Income and Loss*, for rental real estate). The deduction for the employer-equivalent portion of federal self-employment tax paid is claimed as an adjustment to gross income (see Chapter 17).

Foreign income taxes can *either* be deducted as an itemized deduction or used to calculate a foreign tax credit. Taxpayers may choose the more favorable option.

Tests for Deducting Taxes

A taxpayer can deduct taxes only if three tests are met:

1. The tax is imposed on the taxpayer.
2. The taxpayer pays the tax during the year.
3. The tax is a deductible tax (e.g., it is not a special assessment that increases property value.)

A tax may be imposed on a taxpayer who owns property, receives compensation that is taxable at a state or local level, or for other reasons. If one spouse owns real estate and pays the taxes on it, the taxes can be deducted on that spouse's separate return or on a joint return.

In determining whether the tax has been paid during the year, these rules apply:

- A payment that is mailed is treated as paid on the date of mailing, as long as there are sufficient funds to cover the amount of the check.

- A payment made through a pay-by-phone account or similar electronic transfer is treated as paid on the date reported on the account statement.

ALERT: Expired! The option to deduct state and local sales taxes in lieu of state and local income taxes expired as of January 1, 2012. As of this writing, Congress has not extended this provision.

A taxpayer using the accrual method of accounting (which is very rare for an individual) deducts the tax when all the events have occurred to fix the liability and the amount of the payment is certain.

Not all taxes paid are deductible. A tax is deductible only if tax law allows for the deduction. For example, federal income taxes, and the employee's share of Social Security and Medicare taxes (FICA), are *not* deductible. Table 21.1 lists deductible and nondeductible taxes.

The portion of federal estate taxes related to the receipt of income in respect of a decedent (such as benefits in qualified retirement plans and individual

TABLE 21.1 Deductible and Nondeductible Taxes

Type of tax	Deductible	Nondeductible
Fees and charges	Expenses of a business or income-producing property (deducted on Schedule C, *Profit* or *Loss From Business*	Fees and charges for personal purposes (e.g., driver's license, car inspection, parking charges, water bill
Income taxes	State and local income or sales taxes (See the ALERT on this page) Foreign income taxes Employee contributions to certain state benefit funds	Federal income taxes Employee contributions to private or voluntary disability funds
Other taxes	Taxes for a trade or business (deducted on Schedule C) Taxes on property producing rent or royalty income (deducted on Schedule E) Occupational taxes Employer-equivalent portion of self-employment tax paid	Federal excise taxes not on business/income-producing property Per capita taxes Estate, inheritance, legacy, or succession taxes Gift taxes Transfer taxes or stamp taxes Fines and penalties
Personal property taxes	State and local personal property taxes	Customs duties not on business/income-producing property
Real estate taxes	State and local real estate taxes Foreign real estate taxes Tenant's share of real estate taxes paid by a cooperative housing corporation	Taxes for local benefits Trash and garbage pickup fees Rent increases due to higher real estate taxes Homeowner's association charges Real estate taxes that are treated as imposed on someone else

retirement accounts) is deductible, but not as a tax. It is treated as a miscellaneous itemized deduction not subject to the 2%-of-adjusted-gross-income (AGI) floor.

State and Local Taxes

Two types of state and local taxes can be deductible: income taxes and sales taxes. Both types are deductible only as itemized deductions. However, as explained later in this chapter, a taxpayer must choose to deduct either income taxes or sales taxes; both cannot be deducted on the same return.

TIP: Withholding on a taxpayer's state and local income taxes can appear on Form W-2, *Wage and Tax Statement*, Form W-2G, *Certain Gambling Winnings*, Form 1099-MISC, *Miscellaneous Income*, and Form 1099-R, *Distributions from Pensions, Annuities, Retirement or Profit Sharing Plans, IRA's, Insurance Contracts, etc.*

For estimated tax payments, amounts deductible in 2012 include amounts paid in 2012. Therefore, if the fourth installment of 2012 estimated taxes is paid in January 2013, it is deductible in 2013, not in 2012. A prior-year tax refund of state and local income taxes that is applied (usually done through taxpayer election) to the current-year tax can be deducted.

State and Local Income Taxes

All states except Alaska, Florida, Nevada, South Dakota, Texas, Washington, and Wyoming, have state income taxes. Tennessee and New Hampshire tax only interest and dividend income. A handful of municipalities also have local income taxes. A taxpayer can deduct state and local income taxes paid through withholding, estimated taxes, or payments made directly to the state and/or local government (by check, credit/debit card, or via a tax refund).

Example

Gwen paid her fourth installment of 2012 estimated state income taxes on January 10, 2013. She cannot deduct this payment on her 2012 tax return even though it covers her 2012 tax obligation to the state. Instead, she can deduct it on her 2013 return, the year she makes the payment. She can deduct on her 2012 tax return her fourth installment of 2011 estimated state income taxes paid in January 2012.

If Gwen files her 2012 state tax return in 2013 and has her state tax refund credited toward her 2013 liability, the refund amount is deductible as a tax payment made in 2013 (and it may also be taxable on her federal return; see Chapter 10).

Married Couples

Married couples filing a joint federal income tax return deduct the total state and local income taxes for both spouses on their joint return.

Married couples filing separate state, local, and federal income tax returns can deduct only the amount of state and local income taxes that each paid on their respective federal returns.

Married couples filing joint state and local returns and separate federal income tax returns can deduct only the proportionate amount of total taxes relative to the gross income of each spouse. However, each taxpayer may not deduct more than the amount he or she actually paid. If each spouse is **jointly and severally liable** for the full amount of the state income taxes, no apportionment is required. The spouses can deduct on separate federal returns the amount that each spouse actually paid.

DEFINITION: Joint and several liability means that each spouse is liable for the full amount of the tax owed. The taxing authority can pursue either spouse for the full amount owed.

ALERT: A credit or refund of state or local income taxes in a year after they were deducted may be taxable if the taxpayer itemized deductions (see Chapter 10).There is no taxable income if the taxpayer claimed the standard deduction for the year of payment.

Example

Jim and Nancy are married and file a joint state and local income tax return in a state where spouses are not jointly and severally liable for state income taxes. The couple files separate federal tax returns. Jim's AGI for the year was $75,000 and Nancy's was $50,000. In total, the couple's state tax liability for the year was $5,000. Each paid one-half of the state tax liability ($2,500 each) during the year through income tax withholdings. Based on the proportion of income earned, Jim should have paid $3,000 of tax ($75,000/$125,000 × $5,000) and Nancy should have paid only $2,000 ($50,000/$125,000 × $5,000).

Jim may deduct the state and local taxes he paid in proportion to his income, but only to the extent of taxes he actually paid ($2,500). Nancy can deduct only $2,000 in state and local taxes paid on her federal return (even though she actually paid $2,500) because she is liable only for $2,000.

Note: If the couple resided in a state in which they were jointly and severally liable for the entire tax liability, they would not have to go through the apportionment calculation and each could take a deduction for the amount of state and local taxes they actually paid on their respective separate federal return.

The treatment of estimated taxes for spouses who divorce or legally separate is discussed in Chapter 36.

Contributions to State Benefit Funds

An employee may be required to contribute to a state benefit fund providing disability or unemployment insurance benefits. The contribution is automatically withheld from wages and reported on the taxpayer's Form W-2. The IRS has approved the deduction of payments made to these state benefit funds:

- Alaska Unemployment Compensation Fund
- California Nonoccupational Disability Benefit Fund
- New Jersey Nonoccupational Disability Benefit Fund
- New Jersey Unemployment Compensation Fund
- New York Nonoccupational Disability Benefit Fund
- Pennsylvania Unemployment Compensation Fund
- Rhode Island Temporary Disability Benefit Fund
- Washington State Supplemental Workmen's Compensation Fund

A taxpayer's contributions to a private or voluntary disability plan are not deductible.

TIP: Generally, claiming a tax credit instead of an itemized deduction produces the greater tax savings. The credit can be claimed even if the taxpayer uses the standard deduction amount.

Foreign Income Taxes

Foreign income taxes can be deducted or claimed as a foreign tax credit. However, taxpayers cannot claim a deduction or a credit for foreign taxes paid on earnings that are excluded from tax using the foreign earned income exclusion or foreign housing exclusion.

State and Local Sales Taxes

All states other than Alaska, Delaware, Montana, New Hampshire, and Oregon have state sales taxes. Many localities also have sales taxes.

> **TIP:** Use the interactive sales tax calculator supplied by the IRS at http://apps.irs.gov/app/stdc/ to determine the amount of a taxpayer's sales tax deduction.

This is no longer an uncertainty. There are two ways to figure the deductible sales tax amount. Taxpayers can use the method that produces the greater deduction:

1. *Use the actual receipts method*, and rely on receipts to deduct the actual amount of sales tax paid during the year.
2. *Use the IRS optional sales tax table.* (located in the Form 1040 Schedule A instructions). The table determines the taxpayer's deduction based on a taxpayer's state of residence, income (including exempt income), and number of exemptions claimed on the taxpayer's return. Using the table, the taxpayer can add to the amount figured sales tax for certain big-ticket items, such as a car, boat, aircraft, or building materials for the construction of a home or for major home renovations.

A taxpayer who lived in more than one state during the year must apportion the amount of sales tax paid in each state according to the days of residence in each state.

Example

Nick lived in New York for the first 100 days of the year and then relocated to North Carolina. Using the IRS optional sales tax table located in the Schedule A instructions, Nick could deduct 100/365 of the amount shown in the table for New York plus 265/365 of the amount shown for North Carolina.

Real Estate Taxes

Generally, real estate taxes paid to a state or local government or to a foreign government on property owned by the taxpayer and used for personal purposes (not as rental property) are deductible as an itemized deduction. There is no limit to the number of properties for which the deduction can be taken.

Deductible real estate taxes are those levied for the general public welfare. They do *not* include:

- Charges for local benefits and improvements that increase the value of the taxpayer's property (e.g., extending a sewer line to a taxpayer's home)
- Charges for services such as trash collection, even if the amount is paid to the taxing authority (i.e., it is part of the property tax bill)
- Homeowner's association charges

TIP: The lender usually issues an annual statement to a homeowner showing the amount of taxes disbursed from the escrow account. Also, the local tax authority typically sends the homeowner tax statements marked "paid."

If a taxpayer pays a portion of taxes each month along with mortgage payments that are placed in escrow by the lender, the taxpayer cannot deduct any part of the payments. Only the amount of taxes disbursed from escrow to the government taxing authority is deductible, and only in the year when such disbursement occurs.

A divorced or separated taxpayer who pays real estate taxes on the home that continues to be jointly owned with the spouse or former spouse may be able to treat part of the payments as deductible alimony (see Chapter 18).

Tenant-shareholders in a cooperative housing corporation can deduct their share of real estate taxes paid by the corporation for their dwelling unit. The cooperative should provide this information to residents.

Buying or Selling Realty Midyear

When property is bought or sold during the year, the real estate taxes are divided between the buyer and seller according to the number of days of ownership for each person. The seller is treated as owning the property up to, but not including, the date of sale; the buyer is treated as owning the property from the date of sale. Use the worksheet shown in Figure 21.1 to figure the real estate deduction for a buyer or seller.

Example

The Greens' real property tax year for their old and their new home is the same as the calendar year. Payments were due on August 1. The entire year's property tax on their old home, which was sold on May 7, was $3,820. The tax on their new home, which was purchased on May 3, was $4,245. The Greens are treated as having paid a proportionate share of the taxes on the old home even though they did not actually pay them. They can claim only a proportionate share of the taxes on the new home even though they paid the entire amount.

Using the worksheet in Figure 21.1, they can deduct 34.52% of the taxes for the old home. They owned the home for 127 days (January 1 through May 6); 127 days divided by 366 days (in 2012) is 0.3470. Their deduction is $1,329 ($3,829 × 0.3470).

Again using the worksheet, they owned the new home for 243 days (May 3 through December 31); 243 days divided by 366 days is 0.6639. They can deduct 66.39% of the new taxes, or $2,818 ($4,245 × 0.6639).

TIP: Form 1099-S, *Proceeds from Real Estate Transactions*, may be issued to the seller. Box 2 shows the gross proceeds of the sale, including the seller's real estate taxes that the buyer will pay after closing. Real estate taxes paid in advance by the seller that are the liability of the buyer are listed in box 5.

The seller can be treated as paying property taxes for this period even if he or she does not actually pay them, as long as the buyer is personally liable for the tax. The amount of tax must be included in the selling price of the property, and the buyer includes the amount of the seller's tax in his or her cost basis for the property. When this occurs, the settlement statement generally shows the allocation of taxes between the buyer and the seller.

However, in the case of delinquent taxes (amounts owed for years before the year of the sale), the buyer who pays them adds them to the basis of the property. The seller can deduct them but must include them in the selling price.

Worksheet 21-1. Figuring Your Real Estate Tax Deduction
Keep for Your Records

1. Enter the total real estate taxes for the real property tax year . . . . . ______
2. Enter the number of days in the real property tax year that you owned the property . . . . ______
3. Divide line 2 by 365 (for leap years, divide line 2 by 366) . . . . ___.___
4. Multiply line 1 by line 3. This is your deduction. Enter it on Schedule A (Form 1040), line 6 ______

Note. Repeat steps 1 through 4 for each property you bought or sold during the real property tax year. Your total deduction is the sum of the line 4 amounts for all of the properties.

FIGURE 21.1 Worksheet for Figuring Your Real Estate Tax Deduction

A taxpayer who receives a refund or rebate of 2012 real estate taxes in 2012 must reduce the deduction by the amount received. If the refund or rebate relates to payments made in a prior year in which the taxpayer itemized deductions, check to see whether income must be included in income (see Chapter 10).

Personal Property Taxes

Some states charge personal property taxes on certain items. These taxes are deductible if:

- Charged on personal property (such as a car)
- Based only on the value of the item
- Charged on a yearly basis, even if it is collected more or less than once a year

The tax may be called a registration fee for the privilege of using a vehicle on the highway.

Example

Veronica lives in a state that charges a monthly motor vehicle registration tax of 1% of the value of the vehicle, plus 50¢ per hundredweight. She paid $80 (1% of her car's value of $8,000), plus $17 (.50 × 3,400 pounds). The $80 is deductible because it is based on value; the $17 is not deductible because it is based on weight.

Review Questions

1. On December 31, 2012, a taxpayer pays state income taxes by the following methods. Which one **cannot** be deducted on a 2012 return?
   a. The taxpayer mails the check before midnight; the check is received and cashed on January 2, 2013.
   b. The taxpayer delivers the check personally to the state revenue office.
   c. The taxpayer authorizes payment by phone; the bank statement shows the funds were paid on December 31.
   d. The taxpayer pays by a computer transfer; the bank statement shows the funds were paid on January 2, 2013.

2. All of the following taxes are deductible as an itemized deduction (assuming conditions are met) **except**:
   a. Foreign income taxes
   b. State death taxes
   c. Occupational taxes
   d. Personal property taxes

3. Which of the following is a deductible tax?
   a. Homeowner's association fees
   b. Tenant-shareholder's share of real property taxes paid by a cooperative housing corporation
   c. Fines
   d. Employee's share of FICA

4. Which of the following items on which sales tax is paid **cannot** be added to the amount of the sales tax deduction from the IRS table?
   a. Jewelry
   b. Boat
   c. Airplane
   d. Home building materials to renovate a home

5. Which of the following tax payments is deductible?
   a. Special assessments to benefit the entire tax district
   b. Special assessments to benefit the taxpayer's property
   c. Charges for trash collection
   d. Homeowner's association charges

Interest Payments

Interest paid on personal debt generally is not deductible unless the debt is qualified home mortgage debt or a qualified student loan. Interest on personal loans, such as revolving credit agreements or credit cards, cannot be deducted.

Interest related to investments may be deductible up to set limits (generally, the amount of investment income). Interest related to a trade or business may also be deductible.

The deductibility of interest expense depends on how the proceeds of the related loan are used. For example, interest on a personal loan used to make a taxable investment is treated as investment interest, not personal interest, and may be deductible. However, interest on a margin loan (borrowing against investments held in a brokerage account) used to take a vacation is nondeductible personal interest.

Home Mortgage Interest

Interest paid on **acquisition debt** is deductible. Acquisition debt is debt that is incurred to buy, build, or substantially improve a principal residence (main home) or a second home belonging to the taxpayer. Except for grandfathered loans (loans that were taken out on or before October 13, 1987), only the interest on a mortgage up $1 million ($500,000 if married filing separately) can be taken into account. There is no dollar limit on the amount of the interest that can be deducted.

Similarly, interest on home equity debt, including lines of credit secured by the home, may be deductible regardless of how the proceeds are used. The amount of home equity debt cannot exceed the lesser of $100,000 ($50,000 if married filing separately) or the fair market value (FMV) of the home, reduced by any acquisition or grandfathered debt.

Thus, interest on total borrowing of up to $1.1 million ($550,000 if married filing separately) may be deducted.

TIP: Interest on home mortgages obtained on or before October 13, 1987, is not subject to the $1.1 million limit ($550,000 for taxpayers who are married filed separately [MFS]). This is called *grandfathered debt*. For debt acquired after this date, the dollar limits apply to the combined borrowing on the principal residence and the second home.

TIP: A lender who receives $600 or more of mortgage interest from an individual during the year reports the amount of interest paid during the year on Form 1098, *Mortgage Interest Statement*. The $600 limit applies separately to each mortgage, so a taxpayer with a first and second mortgage from the same lender may receive two forms.

ALERT: Even though interest on home equity debt may be deductible for regular tax, it is not deductible for alternative minimum tax (AMT) unless the loan is used to buy, build, or substantially improve a main or second home.

Example

In 2007, the Browns purchased a principal residence for $300,000. They made a down payment of $90,000 and financed the balance with a home mortgage of $210,000. In 2012, the FMV of the home was $280,000, and they obtained a second mortgage for $20,000. If the proceeds of the second mortgage are used to substantially improve the home, the interest is deductible as acquisition debt. If the proceeds are used to pay their child's college tuition, the interest is still deductible, but as home equity debt.

To qualify for the interest deduction, both of these conditions must be met:

1. The taxpayer must itemize deductions.
2. The mortgage or loan must be secured by a home. This means that the lender can foreclose on the home and acquire it if the taxpayer defaults on the loan.

Qualified Home

A *qualified home* is any home owned by the taxpayer and used as a residence. A qualified home must include sleeping, cooking, and toilet facilities, and can be a

- House, either single-family or multi-unit home, such as a duplex
- Condominium
- Cooperative apartment
- Mobile home
- House trailer (with sleeping, cooking, and toilet facilities)
- Boat (with sleeping, cooking, and toilet facilities)

A taxpayer who owns a multi-unit home can treat the unit in which he or she lives as a qualified home.

A taxpayer can have only one *main* home (or principal residence) at a time. Taxpayers who own more than one home can deduct mortgage interest for their main home plus one other home. A taxpayer who owns more than two homes can decide each year which home to consider as the second home for deducting any related mortgage interest.

A taxpayer may consider a vacation home as a second home and deduct the interest on that home, even if the home was unoccupied and the taxpayer spent no personal days in the home. However, if a home is used for both personal purposes and rented out during the year, the tax treatment of expenses depends on the amount of personal use.

- If the taxpayer uses the home as a residence and rents it out for 14 or fewer days during the year, the taxpayer follows the rules for deducting home mortgage interest discussed earlier.

- If the taxpayer uses the home as a residence for the greater of (1) more than 14 days or (2) 10% of the days the property is rented at fair rental value, mortgage interest (and real estate taxes) are allocated between personal and rental usage based on the number of days used for each. See Chapter 7 for more information.

A home owned under a time-share arrangement can be treated as a qualified home only if it meets all the requirements to be considered a qualified home.

A home under construction can be treated as a qualified home for up to 24 months as long as it becomes the taxpayer's qualified home at the time it is ready for occupancy. The 24-month period starts any time on or after the day construction begins.

ALERT: In Sophy v. Commissioner, the tax court held that the dollar limit on deducting mortgage interest also applies on a per-residence basis. Thus, if two co-owners are not married to each other, the total limit on acquisition indebtedness for the home is $1 million (not $2 million). *Sophy*, 138 TC 8 (2012).

Example

In May 2012, Don took out a mortgage to build a home on a lot he owned. Construction started on July 1, 2012. Don can deduct the interest he paid on this acquisition debt starting in July 2012. He can continue to deduct the interest for the balance of the loan as long as the home is completed and he occupies the home by June 30, 2014 (the end of the 24-month period beginning on July 1, 2012). At that time, if (1) the home is not completed, or (2) the home is complete but he does not move in, no further home mortgage interest can be deducted until the home is considered a qualified home.

Special Situations

Certain mortgage-related charges and other situations may affect a taxpayer's deduction. These include:

- *Late payment charges.* When a taxpayer's mortgage payment is late, a fee or charge for this is deductible as part of home mortgage interest if the charge is not for a specific service performed in connection with the mortgage.
- *Mortgage assistance payments.*
  - Under a safe harbor that is in place for tax years 2010, 2011, and 2012, a taxpayer can deduct interest paid through mortgage assistance payments if the taxpayer is receiving assistance under a program designed by a state housing finance agency with funds allocated from the Housing Finance Authority's Hardest Hit Fund or from the Department of Housing and Urban Development's (HUD) Emergency Homeowners' Loan Program. The mortgage interest deduction is limited to the amount of payments the taxpayer actually makes during the year. Taxpayers receiving assistance under these programs should receive Form 1098-MA, *Mortgage Assistance Payments*.
  - However, taxpayers may not take a deduction for interest paid by HUD under Section 235 of the National Housing Act.

TIP: A refund of mortgage interest typically is reported on Form 1098 in box 3. However, if overpayment and refund occur in the same year, the overpayment should not be included in box 1 and the refund should not be reported in box 3.

- *Mortgage interest credit.* A taxpayer who receives a mortgage credit certificate from a state or local government may be eligible for a tax credit (explained in Chapter 31). Deductible mortgage interest is reduced by the amount of any credit claimed.
- *Prepaid interest.* Prepaid interest for a period that extends beyond the current year is deductible only for the period to which it relates. A special rule for points, which are a form of prepaid interest, is explained later in this chapter.
- *Prepayment penalty.* A taxpayer who is charged a penalty for prepaying a mortgage may deduct the penalty as mortgage interest as long as the penalty is not assessed for a specific service related to the loan.
- *Refunds of interest.* A refund of interest paid in an earlier year may result in income if the taxpayer itemized deductions in the year in which it was paid (see Chapter 10 for information about taxable recoveries). If the taxpayer receives a refund in the year the interest was paid, reduce the mortgage interest deduction by the amount of the refund.
- *Reverse mortgages.* With a reverse mortgage, a lender pays the owner of a home while the homeowner continues to live in the home. However, the interest on a reverse mortgage is not due until the homeowner sells or dies or the term of the mortgage ends. Therefore, no interest can be deducted until the interest is paid, which is usually when the loan is paid in full.
- *Sale of a home.* Only interest paid up through the day before the date of sale is deductible mortgage interest.

Deducting Mortgage Interest

Mortgage interest is deducted on Schedule A, *Itemized Deductions,* of Form 1040, *U.S. Individual Income Tax Return.* Use Figure 22.1 to determine whether the home mortgage interest is fully deductible.

Figure 22.2 can be used to calculate the amount of deductible home mortgage interest when a taxpayer's mortgage exceeds the allowable limits.

Points

Points—which may be called loan origination fees, maximum loan charges, loan discount, or discount points—are a form of prepaid interest that are paid in order to reduce the mortgage interest rate. One point represents 1% of the mortgage. Thus, one point on a $100,000 mortgage is $1,000.

As a general rule, a deduction for points is spread over the term of the loan. However, there is an exception to this rule for points paid on certain acquisition debt for a principal residence (explained later in this chapter).

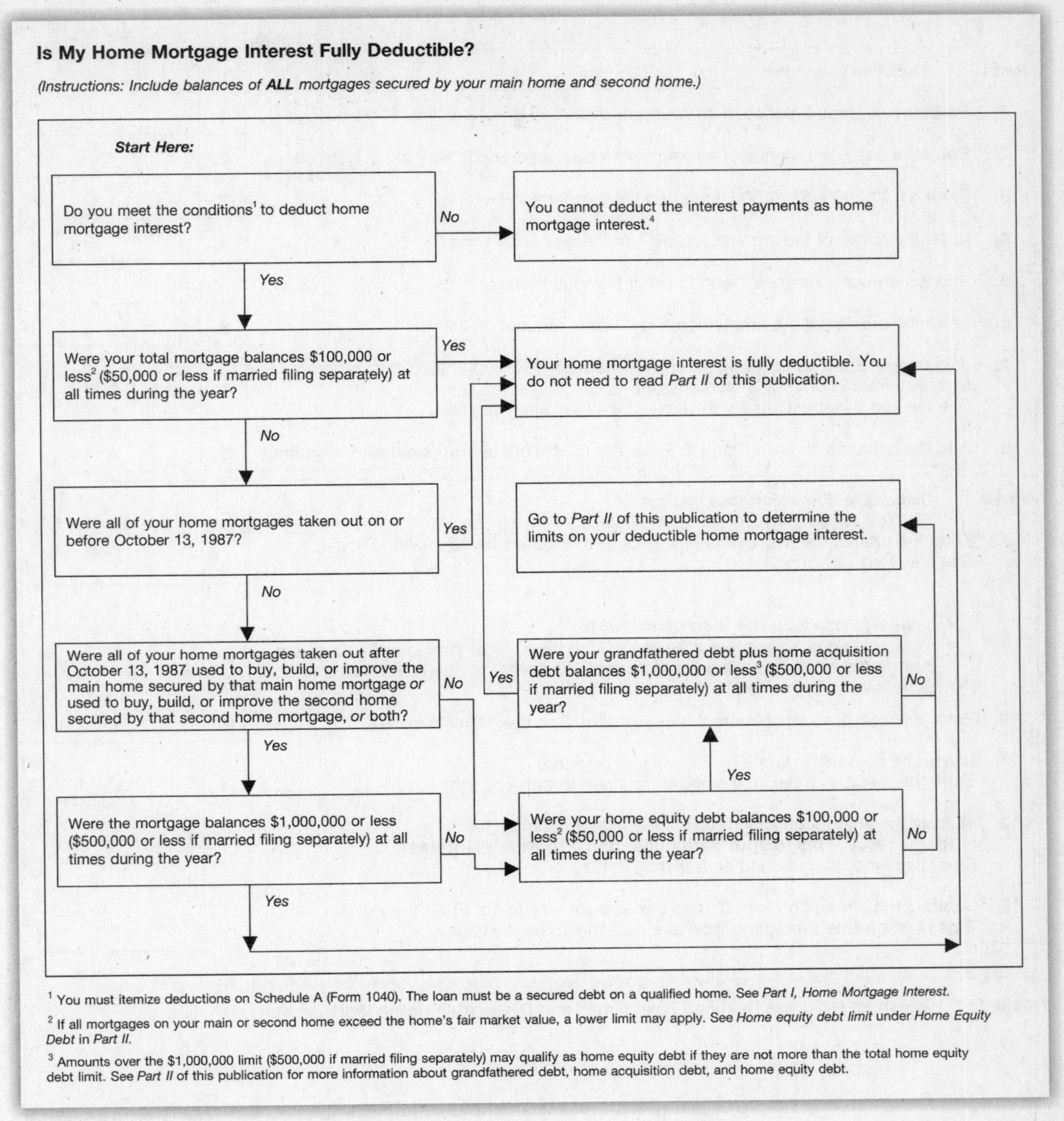

FIGURE 22.1 Is Home Mortgage Interest Fully Deductible?

Example

In January 2012, Vincent buys a vacation home for $400,000, financed with a 30-year fixed mortgage of $360,000. He pays two points, or $7,200 (2% of $360,000). Each year for 30 years (360 months), Vincent can deduct $240 of the points ($7,200 ÷ 360 × 12).

Part I	Qualified Loan Limit		
1.	Enter the average balance of all your grandfathered debt. See line 1 instructions . .	1.	
2.	Enter the average balance of all your home acquisition debt. See line 2 instructions	2.	
3.	Enter $1,000,000 ($500,000 if married filing separately)	3.	
4.	Enter the larger of the amount on line 1 or the amount on line 3	4.	
5.	Add the amounts on lines 1 and 2. Enter the total here	5.	
6.	Enter the smaller of the amount on line 4 or the amount on line 5	6.	
7.	If you have home equity debt, enter the smaller of $100,000 ($50,000 if married filing separately) or your limited amount. See the line 7 instructions for the limit which may apply to you.	7.	
8.	Add the amounts on lines 6 and 7. Enter the total. **This is your qualified loan limit.**	8.	

Part II	Deductible Home Mortgage Interest		
9.	Enter the total of the average balances of all mortgages on all qualified homes. See line 9 instructions	9.	
	• If line 8 is less than line 9, go on to line 10. • If line 8 is equal to or more than line 9, stop here. All of your interest on all the mortgages included on line 9 is deductible as home mortgage interest on Schedule A (Form 1040).		
10.	Enter the total amount of interest that you paid. See line 10 instructions.	10.	
11.	Divide the amount on line 8 by the amount on line 9. Enter the result as a decimal amount (rounded to three places)	11.	× .
12.	Multiply the amount on line 10 by the decimal amount on line 11. Enter the result. **This is your deductible home mortgage interest.** Enter this amount on Schedule A (Form 1040)	12.	
13.	Subtract the amount on line 12 from the amount on line 10. Enter the result. **This is not home mortgage interest.** See line 13 instructions	13.	

FIGURE 22.2 Worksheet to Figure Qualified Loan Limits and Deductible Home Mortgage Interest

A taxpayer who is not eligible to deduct points in the year they are paid or chooses not to deduct them all at once can deduct them ratably over the term of the loan if *all* of these conditions are met:

- The loan is secured by the taxpayer's home. (It need not be a principal residence.)

- The term of the loan does not exceed 30 years. If the loan period is more than 10 years, the terms of the loan are the same as other loans offered in the area for the same or longer period.
- The amount of the loan is $250,000 or less, or the number of points is not more than four (if the loan term is 15 years or less) or six (if the loan term is more than 15 years).
- The taxpayer uses the cash method of accounting.

Deducting Points in the Year Paid

Points paid to purchase a home can be deducted in full in the year paid if *all* of these conditions are met:

- The mortgage is secured by the taxpayer's principal residence. (Deduction in the year of payment does not apply to points on vacation homes.)
- The proceeds of the loan are used to buy or build the home.
- Paying points is an established business practice in the area where the mortgage was obtained.
- The amount of points does not exceed those generally charged in the area and are computed as a percentage of the mortgage. If the points exceed those generally charged, only the usual amount can be deducted in the year of payment; the balance must be deducted ratably over the term of the loan.
- The funds provided by the taxpayer at or before closing (including any points paid by the seller) are at least as much as the points charged and are not borrowed from the lender or mortgage broker.
- The points are identified on Form HUD-1, *Settlement Statement*, as points.
- The points are not paid in place of items that ordinarily are separately stated on the statement, such as appraisal fees, attorney fees, inspection fees, property taxes, and title fees.
- The taxpayer uses the cash method of accounting.
- The points are computed as a percentage of the principal amount.

TIP: Funds provided by the taxpayer at or before closing do not have to be used to pay points. They can be applied toward a down payment, an escrow deposit, earnest money, and other closing costs.

Refinancing

Points paid to refinance an existing mortgage on the home are not fully deductible in the year of payment; they are deductible over the term of the loan. However, additional funds obtained through refinancing used to substantially improve a principal residence allow the homeowner to deduct the portion of the points relating to these funds.

TIP: Even if a taxpayer qualifies to deduct points in the year paid, he or she is not required to do so. Instead, the taxpayer can choose to spread the deduction over the term of the loan, which may be more beneficial to him or her.

Example

In 2003, Mary bought a principal residence and obtained a 25-year mortgage secured by the home. Because of low interest rates in 2012, she refinanced with a 15-year mortgage at a lower interest rate and used all of the proceeds to pay off the first mortgage. She had to pay three points out of pocket to obtain the new loan. All of the points must be deducted ratably over 15 years because the proceeds were used to refinance an existing mortgage, not to buy, build, or substantially improve a principal residence.

If Mary's refinancing provides her with additional funds that she uses to add a new room to her house, the points on the portion of the proceeds used for this purpose can be deducted in 2012 (assuming all of the other conditions are met). The balance of the points is deducted ratably over the remaining 15 years.

Any remaining balance of points can be deducted in the year that a mortgage is paid off early because of a prepayment when the home is sold, refinanced with a different lender, or foreclosed on.

Example

Continuing the previous example, assume that Mary sells her home in 2015, after deducting 36 months of points. She can deduct the remaining points in 2015.

Special Situations

Points Paid by the Seller Loan placement fees (points) paid by the seller to arrange financing for the buyer are not deductible by the seller. They are treated as a selling expense that reduces the amount realized on the sale (i.e., it reduces the gain).

The buyer reduces the basis of the home by the amount of seller-paid points and treats them as if he or she had paid them. The buyer can then deduct the points over the life of the loan or in the year of payment, provided the buyer meets the requirements to deduct points.

Original Issue Discount A taxpayer who does not qualify to deduct points in the year of payment or ratably over the term of the loan must reduce the issue price of the loan by the amount of the points. This reduction is treated as original issue discount (see Chapter 5).

TIP: Even though mortgage insurance premiums technically are not interest, they can be considered interest under the tax law. The Internal Revenue Code section authorizing the deduction (§163(h)(3)(E)) is called "Mortgage insurance premiums treated as interest."

The premiums may also be called funding fees by the Department of Veterans Affairs or guarantee fees by the Rural Housing Service.

Mortgage Insurance Premiums

A taxpayer who cannot pay at least 20% of the purchase price usually has to carry mortgage insurance to protect the lender. Mortgage insurance can be purchased from a private company, the Department of Veterans Affairs, the Federal Housing Administration, or the Rural Housing Service.

Private mortgage insurance premiums can be deducted as home mortgage interest through 2011. To qualify, the insurance contract must have been issued after December 31, 2006, in connection with home acquisition debt.

Before you begin: ✓ See the instructions for line 13 to see if you must use this worksheet to figure your deduction.

1. Enter the total premiums you paid in 2012 for qualified mortgage insurance for a contract issued after December 31, 2006 . . . . . 1. ______
2. Enter the amount from Form 1040, line 38 . . . . . 2. ______
3. Enter $100,000 ($50,000 if married filing separately) . . . . . 3. ______
4. Is the amount on line 2 more than the amount on line 3?
   - ☐ **No.** Your deduction is not limited. Enter the amount from line 1 above on Schedule A, line 13. **Do not** complete the rest of this worksheet.
   - ☐ **Yes.** Subtract line 3 from line 2. If the result is not a multiple of $1,000 ($500 if married filing separately), increase it to the next multiple of $1,000 ($500 if married filing separately). For example, increase $425 to $1,000, increase $2,025 to $3,000; or if married filing separately, increase $425 to $500, increase $2,025 to $2,500, etc. . . . . . 4. ______
5. Divide line 4 by $10,000 ($5,000 if married filing separately). Enter the result as a decimal. If the result is 1.0 or more, enter 1.0 . . . . . 5. ___ . ___
6. Multiply line 1 by line 5 . . . . . 6. ______
7. **Mortgage insurance premiums deduction.** Subtract line 6 from line 1. Enter the result here and on Schedule A, line 13 . . . . . 7. ______

FIGURE 22.3 Mortgage Insurance Premium Deduction Worksheet

Deductibility of the premiums depends on a taxpayer's adjusted gross income (AGI). If AGI is $100,000 or less ($50,000 or less if married filing separately), then the full amount is deductible. The deduction phases out until AGI reaches $109,000 ($54,500 if married filing separately). No deduction can be claimed if AGI exceeds these limits. The phase-out reduces the otherwise deductible amount by 10% for each $1,000 or fraction of $1,000 by which the taxpayer's AGI exceeds $100,000 (10% for each $500 or fraction of $500 for taxpayers filing MFS returns whose AGI exceeds $54,500).

TIP: Mortgage insurance premiums typically are reported on Form 1098 in Box 4. If not, the taxpayer should contact the mortgage insurance issuer to determine the amount of premiums paid.

Use Figure 22.3 to determine the amount of the deduction for mortgage insurance premiums.

If premiums from a private mortgage company or the Federal Housing Administration are prepaid, they must be allocated and deducted over the shorter of the term of the mortgage or 84 months. No allocation is required for premiums for coverage from the Department of Veterans Affairs or the Rural Housing Service.

ALERT: If mortgage insurance premiums have been amortized and the homeowner sells the residence before fully deducting the premiums, the unamortized amount is *not* deductible.

Investment Interest

Interest paid to borrow money that is used to buy property held for investment may be deductible as an investment interest expense. Property purchased for investment can include any property held that produces income. For a cash-basis taxpayer, this interest is deductible when it is paid.

The interest can be paid on many types of loans as long as the loan proceeds are used to produce investment income. A common type of investment interest

TIP: Investment interest expense includes interest allocable to investment income passed through from a passive investment in a partnership, estate, trust, or S corporation.

DEFINITION: A taxpayer can make the **capital gain election** to treat qualified dividends and net capital gain from the disposition of property as investment income. One reason for this election is to allow the taxpayer to utilize investment expense that would not otherwise be deductible. The taxpayer would need to determine which option is better (favorable tax rates for qualified dividends or income to offset investment interest expense). If the taxpayer makes this election, the income subject to the election is not eligible to be taxed at long-term capital gains rates. The election may be revoked only with IRS consent.

TIP: Any investment interest carryover from the prior year is treated as paid or incurred in the current year. Any investment interest that could not be deducted in the current year because of the investment income limitation can be carried to the next year as interest paid or accrued.

is margin interest paid by an investor who buys stock with money borrowed from a broker.

Deductible investment interest does *not* include:

- Interest paid to produce tax-exempt income
- Interest used in determining a taxpayer's income or loss from an active participation rental real estate activity or other passive activity
- Home mortgage interest
- Interest that must be capitalized (e.g., under the uniform capitalization rules)
- Interest expense on debt to purchase certain life insurance, endowment, or annuity contracts

If a taxpayer borrows money and uses the funds to buy both investment and personal-use or business-use property, the interest expense must be allocated based on the funds spent on each type of property. This allocation is known as sourcing or tracing the interest expense.

Investors must limit the deduction for investment interest to the amount of net investment income for the year. Interest expense in excess of net investment income may be carried forward and is subject to the limitation in the year to which it is carried.

Example

Ryan had investment income of $8,000 and investment expenses (other than investment interest) of $500 (after taking into account the 2%-of-AGI floor). His net investment income is $7,500 ($8,000 – $500). The maximum deduction for investment interest expense is limited to net investment income, or $7,500. If Ryan has $7,800 in investment interest expenses, $300 ($7,800 – $7,500) of investment interest expense is not deductible.

Investment interest may be entered directly on the Investment Interest line of Schedule A if all the next conditions are met:

- Investment income from interest and ordinary dividends less any qualified dividends is more than the investment interest expense.
- Investment interest expense is not more than investment income without regard to the **capital gain election**.
- The taxpayer has no other deductible investment expenses.
- There is no carryover of investment interest expense from a prior year.

If any of these qualifications is not met, Form 4952, *Investment Interest Expense Deduction*, must be used to compute the amount of currently deductible investment interest expense and any amounts to be carried over.

Review Questions

1. A taxpayer's mortgage on his personal residence was obtained in 1985 when he bought the home. This mortgage is called:

a. Grandfathered debt

b. Acquisition debt

c. Home equity debt

d. Mortgage debt

2. All of the following can be treated as a qualified home **except**:

a. A condominium

b. A mobile home

c. A large motor boat with no toilet facilities

d. A unit in a two-family home in which the taxpayer resides

3. Which of the following is **not** deductible?

a. A late payment charge on a mortgage

b. Prepaid interest

c. Prepayment penalty

d. Interest paid through mortgage assistance payments under section 235 of the National Housing Act

4. Which of the following is **not** a condition for deducting points in the year of payment?

a. The taxpayer's AGI cannot exceed a set amount.

b. The proceeds of the loan must be used to buy, build, or substantially improve the taxpayer's principal residence.

c. The charging of points must be an established business practice in the area in which the mortgage is obtained.

d. The amount of points cannot exceed those generally charged in the area and are computed as a percentage of the mortgage.

5. For purposes of figuring the deduction for investment interest, which is **not** treated as investment income?

a. Net long-term capital gains

b. Bank interest

c. Qualified dividends which the taxpayer elects to treat as ordinary income

d. Royalties not from a trade or business

Charitable Contributions

Taxpayers who contribute cash or noncash items to a qualified organization may deduct their charitable contributions. The contributions must be made with no expectation of receiving any goods or services in return. Only taxpayers who itemize deductions can deduct their charitable contributions.

Deductions can include cash, securities, and noncash items of value as well as out-of-pocket expenses incurred while performing services for the charitable organization. The amount of the deduction may be limited by a taxpayer's adjusted gross income. However, excess contributions can be carried forward for up to five years.

No deduction is allowed without proper substantiation, the form of which varies depending on the type and amount of contribution involved.

Qualifying Organizations

Only donations to a qualified organization can be deductible. There are five categories of qualified organizations:

1. An organization organized or created in or under the laws of the United States (or its possessions) that is operated for a religious, charitable, educational, scientific, or literary purpose, or for the prevention of cruelty to children or animals. An organization that fosters national or international amateur sports competition may also be qualified.
2. War veterans' organizations, such as posts, auxiliaries, trusts, and foundations, that are organized in the United States or any of its possessions.
3. Domestic fraternal societies, orders, and associations operating under a lodge system. Contributions to these organizations are allowed only to the extent they are used for religious, charitable, educational, scientific, or literary purposes, or for the prevention of cruelty to children or animals.

TIP: Donations to certain foreign charitable organizations may also be deductible under income tax treaties. Contributions to charitable organizations in Canada, Israel, and Mexico are deductible by a taxpayer who has income from sources within the country to which they are made. More information about contributions to Canadian charities is in IRS Pub. 597, *Information on the United States–Canada Income Tax Treaty*. More information about contributions to Israel and Mexico is in IRS Pub. 526, *Charitable Contributions*.

TIP: Charitable organizations such as the Red Cross and the United Way are clearly qualified organizations. However, not all qualified organizations are as well known. Therefore, if in doubt, check IRS Pub. 78, *Cumulative List of Organizations*, which is an online cumulative list of IRS-approved organizations. (Enter "Pub. 78" in the search box at www.irs.gov, or go to www.irs.gov/Charities-&-Non-Profits/Exempt-Organizations-Select-Check.)

4. Nonprofit cemetery companies or corporations, provided donations are not used for the care of a specific lot or mausoleum crypt.
5. The United States or any state, the District of Columbia, a U.S. possession, a political subdivision of a state or U.S. possession, or an Indian tribal government or any of its subdivisions that perform substantial government functions, provided donations are made solely for public purposes.

Table 23.1 presents a list of the types of organizations that do and do not qualify for purposes of charitable contributions.

TABLE 23.1 Examples of Charitable Contributions—A Quick Check

Deductible As Charitable Contributions	Not Deductible As Charitable Contributions
Money or property you give to: • Churches, synagogues, temples, mosques, and other religious organizations • Federal, state, and local governments, if your contribution is solely for public purposes (for example, a gift to reduce the public debt) • Nonprofit schools and hospitals • Public parks and recreation facilities • Salvation Army, Red Cross, CARE, Goodwill Industries, United Way, Boy Scouts, Girl Scouts, Boys and Girls Clubs of America, etc. • War veterans' groups • Expenses paid for a student living with you, sponsored by a qualified organization • Out-of-pocket expenses when you serve a qualified organization as a volunteer	Money or property you give to: • Civic leagues, social and sports clubs, labor unions, and chambers of commerce • Foreign organizations (except certain Canadian, Israeli, and Mexican charities) • Groups that are run for personal profit • Groups whose purpose is to lobby for law changes • Homeowners' associations • Individuals • Political groups or candidates for public office • Cost of raffle, bingo, or lottery tickets • Dues, fees, or bills paid to country clubs, lodges, fraternal orders, or similar groups • Tuition • Value of your time or services • Value of blood given to a blood bank

Deductible Contributions

Only contributions made to or for the use of a qualified organization are deductible. A donation "for the use of" a qualified organization means a gift held in a legally enforceable trust for the organization or in a similar trust arrangement.

Gifts that Benefit the Taxpayer

A taxpayer who makes a contribution and also receives a benefit from the organization can deduct only the amount in excess of the benefit received. A taxpayer who pays more than fair market value (FMV) to an organization for goods or services can deduct only the amount in excess of FMV. The donation must have been made with intent to make a charitable contribution. Thus, a taxpayer who makes a payment to a charitable organization for the main purpose of obtaining services will not be able to claim a charitable deduction.

ALERT: No deduction can be claimed for a donation made to or set aside for a specific person. Thus, a payment made to a hospital for the care of a specific person is not deductible, even though the hospital is a qualified charitable organization.

Example

Gail pays $85 for a ticket to a luncheon held by a charitable organization. The FMV of the luncheon is $25. Gail's deduction is limited to $60 ($85 – $25).

Gail pays $500 at a charity auction entitling her to the use of a ski house for a week. The value of the week's stay is $500. Gail cannot take any deduction for this payment.

Athletic Events If a taxpayer makes a payment to or for the benefit of a college or university that entitles the taxpayer to buy tickets to a sporting event, then only 80% of the payment is deductible.

Example

Evan gives $500 a year for a membership in his alma mater's athletic scholarship program. As a result of the donation he is entitled to receive one season ticket valued at $150. Evan's deduction is $280 ([$500 – $150] × 80%).

If Evan's donation entitled him to purchase, rather than receive, a ticket, his deduction would have been $400 ($500 × 80%).

Charity Benefit Events A taxpayer who pays a qualified organization more than the cost of attending a charity ball, banquet, show, sporting event, or other benefit event can deduct only the amount exceeding the cost of the event, even if the ticket states that the payment is a fully deductible contribution. The cost of the event is the established value of the event or a reasonable value if there is no established value.

Example

Lili pays $50 to see a special theater performance benefitting a qualified organization. The ticket shows: "Contribution—$50." The regular ticket price is $10, so Lili's deduction is $40 ($50 payment – $10 regular ticket price).

Membership Fees or Dues A payment of fees or dues to a qualified organization is deductible only to the extent that it exceeds the value of the benefit received. Annual dues to churches and synagogues are fully deductible; there is no monetary value for the benefit of attending services.

However, a payment to a church or synagogue for a student to attend religious school (i.e., tuition) is not a deductible payment. Rather, it is a nondeductible personal expense.

ALERT: No deduction can be claimed for dues, fees, or assessments paid to a nonqualified organization, such as a country club or other social organization.

Certain benefits received by a taxpayer in return for an annual payment of $75 or less are disregarded:

- Rights or privileges (other than athletic events as discussed earlier), such as free or discounted admission to the organization's facilities or events, free or discounted parking, preferred access to goods or services, and discounts on the purchase of goods and services
- Admission for a member to events open only to members, as long as the cost per person (excluding allocated overhead) in 2012 does not exceed $9.90

Token items, such as calendars, refrigerator magnets, or mugs, are disregarded provided the organization tells the taxpayer that the donation is fully deductible.

A taxpayer must obtain a written statement from an organization to which the taxpayer contributes more than $75 that is part contribution and part payment for goods and services. The statement should indicate that only the payment exceeding the value of goods and services is deductible. The statement should also give the taxpayer a good faith estimate of the value of those goods and services so the amount of the deduction can be determined. However, no statement is required if the goods and services are only a token amount, are the type of disregarded membership benefits (described earlier), or if the organization is a government or religious organization.

Expenses Paid for a Student Living with the Taxpayer

ALERT: No deduction can be claimed for a foreign exchange student who lives in a taxpayer's home under a mutual exchange program entitling the taxpayer's child to live with a family in a foreign country.

A deduction of up to $50 per month can be claimed for any month in which a foreign or American student lives with a taxpayer, as long as all of the following conditions are met for at least 15 days within a month:

- The student is there under a written agreement between the taxpayer and the qualified organization as part of a program to provide educational opportunities for the student.
- The student is not the taxpayer's relative or dependent.
- The student is a full-time student in any grade K–12 in the United States.

Out-of-Pocket Expenses

A taxpayer's out-of-pocket expenses in rendering services to a qualified organization are deductible.

The expenses must be:

- Unreimbursed by the organization
- Directly connected with the services
- Incurred only because of the services
- An expense other than personal, living, or family expenses

Special rules apply to certain types of out-of-pocket expenses:

- *Conventions.* Only a taxpayer who is chosen as a representative or delegate of a qualified organization for a convention can deduct travel, lodging, meals, and other convention-related expenses. A taxpayer attending as a member of the organization cannot deduct these costs.
- *Uniforms.* The cost of uniforms to perform services as a volunteer is deductible only if the uniforms are not suitable for normal everyday use (e.g., the cost of a volunteer candy striper's uniform at a hospital).
- *Foster parents.* The costs related to one's service as a foster care provider are deductible if the taxpayer has no profit motive in providing the care and is not making a profit. The payments also must be made mainly to benefit the organization. Allowable costs include unreimbursed out-of-pocket expenses for food, clothing, and medical care.
- *Car expenses.* A taxpayer can deduct gas and oil paid for driving for charitable purposes. Alternatively, the taxpayer can deduct driving at the rate of 14¢ per mile, plus parking and tolls. A careful record of driving must be retained by the taxpayer in order to claim these expenses.

Example

Julie donates blood to her local blood bank. She cannot deduct the donation, although she can deduct her travel costs to and from the donation site if she maintains a record of her mileage for this purpose.

- *Travel.* The cost of travel is deductible only if there is no significant element of personal pleasure, recreation, or vacation in the travel. It does not matter whether payment for the travel is made directly by the individual or indirectly through the charity. However, a deduction is not prevented merely because the taxpayer enjoys providing services to the organization.

Example

Ian, a troop leader for a youth group, takes the group on a camping trip. He is responsible for setting up camp and providing adult supervision. His travel costs are deductible.

If Ian were to go on an archeological dig sponsored by a charitable organization, but spent only the mornings on the dig and the rest of the day sightseeing, no part of the travel costs would be deductible because the travel would have significant elements of personal pleasure, recreation, and vacation.

If Ian was the organization's representative to a regional meeting and attended the meeting all day, his travel costs would be deductible even if he participated in personal activities at night.

Deductible travel expenses include air, rail, or bus transportation, out-of-pocket car expenses, taxi and other transportation to and from the airport or station. Deductible expenses also include lodging and meals.

ALERT: No deduction can be taken for the value of a taxpayer's services rendered to or for the benefit of the organization. No deduction can be taken for blood donations to the Red Cross or other blood banks. For example, an attorney who performs legal work for her church cannot deduct what she would have charged a client for her services. However, she can deduct any out-of-pocket costs related to the services, such as postage or printing costs.

TIP: Unreimbursed expenses of a foster parent that are not deductible as a charitable contribution may be considered support in determining whether the foster child is the taxpayer's dependent. Thus, while payments for the care of a foster child that the taxpayer hopes to adopt are not made for the benefit of the organization and do not qualify as a charitable contribution, they do count toward the support of the child for purposes of the dependency exemption.

Contributions of Property

Generally, the FMV of property given to a qualified organization is deductible.

TIP: If the organization gives the taxpayer a per diem allowance to cover travel expenses, any payment exceeding the actual amount of travel expenses is income to the taxpayer.

Amount to Deduct

Determining the amount of the deduction depends on the type of property donated and whether the property has increased or decreased in value.

Property that Has Increased in Value When property has increased in value since the taxpayer acquired it, the appreciation (increase in value) may have to be reduced when figuring the deduction, depending on whether the property is ordinary income or capital gain property.

TIP: If an appraisal is required to determine the FMV of the donated property, the cost of the appraisal is deductible as a miscellaneous itemized deduction. The cost of the appraisal is not part of the charitable deduction, although the cost can be deducted as a miscellaneous itemized deduction subject to the 2%-of-adjusted gross income (AGI) limit.

- The FMV of capital gain property is deductible in full unless certain exceptions apply. These exceptions are beyond the scope of this book.
- The FMV of ordinary income property is reduced by the amount that would be ordinary income or short-term capital gain if sold. Thus, the deduction for ordinary income property is generally limited to its basis.

Ordinary income property is the type of property that would produce ordinary income or short-term capital gain if it were sold. Examples of ordinary income property include capital assets (e.g., stocks and bonds) held one year or less, inventory, and works of art created by the taxpayer.

Example

Victoria donates 100 shares of stock in X Corporation that she bought seven months ago for $5,000. The stock is now worth $6,000, but her deduction is limited to $5,000 because the stock was not held for more than one year (making the stock ordinary income property). Her deduction is calculated as the $6,000 FMV minus $1,000 short-term capital gain on the sale.

Capital gain property is property held longer than one year as well as certain real property and depreciable property used in a trade or business and held more than one year.

TIP: A taxpayer who wants to donate property with an FMV less than the taxpayer's basis should consider selling the property and then donating the proceeds to the charity. This allows the taxpayer to both recognize the loss and deduct the cash contribution. (The property cannot be personal-use property for which no loss can be claimed.)

Bargain sales. A sale or exchange of property to an organization at less than the property's FMV is treated as part contribution and part sale or exchange. The bargain sale part may result in taxable gain to the taxpayer, as explained in Pub. 526.

Property that Has Decreased in Value If the FMV of the property at the time of the donation is less than the taxpayer's basis in the property, the donation is limited to the FMV. No loss can be recognized when making a donation.

Contributions Subject to Special Rules

Certain types of property donations have special rules for determining the amount of the deduction and the type of substantiation required for the donation.

Clothing and Household Items Used clothing and household goods may be deducted only at their FMV at the time of the donation, regardless of what the taxpayer paid for them. Determining the value of these items can be challenging. Here are some ways of determining value:

- For used clothing, the value is the price that a buyer of such items would pay in used clothing stores, such as consignment shops.
- IRS Pub. 561, *Determining the Value of Donated Property*, can be helpful. However, note that this publication has not been updated since 2007.

A deduction is allowed at FMV only if the used item is in "good used condition." However, if an item is valued at over $500 by a qualified appraisal, FMV can be used even if the item is not in good used or better condition.

Cars, Boats, and Planes If a taxpayer claims a deduction for more than $500 for donating any of these vehicles, the deduction is limited to the lesser of:

- The gross proceeds from the sale of the vehicle by the organization, OR
- The vehicle's FMV on the date of the donation. If the vehicle's FMV is greater than the taxpayer's basis, the FMV may have to be reduced. This reduction is described in the section earlier in this chapter titled "Property That Has Increased in Value."

TIP: The organization must issue Form 1098-C, *Contributions of Motor Vehicles, Boats, and Airplanes*, to the taxpayer for each donated vehicle with a claimed value more than $500. Copy B of this form must be attached to the taxpayer's return.

However, a donation of a vehicle worth more than $500 is not subject to the deduction limitation (i.e., the full FMV can be deducted) if either of these two exceptions applies:

- The vehicle is used or improved by the organization (e.g., a car donated to Meals on Wheels used by the organization to deliver meals meets this exception).
- The vehicle is given or sold to a needy individual by the organization. This exception does not apply if the organization sells the vehicle at an auction.

If the qualified organization sells the vehicle for $500 or less and neither exception just listed applies, the taxpayer's deduction is the lesser of:

- $500, OR
- The vehicle's FMV on the date of the contribution. If the vehicle's FMV is greater than the basis, then the FMV may have to be reduced. This reduction is described in the section earlier in this chapter titled "Property That Has Increased in Value."

Conservation Contribution A *qualified conservation contribution* is a contribution of an interest in qualified real property to a qualified organization. A *qualified organization* in this case is a governmental unit, publicly supported charity, or organization controlled and operated for the exclusive benefit of a governmental unit or publicly supported charity. The interest in the qualified real property must be used for conservation purposes.

Special rules apply to conservation contributions. See IRS Pub. 561 for more detail.

Other Special Situations Generally, only a donation of an entire interest in property can be deducted. The right to use property is viewed as a contribution of less than the entire interest in property and is not deductible.

A donation of a future interest in tangible personal property, such as furniture, books, jewelry, and cars, is deductible only after the intervening interests in or rights to possession of the property have expired or been turned over to the charity.

Example

Gil owns an antique car that he donates to a museum with the condition that the car remains in his garage. No deduction can be claimed until possession of the car is transferred to the museum.

Special rules also apply to donations of inventory as well as patents and other intellectual property. These rules are explained in IRS Pub. 561.

Nondeductible Contributions

As mentioned earlier in this chapter, some types of contributions are not deductible, including:

- *Contributions to nonqualified organizations.* Donations to nonqualified organizations are not deductible; these include donations made to communist or terrorist organizations, country clubs and other social clubs, and foreign organizations. (There are some exceptions.) However, donations may be deductible as business expenses. For example, a business expense deduction may be allowed for payments to bar associations, chambers of commerce, and civic leagues and associations.
- *Contributions to individuals.* Donations directly to a needy individual, such as a hurricane victim, are not deductible. Only contributions to organizations that benefit victims in general are deductible.
- *Contributions from which the taxpayer benefits.* No deduction is allowed for lobbying, state lotteries, dues to fraternal orders (other than membership dues discussed earlier in this chapter), or amounts paid to parochial or nonprofit day care centers for a child or dependent. No deduction is allowed for contributions to a retirement home that are for room, board, maintenance, or admittance.
- *Value of time and services.* The value of volunteer work is not deductible. The cost of donating a body part, such as a kidney, is not deductible. However, related medical costs may be a medical expense deduction (see Chapter 20).
- *Personal expenses.* Adoption fees paid to an agency are not a charitable contribution. However, they may entitle the taxpayer to an adoption credit (see Chapter 31).

Recordkeeping and Substantiation

Special rules govern what records and other proof must be obtained in order to deduct donations.

Cash Contributions

Cash contributions are donations by cash, check, credit or debit card, electronic funds transfer, or a payroll deduction. No deduction is allowed unless the taxpayer has one of the following to prove the contribution:

- A bank record, such as a canceled check, bank or credit union statement, or credit card statement, showing the name of the qualified organization, the date of the contribution, and the amount of the contribution
- A receipt or letter from the qualified organization showing the name of the qualified organization, the date of the contribution, and the amount of the contribution
- For a payroll deduction, a pay stub, W-2 form, or other document from the employer showing the date of the contribution and the amount of the contribution and a pledge card or other document from the organization that shows the organization's name

Contributions of $250 or More Contributions of $250 or more require a written acknowledgment from the charity or certain payroll deduction records (a pay stub or W-2 form and a pledge card, plus other documentation if these do not show the date of the contribution).

Example

Elsa donates $300 by check to a qualified organization and receives nothing in return. Elsa cannot deduct the contribution unless she obtains a written acknowledgment from the organization; her canceled check is not sufficient documentation.

If more than one donation of $250 or more is made to a particular organization, a separate acknowledgment is required for each donation unless one acknowledgment lists each separate donation (amount and date) and then totals the annual amount.

ALERT: Out-of-pocket expenses are treated like cash contributions. Thus, adequate records of such expenses are necessary. For example, a taxpayer who drives his or her car for charitable purposes must keep a record of the mileage, date, and purpose of each trip. If out-of-pocket expenses are $250 or more, an acknowledgment from the organization is required.

The acknowledgment must meet all of these conditions:

- It is in writing.
- It states the amount of the cash contribution, whether any goods or services were furnished by the organization (other than token or membership benefits), a description of the goods and services and a good faith estimate of their value, and a statement that the only benefit received is an intangible religious benefit (admission to a religious service), if applicable.

- The acknowledgment is received by the earlier of the date that the return is filed or the due date, including extensions, for the filing of the return.

Noncash Contributions

Property donations require special substantiation. The type necessary depends on whether the contribution is:

- Less than $250
- At least $250 but not more than $500
- Over $500 but not more than $5,000
- Over $5,000

Whether the $500 threshold is exceeded is determined by adding all similar items of property made to any organization during the year. When goods or services are received in exchange for the donation, the amount of the donation is reduced by the goods and services. The dollar limit is based on the property's FMV on the date of the donation (or the value reduced by appreciation where applicable).

Donations of Less than $250 A taxpayer must keep a receipt from the organization showing the name of the organization, the date and location of the contribution, and a reasonably detailed description of the property. A written acknowledgment from the charity can serve as a receipt. However, no receipt is required if obtaining a receipt is impractical, such as a taxpayer leaving property at a charity's drop site (e.g., a Goodwill box).

The taxpayer must also keep a written record of each item of property donated, including:

- The name and address of the organization
- The date and location of the contribution
- A description of the property
- The FMV of the property and how it was determined
- The cost or other basis of the property
- The amount claimed as a deduction
- Any terms or conditions attached to the gift

Donations of at Least $250 but Not More than $500 Donations of at least $250 but not more than $500 (including deductible out-of-pocket volunteer expenses) require the name, date, and location of the charitable organization along with a description of the property. Additionally, these donations require a written acknowledgment similar to the type required for certain cash donations. This acknowledgment must indicate whether the goods or services were given for the contribution, a good faith estimate of the value of the goods or services given (if any), and whether the only benefit was a religious benefit. This information should be provided on or before the earlier of the date the return is filed or the due date, including extensions, for filing the return.

Donations Over $500 but Not Over $5,000 In addition to the acknowledgment and written records required for a deduction of at least $250, for donations over $500 but not over $5,000, the taxpayer also needs records to show:

- How the property was acquired (by purchase, gift, etc.).
- The approximate date it was acquired. If the taxpayer created it, then the approximate date of creation.
- The cost or other basis of property held 12 months or less and, if available, the basis of property held more than 12 months. This requirement does not apply to publicly traded securities.

A taxpayer who has reasonable cause for not knowing the date of acquisition or basis should attach to the return an explanation for lacking this information.

Donations Over $5,000 In addition to the information required for a donation over $500, a qualified written appraisal from a qualified appraiser is necessary for donations over $5,000. Details about this requirement are described in Pub. 561.

Form 8283 Form 8283, *Noncash Charitable Contributions*, must be filed if the total of noncash contributions for the year exceeds $500. The amount of the donation dictates which sections of the form must be completed.

When to Deduct Contributions

Contributions are deductible only in the year they are made, regardless of a taxpayer's method of accounting. Special rules apply to certain donations:

- *Borrowed funds.* A contribution made with borrowed funds is deductible, regardless of when the loan is repaid.
- *Checks.* The date of mailing is considered the date of delivery (the date of the donation).
- *Credit card.* The date the donation is charged to the card is the date of the donation, even when the credit card bill is paid in the following year.
- *Option.* An option given to an organization to buy property at a bargain price is not deductible until the organization exercises the option.
- *Pay-by-phone account.* The date that the financial institution pays the organization is the date of donation; this can be after the date that the taxpayer calls the institution to make the donation.
- *Promissory note.* A pledge or other promissory note is not deductible until the actual donation is made.

- *Stock certificate.* The date of mailing or delivery of the certificate to the charity is the date of the donation. A stock certificate given to a transfer agent or issuing corporation for transfer to the name of the organization is not deductible until the stock is transferred on the books of the corporation.

Limits on Deductions

Total donations for the year of 20% or less of a taxpayer's AGI are fully deductible; no limitations apply. Donations exceeding this percentage are subject to the following limits:

- *100% of AGI.* Contributions of conservation easements by farmers and ranchers in tax years 2006 through 2013.
- *50% of AGI.* The total deduction for all contributions made during the year cannot exceed 50% of AGI (a higher limit may apply to donations of certain conservation easements, discussed above). In addition, contributions to 50% limit organizations (most public charities) are limited to 50%.
- *50% of AGI.* Contributions of conservation easements by individual taxpayers other than farmers and ranchers in tax years 2006 through 2013.
- *30% of AGI.* There are two 30% limits. One applies to gifts made to organizations other than to 50% limit organizations, such as veterans' organizations, fraternal societies, nonprofit cemeteries, and certain private nonoperating foundations as well as gifts for the use of any organization that is a 50% limit organization. The other is capital gain property donations to a 50% limit organization. However, a taxpayer can opt to avoid the 30% limit for capital gain property when the FMV of the property is reduced by the amount that would have been long-term capital gain if the property had been sold. See IRS Pub. 526 for more information on making this choice.
- *20% of AGI.* This limit applies to capital gain property donated to or for the use of an organization that is not a 50% limit organization.

Carryovers

Contributions in excess of any AGI limit can be carried forward for up to five years until the excess is used up. Special rules apply to a carryover of an excess conservation property contribution. There is no carryback for excess charitable contributions. Carryovers are explained in IRS Pub. 526.

Carryovers are subject to the same percentage of AGI limit in the carryover year. For example, property subject to the 30% limit in the year in which the contribution is made is subject to a 30% limit in the carryover year.

Carryovers are taken into account only after determining the charitable deduction allowed in the current year. The total amount of contributions a taxpayer may carry over cannot exceed 50% of the taxpayer's AGI.

Example

In 2012, Geoff, whose AGI is $24,000, made a cash donation of $14,000 to a 50% limit organization. His 2012 deduction is limited to $12,000, 50% of his AGI, and $2,000 is carried over to 2013. In 2013, Geoff contributes another $10,000 to a 50% limit organization. Geoff's AGI in 2013 increases to $110,000, so he can deduct the entire 2013 contribution of $10,000 plus the $2,000 carried over from 2012.

However, a carryover of a contribution to a 50%-limit organization must be used before current-year contributions to organizations other than 50%-limit organizations.

Review Questions

1. Which of these organizations is **not** a qualified organization for charitable contribution purposes?
   a. An organization that fosters international amateur sports
   b. A war veterans' post
   c. A church in Brazil
   d. The U.S. government

2. Earl pays $100 to attend a charity theater party. The tickets for this performance normally cost $75. His adjusted gross income is $36,000. How much can Earl deduct as an itemized deduction?
   a. $25
   b. $75
   c. $100
   d. $18,000

3. Which of the following types of out-of-pocket volunteer expenses is **not** deductible?
   a. The cost of attending a convention as a member of the organization
   b. Uniforms to perform services as a volunteer
   c. Driving to and from a school to volunteer in the classroom
   d. Airfare to perform volunteer work full time on an archeological dig

4. Which of the following contributions is deductible?
   a. Donations made to a country club
   b. Contributions to help a neighbor who suffered property damage in a fire
   c. The amount that would be charged by a preparer to do a tax return for her church
   d. Donations made to a special relief fund set up to help victims of Hurricane Sandy

5. In which situation can a charitable deduction be claimed even though the taxpayer has no receipt?
   a. Donations of less than $250 made in the church collection plate
   b. Used clothing of less than $250 put in the Salvation Army drop box
   c. Out-of-pocket volunteer costs of $250 or more
   d. A painting created by the taxpayer and valued at $6,000

6. Which statement concerning charitable contribution amounts in excess of the applicable AGI limit is correct?
   a. Unused amounts can be carried back for two years.
   b. Unused amounts can be carried forward indefinitely.
   c. Unused amounts can be carried forward for up to five years.
   d. Unused amounts are lost forever and cannot be carried back or forward.

7. In which situation must Form 8283 be filed?
   a. Cash donations totaling $8,000 for the year.
   b. A donation of used clothing valued at $350.
   c. Having out-of-pocket volunteer expenses of $200.
   d. A donation of stock valued at $750.

8. Stan donates his old car to a charity. He estimates that it is worth $700, but the charity immediately sells it for $450. What can Stan deduct?
   a. $0.
   b. $450
   c. $500
   d. $700

Nonbusiness Casualty and Theft Losses

A casualty or theft loss that is not covered by insurance or other reimbursement may be deductible as an itemized deduction. The loss is reported on Form 4684, *Casualties and Thefts*, and the total is transferred to Schedule A, *Itemized Deductions*, of Form 1040, *U.S. Individual Income Tax Return*, after accounting for two limitations:

1. Each separate casualty or theft loss is reduced by $100.
2. After this initial reduction, the total amount of all casualty and theft losses is reduced by 10% of adjusted gross income (AGI).

A taxpayer who suffers a disaster loss—which is a casualty loss occurring in an area eligible for federal disaster assistance—can choose to claim the deduction on the current or prior year's return.

A taxpayer who claims a casualty or theft loss must *decrease* the basis of property by both insurance reimbursements and any deductible casualty or theft loss. Amounts spent to restore property after a casualty *increase* the basis of the property.

When insurance or other reimbursements exceed the taxpayer's adjusted basis in the property, a tax gain can result from the loss of or damage to property. However, tax on the gain can be postponed, as explained in Chapter 13.

> **DEFINITION: Sudden** means swift, not gradual or progressive.
>
> **Unexpected** means ordinarily unanticipated and unintended.
>
> **Unusual** means not a day-to-day occurrence and something that is not typical of the activities in which the taxpayer is engaged.

What Is a Casualty?

Losses resulting from a casualty event are deductible. A *casualty* is an identifiable event that is **sudden**, **unexpected**, or **unusual**.

Examples of casualty events include:

- Car accidents
- Earthquakes
- Fires

- Floods
- Government-ordered demolition or relocation of a home that became unsafe due to a federally declared disaster
- Mine cave-ins
- Shipwrecks
- Sonic booms
- Storms, including hurricanes and tornadoes
- Terrorist attacks
- Vandalism
- Volcanic eruptions

Casualty losses from a federally declared disaster (disaster area losses) are explained in the "Disaster Losses" section later in this chapter.

Nondeductible Losses

Not all types of damage or destruction to property are the result of a casualty. No deduction can be taken for losses resulting from gradual or progressive deterioration or for certain other occurrences, including accidental breakage of articles like china or glassware under normal conditions, a car accident caused by the taxpayer's willful negligence or willful act, or a fire the taxpayer willfully set or paid someone to set.

Damage caused by a family pet usually is not deductible. It can be deductible only if it meets the casualty loss definition (sudden, unexpected, and unusual). Thus, damage to an antique Oriental rug from a puppy that is not yet house-broken is not a casualty because the damage is not unexpected or unusual. However, a fire resulting from a pet's knocking over an open container of flammable liquid in the garage may be deductible.

Progressive Deterioration Damage resulting from a steadily operating cause or normal process is not deductible; it is not from a sudden or unexpected event. Examples of nondeductible progressive deterioration include:

- Weakening of a building from normal wind and weather conditions over time.
- Damage to a water heater that bursts from deterioration. (However, any damage caused to other property, such as carpeting and drapes, from the bursting of the water heater is a casualty.)
- Losses due to drought in most cases.
- Termite and moth damage.
- Damage or destruction to trees, shrubs, and other plants from fungus, disease, insects, worms, or similar pests. (However, damage resulting from an unexpected or unusual infestation of beetles or other insects may be a casualty.)

Proof of Casualty Loss

To support a casualty loss deduction, the taxpayer should have records showing:

- The type of casualty, such as a hurricane or car accident, and when it occurred. If the loss is a casualty unique to the taxpayer, such as a car accident, a police report or other documentation can prove the date and nature of the event.
- Proof the loss directly resulted from the casualty.
- Whether a claim for reimbursement exists and whether there is a reasonable expectation of recovery. A taxpayer with insurance coverage who fails to make a claim cannot take a casualty loss.
- The taxpayer was the owner of the property or a lessee contractually liable to the owner for any damage to the property.

TIP: The taxpayer does not have to attach casualty loss records to the return. Records should be retained with the taxpayer's return for the year in which the loss is claimed.

What Is a Theft?

A *theft* is the taking of money or property with the intent to deprive the owner of it. The taking must be illegal under the laws of the state where it occurred, and it must be done with criminal intent. However, the taxpayer does not have to show a conviction for theft. A theft can occur through any of these means:

- Blackmail
- Burglary
- Embezzlement
- Extortion
- Fraud or misrepresentation if this is a theft under state or local law
- Kidnapping for ransom
- Larceny
- Robbery

If property merely disappears or is lost, that does not constitute a theft and no loss can be taken. However, an accidental loss or disappearance may qualify as a casualty if it results from an identifiable event that is sudden, unexpected, or unusual.

Example

A taxpayer wore her diamond pendant necklace while at the park with her three young children. Later that evening when she was at home, she discovered the necklace had disappeared. She did not know where or when this happened. She retraced her steps but did not find the necklace. Because she may have lost the necklace and could not confirm that the necklace was stolen, she cannot claim a theft loss deduction.

TIP: A capital loss resulting from the sale of stock, or from stock becoming completely worthless, is deductible (see Chapter 13).

No deduction can be taken for the decline in value of publicly traded stock, even if the decline results from the disclosure of accounting fraud or other illegal conduct by officers or directors of the corporation.

Ponzi-Type Investment Schemes

Generally, a taxpayer cannot deduct a theft loss if an investment declines in value, even if due to accounting fraud or similar illegal activity. However, losses from a Ponzi-type investment scheme may be treated as a theft loss of income-producing property. Under special rules, a current deduction can be claimed even though claims are pending against the thief or other sources. (See Revenue Ruling 2009-9, Revenue Procedure 2009-20, Revenue Procedure 2011-58, and IRS Pub. 547, *Disasters, Casualties, and Thefts,* for more details about deducting these types of losses.)

TIP: To deduct a theft loss, the taxpayer must be able to prove that the property was stolen. While proof of an actual theft may be difficult to produce, filing a police report may satisfy this requirement.

Theft Loss Proof

To support a theft loss deduction, the taxpayer should have records showing:

- When the taxpayer discovered the property was missing
- That the property was stolen
- Whether a claim for reimbursement was made for which there is a reasonable expectation of recovery
- That the taxpayer was the owner of the property

ALERT: Once the choice is made on how to deduct a lost deposit, it cannot be changed without permission from the IRS.

Loss on Deposits

A taxpayer who loses a deposit in a bank, credit union, or other financial institution because of the institution's insolvency or bankruptcy has three ways to deduct the loss. The taxpayer should consider the pros and cons of each before making a choice.

The three choices to deduct the loss are:

1. *As a casualty loss.* A casualty loss is reported on Form 4684 and then on Schedule A of Form 1040. This option can be used in any year in which the amount of the lost deposit can be reasonably determined. Using this option means that the $100 and 10%-of-AGI limits apply.
2. *As an ordinary loss.* An ordinary loss is reported on Schedule A as a miscellaneous itemized deduction. A taxpayer can claim a maximum of $20,000 ($10,000 if married filing separately) for the year, which is reduced by any expected state insurance proceeds. The loss can be claimed in any year in which the amount of the lost deposit can be reasonably determined. The loss is also subject to the 2%-of-AGI limit for miscellaneous itemized deductions. A taxpayer cannot claim an ordinary loss if any part of the deposit is federally insured.

3. *As a nonbusiness bad debt.* A nonbusiness bad debt deduction cannot be claimed until the year in which the actual loss is determined. This is reported on Form 8949, *Sales and Other Dispositions of Capital Assets,* and then on Schedule D (Form 1040), *Capital Gains and Losses.*

ALERT: When a loss has been deducted as a casualty loss or as an ordinary loss based on an estimate, and the actual amount of the loss turns out to be greater than the estimate, the additional amount can be deducted as a nonbusiness bad debt.

Figuring the Loss

The amount of the loss is based on financial benchmarks and is not dependent on the taxpayer's emotional or sentimental losses. The tax preparer uses three steps to figure the loss:

1. Determine the adjusted basis of the property before the casualty or theft. (Adjusted basis is explained in Chapter 12.)
2. Determine the decrease in the fair market value (FMV) of the property as a result of the casualty or theft.
3. The deductible loss is the smaller of the above two amounts less any insurance or other reimbursement received or expected to be received.

ALERT: Reimbursements exceeding the taxpayer's adjusted basis in the property result in a gain, even if the FMV of the property has declined. Tax on the gain, however, can be postponed by election (see Chapter 13).

Example

Vincent purchased a painting several years ago for $500, which is his adjusted basis in the property. This year, it was destroyed in a storm; the painting was not insured, and Vincent does not expect to receive any reimbursement. The FMV of the painting just before the casualty was $6,000. The casualty loss is $500 (the smaller of adjusted basis before the casualty, or decline in the FMV as a result of the casualty).

Decrease in FMV

The decrease in the FMV is the difference between the property's value immediately before and immediately after the event. For stolen property, the FMV is zero after the theft.

Example

Vincent also purchased another painting several years ago for $6,000, which is his adjusted basis in the property. This year, it too was completely destroyed, and this painting also was not insured. The FMV of the painting just before it was destroyed was $1,000. The casualty loss is $1,000 (the smaller of the adjusted basis before the casualty or the decline in the FMV as a result of the casualty).

Usually an appraisal is needed to determine the change in FMV before and after a casualty. The appraiser should be competent. There are several factors important to determining the accuracy of an appraisal. These factors are considered:

- The appraiser's familiarity with the property before and after the event
- The appraiser's knowledge about sales of similar property in the area

- The appraiser's knowledge of the conditions in the area of a casualty
- The appraiser's method of appraisal

An appraisal used to obtain a federal loan or loan guarantee as a result of a federally declared disaster can be used to establish the loss.

TIP: The cost of an appraisal is not part of the casualty loss. Appraisal fees can be deducted as a miscellaneous itemized deduction (see Chapter 25).

In some cases, taxpayers do not have to obtain an appraisal to determine the decrease in FMV. These cases are discussed next.

Cost of Cleaning Up or Making Repairs The cost of repairing or cleaning up property can be used to show the decrease in FMV if the taxpayer meets all of the following conditions:

- The repairs are actually made.
- The repairs are necessary to bring the property back to precasualty condition.
- The amount spent on repairs is not excessive.
- The repairs only correct the damage (and do not add to the property).
- The value of the property after the repairs is not more than the value of the property before the casualty (i.e., the repairs merely restore the property to precasualty condition).

Landscaping The cost of restoring landscaping to its precasualty condition is a measure of loss. The cost can include removing destroyed or damaged trees and plants (less any salvage received), pruning and other measures to preserve trees and plants, and replanting necessary to restore the property to its value before the casualty.

Car Value Retail values listed in books from various organizations (e.g., *Kelley Blue Book*) can be used to determine a car's value as long as the value reflects the taxpayer's mileage and actual condition of the car. A dealer's offer for the car as a trade-in is not usually a measure of the car's true value.

Insurance and Other Reimbursements

Insurance and other reimbursements are subtracted from the amount figured as the loss. There is no loss to the extent it is covered by insurance or other reimbursements. If there is insurance in place, the taxpayer must make a timely claim for the loss (even though this might raise premiums in the future).

Example

Margo was in a fender bender, which caused $4,500 of damage to her car. Her insurance policy had a $1,000 deductible. She paid $1,000 for the repair to cover the deductible, and her insurance company paid for the remaining cost of the repair. Her loss is limited to $1,000, the portion of the loss not covered by insurance.

Reimbursements that reduce a casualty loss include amounts received from an employer's emergency disaster fund. Reimbursements do not include cash received as gifts, such as from friends and relatives.

Insurance Payments for Living Expenses

When a taxpayer loses the use of his or her main home because of a casualty or when government authorities do not allow a taxpayer access to the taxpayer's main home, insurance payments to cover personal living expenses are not taken into account in determining a casualty loss.

The payments are not included in taxable income if they merely cover the increase in temporary living costs. However, if the payments exceed the temporary increase in living expenses, the excess is taxable. IRS Pub. 547 contains more about insurance payments for living expenses.

Example

The Browns, whose home was severely damaged by a fire, had to live in a motel until repairs were made. Their usual monthly living expenses are $2,000. However, for the period in which they lived in a motel, their temporary monthly living expenses were $3,000.

If their insurance reimburses them $800 per month for the increase in temporary living expenses, the payments are not included in taxable income.

However, if their insurance reimburses them $1,500 per month for the increase in temporary living expenses, $500 per month (the difference between the reimbursement and the increase in living expenses) will be taxable.

Disaster relief for food, medical supplies, and other assistance are not part of the casualty loss reimbursement unless they are replacements for lost or destroyed property. Disaster relief payments for reasonable and necessary personal living expenses resulting from a federally declared disaster are not taxable.

ALERT: A casualty or theft loss to property used in performing services as an employee is deductible as a miscellaneous itemized deduction. The $100 and 10%-of-AGI limits do not apply. Instead, employee business expenses, including a casualty or theft loss to employee property, are subject to a 2%-of-AGI limit.

Deduction Limits

Two limits apply to a casualty or theft loss deduction for personal use property:

1. *The $100 rule.* Reduce each total casualty and theft loss by $100, regardless of the number of items affected.
2. *The 10% rule.* Reduce the *total* of all the casualty and theft losses by 10% of AGI.

The application of the limits is shown in Table 24.1.

TABLE 24.1 How to Apply the Deduction Limits for Personal-Use Property

		$100 Rule	10% Rule
General Application		You must reduce each casualty or theft loss by $100 when figuring your deduction. Apply this rule to personal-use property after you have figured the amount of your loss.	You must reduce your total casualty or theft loss by 10% of your adjusted gross income. Apply this rule to personal-use property after you reduce each loss by $100 (the $100 rule).
Single Event		Apply this rule only once, even if many pieces of property are affected.	Apply this rule only once, even if many pieces of property are affected.
More Than One Event		Apply to the loss from each event.	Apply to the total of all your losses from all events.
More Than One Person— With Loss From the Same Event (other than a married couple filing jointly)		Apply separately to each person.	Apply separately to each person.
Married Couple— With Loss From the Same Event	Filing Joint Return	Apply as if you were one person.	Apply as if you were one person.
	Filing Separate Return	Apply separately to each spouse.	Apply separately to each spouse.
More Than One Owner (other than a married couple filing jointly)		Apply separately to each owner of jointly owned property.	Apply separately to each owner of jointly owned property.

Example

Mitchell's home and car were damaged as a result of a hurricane. The loss on the home and the car is reduced by $100 since they were both damaged in the same event.

Assume the uninsured damage to the home is $11,000 and the uninsured damage to the car is $1,000 (the car's deductible), for a combined loss of $12,000. If Mitchell's AGI is $48,000, his deductible loss is:

Loss after insurance	$12,000
Subtract $100	–$100
Loss after $100 limit	$11,900
Subtract 10% of AGI	–$4,800
Deductible Casualty loss	$7,100

Figuring a Gain

As discussed earlier, gain can result from a casualty or theft loss when reimbursements exceed a taxpayer's adjusted basis.

Example

Martha's diamond bracelet was stolen. She paid $2,500 for it, and it was worth $6,000 before the theft. She had it insured for $4,500 and received the full amount from her insurer. She has a gain of $2,000 ($4,500 insurance proceeds – $2,500 adjusted basis).

Compare the taxpayer's casualty and theft gains and losses (after applying the $100 and 10% limits for losses).

- Gains that exceed losses, and which are not postponed, are treated as capital gains reported on Form 8949 and then on Schedule D.
- Losses that exceed any recognized gains are deductible.

When to Report Gains and Losses

Table 24.2 summarizes when taxpayers can claim a gain or loss on their tax returns.

If a taxpayer is unsure whether part of the casualty or theft loss will be reimbursed, the taxpayer should not deduct that part of the loss until he or she is reasonably certain it will not be reimbursed.

Disaster Losses

An ordinary casualty loss is generally deducted in the year it occurred. However, if the taxpayer has a casualty loss from a federally declared disaster that warranted public and/or individual assistance, then the taxpayer can choose to deduct a loss on the tax return for the year of the loss or for the year immediately preceding the year the disaster occurred. A taxpayer must make the choice by the later of the following dates:

- The due date (without extensions) for filing the return for the year of the disaster
- The due date (with extensions) for filing the return for the preceding tax year

Example

Deidre's home was entirely destroyed by a tornado in March 2013. Her area was designated as a federal disaster area eligible to receive individual assistance. She can deduct the disaster loss on her 2012 return, which is due April 15, 2013. Alternatively, she can wait to deduct it on her 2013 return, which is due April 15, 2014.

TIP: The IRS may extend filing deadlines, postpone estimated tax payments, and provide other relief to victims in federally declared disaster areas. Watch for IRS news releases and other notices or check the IRS Web site for specific guidance.

TABLE 24.2 When to Deduct a Loss

IF you have a loss...	THEN deduct it in the year...
from a casualty,	the loss occurred.
in a federally declared disaster area,	the disaster occurred or the year immediately before the disaster.
from a theft,	the theft was discovered.
on a deposit treated as a:	
• casualty,	• a reasonable estimate can be made.
• bad debt,	• deposits are totally worthless.
• ordinary loss,	• a reasonable estimate can be made.

Receiving Reimbursements

After a deduction has been claimed, a taxpayer may recover stolen property or receive additional reimbursements for damaged property.

Recovered Stolen Property A recovery of stolen property may create income if it is more than the benefit received from the deduction. Refigure the loss using the smaller of the property's adjusted basis or the decrease in the FMV from the time just before it was stolen until the date of recovery. Income is the difference between the refigured loss and the original loss if the refigured loss is less than the original loss. Income from recoveries is explained more fully in Chapter 10 (see "Taxable Recoveries").

Actual Reimbursement Less than Expected A taxpayer who receives less reimbursement than expected may include that difference as a loss on his or her return for the year in which the taxpayer can reasonably expect no more reimbursement.

Example

Armand's car was totaled in a collision in 2011 that was due to the other driver's negligence. Armand did not deduct anything in 2011 because he had a lawsuit pending for the recovery. The suit was settled in 2012 for $4,800, but by the end of 2012, he was unable to collect anything on the settlement, and it was apparent that he would not be able to collect anything in the future. He can deduct his loss on his 2012 tax return.

Actual Reimbursement More than Expected A taxpayer who deducted a loss and then recovers more than anticipated may have income from the recovery (see the earlier section, "Recovered Stolen Property").

Actual Reimbursement as Expected Nothing has to be done in this case because there is no additional loss or income.

Review Questions

1. Which of the following is **not** a casualty?
   a. A terrorist attack
   b. A puppy's damage to carpeting
   c. A tornado
   d. A rare infestation of beetles

2. All of the following can be treated as a theft **except**:
   a. Blackmail
   b. Embezzlement
   c. Lost money
   d. Mugging

3. Which of the following options **cannot** be used to deduct losses on a bank deposit?
   a. Casualty loss
   b. Ordinary loss
   c. Nonbusiness bad debt (short-term capital loss)
   d. Long-term capital loss

4. A taxpayer's car is stolen. The taxpayer paid $22,000 for the car; it was worth $12,000 at the time it was stolen. Insurance paid her $11,000. Her adjusted gross income for the year of the theft is $45,000. What is the amount of the taxpayer's deductible theft loss?
   a. $0
   b. $900
   c. $1,000
   d. $11,000

5. Which of the following is **unique** about a disaster loss?
   a. The $100 limit does not apply.
   b. The deduction can be claimed in the year of the disaster or the prior year.
   c. The 10% limit does not apply.
   d. The amount of the loss is based solely on a decrease in FMV.

6. To prove a theft loss, the taxpayer should be able to show all of the following **except**:
   a. That the property has been stolen.
   b. When the discovery was made that the property was missing.
   c. Whether a claim for reimbursement exists.
   d. The property is worth more at the time of the theft than its adjusted basis.

Miscellaneous Itemized Deductions

Some deductible expenses may be deducted as miscellaneous itemized deductions, most of which are subject to a floor based on the taxpayer's adjusted gross income (AGI). Specifically, only the total of all such deductions exceeding 2% of the taxpayer's AGI is deductible. However, some miscellaneous deductions are fully deductible without regard to this 2% limit.

Miscellaneous itemized deductions for regular income tax purposes are not deductible for purposes of the alternative minimum tax (AMT) (see Chapter 33).

Miscellaneous Itemized Deductions Subject to the 2% Limit

Most miscellaneous itemized deductions are deductible to the extent they exceed the 2% limit. A taxpayer claims a miscellaneous itemized deduction on Schedule A, *Itemized Deductions*. The 2% limit is applied after any other limit for a particular type of expense, such as the 50% limit for business meals (explained in Chapter 26).

Three categories of expenses are subject to the 2% limit:

1. Unreimbursed employee business expenses (see Chapter 26)
2. Tax preparation fees
3. Other expenses

Tax Preparation Fees

Fees paid for income tax preparation of a taxpayer's personal income tax return are deductible in the year the fees are paid.

Example

Jerry paid you $350 to prepare his 2012 Form 1040, *U.S. Individual Income Tax Return*, in April 2013. He can deduct the $350 as a miscellaneous itemized deduction for 2013 (if he is eligible to itemize deductions and to the extent his total miscellaneous itemized expenses exceed the 2% limit).

Deductible tax preparation fees also include the cost of:

- E-filing fees
- Tax books and publications
- Tax preparation software
- Tax advice

Other Expenses

> **TIP:** A taxpayer who receives tax advice from an attorney or other tax professional should request the professional to show this detail on the invoice or statement and the related charges. An invoice showing "For services rendered" does not support a deduction paid for tax advice.

Deductible expenses other than employee business expenses and tax preparation fees that are subject to the 2% limit are reported as other expenses. These fall into three categories:

1. Expenses to produce or collect income that is included in gross income,
2. Expenses to manage, conserve, or maintain property held for producing such income, OR
3. Costs or fees to determine, contest, pay, or claim a refund of any tax.

Appraisal Fees Appraisal fees charged to determine the fair market value of property donated to a tax-exempt organization (see Chapter 23) or to figure a casualty loss deduction (see Chapter 24) are deductible as miscellaneous itemized deductions.

> **TIP:** Annual individual retirement account (IRA) custodial fees are deductible only if they are separately billed and paid from funds outside of the IRA. Fees that are subtracted from the IRA are not deductible.

Investment Expenses Investment expenses (which do not include interest income) include fees, custodial trust administration fees, and other expenses related to the production of taxable investment income. These expenses are deductible as miscellaneous itemized deductions subject to the 2%-of-AGI limit. Investment expenses (exceeding the AGI limit) reduce investment income, against which investment interest expense may be deducted. See definition of net investment income later in this chapter.

Example

Jed has AGI of $100,000, investment income of $9,000, investment interest expense of $11,000, and miscellaneous investment expenses of $3,000 related to the production of his investment income, but no other miscellaneous itemized deductions. He may deduct $1,000 of miscellaneous investment expenses [$3,000 – ($100,000 x 2%)], reducing his net investment income to $8,000 ($9,000 – $1,000). Thus, he may deduct up to $8,000 in investment interest expense. The remaining interest expense of $3,000 ($11,000 – $8,000) may be carried forward to the following year.

Hobby Losses Expenses of an activity not engaged in for profit are deductible only to the extent of income from such activity (see Chapter 11).

Example

Julia, whose hobby is stamp collecting, sells three valuable stamps in 2012 for a total of $11,600. Her hobby-related expenses for the year total $21,300. She must report the $11,600 as "other income" for 2012 (Form 1040, line 21). Of her $21,300 in expenses, only $11,600 is deductible as a miscellaneous itemized deduction, the extent of her income. She cannot deduct the remaining expenses of $9,700 in 2012, nor can she carry these expenses back or forward to another tax year.

Job Search Expenses A taxpayer can deduct certain expenses he or she incurs in looking for a new job in their present occupation. A taxpayer *cannot* deduct expenses when:

- Looking for a job in a new occupation,
- There is a substantial break in time between the ending of the last job and looking for a new one, OR
- The taxpayer is looking for a job for the first time.

Legal Expenses Legal fees and other costs incurred to produce or collect income that is taxable or paid in connection with the determination, collection, or refund of any tax are deductible. Legal fees incurred to do or keep a job, for tax advice related to a divorce, or to collect taxable alimony are deductible as miscellaneous itemized deductions subject to the 2% limit.

> **TIP:** Legal fees related to a discrimination suit are deductible as an adjustment to income on Form 1040, rather than as a miscellaneous itemized deduction. This adjustment can be taken whether the taxpayer itemizes other deductions or not. Such legal fees, which are limited to the amount of the settlement or lawsuit, are reported on Form 1040 line 36 with "UDC" (for "unlawful discrimination claim") written on the line.

The cost of resolving tax matters related to profit or loss from a business (Schedule C, *Profit or Loss From Business*; Schedule C-EZ, *Net Profit From Business*), rentals or royalties (Schedule E, *Supplemental Income and Loss*), and farm income and expenses (Schedule F, *Profit or Loss From Farming*) are deductible on these schedules.

Loss on Deposits There are three ways in which losses of deposits held in a financial institution can be deducted. One way is to claim an ordinary loss for the unrecovered funds, reported as a miscellaneous itemized deduction on Schedule A. Other ways include reporting the loss as a casualty loss or nonbusiness bad debt, discussed in Chapter 24.

Loss on IRAs A taxpayer cannot claim a loss on the decline in account value while funds remain in the IRA. However, a deduction for a loss can be taken if *all three* of these conditions are met:

1. *All* of the funds in *all* of a taxpayer's IRAs are withdrawn (this rule applies separately to traditional and Roth IRAs); AND
2. The taxpayer has basis in the IRA. This can result if the IRA has been funded with after-tax (nondeductible) contributions or if the account is a Roth IRA; AND
3. The amounts distributed from the IRAs are less than the taxpayer's remaining unrecovered basis in the IRAs (applying separately to traditional and Roth IRAs).

Example

Kevin opened a Roth IRA in 2007 with a $4,000 contribution. No other contributions or distributions were made. In 2012, when the account was worth $2,800, he withdrew the entire balance of the account. Assuming he had no other Roth IRAs, he can deduct a loss of $1,200 ($4,000 – $2,800).

Had the IRA been a traditional IRA with zero basis (because all contributions had been previously deducted) instead of a Roth IRA, Kevin would report income of $2,800 (the amount distributed). He might also be subject to the 10% early distribution penalty if he was under age 59½ when the distribution was made. However, he could not deduct a loss for the decline in the account value because he had no basis in the traditional IRA.

Repayment of Income A repayment occurs when an amount of ordinary income reported by a taxpayer in a prior year must be repaid by the taxpayer in the current year. A repayment can be deducted only as a miscellaneous itemized deduction if the repayment does not exceed $3,000. Repayments of $3,000 or less are subject to the 2% limit.

A repayment of more than $3,000 may be deductible without regard to the 2% limit, or claimed as a credit under "claim of right." (See "Repayments of More than $3,000" later in this chapter.)

Repayment of Social Security Benefits Taxable Social Security benefits received by a taxpayer in a prior year that are repaid by the taxpayer in the current year may be deductible (see Chapter 9). As with repayments of other income, the repayment may or may not be subject to the 2% limit, depending on the amount of the repayment.

Other Miscellaneous Deductions Subject to the 2% Limit

TIP: Casualty or theft losses of property used in performing services as an employee are first figured on Section B of Form 4684, *Casualties and Thefts*, before applying the 2% limit.

Examples include:

- *Casualty and theft losses* of property used in performing services as an employee.
- *Investment activity expenses* incurred to produce or collect taxable income and manage or protect property held for earning income. This includes clerical help, office rent, a computer (the cost of which usually must be depreciated and the allowance for the current year claimed as a miscellaneous deduction), and rental fees for a safe deposit box used to store taxable income–producing stocks, bonds, and investment-related papers and documents (and not merely personal jewelry or tax-exempt securities).
- *Fees to collect interest and dividends*, such as fees to a brokerage firm. However, the costs incurred for buying investment property are added to the basis of the property; costs for selling the property are selling fees that reduce the proceeds from the sale.
- *Indirect deductions of pass-through entities.* Partnerships, S corporations, and privately traded mutual funds, such as investment clubs, pass through to owners their share of investment-related expenses. Owners can deduct them as a miscellaneous itemized deduction.
- *Service charges on dividend reinvestment plans (DRIPs)* for holding shares acquired through a plan, collecting and reinvesting dividends, and keeping individual records and providing statements are miscellaneous itemized deductions.

TIP: Partnerships and S corporations report to owners their share of investment-related expenses on Schedule K-1, *Partner's (Shareholder's) Share of Income, Deductions, Credits, Etc.* Non–publicly offered mutual funds report these deductions on Form 1099-DIV, *Dividends and Distributions.*

Deductions Not Subject to the 2% Limit

Some expenses are treated as miscellaneous itemized deductions but are not subject to the 2% limit.

Casualty and Theft Losses on Income-Producing Property

A miscellaneous itemized deduction not subject to the 2% limit can be claimed for income-producing property that is damaged, destroyed, or stolen. The amount of the deduction is limited to what is not reimbursed by insurance. Examples of income-producing property include:

- Artworks
- Metals (gold and silver)
- Securities (stocks, bonds, and notes)
- Vacant lots

Victims of Ponzi-like schemes, such as the one perpetrated by Bernard Madoff, can deduct the investments that are not recovered through insurance or other reimbursements. Generally, the loss is taken in the year the loss is discovered. However, no recovery is allowed for taxes paid on investment income or gains reported in prior years.

> **TIP:** Casualty or theft loss on income-producing property is first figured in Section B of Form 4684. The loss may be included on Form 4797, Sale of *Business Property*, if the taxpayer is otherwise required to file that form. For more details about casualties and thefts, see Chapter 24.

Gambling Losses

While all winnings from gambling activities, including lotteries, bingo, slots, and other games of chance, are fully taxable as "other income" (see Chapter 10), losses are limited to the amount of gambling winnings for the year. Losses cannot be used to reduce or offset the amount of winnings that must be reported as income. In other words, all winnings must be reported as income, and then the losses (not exceeding the amount of winnings) are taken as a miscellaneous itemized deduction; the losses are not simply netted against winnings to determine the amount reported as income.

Example

Sally goes to Las Vegas several times a year to see the shows and gamble. Her winnings from the slot machines total $2,900. Her losses total $4,200. She must report $2,900 as income; she can deduct $2,900 as a miscellaneous itemized deduction not subject to the 2% limit.

To claim a deduction for gambling losses, the taxpayer must have proof of the loss. This requires a record of winnings and losses for the year, which can be kept in a diary or other record. Information in the record should include:

- The date and type of the wager or other gambling activity
- The name and address or location of the gambling establishment (e.g., the number of the table where the taxpayer played baccarat, blackjack, craps, poker, or roulette)
- The names of other persons with the taxpayer, if applicable
- The amount(s) won or lost

The taxpayer should keep copies of lottery tickets and keno tickets validated by the gambling establishment.

> **TIP:** Gambling winnings can be proven by Form W-2G, *Certain Gambling Winnings*; Form 5754, *Statement by Person(s) Receiving Gambling Winnings*; wagering tickets; canceled checks; and statements issued by the gambling establishments. These types of proof, however, do not show the amounts wagered.

Repayments of More than $3,000

A taxpayer who repays an amount greater than $3,000 that had been included in ordinary income in a prior year can deduct the repayment in the year it is made. This deduction is not subject to the 2%-of-AGI limitation.

However, the taxpayer can choose to claim a credit for the year of repayment (instead of a deduction) if the taxpayer appeared to have an unrestricted right to the income when the income was originally reported. If the taxpayer qualifies to make this choice, both methods should be compared to determine which method provides the greater tax benefit.

Method 1. Figure the tax for the year of repayment, claiming a deduction for the repaid amount as a miscellaneous itemized deduction not subject to the 2% limit.

Method 2. Figure the tax for the year of repayment, claiming a credit for the repaid amount. Follow these steps:

- **a.** Figure the tax for the year of repayment without claiming a deduction for the repaid amount.
- **b.** Refigure the tax for the prior year in which the income was received, but excluding the amount the taxpayer repaid.
- **c.** Subtract the tax figured in Step b from the tax shown on the actual return for the prior year.
- **d.** Subtract the amount figured in Step c from the tax figured in Step a.

TIP: Repayments of $3,000 or less are deducted from income in the year repaid as a miscellaneous itemized deduction subject to the 2% limit.

If the first alternative is better, then deduct the repayment as a miscellaneous itemized deduction not subject to the 2% limit. If the second alternative is better, then claim it as a tax credit on Form 1040, line 72 (enter "I.R.C. 1341" in the margin on the Total Payments line of Form 1040).

Other Expenses Not Subject to the 2% Limit

DEFINITION:
Net investment income is determined by reducing gross investment income by investment expenses (other than the investment interest). For this purpose, investment income does not include:

- Alaska Permanent Fund dividends OR
- Qualified dividends or net capital gains, unless elected.

See Pub. 550, *Investment Income and Expenses.*

Other expenses that also may be deductible as miscellaneous itemized deductions not subject to the 2% limit include:

- *Investment interest.* Investment interest is deductible up to the extent of the taxpayer's **net investment income**. (See Chapter 22.) Interest that cannot be deducted may be carried to the following year and treated as paid or accrued in the following year for purposes of the deduction. Form 4952, *Investment Interest Expense Deduction*, may be required.
- *Impairment-related work expenses.* A taxpayer who has a physical or mental disability affecting major life activities (walking, speaking, etc.) can deduct expenses that enable him or her to work as a miscellaneous itemized deduction not subject to the 2% limit. Such expenses include, for example, the cost of attendant care services or a reader for a blind individual.
- *Loss from other activities on Schedule K-1.* Amounts reported in Box 2 of Schedule K-1 (Form 1065-B, *U.S. Return of Income for Electing Large Partnerships*) are not subject to the passive activity loss limitations

(see Chapter 7) and can be deducted as a miscellaneous itemized deduction not subject to the 2% limit.

- *Unrecovered investment in an annuity.* A deduction can be claimed on the final income tax return of a retiree who dies before recovering the tax-free return of his or her investment in an annuity.

TIP: Impairment-related work expenses of a self-employed individual are deducted on Schedule C or other business form, not on Schedule A as a miscellaneous itemized deduction.

Nondeductible Expenses

Not every expense is deductible. Following is a list of expenses that *cannot* be deducted as miscellaneous itemized deductions, although some of these expenses may produce a tax benefit, as indicated.

- *Adoption expenses.* While not deductible as a miscellaneous itemized deduction, adoption expenses may be used to claim a tax credit if all qualifications are met (see Chapter 31).
- *Bank account fees for personal accounts.* Fees charged to write checks or access automated teller machines (ATMs) are nondeductible personal expenses, even if the account pays interest.
- *Campaign contributions and expenses.* No deduction or credit can be claimed for contributing to a political campaign, including advertisements in convention bulletins and admissions to dinners for candidates. A taxpayer who runs for public office or who campaigns for someone else cannot deduct expenses, including registration fees for primary elections and legal fees to defend charges arising from participation in a political campaign.
- *Capital expenses.* Amounts paid to buy property or amounts paid to increase the value or prolong the life of property are not deductible. However, these expenditures are added to the basis of the property, which serves to minimize gain or maximize loss when the property is sold or otherwise disposed of (see Chapter 13).
- *Club dues.* Membership fees in clubs, whether for business, pleasure, recreation, or other social purposes, are not deductible. These include health clubs (unless prescribed by a doctor and deductible as a medical expense, as explained in Chapter 20), airline clubs, and country clubs.
- *Commuting expenses.* Generally, the cost of getting to and from work is not deductible, regardless of the length of the commute. However, the extra cost of hauling tools, instruments, or other work-related items, such as the cost of renting a trailer, is deductible (see Chapter 26).
- *Fines and penalties.* Payments to the government for violating the law, such as fines for parking tickets and penalties that are withheld from the paychecks of public workers for illegal strikes, are not deductible.
- *Home security system.* The cost of the system and monthly monitoring fees to protect a home and its contents are not deductible. However, a portion of the fees may be deductible if home office expenses are deducted (see Chapter 11).

- *Investment-related seminars and meetings.* The cost of attending a seminar, convention, or similar meeting for investment purposes is not deductible. This includes the cost of attending stockholder meetings.
- *Legal fees for personal reasons.* Most personal-related legal fees, such as costs for property claims in a divorce, custody disputes, suits for breach of promise to marry, and preparation of a will, are not deductible. However, legal fees for some personal-related legal matters may be deductible. These include legal fees related to doing or keeping one's job or legal fees related to producing or collecting taxable income. Also, legal fees incurred in lawsuits are deductible if the court award or settlement is taxable. Legal expenses that are deductible as miscellaneous itemized deductions are subject to the 2% limit.
- *Life insurance premiums.* Premiums on insurance covering the taxpayer or spouse are not deductible. However, premiums paid on a policy assigned to a former spouse under a divorce decree or settlement may be deductible alimony (see Chapter 18).
- *Lobbying expenses.* Amounts paid to influence public officials, influence legislation, or influence the public about elections or legislative matters are not deductible. However, amounts paid in connection with the taxpayer's business may be deductible under limited circumstances (see IRS Pub. 529, *Miscellaneous Deductions*).
- *Lost or mislaid cash or property.* Unless the action is a casualty loss (see Chapter 24), no deduction can be claimed.
- *Meals.* The cost of a taxpayer's meals at work, such as a dinner while working late or meals with coworkers, is not deductible, unless the meals are eaten while traveling away from home (see Chapter 26).
- *Personal living expenses.* The cost of food, clothing, and shelter, including personal telephone charges, are not deductible. This includes the cost of a wristwatch, even if required for a job. It also includes vacations or the travel costs of a companion on a business trip (with a limited exception).
- *Professional accreditation fees.* Fees for the initial right to practice accounting, bar exam preparation and admission fees, and fees for initial medical and dental licensing are not deductible.
- *Tax-exempt income expenses.* Expenses to buy or carry tax-exempt securities, such as municipal bonds, are not deductible. Expenses relating to both taxable and nontaxable income must be allocated if the taxpayer cannot identify the expenses for producing each type of income.

Example

Stanley received taxable interest of $12,000 and tax-exempt interest of $1,200. He had investment expenses for the year of $600. He cannot identify the amount of expense for each type of income. The deductible portion of his expenses is $540, which is 90% of $600 (($12,000 – $1,200) ÷ $12,000). This deduction is subject to the 2% limit on miscellaneous itemized deductions.

How to Deduct Miscellaneous Itemized Expenses

A taxpayer must itemize deductions on Schedule A of Form 1040 in order to deduct miscellaneous expenses.

Employee-related expenses first must be figured on Form 2106, *Employee Business Expenses* (or Form 2106-EZ, *Unreimbursed Employee Business Expenses*), explained in Chapter 26. Unreimbursed employee business expenses are then entered on Schedule A.

Tax preparation fees and other expenses subject to the 2% limit are reported directly on Schedule A. These amounts are totaled, and the 2% limit is subtracted to determine the deductible amount.

Other miscellaneous deductions that are not subject to the 2% limit are reported directly on Schedule A in their own section (line 28). They are then included with all other itemized deductions.

ALERT: A deduction for miscellaneous itemized expenses may create or increase the alternative minimum tax (AMT) liability. See Chapter 33.

Self-employed taxpayers and statutory employees (as indicated on the W-2 form) can deduct expenses on Schedule C or C-EZ; self-employed farmers use Schedule F. Miscellaneous expenses related to investments that are not required to be reported on Schedule A, as specified in this chapter, can be deducted on Schedule E.

Job Expenses and Certain Miscellaneous Deductions	21	Unreimbursed employee expenses—job travel, union dues, job education, etc. Attach Form 2106 or 2106-EZ if required. (See instructions.) ▶	21	
	22	Tax preparation fees	22	
	23	Other expenses—investment, safe deposit box, etc. List type and amount ▶	23	
	24	Add lines 21 through 23	24	
	25	Enter amount from Form 1040, line 38 | 25 |		
	26	Multiply line 25 by 2% (.02)	26	
	27	Subtract line 26 from line 24. If line 26 is more than line 24, enter -0-		27

FIGURE 25.1 Schedule A, Job Expenses and Certain Miscellaneous Deductions

Review Questions

1. Which of the following miscellaneous itemized expenses is **not** subject to the 2% limit?
   a. Unreimbursed employee business expenses
   b. The cost of e-filing a state income tax return
   c. Fees to obtain a tax refund
   d. Impairment-related work expenses

2. All of the following can be deducted without regard to the 2% limit **except**:
   a. Amortization of bond premium
   b. Unrecovered investment in an employee annuity
   c. Personal income tax preparation fees
   d. Impairment-related work expenses

3. Gambling losses are deductible:
   a. As an offset to gambling winnings so only the net amount of winnings is reported as income
   b. In full as a miscellaneous itemized deduction subject to the 2% limit
   c. To the extent of gambling winnings, but after taking the 2% limit into account
   d. To the extent of gambling winnings, without regard to the 2% limit

4. Which of the following is deductible as a miscellaneous itemized deduction?
   a. ATM fees on an interest-bearing personal bank account
   b. Loss on a Roth IRA account that has been completely withdrawn, and the taxpayer has no other Roth IRA accounts
   c. Campaign expenses for a candidate seeking reelection
   d. Subway fare to and from work

5. Which of the following miscellaneous itemized deductions is entered directly on Schedule A?
   a. Tax preparation fees for a taxpayer's personal income tax return
   b. A theft of a taxpayer's personal computer
   c. An employee's meal costs while on a business trip
   d. Tax preparation fees related to the preparation of Schedule C

CHAPTER 26

Employee Business Expenses

An employee's deductible business expenses include work-related travel away from home, costs of local transportation, unreimbursed job-related expenses, and job-related education expenses. Employee business expenses are subject to the 2%-of-adjusted-gross-income (AGI) limitation. Thus, only the amount of these expenses (combined with other miscellaneous deductions) that exceeds the 2%-of-AGI limit is actually deductible.

Employee business expenses may be subject to other limitations before applying the 2%-of-AGI limit. For example, generally only 50% of business meals are deductible. Taxpayers deducting employee business expenses generally use either Form 2106, *Employee Business Expenses*, or Form 2106-EZ, *Unreimbursed Employee Business Expenses*. The net amount from Form 2106 (or 2106-EZ) is then entered on Schedule A, *Itemized Deductions*, of Form 1040, *U.S. Individual Income Tax Return*.

Overview of Employee Business Expenses

DEFINITIONS: Ordinary means common and accepted in the employee's industry.

Necessary means helpful and appropriate to the employee's job.

Taxpayers can deduct certain unreimbursed expenses incurred in the course of their employment (i.e., expenses incurred for their job). To be deductible, the expenses must be both **ordinary** and **necessary**. An expense need not be a required expenditure for the business expense to be treated as ordinary and necessary.

Two types of nondeductible costs are *capital expenditures* and *personal expenses*. Capital expenditures are recovered through depreciation over a period of years rather than expensed in the current year (explained in Chapter 12). Personal expenses (e.g., haircuts) are never deductible as employee business expenses and are not added to the basis of any property.

Certain expenses are nondeductible despite appearing ordinary and necessary. These nondeductible expenses include:

- Club dues for membership in certain clubs, such as airline clubs and country clubs

- Commuting to a normal work location, regardless of the length or cost of the commute
- Fines and penalties, including parking tickets on work-related travel
- Professional accreditation fees for the initial right to practice in the accounting, medical, and dental professions, along with bar and certified public accountant exam preparation and admission fees

Travel Away from Home

DEFINITIONS: A **tax home** is generally the regular place of business or post of duty, regardless of where the family home is located.

The **regular place of work** includes the entire city or general area in which the employee's work is located.

The cost of temporary travel away from a taxpayer's **tax home** on business is deductible if (1) the employees are traveling away from their tax home for substantially longer than an ordinary day's work and (2) they need to sleep or rest to meet the demands of the work.

An employee with more than one **regular place of work** uses the main place of work as his or her tax home. Factors to determine the main place of work include the total time spent in each location, the level of business activity in each location, and whether income from each location is significant.

An employee with no regular or main place of business can use the place where he or she lives as the tax home if all three of these conditions are met:

1. Part of the work is performed in the area of the employee's main home and the home is used for lodging while working in the area.
2. Living expenses at the main home are duplicated when away.
3. The main home has not been abandoned (e.g., the employee's family uses the home for lodging).

If all three conditions are met, the taxpayer's home is treated as his or her tax home for purposes of deducting employee travel expenses, instead of using the main place of business as the tax home, such as an office building.

Under some circumstances, meeting two conditions can create a tax home where the taxpayer lives.

Meeting only one condition means the employee is a transient and his or her tax home is wherever the work is performed.

A taxpayer who does not have a regular place of business or post of duty and has no place where he or she regularly lives is considered a transient (or itinerant) worker and the taxpayer's tax home is wherever he or she works. A transient worker *cannot* claim a travel expense deduction because he or she is *never* considered to be traveling away from home.

Example

Calvin, who is single, lives in a rented apartment in Miami and works nearby. His employer sends him to a 12-month executive training program that will be taught in various locations throughout the United States outside of Miami. Calvin will relocate to Chicago when he completes the program and does *not* expect to return to work in Miami. However, during the training program, he frequently returns to his Miami apartment for personal reasons. He does not meet the first condition because he performs no work in Miami. He satisfies conditions 2 and 3 because he has duplicative living costs and has not abandoned his apartment and community contacts in Miami. Because he satisfies two conditions, Calvin's tax home is Miami.

An employee can have a different tax home from his or her family. If so, the employee cannot deduct travel costs to and from the family's home. In addition, a taxpayer cannot deduct meal and lodging costs incurred while at his or her tax home.

ALERT: Spouses can have different tax homes. For example, if one spouse's job is based in New York and the other's is based in Hawaii, the home they share in Colorado is not the tax home of either spouse; each has a different tax home (New York and Hawaii).

Example

Veronica is a truck driver who lives with her family in Kansas City. Veronica's trucking company has its terminal in St. Louis. After long runs, Veronica returns to the terminal in St. Louis and spends a night there before returning to Kansas City. Veronica's tax home is St. Louis. Thus, meals and lodging incurred while in St. Louis are not deductible. In addition, costs of traveling to and from St. Louis and Kansas City are not deductible.

Travel expenses are deductible if incurred and related to a temporary assignment, such as a one-week business trip. Generally, a temporary assignment is one realistically expected to last for one year or less that does in fact end within this period. The meal, lodging, and travel costs associated with traveling between a temporary place of work and the tax home on days off are deductible. However, such expenses are not deductible while the taxpayer is at his or her tax home.

ALERT: Employer payments for living expenses made to an employee on an indefinite assignment are includible in the employee's gross income, even if they are called travel allowances. The payments are reported on the employee's Form W-2, *Wage and Tax Statement*.

Expenses are not deductible if the assignment is indefinite. An *indefinite assignment* is one realistically expected to last more than one year, even if it ends sooner. Costs incurred during a probationary work period are not deductible even if the individual is later hired.

Deductible Travel Expenses

Ordinary and necessary travel expenses generally are deductible. Examples of deductible travel costs can be found in Table 26.1.

Travel costs of a companion, such as a spouse, are not deductible by the employee. However, a taxpayer may deduct the costs of an employee or business associate traveling with the taxpayer for a bona fide reason and if those costs would otherwise be allowable travel expenses.

TABLE 26.1 Deductible Travel Expenses

IF you have expenses for...	THEN you can deduct the cost of...
transportation	travel by airplane, train, bus, or car between your home and your business destination. If you were provided with a ticket or you are riding free as a result of a frequent traveler or similar program, your cost is zero. If you travel by ship, see *Luxury Water Travel* and *Cruise Ships* (under *Conventions*) for additional rules and limits.
taxi, commuter bus, and airport limousine	fares for these and other types of transportation that take you between: • The airport or station and your hotel, and • The hotel and the work location of your customers or clients, your business meeting place, or your temporary work location.
baggage and shipping	sending baggage and sample or display material between your regular and temporary work locations.
car	operating and maintaining your car when traveling away from home on business. You can deduct actual expenses or the standard mileage rate, as well as business-related tolls and parking. If you rent a car while away from home on business, you can deduct only the business-use portion of the expenses.
lodging and meals	your lodging and meals if your business trip is overnight or long enough that you need to stop for sleep or rest to properly perform your duties. Meals include amounts spent for food, beverages, taxes, and related tips. See *Meals* for additional rules and limits.
cleaning	dry cleaning and laundry.
telephone	business calls while on your business trip. This includes business communication by fax machine or other communication devices.
tips	tips you pay for any expenses in this chart.
other	other similar ordinary and necessary expenses related to your business travel. These expenses might include transportation to or from a business meal, public stenographer's fees, computer rental fees, and operating and maintaining a house trailer.

Example

Sue drives to Boston on business and takes her husband, Jeremy. He is not her employee but accompanies her to business lunches and dinners. Her expenses are deductible, but his are not because he is not her employee and there is no bona fide reason for his presence on the trip (even if customers bring their spouses to the meals).

However, as a practical matter, if allocated costs are the same, such as if the cost of a hotel room is the same for a single or double room, then no expense allocation is necessary. Similarly, there is no allocation of the cost of driving (the same cost applies if Sue had gone alone).

All of the travel expenses are deductible if the purpose of the trip is primarily for business. A trip that is part business and part personal must be allocated between the personal and business portions. A trip that is primarily for personal reasons is not deductible. However, any business expenses incurred on the trip are deductible.

Example

Luke works in Sioux Falls and takes a business trip to San Diego for five days. He stops for three days to visit family on his way home. The cost of the entire trip was $2,000. If Luke had not stopped to visit family, the cost of the business trip would have been $1,500. Luke can deduct $1,500, including round-trip transportation to and from San Diego.

There are special rules for trips outside the United States, including conventions abroad. Generally, expenses are fully deductible for trips outside the United States that are entirely for business reasons. Expenses must be allocated on a daily basis for trips outside the United States that are primarily (but not entirely) for business. Expenses are generally nondeductible for travel outside the United States that are primarily for personal reasons. For a complete discussion on the rules of traveling outside the United States, see IRS Pub. 463, *Travel, Entertainment, Gifts, and Car Expenses.*

Meals and Incidental Expenses

Meals are deductible (subject to limits described later) if:

- It is necessary to stop for substantial sleep or rest in order to perform duties while traveling away from home on business. Thus, meals on an out-of-town business trip are deductible, but an employee's lunch costs in town are not deductible, even if away from the office to see customers or vendors; OR
- The meal is business-related entertainment (explained later in this chapter).

Limitations There are certain limitations on the deduction for the cost of business meals.

- *Lavish or extravagant.* No deduction is allowed if a meal is lavish or extravagant under the circumstances.
- *50% limit.* Generally, only 50% of the cost of meals is deductible. The 50% limit applies either to the actual cost of meals or the standard meal allowance (if this is used to substantiate costs rather than keeping track of actual costs). The standard meal and incidental expense allowance in most small localities in the United States is $46 per day (this rate applies from October 1, 2011 through September 30, 2013). Higher rates apply in larger cities, and different rates apply outside the continental

United States (CONUS) (see IRS Pub. 1542, *Per Diem Rates*, for more information on these rates).

- *80% limit.* An employee subject to "hours of service" limits by the Department of Transportation (DOT) can deduct 80% of either the actual cost of meals or the standard meal allowance (rather than 50%). For October 1, 2011, through September 30, 2013, the standard meal and incidental allowance for taxpayers in the transportation industry who regularly travel away from home (such as long-distance truck drivers) is $59 per day ($65 per day for travel outside the continental United States).

Incidental Expenses Incidental expenses are miscellaneous costs, such as tips to porters, hotel maids, and stewards, transportation between the place of lodging and restaurants, and certain mailing costs. Incidental costs do not include laundry and cleaning, lodging taxes, and phone calls.

A taxpayer can choose to deduct $5 per day instead of deducting the actual amount of incidental costs. This option applies only if a taxpayer does not pay or incur any meal costs and no standard meal allowance is claimed.

Entertainment Expenses

Business-related entertainment costs may be deductible (subject to limitations explained later in this chapter). The costs must be ordinary and necessary and the entertainment must be *either*:

- *Directly related* to the active conduct of business, OR
- *Associated* with the active conduct of business

The *directly related* test requires the taxpayer actually to engage in business discussions in a setting where the main purpose of the business entertainment is for the active conduct of business. The business expectation of the entertainment must be more than a general expectation of future income or business benefit. Additionally, entertainment expenses are generally not considered directly related if the entertainment is conducted where there are substantial distractions that can prevent the taxpayer from actively conducting business, such as: a meeting with nonbusiness clients (such as personal or social contacts), a meeting in a social setting (such as a cocktail party), or a meeting in a nonbusiness setting (such as a nightclub or sporting event).

The *associated with* test generally requires a clear business purpose to be considered associated with the business. In addition, the test requires the entertainment to occur before or after a substantial business discussion, such as goodwill entertaining done to cultivate a business relationship. A *substantial business discussion* is a fact-based inquiry that usually requires discussions, meetings, negotiations, or other business transactions.

The rules for deducting entertainment expenses are summarized in Table 26.2.

TABLE 26.2 When Are Entertainment Expenses Deductible?

General rule	You can deduct ordinary and necessary expenses to entertain a client, customer, or employee if the expenses meet the directly-related test or the associated test.
Definitions	• Entertainment includes any activity generally considered to provide entertainment, amusement, or recreation, and includes meals provided to a customer or client. • An ordinary expense is one that is common and accepted in your trade or business. • A necessary expense is one that is helpful and appropriate.
Tests to be met	Directly-related test • Entertainment took place in a clear business setting, or • Main purpose of entertainment was the active conduct of business, and You did engage in business with the person during the entertainment period, and You had more than a general expectation of getting income or some other specific business benefit. Associated test • Entertainment is associated with your trade or business, and • Entertainment directly before or after a substantial business discussion.
Other rules	• You cannot deduct the cost of your meal as an entertainment expense if you are claiming the meal as a travel expense. • You cannot deduct expenses that are lavish or extravagant under the circumstances. • You generally can deduct only 50% of your unreimbursed entertainment expenses (see *50% Limit*).

Limitations There are certain limitations on the deduction for the cost of business-related entertainment.

- *Lavish or extravagant.* No deduction is allowed if the entertainment is lavish or extravagant under the facts and circumstances of the situation.
- *50% limit.* Generally only 50% of the cost of the entertainment is deductible.
- *Dues for clubs and associations.* No deduction is allowed for dues to clubs, such as country clubs, airline clubs, and athletic clubs. However, direct costs incurred at the clubs for business, such as a luncheon for a client, can be deductible (subject to the 50% limit). Dues to professional associations and unions, business or civic organizations (e.g., chamber of commerce), and certain service organizations (e.g., Rotary and Lions) are deductible.
- *Entertainment facilities.* The cost of yachts, hunting lodges, fishing camps, swimming pools, tennis courts, vacation homes, and other facilities used for entertainment are not deductible. Again, direct costs incurred at a facility, such as meals for clients at a hunting lodge, are deductible (subject to the 50% limit).

Business Gifts

Gifts given in the course of an employee's job are deductible. However, the deductible amount of the gift cannot exceed $25 per recipient per year.

Incidental costs, such as gift wrapping, engraving, insuring, and postage, are not part of the $25 limit. Thus, the actual deduction for a gift may exceed $25 when incidental costs are also deducted.

The $25 limit does not apply to items that cost $4 or less and have the business name imprinted on it, such as pens, refrigerator magnets, and plastic bags. The $25 limit does not apply to promotional materials used on the recipient's business premises, such as signs, calendars, or display racks.

Gift or Entertainment

It may be difficult to distinguish between a gift (subject to the $25 limit) and entertainment (subject to the 50% limit). When the circumstances are not clear, use these rules to make this determination:

- Items that may be considered either a gift or entertainment generally will be treated as entertainment.
- Food or beverages intended to be used by the recipient at a later time are a gift.
- Tickets to a theater or sporting event are entertainment if the taxpayer attends. However, as noted, it may be difficult for the taxpayer to meet the rules for deducting entertainment expenses if the taxpayer attends.
    - If the taxpayer does not attend the event along with the recipient, the taxpayer can choose to treat the cost of the tickets either as a gift or as an entertainment expense, depending on which provides the greater deduction.

Local Transportation Expenses

> **ALERT:** The cost of commuting to and from work each day is a *nondeductible* personal expense. Such commuting expenses are not deductible even if a taxpayer works during the commute. Only the extra cost of hauling equipment or instruments, such as a taxpayer renting a trailer and towing it with their truck, can be deductible.

When not traveling away from a tax home, certain local transportation costs can be deductible. These costs include travel by train, bus, taxi, or the employee's car. Deductible travel costs include:

- Visiting clients, customers, vendors, or suppliers
- Going from the workplace to a business meeting
- Getting from one workplace to another within the area of the employee's tax home (e.g., going from a full-time job to a part-time job after hours)
- Going from home to a temporary workplace when a taxpayer has one or more regular places of work

See Figure 26.1 for an explanation of transportation costs that are deductible.

Most employees and self-employed persons can use this chart. (Do not use this chart if your home is your principal place of business. See *Office in the home*.)

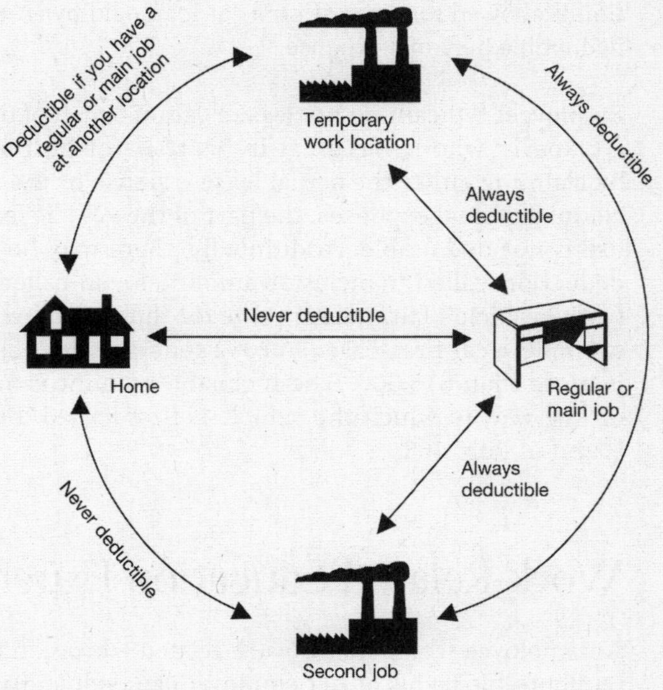

Home: The place where you reside. Transportation expenses between your home and your main or regular place of work are personal commuting expenses.

Regular or main job: Your principal place of business. If you have more than one job, you must determine which one is your regular or main job. Consider the time you spend at each, the activity you have at each, and the income you earn at each.

Temporary work location: A place where your work assignment is realistically expected to last (and does in fact last) one year or less. Unless you have a regular place of business, you can only deduct your transportation expenses to a temporary work location outside your metropolitan area.

Second job: If you regularly work at two or more places in one day, whether or not for the same employer, you can deduct your transportation expenses of getting from one workplace to another. If you do not go directly from your first job to your second job, you can only deduct the transportation expenses of going directly from your first job to your second job. You cannot deduct your transportation expenses between your home and a second job on a day off from your main job.

FIGURE 26.1 When Are Transportation Expenses Deductible?

Car Expenses

An employee who uses his or her personal car for business driving can deduct the cost using one of two ways:

- Deduct actual expenses, including gasoline, oil, repairs, etc. Actual costs include lease payments if the car is leased or depreciation (subject to dollar limits) if the car is owned. The dollar limits are explained in Chapter 11.

ALERT: Taxpayers claiming car expenses should identify their preferred method of claiming expenses. Taxpayers claiming the standard mileage rate must do so in the first year their vehicle is available for use in their business but can choose to use the standard mileage rate or actual expenses in later years. Taxpayers choosing actual expenses in the first year must use this method for every year the vehicle is used in the taxpayer's business.

- Rely on an IRS-set standard mileage rate for the miles driven for business. For 2012, the rate is 55.5¢ per mile.

Whichever method is used, parking and tolls can also be deducted. No deduction is allowed for interest on a car loan paid by an employee as this is a nondeductible personal expense.

Employees typically do not lease a car on behalf of their employers. However, a taxpayer who leases a car in his trade or business can deduct expenses by claiming either the actual lease expense or the standard mileage rate. If claiming actual expenses, the part of the vehicle lease allocated to personal use is not deductible. Additionally, there may be a reduction of the lease deduction, called an inclusion amount, for so-called luxury cars (determined by the vehicle's fair market value for the year in which the lease starts). For example, a car first leased in 2012 generates an inclusion amount if its value is more than $18,500. The inclusion amount is an IRS-set amount based on the year in which the vehicle is first leased. Inclusion amounts can be found in Pub. 463.

Work-Related Education Expenses

TIP: The cost of a teacher's certification in a new state is deductible because a certified teacher is viewed as already meeting the minimum educational requirements in all states. Thus, a teacher certified in one state can deduct any additional courses required to become certified in another state.

An employee who pays for work-related education that is not reimbursed or reimbursable by his or her employer can deduct expenses as a miscellaneous itemized deduction if the education *either*:

- Is required by the employer or by law to keep the present job, salary, or position and serves a bona fide business purpose of the employer, OR
- Maintains or improves job skills for the current position.

However, the education is not deductible if it is necessary to meet minimum education requirements for the current job or is part of a course of study to qualify for a new trade or business. A teacher who is already licensed can deduct the cost of a master's degree, even if it leads to a higher salary. A dentist who takes additional courses to become an orthodontist can deduct the courses; these are not new trade or businesses but merely specializations within a trade or business. However, an accountant cannot deduct the cost of law school because it leads to a new trade or business as a lawyer.

Taxpayers claiming qualifying work-related education expenses generally must be employed while obtaining the education. However, education during a temporary absence that is expected to last one year or less and does in fact last one year or less is deductible if it maintains or improves skills needed in the current occupation. Education during an absence from work of more than one year is considered indefinite and is not deductible even if it maintains or improves skills needed in the occupation from which a taxpayer is absent.

Deductible Expenses

There are no dollar limits on deductible education costs. Examples of deductible expenses include:

- Tuition and fees
- Books, supplies, and lab fees
- Transportation costs, such as travel from a job to a night class

The employee can use the standard mileage rate to figure travel costs if proper records showing miles driven are maintained. The amount of the transportation that is deductible will depend on whether the education is temporary (the education is realistically expected to last one year or less).

TIP: No double tax benefit is allowed for employment-related education. Thus, amounts that are deducted (such as the tuition and fees deduction, discussed in Chapter 16) or are paid with tax-free amounts, such as scholarships or grants, are not deductible as a business expense.

Example

Jack is regularly employed and attends classes three nights a week for 18 months. Because a class program this long is not considered temporary, the costs of traveling from his home to his school are not deductible. However, if Jack traveled directly from work to school, the travel expenses between work and school would be deductible. If the class program was temporary (one year or less), such as a few days or weeks, round-trip travel expenses between his home and the school would be deductible. Travel expenses of traveling from work to school and then to Jack's home also would be deductible. However, travel costs between his home and work are not deductible because these are commuting costs. Commuting costs are never deductible.

Examples of nondeductible education costs include:

- Costs covered by tax-free scholarships or grants.
- Travel as a form of education, even if related to the job. (Thus, a Spanish teacher who spends her summer in Spain to improve her language skills cannot deduct the cost of the trip. However, if she were to take courses in Spain and she meets the tests previously discussed, then her travel and education courses may be deductible.)
- Licensing courses, such as a bar exam preparation course.

Other Work-Related Expenses

Other ordinary and necessary expenses related to the employee's trade or business may be deductible.

Home Office

An employee who works from home may be eligible to deduct a portion of home-related costs (e.g., mortgage interest and real estate taxes or rent, utilities, homeowner's insurance, and other costs) as a home office deduction. To

TIP: A note from an employer stating that the employee works from home for the employer's convenience is helpful but not determinative. Examples of the employer's convenience being shown is if there is no desk for an employee at the company's facilities, or the employee works in a city where the employer has no offices.

qualify, the employee must use a portion of the home regularly and exclusively *and* do so for the convenience of the employer. Working from home after hours or teleworking for personal reasons does not satisfy the requirement that the home office is for the employer's convenience. Also, the space in the home must not be rented to the employer.

The home office deduction rules are explained in Chapter 11.

ALERT: No deduction can be claimed for clothing that is merely distinctive but is still suitable for ordinary use. For example, in Hamper v. Commissioner, a TV anchorwoman could not deduct the wardrobe she bought for on-air appearances because the items could be worn outside of work. The fact that she would not have purchased them "but for" the job did not make them deductible. T.C. Summ. Op. 2011–17.

TIP: The upkeep of deductible uniforms and work clothes is also deductible. This includes laundering (dry cleaning or other special care) and tailoring expenses.

Uniforms and Work Clothes

Clothing and uniforms are deductible if two conditions are met:

- They are worn as a condition of employment, AND
- They are not suitable for everyday wear (ordinary use).

Examples of deductible clothing and accessories include:

- Protective clothing, such as safety shoes or boots, safety glasses, hard hats, and work gloves.
- Military reservist uniforms, if local military regulations prohibit the reservist from wearing them except when on duty as a reservist, but only to the extent that the expenses exceed any allowance or reimbursement received.
- Military fatigues, if local military rules do not allow the fatigues to be worn except when on duty or when traveling to and from duty, but then only to the extent that the expenses exceed any allowances received.
- Scrubs for doctors, nurses, and other hospital workers.
- Theatrical clothing and accessories (costumes), such as items worn by musicians and entertainers, to the extent they are not ordinary clothing.

Tools and Equipment

Tools used on the job are deductible if they are expected to wear out and be thrown away within one year. Tools that have a useful life of more than one year from the date of purchase must be depreciated.

Computers, tablets, and other office equipment used for business are also recovered through depreciation. For more information about depreciating tools and other equipment, see Chapter 11 as well as IRS Pub. 946, *How to Depreciate Property*.

Miscellaneous Expenses

Other job-related costs may be deductible, even though there is no special rule for them. Examples of deductible expenses include:

- Job-hunting costs for a job in the same line of business. If the employee has been out of work for a long time (e.g., a parent returning to the job market after years of child care), the costs may be disallowed.

- Licenses and regulatory payments to state or local governments.
- Subscriptions to periodicals, business books, and business magazines.
- Union and trade association dues.

Recordkeeping and Substantiation

Generally, no deduction is allowed for travel, entertainment, gifts, and car expenses without proper substantiation. The employee must keep certain records and receipts to prove the deductible amounts. The records need not be attached to the return but should be retained in case the IRS questions the deductions.

Table 26.3 shows the types of records needed to back up deductible expenses.

Records

Taxpayers should use an account book, diary, expense account sheet, or similar record to note the date of the expense, the type of expense (e.g., business meal), and other required information shown in Table 26.3.

Documentary Evidence

Documentary evidence includes receipts, canceled checks, credit card statements, and other documents that support the amount of the deduction. Documentary evidence is not needed in any of these situations:

> **TIP:** The records should be kept "contemporaneously," meaning at or near the time the expenses are incurred.

- The employee accounts for meal and lodging expenses to the employer under an accountable plan, and the employee relies on a per diem allowance.
- The expense (other than lodging) is less than $75.
- A receipt is not readily available for a transportation expense (i.e., no receipt for bus fare).

Incomplete or missing records that fail to prove a necessary element (shown in Table 26.3) may be proven by the employee's statement and other supporting evidence. Records that are lost or destroyed through no fault of the employee should be reconstructed to support deductions. For example, if expense receipts or log were destroyed in a fire, the employee should attempt to reconstruct a new record the best he or she can under the circumstances.

Reimbursements

An employee may receive payments from an employer to cover the cost of business expenses. The tax treatment of the reimbursements depends on whether an employee is paid under an accountable or nonaccountable plan.

TABLE 26.3 How to Prove Certain Business Expenses

IF you have expenses for...	THEN you must keep records that show details of the following elements...			
	Amount	**Time**	**Place or Description**	**Business Purpose and Business Relationship**
Travel	Cost of each separate expense for travel, lodging, and meals. Incidental expenses may be totaled in reasonable categories such as taxis, fees and tips, etc.	Dates you left and returned for each trip and number of days spent on business.	Destination or area of your travel (name of city, town, or other designation).	Purpose: Business purpose for the expense or the business benefit gained or expected to be gained. Relationship: N/A
Entertainment	Cost of each separate expense. Incidental expenses such as taxis, telephones, etc., may be totaled on a daily basis.	Date of entertainment. (Also see *Business Purpose.*)	Name and address or location of place of entertainment. Type of entertainment if not otherwise apparent. (Also see *Business Purpose.*)	Purpose: Business purpose for the expense or the business benefit gained or expected to be gained. For entertainment, the nature of the business discussion or activity. If the entertainment was directly before or after a business discussion: the date, place, nature, and duration of the business discussion, and the identities of the persons who took part in both the business discussion and the entertainment activity. Relationship: Occupations or other information (such as names, titles, or other designations) about the recipients that shows their business relationship to you. For entertainment, you must also prove that you or your employee was present if the entertainment was a business meal.
Gifts	Cost of the gift.	Date of the gift.	Description of the gift.	
Transportation	Cost of each separate expense. For car expenses, the cost of the car and any improvements, the date you started using it for business, the mileage for each business use, and the total miles for the year.	Date of the expense. For car expenses, the date of the use of the car.	Your business destination.	Purpose: Business purpose for the expense. Relationship: N/A

Accountable and Nonaccountable Plans

An *accountable plan* is a plan set up by the employer (not the employee) for the purpose of reimbursing employees for certain business-related costs. Under an accountable plan, the employer deducts the business expense and either pays the expense directly (such as when expenses are charged to a corporate credit card) or reimburses the employee for any out-of-pocket expenses. The employer's reimbursement to the employee for the expense is not considered compensation and is not reported on the employee's Form W-2.

To be treated as an accountable plan, the plan must satisfy three requirements:

1. The expense has a business connection; it is paid or incurred in performing services for an employer.

2. The employee must adequately account for the expense to the employer within a reasonable time (usually 60 days).

3. The employee must return any excess reimbursement within a reasonable period of time (usually within 120 days). A reasonable period of time will be found if the employee receives a periodic statement, at least quarterly, that asks for the return or an adequate accounting of the reimbursement and the employee complies within 120 days.

A non-accountable plan is a plan that does not satisfy all three of the elements of an accountable plan. Under a non-accountable plan the reimbursements are reported as compensation to the employee and appear on the employee's Form W-2. The employee then can then deduct expenses as miscellaneous itemized expenses on Schedule A of Form 1040 (subject to the 2%-of-AGI limitation).

Per Diems

An employee who receives reimbursements based on a per diem allowance (a fixed daily allowance) does not need to account to his or her employer for the amount of the expense. However, the employee still must keep records to support the expense (location, date, business purpose, etc.).

ALERT: Per diems cannot be used for adequate accounting if the employee is related to the employer. A *related person* is a spouse, sibling, half sibling, parent, grandparent, child, grandchild; a corporation owned (directly or indirectly) more than 10% by the employee; or certain trusts.

The per diem rates that may be used include:

- *The regular federal per diem rate*, which is the highest rate paid by the federal government to its employees for lodging, meals, and incidental expenses away from home.
- *The standard meal allowance for localities in the continental United States.* The rate is prorated on a 24-hour basis if the travel is less than a full day. Methods of proration are described in IRS Pub. 463.
- *The high-low method.* Under this method, employers who use a per diem method to reimburse employees may use only two rates for travel within the continental United States. This method is used only by employers to pay a travel allowance; it may not be used by employees or self-employed taxpayers. The most current rates and list of high-cost localities can be found in IRS Pub. 1542.

The car expense rates that may be used include:

- *The standard mileage rate for driving on business trips*, which is 55.5¢ per mile in 2012.
- *The fixed and variable rate (FAVR)*, which includes a combination of payments covering fixed and variable costs for car expenses. The employer chooses the method of reimbursements.

The portion of an employee's expenses exceeding the employer's reimbursement under a per diem rate (e.g., the employer reimburses at less than the full per diem rate) can be deducted.

Example

Anna drives 12,000 miles for business in 2012 (assume travel at 1,000 miles per month). Her employer reimburses her under an employer-set mileage rate of 50¢ per mile. She can deduct her excess mileage costs of $660 ([12,000 × (55.5¢ – 50.0¢]).

Reporting Employee Business Expenses

TIP: Business expenses and reimbursements, other than those related to meals and entertainment, are entered in column A, Form 2106 those related to meals and entertainment are entered in column B so that the 50% limitation (or 80% limitation for employees subject to DOT hours of service limits) can be applied.

An employee usually must complete Form 2106 to determine the total deductible portion that is then entered on Schedule A of Form 1040. Form 2106-EZ, which is a simplified version of Form 2106, can be used if the employee is deducting ordinary and necessary job expenses that are not reimbursed by the employer and the employee uses the standard mileage rate to claim any car expenses.

Items entered on Form 2106 include vehicle expenses, such as parking fees, tolls, and transportation; travel expenses away from home; other business expenses; and meals and entertainment. Reimbursements not treated as compensation are also included on this form.

The net amount from Form 2106 is then entered on Schedule A as an unreimbursed employee business expense (see Figure 26.2). These expenses are subject to the 2%-of-AGI limit.

TIP: A taxpayer should not file Form 2106 if none of his or her expenses is deductible because of the 2% limit on miscellaneous itemized deductions.

Example

Harrison has $2,600 of employee business expenses, none of which was reimbursed by his employer. Of this amount, $850 was for business meals, and the remaining $1,750 was for deductible expenses other than meals. Harrison figures a deductible amount on Form 2106 of $2,175 ($1,750 + (50% × $850)). With an adjusted gross income of $42,000 and a 2%-of-AGI threshold of $840 ($42,000 × 2%), Harrison can deduct $1,335, or $2,175 – $840.

Job Expenses and Certain Miscellaneous Deductions	21	Unreimbursed employee expenses—job travel, union dues, job education, etc. Attach Form 2106 or 2106-EZ if required. (See instructions.) ▶	21
	22	Tax preparation fees	22
	23	Other expenses—investment, safe deposit box, etc. List type and amount ▶	23
	24	Add lines 21 through 23	24
	25	Enter amount from Form 1040, line 38 | 25 |	
	26	Multiply line 25 by 2% (.02)	26
	27	Subtract line 26 from line 24. If line 26 is more than line 24, enter -0-	27

FIGURE 26.2 Schedule A, Job Expenses and Miscellaneous Expenses

Review Questions

1. Which of the following job-related expenses are deductible?

a. Commuting costs

b. Initial professional accreditation fees

c. Dues to a trade association

d. Country club membership dues

2. Which statement concerning a tax home is correct?

a. Spouses must have the same tax home.

b. A tax home is always the family's residence.

c. A taxpayer can never use the place where he or she lives as the tax home.

d. A tax home includes the entire city or general area in which the employee's work is located.

3. Which of the following jobs away from home is a temporary assignment for the entire time the taxpayer is at the job?

a. A job expected to last six months that ends within this period

b. A job expected to last one year but lasts for 13 months

c. A job expected to last 14 months but which is completed in 10 months

d. A job expected to last 15 months that lasts for two years

4. Incidental expenses while away from home include all of the following costs **except**:

a. Tips to hotel maids

b. Laundry in the hotel

c. Cab fare between the hotel and a restaurant

d. Mailing costs

5. An employee gives a customer a gift of two tickets to a Broadway show costing $200. The employee does not accompany the customer. What is the maximum deduction?

a. $4

b. $25

c. $100

d. $200

6. The inclusion amount for leased cars used for business is:

a. A deduction limit.

b. An income add-back.

c. The total costs for the cars that can be deducted.

d. An alternative for basing the deduction on the standard mileage rate.

7. What is **not** a requirement for a reimbursement arrangement to be treated as an accountable plan?

a. The expense has a business connection.

b. The employee is required to adequately account for expenses to the employer within a reasonable time.

c. The employee is required to return any excess reimbursement within a reasonable time.

d. The employee adopts a special plan.

Earned Income Credit

The earned income credit (EIC) is a tax credit for certain working individuals with earned income below a threshold amount. The credit reduces tax liability. The EIC is refundable when the amount of the credit exceeds the tax owed for the year. The amount of the EIC depends on the taxpayer's income and the number of qualifying children, if any.

From your perspective as a preparer, you must recognize that the EIC is one of the most frequently miscalculated credits, and the IRS looks closely at this tax credit. You must exercise due diligence in determining a taxpayer's eligibility for the credit and in figuring the credit amount, as the IRS can hold you personally liable for a penalty for each failure.

The IRS will figure a taxpayer's EIC under certain conditions. These rules are not covered here because you, as the preparer, are responsible for accurately figuring and claiming the EIC, when appropriate, for every tax return you prepare.

Overview of the Earned Income Credit

A taxpayer who works at a job or business may be entitled to the earned income credit (EIC), even if the credit is more than the taxes owed. The EIC can be claimed on any return: Form 1040EZ, *Income Tax Return for Single and Joint Filers With No Dependents*; Form 1040A, *U.S. Individual Income Tax Return*; or Form 1040, *U.S. Individual Income Tax Return*.

TIP: A taxpayer must file a return if he or she wishes to claim the EIC, even if income is below the filing threshold for the taxpayer's filing status, there was no tax withheld from the taxpayer's wages, or the taxpayer did not owe any tax (see Chapter 1).

The amount of the EIC varies with the number of the taxpayer's qualifying children, if any, and filing status. For 2012, the maximum EIC, regardless of filing status, is:

- $475 if there is no qualifying child
- $3,169 for one qualifying child
- $5,236 if there are two qualifying children
- $5,891 if there are three or more qualifying children

Who Can Claim the Credit? Rules that Apply to Everyone

A taxpayer claiming the EIC must meet certain tests. There are some tests that all taxpayers claiming the credit must pass. There are also separate tests that apply to taxpayers with qualifying children and without qualifying children. (discussed later in this chapter)

The tests that apply to everyone claiming EIC include:

- Income qualifications
  - AGI limitations
  - Earned income
  - Investment income
- Citizenship or residency
- Social Security Number
- Filing status
- Taxpayer not a qualifying child

Income Qualifications

Adjusted Gross Income In order to qualify for the credit, a taxpayer's adjusted gross income (AGI) cannot exceed a set limit, which depends on the taxpayer's filing status as well as whether the taxpayer has a qualifying child for EIC purposes. This limit is adjusted annually for inflation. A reduced credit is allowed for AGI within the phase-out range and no credit is allowed for AGI above the phase-out range.

For 2012, the phase-out ranges are listed in Table 27.1.

TABLE 27.1 2012 AGI Phase-Out Ranges for the EIC

Filing status	No qualifying child	One qualifying child	Two qualifying children	Three or more qualifying children
Single, qualifying widow(er), or head of household	$7,700–$13,980	$17,090–$36,920	$17,090–$41,952	$17,090–$45,060
Married filing jointly	$12,980–$19,190	$22,300–$42,130	$22,300–$47,162	$22,300–$50,270

Example

Erica files as head of household and has one qualifying child. Her AGI (including earned income of $33,500) in 2012 is $35,000. She can claim the EIC because her AGI is below the limit for her filing status. She does not qualify for the maximum credit amount because her income is within the phase-out range. If her AGI was $40,000, she would not be eligible for any credit because her AGI would exceed the end of the phase-out range.

ALERT: If a married person qualifies to file as head of household and lives in a community property state, the taxpayer's AGI includes any portion of the spouse's wages that are required to be included in the taxpayer's gross income.

Earned Income AGI is one limitation on the amount of credit that can be claimed. However, the taxpayer must also have *earned income* to qualify for the EIC. Only one spouse needs to have earned income when a couple is married and files jointly.

Earned income includes:

- Wages, salary, tips, and other taxable employee pay. Disability income from an employer's disability retirement plan is included as taxable wages until the taxpayer reaches the minimum retirement age. Taxable wages are reported in box 1 of Form W-2, *Wage and Tax Statement.*
- Net earnings from self-employment.
- Gross income received as a statutory employee (see Chapter 4).

TIP: A member of the military can elect to treat nontaxable combat pay as earned income for purposes of the EIC. Nontaxable combat pay is reported in box 12 (code Q) of Form W-2.

Earned income does *not* include interest and dividends, pensions and annuities, Social Security and railroad retirement benefits (including disability benefits), alimony and child support, welfare benefits, workers' compensation benefits, unemployment benefits, nontaxable foster care payments, veterans' benefits (including Department of Veterans Affairs (VA) rehabilitation payments), and nontaxable workfare payments from a state or local agency.

ALERT: A married person who qualifies to file as head of household and lives in a community property state must have earned income of his or her own and cannot treat the spouse's portion of earned income as his or her own for purposes of claiming EIC, even though it is included in AGI.

A taxpayer cannot claim the earned income credit if he or she claims the foreign earned income exclusion on Form 2555, *Foreign Earned Income,* or Form 2555-EZ, *Foreign Earned Income Exclusion.* The credit cannot be claimed if a taxpayer deducts or excludes a foreign housing amount. (For more information, see IRS Pub. 54, *Tax Guide for U.S. Citizens and Resident Aliens Abroad.*)

Investment Income A taxpayer cannot claim the EIC if his or her investment income exceeds a set amount ($3,200 for 2012). Investment income for purposes of the EIC includes, for example:

- Capital gain distributions
- Capital gains in excess of capital losses
- Ordinary and qualified dividends
- Royalties and rental income from personal property
- Passive activity income
- Taxable interest
- Tax-exempt interest

For this purpose, investment income does not include long-term capital gains from the sale of certain business assets. Passive activity income is the total income from all passive activities for the year less the total losses from all passive activities.

Example

Bianca files as head of household and has one qualifying child for EIC. She earned $30,000 in wages, $100 in taxable investment interest, $300 in tax-exempt investment interest, and $3,000 in rental income from personal property. Bianca cannot claim the EIC because her investment income totals $3,400 ($100 + $300 + $3,000), an amount that exceeds the investment income limit.

If a parent elects to report a child's investment income on the parent's return under the kiddie tax rules (see Chapter 34), the child's investment income is added to the parent's investment income when determining eligibility for the EIC.

Use Worksheet 1 in IRS Pub. 596, *Earned Income Credit (EIC)*, to calculate investment income if the taxpayer is filing Schedule E, *Supplemental Income and Loss*, reporting income from the trade or business of renting personal property, or reporting income from Form 8814, *Parent's Election to Report Child's Interest and Dividends*. See Figure 27.1.

Citizenship or Residency

Only a taxpayer who is a U.S. citizen or resident alien for the *entire* year can claim the EIC. However, a taxpayer with a nonresident spouse can claim the EIC if the taxpayer files married filing jointly and the nonresident spouse chooses to be treated as a U.S. resident. As a result of this choice, both the taxpayer and spouse will be taxed on worldwide income.

Social Security Number

To claim the credit, a taxpayer, and the taxpayer's spouse if filing jointly, must have a valid Social Security Number (SSN) for him- or herself *and* for any qualifying child. If the taxpayer, the spouse, or a qualifying child does not have the SSN by the original due date of the return (generally April 15), the return can be filed without claiming the EIC or the taxpayer may request an extension of time to file. If the taxpayer chooses to file the return without claiming the EIC, the return can be amended to claim the EIC once all required SSNs have been obtained.

Filing Status

To be eligible to claim EIC, a married couple who lives together *must* file a joint return. No EIC can be claimed by a taxpayer filing using the married filing separately filing status.

Interest and Dividends

1. Enter any amount from Form 1040, line 8a. . . . . 1.______
2. Enter any amount from Form 1040, line 8b, plus any amount on Form 8814, line 1b. . . . . 2.______
3. Enter any amount from Form 1040, line 9a. . . . . 3.______
4. Enter the amount from Form 1040, line 21, that is from Form 8814 if you are filing that form to report your child's interest and dividend income on your return. (If your child received an Alaska Permanent Fund dividend, use Worksheet 2 in this chapter to figure the amount to enter on this line.) . . . . 4.______

Capital Gain Net Income

5. Enter the amount from Form 1040, line 13. If the amount on that line is a loss, enter -0-. 5.______
6. Enter any gain from Form 4797, Sales of Business Property, line 7. If the amount on that line is a loss, enter -0-. (But, if you completed lines 8 and 9 of Form 4797, enter the amount from line 9 instead.) . . . . 6.______
7. Subtract line 6 of this worksheet from line 5 of this worksheet. (If the result is less than zero, enter -0-.) . . . . 7.______

Royalties and Rental Income from Personal Property

8. Enter any royalty income from Schedule E, line 23d, plus any income from the rental of personal property shown on Form 1040, line 21. . . . . 8.______
9. Enter any expenses from Schedule E, line 20, related to royalty income, plus any expenses from the rental of personal property deducted on Form 1040, line 36. . . . . 9.______
10. Subtract the amount on line 9 of this worksheet from the amount on line 8. (If the result is less than zero, enter -0-.) . . . . 10.______

Passive Activities

11. Enter the total of any net income from passive activities (such as income included on Schedule E, line 26, 29a (col. (g)), 34a (col. (d)), or 40). (See instructions below for lines 11 and 12.) . . . . 11.______
12. Enter the total of any losses from passive activities (such as losses included on Schedule E, line 26, 29b (col. (f)), 34b (col. (c)), or 40). (See instructions below for lines 11 and 12.) . . . . 12.______
13. Combine the amounts on lines 11 and 12 of this worksheet. (If the result is less than zero, enter -0-.) . . . . 13.______
14. Add the amounts on lines 1, 2, 3, 4, 7, 10, and 13. Enter the total. **This is your Investment Income.** . . . . 14.______
15. Is the amount on line 14 more than **$3,150**?
    ☐ **Yes.** You cannot take the credit.
    ☐ **No.** Go to *Step 3* of the Form 1040 instructions for lines 64a and 64b to find out if you can take the credit (unless you are using this publication to find out if you can take the credit; in that case, go to *Rule 7*, next).

Instructions for lines 11 and 12. In figuring the amount to enter on lines 11 and 12, do not take into account any royalty income (or loss) included on line 26 of Schedule E or any amount included in your earned income. To find out if the income on line 26 or line 40 of Schedule E is from a passive activity, see the Schedule E instructions. If any of the rental real estate income (or loss) included on Schedule E, line 26, is not from a passive activity, print "NPA" and the amount of that income (or loss) on the dotted line next to line 26.

FIGURE 27.1 Worksheet 1, Investment Income for the EIC

However, if a married taxpayer lives away from his or spouse, the taxpayer may be eligible to use the head of household filing status rather than married filing separately (see Chapter 2). In this case, a taxpayer filing as head of household may still be eligible to claim the EIC if all other requirements are met.

Taxpayer May Not Be a Qualifying Child of Another Taxpayer

The taxpayer (and spouse if filing jointly) who wants to claim an EIC cannot be a qualifying child of another taxpayer, such as a parent, guardian, or foster parent. The definition of *qualifying child* for this purpose is listed below under "Taxpayers with a Qualifying Child."

> **Example**
>
> Christina and her daughter live with Christina's mother all year. Christina is 22 years old, unmarried, and attends a trade school full time. She has earned income of $5,950 from a part-time job and no other income. Because Christina is a qualifying child of her mother (she meets the relationship, age, residency, and joint return tests), Christina cannot claim the EIC for her daughter, whether her mother claims the EIC or not.

Taxpayers with a Qualifying Child

Besides AGI and earned income, the amount of the EIC depends on the number of qualifying children a taxpayer has.

Child Must Meet Four Tests

A child is the taxpayer's *qualifying child* for purposes of claiming the EIC if four tests are met:

> **DEFINITION:** A child is **permanently and totally disabled** if both the following apply:
>
> 1. The child cannot engage in any substantial gainful activity because of a physical or mental condition, AND
> 2. A doctor determines the condition has lasted or can be expected to last continuously for a year, or can lead to death.

1. *Relationship.* The child must be the taxpayer's child, stepchild, foster child (placed with the taxpayer by an authorized placement agency, court, or state-licensed tax-exempt organization), sibling, half sibling, stepsibling, or any descendant of them (such as a nephew or grandchild). A legally adopted child is treated the same as a child related by blood.
2. *Age.*
   a. The child must be under the age of 19 by the end of the year *and* younger than the taxpayer (or the taxpayer's spouse if filing jointly); OR
   b. The child must be under 24 if the child is a student enrolled full time for any part of each of five calendar months (or taking a full-time on-farm training course) and younger than the taxpayer (or the taxpayer's spouse if filing jointly); OR
   c. The child can be any age if **permanently and totally disabled** at any time during the year.
3. *Residency.* The child must live with the taxpayer in the United States for more than half the year. The United States includes all 50 states and the District of Columbia, but does not include Puerto Rico or any other United States possession. *Home* is any location in which the taxpayer regularly lives, including a homeless shelter. United States military

personnel stationed outside the country on extended active duty are treated as living in the United States for that period for purposes of the EIC. A child who is born or dies during 2012 is treated as living with the taxpayer for the full year if the child lived with the taxpayer more than half the time he or she was alive in 2012. Temporary absences due to special circumstances, such as illness, school attendance, or vacation, are disregarded. A child who has been kidnapped is treated as living with the taxpayer for the full year if the child lived with the taxpayer more than half the part of the year before the kidnapping. This special rule for kidnapping applies until there is a determination of death or the year in which the child would have reached age 18, whichever occurs earlier.

4. *Joint return*. Generally, the child cannot file a joint return. However, this rule does not apply if the joint return is being filed *only* to obtain a tax refund.

ALERT: Where the dependency exemption is released by the custodial parent to the noncustodial parent, there may be a split in these tax benefits. The noncustodial parent may be eligible to claim the child tax credit (and dependency exemption), while the custodial parent may be eligible to claim the remaining tax benefits associated with the released exemption. The noncustodial parent will never be eligible to claim head of household, EIC, child and dependent care credit, or an exclusion for dependent care benefits associated with the released exemption.

Example

Charles's 19th birthday was August 1, 2012. His dad, Harry, cannot claim the EIC for him in 2012, unless Charles is a full-time student or totally and permanently disabled.

John and Julie Edwards are married and are both 21 years old. Julie's brother, Sam, who lives with the Edwardses, is 22 years old and a full-time student. The Edwards cannot claim the EIC for Sam because they are not older than him. If, however, John were 26, the Edwardses could claim the EIC on a joint return; Sam would be younger than John even though he would not be younger than Julie.

Qualifying Child May Not Be Claimed by More than One Person

Child-related tax benefits generally cannot be split among taxpayers. Only one taxpayer can claim the EIC with respect to a qualifying child. When a child can be viewed as the qualifying child of more than one taxpayer, only one such taxpayer can claim the credit. Generally, the person entitled to claim EIC is the person who claims all of the tax benefits related to the qualifying child, including the dependency exemption for the child, the child tax credit, head of household filing status, the credit for child and dependent care expenses, and the exclusion for dependent care benefits.

In divorce situations, the custodial parent is the only parent entitled to claim the EIC, even though the custodial parent may release the dependency exemption to the noncustodial parent with Form 8332, *Release/Revocation of Release of Claim to Exemption for Child by Custodial Parent.* In other words, a noncustodial parent can never claim the EIC even when Form 8332 is executed by the custodial parent.

ALERT: Two taxpayers who have the same qualifying child cannot agree between themselves to divide these benefits. Only one taxpayer can claim the benefits with respect to a qualifying child. Tie-breaker rules determine which taxpayer can claim the benefits. Tie-breaker rules are explained in Chapter 3.

Taxpayers with No Qualifying Child

A taxpayer without a qualifying child can still claim an EIC. The taxpayer must meet all of the rules discussed earlier in this chapter ("Rules that Apply to Everyone"). However, there are four additional rules to meet.

To qualify for the EIC without a qualifying child the taxpayer:

1. Must be at least age 25 but under 65 years old at the end of the tax year. For a married couple filing jointly, only one spouse must meet this age rule. If the taxpayer is filing a joint return with a spouse who died during the year, the taxpayer will meet the age test if the spouse met the age rule at the time of death.

Example

Wesley's spouse died in October 2012 at the age of 64 (she would have been 65 in December 2012). Wesley, who is 68 years old, meets the age test because his wife satisfied it at the time of her death.

2. Cannot be a dependent of another person, whether the other person actually claims the dependency exemption or not.
3. Cannot be a qualifying child of another taxpayer.
4. Must have lived in the United States for more than half the year. Married couples filing jointly must *both* live in the United States for more than half the year (see "Residency" in the "Taxpayers with a Qualifying Child" section earlier in this chapter).

Who Cannot Claim the Credit?

This information has been explained previously in this chapter. However, it is helpful to repeat the situations in which the EIC cannot be claimed.

- A taxpayer whose filing status is married filing separately.
- A taxpayer who is the qualifying child of another taxpayer (under the definition listed under "Taxpayers with a Qualifying Child" earlier in this chapter.
- A taxpayer with a qualifying child cannot claim the EIC as a taxpayer with no qualifying child.

Example

Mike and his child live with Mike's mother, Joanne. Mike's child meets the age, relationship, residency, and joint return test for both Mike and Joanne. Therefore, Mike's child is a "qualifying child" of both Mike and Joanne. Mike's AGI is lower than Joanne's, so Mike allows his mother, Joanne; to claim his child. Because Joanne claims the child as a dependent, only Joanne is allowed to claim the EIC on behalf of the child. Joanne qualifies to claim the EIC with a qualifying child. Because Mike has a qualifying child, he cannot claim the EIC as a taxpayer without a qualifying child. Mike is not eligible to claim the EIC in this case.

- A taxpayer who claims the foreign earned income exclusion or a deduction or exclusion for foreign housing.

- A taxpayer whose EIC was disallowed or reduced in a previous year due to reckless or intentional disregard or fraud may not be eligible for the EIC in the current year. (This is explained later in this chapter.)

In the case of parents who are divorced, separated, or living apart, only the custodial parent can claim the EIC.

Figuring the Credit

The credit is figured by looking up the amount in an IRS table. Like the tax tables used to figure tax liability (explained in Chapter 32), the EIC tables are based on filing status, number of qualifying children, if any, and income determined from an EIC worksheet (explained later).

Earned Income Limit

To claim the EIC, earned income must be *less than* the earned income limit amount for the taxpayer's filing status and number of qualifying children. The earned income limit is shown in Table 27.2.

Earned income, which is taxable income for personal services, was explained earlier in this chapter. Examples of items *not* treated as earned income include:

- Conservation reserve program (CRP) payments if the taxpayer is receiving Social Security retirement or disability benefits at the time such payments are received
- Deferred compensation (income earned in previous years)
- Inmate's income for work performed in a penal institution
- Tax-free scholarships and fellowships

As explained earlier, a taxpayer receiving nontaxable combat pay (box 12 (code Q) of Form W-2), which is ordinarily not taxable, can elect to treat the pay as earned income for purposes of the EIC.

TIP: The election to treat nontaxable combat pay as earned income for EIC purposes should be considered if earned income without combat pay is below $6,210 with no qualifying child, $9,320 with one qualifying child, or $13,090 with two or more qualifying children. If both spouses receive combat pay, one or both can make the election. Check the amount of EIC with and without the addition of combat pay to see whether the election should be made.

TABLE 27.2 2012 Earned Income Limits

Number of qualifying children	Single, qualifying widow(er), or head of household	Married filing jointly
None	$13,980	$19,190
One	$36,920	$42,130
Two	$41,952	$47,162
Three or more	$45,060	$50,270

Example

Brad and Diane are married and have one qualifying child. Brad is in the military and earns $15,000 ($5,000 taxable wages plus $10,000 in nontaxable combat pay). Diane works part time, earning $2,000. Their taxable earned income and AGI are $7,000. By electing to treat the combat pay as taxable, they increase their earned income to $17,000, which increases the EIC from $2,389 to $3,169.

If, however, Brad's combat pay had been $22,000 (giving them an AGI of $29,000), the election would have reduced the couple's EIC to $2,094 and would not have been advisable in this situation.

EIC Worksheets

The taxpayer must complete a worksheet from the form instructions to determine eligibility to claim the credit and the amount of income on which to figure the credit. The Form 1040EZ instructions have one worksheet that can be used by any taxpayer. For taxpayers filing Form 1040 or Form 1040A, there are two worksheets to choose from:

1. *EIC Worksheet A* is used if the taxpayer was not self-employed, a member of the clergy, a church employee with self-employment income, or a statutory employee.
2. *EIC Worksheet B* is used if the taxpayer was self-employed, a member of the clergy, a church employee with self-employment income, or a statutory employee.

TIP: EIC Worksheet B cannot be completed before figuring the taxpayer's self-employment tax on Schedule SE, *Self-Employment Tax*, of Form 1040. This is explained in Chapter 35.

Comprehensive examples of the EIC worksheets are available in IRS Pub. 596.

Claiming the Credit on the Return

The EIC is the amount taken from the EIC table in the instructions to the return. Look up the credit amount based on the amount from the EIC worksheet, the taxpayer's filing status, and number of qualifying children.

Example

Tamika is a single mom who files as head of household and has two qualifying children. Her AGI and earned income from Worksheet A are $26,100. Her EIC, based on the draft version of the 2012 table found in the Form 1040 instructions, is $3,333 (see Figure 27.2).

Reporting the Credit

The credit can be claimed on Form 1040, 1040A, or 1040EZ. A taxpayer with at least one qualifying child must complete Schedule EIC, *Earned Income Credit*, to provide information about the child(ren); the schedule is attached to the return.

If the amount you are looking up from the worksheet is --		And you listed--			
		One Child	Two Children	Three Children	No Children
At Least	But less Than	Your credit is--			
26,050	26,100	1,733	3,344	3,998	0
26,100	26,150	1,725	3,333	3,988	0
26,150	26,200	1,717	3,323	3,977	0
26,200	26,250	1,709	3,312	3,967	0

FIGURE 27.2 Tamika's EIC Based on the 2012 Earned Income Credit (EIC)

Previously Disallowed EIC

A taxpayer whose EIC was disallowed or reduced in a previous year due to reckless or intentional disregard or fraud may not be eligible for the EIC in the current year. There is a waiting period of either 2 or 10 years before the EIC can again be claimed by the taxpayer. The 2-year period applies for an error due to reckless or intentional disregard of the EIC rules; the 10-year period applies in cases of fraud.

A taxpayer whose EIC was previously disallowed or reduced for any reason other than a math or clerical error must complete Form 8862, *Information to Claim Earned Income Credit After Disallowance.* This form must be attached to the return.

Even though a taxpayer's EIC has been reduced or disallowed in an earlier year, Form 8862 does not have to be filed if:

- A taxpayer has filed Form 8862 for a later year and the EIC has been allowed, AND
- The EIC was not reduced or disallowed *again* for any reason other than a math or clerical error.

The taxpayer does not have to file Form 8862 for the current tax year if the taxpayer is claiming the EIC with no qualifying child and the only reason the EIC was reduced or disallowed in an earlier year was because the IRS determined that a claimed child was not in fact the taxpayer's qualifying child.

Paid Preparer Responsibilities

It is the paid preparer's responsibility to exercise due diligence in completing a taxpayer's return on which the EIC is claimed. You must determine if the taxpayer is eligible for the credit and properly figure the amount of the credit. Your failure to meet this due diligence requirement can result in a $500 preparer penalty for each failure.

ALERT: Under final regulations issued in March 2012, paid preparers must complete Form 8867 and submit it with the completed tax return or claim for refund.

Use Form 8867, *Paid Preparer's Earned Income Credit Checklist*, for *each* client claiming an earned income credit. The form goes through the eligibility criteria step by step to help you determine the taxpayer's eligibility for the credit.

Part IV, *Due Diligence Requirements*, of Form 8867 contains a checklist for each of your due diligence requirements:

- You must complete Form 8867 based on information that the taxpayer provided or that you reasonably obtained from interviewing the taxpayer. See Figure 27.3. When filling out Form 8867, you must comply with the knowledge requirement (see below).
- You must complete the appropriate EIC worksheet found in the Form 1040, Form 1040A, or Form 1040EZ instructions.
- You must comply with the knowledge requirements. The instructions state that "you must not know or have reason to know that any information used to determine the taxpayer's eligibility for, and the amount of, the EIC is incorrect. You may not ignore the implications of information furnished to or known by you, and you must make reasonable inquiries if the information furnished appears to be incorrect, inconsistent, or incomplete. At the time you make these inquiries, you must document in your files the inquiries you made and the responses you received."

  You may have a reason to know the taxpayer is not being truthful if the information being relayed by the taxpayer would not make sense to a reasonable tax preparer. A common example of this is when a taxpayer has income that seems too low to support the number of children the taxpayer is claiming on the return or if the taxpayer does not provide consistent answers when going through the questions contained in Form 8867.

  In some cases it may also be reasonable to ask the taxpayer for supporting information such as birth certificates, medical records, or other written information in order to determine eligibility for the EIC.
- You must retain records for three years, including:
  - ☐ Form 8867;
  - ☐ The EIC worksheet;
  - ☐ Your own record of how, when, and from whom the information used to prepare the form and worksheet was obtained; AND
  - ☐ Copies of any documents provided by the taxpayer and on which you relied to complete the worksheet.

The three-year retention requirement now runs from the later of (1) the due date of the return without regard to any filing extension, (2) the date the return or claim for refund was filed (if the return was electronically filed), (3) the date the return or claim for refund was presented to the taxpayer for signature (if the return is not electronically filed), or (4) the date you submitted the part of the return you prepared to the signing preparer (if you are a nonsigning preparer).

Form **8867**

Department of the Treasury
Internal Revenue Service

Paid Preparer's Earned Income Credit Checklist

► **To be completed by preparer and filed with Form 1040, 1040A, or 1040EZ.**

► **Information about Form 8867 and its separate instructions is at *www.irs.gov/form8867*.**

OMB No. 1545-1629

2012

Attachment Sequence No. **177**

Taxpayer name(s) shown on return	**Taxpayer's social security number**

For the definitions of the following terms, see **Pub. 596.**

- **Investment Income**
- **Qualifying Child**
- **Earned Income**
- **Full-time Student**

Part I **All Taxpayers**

1 Enter preparer's name and PTIN ► ______________________________

2 Is the taxpayer's filing status married filing separately? . . . . ☐ **Yes** ☐ **No**

► If you checked **"Yes"** on line 2, **stop;** the taxpayer **cannot** take the EIC. Otherwise, continue.

3 Does the taxpayer (and the taxpayer's spouse if filing jointly) have a social security number (SSN) that allows him or her to work or is valid for EIC purposes? See the instructions before answering ☐ **Yes** ☐ **No**

► If you checked **"No"** on line 3, **stop;** the taxpayer **cannot** take the EIC. Otherwise, continue.

4 Is the taxpayer filing Form 2555 or Form 2555-EZ (relating to the exclusion of foreign earned income)? . . . . ☐ **Yes** ☐ **No**

► If you checked **"Yes"** on line 4, **stop;** the taxpayer **cannot** take the EIC. Otherwise, continue.

5a Was the taxpayer a nonresident alien for any part of 2012? . . . . ☐ **Yes** ☐ **No**

► If you checked **"Yes"** on line 5a, go to line 5b. Otherwise, skip line 5b and go to line 6.

b Is the taxpayer's filing status married filing jointly? . . . . ☐ **Yes** ☐ **No**

► If you checked **"Yes"** on line 5a and **"No"** on line 5b, **stop;** the taxpayer **cannot** take the EIC. Otherwise, continue.

6 Is the taxpayer's **investment income** more than $3,200? See Rule 6 in Pub. 596 before answering ☐ **Yes** ☐ **No**

► If you checked **"Yes"** on line 6, **stop;** the taxpayer **cannot** take the EIC. Otherwise, continue.

7 Could the taxpayer, or the taxpayer's spouse if filing jointly, be a **qualifying child** of another person for 2012? If the taxpayer's filing status is married filing jointly, check "No." Otherwise, see Rule 10 (Rule 13 if the taxpayer does not have a qualifying child) in Pub. 596 before answering . . . . ☐ **Yes** ☐ **No**

► If you checked **"Yes"** on line 7, **stop;** the taxpayer **cannot** take the EIC. Otherwise, go to Part II or Part III, whichever applies.

For Paperwork Reduction Act Notice, see separate instructions. Cat. No. 26142H Form **8867** (2012)

FIGURE 27.3 Form 8867

Form 8867 (2012) Page 2

Part II Taxpayers With a Child

		Child 1	Child 2	Child 3
	Caution. If there is more than one child, complete lines 8 through 14 for one child before going to the next column.			
8	Child's name			
9	Is the child the taxpayer's son, daughter, stepchild, foster child, brother, sister, stepbrother, stepsister, half brother, half sister, or a descendant of any of them?	☐ Yes ☐ No	☐ Yes ☐ No	☐ Yes ☐ No
10	Is either of the following true? • The child is unmarried, or • The child is married, can be claimed as the taxpayer's dependent, and is not filing a joint return (or is filing it only as a claim for refund).	☐ Yes ☐ No	☐ Yes ☐ No	☐ Yes ☐ No
11	Did the child live with the taxpayer in the United States for over half of the year? See the instructions before answering	☐ Yes ☐ No	☐ Yes ☐ No	☐ Yes ☐ No
12	Was the child (at the end of 2012)— • Under age 19 and younger than the taxpayer (or the taxpayer's spouse, if the taxpayer files jointly), • Under age 24, a full-time student, and younger than the taxpayer (or the taxpayer's spouse, if the taxpayer files jointly), or • Any age and permanently and totally disabled?	☐ Yes ☐ No	☐ Yes ☐ No	☐ Yes ☐ No
	► If you checked **"Yes"** on lines 9, 10, 11, **and** 12, the child is the taxpayer's qualifying child; go to line 13a. If you checked **"No"** on line 9, 10, 11, **or** 12, the child is not the taxpayer's qualifying child; see the instructions for line 12.			
13a	Could any other person check **"Yes"** on lines 9, 10, 11, **and** 12 for the child?	☐ Yes ☐ No	☐ Yes ☐ No	☐ Yes ☐ No
	► If you checked **"No"** on line 13a, go to line 14. Otherwise, go to line 13b.			
b	Enter the child's relationship to the other person(s)			
c	Under the tiebreaker rules, is the child treated as the taxpayer's qualifying child? See the instructions before answering	☐ Yes ☐ No ☐ Don't know	☐ Yes ☐ No ☐ Don't know	☐ Yes ☐ No ☐ Don't know
	► If you checked **"Yes"** on line 13c, go to line 14. If you checked **"No,"** the taxpayer **cannot** take the EIC based on this child and cannot take the EIC for taxpayers who do not have a qualifying child. If there is more than one child, see the **Note** at the bottom of this page. If you checked **"Don't know,"** explain to the taxpayer that, under the tiebreaker rules, the taxpayer's EIC and other tax benefits may be disallowed. Then, if the taxpayer wants to take the EIC based on this child, complete lines 14 and 15. If not, and there are no other qualifying children, the taxpayer cannot take the EIC, including the EIC for taxpayers without a qualifying child; do not complete Part III. If there is more than one child, see the **Note** at the bottom of this page.			
14	Does the qualifying child have an SSN that allows him or her to work or is valid for EIC purposes? See the instructions before answering	☐ Yes ☐ No	☐ Yes ☐ No	☐ Yes ☐ No
	► If you checked **"No"** on line 14, the taxpayer **cannot** take the EIC based on this child and cannot take the EIC available to taxpayers without a qualifying child. If there is more than one child, see the **Note** at the bottom of this page. If you checked **"Yes"** on line 14, continue.			
15	Are the taxpayer's **earned income** and **adjusted gross income** each less than the limit that applies to the taxpayer for 2012? See Pub. 596 for the limit			☐ Yes ☐ No
	► If you checked **"No"** on line 15, **stop;** the taxpayer **cannot** take the EIC. If you checked **"Yes"** on line 15, the taxpayer can take the EIC. Complete **Schedule EIC** and attach it to the taxpayer's return. If there are two or three qualifying children with valid SSNs, list them on Schedule EIC in the same order as they are listed here. If the taxpayer's EIC was reduced or disallowed for a year after 1996, see Pub. 596 to see if **Form 8862** must be filed. Go to line 20.			
	Note. If you checked **"No"** on line 13c or 14 but there is more than one child, complete lines 8 through 14 for the other child(ren) (but for no more than three qualifying children). Also do this if you checked **"Don't know"** on line 13c and the taxpayer is not taking the EIC based on this child.			

Form **8867** (2012)

FIGURE 27.3 *(Continued)*

Form 8867 (2012) Page 3

Part III Taxpayers Without a Qualifying Child

16	Was the taxpayer's main home, and the main home of the taxpayer's spouse if filing jointly, in the United States for more than half the year? (Military personnel on extended active duty outside the United States are considered to be living in the United States during that duty period. See Pub. 596.)	☐ **Yes** ☐ **No**
	▶ If you checked **"No"** on line 16, **stop;** the taxpayer **cannot** take the EIC. Otherwise, continue.	
17	Was the taxpayer, or the taxpayer's spouse if filing jointly, at least age 25 but under age 65 at the end of 2012? See the instructions before answering	☐ **Yes** ☐ **No**
	▶ If you checked **"No"** on line 17, **stop;** the taxpayer **cannot** take the EIC. Otherwise, continue.	
18	Is the taxpayer, or the taxpayer's spouse if filing jointly, eligible to be claimed as a dependent on anyone else's federal income tax return for 2012? If the taxpayer's filing status is married filing jointly, check "No"	☐ **Yes** ☐ **No**
	▶ If you checked **"Yes"** on line 18, **stop;** the taxpayer **cannot** take the EIC. Otherwise, continue.	
19	Are the taxpayer's **earned income** and **adjusted gross income** each less than the limit that applies to the taxpayer for 2012? See Pub. 596 for the limit	☐ **Yes** ☐ **No**
	▶ If you checked **"No"** on line 19, **stop;** the taxpayer **cannot** take the EIC. If you checked **"Yes"** on line 19, the taxpayer can take the EIC. If the taxpayer's EIC was reduced or disallowed for a year after 1996, see Pub. 596 to find out if **Form 8862** must be filed. Go to line 20.	

Part IV Due Diligence Requirements

20	Did you complete Form 8867 based on current information provided by the taxpayer or reasonably obtained by you?	☐ **Yes** ☐ **No**
21	Did you complete the EIC worksheet found in the Form 1040, 1040A, or 1040EZ instructions (or your own worksheet that provides the same information as the 1040, 1040A, or 1040EZ worksheet)? . .	☐ **Yes** ☐ **No**
22	If any qualifying child was not the taxpayer's son or daughter, did you ask why the parents were not claiming the child and document the answer?	☐ **Yes** ☐ **No** ☐ **Does not apply**
23	If the answer to question 13a is "Yes" (indicating that the child lived for more than half the year with someone else who could claim the child for the EIC), did you explain the tiebreaker rules and possible consequences of another person claiming your client's qualifying child?	☐ **Yes** ☐ **No** ☐ **Does not apply**
24	Did you ask this taxpayer any additional questions that are necessary to meet your knowledge requirement? See the instructions before answering	☐ **Yes** ☐ **No** ☐ **Does not apply**
	To comply with the EIC knowledge requirement, you must not know or have reason to know that any information used to determine the taxpayer's eligibility for, and the amount of, the EIC is incorrect. You may not ignore the implications of information furnished to or known by you, and you must make reasonable inquiries if the information furnished appears to be incorrect, inconsistent, or incomplete. At the time you make these inquiries, you must document in your files the inquiries you made and the taxpayer's responses.	
25	Did you document the additional questions you asked and your client's answers?	☐ **Yes** ☐ **No** ☐ **Does not apply**

Form **8867** (2012)

FIGURE 27.3 *(Continued)*

Form 8867 (2012) Page **4**

26 Which documents below, if any, did you rely on to determine EIC eligibility for the qualifying child(ren) listed on Schedule EIC? Check all that apply. **Keep a copy of any documents you relied on.** See the instructions before answering. If there is no qualifying child, check box a. If there is no disabled child, check box o.

Residency of Qualifying Child(ren)

- ☐ **a** No qualifying child
- ☐ **b** School records or statement
- ☐ **c** Landlord or property management statement
- ☐ **d** Health care provider statement
- ☐ **e** Medical records
- ☐ **f** Child care provider records
- ☐ **g** Placement agency statement
- ☐ **h** Social service records or statement
- ☐ **i** Place of worship statement
- ☐ **j** Indian tribal official statement
- ☐ **k** Employer statement
- ☐ **l** Other (specify) ▼
- ☐ **m** Did not rely on any documents, but made notes in file
- ☐ **n** Did not rely on any documents

Disability of Qualifying Child(ren)

- ☐ **o** No disabled child
- ☐ **p** Doctor statement
- ☐ **q** Other health care provider statement
- ☐ **r** Social services agency or program statement
- ☐ **s** Other (specify) ▼
- ☐ **t** Did not rely on any documents, but made notes in file
- ☐ **u** Did not rely on any documents

27 If a Schedule C is included with this return, which documents or other information, if any, did you rely on to confirm the existence of the business and to figure the amount of Schedule C income and expenses reported on the return? Check all that apply. **Keep a copy of any documents you relied on.** See the instructions before answering. If there is no Schedule C, check box a.

Documents or Other Information

- ☐ **a** No Schedule C
- ☐ **b** Business license
- ☐ **c** Forms 1099
- ☐ **d** Records of gross receipts provided by taxpayer
- ☐ **e** Taxpayer summary of income
- ☐ **f** Records of expenses provided by taxpayer
- ☐ **g** Taxpayer summary of expenses
- ☐ **h** Bank statements
- ☐ **i** Reconstruction of income and expenses
- ☐ **j** Other (specify) ▼
- ☐ **k** Did not rely on any documents, but made notes in file
- ☐ **l** Did not rely on any documents

▶ You have complied with all the due diligence requirements if you:

1. Completed the actions described on lines 20 and 21 and checked **"Yes"** on those lines,
2. Completed the actions described on lines 22, 23, 24, and 25 (if they apply) and checked **"Yes"** (or **"Does not apply"**) on those lines,
3. Submit Form 8867 in the manner required, **and**
4. Keep all five of the following records for 3 years from the latest of the dates specified in the instructions under *Document Retention*:
   a. Form 8867, Paid Preparer's Earned Income Credit Checklist,
   b. The EIC worksheet(s) or your own worksheet(s),
   c. Copies of any taxpayer documents you relied on to determine eligibility for or amount of EIC,
   d. A record of how, when, and from whom the information used to prepare the form and worksheet(s) was obtained, and
   e. A record of any additional questions you asked and your client's answers.

▶ If you checked **"No"** on line 20, 21, 22, 23, 24, or 25, you have not complied with all the due diligence requirements and may have to pay a $500 penalty for each failure to comply.

Form **8867** (2012)

FIGURE 27.3 *(Continued)*

Review Questions

1. Which of the following is **not** specifically taken into account in determining the EIC?
   a. Tax-free combat pay subject to the taxpayer's election
   b. Earned income
   c. Adjusted gross income
   d. Taxable income

2. Which of the following individuals is **not** a qualifying child for EIC?
   a. A 26-year-old graduate student living with her parents and claimed as their dependent
   b. The taxpayer's 18-year-old child
   c. A 28-year-old child with severe autism (who is found to be permanently and totally disabled) who lives with his parents
   d. The taxpayer's 22-year-old child who is a full-time college student

3. Which of the following filing statuses is ineligible to claim the EIC?
   a. Single
   b. Married filing separately
   c. Head of household
   d. Qualifying widow(er)

4. A taxpayer whose EIC was previously disallowed due to reckless disregard is barred from claiming the credit for:
   a. One year
   b. Two years
   c. Ten years
   d. Permanently

5. Which form must be filed with the return following a disallowance or reduction of EIC for any reason other than a math or clerical error?
   a. Worksheet A
   b. Worksheet B
   c. Form 8862
   d. Form 8867

CHAPTER 28

Child and Dependent Care Credit

The child and dependent care credit is designed to assist working parents with the cost of child care. The credit also helps other working taxpayers who care for someone incapable of self-care. The credit amount depends on the taxpayer's adjusted gross income (AGI), earned income, and whether the taxpayer has one or more qualifying children or other persons for whose care the credit may be claimed.

As a nonrefundable credit, the child and dependent care credit can be used only to the extent of the taxpayer's tax liability. Any unused credit amount is lost and cannot be carried forward to another year.

The credit is coordinated with the exclusion for dependent care assistance. In some cases, a taxpayer must decide whether to use the exclusion or the credit and can choose whichever provides the greater tax savings.

If dependent care is provided in the taxpayer's home by a household employee, the taxpayer may have to pay employment taxes on the wages of the household employee.

Overview of the Child and Dependent Care Credit

A taxpayer who works at a job or business or goes to school may be entitled to the child and dependent care credit. The credit is claimed on Form 2441, *Child and Dependent Care Expenses*, which is attached to Form 1040 or 1040A, *U.S. Individual Income Tax Return*, or Form 1040NR, *U.S. Nonresident Alien Income Tax Return.*

Some key points to remember about the child and dependent care credit are:

- The amount of the credit is reduced as the taxpayer's AGI increases, with a limit of two qualifying children or dependents for whom care is provided.
- The amount of the credit does *not* vary with a taxpayer's filing status. However, if the taxpayer is married, he or she usually must file a joint return to claim the credit. (An exception to this rule is explained later in this chapter.)

- The credit can be claimed only with respect to work-related expenses for the care of a qualifying person. The definition of a qualifying child or other person (explained later in this chapter) is different from the definition used for the dependency exemption and the earned income credit.
- The credit is only for work-related care expenses for the qualifying person up to a set limit, which is $3,000 for one qualifying person and $6,000 for two or more qualifying persons. Expenses that may qualify for dual tax benefits can be used for only one tax benefit of the taxpayer's choosing. For example, a taxpayer cannot claim a dependent care credit for the amount of expenses that were paid or reimbursed by an employer-sponsored dependent care benefit plan.
- The credit is calculated as a percentage of qualifying expenses. The percentage ranges from 35% down to 20%, depending on a taxpayer's AGI, with the percentage declining as the AGI increases. For 2012, the maximum child and dependent care credit, regardless of filing status, is:
  - $1,050 (35% × $3,000) for one qualifying person
  - $2,100 (35% × $6,000) for two or more qualifying persons

Filing Status Requirement

ALERT: A married taxpayer who files as married filing separately cannot claim the child and dependent care credit unless he or she is considered unmarried.

A taxpayer can claim the child and dependent care credit if his or her filing status is married filing jointly, qualifying widow(er) with dependent child, head of household, or single.

A married person who does not file a joint return with his or her spouse can qualify to claim the credit only if he or she is considered unmarried for tax purposes. Generally, an individual who is considered unmarried for tax purposes qualifies to file as head of household. A taxpayer is considered unmarried for tax purposes if *all* of these conditions are met:

- A joint return is not filed.
- The taxpayer's home is the qualifying person's home for more than half the year.
- The taxpayer pays more than half the cost of keeping up the home for the year.
- The spouse does not live in the taxpayer's home for the last six months of the year.

ALERT: Eligible expenses include only amounts incurred for care provided before the child's 13th birthday, not through the end of the year in which the child turns 13. For example, if the taxpayer's son turns 13 on July 26, only eligible expenses incurred through July 25 qualify for the credit.

Qualifying Child or Other Person

A qualifying child or other person for whom the credit can be claimed includes *all* these individuals:

- The taxpayer's qualifying child under age 13 when the care was provided.

- The taxpayer's spouse who is **physically or mentally incapable of self-care** and who lives with the taxpayer for more than half the year.
- A person of any age who is physically or mentally incapable of self-care and who lives with the taxpayer for more than half the year. This person either must be the taxpayer's dependent or would have been a dependent except the person had gross income of $3,800 or more in 2012, the person filed a joint return, or the taxpayer (or taxpayer's spouse) could be claimed as another taxpayer's dependent.

When parents of a qualifying child are separated or divorced, only the custodial parent can claim the dependent care credit, even if the noncustodial parent has qualifying dependent care expenses. This is so even if the noncustodial parent is eligible to claim a dependency exemption for a qualifying child.

DEFINITION: A person is **physically or mentally incapable of self-care** if he or she cannot dress, clean, or feed him- or herself because of a physical or mental condition. A person is also physically or mentally incapable of self-care if he or she requires constant supervision to prevent injuries to self or others.

Earned Income

The taxpayer must have earned income from employee compensation or self-employment in order to claim the child and dependent care credit. If the taxpayer is married, both spouses must have earned income. Earned income is a limitation on the credit in that the amount of the credit is figured based on the *lower* of work-related dependent care expenses (up to the dollar limit explained later in this chapter) or earned income.

As described in Chapter 4, earned income is income from the performance of personal services, such as salaries, wages, tips and earnings from self-employment. Earned income also includes strike benefits and disability pay reported as wages (generally disability from an employer until the normal Social Security retirement age). Nontaxable combat pay can also be treated as earned income if the taxpayer makes this election.

Earned income does *not* include:

- Child support
- Income of nonresident aliens not connected with a U.S. trade or business
- Interest and dividends
- Payments to inmates at penal institutions
- Pensions and annuities
- Scholarships and grants (other than amounts reported as wages on Form W-2, *Wage and Tax Statement*, and paid for teaching or other services)
- Social Security and railroad retirement benefits
- Unemployment compensation
- Nontaxable workfare payments
- Workers' compensation

TIP: A taxpayer must provide the qualifying person's Taxpayer Identification Number (TIN) (usually the Social Security Number [SSN]). For a nonresident or resident alien with no SSN, use the person's Individual Tax Identification Number (ITIN), which can be obtained by filing Form W-7, *Application for IRS Individual Taxpayer Identification Number*. For a child placed with the taxpayer for adoption, use the Adoption Taxpayer Identification Number (ATIN), which can be obtained by filing Form W-7A, *Application for Taxpayer Identification Number for Pending U.S. Adoptions*. The credit will be reduced or disallowed if the tax identification number is incorrect.

TIP: A spouse who is a full-time student or incapable of self-care for only part of the month still treats the full $250/$500 as earned income for that month.

Student-Spouses and Disabled Spouses

A spouse is treated as having earned income if the spouse is a full-time student for some part of at least five calendar months or is physically or mentally incapable of self-care and lived with the taxpayer for more than half the year. This spouse's earned income is treated as being the greater of actual earned income or $250 per month if there is one qualifying person or $500 per month if there are two or more qualifying persons.

When both spouses are full-time students and/or incapable of self-care, only one spouse is treated as having earned income of $250 per month if there is one qualifying person or $500 per month if there are two or more qualifying persons.

TIP: If the taxpayer is a household employer, the taxpayer may be required to pay employment taxes on wages to a caregiver in the home. This includes Social Security and Medicare taxes (FICA), federal unemployment taxes (FUTA), and federal income tax withholding as well as any state-level tax obligations. The taxpayer must also obtain an Employer Identification Number (EIN) under which to report these taxes as an employer. Taxes on household employees are figured on the taxpayer's Schedule H (Form 1040), *Household Employment Taxes*; Form 1040A cannot be filed if the taxpayer is required to file Schedule H. More details about tax obligations are explained in IRS Pub. 503, *Child and Dependent Care Expenses*.

Work-Related Expenses

Expenses for the child and dependent care credit include amounts paid to allow the taxpayer (and spouse if filing jointly) to work and cover the cost of care for a qualifying person.

Work-related expenses are those that enable a taxpayer to work or look for work. For married couples, both spouses must work or look for work (unless one or both spouses are students or incapable of self-care). Work can be full time or part time. Expenses paid to enable a taxpayer to do volunteer work are not eligible for the credit.

Examples of work-related expenses include:

- Fees to a daycare center (as long as the dependent child spends at least eight hours each day in the taxpayer's home). The center must comply with all state and local regulations.
- The cost of day camp (but *not* the cost of overnight camp).
- The cost of transportation provided by the caregiver to or from the place where care is provided. However, transportation cost for the caregiver is not eligible.
- Tuition in nursery school, preschool, or other similar programs. However, tuition for kindergarten and any higher grade, summer school, and tutoring are not eligible. Expenses for before- or after-school care for kindergarten and higher grades are eligible.
- Wages to a housekeeper, babysitter, or au pair for care in the taxpayer's home.

A taxpayer who does not work or look for work for the entire year must prorate expenses on a daily basis.

Example

Simon, a widower, pays $250 each month for the care of his six-year-old daughter so he can work. However, in 2012, if Simon works for only two months and 15 days, his work-related expenses are $625 (2½ months × $250).

Temporary absences from work are disregarded (i.e., treated as work). An absence of two weeks or less is automatically disregarded. An absence of more than two weeks may be considered a temporary absence, depending on the circumstances.

Payments to relatives who are not the taxpayer's dependents can be treated as work-related expenses. Thus, a taxpayer who pays her nondependent mother to care for her child while she works can treat the payments as work-related expenses. However, amounts paid to these individuals cannot be counted as work-related expenses:

- The taxpayer's dependent for whom the taxpayer (or taxpayer's spouse if filing jointly) can claim an exemption.
- The taxpayer's child who is under the age of 19 at the end of the year (whether the child is the taxpayer's dependent or not).
- A person who was the taxpayer's spouse at any time during the year. Thus, for example, if the taxpayer divorces on September 1 and pays his former spouse to care for the couple's child, these payments are not work-related expenses.
- The parent of the taxpayer's qualifying person if the qualifying person is the taxpayer's child and under age 13.

Dollar Limit

When figuring the child and dependent care credit, the maximum amount of qualifying expenses that can be used to figure the amount of the credit is:

- $3,000 if a taxpayer has one qualifying child, OR
- $6,000 if a taxpayer has more than one qualifying child

The dollar limit is reduced if the taxpayer receives dependent care benefits from an employer that are excluded or deducted from income. These benefits reduce the maximum amount of qualifying work-related expenses dollar for dollar.

Example

Harold is a single parent with one qualifying child. He earns a salary of $25,000 a year and pays $2,800 in work-related dependent care expenses. His employer pays an additional $1,200 of dependent care expenses, which is excluded from Harold's gross income. The maximum dollar amount for figuring the credit is $1,800 ($3,000 for one qualifying child – $1,200 of excludable employer-paid benefits). Thus, even though Harold paid $2,800 out of pocket in eligible dependent care costs, only $1,800 can be taken into account in figuring the credit.

TIP: Generally, taxpayers with higher incomes benefit more from contributing to an employer-sponsored dependent care flexible spending account (FSA) than taking a credit for expenses paid with after-tax funds. For example, if a taxpayer is in the 28% tax bracket and pays $3,000 for child care expenses, contributing the $3,000 to a child care FSA creates tax savings of $840 ($3,000 × 28%).

However, if the taxpayer does not contribute to an FSA but pays the $3,000 child care with after-tax funds and claims the credit, the taxpayer's tax savings are $600 ($3,000 expenses × 20% credit rate = $600). It is always best to compare and choose the most advantageous benefit.

Figuring the Credit

The credit is figured by multiplying the amount of qualifying expenses (up to the dollar limit) by a percentage. The percentage depends on the taxpayer's AGI, as shown in Table 28.1.

TABLE 28.1 Applicable Percentage for the Child and Dependent Care Credit

Adjusted Gross Income		**Applicable Percentage**
Over	But not over	
$0	$15,000	35%
$15,000	$17,000	34%
$17,000	$19,000	33%
$19,000	$21,000	32%
$21,000	$23,000	31%
$23,000	$25,000	30%
$25,000	$27,000	29%
$27,000	$29,000	28%
$29,000	$31,000	27%
$31,000	$33,000	26%
$33,000	$35,000	25%
$35,000	$37,000	24%
$37,000	$39,000	23%
$39,000	$41,000	22%
$41,000	$43,000	21%
$43,000	No limit	20%

ALERT: Form 2441 requires the taxpayer to provide the EIN, SSN, or other taxpayer identification number of both the qualifying person *and* the care provider as well as the name and address of the care provider.

TIP: The taxpayer should retain records of work-related expenses, including invoices, canceled checks, and credit card statements. These do not have to be filed with the return but should be kept with the taxpayer's records.

Example

Harold, in the previous example, has $1,800 of work-related dependent care expenses that can be taken into account in figuring the credit. If his AGI is $19,600, the credit percentage is 32%. Therefore, his credit is $576 ($1,800 × 32%).

Reporting the Credit

The credit is figured on Form 2441 and is then attached to Forms 1040, 1040A, or 1040NR. No credit can be claimed by a taxpayer filing Form 1040EZ, *Income Tax Return for Single and Joint Filers With No Dependents.*

The amount of the credit cannot be more than the tax owed by the taxpayer. No portion of the credit is refundable.

Review Questions

1. The maximum amount of the child and dependent care credit for a taxpayer with two qualifying children is:

a. $1,050

b. $2,100

c. $3,000

d. $6,000

2. A taxpayer using the following filing status **cannot** claim the child and dependent care credit:

a. Single

b. Head of household

c. Qualifying widow(er)

d. Married filing separately

3. A taxpayer's child celebrates his 13th birthday on May 15. Only expenses paid for care provided through what date qualify for the child and dependent care credit (assuming other requirements are met)?

a. April 15

b. May 14

c. May 15

d. December 31

4. Which of the following is **not** treated as earned income for purposes of the child and dependent care credit?

a. Disability benefits reported as wages

b. Pensions

c. Nontaxable combat pay elected to be included in income

d. Strike benefits reported as wages

5. Which of the following is **not** a work-related expense for a child under age 13 for purposes of the child and dependent care credit?

a. Overnight camp

b. Day camp

c. Preschool tuition

d. Daycare center costs

6. A taxpayer pays a housekeeper to watch his daughter while he is at work. Which of the following need **not** be included on or attached to the taxpayer's return?

a. Form 2441

b. The housekeeper's SSN

c. Canceled checks of payments to the housekeeper

d. The housekeeper's name and address

CHAPTER 29

Child Tax Credit

A taxpayer who has a qualifying child under age 17 may be eligible for a tax credit of up to $1,000 in 2012. Eligibility for the credit does not depend on the taxpayer's making any payments, as does the child and dependent care credit (Chapter 28). The child tax credit applies to each qualifying child of the taxpayer, and there is no limit on the number of children for whom the credit can be claimed.

However, the credit is subject to an income threshold that may limit high-income taxpayers to a partial credit or to no credit at all.

The child tax credit is not refundable, meaning that it is limited to the taxpayer's tax liability. However, certain taxpayers may qualify for the *additional* child tax credit, which is a refundable tax credit.

The child tax credit should not be confused with the child and dependent care credit (explained in Chapter 28). Depending on the circumstances, a taxpayer may be able to claim *both* the child tax credit and the child and dependent care credit.

Qualifying Child

The credit can be claimed only for a qualifying child, which is the same definition as a qualifying child under the dependency rules (see Chapter 3). However, a child who is a resident of Canada or Mexico and is otherwise a qualifying child for the dependency exemption does not qualify as a dependent for the child tax credit. A qualifying child for the dependent care credit must satisfy these requirements:

- *Relationship.* The child must be the taxpayer's child, stepchild, foster child, sibling, stepsibling, or a descendant of any of them, such as a niece, nephew, or grandchild.
- *Age of child.* The child must be under the age of 17 at the end of the year. The child must also be younger than the taxpayer (and taxpayer's spouse if filing jointly) claiming the child.

Example

Zach is age 18 and supports his nephew, John, who turned 16 on September 20. The age test is satisfied because John is under 17 at the end of the year and is younger than Zach.

- *Support.* The qualifying child cannot have provided more than half of his or her own support for the year.
- *Living with taxpayer.* The qualifying child must have lived with the taxpayer for more than half the year. A child is treated as living with the taxpayer for the full year if the child is born or dies during the year and the taxpayer's home was the child's home for the time he or she was alive.
- *Dependent.* The taxpayer must be allowed the dependency exemption for the qualifying child.
- *Citizenship.* The qualifying child must be either a U.S. citizen, a U.S. national, or a U.S. resident alien. An adopted child who lives with the taxpayer for the full calendar year as a member of the household is treated as meeting the citizenship test. As noted, a child who is a resident of Canada or Mexico is *not* a qualifying child for purposes of the child tax credit even though he or she may qualify as the taxpayer's dependent for the dependency exemption.
- *Joint return.* The qualifying child must not file a joint return unless the return is filed only to claim a refund of all taxes paid and neither spouse would owe taxes if separate returns were filed. In some situations, a child may be the qualifying child of more than one taxpayer. Only one taxpayer can claim the child tax credit. The tie-breaker rules for the dependency exemption apply for the child tax credit as well (see Chapter 3).

ALERT: A custodial parent who releases the dependency exemption for a qualifying child (by filing Form 8332, *Release/Revocation of Release of Claim to Exemption for Child by Custodial Parent*; see Chapter 3) also effectively releases the child tax credit. This allows the noncustodial parent to claim the dependency exemption and the child tax credit, subject to the credit's income restrictions.

Amount of the Credit

The amount of the credit is $1,000 per qualifying child. However, the credit may be reduced in two situations:

1. *The credit exceeds the taxpayer's tax liability.* In this case, the credit is limited to the amount of the tax liability. If there is no tax liability, then no credit allowed. (However, a taxpayer with no tax liability may be eligible for the additional child tax credit, discussed later in this chapter.)
2. *The taxpayer's modified adjusted gross income (MAGI) exceeds a threshold amount based on filing status.* If MAGI falls within the phase-out range, the credit is reduced by $50 for each $1,000 of MAGI over the threshold.

ALERT: For purposes of the child tax credit, MAGI is AGI increased by the foreign earned income exclusion, the exclusion for income from Puerto Rico, or the income exclusion for residents of American Samoa.

Thus, for a taxpayer with no foreign income, MAGI is the same as AGI. Table 29.1 shows the phase-out thresholds.

TABLE 29.1 Modified Adjusted Gross Income Thresholds

Filing Status	MAGI threshold for reducing the credit
Married filing jointly	$110,000
Single, head of household, or qualifying widow(er)	$75,000
Married filing separately	$55,000

Example

Florence is a single parent with one qualifying child and MAGI of $78,000. Because her MAGI is $3,000 over the $75,000 threshold, her $1,000 credit is reduced to $850 ($50 reduction per $1,000 over the threshold × 3). The reduction is based on MAGI, not the number of qualifying children. Thus, if Florence had two qualifying children, her $2,000 credit ($1,000 × 2) would be reduced by the same $150, giving her a credit of $1,850 ($2,000 – $150). With three qualifying children, her $3,000 credit ($1,000 × 3) would be reduced by the same $150; she can claim a credit of $2,850 ($3,000 – $150).

Claiming the Credit

The taxpayer must file Form 1040 or Form 1040A, *U.S. Individual Income Tax Return*, to claim the child tax credit. The credit cannot be claimed on Form 1040EZ, *Income Tax Return for Single and Joint Filers With No Dependents*. The taxpayer must provide the name and tax identification number (usually Social Security Number) of each qualifying child.

The taxpayer must complete one of two worksheets for the child tax credit. Use the *Child Tax Credit* Worksheet in IRS Pub. 972, *Child Tax Credit*, if the taxpayer claims the mortgage interest credit, District of Columbia first-time homebuyer credit, and/or the residential energy efficiency property credit. This worksheet must also be used if the taxpayer is excluding any foreign earned income, income from Puerto Rico, or income from American Samoa. A taxpayer who is not required to complete the worksheet in Pub. 972 must complete the worksheet in the instructions for Form 1040.

Additional Child Tax Credit

The additional child tax credit (ACTC) is not a separate credit or an amount greater than the regular child tax credit. Rather, the ACTC is available to eligible taxpayers whose tax liability prevents them from claiming the child tax credit. The ACTC is refundable, which means it is paid to an eligible taxpayer even if the credit exceeds the taxpayer's tax liability.

TIP: The ACTC cannot exceed the maximum amount of the child tax credit ($1,000). For example, a taxpayer with one qualifying child who receives a child tax credit of $400 cannot receive an ACTC greater than $600.

The ACTC is figured on Form 8812, *Additional Child Tax Credit*. The amount of the ACTC is the lesser of:

- The amount of the child tax credit remaining after reducing the regular tax and any alternative minimum tax (AMT) to zero OR
- 15% of earned income in excess of $3,000

Example

The Johnsons have two qualifying children and MAGI of $28,000. Their child tax credit amount is $2,000. Their earned income is $12,000, and their tax liability is zero. They can claim an additional child tax credit of $1,350 ([$12,000 - $3,000] × 15%).

Taxpayers with three or more qualifying children have two different options to calculate the refundable portion of the child tax credit and may use whichever option results in a greater credit:

- The result of the standard calculation for determining the additional child tax credit OR
- The taxpayer's (employee) portion of Social Security and Medicare taxes in excess of the earned income credit, limited to the amount of the child tax credit remaining after reducing regular tax and AMT to zero.

Earned Income

For purposes of the child tax credit, earned income includes only taxable earned income (i.e., not excluded foreign earned income) plus nontaxable combat pay.

Review Questions

1. Which of the following statements about the child tax credit is correct?

a. There is a maximum credit limit, regardless of the number of qualifying children.

b. The credit can be claimed only with respect to certain expenses on behalf of a qualifying child.

c. The credit applies only for a child under the age of 17 at the end of the year.

d. There is no income limit on eligibility for the credit.

2. Which of the following individuals **cannot** be a qualifying child for the child tax credit, even if under age 17 at the end of the year?

a. Aunt

b. Nephew

c. Grandchild

d. Foster child

3. A taxpayer has four children under the age of 17 and files as head of household. Assuming eligibility tests are met and the taxpayer's MAGI is $80,000, what is the maximum child tax credit that can be claimed (assuming sufficient tax liability)?

a. $1,000

b. $1,500

c. $3,750

d. $4,000

4. The additional child tax credit is the lesser of the child tax credit amount greater than tax liability or 15% of __________ in excess of $3,000.

a. Adjusted gross income

b. Modified adjusted gross income

c. Earned income

d. Taxable income

5. A single taxpayer is the custodial parent of two children under the age of 17, and she claimed the dependency exemption for both of them. Her wages are $48,000, and she has no other income. Her ex-spouse, the noncustodial parent, has earned income of $69,000. Neither parent claims a foreign earned income exclusion. Which parent can claim the child tax credit and for how much?

a. Custodial parent claims $1,000; noncustodial parent claims $1,000.

b. Custodial parent claims $2,000.

c. Noncustodial parent claims $2,000.

d. Neither parent can claim any credit.

Education Credits

A taxpayer may be eligible for an education credit for certain costs of higher (postsecondary) education. There are two education credits: the American Opportunity Tax Credit and the Lifetime Learning Credit.

The American Opportunity Tax Credit applies to the first four years of higher education and is capped at $2,500 per year. However, 40% of the credit can be refundable, which means that a taxpayer can receive a refund even if the available credit exceeds the tax liability. The credit is phased out at higher income levels based on filing status.

The Lifetime Learning Credit is capped at $2,000 per year. Unlike the American Opportunity Tax Credit, which applies to the first four years of higher education only, the Lifetime Learning Credit may be claimed for any level of higher education. However, no part of this credit is refundable. The credit is phased out at higher income levels that are indexed to inflation and based on filing status.

Education credits are coordinated with other education-related tax benefits to ensure that a taxpayer cannot claim a double benefit with respect to the same expenses.

Qualified education expenses may be paid in cash, by credit card, or with the use of borrowed funds (i.e., student loans).

TIP: A taxpayer whose modified adjusted gross income (MAGI) is too high to claim the credit for the qualified education expenses of his or her dependent has the option to waive the dependency exemption. This allows the student to claim the credit (assuming the student has income on which taxes are owed so that the credit can be used). However, if the taxpayer qualifies to claim the student as a dependent but chooses not to do so, the student may claim the education credit but *cannot* claim his or her own exemption.

Requirements for Education Credits

Certain requirements are applicable to both credits, as follows:

- *Credit for taxpayer, spouse, or dependent.* The credit applies to qualified expenses for a taxpayer, spouse, or dependent. A taxpayer who does not claim an exemption on the tax return for a dependent cannot claim an education credit for that dependent. A taxpayer who is claimed on another person's return cannot claim an education credit.
- *Filing status.* The credit cannot be claimed by a married taxpayer filing using the married filing separate filing status.

- *Citizenship or residency.* The taxpayer (and spouse if married) must be a U.S. citizen or resident; a taxpayer who is a nonresident alien for any part of the year and who does not elect to be treated as a resident for tax purposes cannot claim the credit.
- *Reduction for tax-free education benefits.* The amount of qualified expenses taken into account in figuring an education credit must be reduced by tax-free scholarships and other tax-free benefits. Other tax-free benefits include any grants, tax-free distributions from education savings accounts, and tax-free distributions from qualified tuition programs (QTPs), also called 529 plans. Gifts, inheritances, loans, withdrawals from savings accounts, or payments for services do not reduce qualified education expenses.
- *No double benefits.* A taxpayer who is eligible for both an education credit and the above-the-line deduction for tuition and fees based on the same expenses can choose either benefit. A taxpayer who is eligible for both credits with respect to a student should choose the one that provides the greater tax benefit; only one type of credit can be claimed on a return with respect to a specific student. However, the American Opportunity Tax Credit can be claimed for one student and the Lifetime Learning Credit can be claimed for another student in the same year.

TIP: No reduction of qualified education expenses is required for the portion of a scholarship or fellowship that is restricted to costs that are not qualified expenses (such as room and board). Even if use of the money is not restricted, the portion of a taxable scholarship or fellowship does not reduce the amount of qualified expenses on which the credit is figured.

Example

Samantha is a single parent with a son, Jimmy, who is a sophomore in college. Samantha is taking graduate-level courses to advance her career. Assuming she meets all requirements, she can claim an American Opportunity Tax Credit for the college expenses of Jimmy and the Lifetime Learning Credit for her own graduate school expenses.

There are a number of differences between the American Opportunity Tax Credit and the Lifetime Learning Credit. These differences are discussed throughout this chapter and briefly explained in Table 30.1.

American Opportunity Tax Credit

The American Opportunity Tax Credit is calculated as 100% of the first $2,000 of qualified expenses plus 25% of the next $2,000 of qualified expenses, for a maximum credit of $2,500. Of this credit amount, up to 40% ($1,000) is refundable. The credit is available to qualified students annually for up to four years of postsecondary school education.

This credit was passed into law in 2009 to temporarily replace the Hope Credit for tax years 2009 and 2010, and was subsequently extended through tax year 2017. The Hope Credit was more restrictive than the American Opportunity Tax Credit. Under the Hope Credit, the top credit was 100% of the first $1,000 of expenses (as adjusted for inflation) and 50% of the next $1,000 of expenses (as adjusted for inflation). Also, the Hope Credit applied only to the first two years of higher education.

TABLE 30.1 Comparison of Education Credits

Caution. You can claim both the American Opportunity Credit and the Lifetime Learning Credit on the same return—but not for the same student.

	American Opportunity Credit	Lifetime Learning Credit
Maximum credit	Up to $2,500 credit per **eligible student**	Up to $2,000 credit per **return**
Limit on modified adjusted gross income (MAGI)	$180,000 if married filing jointly; $90,000 if single, head of household, or qualifying widow(er)	$120,000 if married filing jointly; $60,000 if single, head of household, or qualifying widow(er)
Refundable or nonrefundable	40% of credit may be refundable	Credit limited to the amount of tax you must pay on your taxable income
Number of years of postsecondary education	Available **ONLY** for the first **4** years of postsecondary education	Available for all years of postsecondary education and for courses to acquire or improve job skills
Number of tax years credit available	Available **ONLY** for **4** tax years per eligible student	Available for an unlimited number of years
Type of degree required	Student must be pursuing an undergraduate degree or other recognized education credential	Student does not need to be pursuing a degree or other recognized education credential
Number of courses	Student must be enrolled at least half time for at least one academic period beginning during the tax year	Available for one or more courses
Felony drug conviction	No felony drug convictions on student's records	Felony drug convictions are permitted
Qualified expenses	Tuition and required enrollment fees. Course-related books, supplies, and equipment **do not** need to be purchased from the institution in order to qualify.	Tuition and required enrollment fees, including amounts required to be paid to the institution for course-related books, supplies, and equipment.
Payments for academic periods	Payments made in 2012 for academic periods beginning in 2011 and in the first 3 months of 2013	

Income Limit

The American Opportunity Tax Credit can be claimed if MAGI does not exceed certain limits, as shown in Table 30.2. MAGI for this purpose is the taxpayer's adjusted gross income increased by the foreign earned income exclusion and certain other foreign items.

TABLE 30.2 MAGI Limits for the American Opportunity Tax Credit

Filing status	Phase-out begins	Phase-out complete
Married filing jointly	$160,000	$180,000
All other (except married filing separately)	$80,000	$90,000

DEFINITION: Academic period means a semester, trimester, quarter, or other period of study (such as summer school session) as determined by the educational institution. If the school uses credit hours or clock hours instead of academic terms, each payment period is treated as an academic period.

Who Is an Eligible Student?

The credit applies only to a student in the first four years of higher education. The student must be pursuing a degree program or other recognized education credential. Moreover, the student must be enrolled in the education program at an eligible educational institution at least half time for at least one **academic period** that begins during the tax year. As with the Hope Credit that it replaced, the American Opportunity Tax Credit requires that the student have no record of a felony drug conviction.

The credit may be claimed in only four tax years for the same student. This four-year credit limit includes any year in which the Hope Credit was claimed. In other words, if the Hope Credit was claimed for two years and the American Opportunity Tax Credit was claimed for two years with respect to the same student, the four-year credit limit is reached.

TIP: When a student takes more than four years to complete college and has claimed the American Opportunity Tax Credit four times, he or she may be eligible to use the Lifetime Learning Credit for expenses in the fifth year and beyond.

Qualified Expenses

Qualified expenses include tuition and fees required for enrollment or attendance at an eligible educational institution (essentially any postsecondary school at which federal financial aid is available).

Qualified expenses also include amounts for books, supplies, and equipment required for a course of study. These items need not be purchased directly from the educational institution as a condition of enrollment or attendance.

Not every education-related expense qualifies for the credit. The following items do *not* qualify:

TIP: Once a qualified expense has been paid, it can be used to figure the credit. Thus, even if a student withdraws from a course, the credit still can be claimed as long as the payment is not refunded. If a partial refund is received, the unrefunded qualified expenses may be used to figure the credit.

- Courses involving sports, games, hobbies, or nondegree courses unless it is part of the student's degree program
- Insurance
- Medical expenses (including student health fees)
- Nonacademic fees (including student activity fees, athletic fees, insurance expenses, or other expenses unrelated to the academic course of instruction)
- Personal expenses
- Room and board
- Transportation

TIP: Refer to Form 1098-T, *Tuition Statement*, which is issued to each enrolled student by the educational institution before January 31 of the following year (January 31, 2013, for 2012).

Figuring and Claiming the Credit

The credit is figured as 100% of the first $2,000 of qualified expenses plus 25% of the next $2,000 of qualified expenses, for a maximum credit of $2,500. Thus, a taxpayer with expenses of $4,000 or more can claim the maximum credit.

The credit phases out when MAGI exceeds the limits discussed earlier in this chapter. The credit is figured on Form 8863, *Education Credits*, which is attached to the return. New for 2012, Form 8863 also asks for information about each eligible student and each educational institution the student attended. The credit cannot be claimed by a taxpayer filing Form 1040EZ, *Income Tax Return for Single and Joint Filers With No Dependents.*

The credit is up to 40% refundable. This means that a taxpayer claiming the maximum credit can receive a refundable credit of up to $1,000.

TIP: A student who is claiming the credit because the parent has waived the dependency exemption for the student cannot treat any part of the credit as refundable. Also, the credit is not available to any student subject to the kiddie tax, even if no kiddie tax is paid. Generally, full-time college students under 24 who have at least one living parent and who did not provide at least half of their own support through earned income are subject to the kiddie tax (see Chapter 34).

Example

Bob is a 21-year-old college senior. He earns approximately $3,500 from a part-time job, some of which he has used to pay tuition costs. He has no other income. Bob's parents also pay for some of his tuition and most of his other expenses. The total cost of his support is $15,000. Although Bob has no unearned income and does not pay kiddie tax, he is subject to the kiddie tax rules and therefore is ineligible for the refundable portion of the American Opportunity Tax Credit.

The American Opportunity Tax Credit is figured on a per-student basis. Thus, a taxpayer with two children in college who meet the requirements for the American Opportunity Tax Credit can claim a credit of up to $2,500 for each student, for a total maximum credit of $5,000.

Lifetime Learning Credit

The Lifetime Learning Credit applies to all postsecondary courses or programs at eligible educational institutions. The Lifetime Learning Credit is 20% of the first $10,000 of qualifying expenses paid for all eligible students, for a maximum credit of $2,000 per tax return per tax year. Thus, regardless of the number of students attending school, the maximum credit that can be claimed is $2,000 per tax return. No part of the credit is refundable.

TIP: Payments made in 2012 for an academic period beginning in the first three months of 2013 can be taken into account when figuring the credit for 2012. Thus, a parent who pays tuition in December 2012 for a child's semester starting in January 2013 can use the tuition in figuring the 2012 credit.

Income Limit

The Lifetime Learning Credit can be claimed if MAGI does not exceed certain limits in 2012, as shown in Table 30.3. MAGI for this purpose is the taxpayer's adjusted gross income increased by the foreign earned income exclusion and certain other foreign items.

TABLE 30.3 MAGI Limits for the Lifetime Learning Credit

Filing status	Phase-out begins	Phase-out complete
Married filing jointly	$104,000	$124,000
All other (except married filing separately)	$52,000	$62,000

TIP: Unlike the American Opportunity Tax Credit, a felony drug conviction will not disqualify a student from the Lifetime Learning Credit.

TIP: Form 1098-T, which is issued by the educational institution to each enrolled student no later than January 31, shows payments received or billed for qualified tuition and related expenses the previous year.

TIP: A taxpayer who is not eligible for either credit or for the tuition and fees deduction (e.g., because MAGI is too high) may be able to deduct education expenses as a miscellaneous itemized deduction if the courses are work-related (see Chapter 26).

Who Is an Eligible Student?

The credit applies for a student in any postsecondary education program. There is no cap on the number of years for which the credit can be claimed, and the credit can also be available to students who take courses to acquire or improve job skills.

The student does not have to be pursuing a degree or other recognized education credential. Thus, the credit can be claimed even if the student takes only one course.

Qualified Expenses

Qualified expenses include tuition and fees required for enrollment or attendance at an eligible institution. Other qualified expenses include books, supplies, and equipment that are required to be paid to the institution as a condition of enrollment. Qualified expenses do *not* include:

- Courses involving sports, games, hobbies, or nondegree courses unless it is part of the student's degree program or helps the student acquire or improve job skills
- Insurance
- Medical expenses (including student health fees)
- Nonacademic fees (such as student activity fees, athletic fees, insurance expenses, or other expenses unrelated to the academic course of instruction
- Personal expenses
- Room and board
- Transportation

Figuring and Claiming the Credit

The credit is 20% of the first $10,000 of qualified expenses, for a maximum Lifetime Learning Credit of $2,000. Thus, a taxpayer with expenses of $10,000 or more can claim the maximum credit.

The credit phases out when MAGI exceeds the limits discussed earlier in this section. The credit is figured on Form 8863, which is attached to the return. New for 2012, Form 8863 also asks for information about each eligible student and each educational institution the student attended. The credit cannot be claimed by a taxpayer filing Form 1040EZ.

The credit is figured on a per-return basis and not on a per-student basis.

Example

The Harrisons are both in graduate school; Mr. Harrison is taking courses toward a master's degree in education to further his teaching career, while Mrs. Harrison is enrolled in an MBA program. The Harrisons spend $12,000 in combined tuition each year. Regardless of the amount of their qualified education costs, the maximum Lifetime Learning Credit that the Harrisons can claim is $2,000 ($10,000 × 20%).

Credit Recapture

When a student receives tax-free educational assistance for, or a refund of, an expense used to figure an education credit, recapture of some or all of the credit may be triggered, meaning that some or all of the credit may need to be repaid.

Figure the education credit as if the assistance or refund was received in the tax year the credit was taken. Then subtract the refigured credit from the credit actually claimed on that return. The difference is the amount of recapture, which is reported as additional tax on the Tax line of the current-year tax return. An amended tax return is not filed.

Example

In August 2012, the McDonalds paid qualified education expenses of $7,000 for their daughter, Megan, who began college in September 2012. They claimed an American Opportunity Tax Credit of $2,500 on their 2012 return, which they filed in February 2013. In March 2013, $4,000 of the tuition was refunded by the school because of a scholarship Megan had won.

The McDonalds refigure the credit using $3,000 ($7,000 payment less the $4,000 refund) to arrive at a credit of $2,250 (100% of $2,000 + 25% of $1,000). Subtracting this from the credit they claimed ($2,500) results in a $250 recapture amount. This amount is reported as additional tax on their 2013 return.

Review Questions

1. In figuring an education credit, the amount of eligible expenses taken into account must be reduced by:
   a. Gifts
   b. Inheritances
   c. Tax-free distributions from 529 plans
   d. Student loans

2. The maximum American Opportunity Tax Credit is:
   a. $1,000
   b. $2,000
   c. $2,500
   d. $10,000

3. Which of the following expenses qualify for the American Opportunity Tax Credit?
   a. Books required for a course of study
   b. Student health fees
   c. Room and board
   d. Transportation

4. Which of the following rules applies to the American Opportunity Tax Credit but not to the Lifetime Learning Credit?
   a. The student must be the taxpayer's dependent (or the taxpayer or spouse).
   b. The student cannot have a felony drug conviction.
   c. The taxpayer, if married, must file a joint return.
   d. The taxpayer (and spouse) cannot be a nonresident alien.

5. In 2011, a taxpayer claimed an American Opportunity Tax Credit. In 2012, the student receives a scholarship and a refund of tuition that had been the basis of the 2011 credit. What should the taxpayer do?
   a. Nothing, because the 2011 return has already been filed.
   b. File an amended return for 2011 to refigure the credit.
   c. Report the recapture amount on the 2012 return as other income on Form 1040 line 21.
   d. Report the recapture amount on the 2012 return as additional tax.

Other Tax Credits

Some tax credits, such as the Child and Dependent Care Credit (Chapter 28) and the Lifetime Learning Credit (Chapter 30), are nonrefundable and cannot exceed a taxpayer's tax liability. In most cases, the portion of a nonrefundable tax credit that exceeds a taxpayer's tax liability is lost forever; only some credits have a carryforward.

Other credits, such as the Earned Income Credit (Chapter 27) and the American Opportunity Credit (Chapter 30), are wholly or partially refundable. They can be used to offset tax. If they exceed the tax, the excess is refunded to the taxpayer.

In addition to the tax credits explained in Chapters 27 through 30, there are a number of other tax credits for individuals. This chapter explains nonrefundable and refundable tax credits not covered in prior chapters. Nonrefundable credits include the credit for qualified retirement savings contributions (Saver's Credit), residential energy efficient property credit, alternative motor vehicle credit, the credit for the elderly or disabled, the foreign tax credit, and the mortgage interest credit. For 2012, the Health Coverage Tax Credit is refundable.

The minimum tax credit, which relates to the alternative minimum tax, is discussed in Chapter 33.

Credit for Qualified Retirement Savings Contributions (Saver's Credit)

The credit for qualified retirement savings contributions, often referred to as the Saver's Credit, is designed to encourage lower-income taxpayers to contribute to a company-sponsored retirement plan, such as a 401(k) plan, or a personal individual retirement account (IRA). The credit is in addition to the tax benefits for making the contributions (the exclusion for wage income contributed to a 401(k) plan or a tax deduction for contributions to a traditional IRA). In effect, this is one of the few instances in the tax law where a taxpayer can "double dip" (i.e., obtain two tax benefits for the same action).

The credit is 10%, 20%, or 50% of contributions or elective deferrals up to $2,000. Thus, the maximum credit is $1,000 (50% of a maximum contribution or elective deferral of $2,000 contribution). However, the amount of the credit depends on the taxpayer's filing status, modified adjusted gross income (MAGI), and amount of the retirement plan contribution(s). The credit is nonrefundable.

Requirements

The taxpayer and/or spouse must make contributions to any of these plans during the tax year:

- A traditional IRA or Roth IRA (other than rollover contributions)
- Elective deferrals to a 401(k) or 403(b) plan (including a designated Roth, a governmental 457 plan, simplified employee pension (SEP) plan, or savings incentive match plan for employees (SIMPLE plan))
- Voluntary employee contributions to a qualified 4974(c) retirement plan (including the federal Thrift Savings Plan)
- A 501(c)(18)(D) plan

The person making the contribution or elective deferral cannot claim the credit if any of these applies:

- The taxpayer was born after January 1, 1995.
- The taxpayer is claimed as a dependent on someone else's return.
- The taxpayer is a full-time student. (The taxpayer is considered a full-time student if during any part of each of five calendar months during the year the taxpayer was enrolled full-time at a school or took a full-time on-farm training program.)
- The taxpayer's MAGI exceeds the income limit.

Income Limit

The credit percentage applied to contributions or elective deferrals depends on a taxpayer's filing status and MAGI. For the Saver's Credit, MAGI is adjusted gross income plus any exclusion or deduction for foreign earned income or income for bona fide residents of Puerto Rico or American Samoa.

The applicable credit percentage can be found in Table 31.1.

TABLE 31.1 2012 Income Limits for the Saver's Credit

Married Filing Jointly		Head of Household		All Other Filers		Credit Percentage
Over	Not over	Over	Not over	Over	Not over	
$0	$34,500	$0	$25,875	$0	$17,250	50%
$34,501	$37,500	$25,876	$28,125	$17,251	$18,750	20%
$37,501	$57,500	$28,126	$43,125	$18,751	$28,750	10%
$57,500		$43,125		$28,750		0%

Example

Craig files as head of household and contributes $3,500 to his IRA in 2012. His MAGI is $30,000. Because his MAGI is over $28,125 but not over $43,125, he can claim a Saver's Credit of $200 (10% of the $2,000 maximum contribution taken into account for purposes of the Saver's Credit).

Reporting the Credit

The credit is figured on Form 8880, *Credit for Qualified Retirement Savings Contributions*, which is attached to Form 1040 or Form 1040A, *U.S. Individual Income Tax Return.* The credit cannot be claimed by a taxpayer filing Form 1040EZ, *Income Tax Return for Single and Joint Filers With No Dependents.*

Adoption Credit

The tax law rewards taxpayers who adopt a child by allowing them to claim a tax credit. For 2012, the credit of up to $12,650 is nonrefundable.

The credit applies only for the adoption of an eligible child. An eligible child is:

- Any child under 18 years old, OR
- A person of any age who is physically or mentally incapable of self-care.

The credit is limited to qualified expenses (defined later). However, in the case of a **child with special needs**, the taxpayer can claim the full amount of the credit without regard to the amount of qualified expenses.

DEFINITION: A **child with special needs** is a U.S. citizen or resident who a U.S. state or the District of Columbia has determined should not be returned to his or her parent's home, and who, in the opinion of the state, is unlikely to be adopted without assistance. Factors used by a state in making this determination include the child's ethnic background, age, whether the child is a member of a minority or sibling group, and whether the child has a medical condition or a physical, mental, or emotional handicap.

Qualified Expenses

Only certain adoption-related expenses qualify for the credit. These qualified adoption expenses include:

- Adoption fees
- Attorney fees
- Court costs
- Readoption expenses to adopt a foreign child
- Travel expenses while away from home (including meals and lodging)

Adoption-related expenses that do *not* qualify for the credit include:

- Costs paid or reimbursed by the taxpayer's employer
- Expenses claimed as a deduction or credit under any other federal tax rule
- Expenses that violate state or federal law
- Surrogate parenting arrangement costs

ALERT: A married person filing separately can claim the credit only if he or she lived apart from the spouse for the last six months of the year, the eligible child lived with the taxpayer for more than half the year, the taxpayer provided more than half the cost of keeping up the home, and the taxpayer uses head of household filing status.

Income Limits

A taxpayer may be eligible for a partial credit or for no credit at all if the taxpayer's MAGI is within or exceeds a MAGI phase-out range. For this purpose, MAGI is generally adjusted gross income (AGI), without regard to adjustments for certain foreign income. The credit limit and phase-out do *not* depend on a taxpayer's filing status; the same limits apply whether the taxpayer is married filing jointly or single. The full credit can be claimed for MAGI of $189,710 or less. The credit phases out for MAGI over $189,710 but less than $229,710. No credit can be claimed when MAGI is $229,710 or more.

When to Claim the Credit

Generally, the credit is claimed in the year in which the adoption becomes final. However, special rules may allow the taxpayer to claim the credit in a year before the adoption is finalized. This depends on whether the adoption is a domestic or foreign adoption.

TIP: If the child is a U.S. citizen or U.S. resident, the adoption credit can be claimed even if the adoption falls through and is never finalized.

For a child who is a U.S. citizen or resident, follow Table 31.2.

TABLE 31.2 When to Claim the Credit for a Child Who Is a U.S. Citizen or Resident

If the taxpayer paid qualifying expenses in . . .	Take the credit in . . .
Any year before the year the adoption becomes final	The year *after* the year of the payment
The year the adoption becomes final	The year the adoption becomes final
Any year after the year the adoption becomes final	The year of payment

For a child who is not a U.S. citizen or resident, follow Table 31.3.

TABLE 31.3 When to Claim the Credit for a Foreign Child

If the taxpayer paid qualifying expenses in . . .	Take the credit in . . .
Any year before the year the adoption becomes final	The year the adoption becomes final
The year the adoption becomes final	The year the adoption becomes final
Any year after the year the adoption becomes final	The year of payment

Carryforward For 2012, the credit is not refundable. There is a five-year carry forward for any unused portion of the credit.

Prior to 2010, there was also a five-year carryforward. However, most taxpayers were able to use up carryforwards in 2010 or 2011 as part of the refundable credit that applied only in these two years. Therefore, it is unlikely that there will be any credit carryforward to claim on a 2012 return.

Reporting the Credit

The credit is figured on Form 8839, *Qualified Adoption Expenses*, which is attached to Form 1040. The credit cannot be claimed on Form 1040A or 1040EZ.

> **ALERT:** Because documents must be attached to the return, the return cannot be e-filed.

In order to claim the credit, the taxpayer must attach certain documentation to the return. For domestic adoptions finalized in the current year or in a previous year and for foreign adoptions finalized in the current year, attach:

- For a domestic or international adoption finalized in the United States, a copy of the adoption order or decree must be attached to Form 8839.
- For adoptions finalized abroad, the child's *Hague Adoption Certificate*, an IH-3 visa, or a foreign adoption decree translated into English is required. If the child's country of origin is not a party to the Hague Convention, then attach a copy of the translated decree or an IR-2 or IR-3 visa.
- If the taxpayer adopts a special needs child, the state determination certificate saying that the child has special needs.

A taxpayer who qualified to claim an adoption credit (original credit or carryforward) but failed to file Form 8839 may file an amended return for each year in which the credit was not claimed.

For a domestic adoption that was not finalized in the current year or in a previous year, refer to the Form 8839 instructions for documentation options.

Residential Energy Credits

The tax law rewards homeowners who make certain energy improvements to their residences by providing two types of nonrefundable credits, the nonbusiness energy property credit and the residential energy efficient property credit. There are no income limits on claiming these credits.

Nonbusiness Energy Property Credit

The nonbusiness energy property credit has changed multiple times since the credit was first introduced in 2006. In 2006, the credit had a $500 maximum ($200 for windows) and was subject to a $500 lifetime maximum. This initial version of the credit was available for the 2006 and 2007 tax years. The credit was then allowed to expire and was not available for the 2008 tax year. The credit was reintroduced in 2009 and was available for the 2009 and 2010 tax years. However, the credit was modified to a $1,500 credit (no limit for windows) and had a $1,500 lifetime maximum without regard to the 2006–2007 version of the credit.

The credit is 10% of eligible costs, for a maximum lifetime credit of $500 ($200 for windows). However, the lifetime maximum rules require the taxpayer to take into account all previous versions of the credit the taxpayer claimed in order to determine eligibility for the credit. Thus, for 2012, the $500 limit is reduced by any nonbusiness energy property credit previously claimed by the taxpayer in 2006–2007 and 2009–2011. Therefore, any taxpayer who claimed a $500 credit in 2006 or 2007 or a $1,500 credit during 2009 or 2010 could not claim any additional credit in 2012, despite making qualified improvements.

Qualified improvements made to a taxpayer's principal residence can be considered when figuring the credit. These include building envelope components (such as doors, windows, insulation, and heat resistant roofs) as well as qualified air conditioners, heaters, stoves that use biomass fuel, and water heaters.

However, special dollar limits apply to certain improvements. This list includes eligible property and any credit limits for particular types of property:

- Advanced main air circulating fans used in natural gas, propane, or oil furnaces: $50
- Natural gas, propane, or oil furnaces or hot water boilers: $150
- Energy-efficient building property (central air conditioners, certain heat pump water heaters, electric heat pumps, and stoves that use biomass fuel): $300
- Exterior doors
- Insulation
- Metal or asphalt roofs with pigmented coatings or cooling granules designed to reduce heat gain

As noted, the lifetime limit for exterior windows (including skylights) is $200.

Example

Theresa and Dave made energy improvements to their home in 2006 that qualified them to receive a $500 nonbusiness energy property credit on their 2006 return. They then made additional improvements to their home in 2007 but were unable to claim any portion of the credit for the 2007 tax year because they had used their entire $500 lifetime maximum in 2006.

In 2010, the couple made additional improvements to their home that qualified them to receive an additional nonbusiness energy property credit of $1,200 on their 2010 return. Theresa and Dave were allowed to claim the $1,200 credit in 2010 because the lifetime maximum rules for this version of the credit did not require them to take into account the amount of credit claimed on their 2006 return. Thus, they were eligible for the full $1,200 in nonbusiness energy property credit on their 2010 return.

In 2011, Theresa and Dave make additional improvements to their home that would qualify them for a nonbusiness energy property credit of $500. However, the couple is not eligible for the credit because they used up their entire $500 lifetime maximum in prior tax years ($500 was claimed in 2006 and $1,200 in 2010). Therefore, they are ineligible for the credit in 2012.

Residential EnergyEfficient Property Credit

This credit is calculated as 30% of eligible costs, such as solar panels and geothermal heat pumps. There is no dollar limit on this credit. If any amount of the credit cannot be used in the current tax year because it exceeds tax liability, the credit can be carried forward to the next tax year. Form 5695, *Residential Energy Credits,* can be used to determine the amount of the carryforward.

This credit can be used for certain energy improvements to a taxpayer's home that is located in the United States; it need not be the taxpayer's principal residence. The credit applies to qualified property which includes:

- Solar electric property.
- Solar water heating property (other than for swimming pools or hot tubs).
- Fuel cell property. (The credit is limited to $500 for each one-half kilowatt of capacity of the property.)
- Small wind energy property.
- Geothermal heat pumps.

In some cases, labor, installation and hardware costs can also be included when figuring the amount of the credit. Taxpayers also can rely on manufacturer's certifications about the energy efficiency of the property.

Reporting the Credits

Both the nonbusiness energy property credit and the residential energy-efficient property credit are claimed on Form 5695, which is attached to Form 1040. The credit(s) cannot be claimed by a taxpayer filing Form 1040A or 1040EZ. See the Form 5695 instructions for additional information on this credit.

ALERT: The taxpayer's basis in his or her residence must be reduced by the amount of any residential energy credit claimed on the tax return.

Foreign Tax Credit

A taxpayer who pays foreign income taxes can choose to take either an itemized deduction (Chapter 21) or nonrefundable tax credit for the foreign taxes. Usually the payment of foreign income tax occurs with a taxpayer who has foreign investments or who has foreign earned income that is not excludable (Chapter 4). The choice of claiming the itemized deduction or credit for foreign taxes is made on a year-by-year basis, depending on which produces the greater tax savings for the current year.

A taxpayer who opts to take the credit generally must complete Form 1116, *Foreign Tax Credit.* The form does not have to be filed, and the credit can be claimed directly on the taxpayer's return, if all of these conditions apply:

- All of the foreign source income was passive (e.g., interest and dividends).

- All of the foreign-source income and foreign tax paid on it was reported to the taxpayer on Forms 1099-INT, *Interest Income,* and 1099-DIV, *Dividends and Distributions.*
- The total foreign taxes are not more than $300 ($600 if married filing jointly).
- The taxpayer elects to report the foreign tax credit directly on the return and not file Form 1116.

When the taxpayer does not make this election, the foreign tax credit claimed on Form 1116 cannot be more than the taxpayer's U.S. tax liability multiplied by a fraction:

$$\frac{\text{Taxable income from sources outside the U.S.}}{\text{Total taxable income from U.S. and foreign sources}}$$

More information about the foreign tax credit can be found in IRS Pub. 514, *Foreign Tax Credit for Individuals.*

Alternative Motor Vehicle Credit

ALERT: A taxpayer who uses a vehicle for both business and personal driving must take the business portion of the credit into account in figuring the general business credit on Form 3800, *General Business Credit.*

In 2012, taxpayers who purchased qualified fuel cell vehicles may be eligible for the fuel cell vehicle credit. This credit is set by the IRS for each type of qualifying vehicle. The credit, which is claimed on Form 8910, *Alternative Motor Vehicle Credit,* is available for qualified vehicles if purchased and placed in service before January 1, 2015.

Credit for the Elderly or Disabled

A taxpayer who is 65 or older, or who is retired on permanent and total disability and has taxable disability income, may qualify for a nonrefundable tax credit. The credit is very limited and is based on age, filing status, Social Security income received, and the taxpayer's adjusted gross income (AGI). As a practical matter, a single person receiving Social Security retirement benefits of $417 or more per month becomes ineligible for this credit because of the Social Security limits explained later.

DEFINITION: Totally and permanently disabled means that the taxpayer is unable to engage in any substantial gainful activity (performance of significant duties in a job or for self-employment) because of a physical or mental condition. A doctor must certify that the condition is expected to last at least 12 months or result in death.

Requirements

The credit can be claimed only by a "qualified individual." This is someone who is either:

- At least 65 years old at the end of the year (someone who was born on January 1, 1948, is treated as being 65 years old at the end of 2012), OR
- Under age 65 but **totally and permanently disabled**, receiving taxable disability income, and has not reached mandatory retirement age.

An eligible taxpayer who is under age 65 must have a doctor complete a statement certifying that he or she is totally and permanently disabled. The statement in the instructions to Schedule R, *Credit for the Elderly or the Disabled*, can be used for this purpose. A veteran can substitute VA Form 21-0172, *Certification of Permanent and Total Disability*, signed by an authorized person at the Department of Veterans Affairs to certify disability.

A taxpayer who obtained a certification for a prior year may not need a new one for the current year. (Follow the instructions in Part II of Schedule R.)

Citizenship In either case, the taxpayer must be a U.S. citizen or resident alien. However, a nonresident alien who is married to a U.S. citizen or resident alien can qualify if each spouse agrees to treat the nonresident alien spouse as a U.S. resident (thus agreeing to be taxed on their worldwide incomes). Similarly, a taxpayer who is a nonresident alien at the start of the year but becomes a resident alien by the end of the year and is married to a U.S. citizen or resident alien can choose to be treated as a U.S. resident alien for the entire year.

Filing Status A married person generally must file a joint return to claim the credit. However, if the taxpayer and spouse did not live in the same household at *any* time during the year, the taxpayer can take the credit on either a joint or separate return. A married person who qualifies to file as head of household (see Chapter 2) can also claim the credit.

Income Limits

Even if a taxpayer meets the eligibility requirements, no credit can be claimed if income exceeds the amounts shown in Table 31.4. The income limit may be based on either AGI or total nontaxable Social Security benefits and other nontaxable pensions. If a taxpayer's income exceeds the limits in either column, then no credit can be claimed.

TABLE 31.4 Income Limits for Credit for the Elderly or Disabled

	THEN even if you qualify, a taxpayer CANNOT take the credit if ...	
IF filing status is ...	**Adjusted gross income[1] is equal to or more than ...**	**OR the total of nontaxable Social Security and other nontaxable pension(s) is equal to or more than ...**
Single, head of household, or qualifying widow(er) with dependent child	$17,500	$5,000
Married filing a joint return and both spouses qualify	$25,000	$7,500
Married filing a joint return and only one spouse qualifies	$20,000	$5,000
Married filing a separate return	$12,500	$3,750

[1] AGI is the amount on Form 1040, line 38, or Form 1040A, line 22.

ALERT: Form 1098-MA, *Mortgage Assistance Payments*, reports mortgage assistance payments made by State Housing Finance Agencies or the Department of Housing and Urban Development (HUD) under various home owner assistance programs. Mortgage assistance payments from public or governmental agencies are not taxable because they are general welfare payments. However, special rules (including a safe harbor) apply for purposes of deducting home interest. See IRS Pub. 936, *Home Mortgage Interest Deduction*, for additional information.

Reporting the Credit

The credit is figured on Schedule R. The credit cannot be claimed on Form 1040EZ.

Mortgage Interest Credit

An eligible low-income taxpayer may claim a nonrefundable tax credit for part of the home mortgage interest paid each year. An eligible taxpayer is a homeowner who has been issued a qualified mortgage credit certificate (MCC) from a state or local government.

If the taxpayer's mortgage loan amount is equal to (or less than) the certified indebtedness amount shown on the MCC, the taxpayer can base the credit on all interest paid on the mortgage during the year.

If the taxpayer's mortgage loan amount is larger than the certified indebtedness amount shown on the MCC, the taxpayer can base the credit on only part of the interest paid during the year. The amount of interest a taxpayer can use to calculate the credit is figured by multiplying the total interest the taxpayer paid during the year on the mortgage by the next fraction:

$$\frac{\text{Certified indebtedness amount on MCC}}{\text{Original amount of taxpayer's mortgage}}$$

TIP: The portion of this nonrefundable tax credit that exceeds tax liability for the year can be carried forward. The carryforward period is limited to three years. If the taxpayer is subject to the $2,000 annual limit because the certificate rate is more than 20%, the carryforward for such taxpayer is limited to the unused portion of the $2,000 limit (or the taxpayer's share of $2,000 if the credit is shared with a co-owner).

The amount of the credit is based on the certificate credit rate. If the certificate credit rate is 20% or less, the credit is the amount of interest determined above multiplied by the credit certificate rate. If the certificate credit rate is more than 20%, the credit cannot exceed $2,000. When two or more people (other than married couples) co-own the home that relates to the MCC, the $2,000 limit must be divided based on the interest in the home held by each person.

The mortgage interest credit is claimed on Form 8396, *Mortgage Interest Credit*, which is attached to Form 1040. The credit cannot be claimed if the taxpayer files Form 1040A or 1040EZ.

More information about the mortgage interest credit can be found in IRS Pub. 530, *Tax Information for Homeowners*.

ALERT: A taxpayer may have to recapture the federal mortgage subsidy if the home is sold or disposed of within nine years after the date of closing on the mortgage loan.

First-Time Homebuyer Credit

A taxpayer may have been entitled to a nonrefundable credit for certain primary residences purchased between April 9, 2008, and December 31, 2008, or a refundable credit for purchases between January 1, 2009, and April 30, 2010. The credit applied to first-time homebuyers and, for a limited time, to longtime residents who subsequently purchased a new main home. The credit is now expired and therefore cannot be claimed on a 2012 return. However, in certain cases, the taxpayer is required to repay some or all of the credit when the property is disposed of or is no longer the taxpayer's principal residence.

ALERT: The first-time homebuyer credit is not available for home purchases made after April 30, 2010. However, information about the credit is shown below as a backdrop to the credit's repayment rules, which are discussed in detail in Chapter 35.

Health Coverage Tax Credit

An eligible taxpayer may claim a tax credit for certain health coverage. The credit is designed to help certain displaced workers obtain health coverage.

The credit is taken on a month-by-month basis and is refundable. The credit is 72.5% of qualified premiums paid each month. The credit is set to expire at the end of 2013.

An eligible taxpayer must meet all of the next conditions as of the first day of the month for which the credit is claimed:

- The taxpayer is an eligible trade adjustment assistance (TAA) recipient, an alternative TAA (ATAA) recipient, reemployment TAA (RTAA) recipient, or Pension Benefit Guaranty Corporation (PBGC) pension recipient. These terms are defined in the instructions to Form 8885, *Health Coverage Tax Credit.*
- The taxpayer is covered by a health plan and pays the premiums (or portion of the premiums) directly to the health plan (including premiums paid to the U.S. Treasury-Health Coverage Tax Credit (HCTC).
- The taxpayer does not have health coverage through Medicare (Parts A, B, or C), Medicaid, Children's Health Insurance Program (CHIP), or the Federal Employees Health Benefits Program (FEHBP), and was not eligible to receive benefits under the U.S. military health system (TRICARE).
- The taxpayer is not imprisoned.
- The taxpayer's employer does not pay 50% or more of the cost of coverage.
- The taxpayer did not receive a 65% COBRA (Consolidated Omnibus Budget Reconciliation Act of 1985) premium reduction from a former employer or COBRA administrator.
- The taxpayer is not claimed as a dependent on another person's return.

The credit applies to coverage paid for the taxpayer and any qualifying family member. Qualifying family members include the spouse and dependents of the taxpayer. For this purpose, a child of divorced or separated parents is considered a dependent of the custodial parent (not the noncustodial parent). Qualifying family members may not have coverage through Medicare (Parts A, B, or C), Medicaid, CHIP, or FEHBP, be eligible to receive benefits under TRICARE, or covered by, or eligible for coverage under, any employer-sponsored health insurance plan.

Qualified family members may continue to be eligible for the HCTC after the eligible individual becomes eligible for Medicare, finalizes a divorce, or dies.

ALERT: Starting in 2014, there is a new refundable health-related tax credit called the premium tax credit. The new credit is designed to enable qualifying taxpayers to offset the cost of premiums paid for health coverage purchased through a health benefit exchange. The eligibility criteria for the premium tax credit are different from the eligibility criteria for the HCTC.

The credit is claimed on Form 8885. Invoices and other proofs of payment must be attached to the form, which is filed with Form 1040. If the taxpayer e-files, a copy of Form 8885 and the required documents must be attached to Form 8453, *U.S. Individual Income Tax Transmittal for an IRS e-file Return*. Form 8453 and the attachments should be mailed to the address shown in the form's instructions.

Details about this tax credit can be found in IRS Pub. 502, *Medical and Dental Expenses Including the Health Coverage Tax Credit*, and the instructions to Form 8885.

Credit for Excess Social Security or Railroad Retirement Tax

ALERT: There is no wage base limit for the Medicare taxes. No refund can be claimed for withholding of Medicare taxes.

A taxpayer who works for more than one employer during the year may have Social Security and/or tier 1 Railroad Retirement tax withheld in excess of the limit for the annual wage base. The excess amount can be claimed as a tax credit on the return. For 2012, the maximum wage base for Social Security or tier 1 Railroad Retirement tax is $110,100; the maximum tax that should have been withheld is $4,624.20 ($110,100 × the Social Security withholding rate for 2012 of 4.2%).

The credit is claimed directly on the tax return.

TIP: A taxpayer who works for one employer and whose employer simply withheld too much tax cannot claim the credit. The taxpayer should ask the employer for an adjustment. If the employer fails to make the adjustment, the taxpayer can file for a refund on Form 843, *Claim for Refund and Request for Abatement*.

Example

From January through May 2012, Henry worked for the XYZ Company, earning $60,000, from which $2,520 in Social Security tax was withheld. In June 2012, he gets a better job and earns $90,000 for the balance of the year, from which $3,780 in Social Security tax was withheld. Henry can claim a tax credit of $1,675.80 ([$2,520 + $3,780] − $4,624.20).

Each spouse figures the credit separately. The wages of one spouse cannot be added to the other spouse's wages.

Review Questions

1. Which statement about the credit for qualified retirement savings contributions is true?
   a. There are no income limits.
   b. The maximum credit is $1,000.
   c. The credit cannot be claimed if the taxpayer deducts IRA contributions on which the credit is figured.
   d. The credit is refundable.

2. A taxpayer installs solar panels on her home at a cost of $20,000. What is the maximum amount of the credit that can be claimed?
   a. $0
   b. $500
   c. $6,000
   d. $20,000

3. In 2012, which statement about the adoption credit is **false**?
   a. The full credit amount can be claimed for adopting a special needs child without regard to the amount of adoption expenses.
   b. The maximum credit is $12,650.
   c. There are no income limits.
   d. The credit may apply to domestic and foreign adoptions.

4. Who **cannot** take the health coverage tax credit (assuming all other eligibility requirements are met)?
   a. A taxpayer who is another person's dependent
   b. An eligible trade adjustment assistance recipient
   c. A reemployment TAA recipient
   d. A Pension Benefit Guaranty Corporation pension recipient

5. A single taxpayer with modified adjusted gross income of $28,000 makes a salary reduction contribution to her employer's 401(k) plan of $3,000. Her retirement Saver's Credit is:
   a. $300
   b. $600
   c. $1,500
   d. $3,000

PART 4

Other Taxes

CHAPTER 32

Figuring the Regular Tax

A taxpayer's regular income tax is based on taxable income, which is gross income reduced by various adjustments (such as individual retirement account [IRA] deductions and alimony), the standard deduction or itemized deductions, and personal and dependent exemptions. Taxable income is calculated before taking into account any tax credits that the taxpayer may claim.

The method used to determine a taxpayer's tax liability depends on whether taxable income equals or exceeds $100,000 and whether taxable income includes certain types of income.

Keep in mind that the regular tax is only a tentative number. The final tax liability depends on whether the taxpayer owes any alternative minimum tax (see Chapter 33), other taxes, and whether the taxpayer qualifies for any tax credits.

Taxable Income

Taxable income is the result of several computations:

- Gross income (Chapters 4–13 and 18), reduced by
- Adjustments to gross income ("above-the-line deductions," Chapters 15–18), reduced by
- The standard deduction or itemized deductions (Chapters 19–26), reduced by
- Personal and dependent exemptions ($3,800 each in 2012; Chapter 3).

Example

Howard is single with income from wages of $32,000 and interest income of $875. He made a tax-deductible contribution to his IRA of $2,500. He claims the standard deduction ($5,950 in 2012) and has no dependents. His taxable income is $20,625 ($32,000 + $875 – $2,500 – $5,950 – $3,800).

ALERT: A taxpayer with taxable income of $100,000 or more must file Form 1040, *U.S. Individual Income Tax Return*, and cannot file Form 1040A or 1040EZ, *Income Tax Return for Single and Joint Filers With No Dependents.*

ALERT: A taxpayer with any of these special tax computations *must* file Form 1040 and cannot file Form 1040A or 1040EZ.

Regular Tax Computation Options

Most taxpayers can use one of two basic methods to figure the regular tax:

1. Tax tables for taxable income under $100,000
2. Tax rate schedule or tax computation worksheet for taxable income of $100,000 or more

There are special tax computations for unique situations:

- Capital gains and qualified dividends
- Unearned income of a child subject to the kiddie tax (Chapter 34)
- Lump-sum distributions
- Income averaging for farmers and fishermen
- Foreign earned income exclusion, foreign housing exclusion or foreign housing deduction

Tax Table

A taxpayer who is not required to make any special computations and who has taxable income under $100,000 may use the tax table found in IRS Pub. 17, *Your Federal Income Tax*. The table is organized by columns for the different filing statuses, as can be seen in the portion of the tax table shown in Table 32.1.

TABLE 32.1 2012 Tax Table

If line 43 (taxable income) is		And you are			
At least	**But less than**	**Single**	**Married filing jointly**	**Married filing separately**	**Head of Household**
32,000			**Your tax is—**		
32,000	32,050	4,369	3,934	4,369	4,184
32,050	32,100	4,376	3,941	4,376	4,191
32,100	32,150	4,384	3,949	4,384	4,199
32,150	32,200	4,391	3,956	4,391	4,206
32,200	32,250	4,399	3,964	4,399	4,214
32,250	32,300	4,406	3,971	4,406	4,221
32,300	32,350	4,414	3,979	4,414	4,229
32,350	32,400	4,421	3,986	4,421	4,236
32,400	32,450	4,429	3,994	4,429	4,244
32,450	32,500	4,436	4,001	4,436	4,251
32,500	32,550	4,444	4,009	4,444	4,259
32,550	32,600	4,451	4,016	4,451	4,266
32,600	32,650	4,459	4,024	4,459	4,274

If line 43 (taxable income) is		And you are			
At least	But less than	Single	Married filing jointly	Married filing separately	Head of Household
32,000		Your tax is—			
32,650	32,700	4,466	4,031	4,466	4,281
32,700	32,750	4,474	4,039	4,474	4,289
32,750	32,800	4,481	4,046	4,481	4,296
32,800	32,850	4,489	4,054	4,489	4,304
32,850	32,900	4,496	4,061	4,496	4,311
32,900	32,950	4,504	4,069	4,504	4,319
32,950	33,000	4,511	4,076	4,511	4,326

Example

Jasmine files as head of household and has taxable income of $32,624. Her taxable income falls between $32,600 and $32,650, so she looks under the column for her filing status (the last column) to find her tax liability of $4,286.

Tax Computation Worksheet

A taxpayer with taxable income of $100,000 or more must use the Tax Computation Worksheet shown in Table 32.2.

TABLE 32.2 Tax Computation Worksheet

Taxable Income If line 43 is	(a) Enter the amount from line 43	(b) Multiplication amount	(c) Multiply (a) by (b)	(d) Subtraction amount	Tax Subtract (d) from (c). Enter the result here and on Form 1040, line 44
At least $100,000 but not over $178,650	$	× 28% (.28)	$	$6,539	$
Over $178,650 but not over $388,350	$	× 33% (.33)	$	$15,472	$
Over $388,350	$	× 35% (.35)	$	$23,239	$

Example

Carlton is single with taxable income of $112,486. Assuming he does not have to make any special computations, he figures his tax using the tax computation worksheet. His tax liability is $24,957, figured by entering taxable income in column (a), multiplying it by 28%, and subtracting $6,539 as shown in Table 32.2. Carlton's tax liability may be rounded off to the nearest whole dollar on his tax return.

Capital Gains and Qualified Dividends

Net long-term capital gains (long-term capital gains, including capital gain distributions in excess of net short-term capital losses) that are reported on Schedule D (Form 1040), *Capital Gains and Losses*, and qualified dividends are taxed under special rules. In 2012, they are taxed at no more than 15%, even if the taxpayer's tax rate on other income is higher than 15%. Taxpayers in the 10% or 15% tax brackets, including all of their capital gains and qualified dividends, pay *zero* tax. Taxpayers whose income is in higher brackets also pay a maximum of 15% on capital gains to the extent such income falls within the 10% and 15% tax brackets. If long-term capital gain brings total taxable income into the 25% or higher bracket, then some of the long-term capital gain will be taxed at 0% and the remaining long-term capital gain will be taxed at 15%. In order to put these favorable tax rules into effect, a taxpayer with such income must figure regular tax using the *Qualified Dividends and Capital Gain Tax* Worksheet from the instructions to Form 1040, as shown in Table 32.3.

Example

For 2012, Samuel has taxable income of $66,000, of which $5,000 is long-term capital gain. He is in the 25% marginal tax bracket. The tax on his long-term capital gain income is $5,000 × 15% = $750. If the long-term capital gain was taxed at ordinary income rates, the tax on his long-term capital gain would be $5,000 × 25% = $1,250. Thus, Samuel saves $500 because of the long-term capital gain rate.

Example

Suppose instead that in 2012 Samuel has taxable income of $21,500, including $5,000 long-term capital gain. In that case, he would be in the 15% marginal tax bracket and tax on his long-term capital gain income is $5,000 × 0% = $0. Likewise, if there were no advantageous rate, tax on the long-term capital gain at ordinary rates would be $5,000 × 15% = $750. Thus, Sam saves $750 because of the long-term capital gain rate.

ALERT: A taxpayer with only a capital gain distribution and/or qualified dividends still must use the worksheet even though no Schedule D is filed.

Example

This time assume that, in 2012, Samuel has total taxable income of $50,000, of which $35,000 is attributable to long-term capital gain. This leaves $15,000 of taxable income that will be taxed as ordinary income. For a single taxpayer, the 15% bracket ends at taxable income of $35,350 (for 2012). Therefore, $20,350 ($35,350 – $15,000) of Samuel's long-term capital gain will be taxed at 0% (i.e., to the extent of the 15% bracket). The remaining $14,650 ($35,000 – $20,350) will be taxed at 15%.

TABLE 32.3 Qualified Dividends and Capital Gain Tax Worksheet—Line 28

Before you begin:	√	Be sure you do not have to file Form 1040 (see the Instructions for Form 1040A, line 10).

1. Enter the amount from Form 1040A, line 27 .... 1. ______

2. Enter the amount from Form 1040A, line 9b .... 2. ______

3. Enter the amount from Form 1040A, line 10 .... 3. ______

4. Add lines 2 and 3 .... 4. ______

5. Subtract line 4 from line 1. If zero or less, enter -0- .... 5. ______

6. Enter the **smaller** of:
- The amount on line 1, or
- $34,500 if single or married filing separately, $69,000 if married filing jointly or qualifying widow(er), or $46,250 if head of household.

.... 6. ______

7. Enter the smaller of line 5 or line 6. .... **7.** ______

8. Subtract line 7 from line 6. This amount is taxed at 0% .... 8. ______

9. Enter the smaller of line 1 or line 4 .... **9.** ______

10. Enter the amount from line 8 .... 10. ______

11. Subtract line 10 from line 9 .... 11. ______

12. Multiply line 11 by 15% (.15) .... 12. ______

13. Use the Tax Table to figure the tax on the amount on line 5. Enter the tax here .... 13. ______

14. Add lines 12 and 13 .... 14. ______

15. Use the Tax Table to figure the tax on the amount on line 1. Enter the tax here .... 15. ______

16. **Tax on all taxable income.** Enter the **smaller** of line 14 or line 15 here and on Form 1040A, line 28 .... 16. ______

A taxpayer who has any gain from unrecaptured section 1250 gain (Chapter 13), section 1202 gain from the sale of qualified small business stock (Chapter 13), or gain from the sale of collectibles, such as art and antiques, must complete the Schedule D Tax Worksheet included in the instructions to Schedule D (Form 1040). The worksheet triggers the special tax rates that apply to these income items:

- 25% for unrecaptured section 1250 gain
- 28% for section 1202 gains and collectibles gains

Amounts determined on the Schedule D Tax Worksheet are then combined to figure the taxpayer's tax liability.

TIP: A taxpayer with a marginal rate lower than 25% or 28% will not be taxed at these higher rates for capital gains income that would otherwise be subject to these higher rates. For example, if a taxpayer in the 15% tax bracket has gain from the sale of a collectible, the gain will be taxed no higher than 15%, not the maximum 28% rate for collectible gains.

Kiddie Tax

To discourage parents from shifting investment (unearned) income to children merely as a way to lower the parents' taxes, the tax law imposes a special tax regime on a child under age 18, at age 18 at the end of the year (unless the child provided more than half of his or her support with earned income), or over age 18 and under age 24 and a full-time student (unless the child provided more than half of his or her support with earned income). The kiddie tax is discussed in detail in Chapter 34.

Tax on Lump-Sum Distributions

DEFINITION: A **lump-sum distribution** is the distribution or payment in one tax year of the taxpayer's entire balance from all of the employer's qualified plans of one kind (e.g., pension, profit-sharing, or stock bonus plans). Distributions from IRAs can *never* be treated as a lump-sum distribution even if taken in a lump sum.

A taxpayer who was born before January 2, 1936, and who receives a **lump-sum distribution** from a qualified retirement plan may elect to use the 10-year average rate option or may elect to treat a portion of the distribution as capital gain taxed at 20%.

The tax on taxable income without the distribution is figured in the usual way, and the tax on the lump-sum distribution is added.

Form 4972, *Tax on Lump-Sum Distributions,* is used to figure the tax on the lump-sum distribution; it is then attached to Form 1040. There are five options for figuring the tax on a lump-sum distribution:

ALERT: Ten-year averaging can be used only once by a taxpayer after 1986.

1. Report the part of the distribution from participation in the plan before 1974 as a capital gain (taxed at 20%) and the part from participation after 1973 as ordinary income.
2. Report the part of the distribution from participation before 1974 as a capital gain (taxed at 20%), and use the 10-year tax option to figure the tax on the part of the distribution from participation after 1973 (using the tax rate schedule in the Form 4972 instructions, which is based on the tax rates for a single taxpayer in 1986).
3. Use the 10-year tax option to figure the tax on the total taxable amount (using the tax rate schedule in the Form 4972 instructions, which is based on the tax rates for a single taxpayer in 1986).
4. Roll over all or part of the distribution. No tax is currently due on the part rolled over. However, the taxpayer must report any part not rolled over as ordinary income.
5. Report the entire taxable part of the distribution as ordinary income on the tax return.

TIP: The taxpayer's tax should be figured, using the various options to which he or she may be entitled, to find the method that produces the least tax. More details about these options are available in IRS Pub. 575, *Pensions and Annuities.*

Income Averaging for Farmers and Fishermen

A taxpayer who is a farmer or fisherman (defined in the instructions to Schedule J [Form 1040], *Income Averaging for Farmers and Fishermen*), can elect to average his or her farm income over the three years prior to the current tax year. Essentially, one-third of the current year's taxable income related to farming is spread over the three prior years; the tax is figured on these amounts and added together to determine the current year's tax liability.

Example

Harold is a full-time farmer with a profit from farming in 2012 of $81,270. Harold elects to use income averaging for his farm income, so $27,090 is treated as taxed in each of these years: 2009, 2010, and 2011.

Schedule J is used to figure tax under the income-averaging election for farmers and fishermen. The averaging applies only to the net income from the farming or fishing activity. Income from other sources continues to be taxed in the usual manner and is not eligible for income averaging.

Foreign Earned Income Tax Worksheet

A taxpayer who claims a foreign earned income exclusion, foreign housing exclusion or foreign housing deduction (see Chapter 4) must figure tax liability using the *Foreign Earned Income Tax* Worksheet in the instructions to Form 1040. The purpose of using the worksheet is to ensure that the so-called stacking rule is in effect. This rule requires nonexcluded income to be stacked on top of excluded income. In other words, the tax rate brackets used to compute the tax are based on the bracket the taxpayer would have been in if the income had not been excluded.

For example, a single individual with $90,000 of excluded foreign earned income and $12,000 in other taxable income (after deductions) is subject to tax at the marginal rate of 28%, not 15%, on the $12,000 of income in excess of the excluded amount.

Tax Liability

The final determination of a taxpayer's tax liability may require some adjustment to the amount of the regular tax already computed.

Step 1. If the taxpayer is subject to the alternative minimum tax (AMT) (Chapter 33), the amount of AMT calculated on Form 6251, *Alternative Minimum Tax*, should be added to the amount of regular tax.

Step 2. Subtract tax credits. These include amounts covered in Chapters 27 through 31.

Step 3. Add additional taxes owed to the regular tax or AMT. These include:

- Penalties on IRAs and certain other tax-advantaged accounts (Chapter 35)
- Self-employment tax (Chapter 11)
- Taxes on household employees (Chapter 35)
- Repayment of the homebuyer credit (Chapter 35)

Step 4. Subtract tax payments. These include:

- Withholding on wages and other withholdings (Chapter 36)
- Estimated tax payments (Chapter 36)
- Tax paid with a filing extension (Chapter 36)
- Refundable credits (earned income credit, the additional child tax credit, and part of the American Opportunity Credit) (see Chapters 27, 29, and 30)

The net result is the tax that is owed.

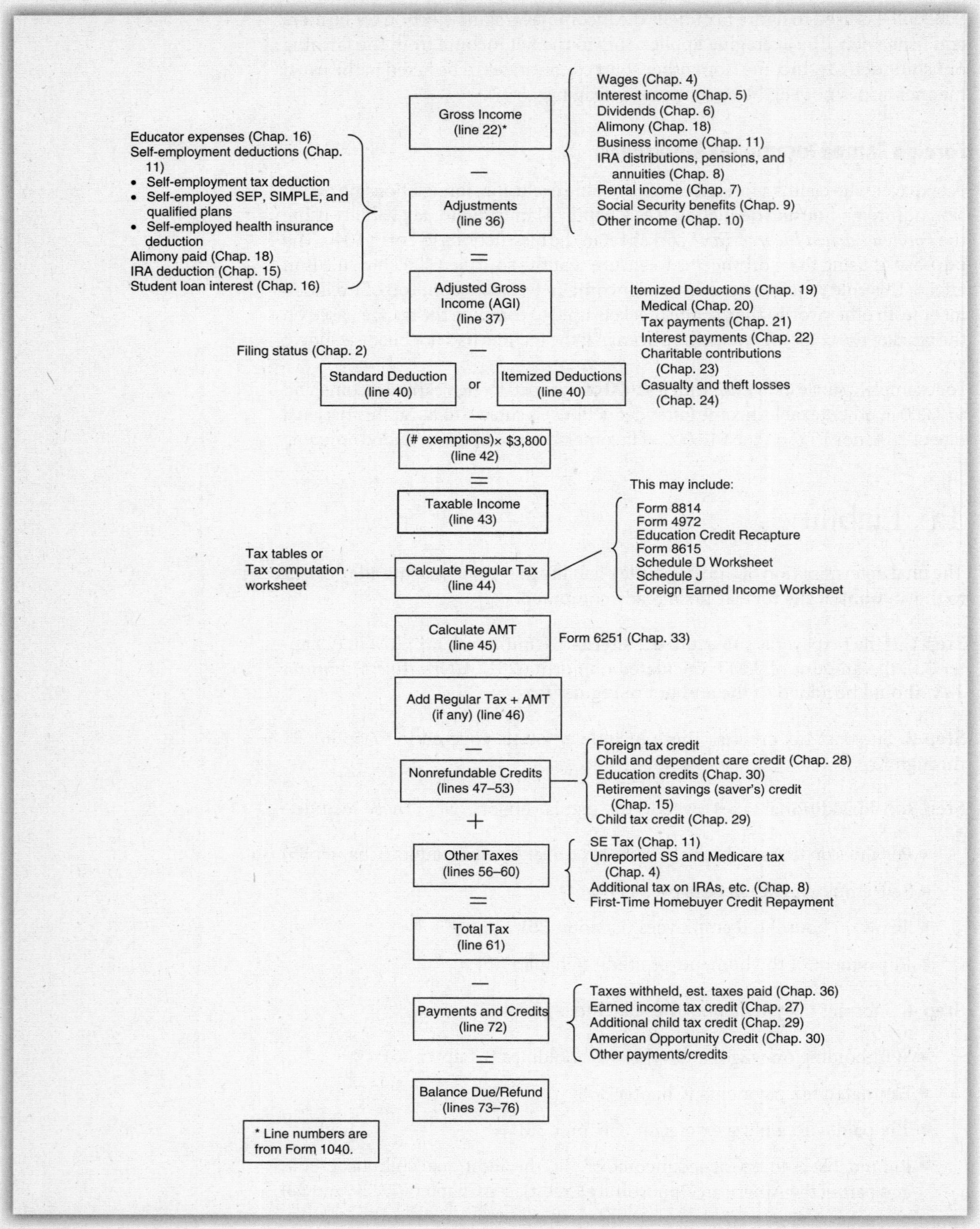

FIGURE 32.1 Tax Calculation

Review Questions

1. Which of the following items is **not** taken into account in figuring taxable income?
   a. Gross income
   b. Adjustments to gross income
   c. Personal and dependency exemptions
   d. Tax credits

2. The tax table **cannot** be used if:
   a. A married person files separately.
   b. Taxable income is $100,000 or more.
   c. Form 1040 is filed.
   d. The taxpayer claims any tax credits.

3. Assume a taxpayer is in the 28% tax bracket. The maximum tax rate on qualified dividends in 2012 is:
   a. 0%
   b. 15%
   c. 25%
   d. 28%

4. A farmer who opts to use income averaging averages income over __________:
   a. 10 years
   b. 5 years
   c. 3 prior years
   d. 3 years including the current year

5. Marcia, a U.S. citizen who works in a foreign country, earned a salary of $110,000 in 2012 and has no other income. She files her return excluding $95,000 under the foreign earned income exclusion. She files her return using the single filing status and claims one personal exemption. What is the marginal tax rate on her taxable income?
   a. 0%
   b. 15%
   c. 28%
   d. 33%

CHAPTER 33

The Alternative Minimum Tax

The alternative minimum tax (AMT) was created to ensure that taxpayers at certain higher income levels pay some amount of tax. A taxpayer who reduces or eliminates the regular tax through various deductions and exclusions still may find himself or herself subject to the AMT.

A taxpayer may have to pay the AMT if taxable income for regular tax purposes (Chapter 32), combined with certain adjustments and tax preference items under the AMT rules (defined later), exceeds a certain threshold.

There is no way to know with certainty before completing a taxpayer's return if he or she is subject to the AMT. Instead, Form 6251, *Alternative Minimum Tax—Individuals*, must be completed to determine whether any AMT liability exists.

Overview of the AMT

The AMT applies to a taxpayer who has certain types of income or deductions that receive favorable treatment for regular tax purposes but are not allowed for AMT purposes. The AMT has its own rules about taxable income and allowable deductions. Some deductions allowed under the regular tax system are not allowed at all under the AMT, while others are allowed only to a limited extent under the AMT. The AMT, which is calculated on Form 6251, adds back or subtracts differences in income and deductions between the regular tax and the AMT to arrive at alternative minimum taxable income (AMTI).

A brief overview of the steps required to calculate AMT follows.

1. Figure AMTI.
   a. For taxpayers who claim the standard deduction, start with adjusted gross income (AGI). For taxpayers who itemize deductions, start with AGI minus itemized deductions. (The standard deduction and personal exemptions are not deductible for AMT purposes.)

      Although a taxpayer with one or more adjustment or preference items (discussed later in this chapter) may be subject to the AMT, it is important to complete Form 6251 to make this determination.
   b. Enter adjustments and preferences to arrive at AMTI.

> **TIP:** Form 6251, Part 1, Line 1, is the starting point for determining AMTI. Line 1 refers to the appropriate line number on Form 1040, *U.S. Individual Income Tax Return*, for the amount to enter.

TIP: While it may seem that a taxpayer with one or more of these triggers would be subject to the AMT, Form 6251 should be completed to make this determination. Also, the taxpayer may have other adjustments that are not covered in this book. The IRS has an AMT Assistant on its website that can be used to make a preliminary determination as to whether a taxpayer is subject to AMT.

2. Figure AMT.

a. Subtract the AMT exemption amount from AMTI (the AMT exemption amount depends on filing status).

b. Compute the tentative minimum tax liability by multiplying AMTI of $175,000 or less ($87,500 or less for married filing separately) by 26%, and amounts over $175,000 ($87,500 for married filing separately) by 28%, and then add these two products.

c. If the result is more than the regular tax before certain credits (discussed later in this chapter), the difference between the amounts is the AMT owed. The taxpayer then pays the AMT in addition to the regular tax.

Another way of viewing the AMT procedure is as follows:

Start with regular taxable income, then
\+ Tax preferences and positive adjustments
− Negative adjustments
= AMTI
− AMT exemption
= Amount subject to tax (AMT base)
× AMT tax rate
= Tentative minimum tax
− Regular income tax
= AMT (if tentative minimum tax is greater than regular income tax)

DEFINITIONS: Tax adjustments and **tax preference items** are changes in the way income or deductions under the regular tax system are treated under the AMT. Both are used to calculate AMTI from a starting point (AGI or AGI less itemized deductions for a taxpayer who itemizes). Adjustments, which are described in section 56 of the Internal Revenue Code, may be added to or subtracted from AGI in calculating AMTI. Preference items, which are described in section 57, are only added back to AGI (increasing AMTI).

Figure AMTI

For a taxpayer who itemizes deductions, the starting point for figuring the AMT is AGI less itemized deductions. For a taxpayer who claims the standard deduction, the starting point is AGI.

This starting point is increased by **tax preference items** and increased or decreased by **tax adjustment items** to arrive at AMTI. Some AMT adjustments are deferral items because of differences in timing between the regular and the alternative tax systems. Tax preference items (or exclusions) are never deductible for the AMT, and therefore are not a matter of timing; they are always added to the starting point to arrive at AMTI.

TABLE 33.1 Adjustment and Preference Items

Item: Alternative Minimum Tax Treatment
■ Standard deduction (deduction not allowed)
■ Personal exemptions (deductions not allowed)
■ Medical and dental itemized deductions (deductible to the extent that qualified medical expenses exceed 10% of AGI)
■ Taxes from Schedule A, *Itemized Deductions* (deductions for state and local income taxes and state and local sales taxes are not allowed)

- Home mortgage interest (deduction is limited to the amount of interest on loans used to buy, build, or substantially improve a first or second home)
- Miscellaneous deductions from Schedule A (deductions are not allowed)
- Recovery of tax (tax refunds included in income for purposes of regular tax are subtracted from income for AMT purposes)
- Investment interest expense (interest expenses attributable to private activity bonds that are deductible for regular tax are added back in calculating AMTI)
- Depletion (depletion deductions must be recalculated for AMT)
- AMT net operating loss (NOL) deduction (NOLs must be recalculated for AMT)
- Interest from specified private activity bonds exempt from regular tax (investment interest from private activity bonds must be added back to income, but interest expense related to the bond may be deducted)
- Qualified small business stock (adjustments must be made for AMT purposes)
- Exercise of incentive stock options (the difference between fair market value and the amount paid must be added to income)
- Sale or other disposition of property (gain or loss from the sale of property must be recalculated for AMT purposes if AMT basis is different than regular tax basis)
- Depreciation on assets placed in service after 1986 (depreciation must be recalculated for AMT; there could be a positive or negative adjustment for AMT purposes)
- A portion of gain from the sale of qualified small business stock is excludaible under regular tax. However, 7% of the excluded amount is added back for AMTI.

Common AMT Triggers

The AMT rules on income and deductions differ from those for regular tax purposes. Under the AMT rules, certain items can trigger or increase AMT liability. Some of the more common triggers include:

- *Personal and dependency exemptions.* These exemptions are not deductible for AMT purposes. Therefore, a taxpayer with numerous dependents could have AMTI that is considerably higher than taxable income for regular tax purposes.
- *Certain itemized deductions.* State and local taxes and miscellaneous itemized deductions are not deductible for AMT purposes. A taxpayer in a high-tax state who pays considerable state income taxes or someone with sizable miscellaneous itemized deductions (such as employee business expenses) may have AMT exposure.

Also, some itemized deductions have different rules for AMT that can increase AMTI. For example, medical expenses that exceed 7.5% of AGI (see Chapter 20) may be deducted for regular tax purposes. However, only the excess over 10% of AGI may be deducted for AMT purposes.

TIP: Taxpayers who claim the standard deduction *cannot* itemize for the AMT. However, certain taxpayers may want to itemize deductions for regular tax purposes, even if the total of their itemized deductions is less than their standard deduction amount. Itemizing for AMT purposes could result in overall tax savings.

ALERT: As of this writing, Congress has not extended the AMT patch for 2012. Legislation has been introduced in Congress that would increase the AMT exemption amounts for 2012 to $78,750 (married filing jointly and qualified widow(er)), $50,600 (single and head of household), and $39,375 (married filing separately). However, this legislation has not been passed or signed into law as of this writing.

The exemption amounts shown in Table 33.2 are for 2011 and are shown for illustration along with the exemption amounts that will be in place if there is not a patch. If there is not a patch, approximately 30 million Americans would be subject to AMT in 2012.

Example

Frank and Abbe live in a state that imposes no state or local income tax. They are married and file jointly. They claim dependent exemptions for their 6 children. Their AGI is $150,000. The personal exemptions total is $30,400 (8 × $3,800), and they claim the standard deduction of $11,900.

Frank and Abbe's regular taxable income is $107,700 ($150,000 – $11,900 – $30,400). However, because personal exemptions and the standard deduction are not allowed for AMT purposes, their AMTI is $150,000.

- *Incentive stock option (ISO).* While the exercise of an ISO is not taxable for regular tax purposes, the spread between the stock and option price is income for purposes of the AMT. (This is explained in detail later in this chapter.)
- *Refinancing a mortgage.* Home mortgage interest generally is deductible for both regular and AMT purposes. However, interest on a mortgage that is used to refinance another mortgage is not deductible for the AMT for any part of the mortgage that is not used to replace acquisition debt. (See Chapter 22 for more information about acquisition debt.)
- *Tax-exempt interest on private activity bonds.* Although interest on private activity bonds issued by state or local municipalities after August 7, 1986 may be exempt from regular tax, interest on these bonds is a preference item and must be included in determining AMTI (except for private activity bonds issued in 2009 and 2010).

Figure AMT

AMT Exemption

A taxpayer can reduce AMTI by an exemption amount based on the taxpayer's filing status. For 2012, the exemption amounts are shown in Table 33.2.

Example

Continuing the Frank and Abbe example from above, their AMTI is $150,000 and the amount of income potentially subject to tax at AMT rates would be $71,250 ($150,000 – $78,750).

TABLE 33.2 AMT Exemption Amount

Filing status	Exemption amount	Exemption amount 2011
Married filing jointly and qualifying widow(er)	$78,750	$74,450
Single and head of household	$50,600	$48,450
Married filing separately	$39,375	$37,225

Phase-Out of Exemption Amount The exemption amount allowed is reduced by 25 cents for each dollar of AMTI over a threshold amount. The threshold amounts and phase-out ranges are different for each filing status. If AMTI is high enough, no exemption amount can be claimed. Table 33.3 shows the threshold amount for the start of the phase-out and the AMTI at which no exemption can be claimed.

TABLE 33.3 Phase-Out of AMT Exemption Amount

Filing status	Start of phase-out	Phase-out complete	Phase-out complete 2011
Married filing jointly or qualifying widow(er)	$150,000	$465,000	$447,800
Single or head of household	$112,500	$314,500	$306,300
Married filing separately	$75,000	$232,500	$223,900

Example

Jimmy is head of household with AMTI of $125,000.

His AMT exemption amount of $50,600 is subject to phase-out. His AMT exemption amount would be $47,475 ($50,600 – [25% × ($125,000 – $112,500)]).

Special Rule for Married Filing Separately Filers A special rule applies when calculating the exemption phase-out for married filing separately (MFS) filers. MFS filers must add to their AMTI the lesser of:

1. The MFS AMT exemption amount for the year, OR
2. 25% of the amount by which AMTI (without taking into account any AMT exemption amount) exceeds the dollar amount that the AMT exemption completely phases out.

Child Subject to the Kiddie Tax A child who is subject to the kiddie tax (Chapter 34) has a special AMT exemption amount. The 2012 AMT exemption for such a child is limited to the sum of the child's earned income plus $6,950. However, this exemption amount cannot exceed the regular AMT exemption amount for the child's filing status.

Example

Erin, age 16, earned $4,000 last summer. She also had $1,100 in interest, dividends, and other unearned income from various accounts and investments given to her by her parents. Her AMT exemption is $10,950 ($4,000 earned income + $6,950).

AMT Tax Rates

There are two tax rates for the AMT:

1. 26% of AMTI up to $175,000 in excess of the exemption amount ($87,500 if married filing separately)
2. 28% on AMTI over $175,000 ($87,500 if married filing separately)

Example

Continue the Jimmy example from above. Jimmy is a head-of-household taxpayer with AMTI of $125,000.

Jimmy's tentative minimum tax is $20,157 (26% × [$125,000 AMTI – $47,475 AMT exemption]).

TIP: Part III of Form 6251 must also be completed by a taxpayer with excluded foreign earned income.

AMT Rates for a Taxpayer with Long-Term Capital Gains and Qualified Dividends To ensure that a taxpayer with long-term capital gains or qualified dividends receives the benefit of the favorable tax rate of a maximum of 15% on this income, a special computation for AMT is required (Part III of Form 6251).

Comparing AMT to the Regular Tax

The amount of any AMT liability is the excess tentative minimum tax over the taxpayer's regular tax. Thus, if a taxpayer's regular tax is $38,000 and the tentative minimum tax is $43,000, the taxpayer's total liability is $43,000 ($38,000 regular tax plus $5,000 AMT).

As a result of numerous AMT patches and modifications by Congress over the past several years, the AMT can be offset by nonrefundable personal tax credits, such as the child and dependent care credit and the Lifetime Learning Credit.

Example

Jon and Sandy have a regular tax liability of $15,000 and a tentative tax liability of $13,000. They also have a $2,000 Lifetime Learning Credit and a $1,000 child and dependent care credit, both nonrefundable credits. Because the AMT patch was extended permanently, they can utilize all of their $3,000 total credit for AMT purposes.

Reporting AMT

The AMT is figured on Form 6251 and attached to the taxpayer's return (or e-filed).

The amount of AMT is entered in the Tax and Credits section of Form 1040. A taxpayer who owes any AMT cannot file Form 1040A or 1040EZ, *Income Tax Return for Single and Joint Filers With No Dependents.*

Minimum Tax Credit

A taxpayer who paid AMT in a previous year as a result of deferral items may be able to claim a minimum tax credit (MTC) in a later year. In other words, deferral items may generate or increase an MTC; exclusion (permanent) items do not because they are *never* deductible for AMT.

TIP: A minimum tax credit cannot be used to reduce AMT liability in the year to which it is carried.

The MTC is figured on Form 8801, *Credit for Prior Year Minimum Tax—Individuals, Estates, and Trusts.* The MTC is limited to the amount that the current-year regular tax exceeds the current-year tentative minimum tax. Unused credits may be carried forward indefinitely (but not back).

TIP: Form 3921, *Exercise of Incentive Stock Option Under Section 422(b)*, is used to report the adjustment for the ISO.

However, a taxpayer with long-term unused MTC from prior years may be entitled to a refundable MTC. For 2012 returns, a long-term MTC is one that arose in 2008 or an earlier tax year. The refundable credit primarily helps a taxpayer who had a large AMT liability in a prior year from the exercise of ISOs. The refundable minimum tax credit is allowed for tax years beginning before January 1, 2013.

Deferral Items

Unlike an exclusion (discussed below), which is never deductible for the AMT, deferral items create differences in timing of income or deductions. A nonexhaustive list of deferral items follows.

- *Incentive stock options.* Included in AMTI is the excess of the fair market value (FMV) of the stock acquired by exercising an ISO over the amount paid for the stock, including any amount paid for the ISO used to acquire the stock. The adjustment applies only if the stock is not sold in the same year it is acquired (i.e., the option is exercised).

Example

Sally exercised an ISO in 2012 to acquire 100 shares of stock in her employer's corporation. She had received the ISO as compensation that was not taxable to her, and she had no basis in the ISO. The exercise price (as reported to her on Form 3921) is $10 per share, and the FMV of the stock (also reported on Form 3921) is $35 per share. Her adjustment for AMT (increasing AMTI) is $2,500 ([$35/share × 100] – [$10/share × 100]).

- *Depreciation.* Depreciation for AMT may differ from depreciation for regular tax purposes if different recovery periods were used for AMT versus the regular tax.
- *Net operating loss deduction.* For AMT purposes, a taxpayer's NOL is refigured to arrive at an alternative tax net operating loss deduction (ATNOLD). This is the sum of the alternative tax NOL carryovers and carrybacks to the current year. However, an ATNOLD cannot offset more than 90% of AMTI.

TIP: The AMT basis of stock acquired by exercising an ISO is increased by any AMT adjustment. This can reduce the gain or increase the loss on the subsequent sale of the stock. For example, a taxpayer exercises an ISO, paying $30 per share when the value is $50 per share. The taxpayer reports an AMT adjustment of $20 per share. Two years later, he sells the stock for $70 per share. For regular tax purposes, his gain is $40 per share ($70 – $30). However, for AMT purposes, his gain is only $20 ($70 – $50) because of his higher AMT basis ($30 per share purchase + $20 per share AMT adjustment).

- *Gain or loss on the disposition of property.* AMT gain or loss on the disposition of property may be different from the gain or loss for regular tax purposes because property can have a different basis for AMT. (See the earlier explanations in connection with increase in the basis of stock acquired by exercising an ISO and depreciation.) The gain or loss from various types of property dispositions (as listed in the instructions to Form 6251) must be refigured for AMT purposes.
- *Intangible drilling costs.* Part of the deduction for these costs is added to AMTI.
- *Other.* This list is not exhaustive. There are adjustments for research and experimentation costs, certain installment sales, tax shelter farm activities, and other items listed in the instructions to Form 6251.

Exclusion Items

TIP: Because of the 90% limitation on the ATNOLD, the carryback and carryforward of unused NOLs is different for regular tax purposes versus AMT purposes. A separate record of ATNOLD carrybacks and carryforwards should be kept.

Tax adjustments that do not have a timing difference are called exclusion items. They affect AMT computations but are not taken into account for purposes of the minimum tax credit. A list of exclusion items follows.

- *Itemized deductions.*
  - Medical expenses are deductible only to the extent they exceed 10% of AGI (compared with 7.5% of AGI for regular tax purposes), so the lesser of 2.5% of AGI or the medical expense deduction must be added to AMTI.
  - No deduction is allowed for state and local income or sales taxes.
  - No deduction is allowed for miscellaneous itemized deductions.
  - The home mortgage interest deduction is allowed only for mortgage proceeds used to buy, build, or substantially improve a home. Thus, an interest deduction on home mortgage proceeds used to take a vacation or pay for college must be added to AMTI. The Form 6251 instructions contain a home mortgage interest worksheet that can be used to determine the amount that is deductible for AMT purposes.
- *Interest on private activity bonds.* Interest received on qualified private activity bonds is not taxable for regular tax purposes but is taxable for AMT purposes (except for interest on such bonds issued in 2009 and 2010).
- *Depletion.* The depletion deduction must be refigured for AMT purposes (as explained in the instructions to Form 6251).
- *Exclusion of gain on the sale of qualified small business stock.* Generally, a taxpayer who has owned qualified small business stock (sometimes referred to as section 1202 stock) for more than five years and sells the stock at a gain must include 7% of the gain as a preference item for AMT purposes.
- *Other adjustments.* This list is not exclusive. There are other adjustments for investment interest expense and tax refunds.

TIP: A taxpayer who previously deducted state income taxes and later receives a refund of those taxes must include that refund in regular taxable income. However, because the state income tax was never deducted for AMT purposes (it is an exclusion item), the refund may be subtracted from income in calculating AMTI.

Review Questions

1. The starting point for figuring AMT for a taxpayer who itemizes deductions is:
   a. Gross income
   b. Adjusted gross income
   c. Adjusted gross income less itemized deductions
   d. Regular tax

2. Which of the following is a deferral item?
   a. Adjustment for incentive stock options
   b. Personal and dependency exemptions
   c. State and local taxes
   d. Interest on private activity bonds

3. A taxpayer is likely to have a refundable minimum tax credit if she has:
   a. A large number of dependents
   b. A large AMT liability in the past from the exercise of ISOs
   c. A large number of any deferral items
   d. A large number of any exclusion items

4. Which of the following would **not** impact the alternative minimum tax?
   a. Medical deductions that exceed 7.5% of AGI but are less than 10% of AGI
   b. Miscellaneous itemized deductions
   c. Charitable contributions
   d. Interest on private activity bonds issued in 2012

The Kiddie Tax

Tax on a child's investment income is figured in a special way. This tax is referred to as the kiddie tax. It is not a separate tax or an additional tax rate. It is merely a tax structure in place to eliminate the opportunity for parents to shift investment income to their child in a lower tax bracket. When the kiddie tax applies, the child's investment income (over a set amount) may be taxed at the parents' highest marginal tax rate.

The kiddie tax does not affect the way in which a child is taxed on his or her earned income from a job or self-employment. It only affects the tax on certain unearned income.

Under certain conditions, parents can elect to include the child's investment income on the parents' return and avoid the need to file a return for the child. This election may or may not be beneficial for the family.

General Rules of the Kiddie Tax

The kiddie tax applies to a child's investment income when all the following apply:

1. The child's investment income exceeds an inflation-adjusted threshold amount ($1,900 in 2012);
2. The child is:
   a. Under age 18 at the end of the year, OR
   b. Age 18 at the end of the year and did not have earned income that was more than half of the child's support, OR
   c. A full-time student over the age of 18 and under age 24 at the end of the year and did not have earned income that was more than half the child's support;
3. The child is required to file a tax return for the tax year (see Chapter 1);
4. At least one of the child's parents was alive at the end of the current tax year; AND
5. The child does not file a joint return for the current tax year.

TIP: Nontaxable (tax-free) income is not taken into account for purposes of the kiddie tax. Thus, tax-exempt interest on municipal bonds and the nontaxable portion of Social Security benefits are not part of the kiddie tax.

If the kiddie tax applies, Form 8615, *Tax for Certain Children Who Have Investment Income of More Than $1,900*, must be attached to the child's tax return, unless the parents qualify and elect to report the child's income on their return (discussed later in this chapter).

Investment Income

The kiddie tax applies only to investment income. Investment income includes all income *other than* wages, salaries, and other amounts received for work performed by the child.

The way in which the child acquires the investments on which the investment income is generated (e.g., by gift, by inheritance, or by purchase) is irrelevant. Examples of investment income include:

- Capital gain distributions
- Capital gains
- Certain distributions from trusts
- Dividends
- Taxable interest
- Taxable part of pension payments
- Taxable part of Social Security benefits

Example

Tiffany, age 16, earned $3,000 from babysitting this year. She also received:

- Taxable interest of $1,200
- Tax-exempt interest of $200 on a municipal bond
- Dividends of $800
- Net capital gains of $150 from the sale of stock

Tiffany's grandparents gifted her the municipal bonds and stock in previous years.

Her investment income is $2,150. The earnings from babysitting ($3,000) and the tax-exempt interest ($200) are not considered investment income for the kiddie tax.

Distributions from a trust that include interest, dividends, and other investment income usually are part of the child's investment income for the kiddie tax. However, if the trust is a "qualified disability trust," these distributions are treated as earned income, not investment income, for purposes of figuring the kiddie tax.

Age Requirements

The kiddie tax applies to a child who is any one of the following:

- Under age 18 at the end of the year, OR
- Age 18 at the end of the year and did not have earned income that was more than half of the child's **support**, OR

- A full-time student over the age of 18 and under age 24 at the end of the year and did not have earned income that was more than half the child's support.

DEFINITION: Support includes amounts spent to provide the child with necessities, including food, housing, clothing, education, medical and dental care, recreation, and transportation. Total support includes amounts spent by the child, the child's parents, and anyone else who provided support. Scholarships are not treated as support if the child is a full-time student.

For purposes of the kiddie tax, special rules apply to children with January 1 birthdays. Use Table 34.1 to determine whether a child with a January 1 birthday is subject to the kiddie tax.

TABLE 34.1 Certain January 1 Birthdays

If a child was born on . . .	Then, at the end of 2012, the child is considered to be ...
January 1, 1995	18[1]
January 1, 1994	19[2]
January 1, 1989	24[3]

[1]This child is not under age 18. The child is subject to the kiddie tax only if the child did not have earned income that was more than half of the child's support.

[2]This child is subject to the kiddie tax only if he or she was a full-time student who did not have earned income that was more than half of his or her support.

[3]This child is not subject to the kiddie tax, and Form 8615 should not be used.

A child does not have to be a dependent in order for the kiddie tax to apply. In some cases, a child who claims his or her own personal exemption may still be subject to the kiddie tax rules.

Tax Treatment of a Child's Income

The filing requirements for a dependent child are explained in Chapter 1. See Table 1.2 in Chapter 1 for a summary of the filing thresholds for dependents in 2012.

The standard deduction for a dependent is also different. For tax year 2012, a dependent's standard deduction is the greater of:

- $950 (the "minimum standard deduction") OR
- $300 plus earned income of up to $5,650

A dependent's standard deduction may not exceed the standard deduction that would otherwise be allowable ($5,950 for a single taxpayer in 2012).

A child's earned income is always taxed at the child's tax rates.

A child's investment income that exceeds the minimum standard deduction amount for a dependent ($950 for 2012) but does not exceed twice the minimum standard deduction amount ($1,900 for 2012) is also taxed at the child's tax rate. Thus, only the amount of a child's investment income that exceeds $1,900 is taxed at the rates that would apply if the income were reported on the parents' return.

ALERT: When figuring the alternative minimum tax for a child subject to the kiddie tax, the exemption amount is $6,950 for 2012. See Chapter 33 for more information.

Some children may benefit from itemizing deductions; see the next section, "Figuring the Tax on the Child's Return," for a discussion of how a child's itemized deductions impact the kiddie tax calculation.

If the tax on a child's taxable income, figured at the child's tax rates (and disregarding the kiddie tax rules), is higher than the tax that would be calculated under the kiddie tax rules, the child is liable for tax using the child's tax rates.

Figuring the Tax on the Child's Return

The kiddie tax is figured on Form 8615. This form is attached to the child's Form 1040 or 1040A, *U.S. Individual Income Tax Return.* A child who files Form 8615 may not file a Form 1040EZ, *Income Tax Return for Single and Joint Filers with No Dependents.*

Itemized Deductions

The child's investment income can be reduced by itemized deductions. Only expenses directly connected to the production of investment income can be claimed as an offset to investment income. These include custodian fees and service charges, service fees to collect taxable income and dividends, and certain investment counsel fees. Because investment expenses are miscellaneous itemized deductions, only amounts in excess of 2% of the child's adjusted gross income (AGI) are actually deductible (see Chapter 25 for more information).

However, because of the way in which income is reported on Form 8615, these deductions may or may not reduce the amount of income subject to the kiddie tax. On Form 8615, a child is allowed to deduct the larger of $1,900 (for 2012) or $950 plus the portion of itemized deductions that is directly related to the production of investment income.

Generally speaking, a child must have at least $950 in deductible investment expenses in order to reduce the amount of investment income subject to the kiddie tax.

Example

Amanda, age 15, has investment income of $7,500 and itemized deductions of $400 (after applying the 2%-of-AGI limitation on miscellaneous itemized expenses) directly connected to her investment income. She has no earned income, and her AGI is $7,500.

Because $1,900 is greater than $1,350 (the sum of $950 plus $400), Amanda may deduct $1,900 from her investment income when determining the amount of income that is subject to the kiddie tax. The amount of Amanda's income that is subject to the kiddie tax is therefore $5,600 ($7,500 – $1,900).

Form 8615 is then used to calculate the child's tentative tax on investment income based on the parents' tax rate. Additional information needed to complete Form 8615 includes the parents' taxable income, the investment income of the child's siblings that is also subject to the kiddie tax, the parents' filing status, and the parents' tax liability.

The child's total tax liability is then calculated, taking into account taxes on the child's earned income (if applicable) and the child's investment income that is not subject to the kiddie tax and is taxed at the child's rates.

Example

Here is a comprehensive example illustrating the key points of the kiddie tax computation on Form 8615. Assume the taxpayers are parents who file jointly and have one child, Khalil, who is 14 years old. Khalil has taxable interest of $3,000, earned income of $1,500, and no itemized deductions.

Khalil's parents have taxable income of $90,000. They do not have any capital gains or qualified dividends.

The income tax tables in the Form 1040 Instructions may be used to calculate the tax liabilities of Khalil and his parents, because they do not have any income taxed at preferential capital gains rates.

The computation of the kiddie tax is shown next.

Khalil's net investment income (the investment income subject to the kiddie tax) is $1,100 ($3,000 investment income – $1,900 base amount).

Khalil's tentative tax on net investment income based on his parents' tax rate is determined in a series of steps as follows:

Khalil's net investment income combined with his parents' taxable income is $91,100 ($1,100 + $90,000).

If Khalil's parents reported his income on their tax return, the total tax liability on $91,100 would be $14,835.

The tax on Khalil's parents' income of $90,000 would be $14,560.

The combined tax liability exceeds the parents' tax liability by $275 ($14,835 – $14,560).

Khalil's tentative tax on his net investment income is therefore $275.

Determine Khalil's tax on his earned income and the net investment income not subject to the kiddie tax, as shown next.

Khalil's AGI is $4,500 ($3,000 investment income + $1,500 earned income).

Khalil's standard deduction is $1,800 ($1,500 earned income + $300).

Khalil's taxable income that is not subject to the kiddie tax is $1,600 ($4,500 AGI – $1,800 standard deduction – $1,100 subject to the kiddie tax).

Khalil's tax on the $1,600 of his earned income plus his net investment income not subject to the kiddie tax is $160.

Khalil's tax liability if the kiddie tax rules are applied is $435 ($275 + $160).

If the kiddie tax rules did not apply, Khalil's taxable income would be $2,700 ($4,500 AGI – $1,800 standard deduction), and his tax liability would be $270.

Because Khalil's tax liability is higher under the kiddie tax rules, he is liable for the amount calculated under the kiddie tax rules. Khalil's tax liability, to be shown on Form 1040, is $435 Figure 34.1 illustrates how Khalil's Form 8615 will be filled out for 2012.

Form **8615** | Department of the Treasury Internal Revenue Service (99)

Tax for Certain Children Who Have Investment Income of More Than $1,900

► Attach only to the child's Form 1040, Form 1040A, or Form 1040NR.
► Information about Form 8615 and its separate instructions is at *www.irs.gov/form8615.*

OMB No. 1545-0074 | **2012** | Attachment Sequence No. **33**

Child's name shown on return: **Khalil** | Child's social security number: **123-45-6789**

Before you begin: If the child, the parent, or any of the parent's other children for whom Form 8615 must be filed must use the Schedule D Tax Worksheet or has income from farming or fishing, see **Pub. 929,** Tax Rules for Children and Dependents. It explains how to figure the child's tax using the **Schedule D Tax Worksheet** or **Schedule J** (Form 1040).

A Parent's name (first, initial, and last). **Caution:** *See instructions before completing.*
Khalil's Father (primary on the parents' joint return)

B Parent's social security number: 987-65-4321

C Parent's filing status (check one):
☐ Single ☑ Married filing jointly ☐ Married filing separately ☐ Head of household ☐ Qualifying widow(er)

Part I Child's Net Investment Income

Line	Description	Box	Amount
1	Enter the child's investment income (see instructions)	1	3,000
2	If the child **did not** itemize deductions on **Schedule A** (Form 1040 or Form 1040NR), enter $1,900. Otherwise, see instructions	2	1,900
3	Subtract line 2 from line 1. If zero or less, **stop;** do not complete the rest of this form but **do** attach it to the child's return	3	1,100
4	Enter the child's **taxable income** from Form 1040, line 43; Form 1040A, line 27; or Form 1040NR, line 41. If the child files Form 2555 or 2555-EZ, see the instructions	4	2,700
5	Enter the **smaller** of line 3 or line 4. If zero, **stop;** do not complete the rest of this form but **do** attach it to the child's return	5	1,100

Part II Tentative Tax Based on the Tax Rate of the Parent

Line	Description	Box	Amount
6	Enter the parent's **taxable income** from Form 1040, line 43; Form 1040A, line 27; Form 1040EZ, line 6; Form 1040NR, line 41; or Form 1040NR-EZ, line 14. If zero or less, enter -0-. If the parent files Form 2555 or 2555-EZ, see the instructions	6	90,000
7	Enter the total, if any, from Forms 8615, line 5, of **all other** children of the parent named above. **Do not** include the amount from line 5 above	7	
8	Add lines 5, 6, and 7 (see instructions)	8	91,100
9	Enter the tax on the amount on line 8 based on the **parent's** filing status above (see instructions). If the Qualified Dividends and Capital Gain Tax Worksheet, Schedule D Tax Worksheet, or Schedule J (Form 1040) is used to figure the tax, check here ► ☐	9	14,835
10	Enter the parent's tax from Form 1040, line 44; Form 1040A, line 28, minus any alternative minimum tax; Form 1040EZ, line 10; Form 1040NR, line 42; or Form 1040NR-EZ, line 15. **Do not** include any tax from **Form 4972** or **8814** or any tax from recapture of an education credit. If the parent files Form 2555 or 2555-EZ, see the instructions. If the Qualified Dividends and Capital Gain Tax Worksheet, Schedule D Tax Worksheet, or Schedule J (Form 1040) was used to figure the tax, check here ► ☐	10	14,560
11	Subtract line 10 from line 9 and enter the result. If line 7 is blank, also enter this amount on line 13 and go to **Part III**	11	275
12a	Add lines 5 and 7 — 12a: 1,100		
b	Divide line 5 by line 12a. Enter the result as a decimal (rounded to at least three places)	12b	× . 1.00
13	Multiply line 11 by line 12b	13	275

Part III Child's Tax—If lines 4 and 5 above are the same, enter -0- on line 15 and go to line 16.

Line	Description	Box	Amount
14	Subtract line 5 from line 4 — 14: 1,600		
15	Enter the tax on the amount on line 14 based on the **child's** filing status (see instructions). If the Qualified Dividends and Capital Gain Tax Worksheet, Schedule D Tax Worksheet, or Schedule J (Form 1040) is used to figure the tax, check here ► ☐	15	160
16	Add lines 13 and 15	16	435
17	Enter the tax on the amount on line 4 based on the **child's** filing status (see instructions). If the Qualified Dividends and Capital Gain Tax Worksheet, Schedule D Tax Worksheet, or Schedule J (Form 1040) is used to figure the tax, check here ► ☐	17	270
18	Enter the **larger** of line 16 or line 17 here and on the **child's** Form 1040, line 44; Form 1040A, line 28; or Form 1040NR, line 42. If the child files Form 2555 or 2555-EZ, see the instructions	18	435

For Paperwork Reduction Act Notice, see your tax return instructions. Cat. No. 64113U Form **8615** (2012)

FIGURE 34.1 Khalil's Form 8615

Parents' Election to Report Child's Interest and Dividends

Parents may elect to include the child's investment income on their tax returns if the child's investment income is less than $9,500 and certain conditions are met (see "Eligibility" later in this section). Doing this avoids the need to file a tax return for the child.

Parents make the election by filing Form 8814, *Parents' Election to Report Child's Interest and Dividends,* with the parents' Form 1040. Parents must file Form 1040 (not 1040A or 1040EZ) to make the election.

The child's income is entered in Part I of Form 8814; the amount of the child's investment income that exceeds $1,900 in 2012 is then entered on the parents' return. Ordinary income is reported on line 21 of Form 1040. Qualified dividends are reported on lines 9a and 9b of Form 1040 or on Schedule B, *Interest and Ordinary Dividends*. Capital gain distributions are reported on line 13 of Form 1040 or on Schedule D, *Capital Gains and Losses.* All amounts reported on a parents' return should be labeled "Form 8814."

> **TIP:** In figuring the kiddie tax on a child, the investment income of all of a parent's children subject to the kiddie tax is taken into account. This results in using the highest rate possible. If the investment income of other children is not available when the child's return is due, reasonable estimates may be used, or the child may obtain an extension of time to file. If reasonable estimates are used, Form 1040X, *Amended U.S. Individual Tax Return,* should be filed when more information becomes available.

Part II of Form 8814 is used to figure the tax on the first $1,900 of a child's interest and dividends. The first $950 is tax free; the next $950 is taxed at a rate of 10%. Therefore, the total tax on the child's first $1,900 of investment income is $95 (see "Impact of Making the Election" later in this section). This amount is added to the parent's tax liability on line 44 of Form 1040, and the box next to 8814 must be checked.

Eligibility

Parents may be able to include the child's investment income on their return if *all* of the following conditions are met:

1. The child is under age 19 (or under age 24 and a full-time student) at the end of the year,
2. The child's only income is from interest and dividends (including capital gain distributions and Alaska Permanent Fund dividends),
3. The child's gross income is less than $9,500,
4. The child is required to file a return (unless the parents make the election),
5. The child does not file a joint return for the year,
6. No estimated tax payments were made by the child for the year,
7. No overpayments of tax by the child from a prior year were applied toward the tax for the current year,
8. The child did not have any withholding of federal income tax, and
9. The parent making the election is the one whose tax rates would be used for figuring the kiddie tax.

> **TIP:** A parent must file a separate Form 8814 for each child for whom an election is made. If more than one Form 8814 is filed, indicate this on line C of Form 8814.

Which Parent Can Make the Election?

The parents' marital status determines which parent can make the election.

- *Married.* The election is made by parents filing jointly, or if filing as married filing separately, then the parent with the higher taxable income makes the election.
- *Unmarried.* A custodial parent who is unmarried, treated as unmarried for federal income tax purposes (head of household), or separated from the child's other parent by a divorce or separate maintenance decree makes the election. The custodial parent is the parent the child spends the greater number of nights with during the year.
- *Custodial parent remarried.* If the custodial parent remarries, he or she can make the election on a joint return with his or her new spouse. If the custodial parent does not file jointly with his or her new spouse, the custodial parent can make the election only if he or she has a higher taxable income than the new spouse. If the new spouse (the child's stepparent) has a higher taxable income than the custodial parent, the new spouse may make the election. The noncustodial parent's return should not be used, and the noncustodial parent may not make the election.
- *Parents unmarried but living together.* When parents who are unmarried live together with the child, only the parent with the higher taxable income can make the election.

Impact of Making the Election

The election can increase the tax owed up to $95 if the child has qualified dividends or capital gain distributions because the preferential capital gain rate that would apply to a child's separate return does not automatically apply to the parent's return. In other words, $950 of the child's income that would ordinarily be taxed at preferential capital gains rates must be taxed at 10% if the election is made.

TIP: Making the election can *increase* the allowable amount of the charitable contribution deduction that the parent can claim. For instance, if the parents' AGI without the election is $120,000, their cash contributions are deductible only to the extent of $60,000 (50% of $120,000). If they make the election and the child's income addition is $10,000, their maximum charitable contribution deduction for cash donations is now $65,000 (50% of [$120,000 + $10,000]).

Example

Jonathan, age 16, had qualified dividends of $1,901. His parents file Form 8814 to include his income on their return. If Jonathan had filed his own return, he would have paid zero tax on this income. The first $950 would have been tax free; the tax on the next $951 would have been zero because of the preferential rates on capital gain distributions and qualified dividends. If the parents include this income on their return, the zero rate does not apply, resulting in the parents paying taxes on the income.

The deductions that parents can claim with respect to a child's income reported on their return are limited. Some of the deductions that the child may have been able to take on his or her return may not be claimed on the parents' return. No deduction can be claimed for:

- The additional standard deduction if the child is blind
- The deduction for the penalty on early withdrawals from timed savings accounts and certificates of deposit

- Itemized deductions that a child may have claimed (e.g., investment expenses or charitable contributions)

The addition of the child's income increases the parents' AGI, which in turn may limit or prevent the parents from claiming deductions and credits on their federal return that phase out at higher income levels. Examples include:

- IRA contribution deduction
- Deduction for student loan interest
- Itemized deductions for medical expenses, casualty losses, and miscellaneous itemized deductions
- Credit for child and dependent care expenses
- Child tax credit
- Education credits
- Earned income credit

The impact of the election on the parents' and child's state income tax returns should also be considered.

ALERT: Making the election can impact the parents' estimated taxes. If such an election is anticipated, factor in the extra tax from inclusion of the child's income on the parents' return when figuring the parents' withholding and estimated taxes. If the parents fail to account for the inclusion of the child's income, there may be a penalty for underpayment of estimated tax.

Review Questions

1. The kiddie tax applies to all of the following types of income **except**:

a. Tips

b. Interest income

c. Dividends

d. Taxable portion of Social Security benefits

2. Which of the following persons is **not** a child who may be subject to the kiddie tax?

a. A child who is 15 years old with investment income.

b. A child who is 17 years old and has earned income that was not more than half of her support.

c. A full-time student, age 22, who did not have earned income that was more than half of his support.

d. A child, age 18, with earned income that was more than half of her support, who is married and files jointly with her spouse.

3. Which itemized deductions of a child can reduce the amount of investment income subject to the kiddie tax?

a. Charitable contributions

b. Unreimbursed employee business expenses

c. Expenses directly connected to the production of investment income

d. Medical expenses

4. The parents of a child subject to the kiddie tax are divorced. The father is unmarried. The mother is remarried. The child lives with the mother, who is the custodial parent, and her new spouse. Which parent can make an election on Form 8814?

a. The father

b. The mother who files jointly with her new spouse

c. The mother who files separately from her new spouse and has lower taxable income than the new spouse

d. Neither the father or mother because they are no longer married to each other and filing jointly

5. Making the election to report a child's interest and dividends on the parent's return (using Form 8814) can be favorable to the parent with respect to:

a. The deduction for student loan interest

b. The deduction for charitable contributions

c. The deduction for medical expenses

d. The credit for child and dependent care expenses

Other Taxes

A taxpayer may owe other types of taxes in addition to the regular tax and alternative minimum tax. A taxpayer who is self-employed may be subject to self-employment taxes (Chapter 11). A taxpayer earning tips that are not reported to the employer may also owe Social Security and Medicare taxes on these unreported tips (Chapter 4).

A taxpayer may owe penalties related to qualified retirement plans, individual retirement accounts (IRAs), and other tax-advantaged accounts, which are paid as additional taxes (Chapter 8). There also may be a recapture of previously claimed tax benefits for an education credit (Chapter 30) and the first-time homebuyer credit (Chapter 14) for certain taxpayers. Those who engage household help may owe employment taxes for their workers.

These other taxes are additional amounts owed and are reported in the Other Taxes section of Form 1040, *U.S. Individual Income Tax Return.*

Self-Employment Tax

To ensure that self-employed individuals earn credits for Social Security and Medicare coverage, they pay self-employment (SE) tax. This tax, which is required under the Self-Employment Contributions Act (SECA), reflects both the employer and employee share of the contribution to Social Security and Medicare, even though a self-employed individual is neither an employer of him- or herself nor an employee.

The net earnings from self-employment, which are the profits reported on Schedule C (Form 1040), *Profit or Loss From Business*, or Schedule F (Form 1040), *Profit or Loss from Farming,* are the basis for SE tax. Net earnings from self-employment are discussed in Chapter 11.

The SE tax is figured on Schedule SE (Form 1040), *Self-Employment Tax,* shown in Figure 35.1. There is both a short version and a long version for computing the tax.

Section A—Short Schedule SE. Caution. Read above to see if you can use Short Schedule SE.

1a	Net farm profit or (loss) from Schedule F, line 34, and farm partnerships, Schedule K-1 (Form 1065), box 14, code A	1a	
b	If you received social security retirement or disability benefits, enter the amount of Conservation Reserve Program payments included on Schedule F, line 4b, or listed on Schedule K-1 (Form 1065), box 20, code Y	1b	( )
2	Net profit or (loss) from Schedule C, line 31; Schedule C-EZ, line 3; Schedule K-1 (Form 1065), box 14, code A (other than farming); and Schedule K-1 (Form 1065-B), box 9, code J1. Ministers and members of religious orders, see instructions for types of income to report on this line. See instructions for other income to report	2	
3	Combine lines 1a, 1b, and 2	3	
4	Multiply line 3 by 92.35% (.9235). If less than $400, you do not owe self-employment tax; **do not** file this schedule unless you have an amount on line 1b . . . . ▶	4	
	Note. If line 4 is less than $400 due to Conservation Reserve Program payments on line 1b, see instructions.		
5	**Self-employment tax.** If the amount on line 4 is: • $110,100 or less, multiply line 4 by 13.3% (.133). Enter the result here and on **Form 1040, line 56,** or **Form 1040NR, line 54** • More than $110,100, multiply line 4 by 2.9% (.029). Then, add $11,450.40 to the result. Enter the total here and on **Form 1040, line 56,** or **Form 1040NR, line 54**	5	
6	**Deduction for employer-equivalent portion of self-employment tax.** If the amount on line 5 is: • $14,643.30 or less, multiply line 5 by 57.51% (.5751) • More than $14,643.30, multiply line 5 by 50% (.50) and add $1,100 to the result. Enter the result here and on **Form 1040, line 27,** or **Form 1040NR, line 27** 6		

For Paperwork Reduction Act Notice, see your tax return instructions. Cat. No. 11358Z **Schedule SE (Form 1040) 2012**

FIGURE 35.1 Short Schedule SE

There is also an optional method (Part II, Section B of Schedule SE) that can be used to pay more tax that would otherwise be due in order to earn Social Security and Medicare credits. More information on this optional method is included in the instructions to Schedule SE. This may be helpful to farmers who have a bad year but want the Social Security and Medicare credits.

For 2012, the Social Security portion of the tax is figured on net earnings up to $110,100. There is no limit on the amount of net earnings taken into account in figuring the Medicare portion of the tax. The tax rates for 2012 are:

- 10.4% for the Social Security portion (after 2012, the rate is set to return to 12.4% rate for 2013)
- 2.9% for the Medicare portion

Chapter 11 explains how to figure the self-employment tax and report it on the return. Chapter 17 explains how to figure the deduction for the employer portion of the tax.

The amount of self-employment tax figured on Schedule SE is entered on line 56 of Form 1040.

Additional Taxes on Qualified Retirement Plans, IRAs, and Qualified Health Plans

Additional taxes related to qualified retirement plans and IRAs are referred to as penalties. These penalties apply because a taxpayer does or fails to do something according to the law. Additional taxes include:

- Early distribution penalty
- Excess contribution penalty
- Excess accumulation penalty
- Prohibited transaction penalty

The rules for these penalties are lengthy. An overview of the rules follows. For more details, see IRS Pub. 575, *Pensions and Annuities*, and IRS Pub. 590, *Individual Retirement Arrangements.*

The penalties are reported on Form 5329, *Additional Taxes on Qualified Plans (including IRAs), and Other Tax-Favored Accounts*, as follows:

- Early distributions—Part I
- Excess contributions—Parts III and IV
- Excess accumulations—Part VIII

The penalty figured on Form 5329 is entered on the appropriate line in the Other Taxes section of Form 1040; attach the form to the return.

TIP: If an exception to the 10% penalty applies, it should be noted on Form 1099-R, *Distributions From Pensions, Annuities, Retirement or Profit-Sharing Plans, IRAs, Insurance Contracts, etc.*, if the issuer is aware of the exception.

Early Distribution Penalty

Funds in retirement plans and IRAs are meant to be used for retirement. However, a taxpayer may need the funds for other reasons. When funds are withdrawn too early (generally, before age 59½), they may be subject to a 10% penalty. However, the penalty does not apply in certain cases.

Some of the exceptions to the penalty apply only to qualified retirement plans, some only to IRAs, and some to both. For example, there is no penalty if distributions are taken from a qualified retirement plan (but not from an IRA) on account of separation from service at age 55 or older (age 50 for qualified public safety employees). Here is a list of the exceptions to the penalty; Table 35.1 shows to which type of plan they apply.

TIP: Distributions from a qualified plan received under a qualified domestic relations order (QDRO) are *not* subject to the 10% premature distribution penalty. However, this exception applies only to qualified plans, *not* to IRA accounts.

- Disability, which must be total and permanent before age 59½.
- Death of the plan participant or IRA owner before age 59½.
- Distributions made as part of a series of substantially equal periodic payments and that run for five years or until the taxpayer is 59½, whichever is later. There are three acceptable methods for calculating the payments.

More information on these methods can be found in Pub. 575 under "Substantially Equal Periodic Payments."

- Separation from employment at age 55 or older.
- Payments to an alternate payee under a QDRO.
- Payments made to a spouse or former spouse incident to divorce.
- Payments of deductible unreimbursed medical expenses to the extent they exceed 7.5% of adjusted gross income (AGI) (even if the taxpayer does not itemize and deduct them).
- Distributions used by certain unemployed taxpayers to pay health insurance premiums.
- Distributions to pay qualified higher education costs.
- Distributions up to $10,000 used for first-time homebuyer costs.
- Distributions that are a qualified reservist distribution for individuals called to active duty for at least 180 days or an indefinite period.
- Distribution due to an IRS levy on qualified retirement plan or IRA account.

If distributions are taken from a Roth IRA before the end of the 5-year period beginning with the first year that the taxpayer's Roth IRA account was set up (or beginning with the first year that any of the taxpayer's Roth IRA accounts

TABLE 35.1 Exceptions to the 10% Early Distribution Penalty

Exception	Applies to qualified retirement plans	Applies to IRAs
Disability	X	X
Death	X	X
Distributions taken in a series of substantially equal periodic payments	X	X
Separation from employment at age 55 or older	X	
Payments to an alternate payee under a QDRO	X	
Payments made to a spouse or former spouse incident to divorce		X
Payments of medical expenses to the extent they exceed 7.5% of AGI (even if the taxpayer does not itemize and deduct them)	X	X
Distributions that are used to pay medical insurance		X
Distributions to pay qualified higher education costs		X
First-time homebuyer costs ($10,000 lifetime maximum per taxpayer)		X
Distributions that are a qualified reservist distribution	X	X
IRS levy	X	X

were set up, if he or she has more than one), the 10% penalty applies to the part of the nonqualified distribution that was included in income. A similar rule applies to in-plan designated Roth account distributions. However, there are certain limited exceptions to this penalty.

Example

Eric, age 58, contributed to a Roth IRA for the first time in February 2013, designating the contribution for the 2012 tax year. The year 2012 marks the first year in the 5-year holding period. Even though Eric turns 59½ in less than two years, he cannot take a distribution from the Roth IRA until this 5-year period is over without incurring the 10% penalty (unless one of the exceptions applies). Thus, he can take penalty-free distributions from the Roth IRA beginning in 2017. If he takes a distribution within the 5-year period, the earnings portion of the distribution is taxable, and the 10% penalty is based on that amount only—not the full amount distributed.

Excess Contributions

The tax code sets limits on annual contributions to qualified retirement plans and IRAs (Chapter 15). When the limits are exceeded, a 6% penalty applies to the excess contribution. For some retirement plans, the company servicing the retirement plan may refund the excess contribution. The penalty is cumulative; it continues to apply each year until the excess has been withdrawn.

Example

Janet, age 48, earned $40,000 and contributed $6,000 to her IRA in 2012. Because Janet is not yet age 50, the maximum allowable contribution she can make is $5,000, so $1,000 is an excess contribution subject to the 6% penalty. Janet can withdraw the excess, plus any earnings on it, by the due date of the return to avoid any penalty. She also can pay the penalty for 2012 and apply the $1,000 toward her 2013 contribution. If she does neither, the 6% penalty applies in 2012, 2013, and beyond until she corrects the error.

TIP: The penalty on excess contributions to Roth IRAs is figured separately from the penalty on other accounts, but both are figured on Form 5329.

Excess Accumulations

A taxpayer usually must start to draw down a traditional IRA or qualified retirement account starting at age 70½. (The first distribution can be postponed until April 1 of the year following the year of attaining age 70½.) A taxpayer who continues to work (and who is not a 5% owner of the business) can postpone distributions from a qualified retirement plan until retirement if allowed by the qualified plan (however, this rule does not apply to IRAs). The amount needed to be drawn annually is called a required minimum distribution (RMD), which generally is calculated as the value of the account as of the previous December 31, divided by the account owner's life expectancy in years as shown in the tables in Appendix C of IRS Pub. 590. See Chapter 8 for more information about RMDs. Failure to take an RMD results in a 50% penalty of the part that was not distributed as required.

TIP: There are no RMDs for the owner of a Roth IRA, and thus there are no excess accumulations or related penalties to the Roth IRA owner. However, a nonspouse beneficiary of an inherited Roth IRA must take RMDs even though they may be tax free.

TIP: A taxpayer who fails to take an RMD may obtain a penalty waiver if the failure was due to reasonable cause. Complete Form 5329 and attach a letter of explanation. In Part VIII of the form, enter "RC" and the amount that the taxpayer wants the IRS to waive. Subtract this amount from the total RMD shortfall. There is no need to pay the "RC" amount unless the IRS rejects the waiver request.

Example

Arthur turns age 70½ in 2012. Generally, he would be required to take the RMD from his IRA by December 31, 2012. However, he can delay the distribution of his first RMD until April 1, 2013. He must take his first RMD from his 401(k) plan by the same date unless he is still employed with the company sponsoring the 401(k) plan and the plan allows active employees to delay RMDs (and Arthur does not own more than 5% of the company). If he does not retire until he is 72, no RMD from his 401(k) plan is required until then. However, IRA distributions cannot be delayed despite continued employment.

Example

Based on Matt's age and the balance of his IRA at the end of 2011, his RMD for 2012 was $4,000. However, he forgot to take the distribution in 2012 and had no valid reason for failing to do so. He will be penalized $2,000—50% of the RMD he should have taken in 2012—and he will report the penalty on Form 5329 (and Form 1040) as an additional tax on IRAs.

Rules for figuring RMDs, along with tables needed to compute RMDs, can be found in IRS Pub. 590.

DEFINITION: A **prohibited transaction** is a transaction between a qualified retirement plan or IRA and a "disqualified person" (e.g., the plan's fiduciary or custodian or the account owner or certain family members of the owner). The following transactions are examples of prohibited transactions between an IRA owner and the owner's IRA that will trigger penalties:

- Borrowing funds from the IRA
- Selling, exchanging, or leasing property to the IRA
- Furnishing goods, services, or facilities
- Transferring or using IRA assets for the benefit of the IRA owner
- Acts of self-dealing or transactions involving a kickback to the owner

Prohibited Transactions

Certain transactions between an IRA owner and the owner's IRA are prohibited. **Prohibited transactions** also apply to qualified retirement plans.

A disqualified person who takes part in a prohibited transaction must correct the transaction *and* must pay an additional tax based on the amount involved in the transaction. The initial tax is 15% of the amount involved for each year (or part of a year) in the taxable period. If the transaction is not corrected within the taxable period, an additional tax of 100% of the amount involved is imposed.

Additional Tax on Qualified Health Plans (HSAs and MSAs)

There are some situations where a taxpayer may owe additional taxes on a health savings account (HSA) or a medical savings account (MSA). These situations are similar to those for retirement plans and IRAs where a taxpayer has made excess contributions or withdrawals for nonmedical purposes.

Excess Contributions

The 2012 contribution limit for an HSA is $3,100 for self-only coverage and $6,250 for family coverage. Individuals who are at least 55 years old by December 31, 2012 may make a catch-up contribution of $1,000. Any amount paid into an HSA in excess of these amounts is generally subject to a 6% penalty that is reported on Form 5329. Like IRAs, the excess is subject to penalties each year it remains in the account.

The penalty can be avoided if the excess plus income is withdrawn by the due date of the return including extensions for the year in which the excess contribution was made.

> **TIP:** If any of the special additional taxes on retirement plans apply, Form 5329 generally must be completed and attached to the return.

If the excess contribution is made by the employer, it will be reported as income to the employee in box 1 of Form W-2, *Wage and Tax Statement.*

Nonqualified Distributions A different penalty applies to distributions used for any purpose other than for qualified medical expenses. Distributions used to pay for nonmedical expenses generally are taxable and are subject to a 20% penalty. If a distribution is used for both qualified medical expenses and nonqualified uses, the penalty applies only to that portion of the distribution that is nonqualified, not to the entire amount distributed.

The penalty is waived if the distribution was made after the HSA account owner dies, becomes disabled, or turns age 65.

> **TIP:** A taxpayer who is at least age 65 can take an HSA distribution and use it for any purpose without incurring the 20% penalty. However, even though the penalty is avoided, the distribution is still subject to taxation, while a qualified distribution is tax-free.

Education Credit and Adjustment Recapture

An education credit (Chapter 30) previously claimed may have to be recaptured if the student receives tax-free educational assistance for, or a refund of, an expense used to figure the credit in a year after the year in which the credit was claimed. Figuring the recapture of the credit is explained in Chapter 30. The recapture amount is reported on the Tax line of the 2012 return; the prior-year return is not amended.

Qualified distributions from a Coverdell education savings account (ESA) or a qualified tuition program (QTP) are tax free. However, when distributions are not used to pay for qualified education costs, the earnings generally are taxable and the taxable amount is reported on Form 1040. These amounts may also be subject to a 10% additional tax. The additional tax on these distributions is figured on Part II of Form 5329, which is attached to the return. (See Figure 35.2.)

Part II **Additional Tax on Certain Distributions From Education Accounts**
Complete this part if you included an amount in income, on Form 1040 or Form 1040NR, line 21, from a Coverdell education savings account (ESA) or a qualified tuition program (QTP).

5	Distributions included in income from Coverdell ESAs and QTPs	5	
6	Distributions included on line 5 that are not subject to the additional tax (see instructions) . . .	6	
7	Amount subject to additional tax. Subtract line 6 from line 5	7	
8	**Additional tax.** Enter 10% (.10) of line 7. Include this amount on Form 1040, line 58, or Form 1040NR, line 56	8	

FIGURE 35.2 Form 5329, Part II

Household Employment Taxes

A taxpayer who employs a worker in his or her home, such as a housekeeper, nanny, au pair, health aide, or chauffeur, is an employer who is responsible for paying employment taxes on wages paid to the worker. These employment taxes are commonly referred to as the nanny tax.

The taxpayer will follow two steps to determine whether any such taxes are due.

Step 1. Determine whether a worker in the household is an employee or an independent contractor. Usually an independent contractor has his or her own business and works only limited hours or days for the homeowner, such as a gardener or pool cleaner. If the worker is an independent contractor, the taxpayer is not responsible for household employment taxes. However, if the worker is an employee, the taxpayer is responsible for these taxes.

Step 2. Determine which taxes that the taxpayer is responsible for. The taxes include:

- *Social Security and Medicare taxes (FICA).* Usually the taxpayer must withhold the employee's share of FICA and pay a like amount as the employer's share of FICA. This tax applies if a taxpayer pays $1,800 or more to a worker during the year (other than a spouse, child under the age of 21, the taxpayer's parent, or any employee under age 18). For 2012, however, the employee's portion of the Social Security tax is reduced to 4.2% on wages up to $110,100; the Medicare portion is 1.45% on all wages. The employer's share is 6.2% for the Social Security portion (the same wage cap applies), plus 1.45% for the Medicare portion of FICA.
- *Federal Unemployment Tax Act (FUTA).* FUTA applies if the taxpayer paid total cash wages of $1,000 or more in any calendar quarter in 2011 or 2012 (other than to a spouse, child under age 21, or a parent). The FUTA tax rate is 6% of the first $7,000 of cash wages paid. (FUTA does not apply to wages in excess of $7,000.) However, the taxpayer can claim a credit of 5.4% for state unemployment taxes, which effectively can reduce the federal tax rate to 0.6%. (However, in some states, the full credit cannot be claimed because these states have not repaid funds borrowed from the federal government to cover unemployment benefits. The instructions to Form 940, *Employer's Annual Federal Unemployment (FUTA) Tax Return* contains a contact list of state unemployment tax agencies.)
- *Federal income tax withholding.* Withholding is required only if the employee requests withholding and the taxpayer agrees to it. (The taxpayer may also have to withhold state income tax.)

The taxpayer must report and pay any taxes due. The taxes are reported on Schedule H (Form 1040), *Household Employment Taxes*, and are entered on the appropriate line in the Other Taxes section of Form 1040 for household employment taxes. A taxpayer who owes these taxes cannot file Form 1040A, *U.S. Individual Income Tax Return*, or Form 1040EZ, *Income Tax Return for Single and Joint Filers With No Dependents.*

TIP: Nonqualified distributions are not subject to penalty if made because of (a) the disability or death of the beneficiary, (b) the receipt by the beneficiary of a tax-free scholarship, (c) attendance by the beneficiary at a U.S. military academy, or (d) included in income because the qualified expenses were taken into account in figuring the American Opportunity Credit or Lifetime Learning Credit. However, even though these distributions are not subject to the penalty, the earnings distributed may be taxable.

TIP: The taxpayer must obtain an Employer Identification Number (EIN) in order to report household employment taxes. The taxpayer's Social Security Number cannot be used for this purpose.

ALERT: The FUTA credit for state unemployment tax may be lower for a taxpayer in some states. Check with the taxpayer's state to determine the credit amount. Contact information for state unemployment tax agencies is in the appendix to IRS Pub. 926, *Household Employer's Tax Guide.*

Agency-Placed Household Employee

There are some situations in which a taxpayer may have a person placed in the household by a placement agency or similar organization. If the agency that placed the worker in the home controls how the worker performs the work, then the worker is not a household employee. If the taxpayer, rather than the agency, controls how the work is done, then the worker may be a household employee.

> **TIP:** Unlike employment taxes related to a business, household employment taxes do not have to be deposited with the government throughout the year. The taxpayer should take household employment taxes into account in figuring estimated taxes for the year to avoid underpayment penalties (see Chapter 36).

Allocated Tips

A taxpayer who receives tips on the job may have some tips allocated to him or her by the employer (see Chapter 4). More specifically, allocated tips arise when a taxpayer worked in a restaurant, cocktail lounge, or similar business that must allocate tips to employees and the tips reported by the taxpayer to the employer were less than the taxpayer's share of 8% of food and drink sales. There are no allocated tips if the employer participates in the IRS's Attributed Tip Income Program (ATIP). The quickest way to know whether a taxpayer has allocated tips is simply to examine box 8 of Form W-2. If it is blank, there are no allocated tips.

> **TIP:** The employer of a household employee is not required to withhold federal income tax but may do so if the employee requests. However, the employer must withhold FICA taxes if he or she pays $1,800 or more to the employee. Any federal income tax withheld is reported on Schedule H and filed with Form 1040.

Allocated tips (or actual tips) are reported as income (discussed in Chapter 4). They are also subject to FICA taxes. The taxpayer figures his or her share of FICA taxes on allocated tips on Form 4137, *Social Security and Medicare Tax on Unreported Tip Income.*

FICA tax on allocated and reported tips is then entered on line 57 of Form 1040; attach the form to the return. Check the box on line 57 to indicate that Form 4137 is being filed.

> **TIP:** A taxpayer with adequate records showing actual tips should report them instead of the allocated tips, even if they are more or less than the amount reported on box 8 of Form W-2.

Uncollected Social Security and Medicare Tax on Wages

Some individuals are treated by companies as independent contractors when, in fact, they should be treated as employees (Chapter 4). Such individuals may be able to file their returns as if they are employees, limiting their payment for FICA tax to the employee share on wages rather than paying both the employer and employee share through self-employment tax.

Form 8919, *Social Security and Medicare Tax on Wages*, is filed if a taxpayer performed services for a company on which no FICA tax was withheld and any of the following applies:

- The taxpayer filed Form SS-8, *Determination of Worker Status for Purposes of Federal Employment Taxes and Income Tax Withholding,* and received a determination letter stating that he or she is an employee of the firm, or has not yet received a response from the IRS.

TIP: A taxpayer with unreported and/or allocated tips may need to make estimated tax payments. Allocated tips, even though reported on Form W-2, are not subject to withholding for income tax or the employee share of FICA. Paying estimated taxes will avoid a penalty on underpayments.

- The taxpayer was designated as a section 530 employee by the employer or by the IRS prior to January 1, 1997.
- The taxpayer received other correspondence from the IRS that states he or she is an employee.
- The taxpayer was previously treated as an employee by the company and is performing services in a substantially similar capacity and under substantially similar direction and control.
- Coworkers performing substantially similar services under substantially similar direction and control are treated as employees.
- Coworkers performing substantially similar services under substantially similar direction and control filed Form SS-8 and received a determination that they were employees.

The FICA tax figured on Form 8919 is reported on the appropriate line in the Other Taxes section of Form 1040 (check the box to indicate that Form 8919 is being filed and attach the form to the return).

First-Time Homebuyer Credit Repayment

A taxpayer who claimed a first-time homebuyer credit may have to recapture some or all of the credit (as discussed in Chapter 14). *Recapture* means reporting it as an additional tax on the 2012 return. The recapture rules depend on when the home was purchased:

- For homebuyers in 2008, the credit is recaptured ratably over 15 years *if the home continues to be owned and used as a principal residence.* This means that if the maximum credit of $7,500 was claimed for the purchase of a home in 2008, $500 must be recaptured (reported as income) each year beginning in 2010. This recapture amount is figured in Part IV of Form 5405, *First-Time Homebuyer Credit and Repayment of the Credit*, and is reported on the appropriate line in the Other Taxes section of Form 1040. (Form 1040A or 1040EZ cannot be filed if there is any recapture.) For more details, see the instructions to Form 5405. If the taxpayer bought the home in 2008, owned the home, and used it as his or her main home during all of 2012, then the taxpayer must continue to repay the credit. In this situation, the taxpayer can report the repayment directly on Form 1040.
- For homebuyers in 2008 who sell the home (or cease using it as their principal residence) before the end of the 15-year recapture period, the remaining credit repayment amount is added to the income tax liability of the taxpayer for the year of sale or cessation of use as a principal residence. The recapture is limited to the amount of gain (if any) on such sale. In figuring gain, the adjusted basis of the home is be reduced by the amount of the first-time homebuyer credit claimed but not yet recaptured. If the reason for the sale or cessation is an **involuntary conversion**, there is no recapture, provided that a new principal residence is acquired within

DEFINITION: An **involuntary conversion** occurs when a taxpayer has property that is destroyed, condemned, or disposed of under threat of condemnation, and the taxpayer is given money or other property in exchange.

a two-year period beginning on the date the first home ceases to be the taxpayer's principal residence. There is no recapture upon the death of the homeowner.

Example

Miryam bought her first home in 2008 and qualified for and claimed the full credit of $7,500 on her return for that year. She continues to live in her home. In 2012, she must include $500 in income (1/15th of $7,500). If she had sold the home in 2012, she would have had to recapture $6,500 ($7,500 – $500 recaptured in 2010 and another $500 recaptured in 2011).

- For homebuyers in 2009 and 2010 (2011 in special cases), full recapture applies if the home is sold or ceases to be used as a principal residence within 36 months of the date of purchase. *Full recapture* means that the entire credit, rather than a ratable amount, must be repaid. However, if the disposition is because of death, involuntary conversion, divorce, or certain other situations there is no recapture. After 36 months, recapture no longer applies regardless of the continued ownership and use of the home.

ALERT: If a home is sold at a loss, there is no recapture of the first-time homebuyer credit.

Example

Same as the example above, except the purchase was made in March 2010 and Miryam claimed a credit of $8,000. In February 2012, she sold her home. Because she sold her home within 36 months of the purchase (and none of the exceptions to recapture applies), she must recapture the full credit amount of $8,000. She will show the recapture amount on Form 1040 (and attach Form 5405).

Review Questions

1. All of the following statements about self-employment tax are correct **except**:

a. It applies to net earnings reported on Schedule C.

b. It applies to net earnings reported on Schedule F.

c. It applies to unallocated tips.

d. It applies to self-employed individuals.

2. Which is **not** a penalty tax related to qualified retirement plans and IRAs?

a. Penalty on certain distributions from Coverdell ESAs

b. Penalty on early distributions

c. Penalty on excess contributions

d. Penalty on excess accumulations

3. Which of the following exceptions to the early distribution penalty applies only to IRAs and **not** to qualified retirement plans?

a. Distributions in a series of substantially equal periodic payments

b. Distributions on account of disability

c. Distributions to pay certain education costs

d. IRS levies

4. Which of the following statements about household employment taxes is **not** correct?

a. FICA applies if the taxpayer pays $1,700 or more to a worker (other than a spouse, child under the age of 21, the taxpayer's parent, or any employee under age 18).

b. Household employment taxes must be deposited with the U.S. Treasury using Form 941.

c. FUTA applies if the taxpayer paid total cash wages of $1,000 or more in any calendar quarter in 2011 or 2012 (other than to a spouse, child under age 21, or a parent).

d. Income tax withholding applies only if the employee requests it and the taxpayer agrees to this.

5. In 2008, a taxpayer claimed a $7,500 first-time homebuyer credit and continues to live in the home. Which of the following statements is correct?

a. The taxpayer must report $500 as recapture (additional tax) on his or her 2012 tax return.

b. The taxpayer is not subject to recapture because he or she still owns the home.

c. The taxpayer is not subject to recapture as long as he or she stays in the home for 36 months, a period that was completed in 2012.

d. The taxpayer must repay the tax credit after 15 years.

6. In 2009, a taxpayer claimed the first-time homebuyer credit. Which situation would require recapture of the credit?

a. The sale of the home at a loss

b. The transfer of the home to a spouse incident to divorce

c. The sale of the home because one owner dies

d. The sale of a home because of a job move

7. Which penalty amount applies if a taxpayer fails to take required minimum distributions?

a. 5%

b. 6%

c. 10%

d. 50%

8. Jake, age 48, wants to roll over $50,000 from his qualified plan with his ex-employer to a traditional IRA. He requests a check for $50,000 and receives $40,000, after withholding, which he uses to open the IRA seven weeks later. Which of the following is the **best** statement describing Jake's situation?

a. As long as Jake deposits the $40,000 check within 60 days, he pays no tax or penalty

b. Jake must pay a 10% penalty on the full distribution because it was not rolled over directly from the qualified plan to the IRA

c. Jake must come up with an additional $10,000 to deposit into the IRA to avoid any tax or penalty

d. Jake did not open the IRA within the prescribed time limit, and therefore he is subject to both tax and penalty on the full distribution.

9. Which of the following is subject to SE tax?

a. Rental income

b. The taxable portion of annuity income

c. Net income from a salaried taxpayer's side business

d. Hobby income

10. The maximum rate that a self-employed taxpayer must pay in SE tax in 2012 is:

a. 7.65%

b. 13.3%

c. 14.3%

d. 15.3%

11. The maximum amount of SE tax a taxpayer can pay in 2012 is

a. $106,800

b. $110,100

c. $11,450.40

d. Unlimited

PART 5

Completion of the Filing Process

CHAPTER 36

Tax Payments and Refund Options

The federal income tax system works primarily on a pay-as-you-go basis. A taxpayer cannot simply wait until filing a return for the year to pay all that is owed. Instead, payments are made throughout the year. The primary means of payment for most taxpayers is withholding from wages, which is mandatory for most individuals. However, there are some voluntary payment options. Taxpayers who cannot satisfy their payment obligation through withholding must pay estimated taxes in four installments.

It is virtually impossible to know precisely what a taxpayer's tax liability will be for the year until completing the return. Thus, a tax payment may be made with the return itself if there is a balance due. If withholdings and estimated tax payment exceed the tax liability, a refund is paid to the taxpayer.

The failure to satisfy tax payment requirements can result in an underpayment penalty. In addition to the underpayment penalty, there are also penalties for late filing, late payments, and other reasons. Additionally, interest may be charged on any outstanding balance due.

Tax Payment and Withholding Information

A taxpayer should track any tax payments made for a particular year, which can include:

- Withholding on wages and supplemental compensation (e.g., bonuses paid in property)
- Mandatory 20% withholding on lump-sum distributions from qualified retirement plans and voluntary withholding on other payments from qualified plans and individual retirement accounts (IRAs)
- Voluntary withholding on Social Security benefits and unemployment benefits
- Backup withholding on interest and dividends
- Estimated taxes

- Tax refunds from the prior year applied toward the current year's tax
- Payment made with a request for a filing extension

> **TIP:** A taxpayer could have tax withholdings shown on Form W-2, *Wage and Tax Statement*, and various 1099-series forms. Also, a taxpayer may have paid estimated taxes recorded on Form 1040-ES, *Estimated Tax for Individuals*. This form should reflect quarterly estimated payments due in April 2012, June 2012, September 2012, and January 2013 (for 2012 taxes). The taxpayer should also review last year's tax return to see whether a refund was applied toward the current year's tax.

Paying a Balance Due

A taxpayer may have a balance due once the return for the year is completed as it will reflect tax liability based on actual income for the year. A balance due occurs when the total payments are not sufficient to cover the total tax liability. There are several ways in which the balance due can be paid when the return is filed:

- *Check or money order.* The taxpayer may remit payment with a personal check or money order made payable to the United States Treasury. Form 1040-V, *Payment Voucher,* is completed as a remittance document with the tax return and should be mailed with the check.
- *Direct debit.* The electronic funds transfer (EFT) method debits the taxpayer's bank account. The taxpayer must provide the bank's routing number and account number. This method is secure, and no fee is charged (unless the taxpayer's bank imposes a fee for the electronic debit).
- *EFTPS.* The Electronic Federal Tax Payment System (EFTPS) allows a taxpayer who has first registered at EFTPS.gov to transfer payments from his or her bank account to the United States Treasury via this online system. Transactions can also be handled by telephone. There is no government fee for using this service.
- *Credit card.* Payment can be charged to a major credit card through an IRS-approved service provider. The IRS does not charge any fee for charging taxes to a credit or debit card, but the service provider may.

> **TIP:** If paying by check, the taxpayer should write his or her daytime phone number, Social Security Number (SSN), and the type of return (e.g., "2012 Form 1040" or "2012 1040EZ") on the check. When filing jointly, the SSN of the spouse listed first on the return should be the SSN written on the check.

Options When Funds Are Not Currently Available

A taxpayer who does not have the funds to write a check or transfer money using EFT or EFTPS and does not want to use a credit card may be able to make the payment under a short-term extension or an installment agreement.

Short-Term Agreement to Pay in Full A taxpayer can request an extension of time in which to make full payment. The extension granted usually is 60 to 120 days. If a taxpayer is able to pay in full within the agreement period, interest and penalties are lower with a short-term agreement to pay in full than with an installment agreement. Asking for this short-term extension avoids the fee for setting up an installment agreement. A taxpayer who fails to make full payment within this period can then ask for an installment agreement for the remaining balance.

> **TIP:** Taxpayers who cannot pay their balance due should not delay filing a return. Filing by the return due date (including extensions) avoids a late filing penalty even if the balance due cannot be paid in full.

Hardship Extension Taxpayers who will face undue financial hardship if they were to pay tax when it is due may file Form 1127, *Application for Extension of Time for Payment of Tax Due to Undue Hardship.* A hardship extension usually is granted for a period of no longer than six months. To be eligible, taxpayers must be able to show that paying the tax is more than an inconvenience and that a substantial financial loss (e.g., selling property at a sacrifice price) will result if the tax owed is paid at this time. There is no cost to apply for a hardship extension, but taxpayers must include a statement of assets and liabilities and an itemized list of income and expenses for three months prior to the return due date. Form 1127 must be filed by the original due date for filing the return. Additionally, no penalty will be assessed if the tax is paid within the time period provided by the extension, but interest will be charged.

TIP: The three approved credit/debit card processors are: Link2Go (www.pay1040.com), RBS WorldPay, Inc. (www.payUSAtax.com and www.valuetaxpayment.com), and Official Payments Corporation (www.officialpayments.com/fed). More information about their fees and other information is available from the IRS at www.irs.gov/efile/article/0,,id=101316,00.html.

Hardship Extension for Unemployed Taxpayers For tax year 2011 returns filed in 2012, eligible unemployed taxpayers may request a six-month grace period on the failure-to-pay penalty. Interest continues to accrue on the late-paid amount. To qualify for this relief:

- The taxpayer must:
  - Have been unemployed for at least 30 consecutive days during 2011 or 2012 (up to the April 17, 2012, filing deadline), OR
  - Have experienced a 25% or more drop in self-employment income in 2011 because of the economy.
- The taxpayer's income may not exceed $100,000 ($200,000 married filing jointly).
- The balance due may not exceed $50,000.
- The entire balance due, including interest and any other penalties that apply, must have been paid by October 15, 2012.

ALERT: Expired! The hardship extension for unemployed taxpayers was limited to tax year 2011 returns filed in 2012.

To request relief, the taxpayer must complete new Form 1127-A, *Application for Extension of Time for Payment of Income Tax for 2011 Due to Undue Hardship*, by the original due date of the return. Unlike the regular hardship extension, documentation of assets, liabilities, income, and expenses is not required.

Installment Agreement A taxpayer who owes $50,000 or less in combined taxes, interest, and penalties and has filed all required tax returns to date can obtain a streamlined installment agreement. A taxpayer who requests a streamlined installment agreement does not have to submit a Collection Information Statement. A taxpayer submits a streamlined request by:

- Applying online at www.irs.gov/individuals/article/0,,id=149373,00.html
- Mailing Form 9465, *Installment Agreement Request*, with the return (for taxpayers who owe $25,000 or less); Form 9465-FS, *Installment Agreement Request* (for taxpayers who owe between $25,000 and $50,000); or Form 2159, *Payroll Deduction Agreement*
- Applying in person at the local IRS office
- Applying over the telephone

Under an installment agreement, taxes must be paid within 72 months or before the collection statute of limitations expires, whichever is earlier. Taxpayers who owe between $25,000 and $50,000 must agree to a direct debit installment agreement in order to participate in the streamlined process.

For taxpayers owing more than $50,000, the streamlined application process does not apply. Such taxpayers must apply using Form 9465-FS and must also file Form 433-F, *Collection Information Statement.*

The IRS cannot reject installment agreement requests for taxpayers owing $10,000 or less who meet the following criteria:

- During the last five years, the taxpayer (and spouse, if filing a joint return) timely filed all income tax returns and paid any income tax due, and did not participate in an installment agreement.
- The IRS determines that the taxpayer cannot pay the entire amount of tax when due, and the taxpayer provided the IRS all necessary information to make that determination.
- The taxpayer agrees to pay the full amount owed within three years and to comply to the tax law while the installment agreement is in effect.

ALERT: Obtaining an installment agreement does not avoid interest and penalties on late payments, which continue to run on the unpaid balance. However, the failure to pay penalty may be reduced because the installment agreement is in place. In some cases, the IRS also can impose a lien on the taxpayer's property during the course of the installment agreement.

The fee for obtaining an installment agreement is:

- $105 for a standard agreement or payroll deduction agreement
- $52 for a direct debit agreement, which is authorization to have the monthly installment amount debited from a taxpayer's bank account
- $43 if the taxpayer's income is below poverty guidelines set by the U.S. Department of Health and Human Services

Offer in Compromise An offer in compromise (OIC) is an agreement between a taxpayer and the IRS that settles a tax liability for less than the full amount owed. The IRS is legally authorized to compromise a tax liability for any of these reasons:

TIP: The fee for obtaining an installment agreement is not paid with the application. Rather, it is added to the tax bill and recouped by the government through the installment payments.

- *Doubt as to liability.* There is doubt as to whether the taxpayer actually owes the tax or about how much exact tax the taxpayer owes. The taxpayer must submit a detailed written statement explaining why the taxpayer believes he or she does not owe the tax. Note: A taxpayer who believes there is doubt as to liability files Form 656-L, *Offer in Compromise (Doubt as to Liability).*
- *Doubt as to collectability.* There is doubt as to whether the taxpayer can pay the full amount owed before the statute of limitations for collection expires. The taxpayer must not be able to pay the taxes in full by liquidating assets or through current installment payment agreement guidelines.
- *Effective tax administration.* There is no doubt the taxpayer owes the tax and no doubt the taxpayer can pay the tax, but collection of the tax would create an economic hardship or would be unfair and inequitable. The taxpayer must submit a detailed written statement explaining his or her special circumstances and why collection would create an economic hardship or would be unfair and inequitable.

In order to be considered for an OIC, a taxpayer must:

- Complete the most current versions of Form 656, *Offer in Compromise*, Form 433-A, *Collection Information Statement for Wage Earners and Self-Employed Individuals*, and/or Form 433-B, *Collection Information Statement for Businesses*, and attach copies of any documentation required with the forms. If the taxpayer is filing Form 656-L, a Collection Information Statement is not required.
- Submit a nonrefundable $150 user fee with Form 656 (unless the taxpayer qualifies for a waiver of the fee under the Low Income Certification guidelines, which are shown on Form 656 Section 4). No user fee is required if the OIC was submitted based solely on doubt as to liability.
- Submit a down payment with Form 656 unless not required because the taxpayer qualifies under the Low Income Certification guidelines. For lump-sum offers, the down payment must equal 20% of the amount of the OIC. For periodic payment offers, the down payment must include the first proposed installment required under the proposed payment schedule, and the taxpayer must continue to make payments while the IRS considers the offer.
- Have filed all required federal tax returns.
- Be current on estimated tax payments for the current year.
- Have filed any required employment tax returns and paid any tax due on time for the two quarters prior to filing the OIC, and be current with deposits for the quarter in which the offer in compromise is submitted.
- Not have an open bankruptcy case.

Obtaining a Refund

When the amount of taxes paid by the taxpayer (total payments) exceeds the tax liability (total tax), the taxpayer is entitled to a refund. A taxpayer may obtain a refund in one of several ways:

- A check from the United States Treasury.
- Direct deposit into one or more eligible accounts or the purchase of U.S. savings bonds.
- Application of some or all of the refund to 2013 estimated taxes. The amount, if any, of the refund applied to 2013 estimated taxes is up to the taxpayer.

Direct Deposits

A taxpayer who wants a refund deposited into his or her bank account simply includes his or her account number and the bank's routing number in the refund section of the return. A taxpayer who wants to split the refund into one or more eligible accounts must file Form 8888, *Allocation of Refund (Including Savings Bond Purchases)*, with the return.

ALERT: When directing a refund to an IRA, HSA, MSA, or Coverdell ESA, the taxpayer should make sure that the custodian will accept it. Also, the taxpayer should tell the custodian to which year the payment should be applied. For example, a direct deposit of a refund to an IRA made in March 2013 may be applied automatically toward a 2013 IRA contribution. A taxpayer who wants the refund to apply to a 2012 IRA contribution must notify the custodian.

Eligible accounts that may be designated include:

- Checking or savings account
- Traditional IRA, Roth IRA, Simplified Employee Pension IRA (SEP-IRA), but not a Savings Incentive Match Plan for Employees IRA (SIMPLE IRA).
- Health savings account (HSA) or Archer medical savings account (MSA)
- Coverdell education savings account (ESA)
- TreasuryDirect online account.

Taxpayers also have the option to purchase Series I U.S. savings bonds directly by filling out Part II of Form 8888. Bond purchases can be made in $50 increments, with a limit of $5,000 per calendar year from a tax refund. Purchases can be made for the taxpayer, the taxpayer's spouse, or someone else named by the taxpayer.

Refund Problems

Refunds paid by check are usually issued within 45 days of the due date of the return. For electronically filed returns, refunds through direct deposits may arrive within three weeks of the acknowledgment date. A taxpayer can check on the status of a refund using Where's My Refund, which is a secure online tracking tool at https://sa1.www4.irs.gov/irfof/lang/en/irfofgetstatus.jsp.

ALERT: A taxpayer who receives a greater refund than shown on the tax return should not cash the check. Instead, the taxpayer should wait for a notice from the IRS explaining the difference and follow the instructions on the notice. If a direct refund deposit is greater than the amount shown on the return, the taxpayer should follow the same process.

A refund that is smaller than the refund shown on the tax return can be cashed; the taxpayer will receive an additional payment at a later date if the IRS erred in issuing the smaller check.

A taxpayer will receive interest on a refund that is not issued within 45 days after the due date of the return. (If a refund is issued within 45 days, no interest is payable for the 45-day period.) Interest may also be issued on additional refund amounts received with an amended return. If a taxpayer receives a larger refund than is owed, however, he or she does not pay interest on the amount that must be returned to the government.

A federal income tax refund may not be paid, or may be partially paid, to a taxpayer if he or she has certain outstanding obligations, such as:

- Federal income taxes not paid in a prior year
- Past-due child support
- State income taxes that were not paid in a prior year
- Student loan debt that is considered in default

The process of applying a federal tax refund to reduce outstanding obligation is called an offset. When a married person files a joint return, the refund can be applied toward obligations of one spouse. The other spouse, if not personally liable for the obligation, can make sure to obtain his or her share of the refund by filing as an injured spouse. Use Form 8379, *Injured Spouse Allocation*, which can be attached to the return. When the form is filed separately, attach copies of W-2s, 1099s, and other relevant forms showing tax payments by the injured spouse.

Taxpayers are eligible to file for allocation as an injured spouse if all of the following apply:

- The taxpayer and spouse filed a joint return.
- The joint return had a refund due, all or part of which was, or is expected to be, applied against a debt of the taxpayer's spouse.
- For purposes of injured spouse, the debt must be a legally enforceable and past-due:
  - Federal tax
  - State income tax
  - State unemployment compensation debt
  - Child or spousal support
  - A federal nontax debt (e.g., a federal student loan)
- The taxpayer is not legally obligated to pay the past-due amount. (The debt is owed only by the taxpayer's spouse.)
- The taxpayer reported income such as wages and taxable interest on the joint return.
- The taxpayer made and reported payments, such as federal income tax withholding or federal estimated tax payments, and/or the taxpayer claimed the Earned Income Credit or other refundable credit on the joint return.

ALERT: Do not confuse the injured spouse allocation with innocent spouse relief. The injured spouse allocation (Form 8379) is made to ensure that the spouse's refund is not used as an offset for the other spouse's past-due obligations. Innocent spouse relief (Form 8857, *Request for Innocent Spouse Relief*) is made to avoid liability for taxes resulting from the other spouse's actions.

Estimated Taxes

A taxpayer must pay estimated taxes if he or she expects to owe at least $1,000 for the year, after subtracting withholding and refundable tax credits. Taxes for this purpose include not only regular tax but also the alternative minimum tax, self-employment tax, and any tax for household employers.

However, under a safe harbor rule, no estimated payments are necessary in the current year (and no estimated tax penalties will be charged), if the total of the taxpayer's payments, including withholding and timely estimated tax payments, are equal to at least the smaller of:

1. 90% of the tax shown on the current year's return OR
2. 100% of the tax shown on the prior year's return. The percentage increases to 110% of the taxes shown on the prior year's return if the taxpayer's adjusted gross income (AGI) in the prior year exceeded $150,000 ($75,000 if filing status for the current year is married filing separately). The prior year's return must have been for a full 12 months. In other words, the taxpayer cannot have filed a short year tax return.

TIP: Different percentages for the safe harbor rule apply to farmers and fishermen. If at least two-thirds of the taxpayer's gross income for 2012 or 2013 is from farming or fishing, substitute $66\frac{2}{3}$% for 90% in (1) of the safe harbor rule.

Example

Sebastian is a single taxpayer who would like to know if he should make estimated tax payments. He has a job and recently got into a rental real estate business. His AGI for 2011 was $53,700, and his tax liability for 2011 was $9,550. Using the 2012 *Estimated Tax* Worksheet in Form 1040-ES, his tax return preparer estimated his 2012 tax liability to be $12,145. Sebastian expects to have $10,000 of federal income tax withheld from his wages.

Because Sebastian expects to owe at least $1,000 for the tax year, he must make estimated tax payments unless he qualifies under the safe harbor. Sebastian's 2012 expected federal income tax withholding ($10,000) is less than 90% of the 2012 tax liability (90% × $12,145 = $10,931). However, Sebastian's 2012 expected federal income tax withholding is greater than 100% of his 2011 tax liability.

Therefore, Sebastian does not need to make estimated payments: 100% of his 2011 tax liability is lower than 90% of the 2012 tax liability, and his 2012 federal income tax withholding is higher than his 2011 tax liability. However, Sebastian's preparer advises him to set money aside, make voluntary estimated payments, or increase his federal income tax withholding through his employer in order to be prepared for his expected balance due.

Also, estimated taxes are not due if the taxpayer had no tax liability in the prior year or was not required to file a return in the prior year.

Figuring Estimated Taxes

Estimated taxes should reflect law changes in effect for the year to which the taxes relate. For example, estimated taxes for 2012 should reflect cost-of-living adjustments to various tax items that apply for that year, including tax brackets, personal and dependency exemptions, and the standard deduction amounts. Taxpayers with interests in pass-through entities, including partnerships, S corporations, trusts, and estates, should take into account projected distributions from these entities as well.

Use the *Estimated Tax* Worksheet in the instructions to Form 1040-ES to figure the quarterly payments for the year. As income, deductions, or other factors change, the payments can be adjusted accordingly.

Estimated taxes are referred to as *quarterly payments* because they are made four times during the year. However, they are not spread evenly over the year. For example, estimated tax payments for tax year 2012 were due on:

- April 17, 2012
- June 15, 2012
- September 17, 2012
- January 15, 2013 (However, this last payment is not due if the taxpayer files a return for 2012 by January 31, 2013, and pays the remaining balance due.)

Estimated taxes can be paid using the same payment options as regular taxes. If paying through check or money order, the payment should be sent with a voucher to the appropriate address listed on the Form 1040-ES instructions.

Penalty for Underpayment of Estimated Taxes

A taxpayer who underpays estimated taxes may be subject to a penalty. The penalty generally is figured separately for each quarterly estimated payment. A taxpayer who receives income unevenly during the year may be able to avoid or lower the penalty by annualizing the income and making unequal payments. The penalty is figured on Form 2210, *Underpayment of Estimated Tax by Individuals, Estates, and Trusts.*

Several ways to figure whether a penalty applies are available. These include:

- *Short method.* This method can be used if the taxpayer made no estimated tax payments (other than federal income tax withholding) or paid the same amount of estimated tax on each of the four payment due dates.
- *Regular method.* This is the basic method and should be used if the short method is not allowed. It must be used if any installments were paid late. It should also be used if a lower penalty would result from treating the federal income tax withheld from income as paid on the dates it was actually withheld instead of in equal amounts on the payment due dates. It should also be used if income varied during the year and the penalty is reduced or eliminated by using the annualized method (in the next bullet point). The annualized method is figured first and then taken into account for the regular method.
- *Annualized method.* A taxpayer with income that varies throughout the year, such as an owner of a seasonable business or an investor with a large capital gain late in the year, can reduce or avoid estimated tax penalties for one or more required installments using this special method. If this situation applies, the taxpayer should fill out Schedule AI, *Annualized Income Installment Method,* which is a part of Form 2210.

The penalty amount is the IRS-set interest rate applicable to the period of the underpayment.

The penalty for underpaying estimated taxes can be waived in certain situations:

- The failure to make estimated payments was caused by a casualty, disaster, or other unusual circumstance, and it would be inequitable to impose the penalty, OR
- The taxpayer retired after reaching age 62 or became disabled during the tax year for which estimated payments were required to be made or in the preceding tax year, and the underpayment was due to reasonable cause and not willful neglect.

To request a waiver, check the appropriate box on Form 2210 and follow the directions in the Form 2210 instructions.

Interest and Penalties

Taxpayers who perform or fail to perform certain actions can be subject to both interest and penalties. Usually the interest and penalties directly relate to the amount of unpaid tax. Interest is compounded daily and usually runs from the last date for making the payment to the date the amount is paid.

Interest

In addition to any penalties that may be owed (as explained in "Tax Penalties" in the next section), interest is owed by the taxpayer to the government on outstanding underpayments. For example, in addition to the failure-to-pay penalty that may apply, interest is charged on tax not paid by the original (unextended) due date of the return. Interest on the tax continues to apply even if a taxpayer obtains a filing extension.

Interest on the failure-to-file penalty, accuracy-related penalties, fraud penalty, and failure-to-pay stamp tax penalty is charged from the date on which the return is required to be filed (including extensions) until the date of payment.

Interest on all other penalties is due only if the penalty is not paid within 21 calendar days (or 10 business days, if the notice is for $100,000 or more) from the date of notice and demand of the penalty; interest starts to run from the date of the notice and demand.

The IRS may owe a taxpayer interest on certain overpayments (see the earlier Refund Problems section). However, no interest is payable on a tax refund issued within 45 days after the due date of the return (or, if the return is filed after the due date, within 45 days after the date of filing the return). However, the IRS is allowed to stop interest on a date it chooses that is within 30 days of issuing a refund. This means that the IRS may owe a taxpayer less than 45 days of interest, even if the refund is issued after 45 days.

Interest is based on a rate set quarterly by the IRS. For individual taxpayers, the same rates apply to both underpayments and overpayments. A list of the IRS interest rates can be found in IRS Notice 746, *Information About Your Notice, Penalty and Interest.* The notice also contains a list of the penalty situations to which interest applies.

Interest can be abated (reduced or forgiven) if an underpayment results from an IRS error or delay. This can arise from erroneous written advice given by the IRS to a taxpayer. A taxpayer seeking abatement must send Form 843, *Claim for Refund and Request for Abatement,* to which a copy of the taxpayer's written request for advice, the written IRS advice, and the written notice of tax adjustments is attached.

Tax Penalties

Numerous tax penalties can apply for various reasons. Here is a brief description of some common tax penalties.

Late Filing and Late Payment Penalty The failure-to-file penalty is usually 5% for each month or part of a month that a return is late, but not more than a total of 25%. (If the penalty is due to fraud, the monthly percentage is 15% instead of 5%.) The penalty is based on the tax not paid by the due date including extensions. For a return filed more than 60 days after the due date, the minimum penalty is the lesser of $135 or 100% of the tax on the return.

The penalty for failure to pay the amount shown as due on the return is ½ of 1% (0.5%) of the unpaid taxes for each month, or part of a month, after the payment due date that the tax is not paid. This penalty does not apply during the automatic six-month extension of time to file period provided at least 90% of tax liability is paid on or before the original due date of the return and the balance is paid when the return is filed.

The penalty for failure to pay the amount shown as due on a notice and demand for payment by the date specified on the notice is ½ of 1% (0.5%) of the amount if the failure lasts for one month or less and an additional 0.5% for each additional month (or part of a month) that the liability remains unpaid.

The penalties for failure-to-pay are increased to 1% for any month the tax remains unpaid after a demand for immediate payment is issued or 10 days after a notice of intent to levy is issued.

A taxpayer who files on time is subject to a failure-to-pay penalty rate of $\frac{1}{4}$ of 1% (0.25%) per month during any month in which the taxpayer has a valid installment agreement in force.

For any month in which both the failure-to-file penalty and the failure-to-pay penalty apply, the penalty for filing late is reduced by the amount of the penalty for paying late for that month, unless the minimum penalty for filing late is charged.

Example

Ben files and pays his $800 balance due on January 20 of the year following the due date of his return, thereby subjecting himself to a failure-to-file penalty and a failure-to-pay penalty. He did not request an extension of time to file. Because Ben is being charged both the failure-to-file and the failure-to-pay penalties, his failure-to-file penalty is reduced by the amount of his failure-to-pay penalty, resulting in a total penalty of 5% per month for the first five months. Ben is assessed a penalty of 0.5% of the monthly balance due for each of the five remaining months that the balance is left unpaid. The penalties are calculated as follows:

Failure-to-pay penalty		
$800 × 0.5% × 10 months =		$40
Failure-to-file penalty		
Failure-to-file penalty = $800 × 5% × 5 months =	$200	
– Failure-to-pay penalty for first 5 months =	–$20	
= Net failure-to-file penalty to be assessed =		$180
Total penalties		
$40 failure-to-pay penalty + $180 failure-to-file penalty =		$220

TIP: The penalty can be avoided by showing reliance on substantial authority, such as court decisions or IRS rulings. The penalty also can be avoided by showing that the position was adequately disclosed on the return and that there was a reasonable basis for the position.

ALERT: Ignorance of the law, or negligence, does not constitute fraud. However, IRS examiners who find strong evidence of fraud will refer the case to the IRS Criminal Investigation Division for possible criminal prosecution. Both civil sanctions and criminal prosecution can be pursued.

Accuracy-Related Penalties Several penalties may be assessed on a taxpayer for reasons related to the accuracy (or inaccuracy) of a tax return. A taxpayer may be penalized 20% of an underpayment due to negligence, disregard of the tax laws and regulations, or if the understatement is substantial. The understatement is substantial if it is more than the greater of 10% of the correct tax due or $5,000.

There is a 40% penalty for an understatement attributable to undisclosed foreign financial assets. For example, if a taxpayer fails to disclose amounts held in a foreign financial account when required to do so on Form 8938, *Statement of Specified Foreign Assets*, any underpayment of tax related to the transaction that gave rise to the income would be subject to the 40% penalty provision, as would any underpayment related to interest, dividends, or other returns accrued on such undisclosed amounts.

Civil Fraud Penalty An underpayment of tax due to fraud results in a penalty of 75% of the underpayment due to fraud. The fraud penalty on a joint return does not apply to a spouse unless some part of the underpayment is due to the fraud of that spouse.

Frivolous Tax Return Penalty In addition to any other penalty that may apply, a taxpayer may be subject to a penalty of $5,000 for filing a frivolous tax return or other frivolous submissions. On a joint return, each spouse may have to pay a penalty of $5,000. A frivolous return penalty may be imposed even if the taxpayer does not owe any tax. A frivolous tax return is one that does not include enough information to figure the correct tax or that contains information clearly showing that what was reported is substantially incorrect. One example of a frivolous return is a return in which the preprinted language above the space for the taxpayer's signature has been altered or crossed out.

Bounced Check Penalty The penalty for a bounced check is 2% of the amount of the check. However, if the check is under $1,250, the penalty is the amount of the check or $25, whichever is less.

Summary Explanation of Penalties and Interest

The second column in Table 36.1 provides a summary of what to expect when the amount of interest or penalty will apply. The third column in the table illustrates the effects of the penalties and interest on a balance due over time.

TABLE 36.1 Summary Table for Interest and Penalties

Type of charge	When interest or penalty applies	Amount of interest or penalty
Interest	Interest is charged on unpaid tax from the original due date of the return until the date of payment (even if the taxpayer was granted an extension of time to file the return)	The interest rate is determined every 3 months and may fluctuate as a result. Interest is compounded daily. Interest also applies to penalties.

Type of charge	When interest or penalty applies	Amount of interest or penalty
Failure-to-file penalty[1]	When a taxpayer fails to file a return by the original or extended due date, the IRS may assess a late filing penalty (also called a failure-to-file penalty). Interest may also apply to penalties.	The penalty is equal to 5% of the unpaid balance, per month or part of a month, up to a maximum of 25% of unpaid tax. (Note: The 5%-per-month penalty increases to 15% per month if the failure to file is due to fraud.) For returns filed more than 60 days after the due date or extended due date, the minimum penalty is equal to the lesser of $135 or 100% of the unpaid tax
Late payment penalty[1]	A late payment penalty generally applies when a taxpayer fails to pay the balance of tax due by the original return due date. Interest may also apply to penalties.	The penalty rate is ½ of 1% per month or part of a month, up to a maximum of 25% of the unpaid tax. The ½-of-1% rate increases to 1% if the tax remains unpaid 10 days after the IRS issues a notice of intent to levy For individuals who file by the due date, the ½-of-1% rate decreases to ¼ of 1% for any month in which an installment agreement is in effect.

[1]Combined failure-to-file and late-payment penalties. If both the failure-to-file and the failure-to-pay penalties apply in any month, the 5% failure-to-file penalty is reduced by the failure-to-pay penalty, so that the combined penalties do not exceed 5% per month.

Review Questions

1. Which of the following tax payment methods may entail a fee?
   a. Federal income tax withholding through an employer
   b. Electronic funds withdrawal
   c. Transfer via EFTPS
   d. Charge to a major credit card

2. Which of the following statements about an installment payment agreement is **not** correct?
   a. A taxpayer must request the installment agreement.
   b. The repayment period usually is 36 months but can be up to 60 months.
   c. Interest or penalties are not charged during the period of the agreement.
   d. There is a fee for obtaining an agreement.

3. Which of the following accounts is **not** an eligible account for purposes of accepting a direct deposit of a tax refund?
   a. 401(k) account
   b. Coverdell education savings account
   c. Health savings account
   d. Checking account

4. Estimated taxes include all of the following taxes **except**:
   a. Self-employment tax
   b. Employment taxes for a household employee
   c. Gift tax
   d. Alternative minimum tax

5. What is the amount of the accuracy-related penalty on a substantial understatement of tax?
   a. 2% of the underpayment
   b. 5% of the underpayment
   c. 20% of the underpayment
   d. 75% of the underpayment

Completing and Filing the Return

The final step in tax return preparation is finalizing and filing the return.

Before the return is signed, tax preparers should verify that it is complete and accurate.

Additional rules apply to e-filed returns. Tax preparers who e-file must ensure that the return is properly submitted to the IRS after the return has been signed. Tax preparers must retain certain records and follow up with taxpayers and the IRS if an e-filed return is rejected.

Completing the Return

Check the Return for Completeness and Accuracy

As the tax return preparer, you must take steps to make sure that the return you have prepared for a taxpayer is accurate and complete. Verify all of the key data on the return, including:

- Taxpayer names, taxpayer identification numbers, and dates of birth
- All numbers entered on the return

Also check that all required forms and schedules have been completed and computed correctly. Review question boxes on forms and schedules (such as the question boxes on Schedule B of Form 1040, *Interest and Ordinary Dividends*) to make sure they have been answered.

TIP: Cross-check entries against information provided on the taxpayer's W-2s, 1099s, K-1s, and other information returns. Make sure that numbers have not been transposed or otherwise entered erroneously.

Explain and Review the Tax Return

Taxpayers should review the return for accuracy before they sign. In many cases, the returns are fairly straightforward. However, you should help taxpayers understand their tax liabilities and answer any questions that taxpayers may have before signing their returns.

Taxpayers whose situations have changed from the prior year, or who have complex returns, may need additional explanation. Taxpayers who did not expect a balance due or who expected a larger refund also benefit from a detailed explanation of their tax return.

Discuss Filing Deadlines and Extensions

Tax law fixes the filing deadline for individual income tax returns, as shown in Table 37.1.

TIP: The taxpayer should retain proof of filing along with a copy of the return. Proof is a registered or certified receipt from the U.S. Postal Service, proof of proper use of an IRS-approved private delivery service, or acknowledgment from the IRS for an e-filed return. Priority mail and delivery confirmation through the U.S. Postal Service is *not* automatic proof to support the timely mailed, timely filed rule.

TABLE 37.1 Filing Deadlines

Basic filing deadline	April 15
Deadline for filers residing abroad	June 15
Extended deadline	October 15

If the filing deadline falls on a Saturday, Sunday, or legal holiday, the deadline is extended to the next business day. For 2012 returns, the filing deadline is April 15, 2013.

A paper return is treated as filed by the due date if it is postmarked on or before the due date by the U.S. Postal Service or an IRS-approved private carrier. The list of private carriers is in the instructions to Form 1040, *U.S. Individual Income Tax Return*. Mailing by the due date is referred to as the "timely mailed, timely filed rule" because it presumes that the return is submitted on time as long as it is properly addressed, postmarked and deposited in the mail by the filing deadline.

To be considered timely filed, an e-filed return can be submitted up to the filing deadline. If an e-filed return submitted by the due date is not accepted by the IRS, the return still will be considered timely filed if the necessary corrections are made and the return is e-filed again and accepted within five days. If the error that caused the rejection cannot be resolved to allow the return to be e-filed, the return must be completed on paper and mailed to the IRS within 10 days. To avoid late filing penalties, these paper returns must include an explanation detailing why the return is being submitted after the due date. Any additions or attachments to the resubmitted return are also considered timely.

An individual taxpayer who cannot file by the original due date *for any reason* can obtain an automatic six-month filing extension. The extended due date is October 15. Thus, the extended due date for 2012 returns is October 15, 2013. Common reasons for requesting an extension include:

- The taxpayer has not received all necessary information for filing (e.g., Schedule K-1, *Partner's Share of Income, Deductions, Credits, etc.* from partnerships).
- The taxpayer has not yet obtained written acknowledgments from charities for contributions made for the year.

To obtain an automatic six-month filing extension, submit Form 4868, *Application for Automatic Extension of Time to File U.S. Individual Income Tax Return*, no later than the regular filing deadline. The form does not require any signature. However, the taxpayer must list the taxes paid for the year through withholding and estimated taxes as well as make a good-faith estimate of the taxes expected to be owed. Paying the outstanding amount is not a requirement for obtaining the extension, but it is advisable for the taxpayer to pay as much as possible to minimize or avoid late payment penalties (see Chapter 36). This is because an extension of time to file the return does not extend the time to pay the tax due. The extension request can be made by any of these means:

- Filing the paper form
- e-filing the form

> **TIP:** A taxpayer living outside of the United States (including someone in the military stationed outside the United States) on the original due date of the return has an automatic two-month filing extension. For 2012 returns, this extends the due date to June 17, 2013 (June 15 falls on a Saturday). For a joint return, only one spouse must meet this requirement for the two-month extension to apply. No special form must be filed, but a statement should be attached to the return explaining the reason for relying on the two-month extension. If the taxpayer needs additional time to file, he or she can obtain another four months by requesting an automatic extension.

Explain Recordkeeping Requirements

Taxpayers should be advised about their recordkeeping requirements and the benefits of retaining records. There are many reasons to retain records, including:

- The records will enable the taxpayer to quickly and accurately file current and future tax returns.
- The records will also support (serve as proof of) items on the tax return in case the return is audited.
- The records may provide information necessary to figure capital gain or loss in the future (e.g., the date property was acquired, cost basis, improvements, and selling costs).

Records can take a variety of forms. The types of records depend in part on the deduction, credit, or other tax item to which they relate. Different types of records include:

> **TIP:** The taxpayer may pay all or part of the estimate of income tax due using a credit or debit card, or the Electronic Federal Tax Payment System (EFTPS) (see Chapter 36).

- *Checks, invoices, bank statements, and other receipts.* For example, invoices or receipts for medical costs should be retained if the taxpayer is deducting medical expenses or claiming tax-free reimbursements from health savings accounts.
- *Written acknowledgments for charitable contributions of $250 or more* (see Chapter 23).
- *Diaries, expense account statements, or other documentation for business travel and entertainment expenses.* For example, a taxpayer who drives her personal car for business must track the mileage and keep other records of business driving (see Chapter 26).
- *Records relating to basis.* For example, a homeowner should retain receipts for capital improvements to a home; the improvements increase the basis of the home and minimize gain when the home is sold.

TIP: Taxpayers should keep records related to the basis of property for as long as the property is owned, plus at least three years after it is sold.

Certain deductions, such as business travel and entertainment expenses, charitable contributions, and business gifts, require specific recordkeeping (substantiation). In the absence of this specific recordkeeping, deductions can be disallowed.

It is advisable to keep these records, along with a copy of the tax return and proof of filing, for at least three years from the due date of the return or the date of filing, if later. This is because the IRS generally has three years within which to audit a return. (This is called the statute of limitations.) However, if there is an omission of gross income of more than 25%, the IRS has six years to examine the return.

Discuss the Significance of Signing a Return

ALERT: A taxpayer may not cross out the perjury statement on the tax return. Doing so can result in a penalty for filing a frivolous return.

Signature Requirements

A tax return is not valid unless it is signed by the taxpayer. On a joint return, *both* spouses must sign the return. Figure 37.1 shows the signature line of form 1040, which states that the return is signed under penalty of perjury, meaning that to the best of the taxpayer's knowledge, the information contained on the return is true, correct, and complete. The taxpayer bears the responsibility to the IRS for the information on the return and the consequences of any misinformation.

The taxpayer should also indicate whether he or she will grant the return preparer the authority to:

ALERT: The tax preparer may still be liable for preparer penalties if they know or have reason to know of certain inaccuracies or omissions on the return.

- Give the IRS any information missing from the return.
- Call the IRS about the processing of the return and the status of a refund or payment.
- Receive copies of notices related to the return.
- Respond to IRS notices about math errors, offsets, and return preparation.

To give this authority, the taxpayer must check the "Yes" box to make you the Third Party Designee. This does *not* authorize a return preparer to receive a refund check or represent the taxpayer before the IRS. Designation lasts until the due date of the following year's return. Thus, designation on a 2012 return runs through April 15, 2014 (the due date for filing the 2013 return).

Sign Here	Under penalties of perjury, I declare that I have examined this return and accompanying schedules and statements, and to the best of my knowledge and belief, they are true, correct, and complete. Declaration of preparer (other than taxpayer) is based on all information of which preparer has any knowledge.			
Joint return? See instructions. Keep a copy for your records.	Your signature	Date	Your occupation	Daytime phone number
	Spouse's signature. If a joint return, **both** must sign.	Date	Spouse's occupation	If the IRS sent you an Identity Protection PIN, enter it here (see inst.)
Paid Preparer Use Only	Print/Type preparer's name	Preparer's signature	Date	Check ☐ if self-employed / PTIN
	Firm's name ▶		Firm's EIN ▶	
	Firm's address ▶		Phone no.	

FIGURE 37.1 Penalty of Perjury Declaration on Form 1040

Tax return preparers must also sign the return and provide their Preparer Tax Identification Number (PTIN). Like taxpayers, tax return preparers also sign under penalty of perjury—which means that to the best of the tax return preparer's knowledge, the information contained on the return is true, correct, and complete.

In addition, the tax preparers must be sure their employer's company name, address, ZIP code, phone number, and employer identification number are entered in the signature section. A self-employed preparer should enter his or her own name and the address, ZIP code, and phone number where he or she can be reached all year, and check the self-employed box.

TIP: In general, to file a return on behalf of any other taxpayer who cannot sign a return due to disease or injury, continuous absence from the United States for 60 days prior to the return due date, or when given permission to do so by the IRS, a person needs authorization through Form 2848, *Power of Attorney and Declaration of Representative*. Attach a copy of this form to the return.

Special Signing Situations

In some cases, the taxpayer may be unable to sign the return him- or herself.

- *Deceased taxpayer.* The person who signs the decedent's final income tax return is the following:
  - If the taxpayer is deceased at the time the return is filed, a **personal representative** (if one has been appointed) must sign the return on the taxpayer's (decedent's) behalf.
  - If the return is a joint return, the surviving spouse must also sign the return.
  - If a personal representative has *not* been appointed, and there is a surviving spouse filing a joint return with the decedent, the surviving spouse can sign for the decedent. The surviving spouse should sign the return and enter: "Filing as surviving spouse."
  - If no personal representative has been appointed and there is no surviving spouse (or a joint return is not filed), anyone who is in charge of the deceased taxpayer's property may sign. The decedent's name, the word "DECEASED," and the date of death should be written across the top of the tax return.
- *Minor child.* On a child's tax return, the parent should sign the child's name in the space provided for the taxpayer and then enter: "By (parent's signature), parent for minor child."
- *Incapacitated spouse.* A spouse can sign the return on behalf of a spouse with an incapacitating medical condition if the ill spouse so requests. The spouse should sign the ill spouse's name and then enter: "By (spouse's name), husband/wife" and attach a statement to the return explaining why the incapacitated spouse could not sign the return but directed the spouse to sign on his or her behalf.
- *Military spouse.* The spouse of a person serving in a combat zone or qualified hazardous duty area can sign a joint return on behalf of his or her spouse. Attach a statement to the return explaining that the military spouse is serving in a combat zone.

DEFINITION: A **personal representative** of an estate includes an executor, administrator, or anyone in charge of the decedent's property. An executor (or executrix) is named in a decedent's will, whereas an administrator (or administratrix) is usually appointed by the court if no will exists, if no executor was named in the will, or if the named executor cannot or will not serve.

E-signatures for filing electronically are discussed later in this chapter.

Joint and Several Liability

Married couples who file jointly are agreeing to joint and several liability for the return. This means that each spouse, alone, is responsible for the entire amount of taxes, interest, and penalties, if any, on the return; the IRS can pursue collection against one or both spouses, up to the extent of the liability (see Chapter 2).

Example:

Mr. and Mrs. Jefferson filed a joint return for 2012 but did not pay the tax due of $3,850. The IRS can collect all or part of the $3,850 from Mr. Jefferson and/or Mrs. Jefferson. However the IRS cannot collect more than the total due ($3,850) from the two combined.

Innocent Spouse Relief

After a tax return has been filed, the IRS may try to collect a tax debt owed on a joint return from one or both spouses. A spouse may be relieved of joint and several liability in limited circumstances by requesting innocent spouse relief. There are three types of innocent spouse relief:

1. *Basic innocent spouse relief.* Relief applies if:
   a. There is an understatement of tax on a joint return due to erroneous items of a spouse or former spouse,
   b. The innocent spouse did not know or have reason to know of the understated tax, AND
   c. Based on the facts and circumstances, it would be unfair to hold the innocent spouse liable for the tax.

Example:

Same as the example above except the $3,850 tax due resulted from an IRS letter audit showing that the couple owed more than what was reported on their return. The IRS seeks to collect the $3,850 from Mrs. Jefferson, who claims basic innocent spouse relief and files for this relief on Form 8857, *Request for Innocent Spouse Relief*. The additional tax due is from Mr. Jefferson's income. When she signed the return, she did not know or have reason to know that the income was understated. Based on these facts, and taking into account all facts and circumstances, it would be inequitable to hold her liable for the tax; she qualifies for innocent spouse relief.

TIP: A tax return preparer can request a hardship exception from mandatory e-filing by submitting Form 8944, *Preparer e-file Hardship Waiver Request*. The waiver request for calendar year 2013 must be submitted between October 1, 2012, and February 15, 2013.

2. *Separation of liability relief.* A spouse who is legally separated or no longer married can obtain relief for the understated tax attributable to the other spouse.
3. *Equitable relief.* When neither of the other two options applies, a spouse can obtain relief from an understatement of tax or an unpaid tax where the circumstances support relief.

A spouse who believes he or she is eligible for such relief must file Form 8857. For relief other than equitable relief, the form must be filed no later than two years after the date that the IRS first starts collection efforts. More information about innocent spouse relief is in IRS Pub. 971, *Innocent Spouse Relief.*

ALERT: If a return is eligible to be filed electronically but is not, a tax return preparer should complete Form 8948, *Preparer Explanation for Not Filing Electronically*, and attach it to the taxpayer's return.

e-filing

e-file Mandate

Specified tax return preparers must submit returns electronically in 2013 if they anticipate filing 11 or more returns for individuals, trusts, and estates during 2013. Preparers working in firms that file 11 or more returns as a firm must e-file the returns they personally prepare, even if they personally prepare fewer than 11 such returns.

TIP: During 2013, the IRS will accept e-filed returns through two different systems. The Legacy system is being phased out, except for emergencies, while the IRS transitions to the modernized e-file platform (MeF). Advantages of using the MeF platform include the ability to file returns year-round, the ability to file some prior-year returns electronically, and faster acknowledgments. During calendar-year 2013, returns for tax years 2010, 2011, and 2012 can be e-filed using MeF. Once the MeF system is fully implemented, the Legacy system will no longer be used.

The application process to become an authorized e-file provider takes approximately 45 days to complete. More information about e-file providers is available online at www.irs.gov.

The fact that a taxpayer's return will be filed using an electronic method (in most situations) should be explained to the taxpayer. Some taxpayers may be unfamiliar or uncomfortable with e-filing; information you provide about the realities and benefits of e-filing should ease their concerns. The benefits include a faster refund, more accurate returns, and secure transmissions. If a taxpayer does not wish to e-file, he or she can opt out of e-filing and mail in a paper return. In this case, specified tax return preparers should complete Form 8948 and attach it to the return.

Some returns are ineligible for e-file under the MeF rules and must be filed on paper. These include:

- Returns on which the adoption credit is claimed (see Chapter 31). This is because additional documentation is required.
- Returns of nonresident aliens.
- Amended returns.
- Returns filed after the extended due date (e.g., after October 15, 2013, for the 2012 return).
- Returns for tax years ending prior to December 31, 2010.
- Returns that are not for calendar-year taxpayers (i.e., fiscal year returns).

Sometimes a return can be e-filed even though the taxpayer is required to mail in one or more forms, schedules, or supporting documents on paper. In this case, the paper forms must be sent along with Form 8453, *U.S. Individual Income Tax Transmittal for an IRS e-file Return.* Two common situations in which this is required is when submitting:

TIP: Tax preparers submitting returns through the MeF platform may be able to submit attachments with Form 8453 electronically (in pdf format) instead of mailing the forms to the IRS. Form 8332 and Form 8283 can be attached and submitted in pdf format.

1. Form 8332, *Release/Revocation of Release of Claim to Exemption for Child by Custodial Parent,* or certain pages from a divorce decree or separation agreement, that went into effect after 1984 and before 2009.

TIP: Most taxpayers are eligible to use the Self-Select PIN (personal identification number) method. However, the Self-Select PIN method may not be used by primary taxpayers under age 16 who have never filed or by secondary taxpayers (spouses) under age 16 who did not file in the immediate prior year. Taxpayers who cannot locate their prior-year adjusted gross income (AGI) or PIN may contact the IRS to request an electronic filing PIN.

TIP: You are permitted to image and store electronically all paper records required to be retained. Details about requirements for acceptable electronic storage can be found in Rev. Proc. 97-22.

2. Form 8283, *Noncash Charitable Contributions*, Section A, *Donated Property of $5,000 or Less and Certain Publicly Traded Securities* (if any statement or qualified appraisal is required) or Section B, *Donated Property Over $5,000 (Except Certain Publicly Traded Securities*, and any related attachments, including any qualified appraisal.

IRS Pub. 1345, *Handbook for Authorized IRS e-file Providers of Individual Income Tax Returns*, contains the list of supporting forms that can be e-filed as well as any limitations that apply to e-filed forms.

Electronic Return Signatures

When e-filing the return, the taxpayer needs a Self-Select PIN or a Practitioner PIN. The Self-Select PIN method requires taxpayers to provide their prior-year AGI amount or prior-year PIN so that the IRS can authenticate individual taxpayers. The Practitioner PIN method does not require taxpayers to provide their prior-year AGI amount or prior-year PIN.

A PIN is a combination of five digits (other than all zeroes) chosen by the taxpayer or generated by the tax return preparer. On a joint return, each spouse needs his and her own PIN.

Form 8879, *IRS e-file Signature Authorization*, is the declaration and signature document used when a tax return is filed by an electronic return originator (ERO) and the taxpayer is using the Practitioner PIN method or is authorizing an ERO to enter or generate the taxpayer's PIN. The form is not filed with the IRS; tax return preparers should retain the completed Form 8879 for three years from the later of the return due date or the date the IRS received the return.

Preparer's Responsibilities for e-filed Returns

In most cases, you will be filing returns electronically. (The e-file mandate for tax return preparers is discussed earlier in this chapter.) In addition to giving each taxpayer a copy of his or her return, there are certain additional responsibilities for e-filing taxpayer returns. These responsibilities are detailed in IRS Pub. 1345. Some key matters to note are discussed next.

Recordkeeping and Documentation You must keep certain records and documents related to each return you e-file through the end of the calendar year, including:

- Form 8453
- Copies of Forms W-2, *Wage and Tax Statement*
- Copies of Forms W-2G, *Certain Gambling Winnings*
- Copies of Forms 1099-R, *Distributions from Pensions, Annuities, Retirement or Profit-Sharing Plans, IRAs, Insurance Contracts, etc.*
- A copy of a signed IRS e-file consent to disclosure form

- A copy of the electronic portion of the return that can be converted into an electronic transmission that the IRS can process
- The acknowledgment file for IRS-accepted returns

Forms 8879 and 8878 must be retained for three years from the due date of the return or the IRS received date, whichever is later. Other recordkeeping and documentation requirements are spelled out in IRS Pub. 1345.

Resubmitting Rejected Returns If a return is rejected, you must take reasonable steps to inform the taxpayer about the rejection within 24 hours and disclose the reasons for rejection. To be considered timely, the resubmitted return must be e-filed and accepted by the IRS within five days. Check the explanation of the error reject codes (ERCs) accompanying the rejection; the explanations are located in IRS Pub. 1346, *Electronic Return File Specifications and Record Layouts for Individual Income Tax Returns & Suggested Solutions*, or at www.irs.gov/efile/article/0,,id=180182,00.html.

The taxpayer can choose not to resubmit the return electronically and instead file a paper return. In order for the paper return to be considered timely if the due date has passed, it must be filed within 10 calendar days after the IRS notification of rejection. Attach an explanation to the return on why it is being filed after the due date and Form 8948.

Advising Taxpayers on Refund Inquiries Refunds are sent to the taxpayer, not to the preparer. The taxpayer can follow up on an anticipated refund by checking "Where's My Refund?" at www.irs.gov. (More information about refunds is in Chapter 36.)

Review Questions

1. An individual taxpayer in the United States who cannot file an income tax return by the due date can obtain an automatic filing extension for what period of time:
   a. Five days
   b. Two months
   c. Four months
   d. Six months

2. Which of the following situations requires the taxpayer to obtain a power of attorney to sign a return?
   a. A minor child
   b. A spouse in the military stationed in a combat zone
   c. A spouse who is outside the United States for 60 days prior to the due date of the return
   d. A spouse who is incapacitated and wants the other spouse to sign

3. How long should tax return preparers retain Form 8879?
   a. One year
   b. Three years
   c. Three years from the later of the return due date or the date the IRS received the return
   d. Seven years

4. Which of the following is **not** a preparer's responsibility for a taxpayer's return?
   a. Receiving a refund check
   b. Retaining certain records related to the client's return
   c. Following procedures after an e-filed return is rejected
   d. Ensuring the return is complete and accurate

5. Which preparer is **not** required to e-file returns?
   a. A preparer who anticipates filing 20 income tax returns for individuals
   b. A preparer who anticipates that her firm will file about 300 tax returns for individuals
   c. A preparer who anticipates the he will file 5 income tax returns for individuals and 10 income tax returns for trusts and estates
   d. A preparer who expects to file 10 income tax returns for individuals.

PART 6

Practices and Procedures

Preparer Responsibilities and Penalties

Beyond preparing clients' tax returns, a tax return preparer also must understand and comply with e-file procedures, safeguard client information, and comply with other IRS rules and regulations. Tax return preparers also must carefully follow the IRS rules for representing taxpayers.

Penalties may be imposed on a tax preparer for actions taken or not taken. Awareness of these penalties and the proper procedures can help a preparer comply with the law and avoid penalties.

> **ALERT:** Electronic return originators (EROs) are prohibited from filing pay-stub returns. Pay-stub filing occurs when a preparer prepares and files a tax return for a taxpayer who presents a pay stub instead of Form W-2, *Wage and Income Statement*. What should a tax return preparer do if a taxpayer says his or her Form W-2 got lost in the mail or was not issued (either by paper or electronically)? Taxpayers should be instructed to contact their employer and request a copy. If the employer will not reissue the form, the taxpayer can file a return with a substitute Form W-2, Form 4852, *Substitute for Form W-2, Wage and Tax Statement*. However, Form 4852 cannot be filed prior to February 14.

Compliance with e-file Procedures

In most cases, the tax preparer must e-file returns, as described in Chapter 37.

Violating e-file procedures, including noncompliance with any provisions of IRS Pub. 3112, *IRS e-file Application and Participation*, can result in warnings or sanctions. The IRS usually issues a warning letter before imposing any sanctions. The IRS classifies infractions as Level One, Level Two, or Level Three.

- *Level One* (reprimand). For infractions that have no adverse impact on the quality of e-filed returns, the IRS usually issues only a written reprimand.
- *Level Two* (suspension). For infractions that do have an adverse impact on the quality of e-filed returns, the IRS may restrict an e-file provider's participation in e-file for one year from the effective date of the sanction. An example of a Level Two infraction includes the continuation of a Level One infraction after the IRS has brought the infraction to the attention of the e-file provider (preparer).
- *Level Three* (expulsion). For infractions that have a significant adverse impact on the quality of e-filed returns, the IRS may suspend the preparer from e-file for two years or, depending on the severity of the infraction, expel the preparer *permanently* from e-file. This may occur if the infraction is fraud or criminal conduct.

TIP: Employers who make their employees' Form W-2 available electronically generally do not e-mail the form because of security reasons. Instead, employers make the form available on a secure online site, allowing employees to view the form and print it for their tax records. Therefore, a taxpayer who claims to have not received a Form W-2 may need to check the employer's website.

Authorization for Tax Representation

The taxpayer can authorize an agent to speak on his or her behalf for certain matters with the IRS. There are three types of authorization:

1. *Limited authorization as a third-party designee* allows the agent to discuss the tax return with the IRS. The agent can provide missing information to the IRS, call the IRS for information about processing the return or the status of a refund, receive copies of notices or transcripts related to the return, and respond to certain IRS notices about math errors, offsets, and tax return preparation. This authorization is made directly on a taxpayer's return. Details about this designation are covered in Chapter 37.
2. *Tax information authorization* gives a person the authority to receive confidential information from the IRS on behalf of the taxpayer. This authorization is discussed in the next subsection, "Form 8821, *Tax Information Authorization.*"
3. *Power of attorney and declaration of representative* is the broadest type of authority to act on a taxpayer's behalf. A taxpayer may authorize an agent, such as a tax return preparer, to have the power to do most actions that a taxpayer could do by him- or herself, including sign any agreements, consents, or other documents. Giving this authorization is discussed later in this section in "Form 2848, *Power of Attorney and Declaration of Representative.*"

TIP: A tax return preparer can appeal e-file sanctions through the Administrative Review Process. The appeals process is explained in IRS Pub. 3112.

Form 8821, *Tax Information Authorization*

The purpose of Form 8821 is to enable a tax return preparer to inspect and/or receive a taxpayer's confidential information for the type of tax (e.g., "Individual Income, 1040") and the years or periods listed on the form (e.g., "2010 through 2012"). The form does *not* authorize a tax return preparer to advocate for a taxpayer's position or to represent the taxpayer before the IRS. The IRS will reject forms that contain general designations, such as "all years," "all periods," or "all taxes."

TIP: The power of attorney is particularly useful when dealing with a taxpayer who is incapacitated or in the military and unavailable to reply to IRS communications while overseas.

Form 8821 instructions list where to mail or fax the form; the address depends on the state in which the taxpayer lives.

A taxpayer can revoke authorization by sending a copy of a previously filed Form 8821. Across the top, the taxpayer should write: "REVOKED." If the taxpayer does not have a copy of the original form, he or she can write a statement indicating that the authority of the appointee (the tax return preparer) is revoked and send the statement to the IRS.

Form 2848, *Power of Attorney and Declaration of Representative*

The purpose of Form 2848 is to authorize an agent, such as a tax return preparer, to perform certain actions in place of the taxpayer, such as signing any agreements, consents, or other documents.

However, when the agent under a power of attorney is an unenrolled tax return preparer (not an enrolled agent, attorney, or CPA), the actions he or she can perform are limited to representation of the taxpayer before customer service representatives, revenue agents, and examination officers with respect to an examination regarding the return the tax return preparer prepared. An unenrolled tax return preparer *cannot*:

- Represent a taxpayer before revenue officers, appeals officers, and other offices of the IRS, such as Collection or Appeals, including the Automated Collection System (ACS) unit
- Execute closing agreements
- Extend the statutory period for tax assessments or collection of tax
- Execute waivers
- Execute claims for refund
- Sign any document on behalf of a taxpayer

Taxpayers can revoke the power of attorney by sending a copy of a previously filed Form 2848, writing "REVOKED" across the top. If the taxpayer does not have a copy of the form, he or she can write a statement indicating that the authority of the agent (the tax return preparer) is revoked and send the statement to the IRS.

The filing of Form 2848 automatically revokes all earlier power(s) of attorney on file with the IRS for the same tax matters and years or periods covered by this document. If a taxpayer does not want to revoke a prior power of attorney, he or she may check a box on Form 2848 to indicate this.

Requesting a Copy or Transcript of a Tax Return

A taxpayer who needs a copy of a previously filed tax return and who cannot obtain a copy from a previous tax return preparer can obtain a copy or transcript of the return from the IRS. To request this information, file:

- Form 4506, *Request for Copy of Tax Return*, to obtain a copy of a return. A fee of $57 per copy applies, so if the taxpayer requests copies for two previous years, the cost is $114. Generally, copies of old returns are available for seven years from filing. The form instructions indicate where and how the form must be filed.
- Form 4506-T, *Request for Transcript of Tax Return*, to obtain a transcript of a return. A transcript is a listing of the entries on the tax return, which may be sufficient for seeking specific information, such as a capital loss carryover. Transcripts are available free of charge for up to three years from filing. The IRS can also provide information reported on Forms W-2 and 1099 for up to 10 years in some cases. Most requests are processed within 30 days.

ALERT: The IRS may take up to 60 days to process a taxpayer's request for a copy of a tax return.

TIP: Preparers can use e-services (at http://tinyurl.com/a7ao7u5) that are not available to the general public. Preparers have access to taxpayer transcripts through the Transcript Delivery Service, which operates on a 24/7 basis.

Safeguarding Taxpayer Information

A taxpayer's information is confidential. By law, a tax preparer must take steps to safeguard taxpayer information. Steps to take include:

- Maintaining a list of all locations in which taxpayer information is stored, including file cabinets and computer servers
- Assessing the risk of unauthorized access to taxpayer information, including computer viruses, natural disasters, and malicious actions by a preparer's employees
- Assessing the impact that unauthorized disclosure can have, including identity theft of the taxpayer and civil and criminal penalties for the tax preparer
- Creating a security plan to address the risks, such as locking cabinets and backing up computer data
- Telling any service providers you use about the security actions you expect them to take
- Testing and monitoring your plan
- Updating your plan as needed

TIP: A tax preparer will *not* be subject to civil or criminal penalties for disclosures made under certain conditions. For example, information may be disclosed pursuant to a court order. The IRC and treasury regulations also contain limited exceptions that allow for specific use or disclosure of information. For example, a preparer may use tax return information of taxpayers whose previous returns were prepared by the preparer to identify specific taxpayers who were affected by a change in tax law and (1) inform them of the law change, (2) advise them whether it would be appropriate for them to file amended returns, and (3) assist them in preparing and filing amended returns.

See IRS Pub. 4600, *Safeguarding Taxpayer Information*, for more details.

Violations of taxpayer confidentiality by a tax return preparer can result in civil and/or criminal penalties listed in the Internal Revenue Code (IRC).

- *Civil charges under section 6713,* Disclosure or Use of Information by Preparers of Returns. Disclosing a taxpayer's information or using the information for any purpose other than to prepare or assist in preparing a return can result in civil penalties of up to $250 per such disclosure or use, up to a maximum of $10,000.
- *Criminal charges under section 7216,* Disclosure or Use of Information by Preparers of Returns. Knowingly or recklessly disclosing a taxpayer's information or using the information for any purpose other than to prepare or assist in preparing a return can result in a criminal conviction. This is a misdemeanor punishable by a fine of up to $1,000 and/or up to one year in jail as well as the costs of prosecution.

Penalties Related to Return Preparation

A tax return preparer can be subject to penalties contained in the IRC related to the preparation of a taxpayer's return. These penalties apply to:

- The understatement of a taxpayer's liability by a tax return preparer
- Other specific actions related to the preparation of a return by a tax return preparer

Section 6694 Penalties

A **tax return preparer** who prepares a return that contains an understatement of a taxpayer's tax liability can be subject to a penalty.

The penalties under section 6694, *Understatement of Taxpayer's Liability by Tax Return Preparer,* are shown in Table 38.1.

Understatements Due to Unreasonable Positions The understatement penalty can be avoided by showing that there is a reasonable basis for the position taken on the return, if such position was not disclosed on the return.

Reasonable Basis The reasonable basis standard does not mean that a position is merely arguable. A reasonable basis means that the preparer has substantial authority for a position taken on the tax return (described in the next paragraph). For example, the tax preparer has a reasonable basis for a position by citing specific provisions of the IRC, Regulations, or Court cases in which the matter is addressed in accordance with the position taken on the tax return. If a position is not disclosed to the IRS and there is no substantial authority for the position, the position will not be considered to have a reasonable basis (see Table 38.2).

Substantial Authority The substantial authority standard is an objective standard involving an analysis of the law and application of the law to relevant facts. The substantial authority standard is less stringent than the more likely than not standard (the standard that is met when there is a greater than 50% likelihood of the position being upheld), but more stringent than the reasonable basis standard. The possibility that a return will not be audited or, if audited, that an item will not be raised on audit is not relevant in determining whether the substantial authority standard (or the reasonable basis standard) is satisfied.

TABLE 38.1 Section 6694 Standards and Penalties for Understatement of Tax Liability

6694(a) General standard for understatement **due to unreasonable positions**	Understatement of a tax liability, and: (1) there was no substantial authority for the position, (2) the preparer knew (or reasonably should have known) of the position, and (3) either the position was not disclosed or there was no reasonable basis for the position.
6694(a) Special standard for tax shelters and reportable transactions	Understatement of a tax liability if the position is related to a tax shelter or reportable transaction, and the position had a 50% or lower chance of success if challenged.
6694(a) Penalty	The greater of $1,000 or 50% of the income from preparing the tax return.
6694(b) Standard for understatement **due to willful or reckless conduct**	Understatement of tax liability and willful, reckless or intentional conduct.
6694(b) Penalty	The greater of $5,000 or 50% of the income derived by the tax return preparer.

DEFINITION: For the purpose of section 6694 penalties, a **tax return preparer** is the signing tax return preparer, the preparer considered to be primarily responsible for all positions on the return or claim for refund giving rise to an understatement. However, a nonsigning preparer who prepares a substantial portion of a return or claim for refund may also be liable for penalties. Whether a schedule, entry, or other portion of a return or claim for refund is a "substantial portion" is determined based on whether the person knows or reasonably should know that the tax attributable to the schedule, entry, or other portion of a return or claim for refund is a substantial portion of the tax required to be shown on the return or claim for refund. A person who gives tax advice on a position that is directly relevant to the determination of the existence, characterization, or amount of an entry on a return or claim for refund can be regarded as having prepared that entry. Finally, the firm that employs the individual preparer may also be subject to penalty if certain conditions are met.

TIP: The penalty for an understatement of tax liability due to an unreasonable position that has not been disclosed on the return can be avoided by showing that the understatement was due to reasonable cause and that the tax return preparer acted in good faith. Factors that the IRS will look at include the nature of the error, the frequency and materiality of errors made by the tax preparer, the tax preparer's normal office practices, and whether the preparer relied on the advice of others or on industry standards. The penalty also can be avoided if there is a final administrative determination or a final judicial decision that there was no understatement of tax liability.

TABLE 38.2 Authorities Used to Determine if Substantial Authority or Reasonable Basis Exists

Regulation Section 1.6662-4(d)(3)(iii)
Provisions of the Internal Revenue Code and other statutory provisions
Regulations (proposed, temporary, and final) construing such statutes
Revenue rulings and revenue procedures
Tax treaties, regulations thereunder, and Treasury Department and other official explanations of such treaties
Court cases
Congressional intent as reflected in committee reports, joint explanatory statements of managers included in conference committee reports, and floor statements made prior to enactment by one of a bill's managers
General explanations of tax legislation prepared by the Joint Committee on Taxation (the Blue Book)
Private letter rulings and technical advice memoranda issued after October 31, 1976
Actions on decisions and general counsel memoranda issued after March 12, 1981 (as well as general counsel memoranda published in pre-1955 volumes of the Cumulative Bulletin)
IRS information or press releases
Notices, announcements, and other administrative pronouncements published by the IRS in the Internal Revenue Bulletin

Determining Whether There Is Substantial Authority There is substantial authority for the tax treatment of an item only if the weight of the authorities supporting the treatment is substantial in relation to the weight of authorities supporting contrary treatment. All authorities relevant to the tax treatment of an item, including the authorities contrary to the treatment, are taken into account when the IRS or a court determines whether substantial authority exists. The weight of authorities is determined in light of the pertinent facts and circumstances. The weight accorded an authority depends on its relevance and persuasiveness and on the type of document providing the authority. For example, a revenue ruling would be given more weight than a private letter ruling. Table 38.2 contains a list of authorities. Conclusions reached in treatises, legal periodicals, legal opinions, or opinions rendered by tax professionals are not authority. The authorities underlying such expressions of opinion where applicable to the facts of a particular case, however, may give rise to substantial authority for the tax treatment of an item.

Understatements Due to Willful or Reckless Conduct The penalty for an understatement due to willful or reckless conduct can be avoided by proving that no rule or regulation was intentionally or recklessly disregarded, that the position represents a good-faith challenge to the validity of the rule or regulation, or that the position has a reasonable basis and that disclosure was adequately made. The penalty can also be avoided if there is a final administrative determination or a final judicial decision that there was no understatement of tax liability.

Example

A taxpayer provided Preparer Trent with detailed check registers reflecting personal and business expenses. One of the expenses was for domestic help, and this expense was identified as personal on the check register. Trent knowingly deducted the expenses of the taxpayer's domestic help as wages paid in the taxpayer's business. Trent is subject to the penalty under section 6694(b).

Example

A taxpayer provided Preparer Ursula with detailed check registers to compute the taxpayer's expenses. Ursula, however, knowingly overstated the expenses on the return. After adjustments by the examiner, the tax liability increased significantly. Because Ursula disregarded information provided in the check registers, she is subject to the penalty under section 6694(b).

Example

Preparer Violeta prepares a taxpayer's return in 2010 and encounters certain expenses incurred in the purchase of a business. Final regulations provide that such expenses incurred in the purchase of a business must be capitalized. One U.S. Tax Court case decided in 2007 had expressly invalidated that portion of the regulations. No courts ruled favorably on the validity of that portion of the regulations, and there are no other authorities existing on the issue. Under these facts, Violeta will have a reasonable basis for the position and will not be subject to the section 6694(b) penalty if the position is adequately disclosed, because the position represents a good-faith challenge to the validity of the regulations.

Section 6695 Penalties

IRC section 6695, *Other Assessable Penalties with Respect to the Preparation of Tax Returns for Other Persons*, imposes various penalties on a tax return preparer who fails to perform certain tasks with respect to a taxpayer's return. These failures include:

- *The failure to furnish a completed copy of the return to the taxpayer* no later than the time the return (or refund claim) is given to the taxpayer for signature. The penalty is $50 per failure, up to a maximum of $25,000 per calendar year.
- *The failure of the tax return preparer to sign the return.* The penalty is also $50 per failure, up to a maximum of $25,000 per calendar year.
- *The failure of the tax return preparer to provide his or her Preparer Tax Identification Number (PTIN).* The penalty is $50 per failure, up to a maximum of $25,000 per calendar year.
- *The failure to retain a copy or list.* The penalty for failure to maintain a list of taxpayer names and identification numbers or failure to make a

TIP: The substantial authority standard means that a position has a 35% to 40% likelihood that it will be upheld. It is possible that there may be substantial authority for more than one position with respect to the same item.

TIP: A tax preparer can avoid a penalty for any of these failures by showing that the failure was due to reasonable cause and not to willful neglect.

copy or list available to the IRS upon request is $50 per failure, up to a maximum of $25,000 per calendar year.

- *The failure to file correct information returns.* The penalty is $50 per failure, up to a maximum of $25,000 per calendar year.
- *Negotiating (cashing or depositing in a preparer's account) a taxpayer's refund check.* The penalty is $500 per check.
- *The failure to exercise due diligence in determining a taxpayer's eligibility for the Earned Income Tax Credit (EITC).* The penalty is $500 per failure.

TIP: A tax return preparer should create a paper trail showing due diligence with respect to the EITC. This means documenting the questions asked by the preparer and the answers provided by the taxpayer, and retaining documents for the record retention period.

Tax return preparers must meet four EITC due diligence requirements when preparing EITC returns:

1. Completion and submission of Form 8867, *Paid Preparer Earned Income Credit Checklist.*
2. Computation of the credit.
3. Knowledge.
4. Record retention.

Of the four requirements, the knowledge requirement is the most challenging for preparers. The knowledge requirement cannot be satisfied merely with software, checklists, or office procedures. To satisfy the knowledge requirement, the tax return preparer:

- Must not know or have reason to know that any information used by in determining the taxpayer's eligibility for, or the amount of, the EITC is incorrect
- May not ignore the implications of information furnished to, or known by, the preparer
- Must make reasonable inquiries if information furnished to, or known by, the preparer appears to be incorrect, inconsistent, or incomplete

IRS publications (such as Pub. 17, *Your Federal Income Tax for Individuals*) are not considered authoritative for "substantial authority" purposes even though they are published by the IRS. The IRS maintains a list of positions that it considers to be adequately disclosed if they are listed on the tax return. In rare cases, a tax return may contain a position that is not adequately disclosed merely by inclusion on the return. Therefore, a separate disclosure is required. A complete discussion of disclosures is beyond the scope of this book. If any disclosures are necessary, they also should be discussed with the client, and a disclosure form should be attached to the return. There are two different methods of disclosure, varying on the situation:

Form 8275, *Disclosure Statement,* is used to disclose tax positions taken by the client that are not adequately disclosed on the tax return. This form also must accompany a reportable transaction, such as a tax shelter in which the client participated.

Form 8275-R, *Regulation Disclosure Statement*, is used if the tax position on the return is contrary to IRS regulations.

In addition, preparers are required to contemporaneously document any additional questions they ask the client, along with the client's responses to those questions. These questions and responses help a preparer determine whether a client is eligible to claim the EITC.

Example

A 22-year-old taxpayer wants to claim two sons, ages 10 and 11, as qualifying children for purposes of the EITC. Preparer Arnold must make additional reasonable inquiries regarding the relationship between the taxpayer and the children, as the age of the taxpayer appears inconsistent with the ages of the children claimed as his sons. Arnold could ask the taxpayer questions such as: Are the children your foster sons or adopted sons? Were you ever married to the children's mother? Did the children's mother live with you? How long have the children lived with you? Arnold should document the questions and answers and retain that information in his files.

Example

Taxpayer asks Preparer Donna to prepare her tax return and tells Donna that she has a Schedule C business, that she has two qualifying children, and that she wants to claim the EITC. Taxpayer indicates she earned $10,000 from her Schedule C business but that she has no expenses. This information appears incomplete because it is very unlikely that someone who is self-employed has no business expenses. Preparer Donna must make additional reasonable inquiries regarding the taxpayer's business to determine whether the information regarding both income and expenses is correct. Donna could ask the taxpayer questions such as: What kind of services do you provide? What training and experience do you have to run a business of this type? Do you have records of the amount of money you received from your clients? How much did you charge your clients? How many clients did you have? Did you use any supplies or equipment? How much do you spend each week on supplies and equipment? Did you provide your own transportation? Donna should document the questions and answers and retain that information in her files.

Aiding and Abetting

A tax return preparer who aids and abets in the understatement of a tax liability may be subject to a penalty of $1,000 per document ($10,000 for corporation documents). The penalty applies to a tax return preparer if all three conditions are met:

1. The tax return preparer aids, assists, procures, or advises with respect to any portion of the preparation or presentation of a return, affidavit, claim, or other document.
2. The tax return preparer knows or has reason to know that the portion will be used in connection with federal taxes.
3. The tax return preparer knows that the portion, if used, will result in an understatement of tax liability for the taxpayer.

ALERT: If a penalty is assessed against a tax preparer, the IRS may refer the case to the Office of Professional Responsibility (OPR) for possible disciplinary action/sanctions under Circular 230, *Regulations Governing Practice Before the Internal Revenue Service* in addition to assessing a penalty under section 6694.

ALERT: The penalty for aiding and abetting can be imposed in addition to any other penalty that may apply, other than the penalties for an understatement of tax liability due to an unreasonable position that was not disclosed or an understatement of tax liability due to willful or reckless conduct. In this case, the penalties under section 6694 (discussed earlier in this chapter) apply instead of the aiding and abetting penalty.

Summary of Penalties

Table 38.3 is a summary of the penalty rules applicable to a tax return preparer.

TABLE 38.3 Statutory Penalties

Internal Revenue Code Section	Description	Penalty	Abatement/ Exception
6694(a)	Understatement of tax liability due to an unreasonable position. Position not disclosed.	The greater of $1,000 or 50% of the income derived by the tax return preparer with respect to the return or claim.	Reasonable cause and preparer acted in good faith. There is a final administrative determination or a final judicial decision that there was no understatement of liability.
6694(b)	Understatement of tax liability due to willful or reckless conduct.	The greater of $5,000 or 50% of the income derived by the tax return preparer with respect to the return or claim. Penalty is reduced to extent a penalty is paid under §6694(a).	Proof that no rule or regulation was intentionally or recklessly disregarded; that the position represents a good-faith challenge to the validity of the rule or regulation; and that the position had a reasonable basis and that disclosure was adequately made. There is a final administrative determination or a final judicial decision that there was no understatement of liability
6695(a)	Failure to furnish a complete copy of the return to the taxpayer not later than the time such return or claim is presented for such taxpayer's signature as required by section 6107(a).	$50 per failure, not to exceed $25,000 per calendar year.	Reasonable cause. No willful neglect.
6695(b)	Failure to sign return.	$50 per failure, not to exceed $25,000 per calendar year.	Reasonable cause. No willful neglect.

Internal Revenue Code Section	Description	Penalty	Abatement/ Exception
6695(c)	Failure to furnish identifying number as required by section 6109(a)(4)	$50 per failure, not to exceed $25,000 per calendar year.	Reasonable cause. No willful neglect.
6695(d)	Failure to retain a completed copy of tax returns or to maintain a list of taxpayer names and ID numbers or failure to make a copy or list available upon request by the Secretary of the Treasury as required by section 6107(b).	$50 per failure, not to exceed $25,000 per return period.	Reasonable cause. No willful neglect.
6695(e)	Failure to file correct information returns, as required by section 6060.	$50 per failure, not to exceed $25,000 per return period.	Reasonable cause. No willful neglect.
6695(f)	Negotiation of check.	$500 per check.	Deposit of check into account held for benefit of the taxpayer.
6695(g)	Failure to be diligent in determining eligibility for EITC.	$500 per failure.	
6701	Aiding and abetting the understatement of tax liability.	$1,000 ($10,000 for corporate returns or documents).	
6713	Improper disclosure or use of information furnished for or in connection with tax preparation.	$250 per disclosure or use, not to exceed $10,000 in any calendar year.	
7216	Improper disclosure or use of tax return information.	Criminal misdemeanor — $1,000 or 1 year imprisonment or both together with costs of prosecution.	

Review Questions

1. For violating e-file procedures, which level of infraction usually results in only a reprimand?

a. Level One

b. Level Two

c. Level Three

d. Any level

2. Which type of authorization for a tax return preparer to act is made directly on a taxpayer's return?

a. Limited authorization as a third-party designee

b. Tax information authorization

c. Power of attorney

d. Declaration of representative

3. A tax return preparer who is unenrolled may be authorized by Form 2848 to:

a. Execute waivers on behalf of a taxpayer.

b. Extend the statutory period for tax assessments.

c. Represent the taxpayer before customer service representatives, revenue agents, and examination officers.

d. Receive refund checks.

4. A penalty of $5,000 or 50% of the income derived by the tax return preparer with respect to the return or claim applies to which action?

a. Understatement of tax liability due to an unreasonable position that has not been disclosed on the return

b. Understatement of tax liability due to willful or reckless conduct

c. Aiding and abetting an understatement of tax liability

d. Failing to sign the tax return

5. The civil penalty for an improper disclosure or use of taxpayer information is:

a. $50 per failure, not to exceed $25,000 per calendar year.

b. $250 per disclosure or use, not to exceed $10,000 in any calendar year.

c. $500 per failure.

d. $1,000.

PART 7

Ethics and Circular 230

Rules Governing Authority to Practice before the IRS

There are very strict rules about who can practice before the IRS. These rules are discussed in Circular 230, *Regulations Governing Practice Before the Internal Revenue Service,* which is a compilation of Treasury regulations. (Circular 230 is available at www.irs.gov/pub/irs-utl/pcir230.pdf)

Circular 230 regulates the individuals who are eligible to practice before the IRS and what actions those individuals are allowed to perform on behalf of taxpayers.

What Is Circular 230?

Federal law gives the Secretary of the Treasury the authority to oversee the practice of representing taxpayers before the Department of the Treasury. Under this authority, the IRS has created Circular 230, a collection of Treasury regulations governing the practice of representatives before the IRS.

Broadly speaking, the IRS allows individuals to practice before it only if they have demonstrated good character, good reputation, and competency to advise and assist taxpayers in presenting their cases. These are the necessary qualifications that enable an individual to provide valuable services to taxpayers.

Two organizations within the IRS help to regulate and oversee the conduct of practice before the IRS:

1. *Office of Professional Responsibility (OPR).* The OPR establishes and enforces standards of competence, integrity, and conduct for tax professionals (enrolled agents, attorneys, certified public accountants, and other individuals and groups covered by Circular 230).
2. *Return Preparer Office (RPO).* The RPO handles the processing of applications for enrollment, administering the competency exam, continuing education activities and all things related to Preparer Tax Identification Numbers (PTINs).

ALERT:
In September 2012, the IRS/Treasury proposed changes to Circular 230. One proposed change clarifies that OPR would have general responsibility for matters related to practitioner conduct and exclusive responsibility for discipline, including disciplinary proceedings and sanctions. As of this writing, the proposed changes have not been finalized.

What Does "Practice before the IRS" Mean?

The phrase "practice before the IRS" has a very broad but specific meaning. According to section 10.2(4) of Circular 230, practice before the IRS consists of:

> All matters connected with a presentation to the Internal Revenue Service or any of its officers or employees relating to a taxpayer's rights, privileges, or liabilities under laws or regulations administered by the Internal Revenue Service. Such presentations include, but are not limited to, preparing documents; filing documents; corresponding and communicating with the Internal Revenue Service; rendering written advice with respect to any entity, transaction, plan or arrangement, or other plan or arrangement having a potential for tax avoidance or evasion; and representing a client at conferences, hearings, and meetings.

This language broadly defines "practice" to encompass all matters connected with a representation to the IRS relating to a taxpayer's rights, privileges, or liabilities under laws and regulations administered by the IRS. It includes preparing or filing documents (such as tax returns), communicating with the IRS, giving written or oral tax advice, and providing representation in matters with the IRS.

Who May Practice Before the IRS?

Six categories of professionals can practice before the IRS:

1. *Attorneys* are members in good standing of the bar of the highest court in a state or the District of Columbia.
2. *Certified public accountants (CPAs)* are accountants who are qualified and licensed by a state, possession, territory, commonwealth, or the District of Columbia to practice as CPAs.
3. *Enrolled agents (EAs)* are individuals who have enrolled with the IRS and have remained in active status.
4. *Enrolled actuaries* are enrolled as actuaries by the Joint Board for the Enrollment of Actuaries. Actuaries are individuals who assess the financial consequences of risks and use mathematics, statistics and financial theory to analyze and determine the financial impact of uncertain future events. However, their practice before the IRS is limited to matters related to sections of the Internal Revenue Code (IRC) within their area of expertise (primarily sections governing employee retirement plans).
5. *Enrolled retirement plan agents*, like EAs, are individuals who have been approved for active enrolled retirement plan agent status by the IRS. However, their practice before the IRS is limited to matters related to sections of the IRC within their area of expertise (primarily sections governing employee retirement plans).

The IRS will allow two other groups limited practice before it:

1. *Supervised preparers* are individuals who do not sign and are not required to sign tax returns as a paid return preparer but are:
   - Employed by attorney or CPA firms, or employed by other recognized firms that are at least 80% owned by attorneys, CPAs, or enrolled agents, and
   - Supervised by an attorney, CPA, enrolled agent, enrolled retirement plan agent, or enrolled actuary who signs the returns prepared by the supervised preparer as the paid tax return preparer.

   Supervised preparers may not sign any tax returns or represent taxpayers before the IRS.

2. *Non–Form 1040 series preparers* are individuals who do not prepare or assist in the preparation of any Form 1040 series tax return or claim for refund (except a Form 1040-PR, *Self-Employment Tax Form—Puerto Rico (Spanish Version).* or Form 1040-SS, *U.S. Self-Employment Tax Return (Including the Additional Child Tax Credit for Bona Fide Residents of Puerto Rico)*) for compensation. Non–Form 1040 series preparers may sign any tax return they prepare or assist in preparing and represent taxpayers before revenue agents, customer service representatives, or similar officers and employees of the IRS (including the Taxpayer Advocate Service) during an examination if the individual signed the tax return or claim for refund for the taxable year under examination.

Others

Individuals are permitted to represent themselves before the IRS; they are not required to have authorized representation when dealing with the IRS. They also can represent immediate family members, including a spouse, child, parent, or sibling.

Other individuals can practice before the IRS in limited circumstances:

- Student attorneys and student CPAs can receive permission to practice before the IRS by virtue of their status as law students or CPA students. Special appearances are discussed in section 10.7(d) of Circular 230.
- A corporate officer can represent the corporation, including a parent, subsidiary, or other affiliated group with proof of authority.
- A partner can represent a partnership with proof of authority.
- A full-time employee can represent his or her employer with proof of authority.
- A fiduciary is effectively the taxpayer of the trust or estate he or she represents and can represent the entity.
- Any other person who obtains authorization from the Office of Professional Responsibility to represent another person for a particular matter. Obtaining authorization is discussed in IRS Pub. 947, *Practice Before the IRS and Power of Attorney*.

DEFINITION: An **examination** is another word for audit, where the IRS critically reviews a taxpayer's return. Examinations are conducted in three different ways: correspondence audits (audits conducted through mail), office audits (audits conducted in an IRS office), and field audits (audits conducted at the taxpayer's home or place of business).

Who Is Eligible to Become an EA?

A person is eligible to become an EA if he or she is at least 18 years old, has demonstrated special tax competence by passing a three-part written examination (the Special Enrollment Examination [SEE]), has a valid PTIN, and has not engaged in any conduct that would justify suspension or disbarment from practice before the IRS.

There are special rules for former IRS employees who want to become EAs; these rules are not discussed here but can be found in section 10.4(d) of Circular 230.

CPAs are regulated by their individual states' boards of accountancy.

TIP: An application to take the SEE is made by filing IRS Form 2587, *Application for Special Enrollment Examination*, with the outside vendor Prometric at www.prometric.com/IRS/default.htm.

What Is the Application Process to Become an EA?

An applicant must apply for the EA designation by filing an application form signed under oath or affirmation and pay a fee. Form 23, *Application for Enrollment to Practice before the IRS*, is the application for an EA; the fee is $30 for a three-year term.

EAs must also undergo a background check. The background check includes a review of the applicant's tax transcript to make sure that he or she has paid taxes due. The failure to timely file or pay taxes can be grounds for denial of enrollment.

TIP: The EA application fee can be paid with a check or money order accompanying the form. Alternatively, the fee can be paid electronically using www.pay.gov.

Compliance and Suitability Check

The IRS may conduct a federal tax compliance and suitability check on EA applicants as a condition of consideration of an application for enrollment. The compliance check is limited to an inquiry to ensure that applicants have filed all required individual and business tax returns and to check whether the applicant has failed to pay or make proper arrangements to pay any federal tax debts. A suitability check is limited to an inquiry to determine if an applicant has engaged in any conduct that would justify suspension or disbarment, including disreputable conduct.

How Do EAs Renew Their Status?

After initial designation as an EA, the designation must be renewed. The renewal period for EAs is every three years.

Renewal for EAs is made on Form 8554, *Application for Renewal of Enrollment to Practice Before the Internal Revenue Service*. The renewal fee is $30.

For an EA's first renewal, he or she must have completed two hours of continuing education (CE) for each month of enrollment, including two hours of ethics each year. After the first renewal, the EA must complete 72 hours of CE over the three-year enrollment cycle, including at least two hours of ethics each year.

CE records must be retained for four years following the date of renewal.

An EA who wants to renew but has not completed all required CE hours can obtain a waiver of CE requirements for certain reasons, including:

- Health
- Extended active military service
- Absence from the United States for an extended period of time because of employment
- Other compelling reason considered on a case-by-case basis

The request for a waiver must be made no later than the last day of the renewal application period. If the waiver is *not* granted, the person will be notified that he or she has been placed on a roster of inactive EAs.

Preparer Tax Identification Numbers

An individual who, for compensation, prepares or assists with all or substantially all of the preparation of a tax return or claim for refund must have a PTIN. The PTIN is obtained online at www.irs.gov/taxpros/article/0,,id=210909,00.html or by filing Form W-12, *IRS Paid Preparer Tax Identification Number (PTIN) Application and Renewal.*

The PTIN must be renewed *every* year on a calendar-year basis; the deadline for renewal for the 2013 tax season for preparing 2012 returns is January 1, 2013. The renewal fee is $63.

ALERT: Certain enrolled retirement plan agents are not required to have PTINs. Those who prepare only forms in the Form 5300 or Form 5500 series do not need PTINs. This exemption is explained further in Notice 2011-91, *Certain Enrolled Retirement Plan Agents Not Required to Obtain a PTIN.*

Review Questions

1. The Office of Professional Responsibility (OPR) is in charge of issuing PTINs. True or false?
2. An individual who wants to represent her child before the IRS must be authorized by the IRS to do so. True or false?
3. Generally, all EAs must pass a competency examination to earn their designations. True or false?
4. The PTIN must be renewed every three years. True or false?

Duties and Restrictions Relating to Practice before the IRS

As a tax return preparer you must comply with the duties and restrictions of limited practice before the IRS. You must adhere to various duties and responsibilities in order to stay in good standing with the IRS and avoid disciplinary actions.

These duties and responsibilities are detailed in Part B of Circular 230, *Regulations Governing Practice Before the Internal Revenue Service.* (Rules for Part A of Circular 230 are discussed in Chapter 39; rules for Part C of Circular 230 are discussed in Chapter 41.) Understanding your obligations as a preparer is just as important as understanding the tax rules you use to prepare returns. This chapter discusses the duties and responsibilities in the same order in which they are presented in Circular 230.

Information to Be Furnished to the IRS—Section 10.20

When an authorized IRS officer or employee makes a lawful and proper request for information, documents, or other materials, you are obligated to submit the records promptly. The only time that you do not have to comply with a request is when you believe in good faith and on reasonable grounds that the records or information is privileged. You generally do not have privilege. Privilege applies to the attorney-client relationship and to some extent can be created by enrolled agents (EAs) and certified public accountants (CPAs) with their clients.

Section 7525 of the Internal Revenue Code provides a limited **privilege** for tax advice furnished by EAs and CPAs. The privilege under section 7525 can be invoked to prevent the disclosure of information in noncriminal tax matters before the IRS or in cases against the IRS in a federal court.

Attorneys can invoke the traditional attorney-client privilege.

DEFINITION:
Privilege applies to attorney-client communications if: the communication in question is made in confidence, in connection with the provision of legal services, to an attorney, and in the context of an attorney-client relationship. There is no privilege for information used to prepare tax returns because that information is intended to be disclosed to a third party—the IRS. With respect to tax advice furnished by an EA or CPA, the same common law protections of confidentiality that apply to a communication between a taxpayer and an attorney also apply to a communication between a taxpayer and any federally authorized tax practitioner, to the extent the communication would be considered a privileged communication if it were between a taxpayer and an attorney.

Knowledge of Client's Omission—Section 10.21

You must advise your client promptly if you know that he or she has not complied with the tax laws or has made an error in or omission from a tax return, document, affidavit, or other paper submitted to the IRS.

You must tell the client about the noncompliance, error, or omission and explain to the client the consequences of the noncompliance, error, or omission. Consequences could include civil and/or criminal penalties.

You should also advise the client of how the noncompliance, error, or omission may be addressed.

TIP: You should document the conversation you have with the client about errors and omissions.

Example

This is the first year Dan has come to your tax practice. He would like you to prepare his current-year tax return. He had prepared his own tax return in the previous year and brought a copy of the return to you for reference. In reviewing Dan's previous return, you notice a large deduction on Schedule C, *Profit or Loss from Business,* relating to Dan's home office that substantially lowered his self-employment tax.

After talking to Dan, you realize that he deducted 100% of his personal rent and utilities as business expenses (instead of the allowable portion that related to his home office). Dan tells you that his office comprises only 15% of the home he rents and he was unaware that he needed to allocate the expenses.

In this situation, you are aware of a substantial error on Dan's prior-year return. Your responsibility as a preparer is to make Dan aware of the error and the possible consequences and penalties that could arise. You do not have to notify the IRS of the error. You also are not required to amend his return, unless he authorizes you to do so.

You are not prohibited from preparing Dan's current-year return, but you should advise Dan to amend the prior-year return and correct the error.

Diligence as to Accuracy—Section 10.22

You *must* exercise due diligence in:

- Preparing, approving, and filing tax returns, documents, affidavits, or other papers for the IRS
- Determining the correctness of oral or written representations made to the client or to the IRS or other Treasury personnel

When using another person's work product, you are *presumed* to have used due diligence as long as you use reasonable care in engaging, supervising, training, and evaluating the person on whose work you relied.

Part of the responsibility of being a tax preparer is using due diligence to ensure the accuracy of the information you are putting on the return. As a paid preparer, you can be held liable for omissions or errors you make in preparing returns, so it is to the benefit of both the preparer and the taxpayer to furnish the most accurate and complete information on the tax return to the best of your ability.

Sometimes you will need to ask the client for additional information in order to ensure that you are interpreting the facts correctly. The next examples are hypothetical and intended to illustrate the exercise of due diligence and asking follow-up questions.

Example

Dave comes to his tax preparer's office in February and asks her to prepare his return. Dave has wage income of $12,000 and states that he provided all the support for his son, Tony. Tony is 26 years old and lived with Dave all year long.

Dave tells his preparer he wants to claim Tony as a dependent because Tony became disabled as a result of a car accident that happened last June. Tony has income of $5,000 that he earned from wages in the first part of the year, and Dave provided more than half of his support.

The tax preparer should ask additional questions in order to determine if Tony meets the definition of permanently and totally disabled (and therefore eligible as Dave's qualifying child). The tax preparer asks about Tony's condition and Dave responds that Tony will recover from his injuries.

As a result of this follow-up question, the tax preparer realizes that Tony does not meet the definition of permanently and totally disabled under the tax law and that Dave is not eligible to claim Tony as a dependent. Because Tony is not considered permanently and totally disabled, he does not meet the age requirement to be considered a qualifying child. The tax preparer might also ask what additional support Tony is receiving, as Dave would have difficulty supporting his son with only $12,000 in wages. Because of Tony's income, he cannot be considered a qualifying relative. Thus, Dave is not eligible to claim Tony as a dependent.

Example

Marilyn goes to her tax preparer's office in March to complete her tax return. She tells the preparer she moved in with her brother Rich last year to help him take care of his son, Matt. Rich is a single parent and makes $7,200 in wages from a part-time job. Marilyn makes $29,000 from wages, and Matt is a qualifying child of both Marilyn and Rich. Marilyn says that she and Rich have agreed that Marilyn will claim Matt as a dependent on her return and she wants to claim the earned income tax credit (EITC) using Matt as her qualifying child.

According to the tie-breaker rules, Marilyn and Rich can choose who will claim Matt since Marilyn's AGI is higher than Rich's.

The tax preparer asks Marilyn if she or Rich have any other sources of income. Marilyn says she received $3,500 of municipal bond interest but since it is tax exempt, she didn't bring you any information about the income.

(continued)

As a result of this follow-up question, the tax preparer realizes that Marilyn's tax-exempt municipal bond interest exceeds the allowable investment income limitation of $3,200 for the EITC. Therefore, Marilyn is not eligible to claim the EITC.

Prompt Disposition of Pending Matters—Section 10.23

You *cannot* unreasonably delay the prompt disposition of any matter before the IRS. In other words, if a preparer or taxpayer has become involved in a matter with the IRS, he or she cannot intentionally delay the time frame in which the matter will be resolved through improper conduct.

Improper conduct includes impeding IRS processes with the intent to reach a more favorable outcome regarding the matter. For example, numerous postponements for scheduled meetings with the IRS solely to avoid reaching a final decision on a tax matter would be improper conduct. Another example would be delayed responses to IRS correspondence and delayed mailing of information to the IRS with intent to delay the receipt of information.

As a tax preparer, you have a responsibility to promptly respond to pending matters with the IRS and to not intentionally delay the resolution process.

Assistance from or to a Disbarred or Suspended Person—Section 10.24

You cannot knowingly accept help (directly or indirectly) from a person under disbarment or suspension from practice before the IRS if the help is related to any matter that would be considered practice before the IRS. This includes preparing tax returns, providing supporting schedules or other information for an audit or collection matters, giving tax advice, or providing representation.

You cannot accept assistance from a former **government employee** if the employee's assistance would violate another part of Circular 230 (section 10.25, discussed next).

DEFINITION:
A government employee is an officer or employee of the U.S. government or any government agency, a state, or the District of Columbia, or a member of Congress or a state legislature.

Practice by Former Government Employees—Section 10.25

A former government employee cannot represent or knowingly assist a taxpayer if the representation would violate any law of the United States.

See section 10.25 for additional restrictions placed on former government employees.

Notaries—Section 10.26

You may *not* act as a notary for any matter in which you are employed as counsel, attorney, or agent or in which you may be in any way interested.

Instead, you must use a disinterested notary, one who is impartial and free of any conflict of interest relating to the matter.

Fees—Section 10.27

DEFINITION: **Unconscionable** is not specifically defined in Circular 230. Generally, it means showing no regard for conscience or affronting the sense of justice, decency, or reasonableness.

You may not charge **unconscionable** fees for practice before the IRS. This can include charging substantial fees in comparison to average fees charged for similar tax matters. Clearly, the term would apply to a preparer who charged $10,000 to an elderly taxpayer where the market rate for the matter ordinarily would be $400.

Special rules apply in the case of contingent fees, which are fees based in whole or in part on the position taken on the tax return or in other tax matters. An example of a contingent fee would be a percentage of a client's tax refund. As a general rule, contingent fees in tax matters are not allowed. Tax matters include tax planning and advice, preparing or filing (or assisting in preparing or filing) tax returns or claims for refund or credit and all other matters of representation of a client before the IRS. Simply stated, tax preparers cannot charge contingent fees for preparing a tax return.

Tax preparers are permitted to charge contingent fees only in these situations:

- Services rendered in connection with an IRS examination or challenge to an original return, or an amended return or claim for refund filed within 120 days of receiving written notice of examination or challenge to the original return.
- Services rendered in connection with the determination of statutory interest or penalties assessed by the IRS in connection with a claim for credit or refund.
- Services rendered in connection with any judicial proceeding arising under the Internal Revenue Code.

DEFINITION: **Client records** include "all documents or written or electronic materials provided to the practitioner, or obtained by the practitioner in the course of the practitioner's representation of the client, that preexisted the retention of the practitioner of the client." (Circular 230, Section 10.28(b))

Return of Client's Records—Section 10.28

You must return **client records** promptly when the client asks for them. These include all records that a client needs to comply with federal tax obligations. You may retain copies of the records returned to the client.

Client records include documents that the client brings to the tax preparer in order to complete the return (such as Form W-2, *Wage and Tax Statement*, and

Form 1099-MISC, *Miscellaneous Income*). You may retain copies of records that are returned to the client.

Client records do not include documents prepared by the tax preparer (or the tax preparer's firm) that are being withheld pending the client's payment of fees.

If the IRS requests client records that never were or are no longer in your possession, you must notify the IRS of this fact and provide information to the IRS about the location of the records. If necessary, you must ask your client about the identity of the person in possession of the requested records.

Example

Lacey had her 2011 tax return prepared by John. This year, Lacey returns and asks John to prepare her 2012 tax return. Lacey brings all of her W-2s and receipts of expenses to John, and he completes the return and related schedules. Lacey refuses to pay John's preparation fee and says that the documents are her records and John cannot withhold them. John is required to return all of Lacey's W-2s and receipts. However, John is not required to furnish the 2012 tax return he prepared for Lacey that she refused to pay for.

If state law allows or permits the retention of a client's records by a preparer in the case of a dispute of fees for services rendered by the preparer, the tax preparer needs to return only the records that must be attached to the taxpayer's return. However, the preparer must allow the client access to review and copy all records necessary to comply with his or her federal tax obligations.

Conflicting Interests—Section 10.29

A conflict of interest exists when the representation of one client is directly adverse to another client or where there is a significant risk that representation of a client will be materially limited by your responsibilities to another client, former client, or third person, or because of your personal interests. You are not permitted to represent a client in these situations.

Even if a conflict exists, you may represent a client if all of these conditions are met:

- You have a reasonable belief that you have the ability to provide competent, diligent representation to each impacted client.
- The assistance is not legally prohibited.
- *Each* affected client waives the conflict by giving informed consent. The informed consent must be confirmed *in writing* no later than 30 days after the consent was made. Written confirmation may take the form of a letter you draft that is subsequently signed by the client.

You must retain copies of the written consent for at least 36 months from the date the representation of the affected clients ends. The documents showing written consent must be provided to the IRS upon request.

Conflicts can exist when representing these clients:

- A husband and a wife going through a divorce
- A client and the client's former spouse
- Multiple shareholders or officers of a dissolving corporation
- All the partners of a newly formed partnership
- A beneficiary of a trust and the fiduciary of the same trust

Example

You have been preparing Kate's and David's tax return for the past five years. They have been married for 10 years, have two children, and have filed joint returns every year since their marriage began.

In January of the current year, Kate came to you by herself and said she wanted to file her return separately. She told you that she and David split up in November of the prior year and were planning on getting a divorce. She tells you that the children lived with her and she provided all of their support after she and David split up; therefore, she is entitled to claim them as dependents.

A week later, David comes to your office and asks you to prepare his separate return. He tells you he wants to claim the children. He tells you that he and Kate are on bad terms and she refuses to file jointly with him.

This is a conflict of interest that could prohibit a preparer from being able to act in the best interest of both Kate and David. Although a preparer would not be prohibited from preparing both Kate's and David's separate returns, the preparer would need to get the written consent of both parties or act as the preparer for either Kate or David, but not both.

ALERT: In September 2012, the IRS/Treasury proposed changes to Circular 230. One proposed change would clarify that it is disreputable conduct for a practitioner to direct tax refund payments (including directing or accepting through electronic means) into an account owned by him- or herself or any other firm or entity with whom the practitioner is associated. This also clarifies that all practitioners are subject to the restriction (not just tax return preparers). As of this writing, the proposed changes have not been finalized.

Solicitation (Including Advertising)—Section 10.30

What is a tax return preparer permitted or prohibited from doing when soliciting new clients?

- You may *not* use or participate in any form of public communication or private solicitation containing false, fraudulent, or coercive statements or claims, or misleading or deceptive statements or claims.
- You may *not* make any uninvited written or oral solicitation of employment in matters related to the IRS if the solicitation violates federal or state law or other applicable rules. You *can* make a lawful solicitation as long as it is identified as a solicitation.

TIP: Not only is negotiating a taxpayer's check prohibited by Circular 230, it is also prohibited by statute. See Chapter 38 for more information.

- You *can* publish or make available a written fee schedule showing fixed rates for specific routine services, hourly rates, the range of fees for particular services, and the fee charged for an initial consultation. However, once the fee schedule has been published, you may not charge more than the published rates for at least 30 calendar days after the last date of publication.

The fee information may be communicated in professional lists, telephone directories, print media, mailings, e-mail, faxes, hand-delivered flyers, radio, television, or any other method. No matter the medium used to communicate, the communication of fee information may not be untruthful, deceptive, or otherwise violate Circular 230. You must retain a record of the fee information dissemination for at least 36 months from the date of the last transmission or use. Information you retain should include:

ALERT: A pattern of conduct is a factor taken into account in determining whether you acted willfully, recklessly, or through gross incompetence.

- For radio and television broadcasting, a recorded broadcast and a record of the actual transmission
- For direct mail and e-commerce communications, a copy of the actual communication, along with a list of the persons to whom the communications were sent

Negotiating Checks—Section 10.31

ALERT: The penalties for violating the provisions of section 10.34 of Circular 230 are assessed independently of the statutory penalties under section 6694 (see Chapter 38). However, even if a statutory penalty applies under section 6694, the IRS will make an independent determination of whether a violation also exists under Circular 230. You may not be subject to a statutory penalty if there is no understatement of tax, but you still may be subject to liability under Circular 230. Remember that the IRS often uses a pattern of conduct to conclude whether a violation exists under Circular 230. However, this same standard is not used in determining whether a statutory penalty applies.

You cannot endorse or otherwise negotiate any check issued to a client by the government with respect to a federal tax liability. Even if the client asks you to do so, you *cannot*:

- Cash checks
- Endorse checks
- Deposit checks into a trust account
- Split refunds via electronic transfers

Example

Your client Patricia owes you $350 for tax return preparation. Her refund is $200. She wants to give you a personal check for $150 and let you deposit her refund check in your account. You cannot do this, no matter how much Patricia insists. A tax preparer can *never* accept a tax refund on behalf of a client, even if the refund were deposited into the client's bank account or handed over to the client.

Practice of Law—Section 10.32

Circular 230 does not authorize you to practice law. Authorization to practice law is handled by state licensing associations.

Best Practices—Section 10.33

Circular 230 encourages you to provide the highest-quality representation for your client for federal tax matters. This is done by adhering to best practices, which include:

- Communicating clearly with the client about the terms of the engagement
- Establishing the facts needed to arrive at a conclusion supported by the law and the facts
- Advising clients about the impact that conclusions can have, including whether clients can avoid accuracy-related penalties if they rely on the advice
- Acting fairly and with integrity (honesty) in practice before the IRS

Best practices are in place in to ensure a high-quality standard for persons who hold a title or designation and to help better serve taxpayers.

DEFINITION: Frivolous for tax purposes means a tax position that is patently improper. An extensive discussion of frivolous arguments is located in the IRS's *Truth About Frivolous Tax Arguments* at www.irs.gov/pub/irs-utl/friv_tax.pdf.

Standards for Tax Returns and Other Documents—Section 10.34

You may not willfully, recklessly, or through gross incompetence sign a tax return or claim for refund that contains a position (or advise a client to take a position on a tax return or claim for refund) that you know or reasonably should have known:

- Lacks a reasonable basis;
- Takes an unreasonable position;
- Willfully attempts to understate tax liability; or
- Recklessly or intentionally disregards rules or regulations.

For other documents, affidavits, and other papers submitted to the IRS, you may not advise a client to take a position that is **frivolous**. You may not advise a client to make a submission to the IRS that is meant to delay or impede tax administration, or that contains or omits information that demonstrates an intentional disregard of rules or regulations.

ALERT: In September 2012, the IRS/Treasury proposed changes to Circular 230. One proposed change would withdraw current section 10.35, "Covered Opinions." New section 10.35 would add a competence standard. Under the competence standard, practitioners must possess the knowledge, skill, thoroughness, and preparation for the matter for which the practitioner is engaged. As of this writing, the proposed changes have not been finalized.

Example

You are preparing Barbara's tax return this year. So far, everything seems to be in order. In discussing her payment options for her balance due of $1,800, she tells you that she would like to invoke her First Amendment right and refuses to pay her tax liability on religious and moral grounds.

(continued)

She supports only half of the government-funded programs currently in existence and says she will pay only half ($900) of the tax liability she owes. She has written a statement to this effect and insists the statement be sent in along with her return and half of the balance due. This is a frivolous argument and incorrect interpretation of the law.

In this case, you should advise Barbara of the penalties for filing frivolous returns and advise her against taking this position. If Barbara refuses to change her stance, you should advise her that you cannot sign or further participate in the preparation of her return because it contains a frivolous position.

DEFINITION: A **covered opinion** is written advice (including electronic communications) by a practitioner on one or more federal tax issues arising from (1) a transaction that the IRS has determined to be a tax avoidance transaction and has been identified by published guidance as a transaction listed in Reg. section 1.6011-4(b)(2); (2) any entity, plan, or arrangement that has the principal purpose of tax avoidance or evasion; or (3) any entity, plan, or arrangement that has a significant purpose of avoidance or evasion if the written advice is a *reliance opinion*, *marketed opinion*, is subject to *conditions of confidentiality*, or is subject to *contractual protection*. These italicized terms are defined in section 10.35(b)(4) through (7) of Circular 230.

A tax practitioner must inform a client about any penalties that are reasonably likely to apply if a position is taken on a return that was advised, prepared, or signed by the practitioner. A practitioner also must inform the client about penalties that may arise for any document, affidavit, or other paper submitted to the IRS. In addition, he or she must explain to the client the opportunity to avoid any penalties by disclosure, if relevant, and of the requirements for disclosure.

When advising a client to take a position on a tax return or other paper submitted to the IRS, you generally can rely, in good faith *without* verification, on the information furnished by the client. However, you cannot ignore the implications of information furnished or made known to you. You must make reasonable inquiries if the information furnished appears to be incorrect, inconsistent, or incomplete.

Example

Andrew comes to your office this year for help in preparing his return. Among the forms he brought is a Form 1099-MISC, *Miscellaneous Income*. The form reports $1,500 of nonemployee compensation. When you ask Andrew about the form and source of the income, he says that he really was more of an employee of the corporation than a contractor, so he was unsure why the corporation issued him this form.

You discuss with Andrew the difference between a contractor and an employee and the tax implications of the different titles such as self-employment tax. Andrew tells you that he doesn't mind if he will owe the extra tax because he was actually paid $5,000, not the $1,500 that was reported on the Form 1099-MISC. At this point, you become aware of the incorrectly reported amounts. You cannot ignore the fact that you know the information is incorrect, and you cannot continue to assist Andrew in the preparation of his return unless the information is correctly reported.

ALERT: In September 2012, the IRS/Treasury proposed changes to Circular 230. One proposed change under section 10.36 would clarify that firm management with principal authority for overseeing a firm's federal tax practice is responsible for establishing procedures to ensure compliance with all provisions of Circular 230. As of this writing, the proposed changes have not been finalized.

Covered Opinions—Section 10.35

Special rules apply to conduct with respect to **covered opinions**. These rules do not apply to oral advice or preliminary written opinions.

Certain advice is excluded from these rules. Excluded advice is discussed in section 10.35(b)(2)(ii) of Circular 230.

Procedures to Ensure Compliance—Section 10.36

A practitioner with principal authority and responsibility for overseeing a firm's practice of preparing returns and other documents for submission to the IRS must take reasonable steps to ensure that the firm has adequate procedures in effect for all members, associates, and employees to comply with Circular 230's requirements for the preparation of tax returns and other documents as well as the preparation of covered opinions.

A practitioner will be subject to discipline if either of the following applies:

- The practitioner, through willfulness, recklessness, or gross incompetence, does not implement adequate procedures to comply with Circular 230, and one or more individuals show a pattern of failing to comply.
- The practitioner knows or should have known that one or more individuals in the firm are engaged in a pattern or practice that does not comply with Circular 230, and the practitioner, through willfulness, recklessness, or gross incompetence, fails to take prompt action to correct the noncompliance.

> **ALERT:** In September 2012, the IRS/Treasury proposed changes to Circular 230. One proposed change would amend section 10.37 so that it applies to all types of written advice. Changes include requiring practitioners to use reasonable efforts to identify and ascertain the facts relevant to written advice and provides that the scope of the written advice and the amount of detail that must be included in the written advice (relevant facts, application of law to the facts, and the conclusion) will depend on the facts and circumstances, such as the type of advice being asked for and the length and nature of the relationship with the client. A heightened standard of review would apply where the practitioner knows or has reason to know that the written advice will be used in promoting, marketing or recommending an investment plan or other arrangement with the principal purpose of tax avoidance. If the amendments are finalized, Circular 230 disclaimers on e-mail and other documents would no longer be required. As of this writing, the proposed changes have not been finalized.

Requirements for Other Written Advice—Section 10.37

A practitioner must follow the standards set forth in Circular 230 with respect to written advice. Different standards apply for covered opinions and other types of written advice.

A practitioner may not give written advice (including electronic communications) concerning federal tax issues:

- Based on unreasonable factual or legal assumptions,
- That unreasonably relies on representations,
- That does not consider all relevant facts that the practitioner knows or should have known, OR
- That takes into account the possibility of an audit or contemplates a settlement.

In the case where a written opinion will be used by someone other than the practitioner in promoting a tax shelter, there is a heightened standard of care in determining whether a preparer has failed to comply with these requirements or not.

Review Questions

1. Because the preparation of a tax return is covered by privilege, you need not turn over records related to return preparation to the IRS. True or false?

2. If you learn that a client has omitted income from a return, you must promptly notify the IRS. True or false?

3. You can receive a contingent fee for preparing a tax return based on the size of the client's refund. True or false?

4. A taxpayer requests records from a preparer that must be attached to his tax return. He has not paid the preparation fees yet. If state law permits retention of client records in cases of nonpayment of fees, the preparer may retain the taxpayer's records. True or false?

5. A conflict of interest may exist if there is a significant risk that representation of a taxpayer may be adverse to the preparer's personal interests. True or false?

6. You may not apply a taxpayer's refund check toward the payment of tax preparation fees by depositing the taxpayer's refund in your bank account. True or false?

7. In preparing written advice for a taxpayer, the practitioner may not take into consideration the chances of being audited in determining whether to recommend a tax position on a return. True or false?

Sanctions for Violating Circular 230

Circular 230, *Regulations Governing Practice Before the Internal Revenue Service*, sets forth the duties and responsibilities of practitioners, including tax return preparers. (Rules for Part A of Circular 230 are discussed in Chapter 39; rules for Part B of Circular 230 are discussed in Chapter 40.)

If the tax return preparer fails to comply with these duties and responsibilities, he or she may be subject to sanctions. Sanctions may result in monetary penalties or disciplinary action which may prevent the tax return preparer from operating as a practitioner.

Sanctions—Section 10.50

The IRS has the authority to take disciplinary action against a tax return preparer for:

1. Incompetence or disreputable conduct (defined later in this chapter),
2. Violating the regulations, OR
3. Having an intent to defraud, willfully and knowingly misleading, or threatening a client or a prospective client.

Disciplinary action can be:

- *Censure.* This is a public reprimand. Censure does not make the tax return preparer ineligible to represent clients. However, it may subject him or her to conditions designed to promote high standards of conduct for the future.
- *Suspension.* This is a period of time during which the tax return preparer may *not* represent clients. After the suspension, the tax return preparer's future client representations may be subject to certain conditions.
- *Disbarment.* This makes the tax return preparer ineligible to represent clients before the IRS. After disbarment from service, the tax return preparer must petition the IRS for reinstatement.

TIP: The IRS rarely institutes a proceeding to suspend or disbar a practitioner without first giving him or her the opportunity to demonstrate or achieve compliance with Circular 230.

ALERT: Practitioners who are censured, suspended, or disbarred are listed by the Office of Professional Responsibility (OPR) on the IRS website at http://tinyurl.com/cnbj2ce.

A practitioner may not assist or accept assistance from anyone who has been suspended or disbarred or aid or abet a suspended or disbarred individual in practicing before the IRS.

Example

Sally Edwards, an EA, is swamped with work and needs assistance. Her neighbor, Harry Jackson, is an EA who has been suspended from practice. She cannot accept help from Harry. If she does, she is subject to disciplinary action.

ALERT: Monetary penalties may be imposed for a single act of prohibited conduct *or* for a pattern of misconduct.

In addition to or instead of a sanction, a monetary penalty may be imposed on a practitioner who engages in conduct subject to sanction. Also, a monetary penalty may be imposed on an employer, firm, or entity if the person acting on its behalf engaged in misconduct and the employer, firm, or entity knew or reasonably should have known of the person's misconduct.

An employer, firm, or other entity knows, or is considered to know, of the prohibited conduct if its principal management knew or should have known about such conduct. The employer or firm also is considered to know about such conduct if it willfully, recklessly, or negligently did not take reasonable steps to ensure compliance with Circular 230.

Example

Barbara, an attorney, owns and operates her own firm that provides return preparation services to the public. Her firm employs 10 attorneys, certified public accountants (CPAs), and enrolled agents (EAs; all practitioners) as well as 15 supervised return preparers. Barbara supervises and directs all of her employees. She has provided specific instructions to staff members regarding how to complete false and misleading forms and schedules to ensure that clients who would otherwise have a balance due obtain refunds. Barbara's firm is considered to know or have reason to know of the prohibited conduct because Barbara, a member of principal management, instructed her staff regarding completion of the forms and schedules in violation of Circular 230. The practitioner's actions subject her firm to a monetary penalty.

TIP: The IRS has said that it will not impose monetary penalties in cases of minor technical violations when there is little or no injury to a client, the public, or the tax administration, and there is little likelihood of repeated similar misconduct.

The amount of the penalty cannot exceed the gross income derived (or to be derived) from the conduct giving rise to the penalty.

Usually, sanctions require a hearing before an administrative law judge. However, a practitioner can consent to a sanction instead of having a hearing or proceeding with an appeal.

The sanction is based on all the relevant facts and circumstances. The IRS has the discretion to impose a monetary penalty in an amount less than the amount allowed by statute. Here are some factors used by the IRS in setting a monetary penalty:

- The level of culpability of the practitioner, firm, or other entity

- Whether the practitioner, firm, or other entity violated a duty owed to a client or prospective client
- The actual or potential injury caused by the prohibited conduct
- The existence of aggravating or mitigating factors

Mitigating factors include whether the practitioner, employer, firm, or other entity:

- Took prompt action to correct the noncompliance after the prohibited conduct was discovered,
- Promptly ceased engaging in the prohibited conduct,
- Attempted to rectify any harm caused by the prohibited conduct, OR
- Undertook measures to ensure that the prohibited conduct would not occur again in the future.

A practitioner who has been subject to disciplinary action can be restored to eligibility to practice before the IRS. OPR may consider a petition for reinstatement for any attorney, CPA, EA, or enrolled actuary censured, suspended, or disbarred from practice before the IRS.

Incompetence and Disreputable Conduct—Section 10.51

Incompetence and disreputable conduct for which a practitioner can be sanctioned include (but are not limited to) these violations:

- Conviction for any criminal offense under federal tax laws
- Conviction for any criminal offense involving dishonesty or breach of trust
- Conviction of any felony under federal or state law that makes the practitioner unfit to practice before the IRS
- Giving false or misleading information, or participating in the giving of false and misleading information to anyone in the Department of the Treasury (including the IRS) or any tribunal in connection with any federal tax matter pending or likely to be pending before them
- Solicitation of employment prohibited by Circular 230 (see Chapter 40), the use of false or misleading representations with the intent to deceive a client or prospective client in order to procure employment, or intimating that the practitioner is able to improperly obtain special consideration or action from the IRS
- Willfully failing to make a federal return or willfully evading, attempting to evade, or participating in any way in evading or attempting to evade any assessment or payment of any federal tax

Example

Tim, a practitioner who failed to file his own tax returns as required by federal tax law, can be charged with disreputable conduct and sanctioned.

- Willfully assisting, counseling, encouraging a client or prospective client in violating, or suggesting to a client or prospective client to violate, any federal tax law, or knowingly counseling or suggesting to a client or prospective client an illegal plan to evade federal taxes or the payment of federal taxes

Example

Simone told her clients they did not have to file federal income tax returns because the Sixteenth Amendment to the United States Constitution was never properly ratified. She can be suspended from practicing before the IRS because she advised clients to evade federal taxes.

- Misappropriation of, or failure to properly or promptly remit, funds received by a client for the payment of taxes or other obligations due to the United States
- Directly or indirectly attempting to influence, or offering or agreeing to attempt to influence, the official action of any officer or employee of the IRS by use of threats, false accusations, duress or coercion, by the offer of any special inducement or promise of an advantage, or by the bestowing of any gift, favor, or thing of value (i.e., bribing)

Example

Charles, a CPA, was acquitted on a criminal charge of bribing an IRS agent. Although Charles was acquitted, he still can be sanctioned under Circular 230. The standard for practice before the IRS is fitness, not criminal culpability.

- Disbarment or suspension from practice as an attorney, CPA, public accountant, or actuary by any state, territory, or possession of the United states, any federal court of record, or any federal agency, body, or board

Example

Melissa was disbarred from the practice of law in her state because of a felony conviction for driving under the influence. She cannot practice before the IRS even though her disbarment is unrelated to federal taxes.

- Knowingly aiding and abetting another person to practice before the IRS during a period of suspension, disbarment, or ineligibility of such other person
- Contemptuous conduct in connection with practice before the IRS, including the use of abusive language, making false accusations or statements, knowing them to be false, or circulating or publishing malicious or libelous matter

- Giving a **false opinion** knowingly, through **reckless conduct**, or through **gross incompetence**, including giving an opinion that is intentionally or recklessly misleading, or engaging in a pattern of providing incompetent opinions on questions arising from federal tax laws
- Willfully failing to sign a tax return prepared by the practitioner when the practitioner's signature is required by federal tax laws, unless the failure is due to reasonable cause and not due to willful neglect
- Willfully disclosing or otherwise using a tax return or tax return information in a manner not authorized by the Internal Revenue Code, contrary to the order of a court of competent jurisdiction, or contrary to the order of an administrative law judge in a proceeding for sanctions against a practitioner or disqualification of an appraiser
- Willfully failing to file on magnetic or other electronic media a tax return prepared by the practitioner when the practitioner is required to so do under federal tax laws, unless the failure is due to reasonable cause and not due to willful neglect

Example

Harlan is a practitioner who annually prepares dozens of federal income tax returns for individuals. He is subject to the e-filing requirements for 2012. If he fails to e-file his clients' returns, he can be subject to sanctions under Circular 230 unless his failure is due to reasonable cause and not due to willful neglect. If he cannot e-file and is eligible for a hardship waiver, he should follow procedures for obtaining a waiver to e-file because of hardship (available on the IRS Web site), to avoid the possibility of sanctions.

- Willfully preparing all or substantially all of, or signing, a tax return or claim for refund when the practitioner does not have a Preparer Tax Identification Number (PTIN)
- Willfully representing a taxpayer before the IRS unless the practitioner is authorized to do so in accordance with Circular 230

DEFINITIONS: A **false opinion** is one resulting from a knowing misstatement of fact or law, from an assertion of a position known to be unwarranted under existing law, from counseling or assisting in conduct known to be illegal or fraudulent, from concealing matters required by law to be revealed, or from consciously disregarding information indicating that material facts expressed in the opinion or offering material are false or misleading.

Reckless conduct is a highly unreasonable omission or misrepresentation involving an extreme departure from the standards of ordinary care that a practitioner should observe under the circumstances.

Gross incompetence is conduct that reflects gross indifference, preparation that is grossly inadequate under the circumstances, and a consistent failure to perform the obligations to the client.

Violations Subject to Sanction—Section 10.52

Sanctions can be imposed if a practitioner willfully violates any regulations contained in Circular 230 (except section 10.33) or recklessly or through gross incompetence (defined earlier in this chapter) violates any of the following (all of which are explained in Chapter 40):

- Standards with respect to tax returns and documents, affidavits and other papers (section 10.34)
- The requirements for covered opinions (section 10.35)
- Procedures to ensure compliance (section 10.36)
- The requirements for other written advice (section 10.37)

ALERT: A pattern of conduct is a factor that will be taken into account in determining whether a practitioner acted knowingly, recklessly, or through gross incompetence.

ALERT: In September 2012, the IRS/Treasury proposed changes to Circular 230. One proposed change would withdraw section 10.35, "Covered Opinions," and replace it with a new competency standard. To accommodate this change, another proposal would remove the sanction for violation of the rules around covered opinions. As of this writing, the proposed changes have not been finalized.

Receipt of Information—Section 10.53

When an officer or employee of the IRS has reason to believe that a practitioner has violated Circular 230, he or she will promptly make a written report of the suspected violation. The report will explain the facts and reasons for the officer's or employee's belief and must be submitted to OPR.

When someone other than an officer or employee of the IRS has reason to believe a practitioner has violated Circular 230, he or she can make an oral or written report of the alleged allegation to OPR or to an officer or employee of the IRS. If the report is made to an officer or employee of the IRS, the officer or employee must make a written report and submit it to OPR.

The IRS and OPR are subject to record retention restrictions. No report should be maintained by the IRS and OPR unless retention is permissible under the applicable records control schedule approved by the National Archives and Records Administration and designated in the Internal Revenue Manual. Reports must be destroyed as soon as possible under an applicable records control schedule. A disciplinary proceeding still is permitted after the destruction of the report, but the use of a copy of the report in a disciplinary proceeding under Circular 230 is not allowed.

Scenarios of Disciplinary Actions

The following scenarios are adapted from ones published by the IRS in Internal Revenue Bulletin 1997-13 available on the IRS website. The scenarios are composites of matters that came to the attention of the IRS and are intended to inform tax practitioners of the types of activity that may result in disciplinary action under Circular 230. (When the scenarios were published, disciplinary action was handled by the Office of Director of Practice [Director]. Today, disciplinary action is handled by OPR.)

False Statements

The practitioner was engaged by a physician to prepare the physician's individual income tax return. When the physician delivered his records, he commented to the practitioner that he hoped he could take a substantial deduction for using his car in his practice. The practitioner did not ask for further substantiation and, on the tax return submitted to the IRS, deducted various automobile expenses: depreciation, insurance, maintenance, gas, and oil. When the tax return was audited, the physician explained to the IRS auditor that he considered his car to be used in his practice because he drove it between his home and office.

Thereafter, the Director called the practitioner's attention to possible violations of Circular 230: lack of due diligence in preparing tax returns in violation of section 10.22(a); and giving false information to the Treasury Department in violation of section 10.51(a)(4). The practitioner asserted that he was entitled to place good-faith reliance on his client's information. However, the practitioner could not cite any authoritative exception to the general rule that commuting expenses are not deductible. Consequently, the Director considered the practitioner to be in violation of section 10.51(a)(4).

Contemptuous Conduct

The practitioner called an IRS revenue officer to discuss his client's case. The revenue officer, after listening to the practitioner's comments, stated that the client could still expect enforcement action. The practitioner then said, "How about my coming down there and jerking you around for a while?" The practitioner added that he "would not mind kicking down the door." The revenue officer terminated the call and notified IRS's Inspection Service. Later in the day, the practitioner called back to apologize.

The Director contacted the practitioner with regard to possible violations of Circular 230: attempting to influence an IRS employee's official action by use of a threat, a violation of section 10.51(a)(9); and contemptuous conduct consisting of abusive language, a violation of section 10.51(a)(12). In response, the practitioner offered little in the way of explanation, stating that he had simply lost his temper.

The Director determined that the practitioner's statements constituted contemptuous conduct in violation of section 10.51(a)(12). Since this was the only such instance involving the practitioner in many years of IRS practice, and in view of the quick apology, the Director determined that a reprimand, with a warning as to future conduct, was the appropriate sanction.

Due Diligence

The practitioner's employees completed clients' tax returns, which the practitioner reviewed and signed as the preparer. In completing a client's individual income tax return, one of the employees accepted the client's characterization of several trips as business trips. The employee made no further inquiry and did not request substantiation. In fact, no business purpose for the trips could be substantiated. The practitioner reviewed and signed the tax return.

The Director contacted the practitioner, stating that the practitioner may have violated the regulations in Circular 230: lack of due diligence in preparing tax returns in violation of section 10.22(a); and giving false information to the Treasury Department in violation of section 10.51(a)(4). The practitioner responded that it would be unfair to hold him responsible for the actions of the employee, who had disregarded the office policy of obtaining substantiation for business trips.

In consideration of the practitioner's office policy, and in the absence of a history of inaccurate returns, the Director was satisfied that the practitioner had not knowingly submitted false information. Therefore, the Director resolved in the practitioner's favor any question with regard to a violation of section 10.51(a)(4). However, the practitioner, as the person who signed the tax return, could not disclaim responsibility for the tax return's accuracy. The Director considered the practitioner to be in violation of section 10.22(a) for failing to exercise due diligence.

Knowledge of Client's Mistake

The client completed the practitioner's tax return preparation questionnaire, indicating that he was separated from his spouse. In reviewing the questionnaire, the practitioner asked the client whether he was "legally separated." The client replied that he was. The practitioner prepared the client's Form 1040, listing the client's filing status as single.

Later the practitioner learned that although the client and the client's spouse had come to terms on a separation agreement, the agreement had not been incorporated into a decree of divorce or separate maintenance. The practitioner, knowing that the client had declined to file an amended tax return in a prior year, did not inform the client of the mistake.

The Director informed the practitioner that his conduct raised a question regarding violation of section 10.21 of Circular 230, which requires a practitioner who knows that his or her client has not complied with the federal revenue laws or has made an error in, or omission from, a tax return or document to advise the client of such noncompliance, error, or omission. The practitioner's assumption that the client would not file an amended tax return did not relieve the practitioner of the duty to advise the client of errors. The practitioner's conduct violated section 10.21, the Director found.

Review Questions

1. Censure prevents a practitioner from representing a client before the IRS. True or false?

2. The IRS can impose a sanction or a monetary penalty but not both for a single violation. True or false?

3. An attorney who is disbarred by her state for a felony unrelated to taxes can continue to practice before the IRS. True or false?

4. A practitioner's failure to file his or her own federal tax returns can result in sanctions. True or false?

5. A tax return preparer can seek the help of an enrolled agent who is under suspension. True or false?

Answers to Review Questions

Chapter 1

1. Sara, who is single, has gross income of $7,000 and self-employment income of $500? Which statement **best** describes her filing situation? Sara:
   a. **Correct. Filing a tax return is mandatory because she has self-employment income of at least $400.**
   b. Incorrect. Filing is not optional because her self-employment income exceeds the $400 threshold.
   c. Incorrect. Even though her gross income is below the basic filing threshold, she is still required to file a tax return.
   d. Incorrect. She should file a tax return because she has a filing requirement.

2. Carlos, who is required to file a tax return, wants to obtain a filing extension. Which of the following actions is required?
   a. Incorrect. While it is advisable to pay as much of the taxes expected to be owed in order to minimize or avoid late payment penalties, full payment is not a prerequisite to obtaining a filing extension.
   b. Incorrect. An extension can be obtained for any reason; no reason is required to be provided with the filing extension request.
   c. Incorrect. While a paid preparer may submit the extension request for Carlos, a taxpayer can obtain the extension on his or her own.
   d. **Correct. The request for the extension must be made no later than the filing deadline.**

3. Harrison, an employee earning $75,000, does not file his return on time and does not obtain a filing extension. He files his return on August 15 and pays his balance due, $4,000 at that time. The $4,000 is 25% of his total tax liability. Harrison is:
   a. Incorrect. While Harrison is subject to a late filing penalty because he did not obtain a filing extension and submitted the return after the original filing deadline, this is not the only penalty owed.
   b. Incorrect. While Harrison is subject to a late payment penalty because he did not pay enough tax by the original filing deadline to avoid this penalty, this is not the only penalty he owes.
   c. **Correct. Harrison is subject to both a late filing penalty and late payment penalty because he failed to file his return on time or obtain a filing extension, and he failed to pay his taxes on time.**
   d. Incorrect. The fact that Harrison actually filed the return within the extension period does not excuse him from late filing penalties, and late payment penalties are due in any event.

4. Ed is a U.S. citizen who is single, age 70, and has gross income of $65,000 (including Social Security benefits of $20,000). He owns his home on which he pays mortgage interest and property taxes. He also makes charitable contributions. Because of these payments, it is beneficial for him to itemize his deductions. Which tax return should he use?
   a. Incorrect. While Ed's filing status as single is permissible on Form 1040EZ, this form is not allowed because he is not under age 65.
   b. Incorrect. Ed he cannot use Form 1040A to itemize deductions.
   c. **Correct. Form 1040 is the only type of return that allows Ed to itemize his personal deductions.**
   d. Incorrect. Form 1040NR is only for nonresident aliens; Ed is a U.S. citizen.

5. Madeline and Owen are U.S. residents who are married, with one dependent child. They do not have enough deductions to itemize. Based on these facts alone, which is the **simplest** tax return they can file?

   a. Incorrect. They cannot file Form 1040EZ because they have a dependent.

   b. Correct. Form 1040A is the simplest form that they can file to claim their dependent and report their income.

   c. Incorrect. While they can choose to file Form 1040, this return is not simpler than Form 1040A.

   d. Incorrect. Form 1040NR is only for nonresident aliens.

6. Louisa, who is 42 years old and files as a head of household, has gross income in 2012 of $12,000. Assuming Louisa is eligible for the earned income tax credit, which of the following statements **best** describes her filing options?

   a. Incorrect. She would be required to file a tax return if her gross income meets the threshold for her filing status, but it does not; her filing threshold is gross income of at least $12,500.

   b. **Correct. If she determines she is eligible for the earned income tax credit, she must file a return to receive a refund for it.**

   c. Incorrect. She cannot obtain a refund for the earned income credit automatically (i.e., without filing a return).

   d. Incorrect. Merely because her filing status is head of household does not mandate the filing of a return; that status depends on gross income.

Chapter 2

1. During the current tax year, Harriet is single from January through October; she marries Charles on November 1. She has no dependents. They each have about the same amount of income and will use the standard deduction. For the current tax year, which filing status is **probably** best for Harriet (and allowable)?

   a. Incorrect. Even though Harriet was single for the greater part of the year, "single" is no longer her filing status because she was not single on December 31.

   b. Correct. Because Harriet was married on December 31 (and is married on the last day of the year), she is treated as married for the entire year. She is probably better off filing jointly than separately.

   c. Incorrect. There can be only one filing status for the year for tax purposes; there cannot be part single/ part married.

   d. Incorrect. While Harriet is eligible to file as married filing separately because she is viewed as married for the entire year, this probably is not the best filing status to use.

2. Stan married Inez several years ago after his first wife died but is separated from Inez under a court order of legal separation. They did not live together during the current year. Stan does not have any children or other dependents. Which filing status is the **most** favorable and allowable?

   a. Incorrect. Because Stan is legally separated, he cannot choose to file a joint return with Inez, even though it may have saved them taxes overall.

   b. Correct. Even though Stan is still married, a legal separation makes him "single" for tax purposes. Since he does not have any dependents, he cannot use any other filing status.

   c. Incorrect. Head of household status, while more favorable than single, is not an option for Stan because he does not have any dependents.

   d. Incorrect. Stan does not qualify to file as a qualifying widow(er) because his wife did not die within the prior two years and he does not have a dependent child.

3. Joan and Edwin are married and have no children or other dependents. Joan, a part-time bookkeeper who earns a comparably modest amount, has large medical expenses that were not covered by insurance. Edwin is a successful Wall Street broker with a comfortable six-figure income. Edwin also pays a large amount of home mortgage interest and real estate taxes. Which permissible filing status for Joan is most likely to result in the **smallest** total tax liability?

   a. Incorrect. While the couple can file jointly, Edwin's high income may prevent the couple from deducting some or all of Joan's medical expenses and could increase the couple's tax bill as compared with the taxes when using a different status.

   b. Correct. Joan can choose to file separately and claim her itemized medical deductions. Since the threshold for the medical deductions is based on her low income, she may substantially reduce or avoid taxes, saving the couple overall.

   c. Incorrect. Since Joan is married and living with Edwin, she does not qualify to file as single.

   d. Incorrect. Since Joan does not qualify to file as single and does not have any dependents, she cannot use head of household status.

4. Ellie, who is single, supports her elderly mother, who resides in a nursing home. Ellie pays all of the costs for her own household as well as more than half the costs for her mother. Her mother receives $10,000 of Social Security benefits and a $3,000 pension that pays the expenses not covered by Ellie. Which filing status is the **most** advantageous (and allowable) for Ellie?

   a. Incorrect. While Ellie qualifies to file as single, this is not the most advantageous filing status that she can use.

   b. Correct. Because Ellie supports her mother, she meets the qualifications for head of household. This status is more advantageous than filing as single.

   c. Incorrect. Ellie does not meet the criteria for a qualifying spouse.

   d. Incorrect. Since Ellie is not married as of the end of the year, she cannot opt to file as married filing separately.

5. Camila has two children who lived with her all year. Her husband, Mark, left the home in August. She has not been able to locate him, and they have not filed for divorce or legal separation. Mark did not work all year, and Camila provided all the support for the home and children. Which filing status can Camila use if she does not wish to file a return together with her husband?

   a. Incorrect. Because Camila is still officially married to Mark, she cannot file as single; she must choose between married filing jointly or married filing separately unless she meets the tests to file as head of household.

   b. Incorrect. In order for Camila to file as head of household, Mark must not have lived in the home for the final six months of the year. Mark left the home in August; thus, he did in fact live in the home for part of the final six months of the year.

   c. Correct. Because Camila is still married to Mark and does not wish to file as married filing jointly, her only remaining option is to file as married filing separately.

   d. Incorrect. If Camila is unable to contact Mark, she will not be able to provide any of Mark's information that is necessary to complete the married filing joint tax return. Furthermore, Camila is not interested in filing jointly with Mark anyway.

6. Margaret, a single mother who has never been married, lost her job in May of 2012. Margaret and her ten-year-old daughter, Samantha, moved in with Margaret's sister, Joanne, that same month and lived with her the rest of the year. Joanne provided more than half of the support for the household during the year. What is Margaret's filing status?

   a. Correct. Because Margaret did not provide more than half of the household support during the year, she is unable to claim the head of household status. Margaret is not married, so the only option left for her is to claim the single status.

   b. Incorrect. Because Margaret did not provide more than half of the household support during the year, she is not eligible to file as head of household. This is true whether Margaret has provided more than half of Samantha's support during the year or not.

   c. Incorrect. Because Margaret is not married, she cannot file as married filing jointly.

   d. Incorrect. Because Margaret is not married, she cannot file as married filing separately.

7. Rose's spouse died in 2011 and she has not remarried. She supports and cares for her 12-year old daughter. What is the filing status for 2012 that typically will be **most** favorable to Rose?

a. Incorrect. While Rose is eligible to file as single because she is not married at the end of the year, this is not the most favorable filing status for her.

b. Incorrect. While Rose is eligible to file as head of household because of her dependent child, this is not the most favorable filing status for her.

c. Correct. Rose can file as a qualifying widow(er) because her spouse died within the prior two years and she has a dependent child who lived with her for the entire year.

d. Incorrect. Rose cannot file as married filing separately because she is not married as of the end of the year.

Chapter 3

1. Art lives with his wife, Marie, who is a full-time homemaker with no outside income. They have no dependents and file a joint return. What is the **maximum** number of personal exemptions that can be claimed on this return?

a. Incorrect. Each taxpayer can claim his or her own exemption, so zero exemptions on the joint return is not correct.

b. Incorrect. Just because Marie does not have any income does not prevent her from using her exemption.

c. Correct. They can claim two exemptions, one for Art and one for Marie.

d. Incorrect. Since the couple does not have any dependents, they cannot claim three exemptions.

2. George lives with his nephew, Sam, who is 18, a U.S. resident, and in school in the United States. George, who is 17, dropped out of school so he could support himself and Sam. Sam does not provide more than half of his own support. George cannot claim his nephew as his qualifying child because:

a. Incorrect. Sam need not be George's child. He is a qualifying child because he is the descendant of George's brother or sister (i.e., his nephew).

b. Correct. The fact that Sam is not older than George prevents George from claiming Sam as his qualifying child.

c. Incorrect. George does not have to demonstrate the amount of support he provides for Sam; it is sufficient that Sam not provide more than half of his own support in order to be his qualifying child.

d. Incorrect. Sam does not have to be a U.S. citizen; he is a U.S. resident.

3. Support items for a qualifying relative include all of the following amounts **except**:

a. Incorrect. Necessities, including food, are support items.

b. Incorrect. Education, including tuition payments, is support.

c. Incorrect. Recreation, which includes a vacation, is treated as support.

d. Correct. The payment of life insurance premiums is *not* treated as support.

4. Natalie lives with her seven-year-old daughter and the daughter's father to whom she is not married. Natalie's AGI is $21,000; the father's AGI is $25,000. Both Natalie and the father qualify for the dependent exemption for Natalie but cannot file a joint return because they are not married. Under IRS rules, which parent, if any, can claim the exemption for the daughter?

a. Incorrect. While Natalie is the custodial parent, tie-breaker rules prevent her from claiming the exemption.

b. Incorrect. The AGI tie-breaker rules apply only if both Natalie and the father actually try to claim the child.

c. Incorrect. The exemption cannot be divided; it is claimed in full by one taxpayer.

d. Correct. Either Natalie or the father can claim the exemption. The AGI tie-breaker rule applies if both of them actually claim the child on their return. If they cannot agree, and they both claim the child, the exemption will go to the father under the AGI tie-breaker rules.

5. John and Phyllis are the divorced parents of Peter, age ten. Peter lives with Phyllis, who has signed a waiver to allow John to claim Peter's exemption. If Phyllis revokes the waiver and gives John the signed statement in 2011, she can claim the exemption for Peter in:

   a. Incorrect. A waiver after 2010 is not effective in the year it is signed.

   b. Correct. The waiver is effective for the year after it is signed, so 2012 is the first year in which Phyllis can claim the exemption.

   c. Incorrect. Phyllis does not have to wait until 2013 to claim the exemption; she can do so in 2012.

   d. Incorrect. The fact that the custodial parent, Phyllis, initially signed a waiver does not preclude her from ever claiming it.

6. Carlos supports his girlfriend and her young child (Carlos is not the child's biological father), both of whom live with him all year. Neither Carlos's girlfriend nor her child has any income. Carlos's girlfriend has not released the dependency exemption to the child's biological father, and the biological father does not provide any support for the child. Carlos can claim a dependency exemption for:

   a. Incorrect. Carlos can claim an exemption for the girlfriend, whom he supports; she does not have any gross income and lives with him for the entire year. But he can also claim an exemption for his girlfriend's child. Because his girlfriend is not required to file a tax return, the child is not considered the qualifying child of any other taxpayer.

   b. Incorrect. Carlos can claim an exemption for his girlfriend's child. Because his girlfriend is not required to file a tax return, the child is not considered the qualifying child of any other taxpayer. And Carlos can claim an exemption for the girlfriend, whom he supports; she does not have any gross income and lives with him for the entire year.

   c. Correct. Carlos can claim an exemption for his girlfriend's child. Because his girlfriend is not required to file a tax return, the child is not considered the qualifying child of any other taxpayer. Carlos can claim an exemption for the girlfriend, whom he supports; she does not have any gross income and lives with him for the entire year.

   d. Incorrect. Carlos is allowed to claim an exemption for both the girlfriend and her child.

7. Mom's only income is Social Security benefits of $18,000 that she uses for her own support. Her three daughters help to support her in this way: Aline contributes $15,000, Betty contributes $10,000, and Carol contributes $3,000. Which daughter, if any, can claim an exemption for Mom?

   a. Incorrect. Carol is ineligible to claim the exemption under a multiple support agreement because she does not contribute more than 10% of Mom's support.

   b. Correct. Either Aline or Betty can claim the exemption because together, they contribute more than half of Mom's support, and Aline and Betty each contribute more than 10% of Mom's support.

   c. Incorrect. The fact that Aline contributes more than Betty does not mean she is the only one eligible to claim the exemption.

   d. Incorrect. The fact that Mom pays for some of her own support does not preclude the daughters, who meet certain requirements, from claiming her as a dependent.

Chapter 4

1. All of the following factors show that a worker is an employee rather than an independent contractor **except**:

   a. Incorrect. The worker is an employee under the company's control because the company tells the employee how to do the job.

   b. Correct. The fact that the worker can profit from an assignment, depending on how the work is done, shows that the worker has a financial stake in the work and is not under the company's control; this helps to show that the worker is an independent contractor.

   c. Incorrect. When a company provides the worker with tools to perform the job, the company demonstrates control, and the worker is more likely an employee.

   d. Incorrect. When a company decides what hours and where the worker will perform duties, the company controls the worker, and the worker is more likely an employee.

2. Cecilia receives vacation pay, sick pay, and employer-paid health coverage. She also receives a year-end bonus. Which of these payments is **not** taxable on Cecilia's 2012 return?
   a. Incorrect. The amount of any vacation pay is taxable.
   b. Incorrect. All of the sick pay used in the year is taxable.
   c. Correct. The amount of employer-paid health coverage is a tax-free fringe benefit.
   d. Incorrect. A year-end bonus is taxable. (There are exceptions when bonuses are deferred, but this does not apply here.)

3. Ann, a server at Joe's Diner who keeps poor records of her tips, reported to Joe that she earned $375 in tips last month. Joe allocated $25 in tips to Ann. Ann reports gross income from tips of:
   a. Incorrect. Because she kept poor records, allocated tips must be added to the tips Ann reported to Joe to determine Ann's total gross income from tips.
   b. Correct. Because she kept poor records, allocated tips must be added to the tips Ann reported to Joe to determine her total gross income from tips.
   c. Incorrect. Because she kept poor records, allocated tips must be added to the tips Ann reported to Joe to determine her total gross income from tips.
   d. Incorrect. Because she kept poor records, allocated tips must be added to the tips Ann reported to Joe to determine her total gross income from tips.

4. Mark is a pastor at a church where he works as an employee. The church pays for his housing with a fair rental value of $15,000. He pays for utilities and does not receive reimbursement. Which statement about this payment is correct?
   a. Incorrect. There is a parsonage allowance for members of the clergy, which includes housing provided to a member such as Mark.
   b. Incorrect. There is a rule making the exclusion for housing for a member of the clergy dependent on income.
   c. Incorrect. If Mark had been reimbursed for the cost of utilities, he could have excluded the reimbursement from gross income.
   d. Correct. While the housing allowance for Mark is tax free, it is still subject to self-employment tax.

5. Greg is out of work in 2012. Which of the following benefits is tax free if he receives them?
   a. Incorrect. Severance pay is treated as taxable wages even though a worker is no longer with the company that pays it.
   b. Incorrect. All unemployment benefits received are includible in gross income.
   c. Correct. Workers' compensation is tax free, regardless of amount.
   d. Incorrect. Supplemental unemployment benefits received from a company-financed fund are taxable but are treated as wages rather than unemployment benefits.

6. Caroline becomes disabled and receives benefits under a disability insurance policy for which she paid the premiums. How are the benefits treated for tax purposes?
   a. Incorrect. All of the benefits would be taxable if Caroline's employer had paid the premiums for the policy.
   b. Correct. Since Caroline paid the premiums, all of the benefits are tax free.
   c. Incorrect. The amount of premiums paid does not affect taxation of benefits if she paid all premiums.
   d. Incorrect. There is no apportionment of benefits (some taxable, some tax free).

7. Fred works for a company that pays him exclusively on commission for sales of its products (insurance policies). His Form W-2 shows $78,000 earned as "Wages, tips, other compensation." He also has unreimbursed employee expenses of $2,400. Which of the following is a true statement about Fred?
   a. Incorrect. Statutory employees do report expenses on Schedule C, but Social Security and Medicare taxes are withheld and shown on Form W-2.
   b. Incorrect. Social Security and Medicare taxes are withheld by the employer and shown on the employee's Form W-2. Therefore, Schedule SE is not filed.
   c. Incorrect. Fred cannot reduce his gross income by his unreimbursed employee expenses.
   d. Correct. Fred is a statutory employee who reports expenses on Schedule C. However, Social Security and Medicare taxes are withheld and shown on Form W-2. Therefore, they should not be reported again on Schedule SE.

8. Jaime is in the military. Which of the following payments is **always** taxable?

   a. Correct. Enlistment and reenlistment bonuses are taxable pay.

   b. Incorrect. Combat pay is nontaxable.

   c. Incorrect. The Basic Housing Allowance is a nontaxable benefit.

   d. Incorrect. Members of the military receive a uniform allowance; it is tax free.

Chapter 5

1. Joann lives in Florida and receives the following payments. Which of these payments is **not** reported as taxable interest on her federal tax return?

   a. Incorrect. The $8 that is not reported on Form 1099-INT is still taxable and must be reported, even if no Form 1099-INT was issued.

   b. Incorrect. Even though they are called "dividends," the payments from a savings and loan association are taxable interest.

   c. Incorrect. The interest on a U.S. Treasury bond is subject to federal income tax; it is exempt from state income tax only.

   d. Correct. Interest on a California state bond is a municipal bond exempt from federal income tax. However, the interest is still reported on the return as tax-exempt interest.

2. Olga had interest of $200 credited to a frozen bank deposit in 2012; she was able to withdraw $180 by the end of the year. For 2012, $180 is reported as interest income. In 2013, Olga is able to withdraw the remaining $20 in interest. How much interest is included in Olga's income in 2013?

   a. Incorrect. Interest income on a frozen account becomes taxable if it is paid out or becomes available for withdrawal by the taxpayer.

   b. Correct. The remaining $20 of interest was available for withdrawal in 2013, so it is taxable to Olga in that year.

   c. Incorrect. The $180 of interest received in 2012 was included in Olga's taxable income in 2012 because the funds were made available.

   d. Incorrect. $180 of the interest was taxable in 2012 and the remaining $20 is taxable in 2013.

3. A taxpayer has a bank account in the Cayman Islands. Assuming this is the taxpayer's only foreign account, which is the correct threshold for FBAR reporting the account to the Treasury?

   a. Incorrect. $1,500 of interest income is the threshold for having to complete Schedule B of Form 1040.

   b. Incorrect. An account value of more than $1,500 does not trigger FBAR reporting.

   c. Incorrect. The threshold for filing is not based on interest, regardless of amount.

   d. Correct. If the account value is more than $10,000, FBAR reporting is required.

4. Gil was subject to backup withholding on his interest income of $1,000. The withholding was $280. Backup withholding on interest means that Gil:

   a. Incorrect. A taxpayer cannot choose to have taxes withheld.

   b. Correct. If backup withholding has been taken on interest income, then the taxpayer can claim a credit for taxes withheld.

   c. Incorrect. Backup withholding is not an additional tax (penalty).

   d. Incorrect. Although there was backup withholding, it does not affect the reporting of interest income on the return; taxable interest reported is $1,000.

5. A grandmother gives her grandchild a $10,000 gift that is used to open a custodial account under the Model Gifts of Securities to Minors Act. The grandchild's father acts as custodian/trustee of the account. Interest on the account for 2012 is $200. Who reports the interest?

   a. Incorrect. The grandmother, who donated the funds, does not report the interest because she has given away the money.

   b. Incorrect. The father does not report the interest even though he acts as the account's custodian or trustee.

   c. Correct. The grandchild reports the interest because his or her Social Security Number is used for a custodial account.

   d. Incorrect. Interest earned in this type of account is not tax free.

6. In 1995, Lidia, age 30, purchased a Series EE bond for $1,000. In 2012, she redeemed it and used all of the proceeds to pay for qualified education expenses of her daughter, who is her dependent. On redemption, she received $1,450, $975 of which is principal and $475 of which is interest. If Lidia's modified adjusted gross income in 2012 is $90,000, how much, if any, of the proceeds are excludable? (Assume Lidia is a single mother filing as head of household.)

   a. **Correct. Because Lidia's MAGI is over $87,850 in 2012, she cannot exclude any interest on redemption of the bond, even though it is used for qualified higher education expenses of her dependent child.**

   b. Incorrect. The full amount of interest, or $475, would be excludable if her MAGI were below $72,850.

   c. Incorrect. The $975 is principal, which is not taxable regardless of MAGI.

   d. Incorrect. The $1,000 is what Lidia paid for the bond; the proceeds do not reflect a recovery of her full investment.

Chapter 6

1. On August 1, Michael buys 100 shares of ABC Corporation, a profitable domestic corporation. On September 1, ABC Corporation declares a dividend. On September 14, Michael sells his shares. To Michael, the dividend is:

   a. **Correct. Michael did not meet the holding period requirement for owning the shares for at least 60 days during the 121-day period starting 60 days before the ex-dividend date, so the dividend is an ordinary dividend to him.**

   b. Incorrect. Although ABC Corporation may have reported the dividend to Michael as a qualified dividend (because it is a domestic corporation), the dividend still will be taxed as an ordinary dividend because the holding period was not met.

   c. Incorrect. Since the distribution was not from a mutual fund, it cannot be considered a capital gain distribution.

   d. Incorrect. Since ABC Corporation was profitable, the dividend was likely a distribution from earnings and profits. Therefore, it cannot be a nondividend, which is paid by companies without earnings and profits.

2. Which of the following is **not** a dividend?

   a. Incorrect. Cash distributions on preferred stock are treated the same as cash distributions on common stock; they are dividends.

   b. **Correct. Dividends from mutual savings banks are treated as interest, not as dividends, even though they are labeled as such.**

   c. Incorrect. Even though distributions are reinvested in additional stock, they are still treated as dividends.

   d. Incorrect. Foreign dividends, including those from such companies as Sony, a Japanese corporation, are dividends and are treated the same as dividends from domestic corporations.

3. What is the tax treatment for capital gain distributions?

   a. Incorrect. Even though capital gain distributions are similar to corporate dividends, they are not taxed like ordinary dividends.

   b. Incorrect. Even though they are subject to the same tax rates as qualified dividends, capital gain distributions are not treated the same as qualified dividends.

   c. **Correct. Capital gain distributions are taxed as long-term capital gains.**

   d. Incorrect. When mutual funds or REITs make capital distributions, they do not receive tax-free treatment.

4. Humphrey bought 100 shares in the DCE Corporation a number of years ago for $5,000. This year, the corporation made a nondividend distribution to him of $600 (reported in Box 3 of Form 1099-DIV). How is the distribution taxed?

   a. Incorrect. A nondividend distribution means that the corporation does not have earnings and profits, and the distribution cannot be taxed as an ordinary dividend.

   b. Incorrect. The dividend was not reported by the DCE Corporation as a qualified dividend and is not taxed as such.

   c. **Correct. The $600 nondividend distribution reduces his stock basis to $4,400 ($5,000 – $600).**

   d. Incorrect. Long-term capital gain on a nondividend distribution results only when basis has been reduced to zero. In this example, if future nondividend distributions exceed $4,400 (his remaining basis), the excess is long-term capital gain.

5. All of the following dividends are tax free **except**:
   a. Incorrect. Dividends on life insurance policies kept by the insurer to pay the premiums are not taxable.
   b. Incorrect. Exempt-interest dividends, as the name implies, are tax free.
   c. Correct. Dividends received from a corporation generally are taxable, regardless of whether the company shows a profit.
   d. Incorrect. Distribution consisting entirely of shareholder basis is tax free. (A return of capital is not taxable.)

6. Geraldo owns 100 shares of stock. His basis is $8,000 (basis of $80 per share). If the corporation splits its stock 2 for 1, he then owns 200 shares, and his total basis of $8,000 is allocated to 200 shares (basis of $40 per share). How much of this is taxable when the split is made?
   a. Correct. There is *no* immediate tax upon a stock split; the existing basis is merely allocated over all of the shares.
   b. Incorrect. The $40 is the amount of the new basis per share.
   c. Incorrect. Even though Geraldo has twice as many shares following the split, half of his basis, or $4,000, is not immediately taxable.
   d. Incorrect. The $8,000 is both the old (pre-split) and new (post-split) basis of the shares, not the taxable amount.

Chapter 7

1. On December 1, 2012, Stan, the landlord of a three-family house, rents out one unit for $800 per month for one year (starting December 1, 2012). The tenant pays him $2,400 —the first month's rent plus a $1,600 security deposit that will be used to pay the last two months' rent. How much of the payment is taxable to Stan in 2012?
   a. Incorrect. There is no tax rule that would make any or all of the income tax free.
   b. Incorrect. While $800 represents the first month's rent (for December), this is not the only amount that is taxable in 2012.
   c. Incorrect. While $1,600 would represent the first month's rent and a one-month security deposit, this is not the full extent of the funds that Stan receives and is taxable on.
   d. Correct. All of the $2,400 is taxable because it includes the current month's rent (December 2012) and an advance payment of two months' rent. It is not a true security deposit.

2. Which of the following is **not** taxable to a landlord?
   a. Correct. A security deposit is not advance rent when it is not a final payment of rent.
   b. Incorrect. Cash payments are not the only types of taxable rent; payments made in property or services are also taxable.
   c. Incorrect. It is true that a landlord has income when a tenant pays his or her expenses.
   d. Incorrect. A payment by the tenant for canceling the lease is taxable to the landlord.

3. What payment is currently deductible?
   a. Incorrect. Replacing the roof is a capital improvement that is not currently deductible.
   b. Incorrect. Putting up a fence is a capital improvement; the cost is recovered through depreciation.
   c. Correct. Fixing a leaky pipe is an ordinary repair cost that is currently deductible.
   d. Incorrect. No current deduction is allowed for installing new appliances because they are capital improvements.

4. Darren rents out his home. What is the maximum rental period that would make the rent tax free?
   a. Incorrect. Ordinarily, all rent is taxable, regardless of the rental period, but there is one exception to this rule.
   b. Incorrect. If the rental period is less than 10% of the time that Darren uses his home, this impacts how Darren can claim deductions for the home.
   c. Correct. The tax law sets a limit of 14 days or less; rental income during this period is tax free.
   d. Incorrect. Even if the rental period is less than the time Darren uses his home, rent is taxable unless it falls within one limited exception.

5. Miriam, a head of household, has $80,000 in wages, $12,000 income from a limited partnership (passive income), and a $30,000 loss from rental real estate activities (passive losses) in which she actively participated. (Her MAGI does not exceed $100,000.) What part of the $30,000 loss can she use in 2012?
   a. Incorrect. She does not have a zero offset because she can use her passive activity losses to offset passive activity income and some nonpassive activity income.
   b. Incorrect. She is not limited to offsetting only the $12,000 in passive activity income.
   c. Incorrect. While there is a $25,000 loss limit for active participants to offset nonpassive activity income, this limit applies only after passive activity income has already been offset.
   d. Correct. She can offset her $12,000 passive income. She can use all of the remaining $18,000 to offset her salary.

6. A landlord owns an apartment building for which he paid $1 million. The purchase contract did not make any allocation for the land, but the most recent tax assessment shows that the building is 80% of the total assessed value. What is the depreciable basis of the building?
   a. Incorrect. Merely because there is no allocation between land and building in the original purchase does not bar depreciation for the building; it is up to the landlord to make an allocation.
   b. Incorrect. The land's basis of $200,000 is not depreciable.
   c. Correct. Because 80% of the assessed value is for the building, then 80% of the landlord's cost (80% of $1 million) is depreciable.
   d. Incorrect. No depreciation can be taken for land, so the full purchase price of $1 million is not depreciable.

Chapter 8

1. This year, Seymour starts to receive a pension from his employer under a defined benefit (pension) plan. The plan was funded entirely by the employer. What portion of the benefits is taxable?
   a. Incorrect. All of the benefits would be tax free if they had been funded entirely with after-tax contributions; this was not the case here.
   b. Incorrect. The simplified method applies to employee annuities when the employee has an investment in the contract, which is not the case here.
   c. Incorrect. The general method applies to commercial annuities (as well as nonqualified employee annuities).
   d. Correct. Since the employee does not have any investment in the plan, all of the benefits are fully taxable.

2. Joan retires and receives a pension for her lifetime. She is 62 years old on the annuity starting date (the total number of anticipated monthly payments for a 62-year-old is 260). Her investment in the contract is $26,000. She receives monthly payments of $1,500. How much of her annual payments of $18,000 is tax free?
   a. Correct. The excludable portion is $1,200 (investment in the contract of $26,000 ÷ 260, [the figure from the table based on her age] × 12 monthly payments).
   b. Incorrect. This amount, $1,500, is what she receives monthly.
   c. Incorrect. The $16,800 is the taxable portion of her annual payments.
   d. Incorrect. The annual payments total $18,000.

3. Which is a lump-sum distribution (assume the recipient was born before January 2, 1936)?
   a. Incorrect. A distribution from an IRA can never be treated as a lump-sum distribution even though it is made in one payment.
   b. Incorrect. By definition, a lump-sum credit or payment from the federal Civil Service Retirement System cannot be treated as a lump-sum distribution.
   c. Correct. A distribution from a participant's entire account in a profit-sharing plan is a lump-sum distribution provided it is made within one taxable year.
   d. Incorrect. Lump-sum treatment does not apply to a total distribution from a 403(b) annuity.

4. Alice, who is now 60 years old, contributed to a Roth IRA on March 12, 2010, for the 2009 plan year. She files her income tax return for 2009 on April 15, 2010. What is the date that the five-year period for tax-free Roth IRA withdrawals begins for Alice?

   a. **Correct. The five-year period starts on the first day of the year for which the contributions were made, which is January 1, 2009.**

   b. Incorrect. The due date (or date of filing) of the 2009 income tax return, April 15, 2010, has no bearing on the five-year period.

   c. Incorrect. The five-year period starts on the first of the year for which the contribution is made (2009), not the year of the contribution (2010).

   d. Incorrect. The date that the taxpayer actually made the contribution (March 12, 2010) does not start the five-year period.

5. Eduardo sells a $100,000 term life policy for $18,000. He paid premiums of $10,000. What taxation results?

   a. Incorrect. There is no taxation only if premiums are equal to or more than sale proceeds.

   b. Incorrect. If this had been a whole life policy with gain equal to or less than the cash surrender value, then all of the gain is ordinary income.

   c. Incorrect. If this had been a whole life policy, then part of the gain in excess of premium payments representing the cash surrender value would have been ordinary income; the balance would have been capital gain. The term policy, however, does not have any cash surrender value.

   d. **Correct. Because it is a term policy, all of the gain is capital gain.**

6. Olivia, age 55, has $100,000 in an IRA (not a Roth) funded entirely by deductible contributions. She wants to convert $50,000 in 2012 to a Roth IRA. What are her tax results?

   a. Incorrect. While there is no tax when funds are rolled over from one IRA to another, this tax-free rollover rule does not apply to conversions to Roth IRAs.

   b. Incorrect. The opportunity to postpone income recognition from Roth IRA conversions applied only to conversions made in 2010.

   c. **Correct. Because the IRA was funded with deductible contributions, all of the conversion amount, or $50,000, is included in her gross income this year.**

   d. Incorrect. Because there is no basis in the IRA (it was funded entirely with deductible contributions), no portion of the $50,000 is excludable from gross income.

Chapter 9

1. In figuring the taxable portion, if any, of Social Security benefits, "income" includes all of the following **except**:

   a. **Correct. Only *half* of Social Security benefits are included in "income."**

   b. Incorrect. All tax-exempt interest is includible in "income."

   c. Incorrect. Pension income must be included in "income."

   d. Incorrect. While an employer's payment of adoption assistance usually is exempt from gross income, it must be included for purposes of figuring "income."

2. What is the maximum portion, if any, of Social Security benefits includible in gross income?

   a. Incorrect. While many taxpayers do not include any benefits in gross income, this is not the maximum amount possible.

   b. Incorrect. Some taxpayers include half of their Social Security benefits in gross income, but this is not the maximum amount possible.

   c. **Correct. Regardless of income, the maximum amount of Social Security benefits that could be included in gross income is 85%.**

   d. Incorrect. There is no situation in which all of Social Security benefits are includible in gross income.

3. As a result of a claim, Julia receives lump-sum payments in 2012 for Social Security benefits that should have been paid to her in 2011. She makes no special election. How is the lump sum taxed?

   a. Incorrect. Benefits may be tax free; it depends on "income" for the appropriate tax year.

   b. Incorrect. The lump-sum payment can be treated as benefits paid in 2011 only if a special election is made.

   c. **Correct. Absent a special election, lump-sum benefits are included entirely in the current year's (2012) benefits for determining taxability.**

   d. Incorrect. A tax credit applies only for the repayment of benefits, which is not the case here.

4. How are Social Security disability benefits treated for tax purposes?

   a. Incorrect. Only SSI payments are always tax free.

   b. Correct. There is no difference between the taxation of Social Security disability benefits and those paid to retirees.

   c. Incorrect. As is the case with Social Security benefits paid to retirees, 85% of the benefits may be taxable only if the taxpayer's "income" exceeds the maximum amount.

   d. Incorrect. Social Security disability payments are *never* fully taxable.

5. Bruce receives Social Security benefits of $12,340, taxable interest of $8,320, wages from a part-time job of $6,250, and tax-exempt interest of $200. What is Bruce's income for purposes of figuring the taxable portion of Social Security benefits?

   a. Incorrect. Tax-exempt interest cannot be excluded from income for purposes of calculating the taxable portion of Social Security benefits, so $20,740 (which is one-half of benefits, plus part-time wages and taxable interest) is not correct.

   b. Correct. Income for purposes of figuring the taxable portion of Social Security benefits is one-half of benefits ($12,340 × 50%), plus part-time wages, plus taxable and tax-exempt interest, or $20,940.

   c. Incorrect. Tax-exempt interest is not excludable for purposes of figuring the taxable portion of benefits, so $26,910 (which excludes the interest as well as including 100% of benefits) is not correct.

   d. Incorrect. Income for purposes of figuring the taxable portion of Social Security benefits does not include all of the benefits, so $27,110 (which is 100% of the benefits, plus part-time wages, taxable interest, and tax-exempt interest) is not correct.

6. Sue receives Social Security benefits of $8,670 on behalf of her dependent child, Tom. Which of the following statements is correct?

   a. Incorrect. Any benefits that may be taxable are based on the income of individual receiving the benefits. Sue's income is not used for this purpose.

   b. Correct. Taxable benefits, if any, are based on Tom's income because the benefits are his, not Sue's.

   c. Incorrect. The benefits belong to Tom and therefore are not taxable to Sue.

   d. Incorrect. The benefits belong to Tom. Therefore, they may be taxed to Tom based on his income, not Sue's.

Chapter 10

1. Mr. Brown, a college student working on a degree in accounting, received the following amounts during the year to pay his expenses:

   $4,000 scholarship used for tuition at State University

   $1,000 scholarship used for fees and books required by the college, and

   $8,000 fellowship used for his room and board

   What amount does Mr. Brown include in taxable income for the year?

   a. Correct. Mr. Brown must include in income the $8,000 fellowship used for room and board. The $4,000 scholarship used for tuition and $1,000 scholarship used for fees and books are not taxable because these amounts are used to pay for qualified education expenses.

   b. Incorrect. The $5,000 representing tuition, fees, and books is a nontaxable scholarship payment because it is used to pay for qualified education expenses. Degree candidates who use scholarship payments to pay for tuition and fees to enroll in an eligible institution and to pay for books required for all students in a course at the eligible institution do not include those payments in income.

   c. Incorrect. Only $8,000 of the total $13,000 is taxable. The $8,000 fellowship for room and board is taxable while the $5,000 for fees, tuition, and books is nontaxable because it is used to pay for qualified education expenses.

   d. Incorrect. Only $8,000 is taxable. The $1,000 of scholarship payments used for fees and books is being paid for qualified education expenses and thus is nontaxable.

2. John, a cash-basis taxpayer, had borrowed $5,000 from his local credit union. He lost his job and was unable to make payments on the loan. The credit union determined legal fees to collect might be more than John owed, so it canceled $3,000 of the balance due. John did not file bankruptcy and was not insolvent. How much does John report as income from cancellation of the debt?

   a. Incorrect. Cancellation of debt income is reported only to the extent of the actual amount canceled, not the underlying amount to which cancellation of debt income applies. As such, only $3,000 of the $5,000 canceled debt would be taxable cancellation of debt income. John remains liable for the remaining $2,000 and is not taxed for the remaining debt he still owes.

   b. Correct. John reports $3,000 of income from the credit union's cancellation of his loan. The canceled debt is taxable because John did not file bankruptcy, he was not insolvent, and the debt would not have been deductible if he paid it.

   c. Incorrect. $3,000 would be taxable because it met the definition of cancellation of debt income. John was not eligible for an exception to reporting this income and thus must report the full amount of the canceled debt.

   d. Incorrect. $8,000 would represent both the full amount of the loan and the discharged amount. As cancellation of debt income only includes canceled debt, only $3,000 would be cancellation of debt income.

3. Sherwood received disability income of $6,000. All premiums on the health and accident policy were paid by his employer and included in Sherwood's income. In addition, he received compensatory damages of $10,000 as a result of inadvertent poisoning at a restaurant. He received no other income during the year. How much income does Sherwood report on his tax return?

   a. Incorrect. The health and accident payments of $6,000 and the compensatory damages for physical injury are not included in income. The health and accident payments are considered as paid by the taxpayer because they were included in income and thus are not taxable. The compensatory damages were paid in regard to a physical injury and thus are not taxable.

   b. Incorrect. The compensatory damages of $10,000 are not taxable because they are paid in regard to a physical injury.

   c. Incorrect. The health and accident payments of $6,000 are not taxable because the employee is considered to have paid the health insurance premiums. While paid with employer contributions, these amounts were included in income and thus are considered paid by the employee.

   d. Correct. Sherwood has $0 reportable income for the year. His disability income of $6,000 is not taxable because he paid tax on the premiums paid by his employer. The $10,000 of compensatory damages is not taxable because it was received because of a physical injury.

4. Lydia, age 28, is single and received $10,000 unemployment benefits from the state. She also received $3,000 from the state to reduce the cost of her winter fuel bill. What amount of income does she report for the year?

   a. Correct. Lydia reports income of $10,000 state unemployment benefits. The $3,000 state aid to reduce her winter fuel bill is not taxable.

   b. Incorrect. Only the state unemployment benefits, not the state winter fuel bill assistance, are taxable. As such, $10,000, not the full $13,000, is taxable to Lydia.

   c. Incorrect. State assistance to reduce the cost of a winter fuel bill is specifically categorized as a nontaxable assistance payment.

   d. Incorrect. Although the $3,000 winter fuel bill assistance is nontaxable, the $10,000 in unemployment compensation is included in income.

5. Which of the following is taxable to the recepient?

a. Incorrect. Gifts of any amount given with no consideration in return are tax free, so the $10,000 gift from mother to daughter is not taxable.

b. Incorrect. Inheritances are tax free, so the $1 million inheritance is not taxable,

c. Correct. Any payment that is not a gift is taxable, so the $100 value of the music player for opening a bank account is included in gross income.

d. Incorrect. A rebate is viewed as a reduction in the purchase price, so the $50 rebate for buying a laptop is not taxable.

Chapter 11

1. All of the following taxpayers file Schedule C **except**:

a. Incorrect. An independent contractor may be a sole proprietor and files a Schedule C (or C-EZ).

b. Incorrect. Schedule C is used by a sole proprietor running a boutique to report income and expenses. (Because of inventory, Schedule C-EZ cannot be filed.)

c. Correct. A farmer who is a sole proprietor files a Schedule F, not a Schedule C.

d. Incorrect. Even though a statutory employee is a technically an employee, he or she reports income and expenses on Schedule C (or C-EZ).

2. Which of the following expenses of a sole proprietor is **not** deducted on Schedule C?

a. Incorrect. Advertising costs are deductible on the line provided for such costs on Schedule C.

b. Incorrect. Work-related education costs are deducted on Schedule C even though there is no dedicated line for these expenses; they are entered in Part V of Schedule C with "other expenses."

c. Incorrect. A business owner's policy for liability and property insurance for the business is deductible on Schedule C.

d. Correct. Health insurance premiums for a policy covering the sole proprietor, spouse, and dependent are deducted from gross income as an adjustment. Premiums paid to cover employees are deductible on Schedule C.

3. The IRS standard mileage rate for a vehicle used for business takes the place of deducting the actual cost of all of the following **except**:

a. Correct. Tolls, as well as parking and interest on vehicle financing, are separately deductible, whether the standard mileage rate or the actual expense method is used to figure the deduction for business driving.

b. Incorrect. Vehicle insurance cannot be deducted separately if the standard mileage rate is used.

c. Incorrect. Depreciation for a vehicle that is owned by the sole proprietor can be claimed only if the actual expense method is used to deduct the cost of business driving.

d. Incorrect. The standard mileage rate is calculated to include registration fees; no separate deduction is allowed.

4. George starts a business in 2012. He pays $7,700 for research, travel, and other costs before he opens his doors. He begins operations on December 31, 2012. What is the most he can deduct in 2012?

a. Incorrect. Even though the business did not start until late in the year, it is not prevented from electing to deduct some start-up costs.

b. Correct. The $5,000 limit applies to start-up costs incurred in 2012. Since the business started at the end of the year, the balance of the costs ($2,700) is amortized over 180 months.

c. Incorrect. If the $7,700 of costs had been incurred in 2011, they would have been fully deductible because of the $10,000 limit applicable for that year.

d. Incorrect. The $10,000 immediate deduction applied only to start-up costs in 2011, and, in any event, the actual costs were not $10,000.

5. Which of the following is **not** "listed property"?

a. Incorrect. Cars, light trucks, and vans weighing 6,000 pounds or less are listed property.

b. Correct. Cell phones had been listed property but were delisted in 2010.

c. Incorrect. Video-recording equipment and similar property is listed property.

d. Incorrect. Desktops and laptops are listed property.

6. Which of the following statements regarding the home office deduction is correct?

a. Incorrect. There is no annual dollar limit on the home office deduction.

b. Incorrect. The home office deduction is composed of both direct expenses and a portion of indirect expenses.

c. Correct. If the deduction is more than the taxable income limit (essentially gross income minus deductions from the office), the excess can be carried forward indefinitely.

d. Incorrect. The home office of a sole proprietor who uses the space to schedule appointments, order supplies, and keep the books is treated as the principal place of business, and expenses for the office can be deductible.

7. Which of the following types of farm income are **not** included on Schedule F?

a. Incorrect. Patronage dividends are farm income reported on Schedule F.

b. Correct. Sales of livestock held for breeding purposes are reported on Form 4797.

c. Incorrect. Even though loans generally are not taxable, Commodity Credit Corporation loans are income to farmers.

d. Incorrect. Sales of crops are the basis type of income from farming activities reported on Schedule F.

8. A sole proprietor has net earnings from SE in 2012 of $56,000. What is the maximum SE tax rate?

a. Incorrect. The 2.9% rate is the Medicare portion of SE tax.

b. Incorrect. The 10.4% is the Social Security portion of SE tax in 2012.

c. Correct. For 2011 and 2012 only, the total SE rate is 13.3%.

d. Incorrect. If the income had been earned in 2010 or 2013, then 15.3% would have been the correct rate.

9. In 2012, a sole proprietor buys used office furniture at a cost of $4,200. He has a net loss from his business activities of $9,600. Which of the following options applies to him for purposes of writing off the cost of the furniture in 2012?

a. Incorrect. Section 179 provides a tax deduction only if a taxpayer is profitable for the year.

b. Incorrect. Bonus depreciation cannot be used for used (preowned) property.

c. Incorrect. Since section 179 and/or bonus depreciation cannot be used, this answer is not correct.

d. Correct. Because the taxpayer has a loss, a section 179 deduction cannot be claimed; because the property is used, bonus depreciation cannot be used.

10. A sole proprietor runs a business from home. In 2012, he has income from the home office activity of $3,300 and expenses for the home office of $6,100. Which of the following statements **best** describes his tax treatment of the home office expenses?

a. Incorrect. As long as the taxpayer meets the rules for claiming a home office deduction, expenses are deductible to the extent of gross income from the home office activity.

b. Incorrect. While it is true that $3,300 ($6,100 – $2,800) is deductible in 2012, the balance is not lost; it can be carried forward indefinitely.

c. Correct. Expenses to the extent of income from the home office activity ($3,300) are deductible in 2012 while the balance can be carried forward indefinitely.

d. Incorrect. The full amount of expenses ($6,100) is not deductible in 2012 because of the gross income limit.

11. In 2012, Sharon started a gift basket business. In 2012, she has income of $7,700 and expenses of $10,440. Assuming that the IRS successfully establishes that this is a hobby activity, how are Sharon's income and expenses reported?

a. Incorrect. She does not report her income and expenses on Schedule C because it is a hobby activity.

b. Correct. She reports all her income and her expenses to the extent of this income as follows: On Form 1040 (line 21) she reports income of $7,700, and on Schedule A she reports expenses of $7,700 (due to the hobby loss limitation).

c. Incorrect. As a hobby activity she reports her $7,700 of hobby income on Form 1040 as other income (line 21) but cannot deduct all of her hobby expenses on Schedule A due to the hobby loss limitation.

d. Incorrect. While she reports her income from the hobby on Form 1040 (line 21), she is not barred from reporting expenses to the extent of income from the activity.

Chapter 12

1. The "basis" of property is the starting point for determining all of the following **except**:

a. Incorrect. Basis is used to figure depreciation on property held for business or investment.

b. Correct. Excise taxes are not based on "basis"; excise taxes may be added to the basis of property.

c. Incorrect. If there is damage or destruction of property due to a casualty event, the starting point for figuring a casualty loss is basis.

d. Incorrect. Gain or loss on the disposition of property is determined by comparing basis to the amount received on the disposition.

2. A taxpayer builds his own personal residence. What **cannot** be added to basis?

a. Correct. While the cost of labor is added to the basis of the home, the value of a taxpayer's own labor cannot be taken into account.

b. Incorrect. The cost of materials can be added to the home's basis.

c. Incorrect. The basis of the home includes the architect's fees.

d. Incorrect. Any payments made to contractors in the construction of the home are added to basis.

3. Which of the following is an **increase** to basis?

a. Incorrect. Residential energy credits for making certain energy improvements to a principal residence are a decrease to basis.

b. Incorrect. A casualty loss is a decrease to basis.

c. Incorrect. The basis of property is decreased by depreciation.

d. Correct. Capital improvements are costs that can be added to the basis of property.

4. Two years ago, Felicia received as a gift from her aunt a bracelet worth $5,000. Her aunt bought it many years ago for $800. If Felicia sells the bracelet for $4,000, her basis for figuring gain or loss is:

a. Incorrect. A zero basis is used only when a taxpayer does not have information to support a different basis.

b. Correct. Because the FMV at the time of the gift was more than the donor's adjusted basis, the taxpayer's basis is the donor's adjusted basis of $800.

c. Incorrect. The sale price of $4,000 is not the basis of the property.

d. Incorrect. The FMV of the property at the time of the gift ($5,000) is not the basis because it was not less than the donor's adjusted basis. FMV would be the basis only if the donor's adjusted basis at the time of the gift was less than FMV and the taxpayer sold the property at a loss.

5. Same facts as in Question 4 except that Felicia inherited the bracelet instead of receiving it as a gift. It is worth $5,000 at the time of the aunt's death. Felicia sells it six months later for $4,000. Her basis for determining gain or loss is:

a. Incorrect. Regardless of records for the decedent, there is a zero basis in inherited property only if the property has no value at the time of death.

b. Incorrect. The decedent's adjusted basis of $800 has no impact on the heir's basis in the property.

c. Incorrect. The fact that the value declined to $4,000 when the inherited property is sold does not impact basis.

d. Correct. For inherited property, the heir gets a stepped-up basis to the property's value on the date of death, which is $5,000.

6. Adelaide sells her personal residence, which she has owned and lived in since 1988. For purposes of determining her gain or loss on the sale, which of the following expenses does **not** increase the basis of her home:
   a. Incorrect. Adding a new roof is a capital improvement that adds to the basis of a home.
   b. Incorrect. Adding aluminum siding to a home is a capital improvement that adds to the basis of the home.
   c. Correct. Repairs, such as painting a room, do not add to the basis of property.
   d. Incorrect. Any extensions or additions to a home, such as a garage, increase the basis because they are capital improvements.

Chapter 13

1. Which of the following is a capital asset?
   a. Incorrect. Property held for sale to customers (i.e., inventory) is not a capital asset.
   b. Incorrect. U.S. government publications are not capital assets.
   c. Correct. Securities, including mutual fund shares, are capital assets.
   d. Incorrect. Real estate used in a business is not a capital asset.

2. Daniel has stock that has declined in value. He can report the loss if he sells it to:
   a. Incorrect. Under the related party rules, a spouse is a related party.
   b. Correct. Under the related party rules, a sale to an in-law (including a mother-in-law) is not treated as a related party sale and the taxpayer can report the loss.
   c. Incorrect. The related party rules apply to descendants, including a taxpayer's child.
   d. Incorrect. The related party rules apply to ancestors, including a taxpayer's parent.

3. On February 1, 2012, a taxpayer buys 10 shares of X Corp. What is the earliest date that the stock can be sold to qualify for long-term treatment?
   a. Incorrect. A long-term holding period of more than one year is not satisfied simply because the sale occurs within the year following the year of purchase.
   b. Incorrect. A sale on February 1, 2013, results in short-term treatment because the stock has been held for only one year.
   c. Correct. For long-term treatment to apply, the stock must be held for at least a year and a day, which is February 2, 2013.
   d. Incorrect. The fact that February 5, 2013, is the settlement date for a sale of stock occurring on February 2, does not impact the holding period.

4. A taxpayer sells stock in 2012. Where is the sale **first** reported by the taxpayer?
   a. Incorrect. While the result of the stock sale will flow onto Schedule D, it is not entered first on this schedule.
   b. Incorrect. The net capital gain (or loss) eventually is reported on Form 1040, but not first (even if the sale is the taxpayer's only capital transaction for the year).
   c. Incorrect. Form 4797 is not used for stock sales; it is used primarily for sales of business property.
   d. Correct. Stock transactions are reported first on Form 8949; results are then transferred to Schedule D.

5. A taxpayer sells 100 shares of X Corp. at a loss on December 15, 2012. Which of the following acquisition dates for acquiring substantially identical stock will **not** trigger the wash sale rule?
   a. Incorrect. The 30-day wash sale period applies to purchases of substantially identical stock within 30 days before the sale, which would be November 15, 2012.
   b. Incorrect. The fact that a purchase of substantially identical stock takes place in the following tax year, January 1, 2013, does not make it extend beyond the wash sale period.
   c. Incorrect. January 14, 2013, is exactly 30 days from the date of the sale at a loss, so it is not beyond the 30-day wash sale period.
   d. Correct. January 15, 2013, is the first day that is outside of the 30-day wash sale period.

6. In 2012, a taxpayer's home is completely destroyed by a tornado. She receives insurance proceeds that exceed the adjusted basis of the home. She decides not to rebuild or buy a new home, relocates to another state, and rents an apartment. Where is the transaction reported?

a. Incorrect. Gain from an involuntary conversion of personal use property must first be reported on Schedule D; it is not reported directly on Form 1040.

b. Incorrect. While losses from a storm (e.g., tornado) are reported on Schedule A of Form 1040, gains are not reported here.

c. Correct. If a taxpayer does not opt to postpone gain from an involuntary conversion of personal use property by acquiring replacement property, then the gain is reported on Schedule D of Form 1040.

d. Incorrect. Form 4797 is for reporting sales and involuntary conversions of business property.

Chapter 14

1. Basis of a home is increased by all of the following **except**:

a. Correct. Points that are fully deductible in the year of payment do not increase basis.

b. Incorrect. Legal fees to buy a home cannot be immediately deducted; they are added to the basis of the home.

c. Incorrect. Surveys of the home made at the time of purchase or any other time are added to basis.

d. Incorrect. There is no deduction for title insurance for the home; the cost is added to basis.

2. Basis of a home is decreased by all of the following **except**:

a. Incorrect. The basis of the home is decreased by any deductible casualty loss that was not covered by insurance.

b. Correct. The basis of the home is increased (not decreased) by assessments for local improvements.

c. Incorrect. If a homeowner claimed the first-time homebuyer credit, the amount of the credit decreases the basis of the home.

d. Incorrect. A subsidy for conservation measures that was excluded from income decreases the basis of the home.

3. A taxpayer, who is single, sells his condo in February 2012. He buys a new home, weds in June 2012, and his new bride moves in at that time. Gain on the sale of his condo is $275,000. Assuming he owned and used the condo as his main home for two out of the last five years, he can:

a. Incorrect. It is correct that the taxpayer can exclude gain of $250,000, but it is not correct that he is free from reporting the balance of the gain.

b. Incorrect. The taxpayer could have excluded his entire gain of $275,000 only if his spouse had lived in the home for at least two years and had not claimed her own exclusion within that period.

c. Incorrect. Even though the taxpayer is married, the full $500,000 for joint filers does not apply in this case; in any event, gain is not $500,000.

d. Correct. Even though the taxpayer is married at the end of the year, the spouse did not live in the home for at least two years, so the maximum exclusion is $250,000; the balance of the gain ($25,000) is taxed as long-term capital gain.

4. Which of the following unforeseen circumstances would **not** entitle a homeowner to a partial home sale exclusion?

a. Incorrect. If a taxpayer has triplets, these multiple births are recognized by the IRS as an unforeseen circumstance.

b. Correct. Even though winning the lottery is an unforeseen event, it is not the type of event that the IRS recognizes as a reason for permitting a partial home sale exclusion.

c. Incorrect. The IRS has allowed a crime victim to move and use the partial home sale exclusion.

d. Incorrect. If a taxpayer loses a job and is unable to pay the household bills, it can be considered an unforeseen circumstance warranting a partial home sale exclusion.

5. On February 1, 2010, Kevin, a single taxpayer, buys a condominium in North Dakota. On April 3, 2011, he suffers a stroke and, following hospitalization, is transferred to a nursing home. While he was living in the nursing home, his daughter, acting under a power of attorney, sells the condo in December 2012 for a gain of $48,000. How is the gain treated?

   a. **Correct. Because he became incapacitated after having owned and lived in the home for at least one year, he can count the time in the nursing home as part of this two-year ownership and use requirement. Therefore, he can fully exclude the gain.**

   b. Incorrect. While he did move because of health reasons, he does not have to figure a partial exclusion due to his move to the nursing home.

   c. Incorrect. The time in the hospital is viewed as a temporary absence and does not impact the home sale exclusion.

   d. Incorrect. The fact that he did not live in the home for the requisite two years does not make his gain fully taxable in this situation because of his move to a nursing home.

Chapter 15

1. Earned income for purposes of an IRA contribution includes all of the following **except**:

   a. Incorrect. Tips are a form of earned income for purposes of making an IRA contribution.

   b. Incorrect. Even though alimony is not earned by the recipient, it is treated as earned income.

   c. **Correct. Unemployment compensation is not treated as earned income for purposes of making an IRA contribution even though it can be received only if a taxpayer worked and earned income in the past.**

   d. Incorrect. Income from self-employment is a form of earned income for the purpose of making an IRA contribution.

2. A taxpayer obtains an extension of time to file her 2012 tax return, but she actually files on April 14, 2013, before the filing deadline. What is the deadline for making a 2012 IRA contribution?

   a. Incorrect. The IRA contribution need not be made by the end of the year to which the contribution relates, such as December 31, 2013, for a 2013 contribution.

   b. Incorrect. The contribution does not have to be made by the date that the return is actually filed (April 14, 2013, in this case).

   c. **Correct. The deadline for making a 2013 IRA contribution is April 16, 2013. This deadline can be used even if the return has already been filed; a deduction can be claimed on the return before the contribution is actually made.**

   d. Incorrect. The deadline for making an IRA contribution is not extended to the extended due date of the 2012 return (October 15, 2013).

3. Roth IRAs are similar to traditional IRAs in all of the following ways **except**:

   a. **Correct. While there is an age limit for contributions to traditional IRAs, there is no maximum age limit for making contributions to Roth IRAs.**

   b. Incorrect. If distributions are taken because of disability, there is no penalty for either traditional or Roth IRAs.

   c. Incorrect. The same contribution limit ($5,000, or $6,000 for those 50 and older by the end of 2012) applies to traditional IRAs and Roth IRAs.

   d. Incorrect. Whether contributing to a traditional IRA or Roth IRA, taxpayers must have earned income.

4. Which of the following statements about a SEP is **not** correct?
   a. Incorrect. The maximum contribution to a SEP is $50,000.
   b. Incorrect. A self-employed individual must make contributions based on the same percentage for all employees. A self-employed individual cannot discriminate in favor of highly compensated employees.
   c. Correct. A SEP can be established by a corporation.
   d. Incorrect. The deadline for making contributions is the due date of the owner's return, including extensions.

5. What is an eligibility requirement for contributing to a health savings account (HSA)?
   a. Incorrect. There is no minimum age requirement to contribute to an HSA.
   b. Correct. In order to contribute to an HSA, the taxpayer must be covered by a high-deductible health plan.
   c. Incorrect. Unlike an IRA, there is no earned income requirement for HSAs.
   d. Incorrect. There are no MAGI limits for contributions to HSAs.

6. What is the maximum contribution for 2012 to a health savings account (HSA) for a taxpayer who has family coverage under a high-deductible health plan?
   a. Incorrect. $2,400 is the minimum deductible for a high-deductible health plan for family coverage in 2012.
   b. Incorrect. $3,100 is the contribution limit for self-only coverage in 2012.
   c. Correct. $6,250 is the maximum contribution to an HSA for family coverage in 2012.
   d. Incorrect. $12,100 is the limit on out-of-pocket expenses for family coverage under a high-deductible health plan in 2012.

Chapter 16

1. A taxpayer is single, graduated college, and is now repaying her student loans. She paid $2,800 in interest on her loans in 2012. Her MAGI before considering any student loan interest deduction is $67,500. How much of an above-the-line deduction can she claim?
   a. Incorrect. She would be allowed no interest deduction if her MAGI exceeded $75,000, which it did not.
   b. Correct. Because her MAGI is within the phase-out range, she must figure a partial deduction.
   c. Incorrect. This amount exceeds the maximum deduction of $2,500.
   d. Incorrect. The full $2,500 deduction limit applies only if her MAGI is below $60,000, which it is not.

2. The student loan interest statement issued by the institution to which interest is paid is:
   a. Incorrect. Form 1099-C is used to report cancellation of debt income.
   b. Incorrect. Form 1099-B is used to report basis in certain stock and mutual funds.
   c. Correct. Form 1099-E is used by the institution to which interest is paid to report student interest. (It is mandatory if the interest is $600 or more.)
   d. Incorrect. Form 1099-T is used to report tuition payments.

3. Which statement concerning the deduction for student loan interest is **not** correct?
   a. Incorrect. It is true that the amount of the deduction depends on modified adjusted gross income.
   b. Incorrect. It is a correct statement that no deduction can be claimed for the repayment of principal on a student loan.
   c. Incorrect. It is true that qualified education expenses must be paid within a reasonable period before or after the loan was obtained
   d. Correct. The deduction can be claimed on Form 1040 or on Form 1040A.

4. Which education-related tax break does **not** depend on MAGI?
   a. Incorrect. The above-the-line deduction for tuition and fees can be claimed only if MAGI is below a set limit.
   b. Incorrect. Education credits (explained more fully in Chapter 30) also have MAGI limits; these limits differ from the limits for the tuition and fees deduction.
   c. Correct. There is no MAGI limit for claiming the deduction for educator expenses.
   d. Incorrect. There is an MAGI limit on eligibility to claim the student loan interest deduction.

5. Which type of expense qualifies for the tuition and fees deduction?
   a. Incorrect. While paying room and board may entitle a taxpayer to a different tax break, these expenses do not qualify for the tuition and fees deduction.
   b. Correct. Activity fees are a qualified expense for purposes of the tuition and fees deduction.
   c. Incorrect. The tuition and fees deduction does not include the cost of student health fees.
   d. Incorrect. No tuition and fees deduction can be claimed with respect to personal living expenses.

6. Which taxpayer does **not** qualify as an educator for purposes of deducting educator expenses up to $250?
   a. Correct. A parent who home-schools her child is not treated as an educator, even if he or she spends more than 900 hours a year.
   b. Incorrect. A principal is specifically listed as a qualified educator for grades K–12.
   c. Incorrect. A classroom aide in grades K–12 (which includes middle school) is treated as an educator for purposes of this deduction.
   d. Incorrect. A teacher in a high school or any other grade from K–12 is a qualified educator as long as the 900-hour requirement is met.

Chapter 17

1. The deduction for a portion of self-employment tax is taken:
   a. Incorrect. While the deduction for a portion of self-employment tax relates to business, it is not a business deduction claimed on Schedule C.
   b. Incorrect. The deduction for a portion of self-employment tax is not taken as a personal miscellaneous itemized deduction on Schedule A.
   c. Correct. The deductible portion of self-employment tax is claimed as an adjustment to gross income directly on Form 1040.
   d. Incorrect. While the deductible portion of self-employment tax is figured on Schedule SE, it is not used to directly reduce self-employment tax.

2. For purposes of deducting health insurance premiums from adjusted gross income, which business owner bases the deduction on compensation?
   a. Correct. A more-than-2% S corporation shareholder can claim the deduction to the extent of W-2 compensation.
   b. Incorrect. A sole proprietor can claim the deduction to the extent of profits from the business.
   c. Incorrect. A general partner's distributive share of partnership income is the limit for deducting health insurance premiums.
   d. Incorrect. Like a general partner, a limited liability company member uses his or her distributive share of business income as the limit for deducting health insurance premiums.

3. A sole proprietor has health insurance for herself and has no employees. In figuring the deductible portion of the premiums, which of the following statements is correct?

   a. Incorrect. While 100% of premiums may be deductible as an adjustment to gross income, there are limits that can result in less than 100% of premiums being deducted.

   b. Incorrect. Net profits shown on Schedule C are only the starting point for figuring the limitations on deducting health insurance premiums as an adjustment to gross income.

   c. Incorrect. While reducing net profits by the employer-equivalent portion of the self-employment tax is necessary, this is not the only adjustment to the net profits limitation on deducting health insurance premiums.

   d. Correct. The deduction limitation requires that net profits be reduced by *both* the employer-equivalent portion of the self-employment tax and a deduction for contributions to a qualified retirement plan for the sole proprietor.

4. A self-employed individual who relocates because of a new business must work in the new location for how long before the individual can deduct moving expenses?

   a. Incorrect. The 12 months is the testing period for employees.

   b. Incorrect. The 24 months is the testing period for self-employed individuals.

   c. Incorrect. Employees, not self-employed individuals, must work 39 weeks within a 12-month period to deduct moving expenses.

   d. Correct. To deduct moving expenses, a self-employed taxpayer must work at least 78 weeks during a 24-month period after the move.

5. Which of the following moving expenses is **not** deductible?

   a. Incorrect. The cost of connecting or disconnecting utilities can be treated as a deductible moving expense.

   b. Correct. No deduction can be taken for any expenses of selling the old home.

   c. Incorrect. The cost of shipping a household pet is part of deductible moving expenses.

   d. Incorrect. The cost of driving to the new home can be deducted using actual costs or an IRS-set standard mileage rate.

Chapter 18

1. Which of the following is **not** a condition for deducting alimony?

   a. Incorrect. It is true that payments must be in cash (including checks).

   b. Correct. There is no income limit for deducting alimony payments.

   c. Incorrect. To be treated as alimony, the obligation to make payments must end on the recipient spouse's death.

   d. Incorrect. If there is a divorce or legal separation, spouses must not be members of the same household.

2. Alimony recapture applies when payments in the third year decrease by more than $15,000 from the second year as a result of:

   a. Correct. Just because the payer spouse has payments reduced because he or she is less able to provide support does not avoid recapture.

   b. Incorrect. There is no recapture if the reduction is due to the death of the recipient spouse.

   c. Incorrect. There is no recapture if the reduction is due to the remarriage of the recipient spouse.

   d. Incorrect. There is no recapture if alimony payments are tied to a portion of business income and that business becomes defunct.

3. Which statement about child support is **not** correct?

   a. Incorrect. Child support is not deductible.

   b. Incorrect. As long as payments are contingent on an event related to the child, such as reaching the age of majority, they are treated as child support.

   c. Incorrect. Child support does not result in income to the recipient-spouse.

   d. Correct. There are no dollar limits on amounts paid as child support.

4. This year, Janet transfers 100 shares of stock to Ben as part of their divorce decree. Janet paid $10,000 for the shares. They are worth $18,000 on the day they are transferred to Ben. He sells the shares six months later for $22,000. What is his gain on the sale of the stock?

   a. Incorrect. There is zero gain recognized when the property is initially transferred. However, when the property is sold, the transferee spouse will recognize the gain on the property.

   b. Incorrect. This assumes that the spouse's basis in the property is $4,000 ($22,000 – $18,000), which is incorrect. The recipient spouse's basis is not determined by the value of the property on the date he or she received it but is instead a carryover basis from the other spouse.

   c. Correct. The recipient spouse's carryover basis is the other spouse's basis ($10,000), so gain is limited to $12,000 ($22,000 – $10,000).

   d. Incorrect. The recipient spouse has some basis in the stock, so the entire amount received ($22,000) is not the gain reported.

5. Sylvia and Joel divorce. Joel obtains custody of their child, Stu, age 16. Sylvia is ordered to pay Joel $500 per month until Stu turns age 18. At that time, her payments decline to $200 per month for the next three years. What, if anything, can Sylvia deduct?

   a. Incorrect. Merely because the payment includes child support and fails to specify the alimony portion does not preclude a deduction.

   b. Correct. Because the payments are reduced when the child reaches age 18, only the portion representing alimony ($500 – $300 = $200 per month) are deductible as long as she makes such payments.

   c. Incorrect. The $500 per month includes nondeductible child support because this amount is reduced by reference to an event of the child (e.g., reaching age 18).

   d. Incorrect. While the $500 per month continues until Stu is age 18, the portion related to Stu is nondeductible child support.

Chapter 19

1. In 2012, Sally, age 45, is single and has no dependents. Her earned income is $45,000. Sally's standard deduction is:

   a. Incorrect. $950 applies to a dependent standard deduction.

   b. Correct. Since Sally is single, not 65 or older, or blind, her standard deduction amount is $5,950.

   c. Incorrect. The standard deduction of $8,700 applies to the head of household filing status.

   d. Incorrect. The standard deduction of $11,900 applies to taxpayers who file using the married filing jointly status or the qualifying widow(er) status.

2. In 2012, Ed, who is single and age 67, fully supports his 90-year-old mother and claims a dependent exemption for her. He can claim a standard deduction of:

   a. Incorrect. Ed is not limited to the standard deduction for a single filer of $5,950 because he is over age 65 and because he may use the head of household filing status.

   b. Incorrect. Although Ed can use the standard deduction amount of $8,700 for qualifying as head of household, this is not the full amount he is entitled to.

   c. Correct. Ed's standard deduction is $10,150, $8,700 as head of household, plus the additional standard deduction of $1,450 because he is at least 65 years old.

   d. Incorrect. Ed cannot increase his total standard deduction amount by an additional amount for his mother's age; only a spouse's age is taken into account.

3. In 2012, Jimmy, who is 21 years old and a full-time college student, earns $2,500 at a summer job. He also has interest income of $250 and capital gain distributions from a mutual fund of $800. His parents claim a dependent exemption for him on their return. Jimmy's standard deduction is:

a. Incorrect. The dependent's standard deduction of $950 applies only if earned income plus $300 is less than this limit.

b. Correct. Jimmy's standard deduction is earned income of $2,500 plus $300, which is greater than $950. Investment income is not considered earned income for purposes of the standard deduction.

c. Incorrect. He cannot use the full standard deduction for a single taxpayer because he is a dependent and he only has $2,500 in earned income.

d. Incorrect. The standard deduction for a dependent cannot exceed the standard deduction for a single taxpayer ($5,950) even if earned income exceeds this amount.

4. Which of the following individuals can use the standard deduction?

a. Incorrect. If one spouse itemizes deductions, the other must itemize as well.

b. Incorrect. A taxpayer who files a return for a short tax year because of a change in the annual accounting period cannot claim the standard deduction.

c. Incorrect. Generally, a nonresident or dual-status alien cannot use the standard deduction.

d. Correct. A dependent can claim the standard deduction, although the amount may be limited.

5. Matt received a certified statement from his optometrist on December 1, 2012, confirming he cannot see better than 20/200. Matt does not itemize deductions. Matt is:

a. Incorrect. Taxpayers who are fully or partially blind on the last day of the tax year may claim an additional standard deduction.

b. Correct. Matt is eligible to claim an additional standard deduction in 2012 because he is certified as partially blind as of the last day of the tax year.

c. Incorrect. Eligibility to claim the additional standard deduction is determined on the last day of each tax year.

d. Incorrect. Full or partial blindness is determined as of the last day of the year.

6. A taxpayer **must** itemize in each of the following situations **except**:

a. Incorrect. Itemizing is required if the taxpayer is married filing separately and the other spouse itemizes deductions.

b. Correct. Even though itemized deductions are greater than the standard deduction amount, itemizing is not mandatory.

c. Incorrect. The taxpayer must itemize deductions if, in the rare situation, he or she has a short year (tax year less than 12 months).

d. Incorrect. Itemizing is required if the taxpayer is a dual-resident alien.

Chapter 20

1. In 2012, Jorge, who is single with no dependents, has AGI of $48,000 and unreimbursed medical costs of $8,900. How much of his medical expenses can be claimed as an itemized deduction?

a. Incorrect. Although Jorge cannot deduct all of his medical costs because of the AGI threshold, he can claim a partial deduction of medical costs.

b. Correct. His deduction is limited to medical costs exceeding 7.5% of AGI ([$48,000 × 7.5%] = $3,600), which means Jorge can deduct $5,300 ($8,900 – $3,600).

c. Incorrect. He cannot deduct all of his medical costs ($8,900) because of the AGI threshold.

d. Incorrect. $3,600 ($48,000 × 7.5%) is his 7.5% of AGI threshold.

2. Edwina can add the medical costs of all of the following people to her own in determining her medical deduction **except**:

a. Incorrect. She can deduct her spouse's medical expenses on a separate return if she pays for them, or on a joint return, regardless of which spouse paid for them.

b. Incorrect. She can deduct expenses for her sister because she is claiming her sister as a dependent under a multiple support agreement.

c. Correct. She cannot add her grandchild's medical costs to her own because the child is not her dependent.

d. Incorrect. She can deduct her dependent son's medical costs and add them to her own costs.

3. Which of the following is **not** a deductible medical expense?

   a. Incorrect. Fees to a chiropractor qualify because they are paid to a medical practitioner.

   b. Correct. The cost of teeth-whitening treatments is not deductible because it is viewed as a cosmetic procedure not required to fix a medical condition.

   c. Incorrect. The cost of a prescribed smoking cessation program is deductible because it treats a medical condition (smoking addiction).

   d. Incorrect. As long as the principal reason for the nursing home stay is for medical reasons, the full fee, including amounts for lodging, and meals, is deductible.

4. Which of the following over-the-counter items is a deductible medical expense?

   a. Correct. Insulin is a deductible medical expense.

   b. Incorrect. Over-the-counter multivitamins are not deductible.

   c. Incorrect. Over-the-counter medications, such as aspirin, are not deductible.

   d. Incorrect. Even though cough syrup may treat a medical condition, such as a cough, it is not deductible if purchased as an over-the-counter medication.

5. Rita, who is 68 years old, pays $3,600 for long-term care insurance in 2012. She is not self-employed. How much of the premiums qualify as a deductible medical expense?

   a. Incorrect. She is not barred for any reason from treating some of the long-term care premiums as deductible.

   b. Incorrect. The limit of $1,310 would apply if she were more than 50 years old but not more than 60.

   c. Correct. Because her age (68) falls within the range of more than 60 but not more than 70, she is limited to $3,500 of premiums as a deductible amount.

   d. Incorrect. She cannot deduct her full premiums of $3,600 because of the dollar limit for her age.

6. Harvey suffers from severe cystic fibrosis. His doctor advised him to install central air conditioning in his home to alleviate his condition by controlling temperature and regulating humidity. It cost him $12,000 and increased the value of his home by $10,000. Assuming the total of his other medical costs already exceed the 7.5% AGI limit, how much of the cost of the air-conditioning installation can Harvey deduct as a medical expense?

   a. Incorrect. While capital expenditures usually are not currently deductible, an exception applies to certain medically related costs.

   b. Correct. Only the excess of the cost of the medical improvement over the increase in the value of the home, or $2,000, is a deductible expense.

   c. Incorrect. The increase in the value of the home by $10,000 **cannot** be included in medical expenses.

   d. Incorrect. The full cost of the expenditure, or $12,000, would be deductible only if the improvement did not increase the value of the home.

Chapter 21

1. On December 31, 2012, a taxpayer pays state income taxes by the following methods. Which one **cannot** be deducted on a 2012 return?

   a. Incorrect. Because the taxpayer had sufficient funds to cover the check mailed before the end of the year, it is deductible in the year of mailing even though the check is cashed in the following year.

   b. Incorrect. Personal delivery is payment on the date of delivery.

   c. Incorrect. Because the bank statement shows the funds were paid on December 31, the payment is deductible in 2012.

   d. Correct. The computer transfer is not treated as payment until it is reported on the account statement, which in this case was January 2, 2013.

2. All of the following taxes are deductible as an itemized deduction (assuming conditions are met) **except**:

   a. Incorrect. Foreign income taxes can be deducted or claimed as a foreign tax credit. However, taxpayers cannot claim a deduction or a credit for foreign taxes paid on earnings that are excluded from tax using the foreign earned income exclusion or foreign housing.

   b. Correct. No deduction can be claimed for state death taxes.

   c. Incorrect. Occupational taxes are deductible.

   d. Incorrect. Personal property taxes based on an item's value are deductible.

3. Which of the following is a deductible tax?

a. Incorrect. Homeowner's association fees are not considered a real estate tax, because they are not based on the assessed value of the property or used for the general community or a governmental purpose and so are not deductible.

b. Correct. A tenant-shareholder can deduct his or her share of real property taxes paid by a cooperative housing corporation.

c. Incorrect. Fines are nondeductible payments.

d. Incorrect. An employee cannot deduct his or her share of FICA withheld from wages.

4. Which of the following items on which sales tax is paid **cannot** be added to the amount of the sales tax deduction from the IRS table?

a. Correct. Even though jewelry can be a big-ticket item, it is not an enumerated one for purposes of adding sales tax to the amount from the table.

b. Incorrect. Sales tax on the purchase of a boat can be added to the amount from the table.

c. Incorrect. The sales tax for buying a plane is an additional deductible amount.

d. Incorrect. Sales tax on home building materials to renovate a home can be deductible in addition to the amount from the IRS table.

5. Which of the following tax payments is deductible?

a. Correct. Special assessments to benefit the entire tax district are considered a general real estate tax, the amount of which paid by the homeowner is deductible.

b. Incorrect. Special assessments to benefit the taxpayer's property are not deductible because they are not levied for the general public welfare.

c. Incorrect. Special fees or charges, including amounts for trash collection, are not deductible.

d. Incorrect. Homeowner's association charges are not taxes that are deductible.

Chapter 22

1. A taxpayer's mortgage on his personal residence was obtained in 1985 when he bought the home. This mortgage is called:

a. Correct. Because the mortgage was obtained on or before October 13, 1987, it is called grandfathered debt.

b. Incorrect. While the mortgage was obtained to buy the home, it is not treated as acquisition debt.

c. Incorrect. The mortgage is not home equity debt because of the date on which it was obtained and the purpose for which the proceeds are used.

d. Incorrect. While it is true that the mortgage is mortgage debt, there is no special category called mortgage debt in the tax law.

2. All of the following can be treated as a qualified home **except**:

a. Incorrect. A condominium is a qualified home.

b. Incorrect. A mobile home with sleeping, cooking, and toilet facilities is a qualified home.

c. Correct. A motor boat lacking toilet facilities cannot be treated as a qualified home.

d. Incorrect. The unit in which the taxpayer resides is a qualified home.

3. Which of the following is **not** deductible?

a. Incorrect. A late payment charge on a mortgage is deductible.

b. Incorrect. Prepaid interest can be deducted, although the deduction usually is spread over the term of the loan.

c. Incorrect. A prepayment penalty on a mortgage is deductible.

d. Correct. A taxpayer cannot deduct interest paid through mortgage assistance payments under section 235 of the National Housing Act.

4. Which of the following is **not** a condition for deducting points in the year of payment?

   a. Correct. There is no AGI limit on deducting points.

   b. Incorrect. It is true that the proceeds of the loan must be used to buy, build, or substantially improve the taxpayer's principal residence.

   c. Incorrect. It is correct that the charging of points must be an established business practice in the area in which the mortgage is obtained.

   d. Incorrect. It is true that the amount of points cannot exceed those generally charged in the area.

5. For purposes of figuring the deduction for investment interest, which is **not** treated as investment income?

   a. Correct. The default rule is that net long-term capital gains are not treated as investment income. Net long-term capital gains are included in investment income only if the taxpayer makes a special election to include them.

   b. Incorrect. Investment income includes interest earned on a bank account or certificate of deposit.

   c. Incorrect. A taxpayer who elects to treat qualified dividends as ordinary income can count the dividends as investment income.

   d. Incorrect. Royalties are treated as investment income as long as they are not derived from a trade or business.

Chapter 23

1. Which of these organizations is **not** a qualified organization for charitable contribution purposes?

   a. Incorrect. An organization that fosters international amateur sports is treated as a qualified organization, even though it involves an international activity.

   b. Incorrect. A war veterans' post is within the category of organizations that are qualified.

   c. Correct. Foreign charities, such as a church in Brazil, do not qualify (with the exception of those in Canada, Israel, and Mexico if certain conditions are met).

   d. Incorrect. The U.S. government and any other state, political subdivision, the District of Columbia, and U.S. possessions are qualified organizations.

2. Earl pays $100 to attend a charity theater party. The tickets for this performance normally cost $75. His adjusted gross income is $36,000. How much can Earl deduct as an itemized deduction?

   a. Correct. The deduction is limited to Earl's payment in excess of the value of the ticket, which is $25 ($100 – $75).

   b. Incorrect. The deduction is not equal to the value of the ticket, or $75.

   c. Incorrect. The deduction is not the amount of Earl's payment of $100. However, if Earl declines to accept the ticket so the organization can give it to someone else, his full payment is deductible.

   d. Incorrect. The 50% of AGI limitation on cash donations, which for Earl is $18,000 (50% of $36,000), is not the amount of the deduction; it is only a limit on the deduction.

3. Which of the following types of out-of-pocket volunteer expenses is **not** deductible?

   a. Correct. The cost of attending a convention as a member of the organization is not deductible; only the cost of attending as a delegate or representative enables a taxpayer to write-off travel costs.

   b. Incorrect. The cost of uniforms to perform services as a volunteer are deductible as long as they are not suitable for normal everyday use.

   c. Incorrect. Driving to and from a school to volunteer in the classroom is deductible based on actual gas and oil costs or at the rate of 14¢ per mile.

   d. Incorrect. As long as there is no significant element of personal pleasure, recreation, or vacation in the travel, then the cost of airfare and other travel expenses are deductible; full-time volunteer work on an archeological dig would seem to meet this requirement.

4. Which of the following contributions is deductible?

   a. Incorrect. Donations to a nonqualified organization, such as a country club, are not deductible.

   b. Incorrect. Contributions directly to an individual, such as those made to help a neighbor who suffered property damage in a fire, are not deductible.

   c. Incorrect. No deduction can be taken for the value of services provided to a qualified charity, such as a preparer's comparable fee to do a tax return.

   d. Correct. As long as the special relief fund set up to help victims of Hurricane Sandy is a qualified organization, then donations to it are deductible.

5. In which situation can a charitable deduction be claimed even though the taxpayer has no receipt?

   a. Incorrect. Cash donations of any amount, even donations of less than $250 made in the church collection plate, must be proved by a canceled check or other acceptable receipt.

   b. Correct. No receipt is required for used clothing of less than $250 that is put in the Salvation Army drop box.

   c. Incorrect. Even out-of-pocket volunteer costs of $250 or more must have documentation, including receipts and an acknowledgment from the organization.

   d. Incorrect. The fact that the donated property is self-created does not alleviate the taxpayer from obtaining required receipts and other documentation.

6. Which statement concerning charitable contribution amounts in excess of the applicable AGI limit is correct?

   a. Incorrect. There is no carryback for excess contribution amounts.

   b. Incorrect. There is no unlimited carryforward for contributions in excess of the applicable AGI limit.

   c. Correct. Unused amounts can be carried forward for up to five years; they are subject to the same applicable AGI limits in the carryforward years.

   d. Incorrect. It is not true that unused amounts are lost forever and cannot be carried back or forward because of the limited carryforward option.

7. In which situation must Form 8283 be filed?

   a. Incorrect. Cash donations of any amount do not require the filing of Form 8283.

   b. Incorrect. A donation of used clothing valued at $350 does not trigger the filing of Form 8283 because the value is below the $500 filing threshold for the form.

   c. Incorrect. Unreimbursed volunteer expenses of any amount need not be reported on the form.

   d. Correct. Any noncash donation valued at over $500 will require the taxpayer to file Form 8283.

8. Stan donates his old car to a charity. He bought the car for $15,000 and now estimates that it is worth $700, but the charity immediately sells it for $450. What can Stan deduct?

   a. Incorrect. The charitable deduction for a donation of property that has decreased in value is generally limited to the lesser of the donor's basis or FMV at the time of contribution. Since both are greater than zero, Stan's deduction is more than $0.

   b. Incorrect. Because the charity sold the vehicle for less than $500, Stan can deduct $500, which is the lesser of $500 or the FMV of the vehicle.

   c. Correct. Because the charity sold the vehicle for less than $500, Stan can deduct $500, which is the lesser of $500 or the FMV of the vehicle.

   d. Incorrect. Stan cannot deduct the value he thought his car was worth, or $700, because the charity sold the car for less than $500. His deduction is limited to $500, which is the lesser of $500 or the FMV of the vehicle ($700).

Chapter 24

1. Which of the following is **not** a casualty?

   a. Incorrect. A terrorist attack is a casualty because it is sudden and unexpected.

   b. Correct. A puppy's damage to carpeting is not a casualty; it can be expected that a puppy might damage carpeting.

   c. Incorrect. A tornado is a storm treated as a casualty.

   d. Incorrect. While most damage to trees and shrubs from infestation is gradual and cannot be treated as a casualty, a rare infestation of beetles, which is unexpected or unusual, can be a casualty.

2. All of the following can be treated as a theft **except**:

   a. Incorrect. Blackmail, which is treated as a theft under state law, is a theft for tax purposes.

   b. Incorrect. Embezzlement can be treated as a theft.

   c. Correct. Missing or lost property, including lost money, is not a theft; only a taking under state law is a theft.

   d. Incorrect. A mugging is a type of robbery, which is a theft.

3. Which of the following options **cannot** be used to deduct losses on a bank deposit?
   a. Incorrect. A loss on a bank deposit can be deducted as a casualty loss, subject to the $100 and 10% limits.
   b. Incorrect. A loss on a bank deposit up to a set dollar limit can be deducted as an ordinary loss.
   c. Incorrect. A taxpayer can opt to deduct a loss on a bank deposit as a nonbusiness bad debt (short-term capital loss).
   d. Correct. There is no rule in the tax law allowing a loss on a bank deposit to be deducted as a long-term capital loss.

4. A taxpayer's car is stolen. The taxpayer paid $22,000 for the car; it was worth $12,000 at the time it was stolen. Insurance paid her $11,000. Her adjusted gross income for the year of the theft is $45,000. What is the amount of the taxpayer's deductible theft loss?
   a. Correct. The amount of the taxpayer's loss is $1,000 (the lesser of $22,000 adjusted basis or $12,000 FMV decreased by the $11,000 insurance reimbursement). However, after applying the $100 and 10%-of-AGI limits, the taxpayer does not have a deductible loss.
   b. Incorrect. While the taxpayer's loss is $1,000, and after applying the $100 limit, the taxpayer would have a $900 loss, the loss cannot be claimed because of the 10%-of-AGI limit.
   c. Incorrect. The taxpayer's loss of $1,000 is not deductible because of the $100 and 10%-of-AGI limits.
   d. Incorrect. The taxpayer's loss is $1,000, not $11,000, and the loss is not deductible because of the $100 and 10% limits.

5. Which of the following is **unique** about a disaster loss?
   a. Incorrect. The $100 limit continues to apply to a disaster loss.
   b. Correct. Only the timing of a disaster loss is different from a regular casualty loss. The deduction can be claimed in the year of the disaster or the prior year.
   c. Incorrect. A disaster loss is subject to the 10% limit.
   d. Incorrect. The measure of a disaster loss is the same as a casualty loss; adjusted basis must be taken into account.

6. To prove a theft loss, the taxpayer should be able to show all of the following **except**:
   a. Incorrect. To prove a theft loss, the taxpayer must be able to show that the taking constitutes a theft under state law (i.e., property has been stolen).
   b. Incorrect. In order to claim a theft loss, the taxpayer must be able to show when the discovery was made that the property was missing.
   c. Incorrect. A theft loss requires a taxpayer to disclose whether a claim for reimbursement exists and whether there is a reasonable expectation of recovery.
   d. Correct. To establish a theft loss, it is not necessary to prove that the property was worth more the taxpayer's adjusted basis at the time of the theft. Instead, the taxpayer must show that he or she owns the property in question.

Chapter 25

1. Which of the following miscellaneous itemized expenses is **not** subject to the 2% limit?
   a. Incorrect. Unreimbursed employee business expenses are subject to the 2% limit after figuring the deductible amount of such expenses on Form 2106, (or Form 2106-EZ).
   b. Incorrect. Fees for e-filing a state income tax return are subject to the 2% limit.
   c. Incorrect. Fees to submit an amended return or file a petition in court to obtain a tax refund are subject to the 2% limit.
   d. Correct. The 2% limit does not apply to impairment-related work expenses.

2. All of the following can be deducted without regard to the 2% limit **except**:
   a. Incorrect. The 2% limit does not apply to amortizable premiums on taxable bonds.
   b. Incorrect. Unrecovered investment in an employee annuity is not subject to the 2% limit.
   c. Correct. Personal income tax preparation fees are deductible only after application of the 2% limit.
   d. Incorrect. Impairment-related work expenses are deductible without regard to the 2% limit.

3. Gambling losses are deductible:

   a. Incorrect. Gambling winnings reported as taxable income cannot be reduced by gambling losses.

   b. Incorrect. Gambling losses are not deductible in excess of winnings.

   c. Incorrect. While it is true that gambling losses are limited to the extent of gambling winnings, the 2% limit does not apply.

   d. Correct. While losses are limited to the extent of gambling winnings, the deductible portion can be claimed without regard to the 2% limit.

4. Which of the following is deductible as a miscellaneous itemized deduction?

   a. Incorrect. ATM fees on a personal bank account are not deductible as a miscellaneous itemized expense, even if the account is interest bearing.

   b. Correct. If all funds in the Roth IRA account have been withdrawn and the taxpayer has no other accounts, the difference between the amount contributed and the amount withdrawn is a loss deductible as a miscellaneous itemized deduction subject to the 2% limit.

   c. Incorrect. Campaign expenses for a candidate, as well as contributions to the campaign, are not deductible. This is so even for a candidate seeking reelection.

   d. Incorrect. Commuting expenses, such as subway fare to and from work, are not deductible.

5. Which of the following miscellaneous itemized deductions is entered directly on Schedule A?

   a. Correct. Tax preparation fees for a taxpayer's personal income tax return do not have to be entered on any other form or schedule before being entered on Schedule A.

   b. Incorrect. Form 4684 must be used first to figure the loss from a theft of a taxpayer's personal computer before entering the amount on Schedule A. See Chapter 24.

   c. Incorrect. An employee's meal costs while on a business trip is first figured on Form 2106 (or Form 2106-EZ) before entering the net amount of employee business expenses on Schedule A.

   d. Incorrect. Tax preparation fees related to the preparation of Schedule C can be deducted on Schedule C rather than on Schedule A.

Chapter 26

1. Which of the following job-related expenses are deductible?

   a. Incorrect. Commuting costs are nondeductible personal expenses; only the additional cost of hauling tools and equipment can be deducted.

   b. Incorrect. No deduction is allowed for initial professional accreditation fees.

   c. Correct. Dues to a trade association are a deductible expense.

   d. Incorrect. Country club membership dues are not deductible but business meals and entertainment at the club may be deductible.

2. Which statement concerning a tax home is correct?

   a. Incorrect. Spouses can have different tax homes.

   b. Incorrect. A job location rather than the family's residence is usually the tax home.

   c. Incorrect. A taxpayer without a regular or main place of business or work can have a tax home at their place of residence if they meet a multiple factor test used in determining tax home.

   d. Correct. A tax home is not limited to a specific address; it includes the entire city or general area in which the employee's work is located.

3. Which of the following jobs away from home is a temporary assignment for the entire time the taxpayer is at the job?

   a. Correct. A temporary assignment must be one that is expected to last one year or less and in fact ends within this period.

   b. Incorrect. Even though the job is expected to last no more than one year, it is not temporary because it in fact lasts for 13 months. However, if the taxpayer realistically expected this job to last for one year or less, then it will be considered temporary for that time period. Once the taxpayer knew the job would last longer than one year, the remaining expenses are not deductible because the job is not considered temporary.

   c. Incorrect. A job expected to last 14 months can never be temporary, even if it is completed in one year or less.

   d. Incorrect. A job expected to last more than one year (15 months) in this case is indefinite; the fact that it lasts for two years does not change anything.

4. Incidental expenses while away from home include all of the following costs **except**:

   a. Incorrect. Tips to hotel maids are incidental expenses.

   b. Correct. Laundry and cleaning in the hotel are not treated as incidental expenses.

   c. Incorrect. The cost of cab fare between the hotel and a restaurant is treated as an incidental travel expense.

   d. Incorrect. Mailing costs while away from home are incidental expenses.

5. An employee gives a customer a gift of two tickets to a Broadway show costing $200. The employee does not accompany the customer. What is the maximum deduction?

   a. Incorrect. $4 is the dollar limit on small items that are exempt from the usual business gift dollar limit.

   b. Incorrect. The dollar limit on business gifts of $25 need not be used here to claim the maximum deduction.

   c. Correct. The employee can choose to treat the tickets as an entertainment expense subject to the 50% limit, so the maximum deduction is $100.

   d. Incorrect. The full amount of the $200 is not deductible whether the employee treats the tickets as a gift or an entertainment expense.

6. The inclusion amount for leased cars used for business is:

   a. Correct. The inclusion amount is a limit placed on the lease deduction for "luxury cars."

   b. Incorrect. Although the effect of the inclusion amount is to increase the taxpayer's taxable income, it does so by limiting the deduction. The inclusion amount is not itself added back to income.

   c. Incorrect. There is no dollar limit on the deduction for cars.

   d. Incorrect. The inclusion amount is not an alternative for figuring the deduction in lieu of using the standard mileage rate.

7. What is **not** a requirement for a reimbursement arrangement to be treated as an accountable plan?

   a. Incorrect. The expense must have a business connection.

   b. Incorrect. The employee must adequately account for expenses to the employer within a reasonable time (usually 60 days).

   c. Incorrect. The employee has to return any excess reimbursement within a reasonable time (usually 120 days).

   d. Correct. It is the employer, not the employee, who sets up an accountable plan.

Chapter 27

1. Which of the following is **not** specifically taken into account in determining the EIC?

   a. Incorrect. Tax-free combat pay can be treated as part of earned income. If the taxpayer makes an election, nontaxable combat pay is part of the income on which the credit is figured.

   b. Incorrect. A taxpayer must have earned income in order to claim the EIC.

   c. Incorrect. Adjusted gross income works as a limitation on the amount of the credit.

   d. Correct. There is no taxable income limit on the credit; taxable income does not factor into any computation for the credit (other than its inclusion in AGI or earned income).

2. Which of the following individuals is **not** a qualifying child for EIC?

   a. Correct. Even though the 26-year-old graduate student living with her parents may be claimed as the parents' dependent, she does not meet the definition of a qualifying child for the EIC.

   b. Incorrect. An 18-year-old child of the taxpayer who is younger than the taxpayer is a qualifying child.

   c. Incorrect. There is no age limit for a child who is permanently and totally disabled.

   d. Incorrect. A parent's qualifying child includes a child under age 24 who is a full-time college student.

3. Which of the following filing statuses is ineligible to claim the EIC?

a. Incorrect. Someone who is single can qualify for the EIC.

b. Correct. A married person filing separately cannot claim the EIC.

c. Incorrect. A head of household filer is eligible for the EIC.

d. Incorrect. A qualifying widow(er) can claim the EIC.

4. A taxpayer whose EIC was previously disallowed due to reckless disregard is barred from claiming the credit for:

a. Incorrect. One year is not the full period in which the EIC cannot be claimed following a reduction or disallowance due to recklessness.

b. Correct. The EIC cannot be claimed for two years if the credit was previously reduced or disallowed due to reckless or intentional disregard.

c. Incorrect. The 10-year disallowance period applies in the case of fraud.

d. Incorrect. There is no permanent bar to claiming the EIC following a disallowance for any reason.

5. Which form must be filed with the return following a disallowance or reduction of EIC for any reason other than a math or clerical error?

a. Incorrect. Worksheet A is used to figure income for taxpayers who are employees.

b. Incorrect. Worksheet B is used to figure income for taxpayers with self-employment income.

c. Correct. Form 8862 must be used following a reduction or disallowance in the EIC due to reckless or intentional disregard or fraud.

d. Incorrect. Form 8867 is a preparer's aid for claiming the EIC on a taxpayer's return.

Chapter 28

1. The maximum amount of the child and dependent care credit for a taxpayer with two qualifying children is:

a. Incorrect. $1,050 is the maximum credit amount for a taxpayer with one qualifying person ($3,000 × 35%).

b. Correct. $2,100 is the maximum credit amount for a taxpayer with two or more qualifying persons ($6,000 × 35%).

c. Incorrect. $3,000 is the maximum amount of work-related expenses taken into account in figuring the credit for one qualifying person.

d. Incorrect. $6,000 is the maximum amount of work-related expenses taken into account in figuring the credit for two or more qualifying persons.

2. A taxpayer using the following filing status **cannot** claim the child and dependent care credit?

a. Incorrect. The credit can be claimed by a taxpayer who files as single.

b. Incorrect. A taxpayer who files as head of household can claim the credit.

c. Incorrect. A taxpayer who files as qualifying widow(er) can claim the credit.

d. Correct. A married taxpayer who files a separate return cannot claim the credit.

3. A taxpayer's child celebrates his 13th birthday on May 15. Only expenses paid for care provided through which date qualify for the child and dependent care credit (assuming other requirements are met)?

a. Incorrect. April 15, the date when individual income tax returns are generally due, has no bearing on whether dependent care expenses qualify.

b. Correct. Only expenses paid through the day before the qualifying child's 13th birthday are eligible expenses for the credit (assuming other requirements are met).

c. Incorrect. Eligible expenses are those that are incurred on the date *before* the child turns age 13, not the child's birth date.

d. Incorrect. Expenses through the end of the year in which the child turns 13 do not qualify once this age limit is met.

4. Which of the following is **not** treated as earned income for purposes of the child and dependent care credit?

   a. Incorrect. Disability benefits reported as wages, typically until the taxpayer reaches the normal retirement age, are treated as earned income.

   b. Correct. Pensions and annuities are not treated as earned income.

   c. Incorrect. While nontaxable combat pay usually is excluded from income, the taxpayer can elect to include the pay in income.

   d. Incorrect. Strike benefits reported as wages are considered earned income.

5. Which of the following is **not** a work-related expense for a child under age 13 for purposes of the child and dependent care credit?

   a. Correct. The cost of overnight camp is cannot be taken into account in figuring the credit

   b. Incorrect. The cost of day camp is an eligible expense.

   c. Incorrect. The cost of any school before kindergarten, including preschool tuition, is an eligible expense.

   d. Incorrect. Work-related expenses include daycare center costs.

6. A taxpayer pays a housekeeper to watch his daughter while he is at work. Which of the following need **not** be included on or attached to the taxpayer's return?

   a. Incorrect. Form 2441 must be completed and attached to the return.

   b. Incorrect. The taxpayer must include the housekeeper's SSN on Form 2441

   c. Correct. While the taxpayer should retain canceled checks of payments to the housekeeper, they do not have to be attached to the return.

   d. Incorrect. Form 2441 requires that the housekeeper's name and address be included.

Chapter 29

1. Which of the following statements about the child tax credit is correct?

   a. Incorrect. There is no limit on the number of qualifying children for whom the credit can be claimed.

   b. Incorrect. There are no special expenditures or outlays required to claim the credit.

   c. Correct. The credit can be claimed only if the qualifying child is under the age of 17 at the end of the year.

   d. Incorrect. The credit is reduced or eliminated if the taxpayer's MAGI exceeds set limits (depending on filing status).

2. Which of the following individuals **cannot** be a qualifying child, even if under age 17?

   a. Correct. An aunt cannot be a qualifying child because this is not a qualifying relationship.

   b. Incorrect. A nephew can be a qualifying child because he is a descendant of a brother or sister.

   c. Incorrect. A grandchild can be a qualifying child because he or she is a descendant of the taxpayer's child.

   d. Incorrect. A foster child is a qualifying child because this is a qualifying relationship.

3. A taxpayer has four children under the age of 17 and files head of household. Assuming eligibility tests are met and the taxpayer's MAGI is $80,000, what is the maximum child tax credit that can be claimed (assuming sufficient tax liability)?

   a. Incorrect. $1,000 is the limit for one qualifying child.

   b. Incorrect. $1,500 is not the correct amount.

   c. Correct. $3,750 is the result of four qualifying children at a maximum credit of $1,000 per child ($4,000), reduced by the taxpayer's MAGI limit. The phase-out range for a taxpayer who files as head of household begins at $75,000. With a MAGI of $80,000, the child tax credit is reduced $50 for every $1,000 over $75,000. The disallowed amount is $50 × 5 = $250, and the credit allowed is $4,000 – $250 = $3,750.

   d. Incorrect. The taxpayer could claim a child tax credit of $4,000 only if his MAGI was below the phase-out range.

4. The additional child tax credit is the lesser of the child tax credit amount greater than tax liability or 15% of _________ in excess of $3,000.

a. Incorrect. Adjusted gross income is used for the child and dependent care credit but not for the child tax credit.

b. Incorrect. Modified adjusted gross income is used as a limitation on the regular child tax credit.

c. Correct. Earned income is used to figure the additional child tax credit.

d. Incorrect. Taxable income does not come into play for the additional child tax credit; however, tax liability can be a factor.

5. A single taxpayer is the custodial parent of two children under the age of 17, and she claimed the dependency exemption for both of them. Her wages are $48,000 and she has no other income. Her ex-spouse, the noncustodial parent, has earned income of $69,000. Neither parent claims a foreign earned income exclusion. Which parent can claim the child tax credit and for how much?

a. Incorrect. The parents do not split the credit between themselves unless each claims a dependency exemption for one of the children.

b. Correct. Because the custodial parent claims the dependency exemption for the children, this parent is eligible for the credit; based on the custodial parent's income, the full credit ($1,000 × 2 qualifying children) is allowed.

c. Incorrect. The noncustodial parent cannot claim the child tax credit unless he or she is entitled to claim dependency exemptions for the qualifying children.

d. Incorrect. Children who are qualifying children of both parents do not bar the parent eligible for the dependency exemption from claiming the child tax credit (subject to income limits).

Chapter 30

1. In figuring an education credit, the amount of eligible expenses taken into account must be reduced by:

a. Incorrect. Gifts do not reduce qualified education expenses.

b. Incorrect. No reduction of qualified education expenses is required when they are paid with an inheritance.

c. Correct. Tax-free education benefits, including distributions from 529 plans, reduce the amount of qualified education expenses used for figuring an education credit.

d. Incorrect. Expenses paid with student loans are not reduced by the amount of the loans.

2. The maximum American Opportunity Tax Credit is:

a. Incorrect. $1,000 is increment of expenses taken into account to figure the American Opportunity Tax Credit.

b. Incorrect. The top Lifetime Learning Credit is $2,000.

c. Correct. The credit is 100% of the first $2,000, plus 25% of the next $2,000, for a maximum credit of $2,500.

d. Incorrect. The amount of expenses taken into account in figuring the Lifetime Learning Credit is $10,000.

3. Which of the following expenses qualify for the American Opportunity Tax Credit?

a. Correct. Books required for a course of study are qualified expenses, whether paid to the educational institution or not.

b. Incorrect. Student health fees cannot be treated as qualified expenses.

c. Incorrect. Room and board are not qualified expenses.

d. Incorrect. Transportation is a personal expense that is not qualified for an education credit.

4. Which of the following rules applies to the American Opportunity Tax Credit but not to the Lifetime Learning Credit?
   a. Incorrect. The student must be the taxpayer's dependent (or the taxpayer or spouse) for purposes of both education credits.
   b. Correct. Although the student cannot have a felony drug conviction to be eligible for the American Opportunity Tax Credit, such a conviction will not disqualify the student for the Lifetime Learning Credit.
   c. Incorrect. The taxpayer, if married, must file a joint return in order to claim either education credit.
   d. Incorrect. Both credits require that the taxpayer (and spouse, if married) be a U.S. citizen or resident alien.

5. In 2011, a taxpayer claimed an American Opportunity Tax Credit. In 2012, the student receives a scholarship and a refund of tuition that had been the basis of the 2011 credit. What should the taxpayer do?
   a. Incorrect. The taxpayer cannot ignore the receipt of the tax-free assistance, even though the 2011 return has been filed.
   b. Incorrect. The taxpayer should not file an amended return for 2011 to refigure the credit.
   c. Incorrect. While the taxpayer must figure a recapture amount, it is not reported on the 2012 return as other income on Form 1040, line 21.
   d. Correct. Report the recapture amount on the 2012 return as additional tax.

Chapter 31

1. Which statement about the credit for qualified retirement savings contributions is true?
   a. Incorrect. Income limits determine whether the taxpayer's percentage for the credit is 50%, 20%, 10%, or zero.
   b. Correct. The maximum credit is $1,000 (50% of contributions or elective deferrals up to $2,000).
   c. Incorrect. The taxpayer can claim *both* the credit and a deduction for IRA contributions on which the credit is figured.
   d. Incorrect. The credit is nonrefundable.

2. A taxpayer installs solar panels on her home at a cost of $20,000. What is the maximum amount of the credit that can be claimed?
   a. Incorrect. While the nonbusiness energy credit for insulation and certain other energy-improvements to the home expired in 2011, the credit for alternative energy improvements to the home continues to apply.
   b. Incorrect. The $500 refers to the credit for fuel cells, which is limited to $500 for each one-half kilowatt of capacity of the property.
   c. Correct. The credit is 30% of eligible costs ($20,000 × 30% = $6,000).
   d. Incorrect. The credit is not the full amount of the solar panels' cost ($20,000), but 30% of that amount ($6,000).

3. In 2012, which statement about the adoption credit is **false**?
   a. Incorrect. The adoption credit for 2012 is refundable.
   b. Incorrect. The maximum credit amount in 2012 is $12,650.
   c. Correct. Income limits may restrict or prevent the claiming of an adoption credit.
   d. Incorrect. The credit is not restricted to adoption of a child who is a U.S. citizen or resident; it can apply to the adoption of a foreign child.

4. Who **cannot** take the health coverage tax credit (assuming all other eligibility requirements are met):
   a. Correct. Even if a taxpayer is a TAA, ATAA, RTAA, or PBGC recipient, he or she is ineligible if claimed as a dependent by another person.
   b. Incorrect. An eligible trade adjustment assistance recipient can claim the credit.
   c. Incorrect. A reemployment TAA recipient is a category of taxpayer who can claim the credit.
   d. Incorrect. A PBGC pension recipient can claim the credit if not on Medicare or covered by certain other health plans.

5. A single taxpayer with modified adjusted gross income of $28,000 makes a salary reduction contribution to her employer's 401(k) plan of $3,000. Her retirement Saver's Credit is:

   a. Correct. Because her MAGI is not more than $28,750, her credit is $3,000 × 10%, or $300.

   b. Incorrect. If her MAGI had been more than $17,250 but not more than $18,750, her credit would have been $600 ($3,000 × 20%).

   c. Incorrect. She would have qualified for a $1,500 credit ($3,000 × 50%) if her MAGI had not exceeded $17,250.

   d. Incorrect. While the $3,000 is excluded from gross income, this full amount is not the amount of the credit.

Chapter 32

1. Which of the following items is **not** taken into account in figuring taxable income?

   a. Incorrect. Gross income is the starting point for determining taxable income.

   b. Incorrect. Adjustments to gross income are subtracted from gross income to help determine taxable income.

   c. Incorrect. Personal and dependency exemptions are taken into account in figuring taxable income.

   d. Correct. Tax credits are not taken into account until *after* the tax is figured on taxable income.

2. The tax table **cannot** be used if:

   a. Incorrect. A married person filing separately is not barred from using the tax tables.

   b. Correct. The tax tables cannot be used once taxable income reaches $100,000.

   c. Incorrect. The tax tables can be used regardless of which income tax form is filed.

   d. Incorrect. Tax credits have nothing to do with figuring the regular income tax, so the tables can be used even if credits are later claimed.

3. Assume a taxpayer is in the 28% tax bracket. The maximum tax rate on qualified dividends in 2012 is:

   a. Incorrect. The zero tax applies only to taxpayers in the 10% or 15% tax bracket.

   b. Correct. The top tax rate on qualified dividends for a taxpayer in any tax bracket above 15% is 15%.

   c. Incorrect. The 25% rate applies to unrecaptured depreciation.

   d. Incorrect. The 28% rate applies to section 1202 gains and collectibles gains.

4. A farmer who opts to use income averaging averages income over ___________:

   a. Incorrect. The 10-year averaging period applies for certain lump-sum gains from qualified retirement plans.

   b. Incorrect. There is no 5-year income averaging option.

   c. Correct. Under farm income averaging, farm income is averaged over the 3 prior years.

   d. Incorrect. The current year is not taken into account for farm income averaging purposes.

5. Marcia, a U.S. citizen who works in a foreign country, earned a salary of $110,000 in 2012 and has no other income. She files her return excluding $95,000 under the foreign earned income exclusion. She files her return using the single filing status and claims one personal exemption. What is the marginal tax rate on her taxable income?

   a. Incorrect. Marcia has some taxable income after claiming the foreign earned income exclusion, standard deduction, and personal exemption, and she is subject to tax at a marginal tax rate that takes into account her foreign earned income as if none of it was excluded.

   b. Incorrect. Under what is known as the stacking rule, Marcia's marginal tax rate is the rate that would have applied if she had not claimed the foreign earned income exclusion.

   c. Correct. Under the stacking rule, Marcia's marginal tax rate is the rate that would have applied if she had not claimed the foreign earned income exclusion. Thus, her marginal bracket is the 28% bracket.

   d. Incorrect. The tax on the income that was not excluded is taxed at 28%, the bracket Marcia would be in if she had not claimed the foreign earned income exclusion.

Chapter 33

1. A taxpayer itemizes deductions. The starting point for figuring AMT is:
   a. Incorrect. While gross income naturally factors into the computation of AMT, it is not the starting point.
   b. Incorrect. Adjusted gross income is the starting point for a taxpayer who claims the standard deduction.
   c. Correct. Adjusted gross income less itemized deductions is the starting point for a taxpayer who itemizes deductions.
   d. Incorrect. Regular tax is used to determine the extent of AMT liability, if any, but is not the starting point for the computation.

2. Which of the following is a deferral item?
   a. Correct. The adjustment for exercising incentive stock options is a deferral item because the difference between AMT and regular tax is due to timing.
   b. Incorrect. Personal and dependency exemptions are treated as exclusion items because they are never deductible for AMT purposes.
   c. Incorrect. State and local taxes, which are not deductible for AMT purposes, are exclusion items because they are never deductible for AMT purposes.
   d. Incorrect. The interest on private activity bonds generally is an exclusion item.

3. A taxpayer is likely to have a refundable minimum tax credit if she has:
   a. Incorrect. While having a large number of dependents can create or trigger AMT, it does not impact the refundable minimum tax credit.
   b. Correct. A taxpayer who had a large AMT liability in the past from the exercise of ISOs may qualify for a refundable minimum tax credit.
   c. Incorrect. While having a large number of any deferral items may create a minimum tax credit, it does not necessarily result in a *refundable* minimum tax credit.
   d. Incorrect. Exclusion items do not create any minimum tax credit.

4. Which of the following would **not** impact the alternative minimum tax?
   a. Incorrect. Only medical deductions above 10% of AGI are deductible for AMT purposes while such deductions over 7.5% are deductible for regular tax purposes.
   b. Incorrect. Miscellaneous itemized deductions are not deductible for AMT purposes.
   c. Correct. Charitable contributions are deductible for *both* the regular tax and the AMT.
   d. Incorrect. While interest on private activity bonds issued in 2012 is exempt from regular tax, it is included in AMTI.

Chapter 34

1. The kiddie tax applies to all of the following types of income **except**:
   a. Correct. The kiddie tax does not apply to earned income, which includes tips for services.
   b. Incorrect. Interest income is investment income subject to the kiddie tax.
   c. Incorrect. Dividends are subject to the kiddie tax.
   d. Incorrect. The taxable portion of Social Security benefits is treated as investment income for purposes of the kiddie tax.

2. Which of the following persons is **not** a child who may be subject to the kiddie tax?
   a. Incorrect. A child who is 15 years old with investment income is subject to the kiddie tax.
   b. Incorrect. The kiddie tax applies to a child who is 17 years old; the exception for children who have earned income that is more than half of his or her support does not apply to children under age 18.
   c. Incorrect. A full-time student, age 22, who did not have earned income that was more than half of his or her support because he or she is under the age of 24 may be subject to the kiddie tax.
   d. Correct. A child (regardless of age or earned income) who files a joint return is not subject to the kiddie tax.

3. Which itemized deductions of a child can reduce the amount of investment income subject to the kiddie tax?

a. Incorrect. While a child subject to the kiddie tax can claim charitable contributions, they do not offset investment income subject to the kiddie tax.

b. Incorrect. While unreimbursed employee business expenses are part of miscellaneous itemized deductions, they do not offset investment income subject to the kiddie tax.

c. Correct. Expenses directly connected to investment income (in excess of the 2%-of-AGI floor) can offset investment income.

d. Incorrect. While a child can claim an itemized deduction for medical expenses, such expenses do not offset investment income for purposes of the kiddie tax.

4. The parents of a child subject to the kiddie tax are divorced. The father is unmarried. The mother is remarried. The child lives with the mother, who is the custodial parent, and her new spouse. Which parent can make an election on Form 8814?

a. Incorrect. The father cannot make the election because he is not the custodial parent.

b. Correct. The mother who files jointly with her new spouse can make the election because she is the custodial parent.

c. Incorrect. The mother who files separately from her new spouse cannot make the election if her taxable income is lower than the taxable income of her new spouse.

d. Incorrect. The parents do not have to be married to each other in order for one of them to make the election.

5. Making the election to report a child's interest and dividends on the parent's return (using Form 8814) can be favorable to the parent with respect to:

a. Incorrect. The election increases the parent's AGI, which can limit the deduction for student loan interest.

b. Correct. The election increases the parent's AGI, which can mean taxpayers who make large charitable contributions that were limited by the 50%-of-AGI rule may be able to claim an increased deduction for charitable contributions.

c. Incorrect. The election increases the AGI threshold for claiming an itemized deduction for medical expenses, thus decreasing the allowable deduction.

d. Incorrect. The election can result in a lower credit for child and dependent care expenses because the credit percentage is tied to AGI.

Chapter 35

1. All of the following statements about self-employment tax are correct **except**:

a. Incorrect. Self-employment tax applies to net earnings reported on Schedule C.

b. Incorrect. A taxpayer with net earnings reported on Schedule F must pay self-employment tax.

c. Correct. Self-employment tax does not apply to unallocated tips. Employees must figure their share of Social Security and Medicare tax on these tips, but the tax is not self-employment tax.

d. Incorrect. Self-employment tax applies to an individual's net earnings from self-employment derived from their trade or business.

2. Which is **not** a penalty tax related to qualified retirement plans and IRAs?

a. Correct. A Coverdell ESA is an education account, not a retirement account, so the penalty on certain distributions from a Coverdell ESA does not relate to retirement plans or IRAs.

b. Incorrect. The penalty on early distributions is from premature withdrawals from qualified retirement plans and IRAs.

c. Incorrect. The penalty on excess contributions applies when too much is added to a qualified retirement plan or IRA.

d. Incorrect. The penalty on excess accumulations applies when insufficient withdrawals are taken from a qualified retirement plan or IRA.

3. Which of the following exceptions to the early distribution penalty applies only to IRAs and not to qualified retirement plans?

a. Incorrect. There is no penalty on early withdrawals taken as a series of substantially equal periodic payments from a qualified retirement plan or IRA.

b. Incorrect. The disability exception applies to both qualified plans and IRAs.

c. Correct. The penalty is avoided only in the case of an IRA when distributions are taken to pay certain education costs.

d. Incorrect. The exception for IRS levies applies to qualified retirement plans and IRAs.

4. Which of the following statements about household employment taxes is **not** correct?

a. Incorrect. It is true that FICA only applies if the taxpayer pays $1,700 or more to a worker (other than a spouse, child under the age of 21, the taxpayer's parent, or any employee under age 18).

b. Correct. Household employment taxes are paid through estimated taxpayer or with the taxpayer's return; there is no requirement to deposit the taxes with the U.S. Treasury.

c. Incorrect. FUTA applies when the taxpayer paid total cash wages of $1,000 or more in any calendar quarter in 2010 or 2011; payments to a spouse, child under age 21, or a parent are not taken into account.

d. Incorrect. There is no mandatory income tax withholding; it applies only if the employee requests it and the taxpayer agrees to this.

5. In 2008, a taxpayer claimed a $7,500 first-time homebuyer credit and continues to live in the home. Which of the following statements is correct?

a. Correct. The taxpayer must report $500 ($7,500 ÷ 15 years) as recapture (additional tax) on his or her 2011 tax return.

b. Incorrect. The ability to avoid recapture applies only if the home was purchased after 2008.

c. Incorrect. A taxpayer who purchased a home after 2008 is not subject to recapture as long as he or she stays in the home for 36 months, a period that was completed in 2011. This rule does not apply to homes bought in 2008.

d. Incorrect. While the repayment period runs for 15 years, it must be repaid ratably over this period. A taxpayer cannot wait 15 years to repay the tax credit.

6. In 2009, a taxpayer claimed the first-time homebuyer credit. Which situation would require recapture of the credit in 2012?

a. Incorrect. There is no recapture of the credit if the home is sold at a loss.

b. Incorrect. The transfer of the home to a former spouse incident to a divorce does not trigger the recapture unless that home is subsequently sold.

c. Incorrect. The death of a homeowner is a reason for not recapturing the first-time homebuyer credit.

d. Correct. There is no exception from the recapture of the first-time homebuyer credit if the sale is motivated by the owner obtaining a new job.

7. Which penalty amount applies if a taxpayer fails to take required minimum distributions?

a. Incorrect. There is no 5% penalty; this percentage defines an owner who cannot postpone receipt of RMDs from a qualified plan until retirement.

b. Incorrect. The 6% penalty applies to excess contributions.

c. Incorrect. The 10% penalty applies to early distributions.

d. Correct. The 50% penalty applies to excess accumulations, which are amounts that should have been taken as RMDs but were not.

8. Jake, age 48, wants to roll over $50,000 from his qualified plan from his ex-employer to a rollover (non-Roth) IRA. He requests a check and receives $40,000, which he subsequently uses to open an IRA 7 weeks later. Which of the following is the **best** statement describing Jake's situation?

a. Incorrect. Even if Jake deposits the $40,000 check into an IRA, the $10,000 that was withheld must also be deposited to avoid tax and penalty.

b. Incorrect. Jake must pay a 10% penalty only on the part of the distribution that is not rolled over

c. Correct. Jake must roll over $50,000 into the IRA to avoid any tax or penalty. Therefore, he must add $10,000 out of pocket (the amount withheld by his ex-employer) to the $40,000 check received from the qualified plan.

d. Incorrect. Jake did roll over $40,000 of the distribution within 60 days, so he is not subject to a tax and or a penalty on that part of the distribution.

9. Which of the following is subject to SE tax?

a. Incorrect. Rental income is not subject to SE tax.

b. Incorrect. Distributions from an annuity, whether taxable or not, are not subject to SE tax.

c. Correct. A taxpayer with a side business is subject to SE tax on income earned from that business.

d. Incorrect. Hobby income is taxable but is not subject to SE tax because it is not self-employment income.

10. The maximum rate that a self-employed taxpayer must pay in SE tax in 2012 is:

a. Incorrect. 7.65% is the rate that an employee pays for Social Security (6.2%) and Medicare (1.45%) in years where there is not a 2-percentage-point payroll tax reduction (years before 2011).

b. Correct. 13.3% is the maximum SE tax rate for 2012, which includes 10.4% for Social Security (6.2% for the employer-equivalent portion and 4.2% for the employee portion) and 2.9% for Medicare (1.45% for each the employer and the employee portions).

c. Incorrect. 13.3% is the maximum SE tax rate for 2012.

d. Incorrect. The maximum rate is reduced from 15.3% to 13.3% for tax years 2011 and 2012.

11. The maximum amount of SE tax a taxpayer can pay in 2012 is:

a. Incorrect. $106,800 was the maximum amount of earnings subject to Social Security tax in 2011.

b. Incorrect. $110,100 is the maximum amount of earnings subject to Social Security tax in 2012.

c. Incorrect. $11,450.40 is the maximum amount of Social Security tax a self-employed taxpayer paid in 2012.

d. Correct. Because Medicare tax is not subject to an earnings limit, the maximum amount of SE tax (which includes both Social Security and Medicare tax) for which a self-employed taxpayer may be liable is theoretically unlimited.

Chapter 36

1. Which of the following tax payment methods may entail a fee?

a. Incorrect. There is no fee for taxpayers who pay their tax liability through federal income tax withholding.

b. Incorrect. A debit direct payment using an electronic funds withdrawal does not entail a fee.

c. Incorrect. There is no government-imposed fee for making a transfer via EFTPS.

d. Correct. While the IRS does not impose a fee for accepting payment by credit card, the service providers may charge a fee.

2. Which of the following statements about an installment payment agreement is **not** correct?

a. Incorrect. The IRS does not offer the agreement; a taxpayer must request one by filing Form 9465.

b. Incorrect. It is true that the repayment period usually is 36 months but can be up to 60 months.

c. Correct. Interest or penalties continue to run during the period of the agreement.

d. Incorrect. There is a fee for obtaining an agreement; the fee varies with certain factors.

3. Which of the following accounts is **not** an eligible account for purposes of accepting a direct deposit of a tax refund?

a. Correct. A direct deposit of a tax refund cannot be made into a 401(k) account.

b. Incorrect. A Coverdell education savings account can accept a direct deposit of a tax refund.

c. Incorrect. A health savings account is an eligible account for accepting a direct deposit of a tax refund.

d. Incorrect. A tax refund can be deposited directly into a checking account.

4. Estimated taxes include all of the following taxes **except**:

a. Incorrect. The self-employment tax is used for purposes of figuring estimated taxes.

b. In correct. Employment taxes for a household employee are part of a taxpayer's estimated taxes.

c. Correct. Even though the gift tax is due on the same date as the income tax, it is not a tax that is taken into account for estimated tax purposes.

d. Incorrect. Estimated taxes include the alternative minimum tax.

5. What is the amount of the accuracy-related penalty on a substantial understatement of tax?

a. Incorrect. The 2% penalty usually applies in the case of a bounced check.

b. Incorrect. The 5% penalty applies per month for the failure to file a return on time.

c. Correct. The accuracy-related penalty is 20% of the underpayment.

d. Incorrect. The penalty of 75% of the underpayment applies in the case of civil fraud.

Chapter 37

1. An individual taxpayer in the United States who cannot file an income tax return by the due date can obtain an automatic filing extension for what period of time:
   a. Incorrect. Five days is the period in which to electronically resubmit a rejected e-filed individual tax return in order for it to be considered timely.
   b. Incorrect. The two-month extension applies for taxpayers who are living outside the United States on the April filing deadline.
   c. Incorrect. The automatic four-month extension applies for taxpayers living outside the United States who need more time after the June filing deadline to submit a return.
   d. Correct. The automatic filing extension period for individuals is six months.

2. Which of the following situations requires the taxpayer to obtain a power of attorney to sign a return?
   a. Incorrect. A parent can sign a minor child's return without any special authorization.
   b. Incorrect. The spouse of someone in the military who is stationed in a combat zone can sign on behalf of the other spouse without authorization but must attach an explanation to the return.
   c. Correct. A spouse who is outside the country for 60 days prior to the return due date must authorize the other spouse to sign the return via a power of attorney form; attach Form 2848 to the return.
   d. Incorrect. The spouse of someone who is incapacitated because of a medical condition can sign on behalf of that spouse as long as that spouse directs the other to sign the return.

3. How long should tax return preparers retain Form 8879?
   a. Incorrect. The form should be retained three years from the later of the return due date or the date the IRS received the return.
   b. Incorrect. The form should be retained three years from the later of the return due date or the date the IRS received the return.
   c. Correct. The form should be retained three years from the later of the return due date or the date the IRS received the return.
   d. Incorrect. The form should be retained three years from the later of the return due date or the date the IRS received the return.

4. Which of the following is **not** a preparer's responsibility for a client's return?
   a. Correct. The refund check is sent to the client, not to the preparer.
   b. Incorrect. The preparer must retain certain records related to the client's return.
   c. Incorrect. The preparer is required to follow certain procedures after an e-filed return is rejected.
   d. Incorrect. The preparer should ensure the return is complete and accurate.

5. Which a preparer is **not** required to e-file returns?
   a. Incorrect. Because the preparer expects to file 11 or more income tax returns for individuals, the returns must be e-filed.
   b. Incorrect. The number of returns that an individual preparer anticipates filing does not control the e-file requirement as long as the preparer's firm meets the requirement.
   c. Incorrect. The e-file requirements for a preparer relate to both income tax returns for individuals and income tax returns for trusts and estates.
   d. Correct. A preparer who expects to file fewer than 11 income tax returns for individuals does not have to e-file them; he or she can choose to do so.

Chapter 38

1. For violating e-file procedures, which level of infraction usually results in only a reprimand?
   a. Correct. Level One infractions, which do not have an adverse impact on the quality of an e-filed return, typically result in only a written reprimand.
   b. Incorrect. Level Two infractions typically result in suspension from the e-file program for one year.
   c. Incorrect. Level Three infractions usually result in suspension for two years or permanent expulsion.
   d. Incorrect. The IRS usually does not issue a reprimand for any level other than Level One.

2. Which type of authorization for a tax return preparer to act is made directly on a taxpayer's return?

   a. **Correct. The limited authorization as a third-party designee is made directly on a taxpayer's return by checking a box and providing the designee's name, phone number, and personal identification number.**

   b. Incorrect. Tax information authorization is made on Form 8821.

   c. Incorrect. Designating an agent to act under a power of attorney is made on Form 2848.

   d. Incorrect. Making a declaration of representative is also made on Form 2848.

3. A tax return preparer who is unenrolled may be authorized by Form 2848 to:

   a. Incorrect. A tax return preparer who is unenrolled cannot execute waivers on behalf of a taxpayer.

   b. Incorrect. A tax return preparer who is unenrolled is not permitted to extend the statutory period for tax assessments.

   c. **Correct. A tax return preparer who is unenrolled can represent the taxpayer before customer service representatives, revenue agents, and examination officers.**

   d. Incorrect. A tax return preparer can never receive a taxpayer's refund checks.

4. A penalty of $5,000 or 50% of the income derived by the tax return preparer with respect to the return or claim applies to which action?

   a. Incorrect. The penalty for an understatement of tax liability due to an unreasonable position that has not been disclosed on the return is $1,000 or 50% of the income derived.

   b. **Correct. The penalty for an understatement of tax liability due to willful or reckless conduct is $5,000 or 50% of the income derived.**

   c. Incorrect. The penalty for aiding and abetting an understatement of tax liability is $1,000 per document.

   d. Incorrect. The penalty for failing to sign the tax return is $50 per failure, not to exceed $25,000 per calendar year.

5. The civil penalty for an improper disclosure or use of taxpayer information is:

   a. Incorrect. The $50 per failure, not to exceed $25,000 per calendar year, applies to the failure to furnish the taxpayer with a copy of the tax return.

   b. **Correct. The civil penalty is $250 per disclosure or use, not to exceed $10,000 in any calendar year.**

   c. Incorrect. The $500 per failure applies to the failure to use due diligence in determining a taxpayer's eligibility for the earned income tax credit.

   d. Incorrect. The $1,000 penalty applies to aiding and abetting an understatement.

Chapter 39

1. The Office of Professional Responsibility (OPR) is in charge of issuing PTINs. True or false?

   True. Incorrect. The Office of Professional Responsibility establishes and enforces standards of competence, integrity, and conduct for tax professionals

   False. Correct. The Return Preparer Office (RPO) oversees the administration of PTINs.

2. An individual who wants to represent her child before the IRS must be authorized by the IRS to do so. True or false?

   True. Incorrect. Only paid professionals require IRS authorization to represent someone before the IRS.

   False. Correct. An individual can represent himself or herself and immediate family members before the IRS without IRS authorization.

3. Generally, all EAs must pass a competency examination to earn their designations. True or false?

   True. Correct. EAs must pass examinations in order to obtain the appropriate designation. (IRS employees may apply for EA designation without taking the SEE exam.)

   False. Incorrect. EAs must pass examinations in order to obtain their designation.

4. The PTIN must be renewed every three years. True or false?

True. Incorrect. The renewal period for EA designation is every three years.

False. Correct. The PTIN must be renewed annually.

Chapter 40

1. Because the preparation of a tax return is covered by privilege, you need not turn over records to the IRS related to return preparation to the IRS. True or false?

True. Incorrect. The preparation of a tax return is not covered by privilege.

False. Correct. As a tax return preparer you do not create privilege by completing a tax return. Privilege may be created in some cases by attorneys and CPAs that complete returns. You must promptly submit records to the IRS if the request is proper and there is no reasonable basis to believe the records are privileged.

2. If you learn that a client has omitted income from a return, you must promptly notify the IRS. True or false?

True. Incorrect. You must advise your client (but not the IRS) promptly if you know there has been an omission from a tax return.

False. Correct. You are not obligated to notify the IRS about an omission on a client's tax return, but you must notify the client immediately.

3. You can receive a contingent fee for preparing a tax return based on the size of the client's refund. True or false?

True. Incorrect. Tax preparation is not a situation in which a contingent fee can be charged.

False. Correct. A contingent fee cannot be charged for tax return preparation. A contingent fee can be charged only in certain limited situations, including services in connection with an examination of an original or amended return, services rendered in connection the determination of statutory interest or penalties, or services rendered in connection with a judicial proceeding arising under the Internal Revenue Code.

4. A taxpayer requests records from a preparer that must be attached to his tax return. He has not paid the preparation fees yet. If state law permits retention of client records in cases of nonpayment of fees, the preparer may retain the taxpayer's records. True or false?

True. Incorrect. You must turn over records needed to be attached to a tax return, regardless of outstanding fees or state law.

False. Correct. You can retain copies of client's records after a request for them has been made. However, records that must be attached to the return must be promptly returned to the taxpayer upon request.

5. A conflict of interest may exist if there is a significant risk that representation of a taxpayer may be adverse to the preparer's personal interests. True or false?

True. Correct. If the preparer's personal interests are adverse to the taxpayer's, then a conflict of interest exists.

False. Incorrect. Conflicts of interest can exist when the preparer's interests differ from those of the taxpayer.

6. You may not apply a taxpayer's refund check toward the payment of tax preparation fees by depositing the taxpayer's refund in your bank account. True or false?

True. Correct. You are prohibited from negotiating a client's check, which includes depositing it in your bank account.

False. Incorrect. You are prohibited from depositing the client's federal tax refund check into your bank account.

7. In preparing written advice for a taxpayer, the practitioner may not take into consideration the chances of being audited in determining whether to recommend a tax position on a return. True or false?

True. Correct. The practitioner may take into consideration only the relevant facts and circumstances and applicable tax law in recommending a tax position for a taxpayer.

False. Incorrect. In preparing written advice, the practitioner may not take into consideration the chances of the taxpayer being audited.

Chapter 41

1. Censure prevents a practitioner from representing a client before the IRS. True or false?

True. Incorrect. A practitioner under censure may represent a client before the IRS.

False. Correct. Censure is a public reprimand that does not impede a practitioner's right to practice.

2. The IRS can impose a sanction or a monetary penalty but not both for a single violation. True or false?

True. Incorrect. A monetary penalty may be imposed in addition to a sanction.

False. Correct. The IRS can choose a sanction, a monetary penalty, or both.

3. An attorney who is disbarred by her state for a felony unrelated to taxes can continue to practice before the IRS. True or false?

True. Incorrect. The fact that the state felony conviction was unrelated to federal tax law is not sufficient to enable the disbarred attorney to continue to practice before the IRS.

False. Correct. If an attorney is disbarred by her state, the practitioner is unfit to practice before the IRS.

4. A practitioner's failure to file his or her own federal tax returns can result in sanctions. True or false?

True. Correct. The willful failure to file a federal tax return when required to do so is considered disreputable conduct for which sanctions can be given.

False. Incorrect. One of the situations evidencing disreputable conduct is a practitioner's failure to file his or her own tax returns when required to do so.

5. A tax return preparer can seek the help of an enrolled agent who is under suspension. True or false?

True. Incorrect. A tax return preparer who seeks the assistance or advice of a suspended or disabarred tax return preparer is subject to disciplinary action.

False. Correct. A tax return preparer may not accept assistance from, or provide assist to, any person who is under disbarment or suspension from practice before the IRS if the assistance relates to a matter constituting practice before the IRS.

IRS Resources

Various IRS forms, publications, and other resources are referred to throughout this book. All of these resources can be found online on the IRS Web site, www.irs.gov. This appendix can help you locate these resources quickly.

All publications, forms, schedules, and related instructions can be downloaded from the IRS Forms and Publications Web site at www.irs.gov/formspubs/index.html.

Often you can locate current-year documents by entering the Web address www.irs.gov/pub/irs-pdf/ followed by "p" for publication, "f" for form, or "i" for form instructions (if not included with the form itself), the publication or form number itself, and ".pdf".

TIP: The IRS Web site can be searched by entering key words in the search box, such as "Form 1040." The site also contains an "Advanced Search" feature, located under the search box, that can be used to narrow results if necessary.

Examples

Enter www.irs.gov/pub/irs-pdf/p17.pdf in your Web browser to directly access the PDF version of IRS Pub. 17, Your Federal Income Tax. Enter www.irs.gov/pub/irs-pdf/f1040.pdf in your Web browser to directly access Form 1040. Enter www.irs.gov/pub/irs-pdf/i1040.pdf in your Web browser to directly access the Form 1040 instructions

ALERT: This formula works in many but not all instances. For example, Form 1040, Schedule A, may be found at www.irs.gov/pub/irs-pdf/f1040sa.pdf. However, www.irs.gov/pub/irs-pdf/f1040a.pdf links to Form 1040A.

The gateway to other IRS information can be found through the IRS electronic Reading Room at www.irs.gov/uac/electronic-reading-room. The Electronic Reading Room contains links to published tax guidance, such as revenue rulings, regulations, and notices. You can also find links to nonprecedential rulings and advice, such as private letter rulings and chief council advice. The Electronic Reading Room also contains links to administrative manuals and instructions (including the Internal Revenue Manual), program plans, and reports, such as art appraisal services, annual summary reports, and training and reference materials, including audit technique guides.

Another helpful resource for IRS documents is the IRS Tax Map, http://taxmap.ntis.gov/taxmap/, where you can also find forms, publications, tax topics, and FAQs on various topics.

Finally, one link you will want to keep handy is the one for Circular 230. It can be found at www.irs.gov/pub/irs-pdf/pcir230.pdf.

INDEX

F

G

M

U

V